Turbo C®:
The Complete Reference

Turbo C®:
The Complete Reference

Herbert Schildt

BORLAND·OSBORNE/McGRAW·HILL

PROGRAMMING SERIES

Osborne **McGraw-Hill**
2600 Tenth Street
Berkeley, California 94710
U.S.A.

For information on translations and book distributors outside of the
U.S.A., write to Osborne **McGraw-Hill** at the above address.

A complete list of trademarks appears on page 893.

Turbo C®: The Complete Reference

1234567890 DODO 898

ISBN 0-07-881346-8

Foreword xiii
Preface xv

CONTENTS

Turbo C has rapidly become the programming tool of choice for C programmers because of the power and simplicity of this language development environment. It has been gratifying to watch the community of professional developers adopt Turbo C as the ideal programming environment.

The latest release of Turbo C, Version 1.5, offers several enhancements over the original package. In particular, professional-level graphics capabilities provide sophisticated graphics and a Borland Graphics Interface that is a standard for all Borland language and applications packages. This newest version of Turbo C also includes a library to manage the multiple libraries and memory modules used in Turbo C development. And making Turbo C even richer in features is the addition of more than 100 new functions.

In *Turbo C: The Complete Reference*, Herb Schildt, the author of the best-selling books *Using Turbo C* and *Advanced Turbo C*, presents an impressive and comprehensive overview of the Turbo C development environment. Extensive coverage of keywords, functions, libraries, and applications are offered. In addition, the new features of the 1.5 release are fully discussed.

Schildt's experience as a writer and a programmer makes this an indispensable guide for all Turbo C programmers.

Philippe Kahn
Chief Executive Officer
Borland International, Inc.

F O R E W O R D

Quite a few Turbo C structure definitions have been presented and discussed in this book. The definitions originate in the Turbo C manuals and disk files. These structure definitions are used with permission from Borland International, Inc., developer of Turbo C.

ACKNOWLEDGMENTS

This book is about Turbo C. Legendary for its speed of compilation and the efficiency of its object code, Turbo C has become one of the most widely used programming languages in the world. This book's purpose is to provide you with a comprehensive source of information about this important programming language.

What's Inside

This guide covers in detail all aspects of the Turbo C language, its integrated development environment, its command line version, and its libraries. The book is divided into five parts:

Part One—The C Language
Part Two—The Turbo C Environment
Part Three—The Turbo C Library
Part Four—Turbo C Applications
Part Five—Software Development Using C

Part One provides a thorough discussion of the keywords, preprocessor directives, and features of the Turbo C language. Part Two discusses the Turbo C development environment. Part Three covers the standard C library. Part Four offers some practical examples of Turbo C programming, including linked lists, AI-based problem solving, and expression parsing. Part Five discusses the Turbo C programming environment, covering topics like interfacing to assembly code, efficiency, porting, and debugging.

Diskette Package

There are many, many working functions and programs contained in this book. If you are like me, you like to have a lot of routines to draw upon, but hate to type them into the computer. Then, if you type something wrong, you spend hours trying to get the program to work. For this reason, I am offering the source code to all the functions and programs contained in this book on a PC-compatible diskette. Just fill in the order blank and mail it, along with your payment, to the address shown. Or, if you're in a hurry, call (217) 586-4021 to place your order. (VISA and MasterCard accepted.)

H. S.
Mahomet, Illinois
December 1987

Diskette Order Form

Please send me _____ copies, at $24.95 each, of the programs in *Turbo C: The Complete Reference* on a PC-compatible diskette. (Foreign orders, please add $5 shipping and handling.)

Name _____

Address _____

City _____ **State** _____ **ZIP** _____

Telephone (_____) _____

Diskette type (check one)   5 1/4 in. _____ 3 1/2 in._____

Method of payment Check _____ VISA_____ MC _____

Credit card number _____

Expiration date _____

Signature _____

Send to: Herbert Schildt
      RR 1, Box 130
      Mahomet, IL 61853

or phone: (217) 586-4021

Osborne/McGraw-Hill assumes NO responsibility for this offer. This is solely an offer of Herbert Schildt and not of Osborne/McGraw-Hill.

The C Language

The first part of this reference guide presents a thorough discussion of the Turbo C programming language. Chapter 1 provides a quick overview of the C language: The more knowledgeable programmer may wish to skip directly to Chapter 2. Chapter 2 examines Turbo C's built-in data types, variables, operators, and expressions. Chapter 3 presents program control statements, and Chapter 4 looks at functions—C's building blocks. Chapter 5 deals with arrays and Chapter 6 discusses pointers. Chapter 7 covers structures, unions, user-defined types, and enumerations; Chapter 8 explores input/output (I/O) functions; and Chapter 9 covers compiler directives and code generation. Chapter 10 discusses Turbo C's memory models. Chapter 11 concludes this section with a discussion of Turbo C's screen and graphics functions.

An Overview of C

This chapter presents the heritage of Turbo C including an overview of the origins, uses, and philosophy of the programming language C.

The Origins of C

Dennis Ritchie invented and first implemented the programming language C on a DEC PDP-11 that used the UNIX operating system. The language is the result of a development process that started with an older language called BCPL, which is still in use, primarily in Europe. Martin Richards developed BCPL, which influenced Ken Thompson's invention of a language called B, which led to the development of C in the 1970s.

For many years the de facto standard for C was the version supplied with the UNIX Version 5 operating system. It is described in *The C Programming Language* by Brian Kernighan and Dennis Ritchie (Prentice-Hall, 1978). The growing popularity of microcomputers led to the creation of a large number of C implementations. In what could almost be called a miracle, at the source code level most of these implementations were highly compatible. However, because no standard existed, there were discrepancies. To rectify this situation, ANSI established a committee in the beginning of the summer of 1983 to create an ANSI standard for the C language. Turbo C fully implements the resulting ANSI standard for C, is a fast, efficient compiler, and provides both an integrated programming environment and the more traditional command-line version to satisfy the needs and desires of a wide variety of programmers.

A Middle-Level Language

C is often called a *middle-level computer language*. This does not mean that C is less powerful, harder to use, or less developed than a high-level language such as BASIC or Pascal; nor does it imply that C is similar to, or presents the problems associated with, assembly language. The definition of C as a middle-level language means that it combines elements of high-level languages with the functionalism of assembly language. Table 1-1 shows how C fits into the spectrum of languages.

Highest level	Ada
	Modula-2
	Pascal
	COBOL
	FORTRAN
	BASIC
Middle level	C
	FORTH
	Macro-assembly language
Lowest level	Assembly language

Table 1-1.   C's Place in the World of Languages

As a middle-level language, C allows the manipulation of bits, bytes, and addresses—the basic elements with which the computer functions. C code is very portable. *Portability* means that it is possible to adapt software written for one type of computer to another. For example, if a program written for an Apple II+ can be moved easily to an IBM PC, that program is portable.

All high-level programming languages support the concept of data types. A *data type* defines a set of values that a variable can store along with a set of operations that can be performed on that variable. Common data types are integer, character, and real. Although C has five basic built-in data types, it is not a strongly typed language like Pascal or Ada. In fact C will allow almost all type conversions. For example, character and integer types may be freely intermixed in most expressions. Traditionally C performs no run-time error checking such as array-boundary checking or argument-type compatibility checking. These checks are the responsibility of the programmer.

A special feature of C is that it allows the direct manipulation of bits, bytes, words, and pointers. This suits it to system-level programming, where these operations are common. Another important aspect of C is that it has only 32 keywords (27 from the Kernighan and Ritchie standard and 5 added by the ANSI standardization committee), which are the commands that make up the C language. (Turbo C contains 11 more keywords to support various enhancements and extensions.) As a comparison, consider that BASIC for the IBM PC contains 159 keywords!

A Structured Language

Although the term *block-structured language* does not strictly apply to C, C is commonly called a structured language because of structural similarities to ALGOL, Pascal, and

Modula-2. (Technically, a block-structured language permits procedures or functions to be declared inside other procedures or functions. In this way the concepts of "global" and "local" are expanded through the use of *scope rules*, which govern the "visibility" of a variable or procedure. Since C does not allow the creation of functions within functions, it is not really block structured.)

The distinguishing feature of a structured language is *compartmentalization* of code and data. Compartmentalization is the language's ability to section off and hide from the rest of the program all information and instructions necessary to perform a specific task. One way of achieving compartmentalization is to use subroutines that employ local (temporary) variables. By using local variables, the programmer can write subroutines so that the events that occur within them cause no side effects in other parts of the program. This capability makes it very easy for C programs to share sections of code. If you develop compartmentalized functions, you only need to know what a function does, not how it does it. Remember that excessive use of global variables (variables known throughout the entire program) may allow bugs to creep into a program by allowing unwanted side effects. (Anyone who has programmed in BASIC is well aware of this problem!)

A structured language allows you a variety of programming possibilities. It directly supports several loop constructs, such as **while**, **do-while**, and **for**. In a structured language the use of **goto** is either prohibited or discouraged and is not the common form of program control as it is in BASIC and FORTRAN. A structured language allows you to indent statements and does not require a strict field concept (as traditional FORTRAN does).

Here are some examples of structured and nonstructured languages:

Structured	Nonstructured
Pascal	FORTRAN
Ada	BASIC
C	COBOL
Modula-2	

Structured languages tend to be modern; nonstructured languages are older. Today it is widely maintained that the clarity of structured languages makes programming and maintenance easier than with nonstructured languages.

The main structural component of C is the function—C's standalone subroutine. In C, functions are the building blocks in which all program activity occurs. They allow the separate tasks in a program to be defined and coded separately, thus allowing your programs to be modular. After a function has been created, you can rely on it to work properly in various situations, without creating side effects in other parts of the program. The fact that you can create standalone functions is extremely critical in larger projects where one programmer's code must not accidentally affect another's.

Another way to structure and compartmentalize code in C is to use code blocks. A *code block* is a logically connected group of program statements that is treated as a unit. In C a code block is created by placing a sequence of statements between opening and closing curly braces. In this example,

```
if(x<10) {
  printf("too low, try again");
  reset_counter(-1);
}
```

the two statements after the **if** and between the curly braces are both executed if **x** is less than 10. These two statements together with the braces are a code block. They are a logical unit: One of the statements cannot execute without the other. Every statement can be either a single statement or a block of statements. Code blocks not only allow many algorithms to be implemented with clarity, elegance, and efficiency but also help the programmer conceptualize the true nature of the routine.

A Programmer's Language

One might respond to the statement, "C is a programmer's language," with the question, "Aren't all programming languages for programmers?" The answer is an unqualified "No!" Consider the classic examples of nonprogrammer's languages, COBOL and BASIC. COBOL was designed to enable nonprogrammers to read and, presumably, understand the program. BASIC was created essentially to allow nonprogrammers to program a computer to solve relatively simple problems.

In contrast, C stands almost alone in that it was created, influenced, and field-tested by real working programmers. The end result is that C gives the programmer what the programmer wants: few restrictions, few complaints, block structures, standalone functions, and a compact set of keywords. It is truly amazing that by using C, a programmer can achieve nearly the efficiency of assembly code, combined with the structure of ALGOL or Modula-2. It is no wonder that C is easily the most popular language among topflight professional programmers.

The fact that C can often be used in place of assembly language contributes greatly to its popularity among programmers. Assembly language uses a symbolic representation of the actual binary code that the computer executes directly. Each assembly language operation maps into a single task for the computer to perform. Although assembly language gives programmers the potential for accomplishing tasks with maximum flexibility and efficiency, it is notoriously difficult to use when developing and debugging a program. Furthermore, since assembly language is unstructured, the final program tends to be spaghetti code—a tangled mess of jumps, calls, and indexes. This lack of structure makes assembly language programs difficult to read, enhance, and maintain. Perhaps more important, assembly language routines are not portable between machines with different central processing units (CPUs).

Initially, C was used for systems programming. A *systems program* is part of a large class of programs that forms a portion of the operating system of the computer or its support utilities. For example, the following are usually called systems programs:

- Operating systems
- Interpreters
- Editors
- Assembly programs
- Compilers
- Database managers

As C grew in popularity, many programmers began to use it to program all tasks because of its portability and efficiency. Because there are C compilers for almost all computers, it is possible to take code written for one machine and compile and run it on another with few or no changes. This portability saves both time and money. In addition, C compilers tend to produce tighter and faster object code than most BASIC compilers, for example.

Perhaps the most significant reason that C is used in all types of programming tasks is that programmers like it! It has the speed of assembly language and the extensibility of FORTH but few of the restrictions of Pascal or Modula-2. Each C programmer can create and maintain a unique library of functions that have been tailored to his or her personality and can be used in many different programs. Because it allows—indeed, encourages—separate compilation, C allows programmers to manage large projects easily and minimize duplication of effort.

Compilers Versus Interpreters

The terms *compiler* and *interpreter* refer to the way in which a program is executed. In theory, any programming language can be either compiled or interpreted, but some languages are usually executed one way or the other. For example, BASIC is usually interpreted and C is usually compiled. (Recently, however, C interpreters have gained in popularity as debugging aids.) The way a program is executed is not defined by the language in which it is written. Interpreters and compilers are simply sophisticated programs that operate on your program source code.

An interpreter reads the source code of your program one line at a time and performs the specific instructions contained in that line. A compiler reads the entire program and converts it into *object code*, which is a translation of the program source code in a form that can be directly executed by the computer. Object code is also called binary code and machine code. Once a program is compiled, a line of source code is no longer meaningful in the execution of the program.

When you use an interpreter, it must be present each time you wish to run your program. For example, in BASIC you have to execute the BASIC interpreter first and then load your program and type RUN each time you want to use it. The BASIC interpreter then examines your program one line at a time for correctness and then executes it. This slow process occurs every time the program runs. By contrast, a compiler converts your program into object code that can be directly executed by your computer. Because the compiler translates your program only once, all you need to do is execute your program directly, usually by the simple process of typing its name. Thus, compilation is a one-time cost, while interpreted code incurs an overhead cost each time a program runs.

The compiling process itself takes extra time, but this is easily offset by the time you save while using the program. Compiled programs run much faster than interpreted programs. The only situation in which this is not true is if your program is very short—less than 50 lines—and does not use any loops.

Two terms that you will often see in this book and in your C compiler manual are *compile time*, which refers to the events that occur during the compilation process, and *run time*, which refers to the events that occur while the program is actually executing. You usually see these terms in discussions of errors, as in the phrases "compile-time errors" and "run-time errors."

The Form of a C Program

Table 1-2 lists the 43 keywords that, combined with the formal C syntax, form the Turbo C programming language.

All C keywords are lowercase. In C uppercase and lowercase are different: **else** is a keyword; ELSE is not. A keyword may not be used for any other purpose in a C program—that is, it may not serve as a variable or function name.

All C programs consist of one or more functions. The only function that absolutely must be present is called

---

The 32 keywords as defined by the proposed ANSI standard

auto	double	int	struct
break	else	long	switch
case	enum	register	typedef
char	extern	return	union
const	float	short	unsigned
continue	for	signed	void
default	goto	sizeof	volatile
do	if	static	while

The Turbo C extended keywords

asm	_cs	_ds	_es
_ss	cdecl	far	huge
interrupt	near	pascal	

Table 1-2. A List of Turbo C Keywords

main( ), and it is the first function called when program execution begins. In well-written C code, **main( )** outlines what the program does. The outline is composed of function calls. Although **main** is technically not part of the C language, treat it as if it were. Don't try to use **main** as the name of a variable because you are likely to confuse the compiler.

The general form of a C program is illustrated in Figure 1-1, where **f1( )** through **fN( )** represent user-defined functions.

The Library and Linking

Technically speaking, it is possible to create a useful, functional C program that consists solely of the statements actually created by the programmer. However, this is rarely done because C does not, within the actual definition of the language, provide any method of performing I/O operations. As a result, most programs include calls to various functions contained in Turbo C's standard library.

Turbo C comes with a standard library that provides functions that perform most commonly needed tasks. When you call a function that is not part of the program you wrote, Turbo C "remembers" its name. Later the *linker* combines the code you wrote with the object code already found in the standard library. This process is called *linking*.

The functions that are kept in the library are in *relocatable* format. This means that the memory addresses for the various machine-code instructions have not been absolutely

```
global declarations
main( )
{
    local variables
    statement sequence
}
f1( )
{
    local variables
    statement sequence
}
f2( )
{
    local variables
    statement sequence
}
    .
    .
    .
fN( )
{
    local variables
    statement sequence
}
```

Figure 1-1.   The general form of a C program

defined; only offset information has been kept. When your program links with the functions in the standard library, these memory offsets are used to create the actual addresses used. There are several technical manuals and books that explain this process in more detail. However, you do not need any further explanation of the actual relocation process to program in Turbo C.

Separate Compilation

Most short C programs are completely contained within one source file. However, as a program gets longer, so does its compile time, and long compile times make for short tempers! Hence, Turbo C allows a program to be broken into pieces and contained in many files and for each file to be compiled separately. Once all files have been compiled, they are linked together, along with any library routines, to form the complete object code. The advantage of separate compilation is that a change in the code of one file does not necessitate the recompilation of the entire program. On all but the simplest projects, the time saved is substantial. (Strategies for separate compilation are covered in detail in Part 5.)

Turbo C's Memory Map

A compiled Turbo C program creates and uses four logically distinct regions of memory that serve specific functions. The first region is the memory that actually holds the code of your program. The next region is the memory where global variables are stored. The remaining two regions are the stack and the heap. The *stack* is used for a great many things while your program executes. It holds the return addresses of function calls, arguments to functions, and local variables. It is also used to save the current state of the CPU. The *heap* is a region of free memory, which your program can use via Turbo C's dynamic allocation functions for things like linked lists and trees.

Although the exact physical layout of each of the four regions of memory differs, based on the way you tell Turbo C to compile your program, the diagram in Figure 1-2 shows conceptually how your C programs appear in memory.

A Review of Terms

The terms that follow will be used frequently throughout the remainder of this book. You should be completely familiar with their meaning.

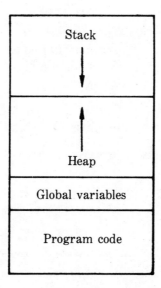

Figure 1-2.   A conceptual memory map of a C program

Source code	The text of a program that a user can read; commonly thought of as the program. The source code is input into the C compiler.
Object code	Translation of the source code of a program into machine code, which the computer can read and execute directly. Object code is the input to the linker.
Linker	A program that links separately compiled functions together into one program. It combines the functions in the standard C library with the code that you wrote. The output of the linker is an executable program.
Library	The file containing the standard functions that can be used by your program. These functions include all I/O operations as well as other useful routines.
Compile time	The events that occur while your program is being compiled. A common occurrence during compile time is a syntax error.
Run time	The events that occur while your program is executing.

Variables, Constants, Operators, and Expressions

Variables and constants are manipulated by operators to form expressions. These are the atomic elements of the Turbo C language. This chapter will examine each element closely.

Identifier Names

Turbo C defines the names that are used to reference variables, functions, labels, and various other user-defined objects as *identifiers*. An identifier in Turbo C can vary from 1 to 32 characters. The first character must be a letter or an underscore with subsequent characters being letters, numbers, or the underscore. Turbo C also allows the $ to be used in an identifier name, but this is nonstandard and is not recommended. Here are some examples of correct and incorrect identifier names:

Correct	Incorrect
count	1count
test23	hi!there
high_balance	high..balance

In C, upper- and lowercase are treated as different. Hence, **count**, **Count**, and **COUNT** are three separate indenti-

fiers. An identifier may not be the same as a Turbo C keyword, and it should not have the same name as functions that
you wrote or that are in the Turbo C library.

Data Types

There are five atomic data types in C: character, integer,
floating point, double floating point, and valueless. The sizes
of these types are shown in Table 2-1.

Values of type **char** are used to hold ASCII characters
or any 8-bit quantity. Variables of type **int** are used to hold
integer quantities. Variables of type **float** and **double** are
used to hold real numbers. (Real numbers have both an integer and a fractional component.)

The **void** type has two uses. The first is explicitly to
declare a function as returning no value; the second is to
create generic pointers. Both of these uses are discussed in
subsequent chapters.

Turbo C supports several *aggregate* types, including
structures, unions, bit fields, enumerations, and user-defined
types. These complex types are discussed in Chapter 7 and
will not be examined here.

Type	Bit Width	Range
char	8	0 to 255
int	16	-32768 to 32767
float	32	3.4E$-$38 to 3.4E$+$38
double	64	1.7E$-$308 to 1.7E$+$308
void	0	valueless

Table 2-1.   Size and Range of Turbo C's Basic Data Types

Type Modifiers

Excepting type **void**, the basic data types may have various *modifiers* preceding them. A modifier is used to alter the meaning of the base type to fit the needs of various situations more precisely. The list of modifiers is shown here:

signed
unsigned
long
short

The modifiers **signed**, **unsigned**, **long**, and **short** may be applied to character and integer base types. However, **long** may also be applied to **double**. Table 2-2 shows all allowed combinations that adhere to the proposed ANSI standard, along with their bit widths and range.

The use of **signed** on integers is redundant but allowed, because the default integer declaration assumes a signed number.

The difference between **signed** and **unsigned** integers is in the way the high-order bit of the integer is interpreted. If a signed integer is specified, the C compiler will generate code that assumes the high-order bit of an integer is to be used as a *sign flag*. If the sign flag is 0, the number is positive; if it is 1, the number is negative. For example:

```
127 in binary is   0 0 0 0 0 0 0 0   0 1 1 1 1 1 1 1
−127 in binary is 1 0 0 0 0 0 0 0   0 1 1 1 1 1 1 1
                  ▲
                  sign bit
```

The reader is cautioned that most computers (including those based on the 8086 family of processors) will use *two's complement* arithmetic, which will cause the representation of −127 to appear different. However, the use of the sign bit is

Type	Bit Width	Range
char	8	−128 to 127
unsigned char	8	0 to 255
signed char	8	−128 to 127
int	16	−32768 to 32767
unsigned int	16	0 to 65535
signed int	16	−32768 to 32767
short int	16	−32768 to 32767
unsigned short int	16	0 to 65535
signed short int	16	−32768 to 32767
long int	32	−2147483648 to 2147483647
signed long int	32	−2147483648 to 2147483647
float	32	3.4E−38 to 3.4E+38
double	64	1.7E−308 to 1.7E+308
long double	64	1.7E−308 to 1.7E+308

Table 2-2.   All Possible Combinations of Turbo C's Basic Types and Modifiers

the same. A negative number in two's complement form has all bits reversed and 1 is added to the number. For example, −127 in two's complement appears like this:

1 1 1 1 1 1 1 1   1 0 0 0 0 0 0 1

Signed integers are important for a great many algorithms, but they only have half the absolute magnitude of their unsigned brothers. For example, here is 32,767:

0 1 1 1 1 1 1 1   1 1 1 1 1 1 1 1

If the high-order bit were set to 1, the number would then be interpreted as −32,768. However, if you declared this to be an

unsigned int, then when the high-order bit is set to 1, the number becomes 65,535.

Access Modifiers

Turbo C has two type modifiers that are used to control the ways in which variables are accessed or modified. These modifiers are called **const** and **volatile**.

Variables of type **const** cannot be changed during execution by your program. For example,

```
const int a;
```

will create an integer variable called **a** that cannot be modified by your program. It can, however, be used in other types of expressions. A **const** variable will receive its value either from an explicit initialization or by some hardware-dependent means.

The modifier **volatile** is used to tell the compiler that a variable's value can be changed in ways not explicitly specified by the program. For example, a global variable's address can be passed to the clock routine of the operating system and used to hold the real-time of the system. In this situation the contents of the variable are altered without any explicit assignment statements in the program. This is important because Turbo C automatically optimizes certain expressions by making the assumption that the content of a variable is unchanging inside that expression. In addition, some optimizations may change the order of evaluation of an expression during the compilation process. The **volatile** modifier will prevent these changes from occurring.

It is possible to use **const** and **volatile** together. For example, if **0x30** is assumed to be the value of a port that is changed by external conditions only, the following declaration would be precisely what you would want to prevent any possibility of accidental side effects:

```
const volatile unsigned char *port=0x30;
```

Declaration of Variables

All variables must be declared before they are used. The general form of declaration is shown here:

type variable—list;

Here, **type** must be a valid C data type and **variable—list** may consist of one or more identifier names with comma separators. Some declarations are shown here, for example:

```
int i, j, l;

short int si;

unsigned int ui;

double balance, profit, loss;
```

Remember, in C, the name of a variable has nothing to do with its type.

There are three basic places where variables will be declared: inside functions, in the definition of function parameters, or outside all functions. These variables are called local variables, formal parameters, and global variables.

Local Variables

Variables that are declared inside a function are called *local variables*. In some C literature, these variables may be referred to as *automatic variables* in keeping with C's use (optional) of the keyword **auto** to declare them. Since the term *local variable* is more generally used, this guide will continue to use it. Local variables may be referenced only by statements that are inside the block in which the variables are declared. Stated another way, local variables are not known outside their own code block. You should remember that a block of code is begun when an opening curly brace is encountered and terminated when a closing curly brace is found.

One of the most important things to understand about local variables is that they exist only while the block of code in which they are declared is executing. That is, a local variable is created upon entry into its block and destroyed upon exit.

The most common code block in which local variables are declared is the function. For example, consider these two functions:

```
func1()
{
   int x;

   x = 10;
}

func2()
{
   int x;

   x = -199;
}
```

The integer variable **x** was declared twice, once in **func1()** and once in **func2()**. The **x** in **func1()** has no bearing on, or relationship to, the **x** in **func2()** because each **x** is known only to the code within the same block as the variable's declaration.

The language contains the keyword **auto**, which can be used to declare local variables. However, since all nonglobal variables are assumed to be **auto** by default, it is virtually never used.

It is common practice to declare all variables needed within a function at the start of that function's code block. This is done mostly to make it easy for anyone reading the code to know what variables are used. However, it is not necessary to do this because local variables may be declared within any code block. To understand how this works, consider the following function:

```
f()
{
  int t;

  scanf("%d", &t);

  if(t==1) {
    char s[80];  /* this is created only upon
                    entry into this block */
    printf("enter name:");
    gets(s);
    process(s);
  }
}
```

Here the local variable s will be created upon entry into the **if** code block and destroyed upon exit. Furthermore, s is known only within the **if** block and may not be referenced elsewhere—not even in other parts of the function that contains it.

The main advantage of declaring a local variable within a conditional block is that memory for it will be allocated only if needed because local variables do not come into existence until the block in which they are declared is entered. Although this is not important in most situations, it can really matter when code is being produced for dedicated controllers (like a garage door opener that responds to a digital security code) where RAM is in very short supply.

Because local variables are created and destroyed with each entry and exit from the block in which they are declared, their content is lost once the block is left. This is especially important to remember in terms of a function call. When a function is called, its local variables are created, and upon its return, they are destroyed. This means that local variables cannot retain their values between calls. (As you will see shortly, however, it is possible to direct the compiler to retain their values through the use of the **static** modifier.)

Unless otherwise specified, storage for local variables is on the stack. The fact that the stack is a dynamic and changing region of memory explains why local variables cannot, in general, hold their values between function calls.

Formal Parameters

If a function is to use arguments, it must declare variables that will accept the values of the arguments. These variables are called the *formal parameters* of the function. They behave like any other local variables inside the function. As shown in the following program fragment, their declaration occurs after the function name and before the function's opening brace.

```
/* return 1 if c is part of string s; 0 otherwise */
is_in(s, c)
char *s;
char c;
{
  while(*s)
    if(*s==c) return 1;
    else s++;

  return 0;
}
```

The function **is_in()** has two parameters: s and c. You must tell C what type of variables these are by declaring them as shown. Once this has been done, they may be used inside the function as normal local variables. Keep in mind that, as local variables, they are also dynamic and are destroyed upon exit from the function.

You must make sure that the formal parameters you declare are the same type as the arguments you will use to call the function. If there is a type mismatch, unexpected results can occur. Unlike many other languages, Turbo C is very robust and will generally do something, even if it is not what you want. There are few run-time errors and no bounds checking. As the programmer, you have to make sure that errors do not occur.

As with local variables, you may make assignments to a function's formal parameters or use them in any allowable C expression. Even though these variables perform the special task of receiving the value of the arguments passed to the function, they can be used like any other local variable.

Global Variables

Unlike local variables, global variables are known throughout the entire program and may be used by any piece of code. They also hold their value during the entire execution of the program. Global variables are created by declaring them outside any function. They may be accessed by any expression regardless of what function the expression is in.

In the following program fragment, the variable **count** has been declared outside all functions. Its declaration occurs before the **main()** function. However, it could have been placed anywhere before its first use, as long as it was not in a function. Common practice is to declare global variables at the top of the program.

```
int count;  /* count is global  */

main()
{
  count = 100;
  func1();
}

func1()
{
  int temp;

  temp = count;
  func2();
  printf("count is %d", count); /* will print 100 */
}

func2()
{
  int count;
```

```
for(count=1; count<10; count++)
  putchar('.');
}
```

Looking closely at this program fragment, it should be clear that although neither **main( )** nor **func1( )** has declared the variable **count**, both may use it. However, **func2( )** has declared a local variable called **count**. When **func2( )** references **count**, it will be referencing only its local variable, not the global one. Remember that if a global variable and a local variable have the same name, all references to that name inside the function where the local variable is declared are to that local variable and have no effect on the global variable. Forgetting this can cause your program to act very strangely, even though it "looks" correct.

Storage for global variables is in a fixed region of memory set aside for this purpose by the compiler. Global variables are very helpful when the same data is used in many functions in your program. You should avoid using unnecessary global variables, however, for three reasons:

1. They take up memory the entire time your program is executing, not just when they are needed.

2. Using a global where a local variable will do makes a function less general because it relies on something that must be defined outside itself.

3. Using a large number of global variables can lead to program errors because of unknown, unwanted, side effects. (This is evidenced in BASIC, where all variables are global.)

A major problem in developing large programs is the accidental changing of a variable's value because it is used elsewhere in the program. This can happen in C if you use too many global variables in your programs.

One of the principal points of a structured language is the compartmentalization of code and data. In C compartmentalization is achieved through the use of local variables and functions. For example, here are two ways to write **mul()** — a simple function that computes the product of two integers:

```
        Two Ways to Write mul()

General                   Specific

-------                   --------
                          int x, y;
mul(x, y)                 mul()
int x, y;                 {
{
    return(x*y);              return(x*y);
}                         }
```

Both functions return the product of the variables **x** and **y**. However, the generalized, or *parameterized*, version can be used to return the product of any two numbers, whereas the specific version can be used to find only the product of the global variables **x** and **y**.

Storage Class Specifiers

Four storage class specifiers are supported by Turbo C. They are

    extern
    static
    register
    auto

These are used to tell the compiler how the variable that follows should be stored. The storage specifier precedes the rest of the variable declaration. Its general form is storage—specifier type var—name;

Each specifier will be examined in turn.

extern

Because C allows separately compiled modules of a large program to be linked together to speed up compilation and aid in the management of large projects, there must be some way of telling all the files about the global variables required by the program. Remember that you can declare a global variable only once. If you try to declare two global variables with the same name inside the same file, Turbo C prints the error message that it does not know which variable to use. The same type of problem occurs if you simply declare all the global variables needed by your program in each file. Although the compiler would not issue any error messages at compile time, you would actually be trying to create two (or more) copies of each variable. The trouble would start when Turbo C attempted to link your modules together. The linker would display an error message because it would not know which variable to use. The solution is to declare all your globals in one file and use **extern** declarations in the other as shown in Table 2-3.

In file two, the global variable list was copied from file one, and the **extern** specifier was added to the declarations. The **extern** specifier tells the compiler that the following variable types and names have already been declared elsewhere. In other words, **extern** lets the compiler know what the types and names are for these global variables without actually creating storage for them again. When the two modules are linked, all references to the external variables are resolved.

When you use a global variable inside a function in the same file as the declaration for the global variable you may

---

File 1	File 2
int x, y;	extern int x, y;
char ch;	extern char ch;
main ()	func22()
{	{
.	x=y/10;
.	}
.	
}	func23( )
{	{
func1()	y=10;
{	}
x=123;	
}	

Table 2-3.   Using Global Variables in Separately Compiled Modules

elect to use **extern**, although you don't have to and it is rarely done. The following program fragment shows the use of this option:

```
int first, last;  /* global definition of first
                     and last */

main()
{
  extern int first;  /* optional use of the
                        extern declaration */
}
```

Although **extern** variable declarations can occur inside the same file as the global declaration, they are not necessary. If the C compiler comes across a variable that has not been declared, the compiler checks whether it matches any of the global variables. If it does, the compiler assumes that the global variable is the one being referenced.

static Variables

The **static** variables are permanent variables within their own function or file. They differ from global variables because they are not known outside their function or file but they maintain their values between calls. This feature can make them very useful when you write generalized functions and function libraries that will be used by other programmers. Because the effect of **static** on local variables is different from its effect on global ones, they will be examined separately.

static Local Variables

When the **static** modifier is applied to a local variable, it causes the compiler to create permanent storage for it in much the same way that it does for a global variable. The key difference between a **static** local variable and a global variable is that the **static** local variable remains known only to the block in which it is declared. In simple terms, a **static** local variable is a local variable that retains its value between function calls.

It is very important to the creation of standalone functions that **static** local variables are available in Turbo C because there are several types of routines that must preserve a value between calls. If **static** variables were not allowed, globals would have to be used, which would open the door to possible side effects. A simple example of how a **static** local variable can be used is illustrated by the **count( )** function in this short program:

```
main()
{
  do {
    count(0);
  } while(!kbhit());
  printf("count called %d times", count(1));
}

count(i)
int i;
{
```

```
static int c=0;

if(i) return c;
else c++;
return 0;
}
```

Sometimes it is useful to know how many times a function has been executed during a program run. While it is certainly possible to use a global variable for this purpose, a better way is simply to have the function in question keep track of this information itself as is done by the **count( )** function. In this example, if **count( )** is called with a value of 0, the counter variable **c** is incremented. (Presumably in a real application, the function would also perform some other useful processing as well.) If **count( )** is called with any other value, it returns the number of times it has been called. Counting the number of times a function is called can be useful during the development stage so that those functions called most frequently can be highly optimized.

Another good example of a function that would require a **static** local variable is a number series generator that produces a new number based on the last one. It would be possible for you to declare a global variable for this value. However, each time the function is used in a program, you would have to remember to declare that global variable and make sure that it did not conflict with any other global variables already declared—a major drawback. Using a global variable would also make this function difficult to place in a function library. A better solution is to declare the variable that holds the generated number to be **static**, as in this program fragment:

```
series()
{
   static int series_num;

   series_num = series_num+23;
   return(series_num);
}
```

In this example, the variable **series_num** stays in existence between function calls, instead of coming and going the way a normal local variable would. This means that each call to **series( )** can produce a new member of the series based on the last number without declaring that variable globally.

You may have noticed something unusual about the function **series( )** as it stands in the example. The static variable **series_num** is never initialized to a known value. This means that the first time the function is called, **series_num** has some random value. While this is acceptable for some applications, most series generators need a well-defined starting point. To do this requires that **series_num** be initialized before the first call to **series( )**, which can easily be done only if **series_num** is a global variable. However, not making **series_num** global was the entire point of making it **static** to begin with. This leads to the second use of **static**.

static Global Variables

When the specifier **static** is applied to a global variable, it instructs the compiler to create a global variable that is known only to the file in which the **static** global variable is declared. This means that even though the variable is global, other routines in other files may have no knowledge of it or alter its contents; thus it is not subject to side effects. For the few situations where a local **static** cannot do the job, you can create a small file that contains only the functions that need the global **static** variable, separately compile that file, and use it without fear of side effects.

To see how a global **static** can be used, the series generator example from the previous section is recoded so that a starting "seed" value can be used to initialize the series through a call to a second function called **series_start( )**. The entire file containing **series( )**, **series_start( )**, and **series_num** follows:

```
/* this must all be in one file - preferably by itself */

static int series_num;

series()
{
   series_num = series_num+23;
   return(series_num);
}

/* initialize series_num */
void series_start(seed)
int seed;
{
   series_num = seed;
}
```

Calling **series_start()** with some known integer value initializes the series generator. After that, calls to **series()** will generate the next element in the series.

The names of local **static** variables are known only to the function or block of code in which they are declared, and the names of global **static** variables are known only to the file in which they reside. This means that if you place the **series()** and **series_start()** functions in a separate file, you can use the functions, but you cannot reference the variable **series_num**. It is hidden from the rest of the code in your program. In fact, you may even declare and use another variable called **series_num** in your program (in another file, of course) and not confuse anything. In essence, the **static** modifier allows variables to exist that are known to the functions that need them, without confusing other functions.

The **static** variables enable you to hide portions of your program from other portions. This can be a tremendous advantage when trying to manage a very large and complex program. The **static** storage specifier lets you create very general functions that can go into libraries for later use.

Register Variables

Turbo C has one last storage specifier that applies only to variables of the types **int** and **char**. The **register** specifier requests Turbo C to keep the value of variables declared with this modifier in the register of the CPU rather than in memory, where normal variables are stored. This means that operations can occur much faster on **register** variables than on variables stored in memory because the values of these variables are actually held in the CPU and do not require a memory access to determine or modify their values. This makes **register** variables ideal for loop control. The **register** specifier can only be applied to local variables and to the formal parameters in a function and are, by default, **auto** variables. Hence, global **register** variables are disallowed. The following is an example of how to declare a **register** variable of type **int** and use it to control a loop. This function computes the result of M^e for integers.

```
int_pwr(m, e)
int m;
register int e;
{
   register int temp;

   temp = 1;

   for(; e; e--) temp *= m;
   return temp;
}
```

In this example, both **e** and **temp** are declared to be **register** variables because both are used within the loop. In general practice, **register** variables are used where they will do the most good, that is, in places where many references will be made to the same variable. This is important because you may not have an unlimited number of register variables in use at one time.

Turbo C supports two register variables at a time. You don't have to worry about declaring too many **register** variables, though, because the compiler automatically makes register variables into nonregister variables when the limit is reached. (This is done to ensure portability of C code across a broad line of processors.) Throughout this book most loop control variables will be **register** variables.

Assignment Statements

The general form of the *assignment statement* is

    variable—name = expression;

where an expression may be as simple as a single constant or as complex as a combination of variables, operators, and constants. Like BASIC and FORTRAN, C uses a single equal sign to indicate assignment (unlike Pascal or Modula-2, which use the := construct). The target, or left part, of the assignment must be a variable, not a function or a constant.

Type Conversion in Assignments

Type conversion refers to the situation in which variables of one type are mixed with variables of another type. When this occurs in an assignment statement, the *type conversion rule* is very easy: The value of the right (expression) side of the assignment is converted to the type of the left side (target variable), as illustrated by this example:

```
int x;
char ch;
float   f;

func()
{
  ch = x;     /* 1 */
  x = f;      /* 2 */
  f = ch;     /* 3 */
  f = x;      /* 4 */
}
```

In line 1, the left, high-order bits of the integer variable **x** are lopped off, leaving **ch** with the lower 8 bits. If **x** was between 256 and 0 to begin with, **ch** and **x** would have identical values. Otherwise, the value of **ch** would reflect only the lower order bits of **x**. In line 2, **x** receives the nonfractional part of **f**. In line 3, **f** converts the 8-bit integer value stored in point format. This also happens in line 4, except that **f** converts an integer value into the floating point format.

When converting from integers to characters, or from long integers to integers, the basic rule is that the appropriate amount of high-order bits will be removed. This means 8 bits will be lost when going from an integer to a character and 16 bits will be lost when going from a long integer to an integer.

Table 2-4 synopsizes these type conversions. You must remember two important points that can affect the portability of the code you write:

1. The conversion of an **int** to a **float**, or a type **float** to **double** and so on, does not add any precision or accuracy. These kinds of conversions change only the form in which the value is represented.

Target Type	Expression Type	Possible Info Loss
signed char	char	If value > 127, then targets will be negative
char	short int	High-order 8 bits
char	int	High-order 8 bits
char	long int	High-order 24 bits
short int	int	None
short int	long int	High-order 16 bits
int	long int	High-order 16 bits
int	float	Fractional part and possibly more
float	double	Precision, result rounded
double	long double	None

Table 2-4.   The Outcome of Common Type Conversions Assuming a 16-bit Word

2. Some C compilers (and processors) always treat a **char** variable as positive, no matter what value it has, when converting it to an integer or float. Other compilers treat **char** variable values greater than 127 as negative numbers when converting (as does Turbo C). Generally speaking, you should use **char** variables for characters and **int**, **short int**, or **signed char** when needed to avoid a possible portability problem in this area.

To use Table 2-4 to make a conversion not directly shown, simply convert one type at a time until you finish. For example, to convert from **double** to an **int**, first convert from a **double** to a **float** and then from a **float** to an **int**.

If you have used a computer language like Pascal, which prohibits this automatic type conversion, you may think that C is very loose and sloppy. However, keep in mind that C was designed to make the life of the programmer easier by allowing work to be done in C rather than assembly language. To do this, C has to allow such type conversions. It is your job to remember the rules.

Variable Initializations

You can give variables in C a value when they are declared by placing an equal sign and a constant after the variable name. This is called an *initialization*, and its general form is

    type variable—name = constant;

Some examples are

```
char ch = 'a';
int first = 0;
float balance = 123.23
```

Global and **static** global variables are initialized only at the start of the program. Local variables, including **static** local variables, are initialized each time the block in which they are declared is entered. All global variables are initialized to zero if no other initializer is specified. Local and register variables that are not initialized have unknown values before the first assignment is made to them.

Constants

Constants in C are fixed values that may not be altered by the program. They can be of any data type, as shown in the example in Table 2-5.

Turbo C supports one other type of constant in addition to those of the predefined data types. This is a string. All string constants are enclosed between double quotes, such as **"this is a test"**. Do not confuse the strings with characters. A single character constant is enclosed by single quotes, such as **'a'**. Because strings are simply arrays of characters, they will be discussed in Chapter 5.

Data Type	Constant Examples
char	'a' '\n' '9'
int	1 123 21000 −234
long int	35000 −34
short int	10 −12 90
unsigned int	10000 987 40000
float	123.23 4.34e−3
double	123.23 12312333 −0.9876324

Table 2-5.   Constant Examples for Data Types

Backslash Character Constants

Enclosing all character constants in single quotes works for most printing characters, but a few, such as the carriage return, are impossible to enter from the keyboard. For these characters, C uses special backslash codes, which are shown in Table 2-6.

You use a backslash code exactly the same way you would use any other character. For example,

```
ch='\t';

printf("this is a test\n");
```

first assigns a tab to **ch** and then prints **this is a test** on the screen followed by a new line.

Code	Meaning
\b	Backspace
\n	New line
\r	Carriage return
\t	Horizontal tab
\"	Double quotation mark
\'	Single quotation mark
\0	Null
\\	Backslash
\v	Vertical tab
\a	Alert
\o	Octal constant
\x	Hexadecimal constant

Table 2-6.   Backslash Codes

Operators

Turbo C is very rich in built-in operators. An *operator* is a symbol that tells the compiler to perform specific mathematical or logical manipulations. There are three general classes of operators in C: arithmetic, relational and logical, and bitwise. In addition, C has some special operators for particular tasks.

Arithmetic Operators

Table 2-7 lists the *arithmetic operators* allowed in C. The operators $+$, $-$, $*$, and $/$ all work the same way in C as they do in most other computer languages. They can be applied to almost any built-in data type allowed by C. When $/$ is applied to an integer or character, any remainder is truncated; for example, **10/3** equals 3 in integer division.

The modulo division operator % also works in C the way that it does in other languages. Remember that the modulo

Operator	Action
$-$	Subtraction, also unary minus
$+$	Addition
$*$	Multiplication
$/$	Division
%	Modulo division
$--$	Decrement
$++$	Increment

Table 2-7.   Arithmetic Operators

division operation yields the remainder of an integer division. However, as such, % cannot be used on type **float** or **double**. The following code fragment illustrates its use:

```
int x, y;

x = 10;
y = 3;

printf("%d", x/y);    /* will display 3 */
printf("%d", x%y);    /* will display 1, the remainder of
                         the integer division */

x = 1;
y = 2;

printf("%d %d", x/y, x%y); /*  will display 0 1 */
```

The reason the last line prints a 0 and 1 is because 1/2 in integer division is 0 with a remainder of 1. 1%2 yields the remainder 1.

The unary minus, in effect, multiplies its single operand by −1. That is, any number preceded by a minus sign switches its sign.

Increment and Decrement

Two very useful operators in C that are not generally found in other computer languages are the increment and decrement operators, ++ and −−. The operation ++ adds 1 to its operand, and −− subtracts 1. For example:

```
x=x+1;  is the same as  ++x;

x=x-1;  is the same as  --x;
```

Both the increment and decrement operators may either precede or follow the operand. For example,

```
x=x+1;
```

can be written as

```
++x;
```

or

```
x++;
```

However, there is a difference when increment and decrement operators are used in expressions. When the operator precedes its operand, C performs the increment or decrement operation before using the operand's value. If the operator follows its operand, C uses the operand's value before incrementing or decrementing it. Consider the following:

```
x = 10;
y = ++x;
```

In this case, **y** is set to 11. However, if the code had been written as

```
x = 10;
y = x++;
```

y would have been set to 10. In both cases, **x** is still set to 11; the difference is when it happens. There are significant advantages in being able to control when the increment or decrement operation takes place.

The precedence of the arithmetic operators is as follows:

highest	++ −−
	− (unary minus)
	* / %
lowest	+ −

Operators on the same precedence level are evaluated by the compiler from left to right. Of course, parentheses may be used to alter the order of evaluation. Parentheses are treated by C in the same way they are treated by virtually all other computer languages: They give the operation or set of operations they enclose a higher precedence level.

Relational and Logical Operators

In the term *relational operator* the word *relational* refers to the relationships that values can have with one another. In the term *logical operator* the word *logical* refers to the ways these relationships can be connected by using the rules of formal logic. Because the relational and logical operators often work together, they will be discussed together here.

The key to the concepts of relational and logical operators is the idea of true and false. In C, "true" is any value other than 0. "False" is 0. Expressions that use relational or logical operators will return 0 for false and 1 for true.

Table 2-8 shows the relational and logical operators. The truth table for the logical operators is shown here using 1's and 0's:

p	q	p && q	p ‖ q	!p
0	0	0	0	1
0	1	0	1	1
1	1	1	1	0
1	0	0	1	0

Both relational and logical operators are lower in precedence than arithmetic operators. This means that an expression like **10 > 1+12** is evaluated as if it were written **10 > (1+12)**. The result is, of course, false.

Several operations can be combined in one expression, as shown here:

```
10>5 && !(10<9) || 3<=4
```

will evaluate true.

Relational Operators

Operator	Action
>	Greater than
>=	Greater than or equal
<	Less than
<=	Less than or equal
==	Equal
!=	Not equal

Logical Operators

Operator	Action
&&	AND
||	OR
!	NOT

Table 2-8.   Relational and Logical Operators

The following list shows the relative precedence of the relational and logical operators:

```
highest  !
         >  >=  <  <=
         ==  !=
         &&
lowest   ||
```

As with arithmetic expressions, it is possible to use parentheses to alter the natural order of evaluation in a relational or logical expression. For example,

```
!1 && 0
```

is false because the ! is evaluated first, and then the && is evaluated. However, when the same expression is parenthesized as shown here, the result is true.

```
!(1 && 0)
```

Remember, all relational and logical expressions produce a result of either 0 or 1. Therefore the following program fragment is not only correct, but also prints the number 1 on the display:

```
int x;

x = 100;
printf("%d", x>10);
```

Bitwise Operators

Unlike many other languages, C supports a complete complement of *bitwise operators*. Since C was designed to take the place of assembly language for most programming tasks, it had to have the ability to support all (or at least many) operations that can be done in assembly language. Bitwise operations are the testing, setting, or shifting of the actual bits in a byte or word, which correspond to C's standard **char** and **int** data types, and variants. Bitwise operators cannot be used on type **float**, **double**, **long double**, **void**, or other more complex types. Table 2-9 lists these operators.

The bitwise AND, OR, and NOT (one's complement) are governed by the same truth table as their logical equivalents except that they work on a bit-by-bit level. The exclusive OR ^ has the truth table shown here:

p	q	p ^ q
0	0	0
1	0	1
1	1	0
0	1	1

Operator	Action
&	AND
|	OR
^	Exclusive OR (XOR)
~	The one's complement (NOT)
>>	Shift right
<<	Shift left

Table 2-9.   The Bitwise Operators

As the table indicates, the outcome of an XOR is true only if exactly one of the operands is true; otherwise it is false.

Bitwise operations most often find application in device drivers, such as modem programs, disk-file routines, and printer routines, because the bitwise operations can be used to mask certain bits, such as parity. (The parity bit is used to confirm that the rest of the bits in the byte are unchanged. It is usually the high-order bit in each byte.)

The bitwise AND is most commonly used to turn bits off. That is, any bit that is 0 in either operand sets the corresponding bit in the outcome to 0. For example, the following function reads a character from the modem port using the function **read—modem()** and resets the parity bit to 0.

```
char get_char_from_modem()
{
    char ch;

    ch = read_modem(); /* get a character from the
                          modem port */
    return(ch & 127);
}
```

Parity is indicated by the eighth bit, which is set to 0 by ANDing it with a byte that has bits 1 through 7 set to 1 and bit 8 set to 0. The expression **ch & 127** means to AND the bits in **ch** with the bits in the number 127. The net result is that the eighth bit of **ch** is set to 0. In the following example, assume that **ch** had received the character 'A' and had the parity bit set:

```
parity bit
  1 1 0 0 0 0 0 1        ch containing an 'A' with parity set
  0 1 1 1 1 1 1 1        127 in binary
& ----------------------  do bitwise AND
  0 1 0 0 0 0 0 1        'A' without parity
```

The bitwise OR, as the reverse of AND, can be used to turn bits on. Any bit that is set to 1 in either operand will cause the corresponding bit in the variable to be set to 1. For example, **128 | 3** is

```
  1 0 0 0 0 0 0 0        128 in binary
  0 0 0 0 0 0 1 1        3 in binary
| ----------------------  bitwise OR
  1 0 0 0 0 0 1 1        result
```

An exclusive OR, usually abbreviated XOR, will turn a bit on only if the bits being compared are different. For example, **127 ^ 120** is

```
  0 1 1 1 1 1 1 1        127 in binary
  0 1 1 1 1 0 0 0        120 in binary
^ ----------------------  bitwise XOR
  0 0 0 0 0 1 1 1        result
```

In general, bitwise ANDs, ORs and XORs apply their operations directly to each bit in the variable individually. For this reason, among others, bitwise operators are not generally used in conditional statements the way relational and logical operators are. For example if, **x=7**, then **x && 8** evaluates to true (1), whereas **x & 8** evaluates to false (0).

Remember: Relational and logical operators always produce a result that is either 0 or 1, whereas the similar bitwise operations may produce any arbitrary value in accordance with the specific operation. In other words, bitwise operations may have values other than 0 or 1, while the logical operators always evaluate to 0 or 1.

The shift operators, $>>$ and $<<$, move all bits in a variable to the right or left as specified. The general form of the shift right statement is

variable $>>$ number of bit positions

and the shift left statement is

variable $<<$ number of bit positions

As bits are shifted off one end, 0's are brought in the other end. Remember: A shift is not a rotate. That is, the bits shifted off one end do not come back around to the other. The bits shifted off are lost, and 0's are brought in.

Bit shift operations can be very useful when decoding external device input, like (D/A) converters, and reading status information. The bitwise shift operators can also be used to perform very fast multiplication and division of integers. A shift right effectively multiplies a number by 2 and a shift left divides it by 2, as shown in Table 2-10.

The 1's complement operator, $\sim$, reverses the state of each bit in the specified variable. That is, all 1's are set to 0, and all 0's are set to 1.

The bitwise operators are used often in cipher routines. If you wished to make a disk file appear unreadable, you could perform some bitwise manipulations on it. One of the simplest methods would be to complement each byte by using the 1's complement to reverse each bit in the byte as shown here:

Original byte	0 0 1 0 1 1 0 0 ----	
		|
After 1st complement	1 1 0 1 0 0 1 1	|-same
		|
After 2d complement	0 0 1 0 1 1 0 0 ----	

	x as Each Statement Executes	Value of x
char x;		
x=7;	0 0 0 0 0 1 1 1	7
x<<1;	0 0 0 0 1 1 1 0	14
x<<3;	0 1 1 1 0 0 0 0	112
x<<2;	1 1 0 0 0 0 0 0	192
x>>1;	0 1 1 0 0 0 0 0	96
x>>2;	0 0 0 1 1 0 0 0	24

Each left shift multiplies by 2. Notice that information has been lost after x<<2 because a bit was shifted off the end.

Each right shift divides by 2. Notice that subsequent divisions do not bring back any lost bits.

Table 2-10.   Multiplication and Division with Shift Operators

Notice that a sequence of two complements in a row always produces the original number. Hence, the first complement would represent the coded version of that byte. The second complement would decode it to its original value.

You could use the **encode()** function shown here to encode a character:

```
char encode(ch)  /* a simple cipher function */
char ch;
{
  return(~ch); /* complement it */
}
```

The ? Operator

Turbo C has a very powerful and convenient operator that can be used to replace certain statements of the if-then-else form. The ternary operator ? takes the general form

Exp1 ? Exp2 : Exp3

where Exp1, Exp2, and Exp3 are expressions. Notice the use and placement of the colon.

The **?** operator works like this. Exp1 is evaluated. If it is true, then Exp2 is evaluated and becomes the value of the expression. If Exp1 is false, then Exp3 is evaluated and its value becomes the value of the expression. For example:

```
x = 10;

y = x>9 ? 100 : 200;
```

In this example, **y** is assigned the value 100. If **x** had been less than 9, **y** would have received the value 200. The same code written using the **if/else** statement would be

```
x = 10;

if(x>9) y = 100;
else y = 200;
```

The **?** operator will be discussed more fully in Chapter 3 in relationship to C's other conditional statements.

The & and * Pointer Operators

A pointer is the memory address of a variable. A pointer variable is a variable that is specifically declared to hold a pointer to its specified type. Pointers have two main functions in C:

1. They provide a very fast means of referencing array elements.

2. They allow C functions to modify their calling parameters.

These topics and uses will be dealt with later. However, the two operators that are used to manipulate pointers will be discussed here.

The first pointer operator is **&**. It is a unary operator that returns the memory address of its operand. (Remember that a unary operator only requires one operand.) For example,

```
m = &count;
```

places into **m** the memory address of the variable **count**.

This address is the computer's internal location of the variable. It has nothing to do with the value of **count**. The operation of the **&** can be remembered as returning "the address of..." Therefore, the above assignment statement could be verbalized as "m receives the address of count."

To better understand the above assignment, assume the variable **count** uses memory location 2000 to store its value. After the above assignment, **m** will have the value 2000.

The second operator, *****, is the complement of the **&**. It is a unary operator that returns the *value of the variable located at the address that follows*. For example, if **m** contains the memory address of the variable **count**,

```
q = *m;
```

places the value of **count** into **q**. For example, if **count** has the value 100, the value of **q** is 100 because 100 is stored at location 2000, which is the memory address that was stored in **m**. The operation of the ***** can be remembered as "at address." In this case, then, the statement could be read as "q receives the value at address m."

Unfortunately, the multiplication sign and the "at address" sign are the same and the bitwise AND and the "address of" sign are the same. These operators have no relationship to each other. Both **&** and ***** have a higher precedence than all other arithmetic operators except the unary minus, with which they are equal.

Variables that will hold pointers must be declared as such. Variables that will hold memory addresses, or pointers as they are called in C, must be declared by putting a * in front of the variable name to indicate to the compiler that it will hold a pointer to that type of variable. For example, to declare a **char** pointer variable called **ch**, you would write

```
char *ch;
```

Here **ch** is not a character but a pointer to a character; there is a big difference. The type of data that a pointer will be pointing to, in this case **char**, is called the *base type* of the pointer. However, the pointer variable itself is a variable that will be used to hold the address to an object of the base type. Hence, a character pointer (or any pointer for that matter) will be of sufficient size to hold an address as defined by the architecture of the computer on which it is running. The key point to remember is that a pointer should be used to point only to data that is of that pointer's base type.

You can mix both pointer and nonpointer directives in the same declaration statement. For example,

```
int x, *y, count;
```

declares **x** and **count** to be integer types, and **y** to be a pointer to an integer type.

Here, the * and & operators are used to put the value 10 into a variable called **target**:

```
main()  /* assignment with * and & */
{
  int target, source;
  int *m;

  source = 10;
  m = &source;
  target = *m;
}
```

The *sizeof* Compile-Time Operator

sizeof is a unary compile-time operator that returns the length, in bytes, of the variable or parenthesized type specifier it precedes. For example,

```
float f;

printf("%f ", sizeof f);
printf("%d", sizeof(int));
```

displays **4 2.**

Remember that to compute the size of a type you must enclose the type name in parentheses. This is not necessary for variable names.

The principal use of **sizeof** is to help generate portable code when that code depends on the size of the built-in data types. For example, imagine a database program that needs to store six integer values per record. To make the database program portable to the widest variety of computers, you must not assume that an integer is 2 bytes; you must determine its actual length using **sizeof**. This being the case, the following routine could be used to write a record to a disk file:

```
/* write a record to a disk file */
put_rec(fp, rec)
file * fp; /* file pointer */
int rec[6];
{
  int size, len;

  size = sizeof(rec);
  len = fwrite(rec, size, 1, fp);
  if(len<>size) printf("write error");
}
```

The key point of this example is that, coded as shown, **put—rec()** will compile and run correctly on any computer—including those with 4-byte integers. Correctly using **sizeof** means that you can use Turbo C to develop code that will ultimately run in a different environment.

The Comma Operator

The comma operator is used to string together several expressions. The left side of the comma operator is always evaluated as **void**. This means that the expression on the right side becomes the value of the total comma-separated expression. For example,

```
x = (y=3, y+1);
```

first assigns **y** the value 3 and then assigns **x** the value 4. The parentheses are necessary because the comma operator has a lower precedence than the assignment operator.

Essentially, the comma causes a sequence of operations to be performed. When it is used on the right side of an assignment statement, the value assigned is the value of the last expression of the comma-separated list. For example:

```
y = 10;
x = (y=y-5, 25/y);
```

After execution, **x** has the value 5 because **y**'s original value of 10 is reduced by 5, and then that value is divided into 25, yielding 5 as the result.

You might think of the comma operator as having the same meaning that the word *and* has in normal English when it is used in the phrase "do this and this and this."

The . and —> Operators

The . (dot) operator and the —> (arrow) operator are used to reference individual elements of structures and unions. Structures and unions are compound data types that can be referenced under a single name. Unions and structures will be thoroughly covered in Chapter 7, but a short discussion of the operators used with them is given here.

The dot operator is used when the structure or union is global or when the referencing code is in the same function as the structure or union declaration. The arrow operator is used when a pointer to a structure or union is used. Suppose you were given the global structure

```
struct employee {
        char name[80];
        int age;
        float wage;
} emp;
```

To assign the value 123.23 to element **wage** of structure **emp**, you would write

```
emp.wage = 123.23;
```

However, the same assignment using a pointer to structure **emp** would be

```
emp->wage = 123.23;
```

There is a very important difference between older versions of C and Turbo C in regard to the way they pass structures and unions to functions. It is important to understand this difference if you will be porting your code to a great many environments. In the older approach, only a pointer to a structure or union is actually passed to a function. (Notice that this is an exception to C's call-by-value method of parameter passing.) However, as specified by the proposed ANSI standard, the entire structure or union is actually passed, making it consistent with the way other type arguments are passed to functions. Since Turbo C follows the ANSI standard, it uses the later approach.

[] and ( )

In C parentheses do the expected job of increasing the precedence of the operations inside them.

Square brackets perform array-indexing. Simply, given an array, the expression within the square brackets provides an index into that array. For example,

```
char s[80];

main()
{
    s[3]='X';
    printf("%c", s[3]);
}
```

first assigns the value 'X' to the fourth element (remember, all arrays in C begin at 0) of array s, and then prints that element.

Precedence Summary

Table 2-11 lists the precedence of all C operators. Note that all operators, except the unary operators and ?, associate from left to right. The unary operators, * & −, and ? associate from right to left.

Expressions

Operators, constants, and variables are the constituents of *expressions*. An expression in C is any valid combination of those pieces. Because most expressions follow the general rules of algebra, they are often taken for granted. However, a few aspects of expressions relate specifically to C and will be discussed here.

Highest	() [] →.
	! ~ ++ −− − (type) * & sizeof
	* / %
	+ −
	<< >>
	< <= > >=
	== !=
	&
	^
	│
	&&
	││
	?
	= += −= *= /=
Lowest	,

Table 2-11.   Precedence of C Operators

Type Conversion in Expressions

When constants and variables of different types are mixed in an expression, they are converted to the same type. Turbo C converts all operands "up" to the type of the largest operand. This is done on an operation-by-operation basis as described in the following type conversion rules:

1. All **char**s and **short int**s are converted to **int**s. All **float**s are converted to **double**s.

2. For all operand pairs, if one of the operands is a **long double**, the other operand is converted to **long double**.

Otherwise, if one of the operands is **double**, the other operand is converted to **double**.

Otherwise, if one of the operands is **long**, the other operand is converted to **long**.

Otherwise, if one of the operands is **unsigned**, the other is converted to **unsigned**.

Once these conversion rules have been applied, each pair of operands is of the same type and the result of each operation is the same as the type of both operands. Please note that rule two has several conditions that must be applied in sequence.

For example, consider the type conversions that occur in Figure 2-1.

First, the character **ch** is converted to an integer and **float f** is converted to **double**. Then the outcome of **ch/i** is converted to a **double** because **f*d** is **double**. The final result is **double** because, by this time, both operands are **double**.

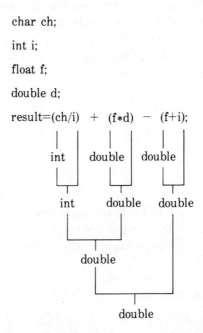

Figure 2-1.   An example of type conversion

Casts

It is possible to force an expression to be of a specific type by using a construct called a *cast*. The general form of a cast is

(*type*) expression

where *type* is one of the standard C data types. For example, if you wished to make sure the expression **x/2** would be evaluated to type **float** you could write it as

```
(float) x/2
```

Casts are often considered operators. As an operator, a cast is unary and has the same precedence as any other unary operator.

Although casts are not used a great deal in programming, there are times when they can be very useful. For example, suppose you wish to use an integer for loop control, yet to perform computation on it requires a fractional part, as in the following program:

```
main() /* print i and i/2 with fractions */
{
   int i;

   for(i=1; i<=100; ++t )
     printf("%d / 2 is: %f", i, (float) i /2);
}
```

Without the cast **(float)**, only an integer division would be performed; but the cast ensures that the fractional part of the answer will be displayed on the screen.

Spacing and Parentheses

To aid readability, an expression in Turbo C may have tabs and spaces in it at your discretion. For example, the following two expressions are the same:

```
x=10/y~(127/x);

x = 10 / y ~(127/x);
```

Use of redundant or additional parentheses does not cause errors or slow down the execution of the expression. You are encouraged to use parentheses to clarify the order of evaluation, both for yourself and for others who may have to read your program later. For example, which of the following two expressions is easier to read?

```
x=y/2-34*temp&127;

x=(y/2) - ((34*temp) & 127);
```

C Shorthand

C has a special shorthand that simplifies the coding of a certain type of assigment statement. For example,

```
x = x+10;
```

can be written, in C shorthand, as

```
x += 10;
```

The operator pair += tells the compiler to assign to **x** the value of **x** plus 10.

This shorthand works for all the binary operators in C (those that require two operands). The general form of the shorthand is

var = var operator expression

is the same as

var operator = expression

For another example,

```
x = x-100;
```

is the same as

```
x -= 100;
```

   You will see shorthand notation used widely in professionally written C programs, and you should become familiar with it.

Program Control Statements

This chapter discusses Turbo C's rich and varied program control statements. These include the loop constructs **while**, **for**, and **do/while**, the **if** and **switch** conditional statements, and **break**, **continue**, and **goto** statements. (Although the **return** statement technically affects program control, its discussion is deferred until the following chapter on functions.) The **exit( )** function is discussed here because it can also affect the flow of a program.

True and False in C

Most program control statements in any computer language, including C, rely on a conditional test that determines what course of action is to be taken. The conditional test produces either a true or false value. Unlike many other computer languages that specify special values for true and false, a true value in C is any nonzero value, including negative numbers. A false value is zero. This approach to true and false is implemented in C primarily because it allows a wide range of routines to be coded extremely efficiently.

C Statements

According to the C syntax, a statement can consist of one of the following: a single statement, a block of statements, or nothing (in the case of empty statements). In the descriptions presented here, the term *statement* is used to mean all three possibilities.

Conditional Statements

Turbo C supports two types of conditional statements: **if** and **switch**. In addition, the **?** operator is an alternative to the **if** in certain circumstances.

if

The general form of the **if** statement is

    if(*expression*) statement;
    else statement;

where **statement** may be either a single statement or a block of statements. (Remember that in C a *block* is a group of statements surrounded by braces.) The **else** clause is optional.

The general form of the **if** with blocks of statements as objects is

```
if(expression) {
    statement sequence
}
else {
    statement sequence
}
```

If the expression is true (anything other than 0), the statement or block that forms the target of the **if** is executed; otherwise, if it exists, the statement or block that is the target of the **else** is executed. Remember, only the code associated with the **if** or the code associated with the **else** executes, never both.

For example, consider the following program, which plays a very simple version of "guess the magic number" game. It prints the message ** **Right** ** when the player guesses the magic number.

```
main()  /* magic number program */
{
  int magic = 123;  /* magic number */
  int guess;

  scanf("%d",&guess);

  if(guess == magic) printf("** Right **");
}
```

This program uses the equality operator to determine whether the player's guess matches the magic number. If it does, the message is printed on the screen.

Taking the magic number program further, the next version illustrates the use of the **else** statement to print a message when the wrong number is tried.

```
main()  /* magic number program - improvement 1 */

{
  int magic = 123;  /* magic number */
  int guess;

  scanf("%d",&guess);
```

```
if(guess == magic) printf("** Right **");
else printf(".. Wrong ..");

}
```

Nested ifs

One of the most confusing aspects of **if** statements in any programming language is nested ifs. A *nested if* is an **if** statement that is the object of either an **if** or an **else**. The reason that nested **if**s are so troublesome is that it can be difficult to know what **else** associates with what **if**. For example:

```
if(x)
  if(y) printf("1");
  else printf("2");
```

To which **if** does the **else** refer?

Fortunately, C provides a simple rule for resolving this type of situation. In C the **else** is linked to the closest **if** that is within the same block and that does not already have an **else** statement associated with it. In this case, the **else** is associated with the **if(y)** statement. To make the **else** associate with the **if(x)**, you must use braces to override its normal association, as shown here:

```
if(x) {
  if(y) printf("1");
}
else printf("2");
```

The **else** is now associated with the **if(x)** because it is no longer part of the **if(y)** object block. Because of C's scope rules, the **else** now has no knowledge of the **if(y)** statement because it is hidden inside a code block. In essence, the **if(y)** and the **else** are no longer in the same block of code.

A further improvement to the magic number program provides the player with feedback on how close each guess is. This is accomplished by using a nested **if**.

```
main()   /* magic number program improvement 2 */
{
  int magic = 123;   /* magic number */
  int guess;

  scanf("%d", &guess);

  if(guess == magic) {
    printf("** Right ** ");
    printf("%d is the magic number", magic);
  }
  else {
    printf(".. Wrong .. ");
    if(guess > magic) printf("Too high");
    else printf("Too low");
  }
}
```

The if-else-if Ladder

A common programming construct is the *if-else-if ladder*. It looks like this:

> if (*expression*)
>   statement;
> else if (*expression*)
>   statement;
> else if (*expression*)
>   statement;
>
>   .
>   .
>   .
>
> else
>   statement;

The conditions are evaluated from the top downward. As soon as a true condition is found, the statement associated with it is executed, and the rest of the ladder is bypassed. If none of the conditions are true, the final **else** is executed. The final **else** often acts as a *default condition;* that is, if all other conditional tests fail, the last **else** statement is performed. If the final **else** is not present, no action takes place if all other conditions are false.

Using an if-else-if ladder the magic number program becomes

```
main()  /* magic number program version 3 */
{
  int magic = 123;  /* magic number */
  int guess;

  scanf("%d", &guess);

  if(guess == magic) {
    printf("** Right ** ");
    printf("%d is the magic number", magic);
  }
  else if(guess > magic)
    printf(".. Wrong .. Too High");
  else printf(".. Wrong .. Too Low");

}
```

The ? Alternative

The ? operator can be used to replace **if/else** statements of the general form

> if(*condition*)
>   expression
> else
>   expression

The key restriction is that the target of both the **if** and the **else** must be a single expression—not another C statement.

The **?** is called a *ternary operator* because it requires three operands and takes the general form

> Exp1 ? Exp2 : Exp3

where Exp1, Exp2, and Exp3 are expressions. Notice the use and placement of the colon.

The value of an **?** expression is determined in this way. Exp1 is evaluated. If it is true, Exp2 is evaluated and becomes the value of the entire **?** expression. If Exp1 is false, Exp3 is evaluated and its value becomes the value of the expression. For example:

```
x = 10;

y = x>9 ? 100 : 200;
```

In this example, **y** is assigned the value 100. If **x** had been less than 9, **y** would have received the value 200. The same code written using the **if/else** statement would be

```
x = 10;

if(x>9) y = 100;
else y = 200;
```

However, the use of the **?** operator to replace **if/else** statements is not restricted to assignments. Remember that all functions (except those declared as void) can return a value. Hence it is permissible to use one or more function calls in a C expression. When the function's name is encountered, the function is, of course, executed so that its return value can be determined. Therefore, it is possible to execute one or more function calls using the **?** operator by placing them in the expressions that form the operands.

For example:

```
main()
{
  int t;

  printf(": ");
  scanf("%d", &t);

  /* print proper message */
  t ? f1(t)+f2() : printf("zero entered");

}
```

```
f1(n)
int n;
{
  printf("%d ",n);
}

f2()
{
  printf("entered");
}
```

In this simple example, if you enter **0**, the **printf()** function is called, and the **zero entered** message appears. If you enter any other number, both **f1()** and **f2()** are executed. It is important to note that the value of the **?** expression is discarded in this example; it is not necessary to assign it to anything.

A word of warning: Turbo C may rearrange the order of evaluation of an expression while performing code optimization. This could cause the functions that form the operands of the **?** operator to execute in a sequence you did not intend.

Using the **?** operator, it is possible to rewrite the magic number program again as shown here:

```
main()  /* magic number program */
{
  int magic = 123;  /* magic number */
  int guess;

  scanf("%d", &guess);
  if (guess == magic) {
      printf("** Right ** ");
      printf("%d is the magic number",magic);
  }
  else
      guess > magic ? printf("High") : printf("Low");
}
```

Here, the **?** operator causes the proper message to be displayed based on the outcome of the test guess>magic.

switch

Although the if-else-if ladder can perform multiway tests, it is hardly elegant. The code can be very hard to follow and can confuse even its author at a later date. For these reasons, Turbo C has a built-in multiple-branch decision statement called **switch**. A variable is successively tested against a list of integer or character constants. When a match is found, a statement or block of statements is executed. The general form of the **switch** statement is

```
switch(variable) {
    case constant1:
            statement sequence
            break;
    case constant2:
            statement sequence
            break;
    case constant3:
            statement sequence
            break;

        .
        .
        .

    default:
            statement sequence
}
```

where the **default** statement is executed if no matches are found. The **default** is optional and, if not present, no action takes place if all matches fail. When a match is found, the statement associated with that **case** is executed until the

break statement is reached or, in the case of the **default** (or last **case** if no **default** is present), the end of the **switch** statement is encountered.

There are three important things to know about the **switch** statement:

1. The **switch** differs from the **if** in that **switch** can test only for equality, whereas the **if** can evaluate a relational or logical expression.

2. No two **case** constants in the same **switch** can have identical values. Of course, a **switch** statement enclosed by an outer **switch** may have **case** constants that are the same.

3. If character constants are used in the **switch** they are automatically converted to their integer values.

The **switch** statement is often used to process keyboard commands, such as menu selection. As shown here, the function **menu( )** displays a menu for a spelling checker program and calls the proper procedures:

```
menu()
{
  char ch;

  printf("1. Check Spelling\n");
  printf("2. Correct Spelling errors\n");
  printf("3. Display Spelling Errors\n");
  printf("Strike Any Other Key to Skip\n");
  printf("      Enter your choice: ");

  ch = getche();  /* read the selection from
                     the keyboard */

  switch(ch) {
    case '1':
      check_spelling();
      break;
    case '2':
      correct_errors();
      break;
    case '3':
```

```
      display_errors();
      break;
    default :
      printf("No option selected");
  }
}
```

Technically, the **break** statements are optional inside the **switch** statement. They are used to terminate the statement sequence associated with each constant. If the **break** statement is omitted, execution continues into the next **case**'s statements until either a **break** or the end of the **switch** is reached. You can think of the **case**s as labels. Execution starts at the label that matches and continues until a **break** statement is found, or the **switch** ends. For example, the function shown here makes use of the "drop through" nature of the **case**s to simplify the code for a device driver input handler:

```
inp_handler()
{
  int ch, flag;

  ch = read_device(); /* read some sort of device */
  flag = -1;

  switch(ch) {
    case 1:  /* these cases have common statement */
    case 2:  /* sequences */
    case 3:
      flag = 0;
      break;
    case 4:
      flag = 1;
    case 5:
      error(flag);
      break;
    default:
      process(ch);
  }
}
```

This routine illustrates two facets of the **switch** statement. First, you can have empty conditions. In this case, the first three constants all execute the same statements:

```
flag = 0;
break;
```

Second, execution continues into the next **case** if no
break statement is present. If **ch** matches 4, **flag** is set to 1
and, because there is no **break** statement, execution continues and the statement **error(flag)** is executed. In this
case, **flag** has the value 1. If **ch** had matched 5, **error(flag)**
would have been called with a **flag** value of −1. The ability to
run **case**s together when no **break** is present enables you to
create very efficient code because it prevents the unwar-
ranted duplication of code.

It is important to understand that the statements associated with each label are not code blocks but *statement
sequences*. (Of course, the entire **switch** statement does define
a block.) This technical distinction is important only in certain special situations. For example, the following code
fragment is in error and will not even compile because it is
not possible to declare an **auto** variable in a statement
sequence:

```
/* this is incorrect */
switch(c) {
  case 1:
    auto int t;
    .
    .
    .
```

However, an **auto** variable could be added as shown
here:

```
/* this is correct */
switch(c) {
  auto int t;
  case 1:
    .
    .
    .
```

Of course, it is possible to create a block of code as one of
the statements in a sequence and declare an **auto** variable
within it as shown here:

```
/* this is correct */
switch(c) {
  case 1:
    if(1) { /* always true, used to create block */
      auto int t;
      .
      .
      .
    }
  .
  .
  .
```

Nested switch Statements

It is possible to have a **switch** as part of the statement sequence of an outer **switch**. Even if the **case** constants of the inner and outer **switch** contain common values there is no conflict. For example, the following code fragment is perfectly acceptable:

```
switch(x) {
  case 1:
    switch(y) {
      case 0: printf("divide by zero error");
              break;
      case 1: process(x,y);
    }
    break;
  case 2:
    .
    .
    .
```

Loops

In Turbo C, and all other modern programming languages, *loops* allow a set of instructions to be performed until a certain condition is reached. This condition may be predefined as in the **for** loop, or open-ended as in the **while** and **do** loops.

for

The general format of C's **for** loop is probably familiar to you because it is found in one form or another in all procedural programming languages. However, in C it has unexpected flexibility and power.

The general form of the **for** statement is

for(*initialization*; *condition*; *increment*) statement;

The **for** statement allows many variants, but there are three major statements:

1. The *initialization* is usually an assignment statement that is used to set the loop control variable.

2. The *condition* is a relational expression that determines when the loop will exit.

3. The *increment* defines how the loop-control variable will change each time the loop is repeated.

These three major sections must be separated by semicolons. The **for** loop continues to execute as long as the condition is true. Once the condition becomes false, program execution resumes on the statement following the **for**.

For a simple example, the following program prints the numbers 1 through 100 on the terminal:

```
main()
{
   int x;

   for(x=1; x<=100; x++) printf("%d ", x);
}
```

In the program, **x** is initially set to 1. Since **x** is less than 100, **printf()** is called, **x** is increased by 1, and **x** is tested to see if it is still less than or equal to 100. This process repeats

until **x** is greater than 100, at which point the loop terminates. In this example, **x** is the *loop-control variable*, which is
changed and checked each time the loop repeats.

Here is an example of a **for** loop that contains multiple
statements:

```
for(x=100; x!=65; x-=5) {
   z = sqrt(x);
   printf("The square root of %d, %f", x, z);
}
```

Both the **sqrt( )** and **printf( )** calls are executed until **x**
equals 65. Note that the loop is *negative running:* **x** was
initialized to 100 and 5 is subtracted from it each time the
loop repeats.

An important point about **for** loops is that the conditional test is always performed at the top of the loop. This
means that the code inside the loop may not be executed at
all if the condition is false to begin with. For example:

```
x = 10;

for(y=10; y!=x; ++y) printf("%d", y);

printf("%d", y);
```

This loop never executes because **x** and **y** are in fact equal
when the loop is entered. Because the conditional expression
is false, neither the body of the loop nor the increment portion of the loop is executed. Hence **y** still has the value 10
assigned to it, and the output is only the number 10 printed
once on the screen.

for Loop Variations

The preceding discussion described the most common form
of the **for** loop. However, several variations increase its
power, flexibility, and applicability to certain programming
situations.

One of the most common variations is achieved by using the comma operator to allow two or more variables to control the loop. (You should recall that the comma operator is used to string together a number of expressions in a sort of "do this and this" fashion. It is described in Chapter 2.) For example, this loop uses the variables **x** and **y** to control the loop, with both variables initialized inside the **for** statement:

```
for(x=0, y=0;x+y<10;++x) {
  y = getchar();
  y = y-'0';        /* subtract the ASCII code for 0
                       from y */
  .
  .
  .
}
```

Here commas separate the two initialization statements. Each time **x** is incremented, the loop repeats and **y**'s value is set by keyboard input. Both **x** and **y** must be at the correct value for the loop to terminate. It is necessary to initialize **y** to 0 so that its value is defined before the first evaluation of the conditional expression. If **y** were not defined it might, by chance or earlier program use, contain a 10, thereby making the conditional test false and preventing the loop from executing.

Another example of using multiple loop-control variables is found in the **reverse( )** function shown here. The purpose of **reverse( )** is to copy the contents of the first string argument back-to-front into the second string argument. If it is called with "hello" in s, upon completion, **r** contains "olleh."

```
/* copy s into r backwards */
void reverse(s, r)
char *s, *r;
{
  int i, j;

  for(i=strlen(s)-1,j=0; i>=0; j++,i--) r[i] = s[j];
  r[j] = '\0'; /* append null terminator */
}
```

The conditional expression does not necessarily involve simply testing the loop-control variable against some target value. In fact, the condition may be any relational or logical statement. This means that you can test for several possible terminating conditions. For example, this function could be used to log a user onto a remote system. In this example, the user is given three tries to enter the password. The loop terminates when either the three tries are used up or the correct password is entered.

```
sign_on()
{
  char str[20];
  int x;
  printf("enter password please:");
  gets(str);
  for(x=0; x<3 && strcmp(str,"password"); ++x) {
    printf("enter password please:");
    gets(str);
  }
  if(x==3) hang_up();
}
```

Remember that **strcmp()** is a standard library function that compares two strings and returns 0 if they match.

Another interesting variation of the **for** loop is created by remembering that each of the three sections of the **for** may consist of any valid C expression. They need not actually have anything to do with what the sections are generally used for. With this in mind, consider the following example:

```
main()
{
  int t;

  for(prompt(); t=readnum(); prompt())
    sqrnum(t);
}

prompt()
{
  printf(": ");
}
```

```
readnum()
{
  int t;

  scanf("%d", &t);
  return t;
}

sqrnum(num)
int num;
{
  printf("%d\n", num*num);
}
```

If you look closely at the **for** loop in **main ( )** you will see that each part of the **for** is composed of function calls that prompt the user and read a number entered from the keyboard. If the number entered is 0, the loop terminates because the conditional expression is false; otherwise the number is squared. Thus, in this **for** loop the initialization and increment portions are used in a nontraditional but completely valid sense.

Another interesting trait of the **for** loop is that pieces of the loop definition need not be there. In fact, there need not be an expression present for any of the sections; they are optional. For example, this loop runs until 123 is entered:

```
for(x=0; x!=123; ) scanf("%d", &x);
```

Notice that the increment portion of the **for** definition is blank. This means that each time the loop repeats, **x** is tested to see if it equals 123, but no further action takes place. If, however, you type 123 at the keyboard, the loop condition becomes false and the loop terminates.

It is not uncommon to see the initialization occur outside the **for** statement. This most frequently happens when the initial condition of the loop-control variable must be computed by some complex means. For example:

```
gets(s);  /* read a string into s */
if(*s) x = strlen(s); /* get the string's length */
```

```
for( ;x<10; ) {
  printf("%d", x);
  ++x;
}
```

Here the initialization section has been left blank and **x** is initialized before the loop is entered.

The Infinite Loop

One of the most interesting uses of the **for** loop is the creation of the infinite loop. Since none of the three expressions that form the **for** loop are required, it is possible to make an endless loop by leaving the conditional expression empty. For example:

```
for(;;) printf(" this loop will run forever.\n");
```

Although you may have an initialization and increment expression, it is more common among C programmers to use the **for(;;)** with no expressions to signify an infinite loop.*

Actually, the **for(;;)** construct does not necessarily create an infinite loop because C's **break** statement, when encountered anywhere inside the body of a loop, causes immediate termination. (The **break** statement is discussed later in this chapter.) Program control then picks up at the code following the loop. For example:

```
ch = '\0';

for(;;) {
  ch = getchar();  /* get a character */
  if(x=='A') break;  /* exit the loop */
}

printf("you typed an A");
```

---

*There is a small but persistent group of C programmers who use the **while(1)** method of creating an infinite loop. They both work equally well. The **for(;;)** method is recommended only because it is the more common form.

This loop runs until 'A' is typed at the keyboard.

for Loops with No Bodies

A statement, as defined by the C syntax, may be empty. This means that the body of the **for** (or any other loop) may also be empty. This fact can be used to improve the efficiency of certain algorithms as well as to create time delay loops.

One of the most common tasks to occur in programming is the removal of spaces from an input stream. For example, a database may allow a query such as "show all balances less than 400." The database needs to have each word of the query fed to it separately, without spaces. That is, the database input processor recognizes "show" but not " show" as a command. The following loop removes any leading spaces from the stream pointed to by **str**:

```
for( ; *str==' '; str++) ;
```

As you can see, there is no body to this loop—and no need for one.

Time delay loops are often used in programs. The following shows how to create one using **for**:

```
for(t=0; t<SOME_VALUE; t++) ;
```

while

The second loop available in C is the **while**. The general form is

　　while(*condition*) statement;

where **statement**, as stated earlier, is either an empty statement, a single statement, or a block of statements that is to be repeated. The *condition* may be any expression, with true being any nonzero value. The loop iterates while the condition is true. When the condition becomes false, program control passes to the line after the loop code.

The following example shows a keyboard input routine that simply loops until 'A' is input:

```
wait_for_char()
{
  char ch;

  ch = '\0';  /* initialize ch */
  while(ch!='A')  ch = getchar();
}
```

First, **ch** is initialized to null. As a local variable, its value is not known when **wait—for—char()** is executed. The **while** loop begins by checking to see if **ch** is not equal to 'A'. Because **ch** was initialized to null beforehand, the test is true and the loop begins. Each time a key is pressed on the keyboard, the test is tried again. Once 'A' is input, the condition becomes false because **ch** equals 'A', and the loop terminates.

As with the **for** loop, **while** loops check the test condition at the top of the loop, which means that the loop code may not execute at all. This eliminates having to perform a separate conditional test before the loop. A good illustration of this is the function **pad()**, which adds spaces to the end of a string up to a predefined length. If the string is already at the desired length, no spaces are added.

```
/* add spaces to the end of a string */
void pad(s, length)
char *s;
int length;
{
  int l;

  l = strlen(s);  /* find out how long it is */

  while(l<length) {
    s[l] = ' ';    /* insert a space */
    l++;
  }

  s[l] = '\0';  /* strings need to be
                   terminated in a null */

}
```

The two arguments to **pad()** are **s**, a pointer to the string to lengthen, and **length**, the number of characters that **s** will be lengthened to. If the string **s** is already equal to or greater than **length**, the code inside the **while** loop never executes. If **s** is less than **length**, **pad()** adds the required number of spaces to the string. The **strlen()** function, which is part of the standard library, returns the length of the string.

Where several separate conditions may be needed to terminate a **while** loop, it is common to have only a single variable forming the conditional expression with the value of this variable being set at various points throughout the loop. For example:

```
void func1()
{
  int working;

  working = 1;    /* i.e., true */

  while(working) {
    working=process1();
    if(working)
      working=process2();
    if(working)
      working=process3();
  }
}
```

Here any of the three routines may be false and cause the loop to exit.

There need not be any statements at all in the body of the **while** loop. For example,

```
while((ch=getchar()) != 'A') ;
```

simply loops until '**A**' is typed at the keyboard. If you feel a bit uncomfortable with the assignment inside the **while** conditional expression, remember that the equal sign is really just an operator that evaluates to the value of the right-hand operand.

do/while

Unlike the **for** and **while** loops that test the loop condition at the top of the loop, the **do/while** loop checks its condition at the bottom of the loop. This means that a **do/while** loop always executes at least once. The general form of the **do/while** loop is

```
do {
    statement;
} while(condition);
```

Although the braces are not necessary when only one statement is present, they are usually used to improve readability and avoid confusion (to the reader), with the **while**.

This **do/while** reads numbers from the keyboard until one is less than or equal to 100.

```
do {
  scanf("%d", &num);
} while(num>100);
```

Perhaps the most common use of the **do/while** is in a menu selection routine. When a valid response is typed, it is returned as the value of the function. Invalid responses cause a reprompt. The following shows an improved version of the spelling-checker menu that was developed earlier in this chapter:

```
menu()
{

  char ch;

  printf("1. Check Spelling\n");
  printf("2. Correct Spelling Errors\n");
  printf("3. Display Spelling Errors\n");
  printf("     Enter your choice: ");
```

```
do {
    ch=getche();   /* read the selection from
                        the keyboard */
    switch(ch) {
      case '1':
        check_spelling();
        break;
      case '2':
        correct_errors();
        break;
      case '3':
        display_errors();
        break;
    }
  } while(ch!='1' && ch!='2' && ch!='3');
}
```

In the case of a menu function, you always want it to execute at least once. After the options have been displayed, the program loops until a valid option is selected.

break

The **break** statement has two uses. The first is to terminate a **case** in the **switch** statement, and is covered earlier in this chapter in the section on the **switch**. The second use is to force immediate termination of a loop, bypassing the normal loop conditional test. This use is examined here.

When the **break** statement is encountered inside a loop, the loop is immediately terminated and program control resumes at the next statement following the loop. For example:

```
main()
{
  int t;

  for(t=0; t<100; t++) {
    printf("%d ", t);
    if(t==10) break;
  }
}
```

This prints the numbers 0 through 10 on the screen and then terminates because the **break** causes immediate exit from the loop, overriding the conditional test **t<100** built into the loop.

The **break** statement is commonly used in loops in which a special condition can cause immediate termination. For example, here pressing one key can stop the execution of the **look—up( )** routine:

```
look_up(name)
char *name;
{
  char tname[40];
  int loc;

  loc=-1;
  do {
    loc = read_next_name(tname);
    if(kbhit()) break;
  } while(!strcmp(tname, name));
  return loc;
}
```

You can use this function to find a name in a database file. If the file is very long and you are tired of waiting, you could strike a key and return from the function early. The **kbhit( )** function returns zero if no key has been hit and nonzero otherwise.

A **break** causes an exit from only the innermost loop. For example,

```
for(t=0; t<100; +=t) {
  count = 1;
  for(;;) {
    printf("%d ", count);
    count++;
    if(count==10) break;
  }
}
```

prints the numbers 1 through 10 on the screen 100 times. Each time the **break** is encountered, control is passed back to the outer **for** loop.

A **break** used in a **switch** statement affects only that **switch** and not any loop the **switch** happens to be in.

exit( )

The function **exit( )**, which is found in the standard library, causes immediate termination of the entire program. Because the **exit( )** function stops program execution and forces a return to the operating system, its use is somewhat specific as a program control device, yet a great many C programs rely on it.

The function **exit( )** is traditionally called with an argument of 0 to indicate that termination is normal. Other arguments are used to indicate some sort of error that a higher-level process will be able to access.

A common use of **exit( )** occurs when a mandatory condition for the program's execution is not satisfied. For example, imagine a computer game in which a color graphics card must be present in the system. The **main( )** function of this game might look like

```
main()
{
  if(!color_card()) exit(1);
  play();
}
```

where **color_card( )** is a user-defined function that returns true if the color card is present. If the card is not in the system, **color_card( )** returns false and the program terminates.

As another example, **exit( )** is used by this version of **menu( )** to quit the program and return to the operating system.

```
menu()
{

   char ch;

   printf("1. Check Spelling\n");
   printf("2. Correct Spelling Errors\n");
   printf("3. Display Spelling Errors\n");
   printf("4. Quit\n");
   printf("        Enter your choice: ");

   do {
       ch = getchar();   /* read the selection from
                             the keyboard */
       switch(ch) {
         case '1':
           check_spelling();
           break;
         case '2':
           correct_errors();
           break;
         case '3':
           display_errors();
           break;
         case '4':
           exit(0);   /* return to OS */
       }
   } while(ch!='1' && ch!='2' && ch!='3');
}
```

continue

The **continue** statement works somewhat like the **break** statement. But instead of forcing termination, **continue** forces the next iteration of the loop to take place, skipping any code in between. For example, the following routine displays only positive numbers:

```
do {
  scanf("%d", &x);
  if(x<0) continue;
  printf("%d ", x);
} while(x!=100);
```

In **while** and **do/while** loops, a **continue** statement causes control to go directly to the conditional test and then continues the looping process. In the case of the **for**, first the increment part of the loop is performed, next the conditional test is executed, and finally, the loop continues. The previous example could be changed to allow only 100 numbers to be printed, as shown here:

```
for(t=0; t<100; ++t) {
  scanf("%d", &x);
  if(x<0) continue;
  printf("%d ", x);
}
```

In the following example, **continue** is used to expedite the exit for a loop by forcing the conditional test to be performed sooner:

```
void code()
{
  char done, ch;

  done = 0;
  while(!done) {
    ch = getchar();
    if(ch=='$') {
      done=1;
      continue;
    }
    putchar(ch+1);   /* shift the alphabet one
                        position */
  }
}
```

You could use this function to code a message by shifting all characters one letter higher; for example, **a** would become **b**. The function terminates when $ is read, and no further output occurs because the conditional test, brought into effect by **continue**, finds **done** to be true and causes the loop to exit.

Labels and goto

Although **goto** fell out of favor some years ago, it has managed to polish its tarnished image a bit recently. This book will not judge its validity as a form of program control. However, no programming situations require the use of **goto**; it is a convenience, which, if used wisely, can be beneficial in certain programming situations. As such, **goto** is not used extensively in this book outside of this section. (In a language like C, which has a rich set of control structures and allows additional control using **break** and **continue**, there is little need for it.) The chief concern most programmers have about the **goto** is its tendency to confuse a program and render it nearly unreadable. However, there are times when the use of the **goto** actually clarifies program flow rather than confuses it.

The **goto** requires a label for operation. A *label* is a valid C identifier followed by a colon. Furthermore, the label must be in the same function as the **goto** that uses it. For example, a loop from 1 to 100 could be written using a **goto** and a label as shown here:

```
x = 1;
loop1:
  x++;
  if(x<100) goto loop1;
```

One good use for the **goto** is to exit from several layers of nesting. For example:

```
for(...) {
  for(...) {
    while(...) {
      if(...) goto stop;
      .
      .
      .
```

```
      }
    }
}

stop:
  printf("error in program\n");
```

Eliminating the **goto** would force a number of additional tests to be performed. A simple **break** statement would not work here because it would exit only from the innermost loop. If you substituted checks at each loop, the code would then look like

```
done=0;
for(...) {
  for(...) {
    while(...) {
      if(...) {
        done=1;
        break;
      }
      .
      .
      .
    }
    if(done) break;
  }
  if(done) break;
}
```

You should use the **goto** sparingly, if at all. But if the code would be much more difficult to read or if execution speed of the code is critical, by all means use the **goto**.

Functions

Functions are the building blocks of C in which all program activity occurs. The general form of a function is

> type-specifier function_name(*parameter list*)
> parameter declarations
> {
>   body of the function
> }

The **type-specifier** specifies the type of value that the function will return using the **return** statement. It can be any valid type. If no type is specified, the function is assumed to return an integer result. The parameter list is a comma-separated list of variable names that receive the values of the arguments when the function is called. A function may be without parameters, in which case the parameter list is empty. However, the parentheses are required even if there are no parameters. The parameter declaration section is used to define the type of the parameters in the list.

The return Statement

The **return** statement has two important uses:

1. It causes an immediate exit from the function it is in. That is, it causes program execution to return to the calling code.
2. It can be used to return the value.

Both of these uses are examined here.

Returning from a Function

There are two ways that a function terminates execution and returns to the caller. One way is when the last statement in the function has executed and, conceptually, the function's ending } is encountered. (Of course, the curly brace isn't actually present in the object code, but you can think of it in this way.) For example, this function simply prints a string backward on the display:

```
void pr_reverse(s)
char *s;
{
  register int t;

  for(t=strlen(s)-1; t>-1; t--) printf("%c", s[t]);
}
```

Once the string has been displayed, there is nothing left for the function to do, so it returns to the place it was called from.

However, not many functions use this default method of terminating their execution. Most functions rely on the **return** statement to stop execution either because a value must be returned or to simplify a function's code and make it more efficient by allowing multiple exit points. It is important to remember that a function may have several **return** statements in it. For example, the function shown here returns either the starting position of the first occurrence of substring **s2** within a string **s1** or −1 if no match is found:

```
find_substr(s1, s2)
char *s1, *s2;
{
  register int t;
  char *p, *p2;

  for(t=0; s1[t]; t++) {
    p = &s1[t];
    p2 = s2;
    while(*p2 && *p2==*p) {
      p++;
      p2++;
    }
    if(!*p2) return t;
  }
  return -1;
}
```

Return Values

All functions, except those of type **void**, return a value. This value is explicitly specified by the **return** statement, or it is 0 if no **return** statement is specified. As long as a function is not declared as **void**, it can be used as an operand in any valid C expression. Therefore, each of the following expressions is valid in Turbo C:

```
x=power(y);

if(max(x,y) > 100) printf("greater");

for(ch=getchar(); isdigit(ch); ) ... ;
```

However, a function cannot be the target of an assignment. A statement such as

```
swap(x, y) = 100;        /* incorrect statement */
```

is wrong. Turbo C will flag it as an error and will not compile a program that contains a statement like this.

Although all functions not of type **void** have return values, when you write programs you generally use three types of functions. The first is simply computational. It is specifically designed to perform an operation on its arguments and return a value based on that operation; it is essentially a "pure" function. Examples of this sort of function are **sqr()** and **sin()**.

The second type of function manipulates information and returns a value that simply indicates the success or failure of the manipulation. An example is **fwrite()**, which is used to write information to a disk file. If the write operation is successful, **fwrite()** returns the number of items successfully written. If an error occurs, the number it returns is not equal to the number of items it was requested to write.

The last type of function has no explicit return value. In essence, the function is strictly procedural and produces no value. An example is **srand()**, which is used to initialize the random number generating function **rand()**. For murky reasons functions that really don't produce an interesting result often return something anyway. For example, **printf( )** returns the number of characters written, but it would be a very unusual program that actually checked this. Therefore, although all functions, except those of type **void**, return values, you don't necessarily have to use them for anything. A common question concerning function return values is, "Don't I have to assign this value to some variable since a value is being returned?" The answer is no. If no assignment is specified, the return value is simply discarded. Consider the following program that uses **mul( )**:

```
main()
{
   int x, y, z;

   x = 10;    y = 20;
   z = mul(x, y);            /* 1 */
   printf("%d", mul(x, y));  /* 2 */
   mul(x, y);                /* 3 */
}

mul(a, b)
int a, b;
{
   return a*b;
}
```

Line 1 assigns the return value of **mul( )** to **z**. In line 2, the return value is not actually assigned, but it is used by the **printf( )** function. Finally, in line 3 the return value is lost because it is neither assigned to another variable nor used as part of an expression.

Scope Rules of Functions

The *scope rules* of a language are the rules that govern whether a piece of code knows about, or has access to, another piece of code or data.

Each function in C is a discrete block of code. A function's code is private to that function and cannot be accessed by any statement in any other function except through a call to that function. (It is not possible, for instance, to use **goto** to jump into the middle of another function.) The code that comprises the body of a function is hidden from the rest of the program, and, unless it uses global variables or data, it can neither affect nor be affected by other parts of the program. In other words, the code and data that are defined within one function cannot interact with the code and data defined in another function because the two functions have a different scope.

Variables that are defined within a function are called *local variables*. A local variable comes into existence when the function is entered and is destroyed upon exit. Therefore, local variables cannot hold their value between function calls. This rule is broken only when the variable is declared with the **static** storage-class specifier. This causes the compiler to treat it like a global variable for storage purposes but still limit its scope to within the function. (Chapter 2 contains a complete discussion of global and local variables.)

All functions in C are at the same scope level. That is, it is not possible to define a function within a function.

Function Arguments

If a function is to use arguments, it must declare variables to accept the values of the arguments. These variables are called the *formal parameters* of the function. They behave like other local variables inside the function and are created upon entry into the function and destroyed upon exit. As shown in the following example, the parameter declaration occurs after the function name and before the function's opening brace:

```
/* return 1 if c is part of string s; 0 otherwise */
is_in(s, c)
char *s;
char c;
```

```
{
  while(*s)
    if(*s==c) return 1;
    else s++;

  return 0;
}
```

The function **is—in( )** has two parameters: s and c. This function returns 1 if the character c is part of the string s and 0 otherwise.

You must make sure that the formal parameters are of the same type as the arguments used to call the function. If there is a type mismatch, no compiler error message will be issued, but unexpected results will occur. (Turbo C will report this type of error if you have used function prototypes, which we will examine later in the chapter.) Unlike many other languages, C is very robust and will generally do something, even if it is not what you want. For example, if a function expects an integer argument but was called with a **float**, the first two bytes of the **float** would be used as the integer value! It is the programmer's responsibility to make sure that errors do not occur.

As with local variables, you can make assignments to a function's formal parameters or use them in any allowable C expression. Even though these variables perform the special task of receiving the value of the arguments passed to the function, they can be used like any other local variable.

Call by Value, Call by Reference

In general, subroutines can be passed arguments in one of two ways. The first way is called *call by value*. This method copies the value of an argument into the formal parameter of the subroutine. Changes made to the parameters of the subroutine have no effect on the variables used to call it.

Call by reference is the second way a subroutine can have arguments passed to it. In this method the *address* of an argument is copied into the parameter. Inside the subroutine, the address is used to access the actual argument used in the call. This means that changes made to the parameter will affect the variable used to call the routine.

With a few exceptions, C uses call by value to pass arguments. This means that you generally cannot alter the variables used to call the function. (You will find out later in this chapter how to "force" a call by reference by using a pointer to allow changes to the calling variables.) Consider the following function:

```
main()
{
   int t=10;

   printf("%d %d", sqr(t), t);
}

sqr(x)
int x;
{
   x = x*x;
   return(x);
}
```

In this example, the value of the argument to **sqr()**, 10, is copied into the parameter **x**. When the assignment **x=x*x** takes place, the only thing modified is the local variable **x**. The variable **t**, used to call **sqr()**, still has the value 10. Hence, the output will be **100 10**.

Remember that only a copy of the value of the argument is passed to that function. What occurs inside the function has no effect on the variable used in the call.

Creating a Call by Reference

Even though C's parameter-passing convention is call by value, it is possible to simulate a call by reference by passing a pointer to the argument. Since this passes the address of the argument to the function, it is then possible to change the value of the argument outside the function.

Pointers are passed to functions just like any other value. Of course, it is necessary to declare the parameters as pointer types. For example, the function **swap ()**, which exchanges the value of its two integer arguments is shown here:

```
void swap(x, y)
int *x, *y;
{
  int temp;

  temp = *x;   /* save the value at address x */
  *x = *y;     /* put y into x */
  *y = temp;   /* put x into y */
}
```

The * operator is used to access the variable pointed to by its operand. (A complete discussion of the * is found in Chapter 2, and Chapter 6 deals exclusively with pointers.) Hence, the contents of the variables used to call the function are swapped.

It is important to remember that **swap( )** (or any other function that uses pointer parameters) must be called with the *addresses of the arguments*. The following program shows the correct way to call **swap( )**:

```
void swap();

main()
{
  int x, y;

  x = 10;
  y = 20;
  swap(&x, &y);
}
```

In this example, the variable **x** is assigned the value 10, and **y** is assigned the value 20. Then **swap( )** is called with the addresses of **x** and **y**. The unary operator **&** is used to produce the address of the variables. Therefore, the addresses of **x** and **y**, not their values, are passed to the function **swap( )**. (Again, the reader is referred to Chapter 2 for a complete discussion of the **&** operator.)

Calling Functions with Arrays

Arrays will be covered in detail in Chapter 5. However, the operation of passing arrays as arguments to functions is dealt with here because it is an exception to the standard call by value parameter-passing convention.

When an array is used as an argument to a function, only the address of the array is passed, not a copy of the entire array. When you call a function with an array name, a pointer to the first element in the array is passed to the function. (Remember that in C an array name without any index is a pointer to the first element in the array.) The parameter declaration must be of a compatible pointer type. There are three ways to declare a parameter that is to receive an array pointer. First, it can be declared as an array, as shown here:

```
void display();
main()  /* print some numbers */
{
   int t[10], i;

   for(i=0; i<10; ++i) t[i]=i;
   display(t);
}
void display(num)
int num[10];
{
   int i;

   for(i=0; i<10; i++) printf("%d ", num[i]);
}
```

Even though the parameter **num** is declared to be an integer array of 10 elements, Turbo C automatically converts it to an integer pointer because no parameter can actually receive an entire array. Only a pointer to an array is passed, so a pointer parameter must be there to receive it.

A second way to declare an array parameter is to specify it as an unsized array, as shown here,

```
void display(num)
int num[];
{
   int i;

   for(i=0; i<10; i++) printf("%d ", num[i]);
}
```

where **num** is declared to be an integer array of unknown size. Since C provides no array boundary checks, the actual size of the array is irrelevant to the parameter (but not to the

program, of course). This method of declaration also actually
defines **num** as an integer pointer.

The final way that **num** can be declared—and the most
common form in professionally written C programs—is as a
pointer, as shown here:

```
void display(num)
int *num;
{
  int i;

  for(i=0; i<10; i++) printf("%d ", num[i]);
}
```

This is allowed because any pointer can be indexed using **[]**
as if it were an array. (Actually, arrays and pointers are very
closely linked.)

All three methods of declaring an array parameter yield
the same result: a pointer.

On the other hand, an array *element* used as an argument is treated like any other simple variable. For example,
the program just examined could have been written without
passing the entire array, as shown here:

```
void display();

main() /* print some numbers */
{
  int t[10], i;

  for(i=0; i<10; ++i) t[i]=i;
  for(i=0; i<10; i++) display(t[i]);
}

void display(num)
int num;
{
  printf("%d ", num);
}
```

As you can see, the parameter to **display( )** is of type **int**.
It is not relevant that **display( )** is called by using an array
element, because only that one value of the array is used.

It is important to understand that when an array is used
as a function argument, its address is passed to a function.
This is an exception to C's call by value parameter-passing

convention. This means that the code inside the function will be operating on and potentially altering the actual contents of the array used to call the function. For example, consider the function **print__upper**, which prints its string argument in uppercase:

```
void print_upper();

main()  /* print string as uppercase */
{
  char s[80];

  gets(s);
  print_upper(s);
}

void print_upper(string)
char *string;
{
  register int t;

  for(t=0; string[t]; ++t)  {
    string[t] = toupper(string[t]);
    printf("%c", string[t]);
  }
}
```

After the call to **print__upper( )**, the contents of array s in **main( )** are changed to uppercase. If this is not what you want to happen, you could write the program like this:

```
void print_upper();

main()  /* print string as uppercase */
{
  char s[80];

  gets(s);
  print_upper(s);
}

void print_upper(string)
char *string;
{
  register int t;

  for(t=0; string[t]; ++t)
    printf("%c", toupper(string[t]));
}
```

In this version, the contents of array s remain unchanged because its values are not altered.

A classic example of passing arrays into functions is found in the standard library function **gets( )**. Although the **gets( )** in Turbo C's library is much more sophisticated and complex, the function shown below will give you an idea of how it works. To avoid confusion with the standard function, this function is called **xgets( )**:

```
/* A very simple version of the standard
   gets() library function. */

void xgets(s)
char *s;
{
   char ch;
   int t;

   for(t=0; t<80; ++t) {
      ch = getche();
      switch(ch) {
         case '\r':
            s[t] = '\0'; /* null terminate the string */
            return;
         case '\b':
            if(t>0) t--;
            break;
         default:
            s[t] = ch;
      }
   }
   s[80] = '\0';
}
```

The **gets( )** function must be called with a character pointer, which can be either a variable that you declare to be a character pointer or the name of a character array, which by definition is a character pointer. Upon entry, **xgets( )** establishes a **for** loop from 0 to 80. This prevents larger strings from being entered at the keyboard. If more than 80 characters are typed, the function returns. Because C has no built-in bounds checking, you should make sure that any variable used to call **xgets( )** can accept at least 80 characters. As you type characters on the keyboard, they are entered in the string. If you type a backspace, the counter **t** is reduced by 1. When you enter a carriage return, a null is placed at the end of the string, signaling its termination. Because the actual array used to call **xgets( )** is modified, upon return it contains the characters typed.

argc and argv—Arguments to main( )

Sometimes it is very useful to pass information to a program when you run it. The general method is to pass information to the **main( )** function by using *command-line arguments*. A command-line argument is the information that follows the program's name on the command line of the operating system. For example, when you compile programs using Turbo C's command line version, you type something like

```
>tcc program_name
```

where **program_name** is the program you wish compiled. The name of the program is passed to Turbo C as an argument.

Two special built-in arguments, **argv** and **argc**, are used to receive command-line arguments. These are the only arguments that **main( )** can have. The **argc** parameter holds the number of arguments on the command line and is an integer. It is always at least 1 because the name of the program qualifies as the first argument. The **argv** parameter is a pointer to an array of character pointers. Each element in this array points to a command-line argument. All command-line arguments are strings; any numbers have to be converted by the program into the proper format. The simple program shown here illustrates the use of command-line arguments; it prints **hello** on the screen, followed by your name if you type it directly after the program name:

```
main(argc,argv)  /* name program */
int argc;
char *argv[];
{
  if(argc!=2) {
    printf("You forgot to type your name\n");
    exit(0);
  }
  printf("Hello %s", argv[1]);
}
```

If you title this program **name** and your name is Tom, to run the program you would type **name Tom**. The output from the program would be **Hello Tom**. For example, if you were logged into drive A, you would see

```
A>name Tom
Hello Tom
A>
```

after running **name**.

Command-line arguments must be separated by a space or a tab. Commas, semicolons, and the like are not considered separators. For example,

```
run Spot, run
```

is composed of three strings, while

```
Herb,Rick,Fred
```

is a single string — commas are not legal separators.

It is important that you declare **argv** properly. The most common method is

```
char *argv[];
```

The empty brackets indicate that it is an array of undetermined length. You can now access the individual arguments by indexing **argv**. For example, **argv[0]** points to the first string, which is always the program's name; **argv[1]** points to the first argument, and so on.

A short example using command-line arguments is the following program called **countdown**. It counts down from a value specified on the command line and beeps when it reaches 0. Notice that the first argument containing the number is converted into an integer using the standard function **atoi()**. If the string "**display**" is present as the second command-line argument, the count will also be displayed on the screen.

```
main(argc, argv)  /* countdown */
int argc;
char *argv[];
{
  int disp, count;

  if(argc<2) {
    printf("You must enter the length of the count\n");
    printf("on the command line.  Try again.\n");
    exit(0);
  }

  if(argc==3 && !strcmp(argv[2],"display")) disp = 1;
  else disp = 0;

  for(count=atoi(argv[1]); count; --count)
    if(disp) printf("%d ", count);

  printf("%c", 7);   /* this will ring the bell on most
                        computers */
}
```

Notice that if no arguments are specified, an error message
is printed. It is common for a program that uses command-
line arguments to issue instructions if an attempt has been
made to run it without the proper information being present.

To access an individual character in one of the command
strings, you add a second index to **argv**. For example, the
following program displays on the screen, one character at a
time, all the arguments with which it was called:

```
main(argc,argv)
int argc;
char *argv[];
{
  int t, i;

  for(t=0; t<argc; ++t) {
    i = 0;
    while(argv[t][i]) {
      printf("%c", argv[t][i]);
      ++i;
    }
  }
}
```

Remember that the first index accesses the string and the
second index accesses that character of the string.

You generally use **argc** and **argv** to get initial commands into your program. In theory, you can have up to
32,767 arguments, but most operating systems do not allow

more than a few. You normally use these arguments to indicate a file name or an option. Using command-line arguments gives your program a very professional appearance and facilitates the program's use in batch files.

Functions Returning Noninteger Values

When the type of a function is not explicitly declared, it is automatically defaulted to **int**. The vast majority of C functions use this default. However, when it is necessary to return a different data type you must use this two-step process:

1. The function must be given an explicit type specifier.

2. The type of the function must be identified before the first call is made to it.

Only in this way can Turbo C generate correct code for functions returning noninteger values.

Functions can be declared to return any valid C data type. The method of declaration is similar to that of variables: The type specifier precedes the function name. The general form of declaration is

```
type—specifier function—name(parameter list)
parameter declarations;
{
    body of function statements;
}
```

The type specifier tells the compiler what type of data the function is to return. This information is critical if the program is going to run correctly, because different data types have different sizes and internal representations.

Before you can use a function returning a noninteger type, its type must be made known to the rest of the program. Unless directed to the contrary, Turbo C assumes that a function is going to return an integer value. If your program calls a function that returns a different type prior to that function's declaration, the compiler mistakenly generates the wrong code for the function call. To prevent this, you must use a special form of declaration statement near the top of your program to tell the compiler what value that function is really returning. To see how this is done examine this short example:

```
float sum();   /* identify the function */

main()
{
   float first, second;

   first = 123.23;
   second = 99.09;
   printf("%f", sum(first,second));
}

float sum(a, b)
float a, b;
{
   return a+b;
}
```

The first function type declaration tells the compiler that **sum()** will return a floating-point data type. This allows the compiler to generate correct code for calls to **sum()**.

The function type declaration statement has the general form

> type—specifier function—name();

If the function takes arguments, it is not necessary to list them in its type declaration. (However, as the next section will explain, listing the types of the arguments increases Turbo C's type-checking capabilities.)

Without the type declaration statement a mismatch occurs between the type of data the function returns and the type of data the calling routine expects. This mismatch produces bizarre and unpredictable results. If both functions are in the same file, Turbo C catches the type mismatch and does not compile the program. If they are in different files, however, the compiler cannot find the error. Type-checking is not done at link time or run time, only at compile time. Therefore, you must be very careful to make sure that both types are compatible.

When a character is returned from a function declared to be of type **int**, the character value is converted to an integer. Because C handles the conversion from character to integer and back again cleanly, a function that returns a character value is often not declared as returning a character value but relies on the default type conversion of characters into integers and back again.

Returning Pointers

Although functions that return pointers are handled the same way as any other type of function, a few important concepts need to be discussed.

Pointers to variables are neither integers nor unsigned integers. They are the memory addresses of a certain type of data. The reason for this distinction lies in the fact that pointer arithmetic is performed relative to the base type. That is, if an integer pointer is incremented, it contains a value that is 2 greater than its previous value (assuming 2-byte words). More generally, each time a pointer is incremented, it points to the next data item of its type. Since data types may be of different lengths, the compiler must know to what type of data the pointer is pointing to make it point to the next data item. (The subject of pointer arithmetic is covered in detail in Chapter 6.)

For example, here is a function that returns a pointer to a string at the place where a character match was found:

```
char *match(c, s);
char c, *s;
{
  int count;

  count=0;
  while(c!=s[count] && s[count]!='\0') count++;
  return(&s[count]);
}
```

The function **match()** attempts to return a pointer to the place in a string where the first match with **c** is found. If no match is found, a pointer to the null terminator is returned. Here is a short program that uses **match()**:

```
char *match();  /* declare match's type */

main()
{
  char s[80], *p, ch;

  gets(s);
  ch = getche();
  p = match(ch,s);
  if(p)   /* there is a match */
    printf("%s ", p);
  else
    printf("no match found");
}
```

This program reads a string and then a character. If the character is in the string, it prints the string from the point of match. Otherwise, it prints **no match found**.

Function Prototypes

As we discussed in the previous section, a function returning a value other than **int** must be declared before its use. In Turbo C you can take this idea one step further by also declaring the number and types of the function's arguments. This expanded definition is called a *function prototype*. Function prototypes are not part of the original UNIX C but were added by the ANSI standardization committee. They enable C to provide stronger type-checking somewhat similar to that provided by languages such as Turbo Pascal. In a strongly typed language, the compiler issues error messages if functions are called with arguments that cause illegal type conversions or with a different number of arguments. Although C is designed to be very forgiving, some type conversions are simply not allowed. For example, it is an error to attempt to convert a pointer into a **float**. Using function prototypes catches this sort of error.

A function prototype takes the general form

type function—name(*arg—type1,*
   arg—type 2, . . . ,arg—typeN);

where *type* is the type of value returned by the function and *arg—type* is the type of each argument.

For example, the following program produces an error message because there is an attempt to call **func( )** with a pointer instead of the **float** required:

```
/* This program uses function prototypes to
   enforce strong type checking in the calls
   to func().

   The program will not compile because of the
   mismatch between the type of the arguments
   specified in the function's prototype and
   the type of arguments used to call the function.
*/

float func(int, float); /* prototype */

main()
{
  int x, *y;

  x = 10;  y = 10;
  func(x, y);  /* type mismatch */
}

float func(x,  y)
int x;
float y;
{
  printf("%f", y/(float)x);
}
```

Using function prototypes not only helps you trap bugs before they occur but also helps verify that your program is working correctly by not allowing functions to be called with mismatched arguments or with an incorrect number of arguments. It is generally a good idea to use prototyping in larger programs or when several programmers are working on the same project.

Classic Versus Modern Parameter Declarations

So far in this book, when parameters have been declared as part of a function declaration, the traditional, or classic, form has been used. However, the ANSI standard (and Turbo C) allows a second, more compact, method of declaration to be used, which is called the modern form. In this method, both the type and the name of the variable are placed in an argument list that follows the function's name and is enclosed in parentheses. That is, the function parameter declaration takes a similar form to the prototype declaration except that the name of the parameter is also included. The modern declaration method takes this general form:

type function_name(*type parm1, type parm2*, . . . ,
   type parmN)
{
   body of function
}

where *type* is the type of the parameter that follows and *parm* is the name of the parameter.

For example, the function **func( )** from the prototype example of the previous section is written like this using the modern parameter declaration method:

```
float func(int x, float y)
{
  printf("%f", y/(float)x);
}
```

From this point forward, this book generally uses the modern declaration convention, but from time to time the classic form is used so that you can become familiar with both. Because so many existing programs have been written in the classic form, you are likely to encounter it quite often.

Recursion

In C, functions can call themselves. A function is *recursive* if a statement in the body of the function calls itself. Sometimes called *circular definition*, recursion is the process of defining something in terms of itself.

Examples of recursion abound. A recursive way to define an integer number is as the digits 0, 1, 2, 3, 4, 5, 6, 7, 8, and 9, plus or minus an integer number. For example, the number 15 is the number 7 plus the number 8; 21 is 9 plus 12; and 12 is 9 plus 3.

For a computer language to be recursive a function must be able to call itself. A simple example is the function **factr()**, which computes the factorial of an integer. The factorial of a number **n** is the product of all the whole numbers between 1 and **n**. For example, 3 factorial is $1 \times 2 \times 3$, or 6. Both **factr()** and its iterative equivalent are shown here:

```
/* Compute the factorial of a number. */
factr(n)  /* recursive */
int n;
{
  int answer;

  if(n==1) return(1);
  answer = factr(n-1)*n;
  return(answer);
}

/* Compute the factorial of a number. */
fact(n)      /* non-recursive */
int n;
{
  int t, answer;

  answer=1;
  for(t=1; t<=n; t++)
    answer=answer*(t);
  return(answer);

}
```

The operation of the nonrecursive version of **fact()** should be clear. It uses a loop starting at 1 and ending at the number and progressively multiplies each number by the moving product.

The operation of the recursive **factr( )** is a little more complex. When **factr( )** is called with an argument of 1, the function returns 1; otherwise it returns the product of **factr(n−1)*n**. To evaluate this expression, **factr( )** is called with **n−1**. This happens until **n** equals 1 and the calls to the function begin returning.

Computing the factorial of 2, the first call to **factr( )** causes a second call to be made with the argument of 1. This call will return 1, which is then multiplied by 2 (the original **n** value). The answer is then 2. You might find it interesting to insert **printf( )** statements into **factr( )** to show the intermediate answers and the level of each call.

When a function calls itself, new local variables and parameters are allocated storage on the stack, and the function code is executed with these new variables from the beginning. A recursive call does not make a new copy of the function. Only the arguments are new. As each recursive call returns, the old local variables and parameters are removed from the stack and execution resumes at the point of the function call inside the function. Recursive functions could be said to "telescope" out and back.

Most recursive routines do not significantly reduce code size or variable storage. The recursive versions of most routines may execute a bit more slowly than the iterative equivalent because of the added function calls; but this is not significant in most cases. Many recursive calls to a function could cause a stack overrun, but this is unlikely. Because storage for function parameters and local variables is on the stack and each new call creates a new copy of these variables, the stack space could become exhausted. However, you probably will not have to worry about this unless a recursive function runs wild.

The main advantage of recursive functions is that they can be used to create versions of several algorithms that are clearer and simpler than their iterative siblings. For example, the QuickSort sorting algorithm is quite difficult to implement in an iterative way. Some problems, especially AI-related ones, also seem to lend themselves to recursive solutions. Finally, some people seem to think recursively more easily than iteratively.

When writing recursive functions, you must have an **if** statement somewhere to force the function to return without the recursive call being executed. If you don't do this, after you call the function, it never returns. This is a very common error when recursive functions are written. Use **printf( )** and **getchar( )** liberally during development so that you can watch what is going on and abort execution if you see that you have made a mistake.

Pointers to Functions

A particularly confusing yet powerful feature of C is the *function pointer*. Even though a function is not a variable, it still has a physical location in memory that can be assigned to a pointer. The address assigned to the pointer is the entry point of the function. This pointer can then be used in place of the function's name. It also allows functions to be passed as arguments to other functions.

To understand how function pointers work, you must understand a little about how a function is compiled and called in Turbo C. As each function is compiled, source code is transformed into object code and an entry point is estab-lished. When a call is made to a function while your program is running, a machine language "call" is made to this entry point. Therefore, a pointer to a function actually contains the memory address of the entry point of the function.

The address of a function is obtained by using the func-tion's name without any parentheses or arguments. (This is similar to the way an array's address is obtained by using only the array name without indices.) For example, consider this program, paying very close attention to the declarations:

```
main()
{
  int strcmp(); /* declare a function */
  char s1[80], s2[80];
  char *p;

  p=(char *)strcmp;

  gets(s1);
  gets(s2);

  check(s1, s2, p);
}
check(a, b, cmp)
char *a, *b;
int (*cmp) ();
{
  printf("testing for equality\n");
  if(!(*cmp) (a, b)) printf("equal");
  else printf("not equal");
}
```

There are two reasons for declaring **strcmp( )** in **main( )**: (1) The program must know what type of value it is returning, in this case an integer, and (2) its name must be known to the compiler as a function. In C there is no way to declare a variable to be a function pointer directly. Instead a character pointer is declared and a cast is used to assign the address of the function to it, as shown in the program. When the function **check( )** is called, two character pointers and one function pointer are passed as parameters. Inside the function **check( )**, the arguments are declared as character pointers and a function pointer. Notice how the function pointer is declared. You must use exactly the same method when declaring other function pointers, except that the return type of the function can be different. The parentheses around the ***cmp** are necessary for the compiler to interpret this statement correctly. Without the parentheses around ***cmp** the compiler would be confused.

Once inside **check( )**, you can see how the **strcmp( )** function is called. The statement

```
(*cmp) (a, b)
```

performs the call to the function, in this case **strcmp()**, which is pointed to by **cmp** with the arguments **a** and **b**. This statement also represents the general form of using a function pointer to call the function it points to.

It is possible to call **check()** using **strcmp** directly, as shown here:

```
check(s1, s2, strcmp);
```

This statement would eliminate the need for an additional pointer variable.

You may be asking yourself why anyone would want to write a program this way. In this example nothing is gained and significant confusion is introduced. However, there are times when it is advantageous to pass arbitrary functions to procedures or to keep an array of functions. The following helps illustrate a use of function pointers. When a compiler is written, it is common for the parser (the part of the compiler that evaluates arithmetic expressions) also to perform function calls to various support routines, for example, the sine, cosine, and tangent functions. Instead of having a large **switch** statement listing all these functions, you can use an array of function pointers with the proper function called. You can get the flavor of this type of use by studying this expanded version of the previous example:

```
#include "ctype.h"

main()
{
   int strcmp();
   int numcmp();
   char s1[80], s2[80];

   gets(s1);
   gets(s2);

   if(isalpha(*s1))
        check(s1, s2, strcmp);
   else
        check(s1, s2, numcmp);

}
```

```
check(a, b, cmp)
char *a, *b;
int (*cmp) ();
{
  printf("testing for equality\n");
  if(!(*cmp) (a, b)) printf("equal");
  else printf("not equal");
}

numcmp(a, b)
char *a, *b;
{
  if(atoi(a)==atoi(b)) return 0;
  else return 1;
}
```

In this program, **check()** can be made to check for either alphabetical or numeric equality by simply calling it with a different comparison function.

Implementation Issues

When you create C functions you should remember a few important things that affect their efficiency and usability. These issues are the subject of this section.

Parameters and General-Purpose Functions

A general-purpose function is one that is used in a variety of situations, perhaps by many different programmers. Typically, you should not base general-purpose functions on global data. All the information a function needs should be passed to it by its parameters. In the few cases in which this is not possible, you should use **static** variables.

Besides making your functions general-purpose, parameters keep your code readable and less susceptible to bugs caused by side effects.

Efficiency

Functions are the building blocks of C and crucial to the creation of all but the most trivial programs. Nothing said in this section should be construed otherwise. In certain specialized applications, however, you may need to eliminate a function and replace it with *in-line code*. In-line code is the equivalent of a function's statements used without a call to that function. In-line code is used instead of function calls only when execution time is critical.

In-line code is faster than a function call for two reasons: (1) A "call" instruction takes time to execute, and (2) arguments to be passed have to be placed on the stack, which also takes time. For almost all applications, this very slight increase in execution time is of no significance. But if it is, remember that each function call uses time that would be saved if the code in the function were placed in line. For example, the following are two versions of a program that prints the square of the numbers from 1 to 10. The in-line version runs faster than the other because the function call takes time.

```
in line                    function call

main()                     main()
{                          {
  int x;                     int x;

  for(x=1; x<11; ++x)        for(x=1; x<11; ++x)
  printf("%d", x*x);         printf("%d", sqr(x));
}                          }

sqr(a)
int a;
{
  return a*a;
}
```

As you create programs, you must always weigh the cost of functions in terms of execution time against the benefits of increased readability, modifiability, and portability.

Arrays

An *array* is a collection of variables of the same type that are referenced by a common name. A specific element in an array is accessed by an index. In C all arrays consist of contiguous memory locations. The lowest address corresponds to the first element; the highest address corresponds to the last element. Arrays may have from one to several dimensions.

Single-Dimension Arrays

The general form of a single-dimension array declaration is

type var—name[*size*];

In C arrays must be explicitly declared so that the compiler can allocate space for them in memory. Here, **type** declares the base type of the array, which is the type of each element in the array. The variable size defines how many elements the array will hold. For a single-dimension array, the total size of an array in bytes is computed as shown here:

total bytes = sizeof(*type*) * length of array

All arrays have 0 as the index of their first element. Therefore, when you write

```
char p[10];
```

you are declaring a character array that has 10 elements,
p[0] through [9]. For example, the following program loads
an integer array with the numbers 0 through 9:

```
main()
{
   int x[10];   /* this reserves 10 integer elements */
   int t;

   for(t=0; t<10; ++t) x[t]=t;
}
```

In C there is no bounds checking on arrays: You could
overwrite either end of an array and write into some other
variable's data, or even into a piece of the program's code. It
is the programmer's job to provide bounds checking when it
is needed. For example, make certain that the character
arrays that accept character input using **gets( )** are long
enough to accept the longest input.

Single-dimension arrays are essentially lists of information of the same type. For example, Figure 5-1 shows how
array **a** appears in memory if it is declared as shown here
and starts at memory location 1000.

```
char a[7];
```

Element	0	1	2	3	4	5	6
Address	1000	1001	1002	1003	1004	1005	1006

Figure 5-1.   A seven-element character beginning at location 1000

Passing Single-Dimension Arrays to Functions

When passing single-dimension arrays to functions, you call the function with the array name without any indexing. This passes the address of the first element of the array to the function. In C it is not possible to pass the entire array as an argument; a pointer is used instead. For example, the following fragment passes the address of **i** to **func1()**:

```
main()
{
  int i[10];

  func1(i);
  .
  .
  .
}
```

If a function is to receive a single-dimension array, you may declare the formal parameter as a pointer, as a sized array, or as an unsized array. For example, to receive **i** into a function called **func1()**, you could declare **func1()** as either

```
func1(str)
int *str;  /* pointer */
{
  .
  .
  .
}
```

or

```
func1(str)
int str[10]; /* sized array */
{
  .
  .
  .
}
```

or

```
func1(str)
int str[]; /* unsized array */
{
    .
    .
    .
}
```

All three methods of declaration are identical because each tells the compiler that a character pointer is going to be received. In the first declaration a pointer is used; in the second the standard array declaration is employed. In the third declaration, a modified version of an array declaration simply specifies that an array of type **int** of some length is to be received. If you give it a little thought, you can see that, as far as the function is concerned, it doesn't matter what the length of the array actually is because C performs no bounds checking. In fact, as far as the compiler is concerned,

```
func1(str)
int str[32];
{
    .
    .
    .
```

also works because the C compiler generates code that instructs **func1()** to receive a pointer; it does not actually create a 32-element array.

Strings

By far the most common use of one-dimensional arrays is for character strings. In C a string is defined to consist of a character array that is terminated by a null. A null is specified as ' \0' and is generally 0. For this reason it is necessary to declare character arrays to be one character longer than the largest string that they are to hold. For example, if you wished to declare an array s that holds a 10-character string, you would write

```
char s[11];
```

This makes room for the null at the end of the string.

Although C does not have a string data type, it still allows string constants. A string constant is a list of characters enclosed between double quotes (for example, **"hello there"** or **"this is a test"**). It is not necessary to add the null to the end of string constants manually; Turbo C does this for you automatically.

Turbo C supports a wide range of string manipulation functions. The most common are

Name	Function
strcpy(s1, s2)	Copies s2 into s1
strcat(s1, s2)	Concatenates s2 onto the end of s1
strlen(s1)	Returns the length of s1
strcmp(s1, s2)	Returns 0 if s1 and s2 are the same; less than 0 if s1<s2; greater than 0 if s1>s2

(These and other string functions are discussed in detail in Part Three of this book.)

The following program illustrates the use of these string functions:

```
#include "string.h"

main()
{
  char s1[80], s2[80];

  gets(s1); gets(s2);

  printf("lengths: %d %d\n", strlen(s1), strlen(s2));

  if(!strcmp(s1, s2)) printf("The strings are equal\n");

  strcat(s1, s2);
  printf("%s\n", s1);
}
```

If this program is run and the strings **"hello"** and **"hello"** are entered, the output is

```
lengths: 5   5
The strings are equal
hellohello
```

It is important to remember that **strcmp( )** returns false if the strings are equal, so be sure to use the ! to reverse the condition, as shown in this example, if you are testing for equality.

Two-Dimensional Arrays

Turbo C allows multidimensional arrays. The simplest form of the multidimensional array is the two-dimensional array. A two-dimensional array is, in essence, an array of one-dimensional arrays. Two-dimensional arrays are declared using this general form:

type array__name[*2d dimension size*][*1st dimension size*];

Hence, to declare a two-dimensional integer array **d** of size 10,20, you would write

```
int d[10][20];
```

Pay careful attention to the declaration: Unlike most other computer languages, which use commas to separate the array dimensions, C places each dimension in its own set of brackets.

Similarly, to access point 3,5 of array **d**, you would use

```
d[3][5]
```

In the following example, a two-dimensional array is loaded with the numbers 1 through 12:

```
main()
{
  int t,i, num[3][4];

  for(t=0;t<3;++t)
    for(i=0;i<4;++i)
      num[t][i]=(t*4)+i+1;
}
```

In this example, **num[0][0]** has the value 1; **num[0][1]**, the value 2; **num[0][2]**, the value 3; and so on. The value of **num[2][3]** is 12.

Two-dimensional arrays are stored in a row-column matrix, where the first index indicates the row and the second indicates the column. This means that the rightmost index changes faster than the leftmost when accessing the elements in the array in the order they are actually stored in memory. See Figure 5-2 for a graphic representation of a two-dimensional array in memory. In essence, the leftmost index can be thought of as a "pointer" to the correct row.

You should remember that storage for all array elements is allocated permanently. In the case of a two-dimensional array, the following formula finds the number of bytes of memory:

bytes = row * column * number of bytes in data type

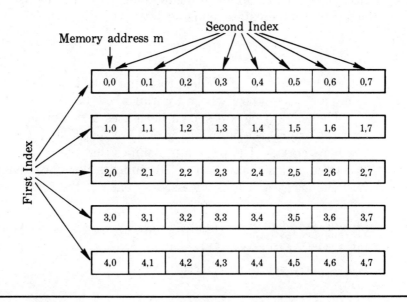

Figure 5-2.   A two-dimensional array in memory

Therefore, assuming 2-byte integers, an integer array with the dimensions 10,5 would have $10 \times 5 \times 2$ or 100 bytes allocated.

When a two-dimensional array is used as an argument to a function, only a pointer to the first element (that is, [0][0]) is actually passed. However, a function receiving a two-dimensional array as a parameter must minimally define the length of the first dimension, because the compiler needs to know the length of each row if it is to index the array correctly. For example, a function that will receive a two-dimensional integer array with dimensions 10,10 would be declared like this:

```
func1(x)
int x[][10];
{
   .
   .
   .
}
```

You can specify the second dimension as well, but it is not necessary. The compiler needs to know the first dimension in order to work on statements such as

```
x[2][4]
```

inside the function. If the length of the rows is not known, it is impossible to know where the third row begins.

The short program shown here uses a two-dimensional array to store the numeric grade for each student in a teacher's classes. The program assumes that the teacher has 3 classes and a maximum of 30 students per class. Notice how the array **grade** is accessed by each of the functions.

```
#define CLASSES  3
#define GRADES   30
int grade[CLASSES][GRADES];

main()   /* class grades program */
{
   char ch;
```

```
    for(;;) {
      do {
        printf("(E)nter grades\n");
        printf("(R)eport grades\n");
        printf("(Q)uit\n");
        ch = toupper(getche());
      } while(ch!='E' && ch!='R' && ch!='Q');

      switch(ch) {
        case 'E':
          enter_grades();
          break;
        case 'R':
          disp_grades(grade);
          break;
        case 'Q':
          exit(0);
      }
    }
}

/* Enter each student's grade. */
enter_grades()
{
  int t, i;

  for(t=0; t<CLASSES; t++) {
    printf("Class # %d:\n", t+1);
    for(i=0; i<GRADES; ++i)
      grade[t][i] = get_grade(i);
  }
}

/* Actually input the grade. */
get_grade(int num)
{
  char s[80];

  printf("enter grade for student # %d:\n", num+1);
  gets(s);
  return(atoi(s));
}

/* Display the class grades. */

disp_grades(int g[] [GRADES])
{
  int t, i;

  for(t=0; t<CLASSES; ++t) {
    printf("Class # %d:\n", t+1);
    for(i=0; i<GRADES; ++i)
      printf("grade for student #%d is %d\n",i+1, g[t][i]);
  }
}
```

Arrays of Strings

It is not uncommon in programming to use an array of strings. For example, the input processor to a database may verify user commands against a string array of valid commands. A two-dimensional character array is used to create an array of strings, with the size of the left index determining the number of strings and the size of the right index specifying the maximum length of each string. For example, the following declares an array of 30 strings, each having a maximum length of 80 characters:

```
char str_array[30][80];
```

To access an individual string is quite easy: You simply specify only the left index. For example, this statement calls **gets()** with the third string in **str_array**:

```
gets(str_array[2]);
```

This is functionally equivalent to

```
gets(&str_array[2][0]);
```

but the previous form is much more common in professionally written C code.

To improve your understanding of how string arrays work, study the following short program that uses one as the basis for a very simple text editor:

```
#include "stdio.h"

#define MAX 100
#define LEN 80

char text[MAX][LEN];

/* A very simple text editor. */
main()
{
  register int t, i, j;
```

```
for(t=0; t<MAX; t++) {
  printf("%d: ", t);
  gets(text[t]);
  if(!*text[t]) break; /* quit on blank line */
}

for(i=0; i<t; i++) {
  for(j=0; text[i][j]; j++) printf("%c", text[i][j]);
  printf("%c", '\n');
}
}
```

This program inputs lines of text until a blank line is entered. Then it redisplays each line.

Multidimensional Arrays

Turbo C allows arrays of greater than two dimensions. The general form of a multidimensional array declaration is

type name[*size1*][*size2*]...[*sizeN*];

Arrays of more than three dimensions are rarely used because of the amount of memory required to hold them. As stated before, storage for all global arrays is allocated permanently at the beginning of the execution of your program. For example, a four-dimensional character array with dimensions 10,6,9,4 would require $10 \times 6 \times 9 \times 4$ or 2160 bytes. If the array were 2-byte integers, 4320 bytes would be needed. If the array were **double** (assuming 8 bytes per **double**), 34,560 bytes would be required. The storage required increases exponentially with the number of dimensions.

A point to remember about multidimensional arrays is that it takes the computer time to compute each index. This means that accessing an element in a multidimensional array is slower than accessing an element in a single-dimension array. For these and other reasons, when large multidimensional arrays are needed, they are often dynamically allocated a portion at a time using Turbo C's dynamic allocation functions and pointers. This approach is called a *sparse array.*

When passing multidimensional arrays into functions, you must declare all but the leftmost dimension. For example, if you declare array **m** as

```
int m[4][3][6][5];
```

A function, **func1()**, which will receive **m**, would look like

```
func1(d)
int d[][3][6][5];
{
    .
    .
    .
```

Of course, you are free to include the first dimension if you like.

Arrays and Pointers

In C, pointers and arrays are closely related. For example, an array name without an index is a pointer to the first element in the array. For example:

```
char p[10];
```

The following statements are identical:

```
p
```

```
&p[0]
```

Put another way,

```
p==&p[0]
```

evaluates true because the address of the first element of an array is the same as the address of the array.

Any pointer variable can be indexed as if it were declared to be an array. For example:

```
int *p, i[10];
p=i;
p[5]=100;  /* assign using index */
(*p+5)=100; /* assign using pointer arithmetic */
```

Both assignment statements place the value 100 in the sixth element of **i**. The first statement indexes **p**; the second uses pointer arithmetic. Either way, the result is the same. (Pointers and pointer arithmetic are dealt with in detail in Chapter 6.)

The same holds true for arrays of two or more dimensions. For example, assuming that **a** is a 10-by-10 integer array, these two statements are equivalent:

```
a
```

```
&a[0][0]
```

Further, the 0,4 element of **a** may be referenced either by array-indexing, **a[0][4]**, or by the pointer, ***(a+4)**. Similarly, element 1,2 is either **a[1][2]** or ***(a+12)**. In general, for any two-dimensional array

a[*j*][*k*] is equivalent to *(a+(j*row length)+k)

Pointers are sometimes used to access arrays because pointer arithmetic is often a faster process than array-indexing. The gain in speed using pointers is the greatest when an array is being accessed in purely sequential fashion.

In this situation, the pointer may be incremented or decremented using Turbo C's highly efficient increment and decrement operators. On the other hand, if the array is to be accessed in random order, the pointer approach may not be much better than array-indexing.

In a sense, a two-dimensional array is like an array of row pointers to arrays of rows. Therefore, one easy way to use pointers to access two-dimensional arrays is by using a separate pointer variable. The following function prints the contents of the specified row for the global integer array **num**:

```
int num[10][10];
.
.
.
pr_row(int j)
{
   int *p, t;

   p = &num[j][0]; /* get address of first
                      element in row j */
   for(t=0; t<10; ++t) printf("%d ", *(p+t));
}
```

This routine can be generalized by making the calling arguments be the row, the row length, and a pointer to the first array element, as shown here:

```
pr_row(int j, int row_dimension, int *p) /* general */
{
   int t;

   p = p + (j * row_dimension);
   for(t=0; t<row_dimension; ++t)
     printf("%d ", *(p+t));
}
```

Arrays of more than two dimensions can be thought of in the same way. For example, a three-dimensional array can be reduced to a pointer to a two-dimensional array, which can be reduced to a pointer to a one-dimensional array. Generally, an n-dimensional array can be reduced to a pointer and an n−1-dimensional array. This new array can be reduced again using the same method. The process ends when a single-dimensional array is produced.

Allocated Arrays

In many programming situations—mailing list programs, for example—it is impossible to know how large an array will be needed. In addition, many types of programs need to use as much memory as is available and still run on machines having only minimal memory. A text editor is an example of this. In these situations, it is not possible to use an array because its dimensions are established at compile time and cannot be changed during execution. The solution is to create a *dynamic array*. A dynamic array uses memory from the region of free memory called the heap and is accessed by indexing a pointer to that memory. (Remember that any pointer can be indexed as if it were an array variable.)

In Turbo C you can dynamically allocate and free memory by using the standard library routines, **malloc()**, which allocates memory and returns a **void** pointer to the start of it, and **free()**, which returns previously allocated memory to the heap for possible reuse. The general forms for calling **malloc()** and **free()** are

```
void *p;

p = malloc(num_bytes);

free(p);
```

Here, **num_bytes** is the number of bytes requested. If there is not enough free memory to fill the request, **malloc()** will return a null. It is important that **free()** be called only with a valid, previously allocated pointer; otherwise the organization of the heap might be damaged, which could cause a program crash. Also, although not technically required, it is best to include the header file **stdlib.h** in any program using

malloc() and **free()** because it contains their prototype declarations.

The code fragment shown here allocates 1000 bytes of memory:

```
char *p;

p = (char *) malloc(1000); /* get 1000 bytes */
```

The **p** points to the first of 1000 bytes of free memory. Notice that a cast is used to convert the **void** pointer returned by **malloc()** into the desired **char** pointer. You generally use a cast to convert the pointer returned by **malloc()** into the type your routine requires.

This example shows the proper way to use a dynamically allocated array to read input from the keyboard using **gets()**:

```
#include "stdlib.h"

/* Print a string backwards using dynamic allocation. */
main()
{
  char *s;
  register int t;

  s = (char *) malloc(80);

  if(!s) {
    printf("memory request failed\n");
    exit(1);
  }

  gets(s);
  for(t=strlen(s)-1; t>=0; t--) printf("%c", s[t]);
  free(s);
}
```

As the program shows, s is tested, before its first use, to ensure that a valid pointer was returned by **malloc()**. This is absolutely necessary to prevent accidental use of a null pointer. (Using a null pointer will almost certainly cause a system crash.) Notice how the pointer s is indexed as an array to print the string backwards.

It is possible to have multidimensional dynamic arrays, but you will need to use a function to access them because there must be some way to define the size of all but the left-most dimension. To do this, a pointer is passed to a function that has its parameter declared with the proper array bounds. To see how this works, study this short example, which builds a table of the numbers 1 through 10 raised to their first, second, third, and fourth powers.

```c
#include "stdlib.h"

/* This program displays various numbers raised to integer
   powers. */
main()
{
  int *p;

  p = (int *) malloc(40*sizeof(int));

  if(!p) {
    printf("memory request failed\n");
    exit(1);
  }

  /* here, p is simply a pointer */
  table(p);
  show(p);
}

/* Build a table of numbers. */
table(int p[4][10]) /* now the compiler thinks that
                       p is an array */
{
  register int i, j;

  for(j=1; j<11; j++)
    for(i=1; i<5; i++) p[i][j] = pwr(j, i);
}

/* Display the table. */
show(int p[4][10])
{
  register int i, j;

  printf("%10s %10s %10s %10s\n","N","N^2","N^3","N^4");
  for(j=1; j<11; j++) {
    for(i=1; i<5; i++) printf("%10d ", p[i][j]);
    printf("\n");
  }
}

/* Raise a to the b power. */
```

```
pwr(int a, int b)
{
  register int t=1;

  for(; b; b--) t = t*a;
  return t;
}
```

The output produced by this program is

N	N^2	N^3	N^4
1	1	1	1
2	4	8	16
3	9	27	81
4	16	64	256
5	25	125	625
6	36	216	1296
7	49	343	2401
8	64	512	4096
9	81	729	6561
10	100	1000	10000

As this program illustrates, by defining a function parameter to the desired array dimensions you can "trick" Turbo C into handling multidimensional dynamic arrays. Actually, as far as the compiler is concerned, you do have a 4,10 integer array inside the functions **show( )** and **table( )**; the difference is that the storage for the array is allocated manually by using the **malloc( )** statement, rather than automatically by using the normal array declaration statement. Also note the use of **sizeof** to compute the number of bytes needed for a 4,10 integer array. This guarantees the portability of this program to computers with different-sized integers.

Array Initialization

Turbo C allows the initialization of global and local arrays at the time of declaration. The general form of array initialization is similar to that of other variables, as shown here:

type-specifier array__name[*size1*]. . .[*sizeN*] = { *value-list* };

The *value-list* is a comma-separated list of constants that are type compatible with **type-specifier**. The first constant is placed in the first position of the array, the second constant in the second position, and so on. The last entry in the list is not followed by a comma. Note that a semicolon does follows the }. In the following example, a 10-element integer array is initialized with the numbers 1 through 10:

```
int i[10] = {1, 2, 3, 4, 5, 6, 7, 8, 9, 10};
```

This means that **i[0]** has the value 1 and **i[9]** has the value 10.

Character arrays that hold strings allow a shorthand initialization in the form

char array__name[*size*] = "string";

For example, this code fragment initializes **str** to the word **hello**.

```
char str[6] = "hello";
```

This is the same as writing

```
char str[6] = {'h', 'e', 'l', 'l', 'o', '\0'};
```

Because all strings in C end with a null, you must make sure that the array you declare is long enough to include it. This is why **str** is six characters long even though **hello** is only five characters. When the string constant is used (as in the previous approach), the compiler automatically supplies the null terminator.

Multidimensional arrays are initialized the same as single-dimensional ones. For example, the following initializes **sqrs** with the numbers 1 through 10 and their squares:

```
int sqrs[10][2] = {
  1,1,
  2,4,
  3,9,
  4,16,
  5,25,
  6,36,
  7,49,
  8,64,
  9,81,
  10,100
};
```

Unsized-Array Initializations

Imagine that you are using array initialization to build a table of error messages as shown here:

```
char e1[12] = "read error\n";
char e2[13] = "write error\n";
char e3[18] = "cannot open file\n";
```

As you might guess, it is very tedious to count the characters in each message manually to determine the correct array dimension. It is possible to let C dimension the arrays automatically by using *unsized arrays*. If the size of the array is not specified in an array initialization statement, the C compiler automatically creates an array big enough to hold all the initializers present. Using this approach, the message table becomes

```
char e1[] = "read error\n";
char e2[] = "write error\n";
char e3[] = "cannot open file\n";
```

Given these initializations, this statement

```
printf("%s has length %d\n", e2, sizeof e2);
```

prints

```
write error
has length 13
```

Aside from being less tedious, the unsized-array initialization method allows any of the messages to be changed without fear of accidentally counting wrong.

Unsized array initializations are not restricted to single-dimension arrays. For multidimensional arrays you must specify all but the leftmost dimensions to allow Turbo C to index the array properly. (This is similar to specifying array parameters.) In this way, you can build tables of varying lengths and the compiler automatically allocates enough storage for them. For example, the declaration of **sqrs** as an unsized array is shown here:

```
int sqrs[][2] = {
  1,1,
  2,4,
  3,9,
  4,16,
  5,25,
  6,36,
  7,49,
  8,64,
  9,81,
  10,100
};
```

The advantage to this declaration over the sized version is that the table may be lengthened or shortened without changing the array dimensions.

A Tic-Tac-Toe Example

This chapter concludes with a longer example that illustrates many of the ways arrays can be manipulated in C.

Two-dimensional arrays are commonly used to simulate board game matrices, as in chess and checkers. Although it is beyond the scope of this book to present a chess or checkers program, a simple tic-tac-toe program can be developed.

The tic-tac-toe matrix will be represented by a 3-by-3 character array. You are always X and the computer is O. When you move, **X** is placed in the specified position of the game matrix. When it is the computer's turn to move, it scans the matrix and puts its **O** in the first empty location of the matrix. (This makes for a fairly dull game. You might find it fun to spice it up a bit!) If it cannot find an empty location, it reports a draw game and exits. The game matrix is initialized to contain spaces at the start of the game. The global array **matrix**, the **main()** function, along with **get__player__move()**, **get__computer__move()**, and **disp__matrix()** are shown here:

```
/* A simple game of Tic Tac Toe. */

#define SPACE ' '

char matrix[3][3] = {  /* the tic tac toe matrix */
  SPACE,SPACE,SPACE,
  SPACE,SPACE,SPACE,
  SPACE,SPACE,SPACE
};

void get_computer_move(), get_player_move(), disp_matrix();

main()
{
  char done;

  printf("This is the game of Tic Tac Toe.\n");
  printf("You will be playing against the computer.\n");

  done=SPACE;
  do {
    disp_matrix();        /* display the game board */
    get_player_move();    /* get your move */
    done=check();         /* see if winner */
    if(done!=SPACE) break; /* winner!*/
    get_computer_move();  /* get computer's move */
    done=check();         /* see if winner */
  } while(done==SPACE);
  if(done=='X') printf("You won!\n");
  else printf("I won!!!!\n");
  disp_matrix(); /* show final positions */
}
```

```c
/* Input the player's move. */
void get_player_move()
{
  int x, y;

  printf("Enter coordinates for your X: ");
  scanf("%d%d",&x, &y);
  x--; y--;
  if(matrix[x][y]!=SPACE) {
    printf("Invalid move, try again.\n");
    get_player_move();
  }
  else matrix[x][y]='X';
}

/* Get the computer's move */
void get_computer_move()
{
  register int t;
  char *p;

  p = (char *) matrix;
  for(t=0; *p!=SPACE && t<9; ++t) p++;
  if(t==9)  {
    printf("draw\n");
    exit(0); /* game over */
  }
  else *p = '0';
}

/* Display the game board. */
void disp_matrix()
{
  int t, i;

  for(t=0; t<3; t++) {
    printf(" %c | %c | %c ", matrix[t][0],
      matrix[t][1], matrix [t][2]);
    if(t!=2) printf("\n---|---|---\n");
  }
  printf("\n");
}

/* See if there is a winner. */
check()
{
  int t;
  char *p;

  for(t=0; t<3; t++) { /* check rows */
    p = &matrix[t][0];
    if(*p==*(p+1) && *(p+1)==*(p+2)) return *p;
  }

  for(t=0; t<3; t++) { /* check columns */
    p = &matrix[0][t];
    if(*p==*(p+3) && *(p+3)==*(p+6)) return *p;
  }
```

```
/* test diagonals */
if(matrix[0][0]==matrix[1][1] && matrix[1][1]==matrix[2][2])
  return matrix[0][0];

if(matrix[0][2]==matrix[1][1] && matrix[1][1]==matrix[2][0])
  return matrix[0][2];

return SPACE;
}
```

The array is initialized to contain spaces because a space
is used to indicate to **get—player—move()** and **get—computer—move()** that a matrix position is vacant. The fact
that spaces are used instead of nulls, for example, simplifies
the matrix display function **disp—matrix()** by allowing the
contents of the array to be printed on the screen without any
translations. Note that the routine **get—player—move()** is
recursive when an invalid location is entered. This is an
example where recursion can be used to simplify a routine
and reduce the amount of code necessary to implement a
function.

In the main loop, each time a move is entered, the function **check()** is called. This function determines if the game
has been won and by whom. The **check()** function will
return an **X** if you have won, or an **O** if the computer has
won. Otherwise, it returns a space. **Check()** works by scanning the rows, the columns, and then the diagonals looking
for a winning configuration.

The routines in this example all access the array **matrix**
differently. You should study them to make sure that you
understand each array operation.

Pointers

The correct understanding and use of pointers is critical to the creation of most successful Turbo C programs, for three reasons:

1. Pointers provide the means by which functions can modify their calling arguments.

2. Pointers are used to support Turbo C's dynamic allocation routines.

3. The use of pointers can improve the efficiency of certain routines.

Pointers are one of C's strongest features, but they are also its most dangerous feature. For example, uninitialized, or "wild," pointers can cause system crash. Perhaps worse, it is very easy to use pointers incorrectly, which causes bugs that are very difficult to find.

Pointers Are Addresses

A *pointer* contains a memory address. Most commonly, the address is the location of another variable in memory. If one variable contains the address of another variable, the first variable is said to point to the second. For example, if a variable at location 1004 is pointed to by a variable at location 1000, the contents of location 1000 will contain the value 1004. This situation is illustrated in Figure 6-1, assuming only the offset portion of the address is used.

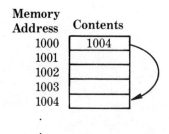

Figure 6-1.   One variable pointing to another

Pointer Variables

If a variable is going to hold a pointer, it must be declared as such. A pointer declaration consists of a base type, an *, and the variable name. The general form for declaring a pointer variable is

    type *name;

where **type** may be any valid C type (also called the base type) and **name** is the name of the pointer variable.

The base type of the pointer defines what type of variables the pointer can point to. Technically, any type of pointer can point anywhere in memory, but all pointer arithmetic is done relative to its base type, so it is important to declare the pointer correctly. (Pointer arithmetic is discussed later in this chapter.)

The Pointer Operators

There are two special pointer operators: * and **&**. The **&** is a unary operator that returns the memory address of its operand. (A unary operator requires only one operand.) For example,

```
m = &count;
```

places into **m** the memory address of the variable **count**. This address is the computer's internal location of the variable. It has nothing to do with the value of **count**. The operation of the **&** can be remembered as returning "the address of." Therefore, the assignment statement above could be verbalized as "m receives the address of count."

To improve your understanding of the assignment, assume the variable **count** uses memory location 2000 to store its value. Also assume that **count** has a value of 100. Then, after the above assignment, **m** will have the value 2000.

The second operator, *, is the complement of the **&**. It is a unary operator that returns the value of the variable located at the address that follows. For example, if **m** contains the memory address of the variable **count**,

```
q = *m;
```

places the value of **count** in **q**. Following through with this example, **q** has the value 100 because 100 is stored at location 2000, which is the memory address that was stored in **m**. The operation of the * can be remembered as "at address." In this case the statement could be read as "q receives the value at address m."

Unfortunately, the multiplication sign and the "at address" sign are the same, and the bitwise AND and the "address of" sign are the same. These operators have no relationship to each other. Both **&** and * have a higher precedence than all other arithmetic operators except the unary minus, with which they are equal.

You must make sure that your pointer variables always point to the correct type of data. For example, when you declare a pointer to be of type **int**, the compiler assumes that any address it holds will point to an integer variable. Because C allows you to assign any address to a pointer variable, the following code fragment compiles with only warning messages but does not produce the desired result.

```
main()
{
  float x,y;
  int  *p;

  p = &x;
  y = *p;
}
```

This does not assign the value of **x** to **y**. Because **p** is declared to be an integer pointer, only 2 bytes of information will be transferred to **y**, not the 4 that normally make up a floating point number.

Pointer Expressions

In general expressions involving pointers conform to the same rules as any other C expression. This section will examine a few special aspects of pointer expressions.

Pointer Assignments

As with any variable, a pointer may be used in the right-hand side of assignment statements to assign its value to another pointer. For example:

```
main()
{
```

```
int x;
int *p1, *p2;

p1 = &x;
p2 = p1;
printf(" %p", p2); /* print the hexadecimal value of the
                      address of x - - not x's value!*/
}
```

The hexadecimal address of **x** is displayed by using the **%p printf( )** format command.

Pointer Arithmetic

Only two arithmetic operations can be used on pointers: addition and subtraction. To understand what occurs in pointer arithmetic, let **p1** be a pointer to an integer with a current value of 2000, and assume that integers are 2 bytes long. After the expression

```
p1++;
```

the contents of **p1** are 2002, not 2001! Each time **p1** is incremented, it points to the next integer. The same is true of decrements. For example,

```
p1--;
```

causes **p1** to have the value 1998, assuming that it previously was 2000.

Each time a pointer is incremented, it points to the memory location of the next element of its base type. Each time it is decremented it points to the location of the previous element. In the case of pointers to characters this appears as "normal" arithmetic. However, all other pointers increase or decrease by the length of the data type they point to. For example, assuming 1-byte characters and 2-byte integers, when a character pointer is incremented, its value increases by 1; however, when an integer pointer is incremented its value increases by 2. The reason for this is that each time a pointer is incremented or decremented, it is done so relative to the length of its base type, so it always points to the next element. More generally, all pointer arithmetic is done relative to the base type of the pointer, so the pointer is always pointing to the appropriate element of the base type. Figure 6-2 illustrates this concept.

You are not limited to increment and decrement, however. You may also add or subtract integers to or from pointers. The expression

```
p1 = p1 + 9;
```

makes **p1** point to the ninth element of **p1**'s type beyond the one it is currently pointing to.

No other arithmetic operations can be performed on pointers. You cannot multiply or divide pointers; you cannot add or subtract two pointers; you cannot apply the bitwise shift and mask operators to them; and you cannot add or subtract type **float** or **double** to pointers.

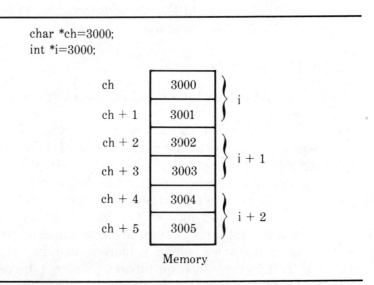

Figure 6-2.   All pointer arithmetic is relative to its base type

Pointer Comparisons

It is possible to compare two pointers in a relational expression. For instance, given two pointers **p** and **q**, the following statement is perfectly valid:

```
if(p<q) printf("p points to lower memory than q\n");
```

There are some special problems associated with **far** pointer comparisons in Turbo C. Because of this, the material presented here is applicable only to **near** or **huge** pointers. (The difficulties with **far** pointers are discussed in Chapter 10 when the Turbo C memory models are explained.)

Pointer comparisons are generally used when two or more pointers are pointing to a common object. As an example, imagine that you are constructing a stack routine to hold integer values. A stack is a list that uses "first in, last out" accessing. It is often compared to a stack of plates on a table—the first one set down is the last one to be used. Stacks are used frequently in compilers, interpreters, spreadsheets, and other system-related software. To create a stack you need two routines: **push( )** and **pop( )**. The **push( )** function is used to place values on the stack, and **pop( )** takes them off. Memory for the stack is allocated from the heap. The variable **tos** holds the memory address of the top of the stack and is used to prevent stack underflows. Once the stack has been initialized, **push( )** and **pop( )** may be used as a stack for integers. These routines are shown here with a simple **main( )** function to drive them:

```
#include "stdlib.h"

int *p1, *tos;

main()
{
  int value;

  p1 = (int *) malloc(50*sizeof(int));
  if(!p1) {
    printf("allocation failure\n");
    return;
  }
```

```
tos = p1;   /* let tos hold top of stack */

do {
  scanf("%d", &value);
  if(value!=0) push(value);
  else printf("this is it %d\n", pop());
} while(value!=-1);
}

push(int i)
{
  p1++;
  if(p1==(tos+50)) {
    printf("stack overflow");
    exit(1);
  }
  *p1 = i;
}

pop()
{
  if((p1)==tos) {
    printf("stack underflow");
    exit(1);
  }
  p1--;
  return *(p1+1);
}
```

Both the **push()** and **pop()** functions perform a relational test on the pointer **p1** to detect limit errors. In **push()**, **p1** is tested against the end of stack by adding 50 (the size of the stack) to **tos**. In **pop()**, **p1** is checked against **tos** to be sure that a stack underflow has not occurred.

In **pop()**, the parentheses are necessary in the **return** statement. Without them, the statement would look like

```
return *p1 + 1;
```

which would return the value at location **p1** plus one, not the value of the location **p1+1**. When using pointers you must be very careful to use parentheses to ensure correct order of evaluation.

Turbo C's Dynamic Allocation Functions

Once compiled, all C programs organize the computer's memory into four regions, which hold program code, global data, the stack, and the heap. The heap is an area of free memory that is managed by C's dynamic allocation functions **malloc( )** and **free( )**.

The **malloc( )** function allocates memory and returns a character pointer to the start of it, and **free( )** returns previously allocated memory to the heap for possible reuse. The general forms for **malloc( )** and **free( )** are

```
void *malloc(num_bytes);

free(void *p);
```

Here, *num—bytes* is the number of bytes requested. If there is not enough free memory to fill the request, **malloc( )** returns a null. It is important that **free( )** be called only with a valid, previously allocated pointer; otherwise the organization of the heap could be damaged, which might cause a program crash.

The code fragment shown here allocates 1000 bytes of memory:

```
char *p;

p = (char *) malloc(1000); /* get 1000 bytes */
```

After the assignment, **p** points to the first of 1000 bytes of free memory. Notice that you must use a type cast with **malloc( )** so that the pointer is converted to the proper type. As another example, this fragment allocates space for 50 integers. It uses **sizeof** to ensure portability.

```
int *p;

p = (int *)malloc(50*sizeof(int));
```

Since the heap is not infinite, whenever you allocate memory, it is imperative to check the value returned by **malloc()** to make sure that it is not null before using the pointer. Using a null pointer will almost certainly crash the computer. The proper way to allocate memory and test for a valid pointer is illustrated in this code fragment:

```
if(!(p=malloc(100)) {
  printf("Out of memory.\n");
  exit(1);
}
```

Of course, you can substitute some other kind of error handler in place of the **exit()**. The point is that you do not want the pointer **p** to be used if it is null.

You should include the header file **stdlib.h** at the top of any file that uses **malloc()** and **free()** because it contains their prototypes.

Later in this book you will see pointers and dynamic allocation used to create linked lists, sparse arrays, and the like.

Pointers and Arrays

There is a close relationship between pointers and arrays. Consider this fragment:

```
char str[80], *p1;

p1 = str;
```

Here, **p1** has been set to the address of the first array element in **str**. If you wished to access the fifth element in **str** you could write

```
str[4]
```

or

```
*(p1+4)
```

Both statements return the fifth element. Remember, arrays start at zero, so a four is used to index **str**. You would also add four to the pointer **p1** to get the fifth element, because **p1** currently points to the first element of **str**. (Remember that an array name without an index returns the starting address of the array, which is the first element.)

In essence C allows two methods of accessing array elements. This is important because pointer arithmetic can be faster than array-indexing. Since speed is often a consideration in programming, the use of pointers to access array elements is very common in C programs.

To see an example of how pointers can be used in place of array-indexing, consider these two versions of **puts( )** —one with array-indexing and one with pointers. The **puts( )** function can be used to write a string to the standard output device.

```
puts(char *s)   /* with arrays */
{
   register int t;

   for(t=0; s[t]; ++t) putch(s[t]);

}
```

```
puts(char *s)   /* with pointers */
{
   while(*s) putch(*s++);
}
```

Most professional C programmers would find the second version easier to read and understand. In fact, the pointer version is the way routines of this sort are commonly written in C.

Sometimes novice C programmers make the mistake of thinking that they should never use array-indexing because pointers are much more efficient. But this is not the case. If the array is going to be accessed in strictly ascending or descending order, pointers are faster and easier to use. However, if the array is going to be accessed randomly, array-indexing is better because it will generally be as fast as evaluating a complex pointer expression and is easier to program and understand. Also, when you use an array, you let the compiler do some of the work for you.

Pointers to Character Arrays

Many string operations in C are generally performed by using pointers and pointer arithmetic, because strings tend to be accessed in a strictly sequential fashion.

For example, here is a version of **strcmp()**, which is found in the Turbo C library:

```
strcmp(char *s1,char *s2)   /* with pointers */
{
  while(*s1)
    if(*s1-*s2)
      return *s1-*s2;
    else {
      s1++;
      s2++;
    }
  return '\0'; /* equal */
}
```

Remember, all strings in C are terminated by a null, which is a false value. Therefore, a statement such as

```
while (*s1)
```

is true until the end of the string is reached. Here, **strcmp()** will return 0 if **s1** is equal to **s2**. It returns less than 0 if **s1** is less than **s2**; otherwise it returns greater than 0.

Most string functions resemble the **strcmp()** with pointers where loop control is concerned. It is faster, more efficient, and easier to understand than using array indexing.

In the **strcmp( )** function, both **s1** and **s2** are local variables. They could be altered with no side effects on the calling variables. But be careful. Examine the following program closely:

```
main()  /* this program is not correct */
{
  char *p1, s[80];

  p1 = s;
  do {
    gets(s);  /* read a string */

    /* print the decimal equivalent of each
        character */
    while(*p1) printf(" %d", *p1++);

  } while(!strcmp(s, "done"));
}
```

Can you find the error?

The problem is that **p1** is assigned the address of **s** only once. The first time through the loop, **p1** does point to the first character in **s**. The second time through, however, it continues from where it left off, because it is not reset to the start of the array **s**. This next character may be part of the second string, another variable, or a piece of the program! The proper way to write this program is

```
main()  /* this program is correct */
{
  char *p1, s[80];

  do {
    p1 = s;
    gets(s);  /* read a string */

    /* print the decimal equivalent of each
        character */
    while(*p1) printf(" %d", *p1++);

  } while(!strcmp(s, "done"));
}
```

Here, each time the loop iterates, **p1** is set to the start of the string.

Arrays of Pointers

Pointers may be arrayed like any other data type. The declaration for an **int** pointer array of size 10 is

```
int *x[10];
```

To assign the address of an integer variable called **var** to the third element of the pointer array, you would write

```
x[2]=&var;
```

To find the value of **var**, you would write

```
*x[2]
```

If you want to pass an array of pointers into a function, you can use the same method used for other arrays—simply call the function with the array name without any indexes. For example, a function that will receive array **x** would look like

```
display_array(q)
int *q[];
{
  int t;

  for(t=0; t<10; t++)
    printf("%d ", *q[t]);

}
```

Remember, **q** is not a pointer to integers but to an array of pointers to integers. Therefore it is necessary to declare the parameter **q** as an array of integer pointers as shown here. It may not be declared as simply an integer pointer because that is not what it is.

A common use of pointer arrays is to hold pointers to error messages. You can create a function that outputs a message given its code number, as shown here.

```
serror(int num)
{
  static char *err[] = {
    "cannot open file\n",
    "read error\n",
    "write error\n",
    "media failure\n"
  };

  printf("%s", err[num]);
}
```

As you can see, **printf()** inside **serror()** is called with a character pointer that points to one of the various error messages indexed by the error number passed to the function. For example, if **num** is passed a 2, the message "write error" is displayed.

It is interesting to note that the command-line argument **argv** is an array of character pointers.

Pointers to Pointers

An array of pointers is the same as *pointers to pointers*. The concept of arrays of pointers is straightforward because the indexes keep the meaning clear. However, pointers to pointers can be very confusing.

A pointer to a pointer is a form of multiple indirection, or a chain of pointers. Consider Figure 6-3.

In the case of a normal pointer, the value of the pointer is the address of the variable that contains the value desired. In the case of a pointer to a pointer, the first pointer contains the address of the second pointer, which points to the variable, which contains the value desired.

Multiple indirection can be carried on to whatever extent desired, but there are few cases where using more than a pointer to a pointer is necessary or even wise. Excessive indirection is difficult to follow and promotes conceptual errors. (Do not confuse multiple indirection with linked lists, which are used in databases and the like.)

A variable that is a pointer to a pointer must be declared as such. This is done by placing an additional asterisk in front of its name. For example, this declaration tells the compiler that **newbalance** is a pointer to a pointer of type **float**.

```
float **newbalance;
```

It is important to understand that **newbalance** is not a pointer to a floating point number but a pointer to a **float** pointer.

In order to access the target value indirectly pointed to by a pointer to a pointer the asterisk operator must be applied twice, as shown in this short example:

```
main()
{
   int x, *p, **q;

   x = 10;
   p = &x;
   q = &p;

   printf("%d", **q); /* print the value of x */
}
```

Here, **p** is declared as a pointer to an integer and **q** as a pointer to a pointer to an integer. The call to **printf()** prints the number 10 on the screen.

Initializing Pointers

After a pointer is declared, but before it has been assigned a value, it contains an unknown value. Should you try to use the pointer before giving it a value, you will probably crash not only your program but also the operating system of your computer —a very nasty type of error!

By convention, a pointer that is pointing nowhere should be given the value null to signify that it points to nothing. However, just because a pointer has a null value does not

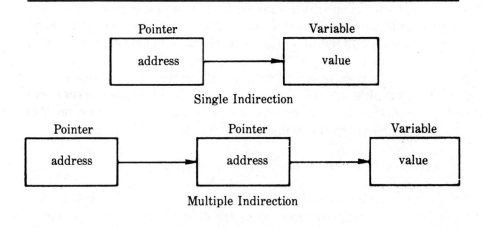

Figure 6-3.   Single and multiple indirection

make it "safe." Should you use a null pointer on the left side of an assignment statement you still risk crashing your program or operating system.

Because a null pointer is assumed to be unused, you can use the null pointer to make many of your pointer routines easier to code and more efficient. For example, you could use a null pointer to mark the end of a pointer array. If this is done, a routine that accesses that array will know that it has reached the end when the null value is encountered. This type of approach is illustrated by the **search()** function shown here:

```
/* look up a name */
search(char *p[], char *name)
{
  register int t;

  for(t=0; p[t]; ++t)
    if(!strcmp(p[t], name)) return t;

  return -1; /* not found */
}
```

The **for** loop inside **search()** runs until either a match or a null pointer is found. Because the end of the array is marked with a null, the condition controlling the loop fails when it is reached.

It is common in professionally written C programs to initialize strings. You saw an example of this in the **serror()** function in the previous section. Another variation on this theme is the following type of string declaration:

```
char *p = "hello world\n";
```

As you can see, the pointer **p** is not an array. The reason this sort of initialization works has to do with the way Turbo C operates. All C compilers create what is called a *string table*, which is used internally by the compiler to store the string constants used by the program. Therefore, this declaration statement places the address of "**hello world**" into the pointer **p**. Throughout the program **p** can be used like any other string. For example, the following program is perfectly valid:

```
char *p="hello world";

main()
{
   register int t;

   /* print the string forward and backwards */
   printf(p);
   for(t=strlen(p)-1; t>-1; t--) printf("%c", p[t]);
}
```

Pointers to Functions

In Chapter 4 you were introduced to a particularly confusing yet powerful feature of C, the *function pointer*. Even though a function is not a variable, it still has a physical location in memory that can be assigned to a pointer. A function's address is the entry point of the function. Because of this a function pointer can be used to call a function. In this section, we will look at another use for the function pointer.

In certain types of programs the user can select one option from a long list of possible actions. For example, in an accounting program, you may be presented with a menu that has 20 or more selections. Once the selection has been made, the routine that routes program execution to the proper function can be handled two ways. First and most commonly, a **case** statement can be used. However, in applications that demand the highest performance there is a better way. An array of pointers can be created with each pointer in the array containing the address of a function. The selection made by the user is decoded and is used to index into the pointer array, causing the proper function to be executed. This method can be very fast.

To see how an array of function pointers can be used as described, imagine that you are implementing a very simple inventory system that is capable of entering, deleting, and reviewing data, as well as exiting to the operating system. If the functions that perform these activities are called **enter( )**, **delete( )**, **review( )**, and **quit( )**, respectively, the following fragment correctly initializes an array of function pointers to these functions:

```
int enter(), delete(), review(), quit();

int *options[] = {
  (int *) enter,
  (int *) delete,
  (int *) review,
  (int *) quit
} ;
```

The type casts are used to prevent compiler warning messages from occurring but are not technically necessary.

Although the actual inventory routines are not developed, the following program illustrates the proper way to execute the functions by using function pointers. Notice how

the **menu( )** function automatically returns the proper index
to the pointer array.

```
int enter(), delete(), review(), quit();

int *options[] = {
  (int *) enter,
  (int *) delete,
  (int *) review,
  (int *) quit
} ;

main()
{
  int i;

  i = menu(); /* get user's choice */

  process(options[i]);  /* execute it */
}

menu()
{
  char ch;

  do {
    printf("1. Enter\n");
    printf("2. Delete\n");
    printf("3. Review\n");
    printf("4. Quit\n");
    printf("Select a number: ");
    ch = getche();
    printf("\n");
  } while(!strchr("1234", ch));
  return ch-49; /* convert to an integer equivalent */
}

process(int (*f) ())
{
  (*f)();
}

enter()
{
  printf("in enter()");
}

delete()
{
  printf("in delete");
}

review()
{
  printf("in review");
}
```

```
quit()
{
  printf("in quit");
  exit(0);
}
```

The program works like this. The menu is displayed, and the user enters the number of the selection desired. Since the number is in ASCII, 49 (the decimal value of 0) is subtracted from it in order to convert it into a binary integer. This value is then returned to **main()** and is used as an index to **options**, the array of function pointers. Next, the call to **process()** is made and the proper function is executed.

Using arrays of function pointers is very common, not only in interpreters and compilers but also in database programs because often these programs provide a large number of options and efficiency is important.

Problems with Pointers

Pointers are a mixed blessing. They give you tremendous power and are necessary for many programs. But when a pointer accidentally contains a wrong value, it can be the most difficult bug to track down. The pointer itself is not the problem; the problem is that each time you perform an operation using it, you are reading or writing to some unknown piece of memory. If you read from it, the worst that can happen is that you get garbage. If you write to it, however, you write over other pieces of your code or data. This may not show up until later in the execution of your program and may lead you to look for the bug in the wrong place. There may be little or no evidence to suggest that the pointer is the problem.

Because pointer errors are such nightmares, you should do your best never to generate one. A few of the more common errors are discussed here.

The classic example of a pointer error is the uninitialized pointer. For example:

```
main()  /* this program is wrong */
{
  int x, *p;

  x = 10;
  *p = x;
}
```

This program assigns the value 10 to some unknown memory location. The pointer **p** has never been given a value, therefore it contains a garbage value. This type of problem often goes unnoticed when your program is very small because the odds are in favor of **p** containing a "safe" address—one that is not in your code, data area, or operating system. However, as your program grows, so does the probability of **p** having a pointer into something vital. Eventually your program stops working. The solution to this sort of trouble is always to make sure that a pointer is pointing at something valid before it is used.

A second common error is caused by a simple misunderstanding of how to use a pointer. For example:

```
main()  /* this program is wrong */
{
  int x, *p;

  x = 10;
  p = x;
  printf("%d", *p);

}
```

The call to **printf()** does not print the value of **x**, which is 10, on the screen. It prints some unknown value because the assignment

```
p = x;
```

is wrong. The statement has assigned the value 10 to the pointer **p**, which was supposed to contain an address, not a value. To make the program correct, you should write

```
p = &x;
```

The fact that pointers can cause very tricky bugs if handled incorrectly is no reason to avoid using them. Simply be careful, and make sure that you know where each pointer is pointing before you use it.

Structures, Unions, and User-Defined Types and Enumerations

SEVEN

The C language gives you five ways to create custom data types:

1. The *structure*, which is a grouping of variables under one name, is sometimes called a *conglomerate* data type.

2. The *bit field* is a variation of the structure and allows easy access to the bits within a word.

3. The *union* enables the same piece of memory to be defined as two or more different types of variables.

4. The *enumeration*, which is a list of symbols, is an extension added by the proposed ANSI standard.

5. The **typedef** keyword simply creates a new name for an existing type.

Structures

In C, a structure is a collection of variables that are referenced under one name, which provides a convenient means of keeping related information together. A *structure definition* forms a template that can be used to create structure variables. The variables that comprise the structure are called *structure elements*. All the elements in the structure are generally related to each other logically. For example, the name and address information found in a mailing list is normally represented as a structure.

To understand structures, it is best to begin with an example. The following code fragment declares a structure template that defines the name and address fields. The keyword **struct** tells the compiler that a structure template is being defined.

```
struct addr {
  char name[30];
  char street[40];
  char city[20];
  char state[2];
  unsigned long int zip;
};
```

The definition is terminated by a semicolon because a structure definition is a statement. The structure tag **addr** identifies this particular data structure and is its type specifier.

At this point in the code, *no variable has actually been declared*. Only the form of the data has been defined. To declare an actual variable with this structure, you write

```
struct addr addr_info;
```

This declares a structure variable of type **addr** called **addr—info**. When you define a structure, you are essentially defining a complex variable type composed of the structure elements. Not until you declare a variable of that type does one actually exist.

Name	30 bytes	
Street	40 bytes	
City	20 bytes	addr—info
State	3 bytes	
Zip	4 bytes	

Figure 7-1.   The structure of **addr—info** in memory

Turbo C automatically allocates sufficient memory to accommodate all the variables that comprise a structure variable. Figure 7-1 shows how **addr—info** would appear in memory assuming 1-byte characters and 2-byte integers.

You may also declare one or more variables at the same time that you define a structure. For example,

```
struct addr {
  char name[30];
  char street[40];
  char city[20];
  char state[2];
  unsigned long int zip;
} addr_info, binfo, cinfo;
```

defines a structure type called **addr** and declares variables **addr—info, binfo,** and **cinfo** of that type.

If you need only one structure variable, the structure name is not needed. This means that

```
struct {
  char name[30];
  char street[40];
  char city[20];
  char state[2];
  unsigned long int zip;
} addr_info;
```

declares one variable named **addr—info** as defined by the structure preceding it.

The general form of a structure definition is

```
struct structure—name {
    type variable—name;
    type variable—name;
    type variable—name;

    .

    .

    .

} structure—variables;
```

The **structure—name** is the name of the structure, not a variable name. The **structure—variables** are variable names in a comma-separated list.

Referencing Structure Elements

Individual structure elements are referenced by using the . (sometimes called the "dot") operator. For example, the following code assigns the zip code 12345 to the **zip** field of the structure variable **addr—info** declared earlier:

```
addr_info.zip = 12345;
```

The structure variable name followed by a period and the element name references that individual structure element. All structure elements are accessed in the same way. The general form is

```
structure—name.element—name
```

Therefore, to print the zip code to the screen, you could write

```
printf("%d",addr_info.zip);
```

This prints the zip code contained in the **zip** field of the structure variable **addr—info**.

In the same fashion, the character array **addr—info. name** can be used to call **gets( )** as shown here:

```
gets(addr_info.name);
```

This passes a character pointer to the start of element **name**.

To access the individual elements of **addr—info.name**, you could index **name**. For example, you could print the contents of **addr—info.name** one character at a time by using this code:

```
register int t;

for(t=0; addr_info.name[t]; ++t) putche(addr_info.name[t]);
```

Arrays of Structures

Perhaps the most common use of structures is in *arrays of structures*. To declare an array of structures, you must first define a structure and then declare an array variable of that type. For example, to declare a 100-element array of structures of type **addr**, which had been defined earlier, you would write

```
struct addr addr_info[100];
```

This creates 100 sets of variables that are organized as defined in the structure type **addr**.

To access a specific structure, index the structure name. For example, to print the zip code of the third structure, you would write

```
printf("%d",addr_info[2].zip);
```

Like all array variables, arrays of structures begin their indexing at 0.

An Inventory Example

To understand how structures and arrays of structures are used, consider a simple inventory program that uses an array of structures to hold the inventory information. The functions in this program interact with structures and their elements in various ways to illustrate structure use.

In this example, the information to be stored includes

item name
cost
number on hand

You can define the basic data structure, called **inv**, to hold this information as

```
#define MAX 100

struct inv {
  char item[30];
  float cost;
  int on_hand;
} inv_info[MAX];
```

In the **inv** structure, **item** holds each inventoried item's name. The element **cost** contains the item's cost, and **on_hand** represents the number of items currently available.

The first function needed for the program is **main( )**.

```
main()
{
  char choice;

  init_list(); /* initialize the structure array*/
  for(;;) {
    choice = menu_select();
    switch(choice) {
      case 1: enter();
        break;
```

```
      case 2: delete();
        break;
      case 3: list();
        break;
      case 4: exit(0);
    }
  }
}
```

In **main( )**, the call to **init—list( )** prepares the structure array for use by putting a null character into the first byte of the item name field. The program assumes that a structure variable is not in use if the name field is empty. The **init— list( )** function is written as

```
/* Initialize the structure array. */
void init_list()
{
  register int t;

  for(t=0; t<MAX; ++t) inv_info[t].item[0] = '\0';
}
```

The **menu—select( )** function will display the option messages and return the user's selection.

```
/* Input the user's selection. */
menu_select()
{
  char s[80];
  int c;

  printf("\n");
  printf("1. Enter a item\n");
  printf("2. Delete a item\n");
  printf("3. List the inventory\n");
  printf("4. Quit\n");
  do {
    printf("\nEnter your choice: ");
    gets(s);
    c = atoi(s);
  } while(c<0 || c>4);
  return c;
}
```

The **enter( )** function prompts the user for input and places the information entered into the next free structure. If the array is full, the message **list full** is printed on the screen. The **find—free()** function searches the structure array for an unused element.

```
/* Input the inventory information. */
void enter()
{
  int slot;
  slot = find_free();
  if(slot==-1) {
    printf("\nlist full");
    return;
  }

  printf("enter item: ");
  gets(inv_info[slot].item);

  printf("enter cost: ");
  scanf("%f", &inv_info[slot].cost);

  printf("enter number on hand: ");
  scanf("%d%*c",&inv_info[slot].on_hand);
}

/* Return the index of the first unused array
   location or -1 if the no free locations exist.
*/
find_free()
{
  register int t;

  for(t=0;inv_info[t].item[0] && t<MAX;++t) ;
  if(t==MAX) return -1; /* no slots free */
  return t;
}
```

Notice that **find—free()** returns a −1 if every structure array variable is in use. This is a "safe" number to use because there cannot be a −1 element.

The **delete()** function requires the user to specify the number of the item that needs to be deleted. The function then puts a null character in the first character position of the **item** field.

```
/* Delete an item from the list. */
void delete()
{
  register int slot;
```

```
    char s[80];
    printf("enter record #: ");
    gets(s);
    slot=atoi(s);
    if(slot>=0 && slot < MAX) inv_info[slot].item[0]='\0';
}
```

The final function the program needs is **list( )**. It prints the entire inventory list on the screen.

```
/* Display the list on the screen. */
void list()
{
  register int t;

  for(t=0;t<MAX;++t) {
    if(inv_info[t].item[0]) {
      printf("item: %s\n",inv_info[t].item);
      printf("cost: %f\n",inv_info[t].cost);
      printf("on hand: %d\n\n",inv_info[t].on_hand);
    }
  }
  printf("\n\n");
}
```

The complete listing for the inventory program is shown here. If you have any doubts about your understanding of structures, you should enter this program into your computer and study its execution by making changes and watching their effect.

```
/*A simple inventory program using an array of structures */

#define MAX 100

struct inv {
  char item[30];
  float cost;
  int on_hand;
} inv_info[MAX];

void init_list(), list(), delete(), enter();

main()
{
  char choice;

  init_list(); /* initialize the structure array*/
  for(;;) {
    choice = menu_select();
```

```
      switch(choice) {
        case 1: enter();
          break;
        case 2: delete();
          break;
        case 3: list();
          break;
        case 4: exit(0);
      }
   }
}

/* Initialize the structure array. */
void init_list()
{
   register int t;

   for(t=0; t<MAX; ++t) inv_info[t].item[0] = '\0';
}

/* Input the user's selection. */
menu_select()
{
   char s[80];
   int c;

   printf("\n");
   printf("1. Enter a item\n");
   printf("2. Delete a item\n");
   printf("3. List the inventory\n");
   printf("4. Quit\n");
   do {
     printf("\nEnter your choice: ");
     gets(s);
     c = atoi(s);

   } while(c<0 || c>4);
   return c;
}

/* Input the inventory information. */
void enter()
{
   int slot;
   slot = find_free();
   if(slot==-1) {
     printf("\nlist full");
     return;
   }

   printf("enter item: ");
   gets(inv_info[slot].item);

   printf("enter cost: ");
   scanf("%f", &inv_info[slot].cost);
```

```
    printf("enter number on hand: ");
    scanf("%d%*c",&inv_info[slot].on_hand);
}

/* Return the index of the first unused array
   location or -1 if the no free locations exist.
*/
find_free()
{
  register int t;

  for(t=0;inv_info[t].item[0] && t<MAX;++t) ;
  if(t==MAX) return -1; /* no slots free */
  return t;
}

/* Delete an item from the list. */
void delete()
{
  register int slot;
  char s[80];
  printf("enter record #: ");
  gets(s);
  slot=atoi(s);
  if(slot>=0 && slot < MAX) inv_info[slot].item[0]='\0';
}

/* Display the list on the screen. */
void list()
{
  register int t;

  for(t=0;t<MAX;++t) {
    if(inv_info[t].item[0]) {
      printf("item: %s\n",inv_info[t].item);
      printf("cost: %f\n",inv_info[t].cost);
      printf("on hand: %d\n\n",inv_info[t].on_hand);
    }
  }
  printf("\n\n");
}
```

Passing Structures to Functions

So far, all structures and arrays of structures used in the
examples have been assumed to be either global or defined
within the function that uses them. In this section special

consideration will be given to passing structures and their elements to functions.

Passing Structure Elements to Functions

When you pass an element of a structure variable to a function, you are actually passing the value of that element to the function. Therefore, you are passing a simple variable (unless, of course, that element is complex, such as an array of characters). For example, consider this structure:

```
struct fred {
  char x;
  int y;
  float z;
  char s[10];
} mike;
```

Here are examples of each element being passed to a function:

```
func(mike.x);  /* passes character value of x */

func2(mike.y); /* passes integer value of y */

func3(mike.z); /* passes float value of z */

func4(mike.s); /* passes address of string s */

func(mike.s[2]); /* passes character value of s[2] */
```

However, if you wished to pass the address of individual structure elements to achieve call-by-value parameter passing, you would place the **&** operator before the structure name. For example, to pass the address of the elements in the structure **mike**, you would write

```
func(&mike.x);  /* passes address of character x */

func2(&mike.y); /* passes address of integer y */

func3(&mike.z); /* passes address of float z*/
```

```
func4(mike.s); /* passes address of string s */

func(&mike.s[2]); /* passes address of character s[2] */
```

Notice that the **&** operator precedes the structure name not the individual element name. Note also that the string element s already signifies an address, so no **&** is required.

Passing Entire Structures to Functions

When a structure is used as an argument to a function, the entire structure is passed using the standard call-by-value method. This means that any changes made to the contents of the structure inside the function to which it is passed do not affect the structure used as an argument.

When using a structure as a parameter the most important thing to remember is that the type of the argument must match the type of the parameter. For example, both the argument **arg** and the parameter **parm** are declared to be of the same type of structure.

```
main()
{
  struct {
    int a,b;
    char ch;
  } arg;

  arg.a=1000;

  f1(arg);
}

f1(parm)
struct {
  int x,y;
  char ch;
} parm;
{
  printf("%d",parm.x);
}
```

This program prints the number 1000 on the screen. Although it is not technically wrong to use parallel structure declarations of this type, a better approach—and one that requires less work on your part—is to define a structure globally and then use its name to declare structure variables and parameters as needed. Using this method, the same program becomes

```
/* define a structure type */
struct struct_type {
  int a,b;
  char ch;
} ;

main()
{
  struct struct_type arg;  /* declare arg */

  arg.a=1000;

  f1(arg);
}
f1(parm)
struct struct_type parm;
{
  printf("%d",parm.a);
}
```

This method not only saves some programming effort, but also helps ensure that the arguments and the parameters do, in fact, match.

Structure Pointers

Turbo C allows pointers to structures the same way it does to other types of variables. However, there are some special aspects to structure pointers that you must keep in mind.

Declaring a Structure Pointer

Structure pointers are declared by placing the * in front of a structure variable's name. For example, assuming the previously defined structure **addr**, the following declares **addr_pointer** to be a pointer to data of that type:

```
struct addr *addr_pointer;
```

Using Structure Pointers

There are two primary uses for structure pointers: (1) to achieve a call-by-reference call to a function and (2) to create linked lists and other dynamic data structures using Turbo C's allocation system. This chapter will be concerned only with the first; the second use will be covered later in the book.

There is one major drawback to passing all but the simplest structures to functions: the overhead needed to push (and pop) all the structure elements onto the stack. In simple structures with few elements this overhead is not too important, but if several elements are used or some of the elements are arrays, run-time performance may degrade to unacceptable levels. The solution to this problem is to pass only a pointer to a function.

When a pointer to a structure is passed to a function only the address of the structure is pushed (and popped) on the stack. This means a very fast function call can be executed. Also, because the function references the actual structure and not a copy, it can modify the contents of the actual elements of the structure used in the call.

To find the address of a structure variable, the **&** operator is placed before the structure's name. For example, given the following fragment,

```
struct bal {
  float balance;
  char name[80];
} person;

struct bal *p;  /* declare a structure pointer */
```

then

```
p = &person;
```

places the address of the structure **person** into the pointer **p**. To reference the **balance** element you would write

```
(*p).balance
```

The parentheses are necessary around the pointer because the "dot" operator has a higher priority than the *.

Actually, two methods can be used to reference an element in a structure that has been given a pointer to it. The first method discussed uses *explicit pointer references* and is considered archaic by today's standards. However, because some older C code may use this approach, it is important to be familiar with it. Also, it lays important groundwork that helps you understand the more common method. The second method of accessing elements of structures given a pointer to the structure is the —> operator, which is essentially a shorthand for the first method.

To see how a structure pointer can be used, examine this simple program that prints the hours, minutes, and seconds on your screen by using a software delay timer:

```
/* display a software timer */

struct tm {
  int hours;
  int minutes;
  int seconds;
};
main()  /* version 1 - explicit pointer references */
{
  struct tm time;

  time.hours = 0;
  time.minutes = 0;
  time.seconds = 0;

  for(;;) {
    update(&time);
```

```
        display(&time);
    }
}
update(struct tm *t)
{
    (*t).seconds++;
    if((*t).seconds==60) {
        (*t).seconds=0;
        (*t).minutes++;
    }
    if((*t).minutes==60) {
        (*t).minutes=0;
        (*t).hours++;
    }
    if((*t).hours==24) (*t).hours = 0;
    delay();
}
display(struct tm *t)
{
    printf("%d:",(*t).hours);
    printf("%d:",(*t).minutes);
    printf("%d\n",(*t).seconds);
}

delay()
{
    long int t;
    for(t=1;t<128000;++t) ;
}
```

The timing of this program is adjusted by varying the loop count in **delay( )**.

A global structure called **tm** is defined but no variable is declared. Inside **main( )**, the structure variable, **time**, of type **tm** is declared and initialized to 00:00:00. This means that **time** is known directly only to the **main( )** function.

The functions **update( )**, which changes the time, and **display( )**, which prints the time, are passed the address of **time**. In both functions the argument is declared to be a pointer to a structure of type **tm** so that the compiler will know how to reference the structure elements.

Each structure element is actually referenced by a pointer. For example, if you wanted to set the hours back to zero when 24:00:00 was reached, you would write

```
if((*t).hours==24) (*t).hours = 0;
```

This line of code tells the compiler to take the address of **t** (which is **time** in **main()**) and assign 0 to its element called **hours**. (Remember that parentheses are necessary around the ***t** because the dot operator has a higher priority than the ***.**)

Today, you seldom, if ever, see references made to a structure's elements with explicit use of the * operator. Because this type of operation is so common, C defines a special operator to perform it. It is the —>, which most C programmers call the *arrow operator*. It is formed by a minus sign followed by a greater-than sign. The arrow is used in place of the dot operator when accessing a structure element given a pointer to the structure. For example,

```
(*t).hours
```

is the same as

```
t->hours
```

Therefore, **update()** could be rewritten as

```
update(struct tm *t)
{
  t->seconds++;

  if(t->seconds==60) {
    t->seconds=0;
    t->minutes++;
  }

  if(t->minutes==60) {
    t->minutes=0;
    t->hours++;
  }

  if(t->hours==24) t->hours = 0;

  delay();

}
```

Remember that you use the dot operator to access structure elements when operating on the structure itself. When you have a pointer to a structure, the arrow operator should be used.

As a final example of using structure pointers, the following program illustrates how a general purpose integer input function can be designed. The function **input_xy()** allows you to specify the **x** and **y** coordinates at which a prompting message will be displayed and then inputs an integer value. To accomplish these things it uses the structure **xyinput**.

```c
/* A generalized input example using structure pointers. */
struct xyinput {
  int x, y; /* screen location for prompt */
  char message[80]; /* prompting message */
  int i; /* input value */
} ;

void input_xy();

main()
{
  struct xyinput mess;

  mess.x = 10; mess.y = 10;
  strcpy(mess.message, "enter an integer: ");

  clrscr();

  input_xy(&mess);

  printf("your number squared is: %d", mess.i*mess.i);
}

/* Display a prompting message at the specified location
   and input an integer value.
*/
void input_xy(struct xyinput *info)
{
  gotoxy(info->x, info->y);

  printf(info->message);
  scanf("%d", &info->i);
}
```

This program uses the functions **clrscr( )** and **gotoxy( )**, which are provided by Turbo C beginning with Version 1.5. If you have an earlier version you will have to call the proper BIOS routines manually by using **int86( )**.

Arrays and Structures Within Structures

A structure element can be either simple or complex. A simple element is any of the built-in data types, such as integer or character. You have already seen one complex element: the character array used in **addr—info**. Other complex data types are single- and multidimensional arrays of the other data types and structures.

A structure element that is an array is treated as you might expect from the earlier examples. Consider this structure, for example:

```
struct x {
  int a[10][10]; /* 10 x 10 array of ints */
  float b;
} y;
```

To reference integer 3,7 in **a** of structure **y**, you would write

```
y.a[3][7]
```

When a structure is an element of another structure, it is called *nested structure*. For example, here the structure variable element **address** is nested inside **emp**:

```
struct emp {
  struct addr address;
  float wage;
} worker;
```

The **addr** is the structure defined previously, and a structure **emp** has been defined as having two elements. The first element is the structure of type **addr**, which contains an employee's address, and **wage**, which holds the employee's wage. The following code fragment assigns $35,000 to the **wage** element of **worker** and 98765 to the **zip** field of **address**:

```
worker.wage = 35000.00;
worker.address.zip = 98765;
```

The elements of each structure are referenced from outermost to innermost.

Bit Fields

Unlike most other computer languages, C has a built-in method to access a single bit within a byte. This can be useful for three reasons:

1. If storage is limited, you can store several *boolean* (true-false) variables in one byte.

2. Certain device interfaces transmit information encoded into bits within 1 byte.

3. Certain encryption routines need to access the bits within a byte.

Although all these functions can be performed using bytes and the bitwise operators, a bit field can add more structure and efficiency to your code. It might also make it more portable.

The method C uses to access bits is based on the structure. A bit field is really just a special type of structure element that defines how long, in bits, it is to be. The general form of a bit field definition is

```
struct struc__name {
    type name 1 : length;
    type name 2 : length;
      .
      .
      .
    type name 3 : length;
}
```

A bit field must be declared as either **int**, **unsigned**, or **signed**. Bit fields of length 1 should be declared as **unsigned** because a single bit cannot have a sign.

For example, consider the following structure definition:

```
struct device {
  unsigned active : 1;
  unsigned ready : 1;
  unsigned xmt_error : 1;
} dev_code;
```

This structure defines three variables of 1 bit each. The structure variable **dev__code** might be used to decode information from the port of a tape drive, for example. The following code fragment writes a byte of information to the (imaginary) tape and checks for errors using **dev__code** from above:

```
wr_tape(char c)
{
  while(!dev_code.ready) rd(&dev_code); /* wait */

  wr_to_tape(c); /* write out byte */

  while(dev_code.active) rd(&dev_code); /* wait till
         info is written */

  if(dev_code.xmt_error) printf("write error");
}
```

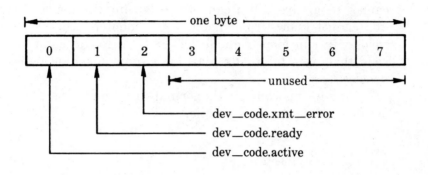

Figure 7-2.   The bit field variable **dev—code** in memory

Here, **rd( )** returns the status of the tape drive and **wr—to— tape( )** actually writes the data.

Figure 7-2 shows what the bit variable **dev—code** looks like in memory.

As you can see from the previous example, each bit field is accessed using the dot operator. However, if the structure is referenced through a pointer, you must use the —> operator.

You do not have to name each bit field. This makes it easy to reach the bit you want and pass up unused ones. For example, if the tape drive also returned an end-of-tape flag in bit 5, you could alter structure **device** to accommodate this by using

```
struct device {
  unsigned active : 1;
  unsigned ready : 1;
  unsigned xmt_error : 1;
  unsigned : 2;
  unsigned EOT : 1;
} dev_code;
```

Bit field variables have certain restrictions. You cannot take the address of a bit field variable. Bit field variables cannot be arrayed. You cannot overlap integer boundaries. You cannot know, from machine to machine, whether the fields will run from right to left or from left to right; any code that uses bit fields may have some machine dependencies.

Finally, it is valid to mix normal structure elements with bit field elements. For example,

```
struct emp {
  struct addr address;
  float pay;
  unsigned lay_off:1;   /* lay off or active */
  unsigned hourly:1:    /* hourly pay or wage */
  unsigned deductions:3: /* IRS deductions */
};
```

defines an employee record that uses only 1 byte to hold three pieces of information: the employee's status, whether the employee is salaried, and the number of deductions. Without the use of the bit field, this information would have taken three bytes.

Unions

In C, a **union** is a memory location used by several variables, which may be of different types. The **union** definition is similar to that of a structure, as shown in this example:

```
union union_type {
  int i;
  char ch;
} ;
```

Like a structure definition, this definition does not declare any variables. You may declare a variable either by placing its name at the end of the definition or by using a separate declaration statement. To declare a **union** variable **cnvt** of type **union__type** using the definition just given, you would write

```
union union_type cnvt;
```

In **union cnvt**, both integer **i** and character **ch** share the same memory location. (Of course, **i** occupies 2 bytes and **ch** uses only 1.) Figure 7-3 shows how **i** and **ch** share the same address.

When a **union** is declared, the compiler automatically creates a variable large enough to hold the largest variable type in the **union**.

To access a **union** element you use the same syntax that you would use for structures: the dot and arrow operators. If you are operating on the **union** directly, use the dot operator. If the **union** variable is accessed through a pointer, use the arrow operator. For example, to assign the integer 10 to element **i** of **cnvt**, you would write

```
cnvt.i = 10;
```

Using a **union** can help you produce machine-independent (portable) code. Because Turbo C keeps track of the

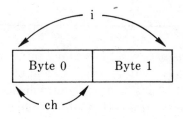

Figure 7-3.   How **i** and **ch** use the union **cnvt**

actual sizes of the variables that make up the **union**, no machine dependencies are produced. You need not worry about the size of an integer, character, **float**, or whatever.

Unions are frequently used when type conversions are needed. For example, the standard library function **putw()** writes the binary representation of an integer to a disk file. Although there are many ways to code this function, the one shown here uses a **union**. First, a **union** composed of one integer and a 2-byte character array is created:

```
union pw {
   int i;
   char ch[2];
};
```

Now **putw()** is written using the **union**:

```
putw(word, fp)    /* putw with union */
union pw word;
FILE *fp;
{
   putc(word->ch[0]); /* write first half */
   putc(word->ch[1]); /* write second half */
}
```

Although called with an integer, **putw()** can still use the standard function **putc()** to write an integer to a disk file. Because the function thinks it is receiving a **union**, both halves of the integer can be written out easily.

Enumerations

An *enumeration* is a set of named integer constants that specify all the legal values that a variable of its type can have. Enumerations are not uncommon in everyday life. For example, an enumeration of the coins used in the United States is

penny, nickel, dime, quarter, half-dollar, dollar

Enumerations are defined like structures, by using the keyword **enum** to signal the start of an enumeration type. The general form is

enum enum—type—name { enumeration list } variable—list;

Both the enumeration name **enum—type—name** and the **variable—list** are optional. The enumeration type name is used to declare variables of its type. The following fragment defines an enumeration called **coin** and declares **money** to be of that type:

```
enum coin { penny, nickel, dime, quarter,
            half_dollar, dollar};

enum coin money;
```

Given this definition and declaration, the following types of statements are perfectly valid:

```
money = dime;

if(money==quarter) printf("is a quarter\n");
```

The key point to understand about an enumeration is that each of the symbols stands for an integer value and can be used in any integer expression. For example,

```
printf("the number of nickels in a quarter is %d ", quarter+2);
```

is perfectly valid.

Unless initialized otherwise, the value of the first enumeration symbol is 0, the second is 1, and so forth. Therefore,

```
printf("%d %d",penny, dime);
```

displays **0 2** on the screen.

It is possible to specify the value of one or more of the symbols by using an initializer. This is done by following the symbol with an equal sign and an integer value. Whenever an initializer is used, symbols that follow it are assigned values greater than the previous initialization value. For example, the following assigns the value of 100 to **quarter**:

```
enum coin { penny, nickel, dime, quarter=100,
            half_dollar, dollar};
```

Now the values of these symbols are

penny	0
nickel	1
dime	2
quarter	100
half—dollar	101
dollar	102

It is commonly assumed that the symbols of an enumeration can be input and output directly, but this is not true. For example, the following code fragment will not perform as desired:

```
/* this will not work */

money = dollar;

printf("%s", money);
```

Remember that the symbol **dollar** is simply a name for an integer; it is not a string. Hence, it is not possible for **printf()** to display the string "dollar." Likewise, you cannot give an enumeration variable a value by using the string equivalent. That is, this code does not work:

```
/* this code will not work */

money = "penny";
```

Actually, creating code to input and output enumeration symbols is quite tedious (unless you are willing to settle for their integer values). For example, the following code is needed to display, in words, the kind of coins that **money** contains:

```
switch(money) {
  case penny: printf("penny");
        break;
  case nickel: printf("nickel");
        break;
  case dime: printf("dime");
        break;
  case quarter: printf("quarter");
        break;
  case half_dollar: printf("half_dollar");
        break;
  case dollar: printf("dollar");
}
```

Sometimes it is possible to declare an array of strings and use the enumeration value as an index to translate an enumeration value into its corresponding string. For example, this code also outputs the proper string:

```
char name[]={
  "penny",
  "nickel",
  "dime",
  "quarter",
  "half_dollar",
  "dollar"
};
printf("%s", name[(int)money]);
```

Of course, this works only if no symbol initializations are used, because the string array must be indexed starting at 0. The cast that precedes **money** is necessary to avoid warning errors because **money** is technically not an integer variable but an enumeration variable.

Since enumeration values must be converted manually to their human-readable string values for console I/O, they are most useful in routines that do not make such conversions. For example, an enumeration is commonly used to define a compiler's symbol table.

Using sizeof to Ensure Portability

You have seen that structures, unions, and enumerations can be used to create variables of varying sizes, and that the actual size of these variables may change from machine to machine. The **sizeof** unary operator is used to compute the size of any variable or type and can help eliminate machine-dependent code from your programs.

For example, Turbo C has the following sizes for these data types:

Type	Size in Bytes
char	1
int	2
long int	4
float	4
double	8

Therefore, the following code will print the numbers **1**, **2**, and **4** on the screen:

```
char ch;
int i;
float f;

printf("%d",sizeof(ch));

printf("%d",sizeof(i));

printf("%d",sizeof(f));
```

The **sizeof** operator is a compile-time operator: All the information necessary to compute the size of any variable is known at compile time. For example, consider the following:

```
union x {
  char ch;
  int i;
  float f;
} tom;
```

The **sizeof(tom)** will be 4. At run-time, it does not matter what the **union tom** is *actually* holding; all that matters is the size of the largest variable it can hold because the **union** must be as large as its largest element.

Keep in mind that Turbo C will align data on word boundaries. This means that a conglomerate data type may be slightly larger than the sum of its parts. Manually adding up the lengths of the elements of a structure, for example, may not yield its correct size.

typedef

Turbo C allows you to define new data type names by using the **typedef** keyword. You are not actually creating a new data class; you are defining a new name for an existing type. This process can help make machine-dependent programs more portable; only the **typedef** statements need to be changed. It can also help you document your code by allowing descriptive names for the standard data types. The general form of the **typedef** statement is

    typedef type name;

where **type** is any allowable data type and **name** is the new name for this type. The new name you define is an addition to, not a replacement for, the existing type name.

For example, you could create a new name for **float** by using

```
typedef float balance;
```

This statement tells the compiler to recognize **balance** as another name for **float**. Next you could create a **float** variable by using **balance**:

```
balance over_due;
```

Here **over—due** is a floating point variable of type **balance**, which is another word for **float**.

You can use also **typedef** to create names for more complex types. For example:

```
typedef struct  {
  float due;
  int over_due;
  char name[40];
} client;

client clist[NUM_CLIENTS]; /* define array of
                structures of type client */
```

Using **typedef** can help make your code easier to read and more portable. However, you should remember that you are *not* creating any new data types.

Input, Output, and Disk Files

Input and output in C are accomplished through the use of library functions; there are no C keywords that perform I/O operations. The ANSI standard, which is followed by Turbo C, defines one complete set of I/O functions. However, the old UNIX standard defines a second system of routines that handle I/O operations. The first method, defined by both standards, is called the *buffered file system* (sometimes the term *formatted* or *high-level* is used). The second is the *unbuffered file system* (sometimes the term *unformatted* or *UNIX-like* is used) and is defined only by the UNIX standard.

The ANSI standard's failure to define the unbuffered file system is justified by several arguments, including the fact that the two file systems are largely redundant. However, because both file systems are currently in widespread use, Turbo C supports both approaches. This chapter will cover both, but the greatest emphasis will be placed on the ANSI standard I/O system because use of the unbuffered system is expected to decline. New code should be written using the ANSI I/O functions.

The purpose of this chapter is to present an overview of I/O in Turbo C and to illustrate the way the core functions of

each file system work together. The Turbo C library contains
a rich and diverse assortment of I/O routines—more than
can be covered here. However, the functions presented in this
chapter are sufficient for all but the most unusual circumstances. The remainder of the I/O functions are covered in
Part Three of this guide.

During this discussion, keep in mind that the prototype
declarations and several predefined types and constants for
the Turbo C buffered I/O library functions are found in the
file **stdio.h**. The header file **io.h** is used for unbuffered file
routines.

Streams and Files

Before beginning our discussion of Turbo C's I/O system, it is
important to understand the difference between the terms
streams and *files*. The C I/O system supplies a consistent
interface to the C programmer independent of the actual
device being accessed. That is, the C I/O system provides a
level of abstraction between the programmer and the device
being used. This abstraction is called a stream; the actual
device is a file. It is important to understand how they
interact.

Streams

The buffered file system is designed to work with a wide
variety of devices, including terminals, disk drives, and tape
drives. Even though each device is very different, the buffered file system transforms each into a logical device called
a stream. All streams are similar in behavior. Because
streams are largely device-independent, the functions that
write to a disk file can also write to the console. There are
two types of streams: text and binary.

Text Streams

A *text stream* is a sequence of characters organized into lines terminated by a newline character. The proposed ANSI standard states that the newline character is optional depending on the implementation. In a text stream, certain character translations may occur as required by the host environment. For example, a newline may be converted to a carriage return, linefeed pair. This is what Turbo C does. Therefore, there may not be a one-to-one relationship between the characters that are written or read and those in the external device. Also, because of possible translations, the number of characters written or read may not be the same as those found in the external device.

Binary Streams

A *binary stream* is a sequence of bytes that have a one-to-one correspondence to those found in the external device. That is, no character translations will occur. Also, the number of bytes written or read will be the same as the number found in the external device. The proposed standard does specify, however, that a binary stream may have an implementation-defined number of null bytes appended to its end. These null bytes might be used to pad the information so that it fills a sector on a disk, for example.

Files

In C, a *file* is a logical concept that can be applied to everything from disk files to terminals. A stream is associated with a specific file by performing an open operation. Once a file is open, information can be exchanged between it and your program.

Not all files have the same capabilities. For example, a disk file can support random access, but a terminal cannot.

This illustrates an important point about the C I/O system: All streams are the same but all files are not.

If the file can support random access (sometimes referred to as *position requests*), opening that file initializes the *file-position indicator* to the start of the file. As each character is read from or written to the file, the position indicator is incremented, ensuring progression through the file.

A file is disassociated from a specific stream, by a close operation. On streams opened for output, closing a stream causes any contents of its associated buffer to be written to the external device. This process is generally called *flushing* the stream, and it guarantees that no information is accidentally left in the disk buffer. All files are closed automatically when your program terminates normally by calling **main( )** to return to the operating system or by calling **exit( )**. Files are not closed if a program terminates through a call to **abort( )** or, obviously, if it crashes.

At the beginning of a program's execution three predefined text streams are opened. They are **stdin**, **stdout**, and **stderr**, and they refer to the standard I/O device connected to the system. Version 1.5 of Turbo C also opens **stdprn** (standard printer) and **stdaux** (standard auxiliary device). For most systems **stdaux** is the console. Remember, however, that most operating systems, including DOS, allow I/O redirection, so routines that read or write to these files can be redirected to other devices. (Redirection of I/O is a process whereby information that would normally go to one device is rerouted to another device by the operating system.) You should never try explicitly to open or close these files.

Each stream that is associated with a file has a file control structure of type **FILE**. This structure is defined in the header **stdio.h**. You must not make modifications to this file control block.

Conceptual Versus Actual

As far as the programmer is concerned, all I/O takes place through streams, which are sequences of characters. All streams are the same. The file system links a stream to a file, which is any external device capable of I/O. Because different devices have differing capabilities, all files are not the same. However, these differences are minimized for the programmer by the C I/O system, which converts the raw information coming from the device into a stream (and vice versa). Aside from the limitation that only certain types of files support random access, the programmer need not worry about the actual physical device and is free to concentrate on the logical device—the stream.

If this approach seems confusing or strange, look at it in the context of languages like BASIC or FORTRAN, in which each device supported by the implementation has its own completely separate file system. In C's approach, the programmer need think only in terms of streams and use only one file system to accomplish all I/O operations.

Console I/O

Console I/O refers to operations that occur at the keyboard and screen of your computer. Generally, console I/O is performed by using a special case of the buffered file system. Because input and output to the console is such a common affair, a subsystem of the buffered file system was created to deal exclusively with console I/O. Technically, these functions direct their operations to the standard input and standard output of the system. In many operating systems, including DOS, the console I/O can be redirected to other devices. For simplicity of discussion, however, it is assumed that the console will be the device used since it is the most common.

getche() and putchar()

The simplest of the console I/O functions are **getche()**, which reads a character from the keyboard, and **putchar()**, which prints a character to the screen. The **getche()** function waits until a key is pressed and then returns its value. The key pressed is also "echoed" to the screen automatically. The **putchar()** function writes its character argument to the screen at the current cursor position.

The following program inputs characters from the keyboard and prints them in reverse case. That is, uppercase prints as lowercase, and lowercase as uppercase. The program halts when a period is typed.

```
#include "stdio.h"
#include "ctype.h"

main()  /* case switcher */
{
  char ch;

  do {
    ch = getche();
    if(islower(ch)) putchar(toupper(ch));
    else putchar(tolower(ch));
  } while (ch!='.'); /* use a period to stop*/
}
```

There are two important variations on **getche()**. The first is **getchar()**, which is the original, UNIX-based character input function. The trouble with **getchar()** is that it buffers input until a carriage return is entered. The reason for this is that the original UNIX systems line-buffered terminal input—that is, you had to enter a carriage return for anything you had just typed actually to be sent to the program. This line-buffering leaves one or more characters waiting in the input queue after **getchar()** returns. This effect is quite annoying in today's interactive environments, and the use of **getchar()** is not recommended. It is supported by Turbo C only to ensure portability with UNIX-based programs. You may want to play with **getchar()** a little to understand its effect better.

A second, more useful, variation on **getche()** is **getch()**, which operates like **getche()** except that the character you type is not echoed to the screen. You can use this fact to create a rather humorous (if disconcerting) program to run on some unsuspecting end user. The program, shown here, displays what appears to be a standard DOS prompt and waits for input. However, every character the user types is displayed as the next letter in the alphabet. That is, an **A** becomes **B**, and so forth.

```
/* This program appears to act as a DOS gone wild.  It
   displays the DOS prompt and but displays every character
   the user types as the next letter in the alphabet.
*/

#include "stdio.h"

main()
{
  char ch;

  do {
    printf("C>");
    for(;;) {
      ch = getch(); /* read chars without echo */
      if(ch=='\r' || ch==1) {
        printf("\n");
        break;
      }
      putchar(ch+1);
    }
  } while(ch!=1) ; /* exit on control-A */
}
```

Use this program with caution; it has been known to cause panic in novice computer users!

gets() and puts()

On the next step up, in terms of complexity and power, are the functions **gets()** and **puts()**. They enable you to read and write strings of characters at the console.

The **gets( )** function reads a string of characters entered at the keyboard and places them at the address pointed to by its character pointer argument. You may type characters at the keyboard until you strike a carriage return. The carriage return does not become part of the string; instead a null terminator is placed at the end and **gets( )** returns. In fact, it is impossible to use **gets( )** to obtain a carriage return (**getchar( )** can do so, though). Typing mistakes can be corrected by using the backspace before pressing ENTER. The **gets( )** function is declared as

    char *gets(*char* *s*)

where *s* is a character array. As an example, the following program reads a string into the array **str** and prints its length:

```
main()
{
  char str[80];

  gets(str);
  printf("length is %d", strlen(str));
}
```

The **gets( )** function returns a pointer to *s*.

The **puts( )** function writes its string argument to the screen followed by a newline. It is declared as

    char *puts(*char* *s*)

It recognizes the same backslash codes as **printf( )**, such as \t for tab. A call to **puts( )** requires far less overhead than the same call to **printf( )** because **puts( )** can output only a string of characters; it cannot output numbers or do format conversions. Since **puts( )** takes up less space and runs faster than **printf( )**, it is often used when highly optimized code is needed. The **puts( )** function returns a pointer to its string argument. The following statement writes **hello** on the screen:

```
puts("hello");
```

The simplest functions that perform console I/O operations are summarized in Table 8-1.

Formatted Console I/O

In addition to the simple console I/O functions, the Turbo C standard library contains two functions that perform formatted input and output on the built-in data types: **printf()** and **scanf()**. The term *formatted* refers to the fact that these functions can read and write data in various formats that are under your control. The **printf()** function is used to write data to the console; **scanf()**, its complement, reads data from the keyboard. Both **printf()** and **scanf()** can operate on any of the built-in data types, including characters, strings, and

Function	Operation
getchar()	Reads a character from the keyboard; waits for carriage return
getche()	Reads a character with echo; does not wait for carriage return
getch()	Reads a character without echo; does not wait for carriage return
putchar()	Writes a character to the screen
gets()	Reads a string from the keyboard
puts()	Writes a string to the screen

Table 8-1.   The Basic Console I/O Functions

numbers. Although you have been using these functions since the start of this book, they will be examined in detail here.

printf()

The **printf()** is declared as

printf (*"control string",argument list*);

The control string consists of two types of items. The first type contains characters that will be printed on the screen. The second type contains format commands that define the way the arguments are displayed. A format command begins with a percent sign and is followed by the format code. The format commands are shown in Table 8-2. There must be exactly the same number of arguments as there are format

Code	Format
%c	A single character
%d	Decimal
%i	Decimal
%e	Scientific notation
%f	Decimal floating point
%g	Uses %e or %f, whichever is shorter
%o	Octal
%s	String of characters
%u	Unsigned decimal
%x	Hexadecimal
%%	Prints a % sign
%p	Displays a pointer
%n	The associated argument shall be an integer pointer into which is placed the number of characters written so far

Table 8-2.   Format Codes of **printf()**

commands, and the format commands and arguments are matched in order. For example, this **printf( )** call

```
printf("Hi %c %d %s", 'c', 10, "there!");
```

displays: **Hi c 10 there!**.

The format commands may have modifiers that specify the field width, the number of decimal places, and a left-justification flag. An integer placed between the % sign and the format command acts as a *minimum-field width specifier*. This pads the output with blanks or zeros to ensure that it is at least a certain minimum length. If the string or number is greater than that minimum, it will be printed in full even if it overruns the minimum. The default padding is done with spaces. If you wish to pad with zeros, place **0** before the field-width specifier. For example, **%05d** will pad a number of less than five digits with zeros so that its total length is five.

To specify the number of decimal places printed for a floating point number, place a decimal point after the field-width specifier, followed by the number of decimal places you wish to display. For example, **%10.4f** will display a number at least ten characters wide with four decimal places. When this is applied to strings or integers the number following the period specifies the maximum field length. For example, **%5.7s** will display a string that will be no less than five characters and no more than seven. If the string is longer than the maximum field width, the characters will be truncated off the end.

By default, all output is *right-justified:* If the field width is larger than the data printed, the data will be placed on the right edge of the field. You can force the information to be left-justified by placing a minus sign directly after the %. For example, **%−10.2f** will left-justify a floating point number with two decimal places in a ten-character field.

There are two format command modifiers that allow **printf( )** to display **short** and **long** integers. These modifiers may be applied to the **d**, **i**, **o**, **u**, and **x** type specifiers. The **l** modifier tells **printf( )** that a **long** data type follows. For example, **%ld** means that a **long int** is to be displayed. The **h** modifier instructs **printf( )** to display a **short int**. Therefore, **%hu** indicates that the data is the **short unsigned int** type.

The l modifier may also prefix the floating point commands of **e**, **f**, and **g**, and it indicates that a **double** follows.

With **printf( )**, you can output virtually any format of data you desire. Figure 8-1 shows some examples.

scanf( )

The general-purpose console input routine is **scanf( )**. It reads all the built-in data types and automatically converts numbers into the proper internal format. It is like the reverse of **printf( )**. The general form of **scanf( )** is

scanf(*"control string"*, *argument list*);

The control string consists of three classifications of characters.

1. Format specifiers

2. White-space characters

3. Non-white-space characters

printf( ) statement	Output
("%−5.2f",123.234)	123.23
("%5.2f",3.234)	3.23
("%10s","hello")	hello
("%−10s","hello")	hello
("%5.7s","123456789")	1234567

Figure 8-1.   Some **printf( )** examples

Code	Meaning
%c	Read a single character
%d	Read a decimal integer
%i	Read a decimal integer
%e	Read a floating point number
%f	Read a floating point number
%h	Read a short integer
%o	Read an octal number
%s	Read a string
%x	Read a hexadecimal number
%p	Read a pointer
%n	Receive an integer value equal to the number of characters read so far

Table 8-3.   Format Codes of **scanf( )**

The input format specifiers are preceded by a % sign and tell **scanf( )** what type of data is to be read next. These codes are listed in Table 8-3. For example, **%s** reads a string, while **%d** reads an integer.

A white-space character in the control string causes **scanf( )** to skip over one or more white-space characters in the input stream. A white-space character is either a space, a tab, or a newline. In essence, one white-space character in the control string causes **scanf( )** to read, but not store, any number (including zero) of white-space characters up to the first non-white-space character.

A non-white-space character causes **scanf( )** to read and discard a matching character. For example, "**%d,%d**" causes **scanf( )** to read an integer, read and discard a comma, and finally read another integer. If the specified character is not found, **scanf( )** will terminate.

All the variables used to receive values through **scanf( )** must be passed by their addresses. This means that all arguments must be pointers to the variables used as arguments. This is C's way of creating a "call by reference," and it allows a function to alter the contents of an argument. For example, if you wish to read an integer into the variable **count**, you use the following **scanf( )** call:

```
scanf("%d", &count);
```

Strings are read into character arrays, and the array name, without any index, is the address of the first element of the array. To read a string into the character array **address**, you would use

```
scanf("%s", address);
```

In this case, **address** is already a pointer and need not be preceded by the & operator.

The input data items must be separated by spaces, tabs, or newlines. Punctuation marks such as commas, semicolons, and the like do not count as separators. This means that

```
scanf("%d%d", &r, &c);'
```

accepts an input of **10 20**, but fails with **10,20**. As in **printf( )**, the **scanf( )** format codes are matched in order with the variables receiving input in the argument list.

An * placed after the % and before the format code reads data of the specified type but suppresses its assignment. Thus, given the input **10/20**,

```
scanf("%d%*c%d", &x, &y);
```

places the value 10 into **x**, discards the division sign, and gives **y** the value 20.

The format commands can specify a maximum field-length modifier. This is an integer number placed between the % and the format command code that limits the number of characters read for any field. For example, if you wish to read no more than 20 characters into **str**, you write

```
scanf("%20s", str);
```

If the input stream is greater than 20 characters, a subsequent call to input begins where this call leaves off. For example, if

ABCDEFGHIJKLMNOPQRSTUVWXYZ

is entered as the response to the **scanf( )** call in this example, only the first 20 characters, or up to the **T**, are placed into **str** because of the maximum size specifier. The remaining characters, **UVWXYZ**, have not yet been used. If another **scanf( )** call is made, such as

```
scanf("%s", str);
```

then **UVWXYZ** are placed into **str**. Input for a field may terminate before the maximum field length is reached if a white space is encountered. In this case, **scanf( )** moves on to the next field.

Although spaces, tabs, and newlines are used as field separators, when reading a single character they are read like any other character. For example, with an input stream of **x y**,

```
scanf("%c%c%c", &a, &b, &c);
```

will return with the character **x** in **a**, a space in **b**, and the character **y** in **c**.

Be careful: If you have any other characters in the control string—including spaces, tabs, and newlines—those characters will be used to match and discard characters from the input stream. Any character that matches is discarded. For example, given the input stream **10t20**,

```
scanf("%st%s", &x, &y);
```

will place 10 into **x** and 20 into **y**. The **t** is discarded because
of the **t** in the control string. For another example,

```
scanf("%s ", name);
```

will *not* return until you type a character *after* you type a
white-space character. This is because the space after the %s
has instructed **scanf( )** to read and discard spaces, tabs, and
newline characters.

You may not use **scanf( )** to display a prompting message. Therefore, all prompts must be explicitly done prior to
the **scanf( )** call.

The Buffered I/O System

The buffered I/O system is composed of several interrelated
functions. The most common are shown in Table 8-4. These
functions require that the header file **stdio.h** be included in
any program in which they are used.

The File Pointer

The common thread that ties the buffered I/O system
together is the *file pointer*. A file pointer is a pointer to
information that defines various things about the file, including its name, status, and current position. In essence, the file
pointer identifies a specific disk file and is used by the
stream associated with it to tell each of the buffered I/O
functions where to perform operations. A file pointer is a
pointer variable of type **FILE**, which is defined in **stdio.h**.

Name	Function
fopen()	Opens a stream
fclose()	Closes a stream
putc()	Writes a character to a stream
getc()	Reads a character from a stream
fseek()	Seeks to specified byte in a stream
fprintf()	Is to a stream what printf() is to the console
fscanf()	Is to a stream what scanf() is to the console
feof()	Returns true if end of file is reached
ferror()	Returns true if an error has occurred
rewind()	Resets the file position locator to the beginning of the file
remove()	Erases a file

Table 8-4.   The Most Common Buffered-File System Functions

fopen( )

The **fopen( )** function opens a stream for use and links a file with that stream. Most often (always for the purposes of this discussion) the file is a disk file. The **fopen( )** function is declared as

FILE *fopen(*char *filename, *mode*);

where *mode* is a string containing the desired open status. The legal values for *mode* in Turbo C are shown in Table 8-5. The *filename* must be a string of characters that provides a valid file name for the operating system and may include a path specification.

Mode	Meaning
"r"	Open a text file for reading
"w"	Create a text file for writing
"a"	Append to a text file
"rb"	Open a binary file for reading
"wb"	Create a binary file for writing
"ab"	Append to a binary file
"r+"	Open a text file for read/write
"w+"	Create a text file for read/write
"a+"	Open or create a text file for read/write
"r+b"	Open a binary file for read/write
"w+b"	Create a binary file for read/write
"a+b"	Open or create a binary file for read/write
"rt"	Open a text file for reading
"wt"	Create a text file for writing
"at"	Append to a text file
"r+t"	Open a text file for read/write
"w+t"	Create a text file for read/write
"a+t"	Open or create a text file for read/write

Table 8-5.   The Legal Values to the **fopen()** *mode* Parameter

As Table 8-5 shows, a file can be opened in either text or binary mode. In text mode, carriage-return-linefeed sequences are translated to newline characters on input. On output, the reverse occurs: Newlines are translated to carriage-return-linefeed sequences. No such translations occur on binary files.

If you wish to open a file for writing with the name **test**, you write

```
fp = fopen("test", "w");
```

where **fp** is a variable of type **FILE** *. However, you usually see it written like this:

```
if ((fp = fopen("test", "w"))==NULL) {
   puts("cannot open file\n");
   exit(1);
}
```

This method detects any error in opening a file, such as a write-protected or full disk, before attempting to write to it. A null, which is 0, is used because no file pointer will ever have that value. **NULL** is a macro defined in **stdio.h**.

If you use **fopen( )** to open a file for writing, any preexisting file by that name is erased and a new file started. If no file by that name exists, one is created. If you want to add to the end of the file, you must use mode **a**. If the file does not exist, it will be created. Opening a file for read operations requires an existing file. If no file exists an error is returned. If a file is opened for read/write operations it is not erased if it exists; if no file exists, one is created.

putc( )

The **putc( )** function is used to write characters to a stream that was previously opened for writing using the **fopen( )** function. The function is declared as

int putc(*int ch*, FILE *fp*);

where *fp* is the file pointer returned by **fopen( )** and *ch* is the character to be output. The file pointer tells **putc( )** which disk file to write to. For historical reasons, *ch* is formally called an **int**, but only the low-order byte is used.

If a **putc( )** operation is a success, it returns the character written. If **putc( )** fails an **EOF** is returned. **EOF** is a macro defined in **stdio.h** that stands for end-of-file.

getc( )

The **getc( )** function is used to read characters from a stream opened in read mode by **fopen( )**. The function is declared as int getc(FILE *fp);

where *fp* is a file pointer of type **FILE** returned by **fopen()**. For historical reasons, **getc()** returns an integer, but the high-order byte is 0.

The **getc()** function returns an **EOF** mark when the end of the file is reached. To read a text file to the end, you could use the following code:

```
ch = getc(fp);

while(ch!=EOF) {
  ch = getc(fp);
}
```

As stated earlier, the buffered file system can also operate on binary data. When a file is opened for binary input, an integer value equal to the **EOF** mark may be read. This would cause the routine just given to indicate an end-of-file condition even though the physical end of the file had not been reached. To solve this problem, Turbo C includes the function **feof()**, which is used to determine the end of the file when reading binary data. The **feof()** function takes a file pointer argument and returns 1 if the end of the file has been reached or 0 if it has not. Therefore, the following routine reads a binary file until the end-of-file mark is encountered.

```
while(!feof(fp)) ch = getc(fp);
```

This method can be applied to text files as well as binary files.

fclose( )

The **fclose()** function is used to close a stream that was opened by a call to **fopen()**. *You must close all streams before your program terminates!* It writes any data still remaining in the disk buffer to the file and does a formal operating-system-level close on the file. Failure to close a stream invites all kinds of trouble, including lost data, destroyed files, and possible intermittent errors in your program. An **fclose()** also frees the file control block associated with the stream and makes it available for reuse. There is an operating system limit to the number of files you can have open at any one time, so it may be necessary to close one file before opening another.

The **fclose()** function is declared as

int fclose(FILE *fp*);

where *fp* is the file pointer returned by the call to **fopen()**. A return value of 0 signifies a successful close operation; any other value indicates an error. You can use the standard function **ferror()** (discussed next) to determine and report any problems. Generally, **fclose()** will fail only when a diskette has been prematurely removed from the drive or if there is no more space on the diskette.

ferror( ) and rewind( )

The **ferror()** function is used to detemine whether a file operation has produced an error. The function **ferror()** has the declaration

int ferror(FILE *fp*)

where *fp* is a valid file pointer. It returns true if an error has occurred during the last file operation; it returns false otherwise. Because each file operation sets the error condition, **ferror()** should be called immediately after each file operation; otherwise an error may be lost.

The **rewind()** function resets the file position locator to the beginning of the file specified as its argument. The declaration is void rewind(FILE *_fp_)

where _fp_ is a valid file pointer.

Using fopen( ), getc( ), putc( ), and fclose( )

The functions **fopen( )**, **getc( )**, **putc( )**, and **fclose( )** comprise
the minimal set of file routines. A simple example of using
putc( ), **fopen( )**, and **fclose( )** is the program **ktod** below. It
simply reads characters from the keyboard and writes them
to a disk file until a dollar sign is typed. The filename is
specified from the command line. For example, if you call
this program **ktod**, typing **ktod test** allows you to enter lines
of text into the file called **test**.

```
#include "stdio.h"

main(argc, argv)  /* ktod - key to disk */
int argc;
char *argv[];
{
  FILE *fp;
  char ch;

  if(argc!=2) {
    printf("You forgot to enter the filename\n");
    exit(1);
  }

  if((fp=fopen(argv[1],"w")) == NULL) {
    printf("cannot open file\n");
    exit(1);
  }

  do {
    ch = getchar();
    putc(ch, fp);
  } while (ch!='$');

  fclose(fp);

}
```

The complementary program **dtos** will read any ASCII
file and display the contents on the screen.

```
#include "stdio.h"

main(argc, argv)     /* dtos - disk to screen */
int argc;
char *argv[];
{
  FILE *fp;
  char ch;

  if(argc!=2) {
    printf("You forgot to enter the filename\n");
    exit(1);
  }

  if((fp=fopen(argv[1], "r")) == NULL) {
    printf("cannot open file\n");
    exit(1);
  }

  ch=getc(fp);    /* read one character */

  while (ch!=EOF) {
    putchar(ch); /* print on screen */
    ch = getc(fp);
  }

  fclose(fp);
}
```

The following program copies a file of any type. Notice that the files are opened in binary mode and the **feof()** is used to check for end-of-file. (No error checking is performed on output, but in a real-world situation it would be a good idea. Try to add some as an exercise.)

```
/* This program will copy a file to another. */
#include "stdio.h"

main(argc, argv)
int argc;
char *argv[];
{
  FILE *in, *out;
  char ch;

  if(argc!=3) {
    printf("You forgot to enter a filename\n");
    exit(1);
  }

  if((in=fopen(argv[1], "rb")) == NULL) {
    printf("cannot open source file\n");
    exit(1);
```

```
  }
  if((out=fopen(argv[2], "wb")) == NULL) {
    printf("cannot open destination file\n");
    exit(1);
  }

  /* this code actually copies the file */
  while(!feof(in)) {
    ch = getc(in);
    if(!feof(in)) putc(ch, out);
  }

  fclose(in);
  fclose(out);
}
```

getw( ) and putw( )

In addition to **getc( )** and **putc( )**, Turbo C supports two additional buffered I/O functions: **putw( )** and **getw( )**. They are used to read and write integers to and from a disk file. These functions work exactly the same as **putc( )** and **getc( )**, except that instead of reading or writing a single character they read or write an integer. For example, the following code fragment writes an integer to the disk file pointed to by **fp**:

```
putw(100, fp);
```

fgets( ) and fputs( )

Turbo C's buffered I/O system includes two functions that can read and write strings from streams: **fgets( )** and **fputs( )**. Their declarations are

> char *fputs(*char *str*, FILE *fp*);
> char *fgets(*char *str*, *int length*, FILE *fp*);

The function **fputs( )** works exactly like **puts( )** except that it writes the string to the specified stream. The **fgets( )** function reads a string from the specified stream until either a newline character or *length−1* characters have been read. If a newline is read, it will be part of the string (unlike **gets( )**). However, if **fgets( )** is terminated, the resultant string will be null-terminated.

fread( ) and fwrite( )

The buffered I/O system provides two functions, **fread()** and **fwrite()**, that allow the reading and writing of blocks of data. Their declarations are

> int fread(*void* *buffer*, *int num—bytes*, *int count*, FILE *fp*)
> int fwrite(*void* *buffer*, *int num—bytes*, *int count*, FILE *fp*);

In the case of **fread()**, *buffer* is a pointer to a region of memory that receives the data read from the file. For **fwrite()**, *buffer* is a pointer to the information to be written to the file. The number of bytes to be read or written is specified by *num—bytes*. The argument *count* determines how many items (each being *num—bytes* in length) will be read or written. Finally, *fp* is a file pointer to a previously opened stream.

As long as the file has been opened for binary data, **fread()** and **fwrite()** can read and write any type of information. For example, this program writes a **float** to a disk file:

```
/* write a floating point number to a disk file */
#include "stdio.h"

main()
{
  FILE *fp;
  float f=12.23;

  if((fp=fopen("test","wb"))==NULL) {
    printf("cannot open file\n");
    return;
  }

  fwrite(&f, sizeof(float), 1, fp);

  fclose(fp);
}
```

As this program illustrates, the buffer can, and often is, simply a variable. One of the most useful applications of **fread()** and **fwrite()** involves the reading and writing of arrays (or structures). For example, this fragment writes the contents of the floating point array **balance** to the file **balance** using a single **fwrite( )** statement:

```
#include "stdio.h"

main()
{
  FILE *fp;
  float balance[100];

  if((fp=fopen("balance","w+"))==NULL) {
    printf("cannot open file\n");
    return;
  }
  .
  .
  .
  /* this saves the entire balance array in one step */
  fwrite(balance, sizeof(balance), 1, fp);
  .
  .
  .
  fclose(fp);
}
```

Later in this book you will see several other, more complex examples of how these functions can be used.

fseek( ) and Random Access I/O

You can perform random read and write operations using the buffered I/O system with the help of **fseek( )**, which sets the file position locator. The declaration of the function is

int fseek(FILE *fp, long int num_bytes, int origin);

where *fp* is a file pointer returned by a call to **fopen( )**; *num_bytes*, a long integer, is the number of bytes from *origin* to make the current position, and *origin* is one of the following macros:

Origin	Macro Name
Beginning of file	SEEK_SET
Current position	SEEK_CUR
End of file	SEEK_END

The macros are defined as integer values with **SEEK_SET** being 0, **SEEK_CUR** being 1, and **SEEK_END** being 2. To seek *num_bytes* from the start of the file, *origin* should be **SEEK_SET**. To seek from the current position use **SEEK_CUR**, and to seek from the end of the file use **SEEK_END**.

Remember that *offset* must be a **long int** to support files larger than 64K bytes.

The use of **fseek()** on text files is not recommended because the character translations cause position errors. Use of **fseek()** is suggested only for binary files.

For example, you could use the following code to read the 234th byte in a file called **test**:

```
func1()
{
  FILE *fp;

  if((fp=fopen("test", "rb")) == NULL) {
    printf("cannot open file\n");
    exit(1);
  }

  fseek(fp, 234L, 0);
  return getc(fp);    /* read one character */
                      /* at 234th position */

}
```

Notice that the L modifier has been appended to the constant 234 to force the compiler to treat it as a **long int**. A cast would accomplish the same thing. (Trying to use a regular integer will, of course, cause errors when a long integer is expected.)

A return value of 0 means that **fseek()** succeeded. A nonzero value indicates failure.

A more interesting example is the following DUMP program, which uses **fseek( )** to let you examine the contents in both ASCII and hexadecimal of any file you choose. You can look at the file in 128-byte "sectors" as you move about in either direction. The output displayed is similar in style to the format used by DEBUG when given the **D** (dump memory) command. You exit the program by typing a −1 when prompted for the sector. Notice the use of **fread( )** to read the file. At the end-of-file mark, less than **SIZE** number of bytes are likely to be read, so the number returned by **fread( )** is passed to **display( )**. (Remember that **fread( )** returns the number of items actually read.) Enter this program into your computer and study it until you are certain how it works:

```c
/* DUMP: A simple disk look utility using fseek. */
#include "stdio.h"
#include "ctype.h"

#define SIZE 128

char buf[SIZE];
void display();

main(argc, argv)
int argc;
char *argv[];
{
  FILE *fp;
  int sector, numread;

  if(argc!=2) {
    printf("usage: dump filename\n");
    exit(1);
  }

  if((fp=fopen(argv[1], "rb"))==NULL) {
    printf("cannot open file\n");
    exit(1);
  }

  do {
    printf("enter sector: ");
    scanf("%ld", &sector);
    if(sector>=0) {
      if(fseek(fp, sector*SIZE, SEEK_SET)) {
        printf("seek error\n");
      }
      if((numread=fread(buf, 1, SIZE, fp)) != SIZE) {
        printf("EOF reached\n");
      }
      display(numread);
    }
  } while(sector>=0);
}
```

```
/* Display the contents of a file. */
void display(int numread)
{
  int i, j;

  for(i=0; i<numread/16; i++) {
    for(j=0; j<16; j++) printf("%3X", buf[i*16+j]);
    printf("  ");
    for(j=0; j<16; j++) {
      if(isprint(buf[i*16+j])) printf("%c", buf[i*16+j]);
      else printf(".");
    }

    printf("\n");
  }
}
```

Notice that the library function called **isprint( )** is used to determine which characters are printing characters. The **isprint( )** function returns true if the character is printable and false otherwise. The **isprint( )** function requires the use of the header file called **ctype.h**, which is included near the top of the program. A sample output with DUMP used on itself is shown in Figure 8-2.

```
A:\>dump dump.c
enter sector: 0
2F 2A 20 44 55 4D 50 3A 20 41 20 73 69 6D 70 6C   /* DUMP: A simpl
65 20 64 69 73 6B 20 6C 6F 6F 6B 20 75 74 69 6C   e disk look util
69 74 79 20 75 73 69 6E 67 20 66 73 65 65 6B 20   ity using fseek
2A 2F  D  A 23 69 6E 63 6C 75 64 65 20 22 73 74   */..#include "st
64 69 6F 2E 68 22  D  A 23 69 6E 63 6C 75 64 65   dio.h"..#include
20 22 63 74 79 70 65 2E 68 22  D  A  D  A 23 64   "ctype.h"....#d
65 66 69 6E 65 20 53 49 5A 45 20 31 32 38  D  A   efine SIZE 128..
 D  A 63 68 61 72 20 62 75 66 5B 53 49 5A 45 5D   ..char buf[SIZE]
enter sector: 2
20 70 72 69 6E 74 66 28 22 75 73 61 67 65 3A 20     printf("usage:
64 75 6D 70 20 66 69 6C 65 6E 61 6D 65 5C 6E 22   dump filename\n"
29 3B  D  A 20 20 20 20 65 78 69 74 28 31 29 3B   );..    exit(1);
 D  A 20 20 7D  D  A  D  A 20 20 69 66 28 28 66   .. }.... if((f
70 3D 66 6F 70 65 6E 28 61 72 67 76 5B 31 5D 2C   p=fopen(argv[1],
20 22 72 62 22 29 29 3D 3D 4E 55 4C 4C 29 20 7B   "rb"))==NULL) {
 D  A 20 20 20 20 70 72 69 6E 74 66 28 22 63 61   ..    printf("ca
6E 6E 6F 74 20 6F 70 65 6E 20 66 69 6C 65 5C 6E   nnot open file\n
enter sector:
```

Figure 8-2.   Sample output from DUMP program

stdin, stdout, and stderr

Whenever a Turbo C program starts execution, three streams are opened automatically. They are standard input (**stdin**), standard output (**stdout**), and standard error (**stderr**). Version 1.5 also opens **stdprn** and **stdaux**. Normally these refer to the console, but they may be redirected by the operating system to some other stream device. Because these are file pointers the buffered I/O system can use them to perform I/O operations on the console. For example, **putchar()** could be defined as

```
putchar(c)
char c;
{
   putc(c, stdout);
}
```

In general, **stdin** is used to read from the console and **stdout** and **stderr** are used to write to the console. You may use **stdin**, **stdout**, and **stderr** as file pointers in any function that uses a variable of type **FILE ***.

Keep in mind that **stdin**, **stdout**, and **stderr** are not variables, but constants, and as such may not be altered. Just as these file pointers are created automatically at the start of your program, they are closed automatically at the end; do not try to close them.

fprintf( ) and fscanf( )

In addition to the basic I/O functions, the buffered I/O system includes **fprintf()** and **fscanf()**. These functions behave exactly like **printf()** and **scanf()** except that they operate with disk files. The declarations of **fprintf()** and **fscanf()** are

fprintf(*fp, "control string", argument list*);
fscanf(*fp, "control string", argument list*);

where *fp* is a file pointer returned by a call to **fopen()**. Except for directing their output to the file defined by *fp*, they operate exactly like **printf()** and **scanf()** respectively.

To illustrate how useful these functions can be, the following program maintains a simple telephone directory in a disk file. You can enter names and numbers or look up a number given a name.

```
/* A simple telephone directory */

#include "stdio.h"

void add_num(), lookup();

main()  /* fscanf - fprintf example */
{
  char choice;

  do {
    choice = menu();
    switch(choice) {
      case 'a': add_num();
        break;
      case 'l': lookup();
        break;
    }
  } while (choice!='q');

}

/* display menu and get request */
menu()
{
  char ch;

  do {
    printf("(A)dd, (L)ookup, or (Q)uit: ");
    ch = tolower(getche());
    printf("\n");
  } while(ch != 'q' && ch != 'a' && ch != 'l');

  return ch;
}

/* add a name and number to the directory */
void add_num()
{
  FILE *fp;
  char name[80];
  int a_code, exchg, num;

  /* open it for append */
  if((fp=fopen("phone","a")) == NULL) {
    printf("cannot open directory file\n");
    exit(1);
  }
```

```
printf("enter name and number: ");
  fscanf(stdin, "%s%d%d%d", name, &a_code, &exchg, &num);
fscanf(stdin, "%*c"); /* remove CR from input stream */
/* write to file */
fprintf(fp,"%s %d %d %d\n", name, a_code, exchg, num);

  fclose(fp);
}

/* find a number given a name */
void lookup()
{
  FILE *fp;
  char name[80], name2[80];
  int a_code, exchg, num;

  /* open it for read */
  if((fp=fopen("phone","r")) == NULL) {
    printf("cannot open directory file\n")`.
    exit(1);
  }

  printf("name? ");
  gets(name);

  /* look for number */
  while(!feof(fp)) {
    fscanf(fp,"%s%d%d%d", name2, &a_code, &exchg, &num);
    if(!strcmp(name, name2)) {
      printf("%s: (%d) %d-%d\n",name, a_code, exchg, num);
      break;
    }
  }
  fclose(fp);
}
```

Enter this program and run it. After you have entered a couple of names and numbers, examine the file **phone**. As you would expect, it appears just the way it would if the information had been displayed on the screen using **printf()**.

A word of warning: Although **fprintf()** and **fscanf()** are often the easiest way to write and read assorted data to disk files, they are not always the most efficient. Because formatted ASCII data is being written just as it would appear on the screen, instead of in binary, you use extra overhead with each call. If speed or file size is a concern, you should probably use **fread()** and **fwrite()**.

Erasing Files

The **remove()** function erases the specified file. Its declaration is int remove(*char *filename*);

It returns 0 on success, nonzero on failure.

Unbuffered I/O — The UNIX-Like File Routines

Because C was originally developed under the UNIX operating system, a second disk-file I/O system was created. It uses functions that are separate from the buffered-file system functions. The low-level UNIX-like disk I/O functions are shown in Table 8-6. These functions all require that the header file **io.h** be included near the beginning of any program that uses them.

The disk I/O subsystem that comprises these functions is called the *unbuffered I/O system* because the programmer must provide and maintain *all* disk buffers; the routines do not do it automatically. Unlike the functions **getc( )** and **putc( )**, which write and read characters from or to a stream of data, the functions **read( )** and **write( )** read or write one

Name	Function
read()	Reads a buffer of data
write()	Writes a buffer of data
open()	Opens a disk file
close()	Closes a disk file
lseek()	Seeks to the specified byte in a file
unlink()	Removes a file from the directory

Table 8-6.   The UNIX-Like Unbuffered I/O Functions

complete buffer of information with each call. (This is similar to **fread( )** and **fwrite( )**.)

As stated at the beginning of this chapter, the unbuffered file system is not defined by the proposed ANSI standard. This implies that programs that use it will have portability problems at some point in the future. The unbuffered file system's use is expected to diminish over the next few years, but it is included in this chapter because many existing C programs use it, and it is supported by virtually all existing C compilers.

open( ), creat( ), and close( )

Unlike the high-level I/O system, the low-level system does not use file pointers of type **FILE** but file descriptors, called *handles*, of type **int**. The declaration of **open( )** is

   int open(*char *filename, int mode, int access*);

where *filename* is any valid file name and *mode* is one of the following macros defined in **fcntl.h**.

Mode	Effect
O—RDONLY	Read-only
O—WRONLY	Write-only
O—RDWR	Read/write

Turbo C also allows some options to be added to these basic modes, so consult your manual.

The *access* parameter relates only to UNIX environments and is included for compatibility. Turbo C also defines a DOS-specific version called **—open( )** that is declared as

   int —open(*char *filename, int mode*);

thus bypassing the *access* parameter altogether. In the examples in this chapter, *access* will be set to 0.

A successful call to **open( )** returns a positive integer. A return value of −1 means that the file cannot be opened.

You usually see the call to **open( )** like this:

```
if((fd=open(filename, mode, 0)) == -1)  {
  printf("cannot open file\n");
  exit(1);
}
```

If the file specified in the **open( )** statement does not appear on the disk, the operation fails and does not create the file.

The declaration of **close( )** is

int close(*int fd*);

If **close( )** returns a −1, it was unable to close the file. This could occur if the diskette were removed from the drive, for example.

A call to **close( )** releases the file descriptor so that it can be reused for another file. There is always some limit to the number of open files that can exist simultaneously, so you should **close( )** a file when it is no longer needed. More importantly, a close operation forces any information in the internal disk buffers of the operating system to be written to disk. Failure to close a file usually leads to loss of data.

You use **creat( )** to create a new file for write operations. The declaration of **creat( )** is

int creat(*char *filename, int access*);

where *filename* is any valid file name. The *access* argument is used to specify access modes and mark the file as being either binary or text.

Because **creat( )**'s use of *access* relates to the UNIX environment, Turbo C provides a special MS-DOS version called **__creat( )**, which takes a file attribute byte for *access* instead. In DOS, each file is associated with an attribute byte that specifies various bits of information. Table 8-7 shows how this attribute byte is organized.

The values in the table are additive. That is, if you wish to create a read-only hidden file, you would use the value 3 (1 + 2) for *access*. Generally, to create a standard file, *access* will be 0.

write( ) and read( )

Once a file has been opened for writing, it can be accessed by **write( )**. The declaration of the **write( )** function is

    int write(*int fd, void *buf, int size*);

Each time a call to **write( )** is executed, *size* characters are written to the disk file specified by *fd* from the buffer pointed to by *buf*.

Because the **write( )** function can write a partially full buffer, the entire contents of the buffer aren't automatically written to disk. The function returns the number of bytes

Bit	Value	Meaning
0	1	Read-only file
1	2	Hidden file
2	4	System file
3	8	Volume label name
4	16	Subdirectory name
5	32	Archive
6	64	Unused
7	128	Unused

Table 8-7.   The Organization of the DOS Attribute Byte

written after a successful write operation. Upon failure a −1 is returned.

The function **read( )** is the complement of **write( )**. Its declaration is

   int read(*int fd, void *buf, int size*);

where *fd, buf,* and *size* are the same as for **write( )** except that **read( )** will place the data read into the buffer pointed to by *buf.* If **read( )** is successful, it returns the number of characters actually read. It returns 0 at the physical end of the file, and −1 if errors occur.

The program shown here illustrates some aspects of the unbuffered I/O system. It reads lines of text from the keyboard, writes them to a disk file, and then reads them back.

```
#include "fcntl.h"
#include "io.h"

#define BUF_SIZE   128

main()   /* read and write using unbuffered I/O */
{
  char buf[BUF_SIZE];
  int fd1, fd2, t;

  if((fd1=_creat("oscar",  O_WRONLY ))==-1) { /* open for write */
    printf("cannot open file\n");
    exit(1);
  }

  input(buf, fd1);

  /* now close file and read back */
  close(fd1);

  if((fd2=open("oscar", 0, O_RDONLY))==-1) { /* open for write */
    printf("cannot open file\n");
    exit(1);
  }

  display(buf,fd2);
  close(fd2);
}

input(buf, fd1)
char *buf;
int fd1;
{
  register int t;

  do {
    for(t=0; t<BUF_SIZE; t++) buf[t]='\0';
    gets(buf); /* input chars from keyboard */
```

```
      if(write(fd1, buf, BUF_SIZE)!=BUF_SIZE) {
        printf("error on write\n");
        exit(1);
      }
  } while (strcmp(buf, "quit"));
}


display(buf, fd2)
char *buf;
int fd2;
{
  for(;;) {
    if(read(fd2, buf, BUF_SIZE)==0) return;
    printf("%s\n",buf);
  }
}
```

unlink( )

If you wish to remove a file from the directory, use **unlink( )**.
Although **unlink( )** is considered part of the UNIX-like I/O
system, it removes any file from the directory. The standard
form of the call is

   int unlink(*char *filename*);

where *filename* is a character pointer to any valid file name.
The **unlink( )** function returns an error (usually −1) if it was
unable to erase the file. This could happen if the file was not
present on the diskette to begin with, or if the diskette was
write-protected.

Random Access Files and lseek

Turbo C supports random access file I/O under the unbuffered
I/O system via calls to **lseek( )**. Its declaration is

   long lseek(*int fd, long num__bytes, int origin*);

where *fd* is a file descriptor returned by a **creat( )** or **open( )**
call. The *num__bytes* must be a **long int**. *Origin* must be one of
the following macros:

Origin	Name
Beginning of file	SEEK__SET
Current position	SEEK__CUR
End of file	SEEK__END

To seek *num__bytes* from the start of the file, *origin* should be **SEEK__SET**. To seek from the current position, use **SEEK__CUR**; to seek from the end of the file, use **SEEK__ END**.

The **lseek( )** function returns *offset* on success. Therefore, **lseek( )** will be returning a **long** integer and must be declared as such at the top of your program. Upon failure, **lseek( )** returns −1L.

A simple example using **lseek( )** is the DUMP program developed earlier and recoded for the UNIX-like I/O system. It not only shows the operation of **lseek( )** but also illustrates many of the unbuffered I/O functions.

```
#include "stdlib.h"
#include "io.h"
#include "ctype.h"
#include "fcntl.h"    /* defines O_RDONLY */

#define SIZE  128

char buf[SIZE];
void display();

main(argc, argv)  /* read buffers using lseek() */
int argc; char *argv[];
{
  char s[10];
  int fd, sector, numread;
  long pos;

  if(argc!=2) {
    printf("You forgot to enter the file name.");
    exit(1);
  }

  if((fd=open(argv[1], O_RDONLY, 0))==-1) { /* open for read */
    printf("cannot open file\n");
    exit(1);
  }
  do {
    printf("\n\nbuffer: ");
    gets(s);

    sector = atoi(s); /* get the sector to read */

    pos = (long) (sector*SIZE);
```

```
      if(lseek(fd, pos, SEEK_SET)!=pos)
        printf("seek error\n");

      if((numread=read(fd, buf, SIZE))!=SIZE)
        printf("EOF reached\n");
      display(numread);
    } while(sector>=0);
  close(fd);
}

void display(int numread)
{
  int i, j;

  for(i=0; i<numread/16; i++) {
    for(j=0; j<16; j++) printf("%3X", buf[i*16+j]);
    printf("   ");
    for(j=0; j<16; j++) {
      if(isprint(buf[i*16+j])) printf("%c", buf[i*16+j]);
      else printf(".");
    }
    printf("\n");
  }
}
```

Choosing an Approach

The buffered I/O system defined by the ANSI standard is recommended for new projects. Because the ANSI standard committee has elected not to standardize the UNIX-like unbuffered I/O system, it cannot be recommended for future projects. However, existing code should be maintainable for a number of years. There is probably no reason to rush into a rewrite at this time.

Within the buffered I/O system, you should use text mode and **getc( )** and **putc( )** when you are working with character files, such as the text files created by a word processor. However, when it is necessary to store binary data or complex data types, you should use binary files and **fread( )** and **fwrite( )**.

A final word of warning: Never try to mix I/O systems inside the same program. Because the way they approach files is different, they could accidentally interfere with each other.

The Turbo C
Preprocessor and
Compiler Options

The source code for a C program can include various instructions to the compiler. Although not actually part of the Turbo C language, these *preprocessor directives* expand the scope of the C programming environment. This chapter will examine Turbo C's preprocessing directives and built-in macros.

The Turbo C Preprocessor

The C preprocessor defined by the proposed ANSI standard contains the following directives:

```
#define
#error
#include
#if
#else
#elif
#endif
#ifdef
#ifndef
#undef
#line
#pragma
```

All preprocessor directives begin with a # sign. Turbo C supports all these directives, and each will be examined in turn.

#define

The **#define** directive is used to define an identifier and a character string that is substituted for the identifier each time it is encountered in the source file. The identifier is called a *macro-name* and the replacement process is called *macro-substitution*. The general form of the directive is

    #define macro-name string

Notice that there is no semicolon in this statement. There can be any number of spaces between the identifier and the string, but once the string begins, it is terminated only by a newline.

For example, if you wish to use TRUE for the value 1 and FALSE for the value 0, then you would declare two macro **#define**s:

```
#define TRUE 1
#define FALSE 0
```

This causes the compiler to substitute a 1 or a 0 each time TRUE or FALSE is encountered in your source file. For example, the following will print **0 1 2** on the screen:

```
printf("%d %d %d",FALSE, TRUE, TRUE+1);
```

Once a macro-name has been defined, it can be used as part of the definition of other macro-names. For example, this code defines the names ONE, TWO, and THREE to their respective values:

```
#define ONE      1
#define TWO      ONE+ONE
#define THREE    ONE+TWO
```

It is important to understand that macro-substitution is simply replacing an identifier with its associated string. Therefore, if you wished to define a standard error message you might write something like

```
#define E_MS "standard error on input\n"
    .
    .
    .
printf(E_MS);
```

Turbo C actually substitutes the string "**standard error on input \n**" when the identifier **E—MS** is encountered. To the compiler, the **printf( )** statement actually appears to be

```
printf("standard error on input\n");
```

No text substitutions occur if the identifier occurs within a string. For example,

```
#define XYZ this is a test
    .
    .
    .
printf("XYZ");
```

does not print **this is a test** but **XYZ**.

If the string is longer than one line, it can be continued on the next line by placing a backslash at the end of the line, as shown in this example:

```
#define LONG_STRING "this is a very long \
string that is used as an example"
```

It is common practice among C programmers to use capital letters for defined identifiers. With this convention anyone reading the program knows at a glance that a macro-substitution will take place. It is best to put all #**define**s at the start of the file or, perhaps, in a separate include file, rather than sprinkling them throughout the program.

The most common use of macro-substitutions is to define names for "magic numbers" that occur in a program. For example, you may have a program that defines an array and has several routines that access the array. Instead of "hard-coding" the array's size with a constant, it is better to define a size and use that name whenever the size of the array is needed. If the size of the array changes, you only have to change it in one place in the file and recompile. For example:

```
#define MAX_SIZE 100

float balance[MAX_SIZE];
```

The #**define** directive has another powerful feature: The macro-name can have arguments. Each time the macro-name is encountered, the arguments associated with it are replaced by the actual arguments found in the program. For example:

```
#define MIN(a,b)  (a<b) ? a : b
main()
{
  int x, y;

  x = 10;
  y = 20;
  printf("the minimum is: %d", MIN(x, y));
}
```

When this program is compiled, the expression defined by **MIN(a,b)** is substituted, except that **x** and **y** are used as the operands. That is, the **printf()** statement is substituted to look like this:

```
printf("the minimum is: %d",(x<y) ? x : y);
```

If you are not very careful in defining macros that take arguments, there can be some surprising results. For example,

```
/* This program will give the wrong answer. */

#define EVEN(a) a%2==0 ? 1 : 0

main()
{
  if(EVEN(9+1)) printf("is even");
  else printf("is odd");
}
```

does not work correctly because of the way the macro-substitution is made. When Turbo C compiles this program, the **EVEN(9+1)** is expanded to

```
9+1%2==0 ? 1 : 0
```

Because the % (modulus) operator takes precedence over the plus operator, the modulus operation is first performed on the 1 and that result is added to 9, which of course does not equal 0. To fix the trouble, there must be parentheses around **a** in the macro definition of **EVEN** as is shown in this corrected version of the program:

```
#define EVEN(a) (a)%2==0 ? 1 : 0

main()
{
  if(EVEN(9+1)) printf("is even");
  else printf("is odd");
}
```

Now the **9+1** is evaluated before the modulus operation. In general, it is a good idea to surround macro parameters with parentheses to avoid unforeseeable troubles like the one just described.

The use of macro-substitutions in place of real functions has one major benefit: It increases the speed of the code because a function call incurs no overhead. However, this increased speed is paid for with an increase in the size of the program because of duplicated code.

#error

The **#error** directive forces Turbo C to stop compiling when it is encountered. It is used primarily for debugging. The general form of the directive is

    #error error-message

The **error-message** is not between double quotes. When the compiler encounters this directive, it displays the following information and terminates compilation:

    Fatal: filename linenum Error directive: error-message

#include

The **#include** directive instructs the compiler to include another source file with the one that has the #include directive in it. The source file, to be read, must be enclosed between double quotes or angle brackets. For example, the two directives

```
#include "stdio.h"
#include <stdio.h>
```

both instruct Turbo C to read and compile the header for the disk file library routines.

It is valid for included files to have **#include** directives in them. These are called *nested includes*. For example, this program, shown with its include files, includes a file that includes another file:

```
The program file:
        main()
        {
        #include "one"
        }
```

```
Include file "one":
      printf("This is from the first include file.\n");
      #include "two"

Include file "two":
      printf("This is from the second include file.\n");
```

If explicit path names are specified as part of the file-name identifier, only those directories will be searched for the included file. If the file name is enclosed in quotes, the current working directory is searched first. If the file is not found, any directories specified on the command line are searched. If the file has still not been found, the standard directories, as defined by the implementation, are searched.

If no explicit path names are specified and the file name is enclosed by angle brackets, the file is first searched for in the directories specified in the compiler command line by using the −I option, or in those specified in the integrated environment by using the options menu. If the file is not found, the standard directories are searched. At no time is the current working directory searched (unless the current working directory is specified in a −I path).

Conditional Compilation Directives

Several directives allow you to compile selected portions of your program's source code. This process is called *conditional compilation* and is used widely by commercial software houses that provide and maintain many customized versions of one program.

#if, #else, #elif, and #endif

The general idea behind the **#if** is that if the constant expression following the **#if** is true, the code between it and an **#endif** is compiled; otherwise the code is skipped. The **#endif** directive is used to mark the end of an **#if** block.

The general form of **#if** is

```
#if constant-expression
    statement sequence
#endif
```

If the constant expression is true, the block of code is compiled; otherwise it is skipped. For example:

```
/* simple #if example */

#define MAX 100
main()
{
#if MAX>99
  printf("compiled for array greater than 99\n");
#endif
}
```

This program displays the message on the screen because, as defined in the program, **MAX** is greater than 99. This example illustrates an important point. The expression that follows the **#if** is *evaluated at compile time*. Therefore, it must contain only identifiers that have been previously defined and constants; no variables can be used.

The **#else** works in much the same way as the **else** that forms part of the C language: It provides an alternative if the **#if** fails. The previous example can be expanded as shown here:

```
/* simple #if/#else example */

#define MAX 10
main()
{
#if MAX>99
  printf("compiled for array greater than 99\n");
#else
  printf("compiled for small array\n");
#endif
}
```

In this case, **MAX** is defined to be less than 99 so the **#if** portion of the code is not compiled, but the **#else** alternative is. Therefore, the message **compiled for small array** is displayed.

Notice that the **#else** is used to mark both the end of the **#if** block and the beginning of the **#else** block. This is necessary because there can be only one **#endif** associated with any **#if**.

The **#elif** directive means "else if" and is used to establish an if-else-if ladder for multiple compilation options. The **#elif** is followed by a constant expression. If the expression is true, that block of code is compiled and no other **#elif** expressions are tested. Otherwise, the next in the series is checked. The general form is

```
#if expression
    statement sequence
#elif expression 1
    statement sequence
#elif expression 2
    statement sequence
#elif expression 3
    statement sequence
#elif expression 4
    .
    .
    .
#elif expression N
    statement sequence
#endif
```

For example, this fragment uses the value of **ACTIVE_ COUNTRY** to define the currency sign:

```
#define US 0
#define ENGLAND 1
#define FRANCE 2

#define ACTIVE_COUNTRY US

#if ACTIVE_COUNTRY==US
  char currency[] = "dollar";
#elif ACTIVE_COUNTRY==ENGLAND
  char currency[] = "pound";
#else
  char currency[] = "franc";
#endif
```

The **#if** and **#elif** directives can be nested with the **#endif**, **#else**, or **#elif** associating with the nearest **#if** or **#elif**. For example, the following is perfectly valid:

```
#if MAX>100
    #if SERIAL_VERSION
        int port = 198;
    #elif
        int port = 200;
    #endif
#else
    char out_buffer[100];
#endif
```

In Turbo C (but not ANSI C) you can use the **sizeof** compile-time operator in an **#if** statement. For example, this fragment determines whether a program is being compiled for a small or large data model (memory models are discussed in Chapter 10):

```
#if (sizeof(char *) == 2)
  printf("Program compiled for small model.");
#else
  printf("Program compiled for large model.");
#endif
```

#ifdef and #ifndef

Another method of conditional compilation uses the directives **#ifdef** and **#ifndef**, which mean "if defined" and "if not defined," respectively.

The general form of **#ifdef** is

    #ifdef macro-name
       statement sequence
    #endif

If the **macro-name** has been previously defined in a **#define** statement, the statement sequence between the **#ifdef** and **#endif** is compiled.

The general form of **#ifndef** is

```
#ifndef macro-name
    statement sequence
#endif
```

If **macro-name** is currently undefined by a **#define** statement, the block of code is compiled.

Both the **#ifdef** and **#ifndef** can use an **#else** statement but not the **#elif**.

For example,

```
#define TED 10

main()
{
#ifdef TED
  printf("Hi Ted\n");
#else
  printf("Hi anyone\n");
#endif
#ifndef RALPH
  printf("RALPH not defined\n");
#endif
}
```

prints **Hi Ted** and **RALPH not defined**. However, if **TED** were not defined, **Hi anyone** would be displayed, followed by **RALPH not defined**.

You may nest **#ifdef**s and **#ifndef**s to any level in the same way that you can nest **#if**s.

#undef

The **#undef** directive is used to remove a previously defined definition of the macro-name that follows it. The general form is

```
#undef macro-name
```

For example:

```
#define LEN 100
#define WIDTH 100

char array[LEN][WIDTH];

#undef LEN
#undef WIDTH
/* at this point both LEN and WIDTH are undefined */
```

Both **LEN** and **WIDTH** are defined until the **#undef** statements are encountered.

The principal use of **#undef** is to allow macro-names to be localized only to those sections of code that need them.

#line

The #**line** directive changes the contents of __LINE__ and __FILE__, which are predefined macro-names in Turbo C. The __LINE__ macro contains the line number of the line currently being compiled and __FILE__ contains the name of the file being compiled. The basic form of the #**line** command is

> #line number ["*filename*"]

where **number** is any positive integer, and the optional *filename* is any valid file identifier. The line number is the number of the current source line, and the file name is the name of the source file. The #**line** directive is primarily used for debugging purposes and special applications.

For example, the following specifies that the line count will begin with 100. The **printf( )** statement displays the number 102 because it is the third line in the program after the #**line 100** statement.

```
#line 100    /* reset the line counter */
main()       /* line 100 */
{            /* line 101 */
  printf("%d\n", __LINE__);   /* line 102 */
}
```

#pragma

The #**pragma** directive is defined by the ANSI standard to be an implementation-defined directive that allows the compiler's creator to give various instructions to the compiler. The general form of the #**pragma** directive is

#pragma name

where **name** is the name of the #**pragma** you want. Turbo C defines two #**pragma** statements: **warn** and **inline**.

The **warn** directive causes Turbo C to override warning message options. It takes the form

#pragma warn setting

where **setting** is one of the various warning error options. These options are discussed in Part Two of this book. For most applications you will not need to use this #**pragma**.

The second #**pragma** is **inline**. It has the general form

#pragma inline

This tells Turbo C that in-line assembly code is contained in the program. For the greatest efficiency, Turbo C needs to know this in advance.

Predefined Macro Names

The proposed ANSI standard specifies five built-in predefined macro-names. They are

```
__LINE__
__FILE__
__DATE__
__TIME__
__STDC__
```

Turbo C defines these additional built-in macros:

```
__CDECL__
__COMPACT__
__HUGE__
__LARGE__
__MEDIUM__
__MSDOS__
__PASCAL__
__SMALL__
__TINY__
__TURBOC__
```

The **__LINE__** and **__FILE__** macros are discussed in the **#line** discussion. The others will be examined
here.

The **__DATE__** macro contains a string of the form
month/day/year, which is the date the source file is translated into object code.

The length of time since the beginning of the compilation
of the source code into object code is contained as a string in
__TIME__. The form of the string is *hour:minute:second*.

The macro **__STDC__** contains the decimal constant
1. This means that the implementation is a standard-con-
forming implementation. If it contains any other number, the
implementation must vary from the standard.

The **__CDECL__** macro is defined if the standard C calling convention is used—that is, if the Pascal option is not in use. If this is not the case, the macro is undefined.

Only one of these macros is defined, based on the memory model used during compilation: __TINY__, __SMALL__, __COMPACT__, __MEDIUM__, __LARGE__, and __HUGE__.

The __MSDOS__ macro is defined with the value 1 in all situations when using the MSDOS version of Turbo C.

The __PASCAL__ macro is defined only if the Pascal calling conventions are used to compile a program. Otherwise it is undefined.

Finally, __TURBOC__ contains the version number of Turbo C. It is represented as a hexadecimal constant. The two rightmost digits represent the minor revision numbers; the leftmost represents the major revision. For example, the number 202 represents Version 2.02.

The following program illustrates the use of some of these macros (its output is shown in Figure 9-1).

```
main()
{
  printf("%s %d %s %s\n", __FILE__, __LINE__, __DATE__,
         __TIME__);

  printf("Program being compiled using the ");
#ifdef __TINY__
  printf("tiny model");
#endif
#ifdef __SMALL__
  printf("small model");
#endif
#ifdef __COMPACT__
  printf("compact model");
#endif
#ifdef __MEDIUM__
  printf("medium model");
#endif
#ifdef __LARGE__
  printf("large model");
#endif
#ifdef __HUGE__
  printf("huge model");
#endif
  printf("\n");

  printf("Using version %X of Turbo C.", __TURBOC__);
}
```

```
example.c 5 Oct 23 1987 15:43:36
Program being compiled using the small model
Using version 150 of Turbo C.
```

Figure 9-1.   The output from the predefined macros demonstration program

For the most part, these built-in macros are used in fairly complex programming environments when several different versions of a program —perhaps running on different computers —are developed or maintained.

Turbo C's Memory Models

One of Turbo C's most confusing aspects is not its fault! For reasons that will become clear, you can compile a Turbo C program using any of the six different memory models defined by the 8086 family of processors. Each model organizes the memory of the computer differently and governs the size of the program's code, or data, or both. It also determines how quickly your program will execute. Because the model used has a profound effect on a program's speed of execution and the way a program accesses the system resources, this chapter discusses in detail the various memory models and concludes with a program that lets you inspect and change any part of the RAM in your system.

This chapter is specifically for Turbo C on the 8086 family of processors. It may not be applicable to other types of processors.

The 8086 Family of Processors

Before you can understand the way the various memory models work you need to understand how the 8086 family of processors addresses memory. (For the rest of this chapter, the CPU will be called the 8086, but the information applies to all processors in this family, including the 8088, 80186, 80286, and 80386.)

The 8086 contains 14 registers into which information is placed for processing or program control. The registers fall into the following categories:

- General purpose registers
- Base pointer and index registers
- Segment registers
- Special purpose registers

All the registers in the 8086 CPU are 16 bits (2 bytes) wide.

The *general purpose registers* are the "workhorse" registers of the CPU. Values are placed in these registers for processing, including arithmetic operations, such as adding or multiplying; comparisons, including equality, less than, greater than, and the like; and branch (jump) instructions. Each of the general purpose registers can be accessed either as a 16-bit register or as two 8-bit registers.

The *base pointer and index registers* are used to provide support for such things as relative addressing, the stack pointer, and block move instructions.

The *segment registers* are used to support the 8086's segmented memory scheme. The **CS** register holds the current code segment, the **DS** holds the current data segment, the **ES** holds the extra segment, and the **SS** holds the stack segment.

The *special purpose registers* are the flag register, which holds the state of the CPU, and the instruction pointer, which points to the next instruction for the CPU to execute.

Figure 10-1 shows the layout of the 8086 registers.

Address Calculation

The 8086 has a total address space of one megabyte (more for the more powerful CPUs in the family). To access a megabyte of RAM requires at least a 20-bit address. However, on the 8086 no register is larger than 16 bits. This means that the 20-bit address must be divided between two registers. Unfortunately, the way the 20 bits are divided is a little more complex than one would ordinarily assume.

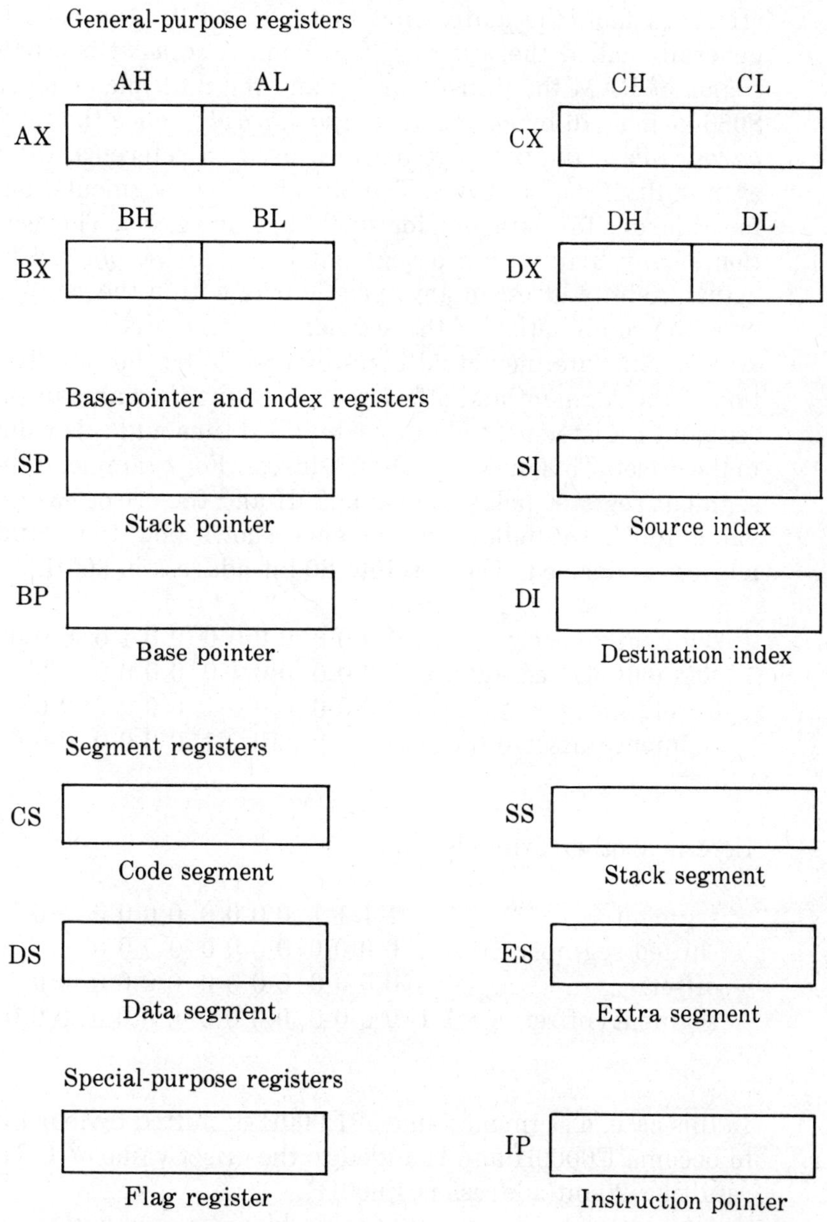

General-purpose registers

AX [AH | AL]   CX [CH | CL]

BX [BH | BL]   DX [DH | DL]

Base-pointer and index registers

SP [   ]   SI [   ]

Stack pointer   Source index

BP [   ]   DI [   ]

Base pointer   Destination index

Segment registers

CS [   ]   SS [   ]

Code segment   Stack segment

DS [   ]   ES [   ]

Data segment   Extra segment

Special-purpose registers

[   ]   IP [   ]

Flag register   Instruction pointer

Figure 10-1.   The 8088 CPU registers

In the 8086, all addresses consist of a segment and an offset. In fact, the addressing method used by the 8086 is generally called the *segment:offset* form. A *segment* is a 64K region of RAM that must start on an even multiple of 16. In 8086 jargon, 16 bytes is called a *paragraph*; hence the term *paragraph boundary* is sometimes used to reference these even multiples of 16 bytes. The 8086 has four segments: one for code, one for data, one for stack, and one extra. The location of any byte within a segment is called the *offset*. The actual 20-bit address of any specific byte within the computer is the combination of the segment and the offset.

To calculate the actual byte referred to by the combination of the segment and offset you first shift the value in the segment register to the left by 4 bits and then add this value to the offset. This makes a 20-bit address. For example, if the segment register holds the value 20H and the offset has the value 100H, the following sequence shows how the actual address is derived. The absolute 20-bit address is 300H.

```
segment register:      0 0 0 0  0 0 0 0  0 0 1 0  0 0 0 0
segment shifted:0 0 0 0  0 0 0 0  0 0 1 0  0 0 0 0
offset:                0 0 0 0  0 0 0 1  0 0 0 0  0 0 0 0
segment+offset: 0 0 0 0  0 0 0 0  0 0 1 1  0 0 0 0  0 0 0 0
```

Here is another example:

```
segment:               1 1 1 1  0 0 0 0  0 0 0 0  0 0 0 0
shifted segment:1 1 1 1  0 0 0 0  0 0 0 0  0 0 0 0
offset:                0 0 0 0  0 0 0 0  0 0 0 0  0 0 0 1
segment+offset: 1 1 1 1  0 0 0 0  0 0 0 0  0 0 0 0  0 0 0 1
```

In this case, a segment value of F000H is shifted by four bits to become F0000H and is added to the offset value of 1. The resulting 20-bit address is F0001H.

As long as you are accessing addresses only within the segment currently loaded in a segment register, you need to load only the offset of the address into a register. However, if you want to access an address not in the current segment, you must load both the segment and the offset of the desired address.

In the 8086, addresses are most commonly referred to in *segment:offset* form. In this form the outcome of the foregoing example is 0020:0100H. Many segment:offset addresses can describe the same byte because the segments overlap each other. For example, 0000:0010 is the same as 0001:0000.

16- Versus 20-bit Pointers

As stated in the previous section, you need load only a 16-bit address to access memory within the segment already loaded into one of the segment registers. However, if you wish to access memory outside that segment, you must load both the segment and the offset with the proper values into their respective registers. This effectively means that a 20-bit address is required. However, to load a 20-bit address implies loading both its 16-bit segment value and its 16-bit offset value. Thus, 20-bit addresses make your programs run much slower, but they also allow you to have larger programs or data. The exact way these things are affected is the subject of the next section.

Memory Models

As stated, Turbo C for the 8086 family of processors can compile your program six different ways, and each way organizes the memory in the computer differently. The six models are called tiny, small, medium, compact, large, and huge. Let's look at how these differ.

Tiny Model

The tiny model compiles a C program so that all the segment registers are set to the same value and all addressing is done using 16 bits. This means that the code, data, and stack must all fit within the same 64K segment. This method of compilation produces the smallest, fastest code. Generally, programs compiled using this version can be converted into .COM files using the DOS command EXE2BIN. The tiny model produces the fastest run-times.

Small Model

The small model is Turbo C's default mode of compilation and is useful for a wide variety of tasks. Although all addressing is done using only the 16-bit offset, the code segment is separate from the data, stack, and extra segments, which are in their own segment. The total size of a program compiled this way is 128K split between code and data. The addressing time is the same as for the tiny model, but the program can be twice as big. Most programs you write will fit into this model. The small model produces run-times that nearly equal those of the tiny model.

Medium Model

The medium model is for large programs where the code exceeds the one-segment restriction of the small model. The code may use multiple segments and requires 20-bit pointers, but the stack, data, and extra segments are in their own segment and use 16-bit addressing. This is good for large programs that use little data. Your programs will run more slowly as far as function calls are concerned, but references to data will be as fast as in the small model.

Compact Model

The complement of the medium model is the compact model. In this version, program code is restricted to one segment, but data may occupy several segments. This means that all accesses to data require 20-bit addressing, but the code uses 16-bit addressing. This is good for programs that require large amounts of data but little code. Your program will run as fast as in the small model, except when referencing data.

Large Model

The large model allows both code and data to use multiple segments. However, the total static data, such as an array, is limited to 64K. This model is used when you have large code and data requirements. It also runs much more slowly than any of the other versions.

Huge Model

The huge model is the same as the large model except that no total static data can exceed 64K. This makes run-time speed even slower than in the large model.

Selecting a Model

Generally, you should use the small model unless there is a reason to do otherwise. Select the medium model if you have a lot of program but not much data. Use the compact model if you have a lot of data but not much program. If you have a lot of both code and data, use the large model, unless you need static data in excess of 64K, in which case you will need to use the huge model. Remember, both the large and huge models have substantially slower run-times than the others.

The Memory Model Compiler Options

Turbo C compiles your program using the small model by default. To use a different model you must give the compiler the proper instructions. In the integrated environment version, you select the memory model by using the Options/Compiler menu path. For the command-line version, you use one of the following command-line options:

Option	Memory Model
−mc	Compact
−mh	Huge
−ml	Large
−mm	Medium
−ms	Small (default)
−mt	Tiny

Overriding a Memory Model

How unfortunate that even a single reference to data in another segment would require you to use the compact rather than the small model, for example, causing the execution speed of the entire program to degrade even though only an isolated part of it actually needs a 20-bit pointer. In general, this sort of situation arises in a variety of ways. For example, it is necessary to use 20-bit addressing to access the video RAM to enable the graphics functions to write directly to it. The solution to this and other related problems is the *segment override* type modifiers, which are enhancements provided by Turbo C. They are **far**, **near**, and **huge**. These modifiers may be applied only to pointers or functions. When they are applied to pointers they affect the way data is accessed. When applied to functions they affect the way you call or return from the function.

These modifiers follow the base type and precede the variable name. For example, the following declares a **far** pointer called **f_pointer**:

```
char far *f_pointer;
```

Let's look at these type modifiers now.

far

The most used memory model override is **far** because it is very common to want to access some region of memory that is (or may be) outside the data segment. However, if the program is compiled for one of the large data models, all access to data becomes very slow. The solution to this problem is to declare the pointers explicitly to memory outside the current data segment as **far** and compile using the small memory model. In this way, only references to objects actually outside the default data segment incur the additional overhead.

The use of **far** functions is less common and is generally restricted to specialized programming situations in which a function lies outside the current code segement, such as a ROM-based routine. In these cases, the use of **far** ensures the proper calling and returning sequences are used.

There are two very important things to remember about **far** pointers in Turbo C:

1. Pointer arithmetic affects only the offset. This means that as a **far** pointer with the value 0000:FFFF is incremented, its new value will be 0000:0000, not 0001:FFF0. The value of the segment is never changed.

2. Two **far** pointers should not be used in a relational expression because only their offsets will be checked. It is possible to have two different pointers actually contain the same physical address but have different segments

and offsets. If you need to compare 20-bit pointers, you must use **huge** pointers. However, the == and != operators do use the full 20-bit address so that a null pointer can be detected.

near

A **near** pointer is a 16-bit offset that uses the value of the appropriate segment to determine the actual memory location. The **near** modifier forces Turbo C to treat the pointer as a 16-bit offset to the segment contained in DS. You use a **near** modifier when you have compiled a program using either the medium, large, or huge memory model and want to override the default.

Using **near** on a function causes that function to be treated as if it were compiled using the small code model. When a function is compiled using either the tiny, small, or compact models, all calls to the function place a 16-bit return address on the stack. Compiling with a large code model causes a 20-bit address in segment:offset form to be pushed on the stack. Therefore, in programs that are compiled for the large code model, a highly recursive function should be declared as **near** to conserve stack space and speed execution time.

huge

The **huge** pointer is like the **far** pointer with two additions:

1. Its segment is normalized so that comparisons between **huge** pointers are meaningful.

2. When a **huge** pointer is incremented, both the segment and the offset may change; it does not suffer from a "wraparound" problem as do **far** pointers.

Turbo C's Segment Specifiers

In addition to **far**, **near**, and **huge**, Turbo C supports the four addressing modifiers _cs, _ds, _ss, and _es. When these type modifiers are applied to a pointer's declaration, they cause the pointer to become a 16-bit offset into the specified segment. That is, given this statement,

```
int _es *ptr;
```

ptr will contain a 16-bit offset into the extra segment. The use of these modifiers is generally reserved for only the most exotic applications. You will most likely never need to use them.

A Memory Display and Change Program

Now that you understand how the memory models work in Turbo C, it is time to put this knowledge to use. The simple memory display and change program that follows allows you to examine any byte in RAM and, if desired, alter its value. The program uses the segment override **far** so that you can access any address in memory.

The display—mem Function

The first function needed is **display—mem( )**, which is used to display the contents of memory at the address requested by the user. It first asks for the 20-bit address to be entered in hexadecimal form and then displays the contents of 256 bytes, beginning with the specified address. The output is arranged with 16 values per line and 16 lines. The address of each line is shown on the left. The **display—mem( )** function is shown here:

```
/* Displays 256 bytes of memory starting at specified
   address.
*/
void display_mem()
{
  register int i;
  unsigned char ch;
  unsigned char far *p;
  char s[80];

  /* get a 20 bit address */
  printf("beginning address (in hex): ");
  scanf("%p%*c", &p);

  printf("%p: ", p); /* print address */
  for(i=1; i<=256; i++) {
    ch =  *p;
    printf("%02x ", ch); /* display in hex */
    p++;
    if(!(i%16)) { /* every 16 bytes use new line */
      printf("\n");
      if(i!=256) printf("%p: ", p); /* print address */
    }
  }
}
```

The change—mem() Function

The second function required by the program is called **change—mem( )**. It is used to change the contents of a specified byte. It operates by requesting the 20-bit address of the contents to be changed and then prompting for the new value. The **change—mem( )** function is shown here:

```
/*  Change the contents of a byte of memory. */
void change_mem()
{
  unsigned char far *p;
  char s[80];
  char value;

  /* get a 20-bit address */
  printf("Enter address to change (in hex): ");
  scanf("%p%*c", &p);
  printf("Enter new value (in hex): ");
  scanf("%x", &value);
```

```
  /* change the value */
  *p = (unsigned char) value;
}
```

The Entire Memory Display
and Change Program

The entire memory display and change program is shown
here. It operates by prompting for input using the |< symbol.
Press D to display memory, C to change it, and Q to exit the
program.

```
/* Display and/or change memory program. */

#include "stdlib.h"

void display_mem(), change_mem();

main()
{
  char ch;

  for(;;) {
    printf("|< "); /* display the prompt symbol */
    ch = getche(); /* read command */
    printf("\n");
    switch(tolower(ch)) {
      case 'd': display_mem();
        break;
      case 'c': change_mem();
        break;
      case 'q': exit(0);
    }
  }
}

/* Displays 256 bytes of memory starting at specified
   address.
*/
void display_mem()
{
  register int i;
  unsigned char ch;
  unsigned char far *p;
  char s[80];

  /* get a 20 bit address */
  printf("beginning address (in hex): ");
  scanf("%p%*c", &p);
```

```
  printf("%p: ", p); /* print address */
  for(i=1; i<=256; i++) {
    ch = *p;
    printf("%02x ", ch); /* display in hex */
    p++;
    if(!(i%16)) { /* every 16 bytes use new line */
      printf("\n");
      if(i!=256) printf("%p: ", p); /* print address */
    }
  }
}

/*  Change the contents of a byte of memory. */
void change_mem()
{

  unsigned char far *p;
  char s[80];
  char value;

  /* get a 20-bit address */
  printf("Enter address to change (in hex): ");
  scanf("%p%*c", &p);
  printf("Enter new value (in hex): ");
  scanf("%x", &value);

  /* change the value */
  *p = (unsigned char) value;
}
```

A sample of the program's output is shown here:

```
|< d
beginning address (in hex): e001a
000E:001A: 70 02 45 14 70 02 59 ec 00 f0 3d 04 00 e0 0d 21
000E:002A: 00 f0 66 52 00 e0 0d 21 00 f0 0d 21 00 f0 5d 02
000E:003A: 00 e0 0d 21 00 f0 0d 21 00 f0 0d 21 00 f0 0d 21
000E:004A: 00 f0 0d 21 00 f0 0d 21 00 f0 0d 21 00 f0 0d 21
000E:005A: 00 f0 0d 21 00 f0 0d 21 00 f0 0d 21 00 f0 0d 21
000E:006A: 00 f0 0d 21 00 f0 0d 21 00 f0 0d 21 00 f0 0d 21
000E:007A: 00 f0 0d 21 00 f0 0d 21 00 f0 0d 21 00 f0 0d 21
000E:008A: 00 f0 0d 21 00 f0 0d·21 00 f0 0d 21 00 f0 0d 21
000E:009A: 00 f0 0d 21 00 f0 00 00 00 00 00 00 00 00 00 00
000E:00AA: 00 00 00 00 00 00 00 00 00 00 00 00 00 00 00 00
000E:00BA: 00 00 00 00 00 00 0d 21 00 f0 0d 21 00 f0 0d 21
000E:00CA: 00 f0 0d 21 00 f0 0d 21 00 f0 0d 21 00 f0 0d 21
000E:00DA: 00 f0 0d 21 00 f0 a3 01 7a 0e 5c 21 00 f0 0d 21
000E:00EA: 00 f0 0d 21 00 f0 d1 05 7a 0e 65 21 00 f0 59 06
000E:00FA: 7a 0e 0d 21 00 f0 00 00 00 00 00 00 00 00 00 00
000E:010A: 00 00 00 00 00 00 00 00 00 00 00 00 00 00 00 00
|< c
Enter address to change (in hex): e001b
Enter new value (in hex): 00
```

```
|< d
beginning address (in hex): e001a
000E:001A:  70 00 45 14 70 02 59 ec 00 f0 3d 04 00 e0 0d 21
000E:002A:  00 f0 66 52 00 e0 0d 21 00 f0 0d 21 00 f0 5d 02
000E:003A:  00 e0 0d 21 00 f0 0d 21 00 f0 0d 21 00 f0 0d 21
000E:004A:  00 f0 0d 21 00 f0 0d 21 00 f0 0d 21 00 f0 0d 21
000E:005A:  00 f0 0d 21 00 f0 0d 21 00 f0 0d 21 00 f0 0d 21
000E:006A:  00 f0 0d 21 00 f0 0d 21 00 f0 0d 21 00 f0 0d 21
000E:007A:  00 f0 0d 21 00 f0 0d 21 00 f0 0d 21 00 f0 0d 21
000E:008A:  00 f0 0d 21 00 f0 0d 21 00 f0 0d 21 00 f0 0d 21
000E:009A:  00 f0 0d 21 00 f0 00 00 00 00 00 00 00 00 00 00
000E:00AA:  00 00 00 00 00 00 00 00 00 00 00 00 00 00 00 00
000E:00BA:  00 00 00 00 00 00 0d 21 00 f0 0d 21 00 f0 0d 21
000E:00CA:  00 f0 0d 21 00 f0 0d 21 00 f0 0d 21 00 f0 0d 21
000E:00DA:  00 f0 0d 21 00 f0 a3 01 7a 0e 5c 21 00 f0 0d 21
000E:00EA:  00 f0 0d 21 00 f0 d1 05 7a 0e 65 21 00 f0 59 06
000E:00FA:  7a 0e 0d 21 00 f0 00 00 00 00 00 00 00 00 00 00
000E:010A:  00 00 00 00 00 00 00 00 00 00 00 00 00 00 00 00
```

Turbo C's Screen and Graphics Functions

Although the ANSI standard for C does not define screen or graphics functions, these functions are obviously important to most contemporary programming tasks. They are not defined by the ANSI standard because there are wide differences between the capabilities and interfaces of different types of hardware. However, since Turbo C is designed to run on the IBM line of microcomputers, it provides a comprehensive set of screen-handling and graphics functions for these machines, beginning with Version 1.5. This chapter presents an overview of both screen and graphics functions, along with some short sample programs that illustrate their use. The screen and graphics systems are so large that it is not possible to discuss every function in detail here. However, this chapter will explain the way the systems operate and give you a taste of their capabilities. (All the screen and graphics functions are discussed thoroughly later in the book.)

If you already know how to use Turbo Pascal Version 4 screen and graphics routines, you will feel at home with Turbo C's because the approach and interface are essentially the same. This common interface is a large advantage when you program in more than one language.

This chapter begins with a brief discussion of the various video modes available for the PC line of computers. It then explores the functions that control the screen in text mode before moving on to the graphics routines.

The PC Video Adapters and Modes of Operation

As you probably know, several different types of video adapters are currently available for the PC line of computers. The most common are the Monochrome, the CGA (Color Graphics Adapter), PCjr, and the EGA (Enhanced Graphics Adapter). Together, these adapters support 16 different modes of video operation. These video modes are synopsized in Table 11-1. As you can see by looking at the table, some modes are for text and some are for graphics. In a text mode only text can be displayed. The smallest user-addressable part of the screen in a text mode is one character. The smallest user-addressable part of the screen in a graphics mode is one pixel. (Actually, the term *pixel* originally referred to the smallest individual phospher element on the video monitor

Mode	Type	Dimensions	Adapters
0	Text, b/w	40×25	CGA, EGA
1	Text, 16 colors	40×25	CGA, EGA
2	Text, b/w	80×25	CGA, EGA
3	Text, 16 colors	80×25	CGA, EGA
4	Graphics, 4 colors	320×200	CGA, EGA
5	Graphics, 4 grey tones	320×200	CGA, EGA
6	Graphics, b/w	640×200	CGA, EGA
7	Text, b/w	80×25	Monochrome
8	Graphics, 16 colors	160×200	PCjr
9	Graphics, 16 colors	320×200	PCjr
10	Graphics, 4 colors PCjr, 16 colors EGA	640×200	PCjr, EGA
13	Graphics, 16 colors	320×200	EGA
14	Graphics, 16 colors	640×200	EGA
15	Graphics, 4 colors	640×350	EGA

Table 11-1.   Video Modes for IBM Microcomputers

that can be individually energized by the scan beam. However, in recent years, use of the term has been generalized to refer to the smallest addressable point on a graphics display.)

In both the text and graphics modes, individual locations on the screen are referenced by their row and column numbers. In the graphics modes the upper left corner of the screen is location 0,0. For unknown reasons, in text modes the upper left corner is 1,1.

The text screen examples shown in this chapter use video mode 3, 80-column color mode. The graphics routines use EGA mode 16. If your hardware does not support one or both of these modes, you will have to make the appropriate changes to the examples.

The Text Screen Functions

Turbo C supports a complete set of text screen functions that fall into the following categories:

- Basic input and output
- Screen manipulation
- Attribute control
- Screen status

These functions require the header file **conio.h** to be included with any program that uses them. This file contains several variables, types, and constants used by the functions, as well as their function prototypes.

Windows

The Turbo C text functions operate through windows. Fortunately, the default window is the entire screen, so you don't need to worry about creating any special windows to use the text and graphics routines. However, it is important to understand the basic concept of windows to get the most from the Turbo C screen functions.

A window is a portal that your program uses to send messages to the user. A window can be as large as the entire screen or as small as a few characters. In sophisticated software it is not uncommon for the screen to have several active windows at once—one for each separate task performed by the program.

Turbo C lets you define the location and dimensions of a window. After you define a window, Turbo C's routines that manipulate text affect only the window you have defined, not the entire screen. For example, Turbo C's **clrscr()** function clears the active window, not the entire screen. (Unless, of course, the active window is the entire screen, as it would be by default.) In addition, all position coordinates are relative to the active window instead of the screen.

One of the most important aspects of Turbo C's windows is that output is automatically prevented from spilling past the boundaries of a window. If some output would exceed a boundary, only the part that will fit is displayed; the rest is *clipped*. Clipped output is not considered an error by the Turbo C screen functions.

The subject of windows will be resumed later in this chapter after the basic screen control functions have been discussed.

Basic Input and Output

Because the standard C output routines, such as **printf()**, are not designed for use in a window-oriented screen environment, Turbo C has created some new functions that recognize windows. Some existing functions have also been modified to operate correctly inside a window. When you are using the default window, which is the entire screen, it does not matter significantly whether you use the window-based I/O functions or the standard functions. However, if you are using a smaller window, you will want to use the window-oriented functions because they automatically prevent text from being written outside the active window. The new or modified text I/O functions are shown in Table 11-2.

The **cprintf( )** function operates exactly like **printf( )** except that it recognizes Turbo C's window system. The **cputs( )** function corresponds to **puts( )** in like fashion. It differs from **puts( )** only in the fact that it recognizes windows. The functions automatically prevent output that is too big to fit in the active window from spilling over to another part of the screen. (The standard I/O functions, such as **printf( )**, do not prevent this.) The same is true for the modified function **putch( )**. It will not allow a character to be written outside the current window. The function **getche( )** has been modified so that it will not receive input outside the active window. Finally, **cgets( )** has been modified to recognize Turbo C's windows.

One other thing to understand about these basic I/O functions is that they are not redirectable. That is, Turbo C's (and ANSI C's) standard I/O functions allow output to be

Function	Purpose
cprintf( )	Writes formatted output to the active window
cputs( )	Writes a string to the active window
putch( )	Outputs a character to the active window
getche( )	Inputs a character from the active window
cgets( )	Inputs a string from the active window

Table 11-2.   Text I/O Functions for Use with Windows

redirected to or from a disk file or auxiliary device. This is not the case with the window-based text screen functions.

The Screen Manipulation Functions

Turbo C's text screen manipulation functions are shown in Table 11-3.

The **clrscr()** function clears a text window. Its prototype is

    void clrscr(*void*)

The **clreol()** function clears, from left to right, a line from the current cursor position to the end of the window. Its prototype is

    void clreol(*void*)

The companion functions **delline()** and **insline()** are used to delete a line and insert a blank line respectively.

Functions	Purpose
clrscr()	Clears the active window
clreol()	Clears from the cursor to the end of the current line
delline()	Deletes the line the cursor is on
gettext()	Copies part of the screen into a character buffer
gotoxy()	Sends the cursor to the specified location
insline()	Inserts a blank line below the current cursor position
movetext()	Copies text from one part of the screen to another
puttext()	Copies text from a buffer onto the screen
textmode()	Sets the screen's text mode
window()	Defines and activates a window

Table 11-3.   Turbo C Text Screen Manipulation Functions

Their prototypes are

> void delline(*void*)
> void insline(*void*)

A call to **delline( )** deletes the line the cursor is on and moves up all lines below that line. A call to **insline( )** inserts a new, blank line just below the line that currently holds the cursor, and moves all lines below it down one line.

One of the most useful functions is **gotoxy( )**, which is used to position the cursor within the active window. Its prototype is

> void gotoxy(*int x, int y*)

Here, x and y specify the coordinate at which the cursor will be positioned. If either coordinate is out of range, no action is taken.

No matter how a window is sized or positioned, the upper left corner is always 1,1. Assuming that the entire screen is being used, in 80-column text modes the valid range for x is 1 through 80; for y it is 1 through 25.

The companion functions **gettext( )** and **puttext( )** are used to copy text from the screen to a buffer and from a buffer to the screen, respectively. Their prototypes are

> int gettext(*int left, int top, int right, int bottom,*
>   *void *buffer*)
> int puttext(*int left, int top, int right, int bottom,*
>   *void *buffer*)

For **gettext( )** you specify the coordinates of the upper left corner and lower right corner of the region of the screen you want. The pointer **buffer** must point to a region of memory large enough to hold the text. The size of the buffer is computed with this formula:

> size in bytes = rows * columns * 2

Each character displayed on the screen requires two bytes of video memory. The first byte holds the actual character, the second holds its *screen attribute*. This is the reason that the number of bytes required to hold the text is twice as large as the number of characters. For example, if you called **gettext()** with 1,1 for the first coordinate pair and 10,10 for the second, you would need **10*10*2** (200) bytes of storage. Both functions return 0 if one or more coordinates is out of range; otherwise they return 1.

To copy text already in a buffer back to the screen, you call **puttext()** with the coordinates of the upper left and lower right corners of the region that will receive the text along with a pointer to the buffer that holds it.

If you want to copy text from one part of the screen to another, using the **movetext()** function is more efficient than calling **gettext()** and then **puttext()**. The prototype for **movetext()** is

> int movetext(*int top, int left, int right, int bottom,*
> *int newtop, int newleft*)

The function **movetext()** returns 0 if one or more coordinates is out of range; otherwise it returns 1.

The **window()** function activates a text window of specified dimensions. Its prototype is

> void window(*int left, int top, int right, int bottom*)

If any coordinate is invalid, **window()** takes no action. Once a call to **window()** has been successfully completed, all references to location coordinates are interpreted relative to the window not the screen. For example, this fragment of code creates a window and writes a line of text at location 2,3 inside that window.

```
window(10, 10, 60, 15);
gotoxy(2, 3);
cprintf("at location 2, 3");
```

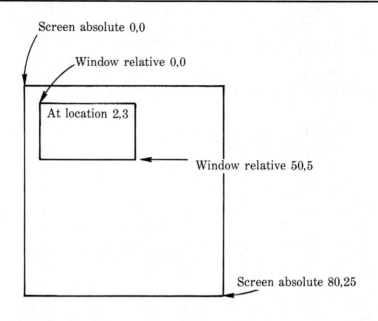

Figure 11-1.   Illustration of relative coordinates inside a window

The action of this fragment is illustrated in Figure 11-1.

It is important to understand that coordinates used to call **window()** are screen absolute—not relative to the currently active window. In this way you can use multiple windows that are not nested inside each other.

The following program first draws a border around the screen (for perspective) and then creates two separate windows with borders. The position of the text inside each window is specified by **gotoxy()** statements that are relative to each window.

```
/* A text window demonstration program */
#include "conio.h"

void border(int, int, int, int);
```

```
main()
{
  clrscr();

  /* draw a border around the screen for perspective */
  border(1, 1, 79, 25);

  /* create first window */
  window(3, 2, 40, 9);
  border(3, 2, 40, 9);
  gotoxy(3, 2);
  cprintf("first window");

  /* create a second window */
  window(30, 10, 60, 18);
  border(30, 10, 60, 18);
  gotoxy(3, 2);
  cprintf("second window");
  gotoxy(5, 4);
  cprintf("hello");

  getche();
}

/* Draws a border around a text window. */
void border(int startx, int starty, int endx, int endy)
{
  register int i;

  gotoxy(1, 1);
  for(i=0; i<=endx-startx; i++)
    putch('-');

  gotoxy(1, endy-starty);
  for(i=0; i<=endx-startx; i++)
    putch('-');

  for(i=2; i<endy-starty; i++) {
    gotoxy(1, i);
    putch('|');
    gotoxy(endx-startx+1, i);
    putch('|');
  }
}
```

Text Attribute Control

It is possible to change video modes, control the color of the text and background, and set the display to high or low intensity. The functions that do these things are shown in Table 11-4 and are applicable to all video adapters with the exception of the monochrome adapter, which supports only one mode and one color.

Function	Purpose
highvideo( )	Displays text in high intensity
lowvideo( )	Displays text in low intensity
normvideo( )	Displays text in the original intensity
textattr( )	Sets the color of the text and the color of the background at the same time
textbackground( )	Sets the background color
textcolor( )	Sets the color of the text
textmode( )	Sets the video mode

Table 11-4.   Text Attribute Functions

The functions **highvideo( )** and **lowvideo( )** set the display to high-intensity and low-intensity video, respectively. Their prototypes are

    void highvideo(*void*)
    void lowvideo(*void*)

The function **normvideo( )** returns the display to the way it was before the program began execution. Its prototype is

    void normvideo(*void*)

The **textcolor( )** function determines the color of subsequent text displayed. It can also be used to make the text blink. The prototype of **textcolor( )** is

    void textcolor(*int color*)

The argument *color* may have the values 0 through 15 with each corresponding to a different color. However, the macro

Macro	Integer Equivalent
BLACK	0
BLUE	1
GREEN	2
CYAN	3
RED	4
MAGENTA	5
BROWN	6
LIGHTGRAY	7
DARKGRAY	8
LIGHTBLUE	9
LIGHTGREEN	10
LIGHTCYAN	11
LIGHTRED	12
LIGHTMAGENTA	13
YELLOW	14
WHITE	15
BLINK	128

Table 11-5.   Color Macros and Integer Equivalents for Text

names defined in **conio.h** for each of these colors are easier to remember. These macros and their integer equivalents are shown in Table 11-5.

It is important to understand that a change in the color of the text affects only subsequent write operations; it does not change any text currently displayed on the screen.

To make text blink you must OR the value 128 (BLINK) with the color you desire. For example, this fragment causes subsequent text output to be green and blinking.

```
textcolor(GREEN | BLINK)
```

The function **textbackground()** is used to set the background color of a text screen. As with **textcolor()**, a call to

textbackground() affects only the background color of subsequent write operations. Its prototype is

void textbackground(*int color*)

The value for *color* must be in the range 0 through 6. This means that only the first seven colors shown in Table 11-5 can be used for background.

The function **textattr()** sets both the text and background colors. Its prototype is

void textattr(*int attribute*)

The value of *attribute* represents an encoded form of the color information as shown here:

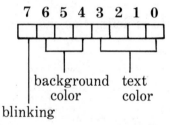

If bit 7 is set, the text will blink. Bits 6 through 4 determine the background color. Bits 3 through 0 set the color for the text. The easiest way to encode the background color into the attribute byte is to multiply the number of the color you desire by 16 and then OR that with the text color. For example, to create a green background with blue text you would use **GREEN * 16 | BLUE**. To cause the text to blink, OR the text color, background color, and BLINK (128) together. For example, this causes the text to be red and blinking with a blue background.

```
textattr(RED | BLINK | BLUE*16);
```

The **textmode()** function is used to change the video mode. Its prototype is void textmode(*int mode*)

The argument *mode* must be one of the values shown in Table 11-6. You may use either the integer value or the macro name. (The macros are defined in **conio.h.**)

The Text Screen Status Functions

Turbo C provides three text mode functions that return the status of the screen. They are shown in Table 11-7.

The **gettextinfo( )** function returns the status of the current window in a structure of type **text_info**, which is defined in **conio.h**. The prototype of **gettextinfo( )** is

void gettextinfo(*struct text_info *info*)

The structure **text_info** is defined as shown here:

```
struct text_info {
    unsigned char winleft;       /* left X coordinate */
    unsigned char wintop;        /* top Y coordinate */
    unsigned char winright;      /* right X coordinate */
    unsigned char winbottom;     /* bottom Y coordinate */
    unsigned char attribute;     /* text attribute */
    unsigned char normattr;      /* normal attribute */
    unsigned char currmode;      /* current video mode */
    unsigned char screenheight;/* height of screen in lines */
    unsigned char screenwidth;  /* width of screen in chars */
    unsigned char curx;          /* cursor's X coordinate */
    unsigned char cury;          /* cursor's Y coordinate */
};
```

When you use **gettextinfo( )**, remember to pass a pointer to a structure of type **text_info** so that the elements of the structure can be set by the function. Do not try to pass the structure variable itself. For example, this fragment illustrates how to call **gettextinfo( )** properly.

```
struct text_info screen_status;

gettextinfo(&screen_status);
```

Macro Name	Integer Equivalent	Description
BW40	0	40 column black and white
C40	1	40 column color
BW80	2	80 column black and white
C80	3	80 column color
MONO	7	80 column monochrome
LAST	−1	Previous mode

Table 11-6.   Text Video Modes

The directvideo Variable

For IBM PCs and 100 percent compatibles, it is possible to bypass the DOS and ROM-BIOS screen output routines and,

Function	Purpose
gettextinfo( )	Returns information about the current text window
wherex( )	Returns the x coordinate of the cursor
wherey( )	Returns the y coordinate of the cursor

Table 11-7.   Text Screen Status Functions

instead, place output directly into the video RAM. Using this method produces the fastest possible output operations. However, for computers that are not hardware compatible with the PC line but are BIOS compatible, the direct video RAM output cannot be used. To allow for this possibility, Turbo C provides a variable called **directvideo**, which controls how output is performed. When **directvideo** is true, as it is by default, all screen output is performed via direct video RAM accesses. To cause the BIOS routines to be used rather than writing directly to the video RAM, set **directvideo** to 0 (false).

A Short Demonstration Program

The following program illustrates the use of several of the text screen functions. Its output is shown in Figure 11-2.

```
#include "conio.h"

main()
{
  register int i, j;

  textmode(C80); /* 80 column text mode */

  clrscr(),

  /* demonstrate the gotoxy() function */
  for(i=1, j=1; j<24; i++, j++) {
    gotoxy(i, j);
    cprintf("X");
  }
  for(; j>0; i++, j--) {
    gotoxy(i, j);
    cprintf("X");
  }

  /* examples of different foreground and background colors */
  textbackground(LIGHTBLUE);
  textcolor(RED);
  gotoxy(40, 12);
  cprintf("This is red with a light blue background.");

  gotoxy(45, 15);
  textcolor(GREEN | BLINK);
  textbackground(BLACK);
  cprintf("This is blinking green on black.");

  getch();

  /* an example of movetext() */
  /* this moves the "inverted peak" of the X's to the
     top of the screen
```

```
*/
movetext(20, 20, 28, 24, 20, 1);
getch();
textmode(LAST);
}
```

Turbo C's Graphics Functions

Turbo C's graphics functions can be grouped into the following categories:

- Video adapter mode control
- Basic graphing
- Text output
- Screen status
- Screen manipulation

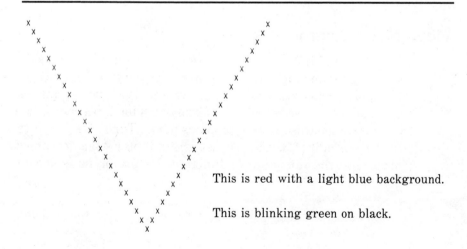

This is red with a light blue background.

This is blinking green on black.

Figure 11-2.   Sample output from text screen control functions

The graphics functions require that the header **graphics.h** be included in any program that uses them.

Keep in mind that the computer must be equipped with a graphics video adapter in order to use Turbo C's graphics routines. This means that systems with only a monochrome adapter will not be able to display graphics output. The examples shown here all use EGA mode 16 (640×350, 16 colors). If you do not have an EGA, you will have to make the appropriate alterations to the examples.

Viewports

All of Turbo C's graphics functions operate through *viewports*. Viewport is really just another name for window, and a graphics viewport has essentially the same qualities as a text window. By default the entire screen is the viewport. However, you can create viewports of other dimensions. You will see how to do this later in this chapter. However, as you read through the following discussions, keep in mind that all graphics output is relative to the current viewport, which is not necessarily the same as the screen.

Video Mode Control Functions

Before any of the graphics functions can be used, it is necessary to put the video adapter into one of the graphics modes. By default, the vast majority of systems that have graphics video adapters use 80-column text mode 3 for DOS communications. Since this is not a graphics mode, Turbo C's graphics functions cannot work. To set the adapter to a graphics mode, use the **initgraph()** function. Its prototype is shown here:

> void far initgraph(*int far *driver, int far *mode, char far *path*);

The **initgraph( )** function loads into memory a graphics driver that corresponds to the number pointed to by *driver*. Without a graphics driver loaded into memory, no graphics functions can operate. The *mode* parameter points to an integer that specifies the video mode used by the graphics functions. Finally, you can specify a path to the driver in the string pointed to by *path*. If no path is specified, the current working directory is searched.

The graphics drivers are contained in .BGI files, which must be available on the system. However, you need not worry about the actual name of the file because you only have to specify the driver by its number. **graphics.h** defines several macros that you can use for this purpose. They are shown here:

Macro	Equivalent
DETECT	0
CGA	1
MCGA	2
EGA	3
EGA64	4
EGAMONO	5
RESERVED	6
HERCMONO	7
ATT400	8
VGA	9
PC3270	10

When you use **DETECT**, **initgraph( )** automatically detects the type of video hardware present in the system and selects the video mode with the greatest resolution.

The value of *mode* must be one of the graphics modes shown in Table 11-8. Notice that the value pointed to by *mode* is *not* the same as the value recognized by the BIOS routine that actually sets the mode. Instead the value used to call BIOS to initialize a video mode is created by **initgraph( )**

Driver	Mode	Equivalent	Resolution
CGA	CGAC0	0	320×200
	CGAC1	1	320×200
	CGAC2	2	320×200
	CGAC3	3	320×200
	CGAHI	4	640×200
MCGA	MCGAC0	0	320×200
	MCGAC1	1	320×200
	MCGAC2	2	320×200
	MCGAC3	3	320×200
	MCGAMED	4	640×200
	MCGAHI	5	640×480
EGA	EGALO	0	640×200
	EGAHI	1	640×350
EGA64	EGA64LO	0	640×200
	EGA64HI	1	640×350
EGAMONO	EGAMONOHI	3	640×350
HERC	HERCMONOHI	0	720×348
ATT400	ATT400C0	0	320×200
	ATT400C1	1	320×200
	ATT400C2	2	320×200
	ATT400C3	3	320×200
	ATT400CMED	4	640×200
	ATT400CHI	5	640×400
VGA	VGALO	0	640×200
	VGAMED	1	640×350
	VGAHI	2	640×480
PC3270	PC3270HI	0	720×350

Table 11-8.   Turbo C Graphics Drivers and Modes Macros

using both the driver and the mode. For example, to cause the graphics system to be initialized to CGA four-color, 320×200 graphics, you would use this fragment (equivalent to BIOS video mode 4). It assumes that the graphics driver's .BGI file is in the current working directory.

```
#include "graphics.h"
   .
   .
   .
int driver, mode;

driver = CGA;
mode = CGAC0;

initgraph(&driver, &mode, "");
```

CGA four-color graphics gives you four palettes to choose from and four colors per palette. The colors are numbered 0 through 3, with 0 always being the background color. The palettes are also numbered 0 through 3. To select a palette, set the *mode* parameter equal to **CGACx** where **x** is the palette number. The palettes and their associated colors are shown in Table 11-9.

In EGA/VGA 16-color mode, a palette consists of 16 colors selected from a possible 64 colors.

To change the palette, use the **setpalette( )** function, whose prototype is

void far setpalette(*int index, int color*)

The operation of this function is a little difficult to understand at first. In essence, it associates the value of *color* with

	Color Number			
Palette	**0**	**1**	**2**	**3**
0	background	green	red	yellow
1	background	cyan	magenta	white
2	background	lightgreen	lightred	yellow
3	background	lightcyan	lightmagenta	white

Table 11-9.   Palettes and Colors in Video Mode 4

VGA Codes (Background Only)		EGA and VGA	
Macro	**Value**	**Macro**	**Value**
BLACK	0	EGA_BLACK	0
BLUE	1	EGA_BLUE	1
GREEN	2	EGA_GREEN	2
CYAN	3	EGA_CYAN	3
RED	4	EGA_RED	4
MAGENTA	5	EGA_MAGENTA	5
BROWN	6	EGA_BROWN	20
LIGHTGRAY	7	EGA_LIGHTGRAY	7
DARKGRAY	8	EGA_DARKGRAY	56
LIGHTBLUE	9	EGA_LIGHTBLUE	57
LIGHTGREEN	10	EGA_LIGHTGREEN	58
LIGHTCYAN	11	EGA_LIGHTCYAN	59
LIGHTRED	12	EGA_LIGHTRED	60
LIGHTMAGENTA	13	EGA_LIGHTMAGENTA	61
YELLOW	14	EGA_YELLOW	62
WHITE	15	EGA_WHITE	63

Table 11-10.   Color Codes for the **setpalette( )** Function

an index into a table that Turbo C uses to map the color actually shown on the screen with that being requested. The values for the color codes are shown in Table 11-10.

For CGA modes, only the background color can be changed. The background color is always index 0. So, for CGA modes, this fragment changes the background color to green.

```
setpalette(0, GREEN);
```

The EGA can display 16 colors at a time with the total number of different colors being 64. You can use **setpalette( )** to map a color onto one of the 16 different indexes. For example, this fragment sets the value of color 5 to cyan.

```
setpalette(5, EGA_CYAN);
```

If you call **setpalette( )** with invalid arguments, a −1L is returned.

When you want to set all the colors in an EGA/VGA palette, it is easier to use the **setallpalette( )** function, which has the prototype

void far setallpalette(*struct palettetype far *pal*)

Here *palettetype* is defined as

```
struct palettetype {
  unsigned char size;
  signed char colors[16];
}
```

You must set *size* to the number of colors in the palette and then load the color for each index into its corresponding element in the array *colors*.

You can set just the background color with **setbkcolor( )**. Its prototype is

void far setbkcolor(*int color*)

The value of *color* must be one of the following:

Number	Color
0	Black
1	Blue
2	Green
3	Cyan
4	Red
5	Magenta
6	Brown
7	Lightgray
8	Darkgray
9	Lightblue
10	Lightgreen
11	Lightcyan
12	Lightred
13	Lightmagenta
14	Yellow
15	White

To stop using a graphics video mode and return to a text mode, use either **closegraph()** or **restorecrtmode()**. Their prototypes are

```
void far closegraph()
void far restorecrtmode()
```

The **closegraph()** function should be used when your program is going to continue executing in text mode. It frees memory used by the graphics functions and resets the video mode to what it was before the first call to **initgraph()**. If your program is terminating, you can use **restorecrtmode()** because it resets the video adapter to the mode it was in before the first call to **initgraph()**.

The Basic Graphing Functions

The most fundamental graphing functions are those that draw a point, a line, and a circle. In Turbo C these functions are called **putpixel()**, **line()**, and **circle()**, respectively. Their prototypes are

void far plot(*int x, int y, int color*)
void far draw(*int startx, int starty, int endx, int endy*)
void far circle(*int x, int y, int radius*)

The **putpixel()** function writes the specified color to the location determined by *x* and *y*. The **line()** function draws a line from the location specified by *startx, starty* to *endx, endy* in the current drawing color. The **circle()** function draws a circle of radius *radius* in the current drawing color, with the center at the location specified by *x,y*. If any of the coordinates are out of range, no action is taken.

You can set the current drawing color using **setcolor()**. Its prototype is

void far setcolor(*int color*)

The value of *color* must be in the range valid for the current graphics mode.

You can fill any enclosed shape using the **floodfill()** function. Its prototype is

void far floodfill(*int x, int y, int bordercolor*)

To use this function to fill an enclosed shape, call it with the coordinates of a point inside the shape and the color of the lines that make up the shape (its border). You must make sure that the object you are filling is completely enclosed. If it isn't, some areas outside the shape will get filled as well.

What the object is filled with is determined by the current fill pattern and fill color. The background color is used by default. However, you can change the way objects are filled using **setfillstyle( )**. Its prototype is

void far setfillstyle(*int pattern, int color*)

The values for *pattern* are shown here along with their macro equivalents (defined in **graphics.h**):

Macro	Value	Meaning
EMPTY—FILL	0	Fill with background color
SOLID—FILL	1	Fill with solid color
LINE—FILL	2	Fill with lines
LTSLASH—FILL	3	Fill with light slashes
SLASH—FILL	4	Fill with slashes
BKSLASH—FILL	5	Fill with backslashes
LTBKSLASH —FILL	6	Fill with light back slashes
XHATCH—FILL	8	Fill with hatching
INTERLEAVE —FILL	9	Fill with interleaving
WIDEDOT—FILL	10	Fill with widely spaced dots
CLOSEDOT —FILL	11	Fill with closely spaced dots
USER—FILL	12	Fill with custom pattern

You can define a custom pattern using **setfillpattern( )**, which is described in Part Three.

The following program demonstrates these basic graphics functions. As you will see by looking at the program, the function **box( )** is used to draw a box in a specified color

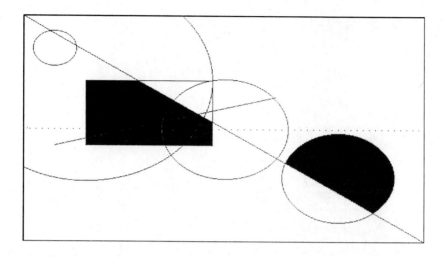

Figure 11-3.   Output from points, lines, and circles
demonstration program

given the coordinates of the upper left and lower right
corners. It is an example of how higher-level graphics functions can be easily constructed from the core of routines provided by Turbo C. The output of the program is shown in
Figure 11-3.

```c
/* Points, lines, circles, and fills demonstration program. */
#include "graphics.h"
#include "conio.h"

void border(void), box(int, int, int, int, int);

main()
{
  int driver, mode;

  register int i;

  driver = VGA;
  mode = VGAMED;
  initgraph(&driver, &mode, "");
```

```
    border();

    setcolor(1);
    line(0, 0, 639, 349);

    box(100, 100, 300, 200, 1);

    setcolor(2);
    floodfill(110, 110, 1); /* fill part of a box */
    setcolor(1);
    line(50, 200, 400, 125);

    /* some points */
    for(i=0; i<640; i+=10) putpixel(i, 175, 5);

    /* line some circles */
    circle(50, 50, 35);
    circle(320, 175, 100);
    circle(500, 250, 90);
    circle(100, 100, 200);

    setfillstyle(SOLID_FILL, GREEN);
    floodfill(500, 250, 1); /* fill part of a circle */

    getch(); /* wait until keypress */
    restorecrtmode();
}

/* Draw a border around the screen for perspective. */
void border()
{
    line(0, 0, 639, 0);
    line(0, 0, 0, 349);
    line(0, 349, 639, 349);
    line(639, 0, 639, 349);
}

/* Draw a box given the coordinates of its two corners. */
void box(int startx, int starty, int endx, int endy,
         int color)
{
    setcolor(color);

    line(startx, starty, startx, endy);
    line(startx, starty, endx, starty);
    line(endx, starty, endx, endy);
    line(endx, endy, startx, endy);
}
```

Text Output in Graphics Mode

Although you can use the standard screen output functions
such as **printf()** to display text while in a graphics mode, in
many situations it is better to use the function **outtext()**,
which is designed for this purpose. Its prototype is

void far outtext(*char *str*)

This function outputs the string pointed to by *str* at the current position. (In graphics modes, there is no visible cursor, but the current position on the screen is maintained as if there were an invisible cursor.) In the *Turbo C User's Guide*, this position is called CP. The principle advantage to using **outtext( )** is that it can output text in different fonts, sizes, or directions in which the text is printed.

To change the style, size, or direction of the text, use **settextstyle( )**. Its prototype is

void far settextstyle(*int font, int direction, int charsize*)

The *font* parameter determines the type of font used. The default is the hardware-defined 8×8 bit-mapped font. You can give *font* one of these values. (The macros are defined in **graphics.h**).

Font	Value	Meaning
DEFAULT_FONT	0	8×8 bit-mapped
TRIPLEX_FONT	1	Stroked triplex
SMALL_FONT	2	Small stroked font
SANSSERIF	3	Stroked sans serif
GOTHIC_FONT	4	Stroked gothic

The direction in which the text will be displayed, from either left to right or bottom to top, is determined by the value of *direction*, which may be either **HORIZ_DIR** (0) or **VERT_DIR** (1).

The *charsize* parameter is a multiplier that increases the character size. It may have a value of 0 through 10.

The following program illustrates the use of the **settextstyle( )** function:

```
/* Demonstrate some different text fonts and sizes. */

#include "graphics.h"
#include "conio.h"
```

```
main()
{
  int driver, mode;
  register int i;

  driver = VGA;
  mode = VGAMED;
  initgraph(&driver, &mode, "");

  outtext("Normal ");

  /* Gothic font, twice normal size */
  settextstyle(GOTHIC_FONT, HORIZ_DIR, 2);
  outtext("Gothic ");

  /* Triplex font, twice normal size */
  settextstyle(TRIPLEX_FONT, HORIZ_DIR, 2);
  outtext("Triplex ");

  /* Sans serif font, 7 times normal size*/
  settextstyle(TRIPLEX_FONT, HORIZ_DIR, 7);
  outtext("Sans serif");

  getch();
  restorecrtmode();
}
```

To put text at a specific viewport location, use the **out-textxy()** function. Its prototype is

void far outtext(*int x, int y, char *str*)

The string is written at the specified viewport coordinates. If either *x* or *y*, or both, is out of range, no output is displayed.

Graphics Mode Status

You can use several functions to get information about the graphics screen. The three most important are examined in this section. The first, **getviewsettings()**, loads a structure with assorted information about the current viewport. Its prototype is

void far getviewsettings(*struct viewporttype far *info*)

The structure **viewporttype** is found in **graphics.h** and is defined as shown here:

```
struct viewporttype {
  int left, top, right, bottom;
  int clipflag;
}
```

The fields **left**, **top**, **right**, and **bottom** hold the coordinates of the upper left and lower right corners of the viewport. When **clipflag** is 0, there is no clipping of output that overruns the viewport boundaries. Otherwise, clipping is performed to prevent boundary overrun.

For information about the current graphics text settings use **gettextsettings( )**, whose prototype is

void far gettextsettings(*struct textsettingstype far *info*)

The structure **textsettingstype** is defined in **graphics.h** and is shown here:

```
struct textsettingstype {
  int font;          /* font type */
  int direction;     /* horizontal or vertical */
  int charsize;      /* size of characters */
  int horiz;         /* horizontal justification */
  int vert;          /* vertical justification */
};
```

The font element contains one of these values (as defined in **graphics.h**):

Value	Font
0	Default 8×8 bit-mapped font
1	Stroked triplex font
2	Stroked small font
3	Stroked sans serif font
4	Stroked gothic font

The **direction** element is set to either **HORIZ_DIR** (the default) for horizontal text or **VERT_DIR** for vertical text. The **charsize** element is a multiplier used to scale the size of the output text. The values of **horiz** and **vert** indicate how text is justified relative to the current position (CP). The values will be one of the following (the macros are defined in **graphics.h**):

Macro	Value	Meaning
LEFT_TEXT	0	CP at left
CENTER_TEXT	1	CP in the center
RIGHT_TEXT	2	CP at right
BOTTOM_TEXT	3	CP at the bottom
TOP_TEXT	4	CP at the top

Another graphics status function is **getpixel()**, which returns the color of a specified pixel. Its prototype is

int far getpixel(*int x, int y*);

It returns the current color at the specified x,y location.

The Graphics Screen Manipulation Functions

There are six graphics functions that allow you to manipulate the screen and one function that allows you to create graphics windows. These functions are shown in Table 11-11. The prototypes for these functions are

void far clearviewport(*void*)
void far getimage(*int left, int top, int right, int bottom, void far *buf*)
unsigned far imagesize(*int left, int top, int right, int bottom*)
void far putimage(*int left, int top, void far *buf, int op*)
void far setactivepage(*int pagenum*)
void far setviewport(*int left, int top, int right, int bottom, int clipflag*);
void far setvisualpage(*int pagenum*)

Function	Purpose
clearviewport( )	Clears the active viewport
getimage( )	Copies part of a viewport to a buffer
imagesize( )	Returns the number of bytes needed to save an image
putimage( )	Copies a buffer to the viewport
setactivepage( )	Determines which page will be affected by the graphics routines
setviewport( )	Creates a graphics window
setvisualpage( )	Determines which page is displayed

Table 11-11.   Regular Graphics Screen Control Functions

For some video modes, there is enough memory in video adapters to have two or more complete screens' worth of information stored at the same time. The RAM that holds the information displayed on the screen is called a *page*. By default, DOS always uses page 0. However, you can use any of the video pages supported by your hardware, switching between them as desired. Although only one screen's worth of data can be displayed at one time, it is occasionally useful to build an image as a background task in a page that is not currently displayed so that it is ready without delay when needed. To activate the image, simply switch to that display page. This method is particularly useful in cases where complex images take a long time to construct.

To support this sort of approach, Turbo C supplies the functions **setactivepage( )** and **setvisualpage( )**. The **setactivepage( )** function determines the video page to which the output of Turbo C's graphics functions will be directed. Turbo C uses video page 0 by default. If you call **setactivepage( )** with another page, subsequent graphics output is written to the new page, not necessarily to the one currently displayed. To display pages other than 0, use the **setvisual-**

page() function. For example, to display video page 1 you would call **setvisualpage()** with an argument of 1.

The **getimage()** and **putimage()** functions are used to copy a region of the graphics window into a buffer and **putimage()** is used to put the contents of a buffer onto the screen. The function **getimage()** copies the contents of a rectangular portion of the screen defined by its upper left and lower right coordinates to the buffer pointed to by *buf*. The size of the buffer in bytes for a given region is returned by the **imagesize()** function. Use **putimage()** to display a buffer of graphics data previously stored using **getimage()**. You need to specify only the upper left coordinates of the place where you want the image displayed. The value of *op* determines exactly how the image is written to the screen. Its valid enumerated values are

Name	Value	Meaning
COPY_PUT	0	Copy as is
XOR_PUT	1	Exclusive-OR with destination
OR_PUT	2	Inclusive-OR with destination
AND_PUT	3	AND with destination
NOT_PUT	4	Invert source image

The following program demonstrates the **getimage()**, **imagesize()**, and **putimage()** functions. Its output is shown in Figure 11-4.

```
/* This program demonstrates how a graphics image can be
   moved using getimage(), imagesize(), and putimage().
*/
#include "conio.h"
#include "graphics.h"
#include "stdlib.h"

void box(int, int, int, int, int);

main()
{
  int driver, mode;
  unsigned size;
  void *buf;
```

```
driver = VGA;
mode = VGAMED;
initgraph(&driver, &mode, "");

box(20, 20, 200, 200, 15);

setcolor(RED);
line(20, 20, 200, 200);
setcolor(GREEN);
line(20, 200, 200, 20);
getch();

/* move the image */

/* first, get the image's size */
size = imagesize(20, 20, 200, 200);
if(size !=-1) { /* alloc memory for the image */
  buf = malloc(size);
  if(buf) {
    getimage(20, 20, 200, 200, buf);
    putimage(100, 100, buf, COPY_PUT);
    putimage(300, 50, buf, COPY_PUT);
  }
}
outtext("press a key");
getch();
restorecrtmode();
}

/* Draw a box given the coordinates of its two corners. */
void box(int startx, int starty, int endx, int endy,
         int color)
{
  setcolor(color);

  line(startx, starty, startx, endy);
  line(startx, starty, endx, starty);
  line(endx, starty, endx, endy);
  line(endx, endy, startx, endy);
}
```

You can create windows in graphics mode in much the same way they are created in text mode. As stated earlier, all the graphics output is relative to the coordinates of the active viewport. This means the coordinate of the upper left corner of the window is 0,0 no matter where the viewport is on the screen.

The function you use to create a graphics viewport is called **setviewport( )**. To use it, you specify the coordinates of the upper left and lower right corners of the screen. If the *clipflag* parameter is nonzero, output that would exceed the viewport's boundaries is automatically truncated. With clipping turned off, output can overrun the viewport. Keep in mind, however, that the clipping of output is not considered

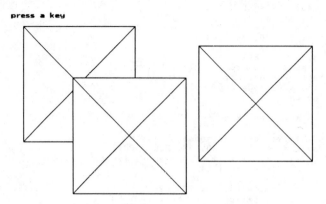

Figure 11-4.   Output from move image demonstration program

an error condition by Turbo C. The following program illustrates how to create a viewport and the clipping of output. The output is shown in Figure 11-5.

```
/* This program illustrates the use of setviewport(). */

#include "conio.h"
#include "graphics.h"

void box(int, int, int, int, int);

main()
{
  int driver, mode;

  driver = VGA;
  mode = VGAMED;
  initgraph(&driver, &mode, "");

  /* frame the screen for perspective */
  box(0, 0, 639, 349, WHITE);

  setviewport(20, 20, 200, 200, 1);
  box(0, 0, 179, 179, RED);

  /* Attempt to draw a line past the edge of the
     viewport.
  */
```

```
setcolor(WHITE);
line(0, 100, 400, 100);

outtextxy(20, 10, "press a key");
getch();
restorecrtmode();
}

/* Draw a box given the coordinates of its two corners. */
void box(int startx, int starty, int endx, int endy,
         int color)
{
setcolor(color);

line(startx, starty, startx, endy);
line(startx, starty, endx, starty);
line(endx, starty, endx, endy);
line(endx, endy, startx, endy);
}
```

As you can see, the line is clipped at the edge of the viewport
when an attempt is made to draw outside the active viewport
boundaries.

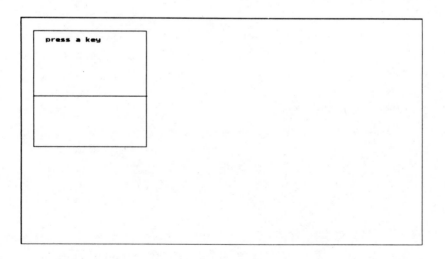

Figure 11-5.   Sample output from graphics viewpoint
demonstration program

The Turbo C Environment

Part Two of this guide to Turbo C explores the Turbo C programming environment, including the operation of both integrated and command line versions. Part Two also examines the Turbo C built-in editor and the various compiler options.

P
A
R
T

T
W
O

The Turbo C Integrated
Programming Environment

The integrated development environment, or IDE for short, makes it possible to edit, compile, link, and run a program without ever leaving the Turbo C environment. This capability promotes extremely fast recompilation cycles, which facilitate and speed up the creation, testing, and debugging of software.

Executing Turbo C

To execute the integrated version of Turbo C you simply type TC followed by a carriage return at the DOS prompt. When Turbo C begins execution you see the screen shown in Figure 12-1. This is called the main menu screen and consists of four parts, in order from top to bottom:

- The main menu
- The editor status line and window
- The compiler message window
- The "hot key" quick reference line

To exit Turbo C you press ALT-X.

The rest of this chapter examines each of these areas.

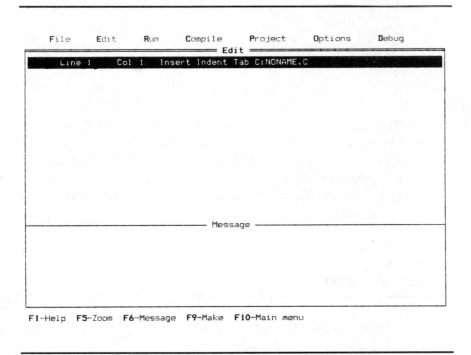

File   Edit   Run   Compile   Project   Options   Debug
━━━━━━━━━━━━━━━━━━━━━━━━━━ Edit ━━━━━━━━━━━━━━━━━━━━━━━━
Line 1   Col 1   Insert Indent Tab C:NONAME.C

──────────────────────────────── Message ────────────────────────────────

F1-Help   F5-Zoom   F6-Message   F9-Make   F10-Main menu

Figure 12-1.   Turbo C opening screen

The Main Menu

The main menu is used either to instruct Turbo C to do
something, such as execute the editor or compile a program,
or to set an environmental option. There are two ways to
make a main menu selection.

1. You can use the arrow keys to move the highlight to
the item you want and then press ENTER.

2. You can simply type the first letter of the menu item you want. For example, to select **Edit** you would type **E**. You may enter the letters in either upper- or lowercase.

Table 12-1 summarizes what each menu selection does.

Most of the main menu options have their own sub-menus, which are presented as a pull-down menu beneath the main menu. For example, if you move the highlight to **File** and press ENTER, you activate the **File** pull-down window as shown in Figure 12-2. Some of the submenus have further options of their own, in which case another pull-down menu is displayed. The number of menus and submenus presented varies according to the needs of each main option.

To make a selection from a pull-down menu, either you move the highlight to the option you desire by using the arrow keys and press ENTER, or you type the capitalized letter of the selection. (This is generally, but not always, the

Item	Options
File	Loads and saves files, handles directories, invokes DOS, and exits Turbo C
Edit	Invokes the Turbo C editor
Run	Compiles, links, and runs the program currently loaded in the environment
Compile	Compiles the program currently in the environment
Make	Manages multifile projects
Options	Sets various compiler and linker options
Debug	Sets various debug options

Table 12-1.   Summary of the Main Menu Items

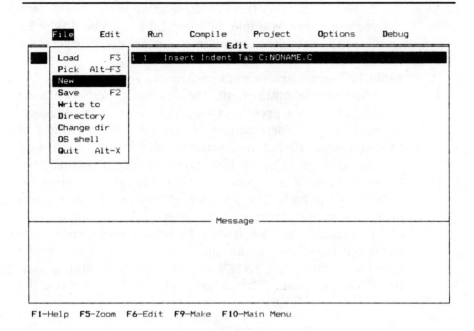

| File | Edit | Run | Compile | Project | Options | Debug |

```
╔══════════════════════════════════ Edit ════════════════════════════╗
║ Load     F3  │1  1   Insert Indent Tab C:NONAME.C                    ║
║ Pick  Alt-F3 │                                                       ║
║ New          │                                                       ║
║ Save     F2  │                                                       ║
║ Write to     │                                                       ║
║ Directory    │                                                       ║
║ Change dir   │                                                       ║
║ OS shell     │                                                       ║
║ Quit   Alt-X │                                                       ║
```

Message

F1-Help F5-Zoom F6-Edit F9-Make F10-Main Menu

Figure 12-2.   The File pull-down window

first letter of the selection.) To exit a pull-down menu you press ESC.

Each of the main options and their suboptions are examined next.

File

The **File** option has nine suboptions. They are

Load
Pick

New
Save
Write to
Directory
Change dir
OS shell
Quit

The **Load** option prompts you for a file name and then loads that file into the editor. **Pick** displays a menu that contains a list of the last eight files that you loaded into the IDE. You use the arrow keys to move the highlight until it is on the file you wish to load and press ENTER to load the file. **New** lets you edit a new file. It erases the current contents of the editor. If the previous file has been changed but not yet saved to disk, the **New** option first asks if you want it to save the file before erasing it. The **Save** option saves the file currently in the editor. The **Write to** option lets you save a file using a different file name. This is especially useful when you use the **New** command to begin editing a new file. The **New** command causes the file name NONAME.C to be used. You can use **Write to** to establish the proper name for the file. The **Directory** option displays the contents of the current working directory. You may specify a mask or use the default *.* mask. The **Change dir** command displays the path name of the current working directory and allows you to change it to another if you desire. The **OS shell** option loads the DOS command processor and lets you execute DOS commands. You must type **EXIT** to return to Turbo C. The **Quit** option quits Turbo C. (Remember that you can also use the ALT-X key combination to exit Turbo C.)

Edit

Selecting the **Edit** option activates Turbo C's built-in editor. The operation of the editor is the subject of Chapter 13.

Run

The **Run** option attempts to compile, link, and execute the program that is currently in the editor. If you have specified a project file, **Run** invokes the project-make process to recreate the program. There are no other options associated with **Run**.

Compile

There are five options under the **Compile** main menu selection:

        Compile to OBJ
        Make EXE file
        Link EXE file
        Build all
        Primary C file

The first option allows you to compile the file currently in the editor (or an alternate primary file) to an *.OBJ file*, which is a relocatable object file that is ready to be linked into an .EXE file that can be executed. The second option compiles your program directly into an executable file. The third option links the current .OBJ and library files. The **Build all** option recompiles and links all files in a project whether they are out of date or not. The final option lets you specify a primary file to be compiled instead of the one that happens to be loaded into the editor.

Project

The **Project** option is used to aid in the development and maintenance of large, multifile programs. Although the subject of projects and the associated **Make** utility is discussed in Part Five, a brief overview is given here.

There are three options under the **Project** main menu selection:

Project name
Break make
Clear project

The **Project name** option lets you specify the name of a project file that contains the names of the files that comprise the project. These files will then be compiled (if necessary) and linked to form the final executable program. For example, if a project file contains the file names FILE1.C, FILE2.C, and FILE3.C, all three files will be compiled and linked to form the program. A project file is essentially the IDE version of a make file used by the standalone **Make** utility. In fact, the Turbo C user's guide refers to the process of building the final executable program as a *make*. All project files must have the extension .PRJ.

The **Break make** option lets you specify what type of conditions cause a project-make to stop. You can specify to stop the make on warnings, errors, fatal errors, or before linking.

The **Clear project** option removes the project file name from the system and resets the message window.

Options

The **Options** selection determines the way the integrated development environment operates. It includes the following options:

Compiler
Linker
Environment
Directories
Args

Retrieve options
Store options

Each of these entries produces another pull-down window with a list of related options. Because compiler, linker, and IDE options are so numerous and complex, all of Chapter 15 is dedicated to a discussion of them. No further explanation is given here.

Debug

The **Debug** option lets you set the way Turbo C displays compiler and linker error messages and shows the amount of memory available for compilation. The selections you can choose from in this menu are

Track messages
Clear messages
Keep messages

When working in the IDE, if a syntax error is found in your program, Turbo C prints the appropriate error message in the message window and then highlights the line of source code that contains the error. In the Turbo C user manuals this process is called *error tracking*. By default, only the current file is tracked in this way even if errors are found in another file, such as an include file. You can have Turbo C track all errors by switching the **Track messages** option to **All**. You can turn off error tracking by switching it to **Off**.

The **Clear** option clears the message window.

The **Keep messages** option is off by default. Turning it on causes Turbo C to save all error messages, appending new ones to the end. Error messages are normally removed before each new compile.

The Edit and Message Windows

Immediately below the main menu are the edit and message windows. The edit window is used by Turbo C's text editor. The message window is beneath the edit window and is used to display various compiler or linker messages.

The Hot Keys

At the bottom of the screen are shown the active "hot keys." These keys are ready for use whenever you need them. The F10 key always returns you to the main menu. The other keys are discussed here.

Help

The online help system is activated by pressing F1. It is *context sensitive*, which means that Turbo C will display information that is related to what you are currently doing. You may also select a help topic manually by pressing F1 a second time. You are shown a list of topics from which to choose. To exit the help system, press the ESC key.

Switching Windows and Zoom

By pressing the F5 key you can enlarge either the edit or message windows to encompass the full size of the screen. This feature somewhat simulates the zoom lens of a camera; hence the name. The F5 key is a toggle, so pressing it again returns the edit and message windows to their regular size.

The window that is enlarged is determined by using the F6 key. The F6 key is a toggle that switches between the edit and message windows. Pressing it once selects the message window; pressing it again returns control to the edit window. You select the message window to examine the various messages generated by the compiler.

Make

The **Make** key is F9. The **Make** option provides a simple way to compile programs consisting of multiple source files. You will see it in use later in this book.

The ALT-X Key Combination

You can exit Turbo C at any time by pressing the ALT-X key combination.

The TCINST Program

Although Turbo C needs no special installation to use it other than simply copying it to work disks or to a hard disk, it is possible to alter the default settings of various attributes and options in the integrated development environment. Included with Turbo C for this purpose is an installation program called TCINST. It is important to understand that you must use the version of TCINST that corresponds to the specific version of your copy of Turbo C. That is, the TCINST that came with Version 1.0 of Turbo C cannot be used to install Version 1.5, for example.

To execute the program you simply type **TCINST** from

the command line. When it begins to execute you see a menu with seven selections:

Turbo C directories
Editor commands
Setup environment
Display mode
Colors
Resize windows
Quit/save

Each of these options is discussed in this section.

Turbo C Directories

After selecting the **Turbo C directories** option you are presented with a menu consisting of five entries:

Include directories
Library directories
Output directory
Turbo C directory
Pick file name

If you select the **Include directories** option, you can specify a list of directories to be searched for your include files. The list can be up to 127 characters long, and the file names must be separated by semicolons.

If you select the **Library directories** option, you can specify a list of directories to be searched for your library files. This list can also be up to 127 characters long with the file names separated by semicolons.

Selecting the **Output directory** option allows you to specify the directory used for output. The file and path name must not be longer than 63 characters.

You can specify where Turbo C looks for its help files and the TCCONFIG.TC file by using the **Turbo C directory** option. This file and path name must not be longer than 63 characters. Finally, you can specify the path for pick files using the **Pick file name** option.

Editor Commands

You can customize the Turbo C editor by selecting the **Editor commands** option, which produces the screen shown in Figure 12-3.

Using this option it is possible to customize the Turbo C editor so that it reponds like your own favorite editor. To

```
                              Install Editor
Command name            Primary                  Secondary

New Line              * <CtrlM>                 · <CtrlM>
Cursor Left           * <CtrlS>                 · <Lft>
Cursor Right          * <CtrlD>                 · <Rgt>
Word Left             * <CtrlA>                 · <CtrlLft>
Word Right            * <CtrlF>                 · <CtrlRgt>
Cursor Up             * <CtrlE>                 · <Up>
Cursor Down           * <CtrlX>                 · <Dn>
Scroll Up             * <CtrlW>                 ·
Scroll Down           * <CtrlZ>                 ·
Page Up               * <CtrlR>                 · <PgUp>
Page Down             * <CtrlC>                 · <PgDn>
Left of Line          * <CtrlQ><CtrlS>          · <Home>
Right of Line         * <CtrlQ><CtrlD>          · <End>
Top of Screen         * <CtrlQ><CtrlE>          · <CtrlHome>
Bottom of Screen      * <CtrlQ><CtrlX>          · <CtrlEnd>
Top of File           * <CtrlQ><CtrlR>          · <CtrlPgUp>
Bottom of File        * <CtrlQ><CtrlC>          · <CtrlPgDn>
Move to Block Begin   * <CtrlQ><CtrlB>          ·
Move to Block End     * <CtrlQ><CtrlK>          ·

←↑↓→-select  PgUp-PgDn-page  ↵-modify  R-restore factory defaults  ESC-exit
F4-Key modes:  (*)-WordStar-like  (↓)-Ignore case  (·)-Verbatim
```

Figure 12-3.   The Editor commands screen of TCINST

alter the keystroke sequence associated with an editor command, position the highlight on the command you wish to change and press ENTER. You are prompted for the keystroke sequence. You then enter the exact sequence you want and press ENTER. The new sequence is now associated with command.

Although quite flexible, you must follow certain rules when customizing the editor commands:

1. No command sequence can be longer than six keystrokes. All special keys, such as ALT, the arrow keys, and the function keys count as two keystrokes.

2. The first character must be a control key or special key, not an alphanumeric key.

3. To enter an escape, press CTRL-[; for a backspace, press CTRL-H; and for ENTER, press CTRL-M.

4. It is best not to use any of Turbo C's hot keys as editor commands.

Setup Environment

The entries under the **Setup environment** selection are used to set the state of certain options in the default operation of the Turbo C editor. The nine settings that can be controlled are

Option	Default
Backup source files	ON
Edit auto save	OFF
Config auto save	OFF
Zoom state	OFF
Insert mode	ON
Autoindent mode	ON
Use tabs	ON
Tab size	8
Screen size in lines	25

By default the Turbo C editor creates backup copies of your source file each time you edit. This is generally a good idea unless you are very cramped for disk space. In this situation you can turn the **Backup source files** off.

When **Edit auto save** is on, the editor automatically saves your source file to disk each time you run the program or use the OS shell command. If it is off, your file is saved only when you specifically command it.

When **Config auto save** is on, any changes made to the configuration file are automatically saved each time you run a program, use the OS shell command, or exit Turbo C. If it is off, the configuration is saved only on your command.

If **Zoom state** is on, the editor window occupies the entire screen.

When **Insert mode** is on, entering characters in the middle of a line causes the existing characters to be pushed over. If **Insert mode** is off, the existing characters are over-written instead.

When **Autoindent mode** is on, the cursor is placed at the current indentation level after you press ENTER. If it is turned off, the cursor always returns to column 1.

When **Use tabs** is on, the editor actually uses the tab character when you press TAB. If it is off, the editor uses the corresponding number of spaces. You can adjust the default tab size using the **Tab size** option.

Finally, if you have an EGA or VGA video adapter, you can tell Turbo C to use a 43-line display. If you have a VGA, you can use a 50-line display. These settings are specified using the **Screen size** option.

Display Mode

The **Display mode** option is used to determine how Turbo C communicates with the video controller in your computer.

Turbo C normally senses the type of video adapter that is installed in your computer and uses the proper mode. You can override this by using the **Display mode** option. You can tell Turbo C to use one of the following video modes: default (Turbo C decides), color, black and white, or monochrome.

The **Display mode** option also performs a test of your video hardware. There are various ways to write to the screen. Depending on how your system is set up you may experience "snow" when using the fastest method. The **Screen mode** option allows you to test for snow based on the type of video adapter you have.

Colors

The **Colors** option lets you select the color scheme used by Turbo C when running in a color environment. There are three built-in color options: the default set, the turquoise set, and the magenta set. In addition, you can define your own color scheme for every part of the Turbo C user interface. To do this you select the **Customize Colors** option. You are asked what area you wish to modify. For example, if you select the main menu, you are shown another menu that lets you select the part of the main menu you wish to change. Your screen will look like Figure 12-4. When you have selected what you wish to change, you are shown a table of color options. As you try each option, the partial view of the main menu will change to reflect each different color scheme.

Resize Windows

It is possible to change the size of the edit and message windows relative to each other by using the **Resize windows** option. After selecting this option you can use the arrow keys to move the line that separates the two windows.

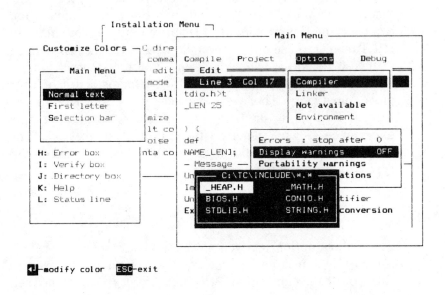

Figure 12-4.   Selecting Customize Colors with TCINST

Quit

The **Quit** option terminates the installation program. You are asked whether you want the changes you made while running the program to be written into Turbo C and become its default mode of option. If you do, answer **yes**. You should probably answer **no** at this time.

The Turbo C Text Editor

This chapter discusses the text editor supplied with Turbo C's integrated programming environment. Its operation is similar to both Micropro's WordStar program and the editors provided by Turbo Pascal, Turbo Prolog, and SideKick. The Turbo C editor contains about 50 commands and is quite powerful.

Editor Commands

With few exceptions, all editor commands begin with a control character. Many are then followed by another character. For example, the sequence CTRL-Q F is the command that tells the editor to find a string. (This book uses the abbreviation CTRL to stand for control.) This means that you type a CTRL-Q and then an F in either upper- or lowercase.

Invoking the Editor and Entering Text

When Turbo C begins, it waits at the sign-on message until you press a key. After that the main menu option **File** is highlighted. To invoke the editor you either use the cursor keys to move the highlight to **Edit** or you simply type an **e**. To leave the editor, press the F10 key.

When you invoke the editor, the top line is highlighted. This is the *editor status line*, which tells you various things about the state of the editor and the file you are editing. The first two items **Line** and **Col** display the line number and column of the cursor. The **Insert** message means that the editor is in insert mode. That is, as you enter text it will be inserted in the middle of what (if anything) is already there. The opposite is called *overwrite;* in this mode of operation new text replaces existing text. You can toggle between these two modes by pressing INS. The **Indent** message means that autoindentation is on. You will see how this works shortly. You toggle the indentation mode by using CTRL-O I. The **Tab** message means that you can insert tabs by using the TAB key. This is toggled by using the sequence CTRL-O T. At the end of the line the name of the file you are editing is displayed.

As soon as you invoke the editor it is ready to accept text. If you make mistakes you can use the BACKSPACE key to correct them. Try entering the lines

    This is a
    test of the Turbo C
    editor.

Your screen now looks like Figure 13-1. Notice the position of the cursor and the values associated with **Line** and **Col**.

You can use the arrow keys to move the cursor around in the file. As you move the cursor, the line and column numbers are updated to reflect its current position.

If you put the cursor in the middle of a line and enter more text, the existing line is moved to the right instead of being overwritten. This is what happens when the editor is in insert mode. For example, if you move the cursor to the start of the second line of text entered from the previous example, and type **good**, the screen looks like Figure 13-2. If you toggle the editor into overwrite mode, the original line would be replaced.

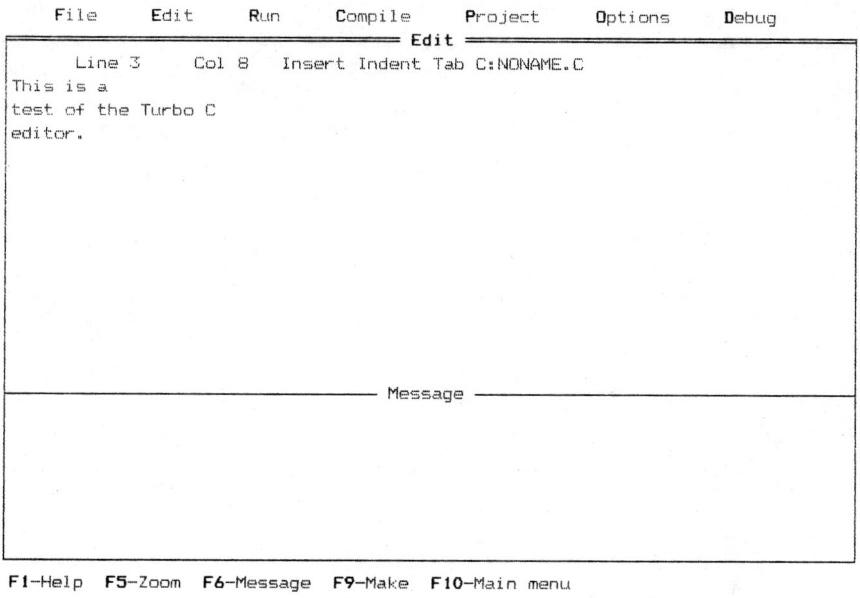

```
     File     Edit     Run     Compile     Project     Options     Debug
========================================= Edit =========================================
     Line 3     Col 8     Insert Indent Tab C:NONAME.C
This is a
test of the Turbo C
editor.




                                                             
                                                             
                                                             
                                                             
                                                             
                                                             
                                                             
                                                             
--------------------------------------- Message ----------------------------------------




                                                             
                                                             
                                                             
                                                             
----------------------------------------------------------------------------------------
F1-Help  F5-Zoom  F6-Message  F9-Make  F10-Main menu
```

Figure 13-1.   Editor screen with text entered

Deleting Characters, Words, and Lines

You can delete a single character two ways: with the BACK-SPACE key or with DEL. The BACKSPACE key deletes the character immediately to the left of the cursor, while DEL deletes the character the cursor is under.

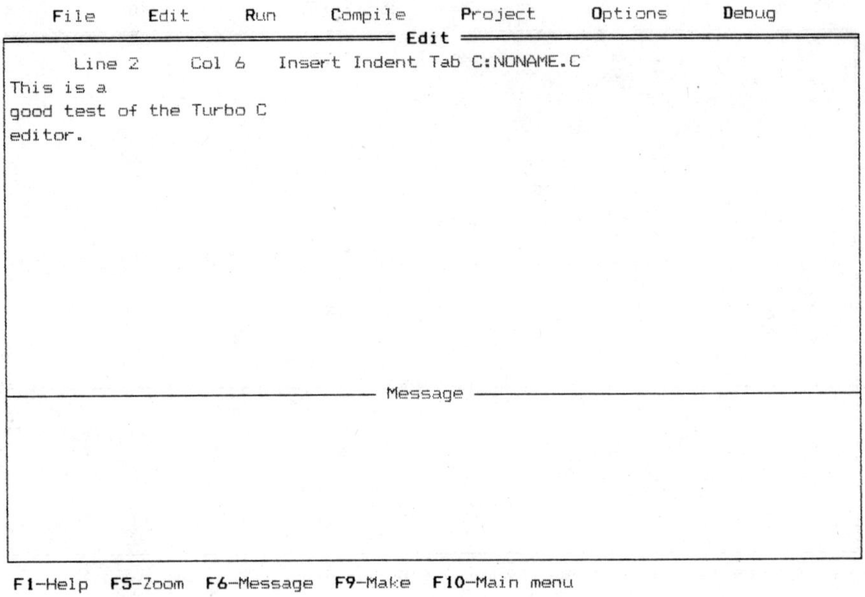

```
     File      Edit      Run      Compile      Project      Options      Debug
════════════════════════════════════════════ Edit ════════════════════════════
    Line 2      Col 6     Insert Indent Tab C:NONAME.C
This is a
good test of the Turbo C
editor.




                                  ─ Message ─



 F1─Help  F5─Zoom  F6─Message  F9─Make  F10─Main menu
```

Figure 13-2.   An example of text insertion

You can delete the entire word to the right of the cursor by typing CTRL-T. A word is any set of characters delimited by one of the following characters:

space $ / − + * ' ^ [ ] ( ) . ; , < >

You can remove an entire line by typing CTRL-Y. It does not matter where the cursor is positioned in the line; the entire line is deleted.

If you wish to delete from the current cursor position to the end of the line, type the sequence CTRL-Q Y.

Moving, Copying, and Deleting Blocks of Text

The Turbo C editor allows you to manipulate a block of text by moving or copying it to another location or deleting it altogether. To do any of these things you must first define the block. You do this by moving the cursor to the start of the block and typing the sequence CTRL-K B. Next, move the cursor to the end of the block and type the sequence CTRL-K K. The block that you have defined will be highlighted (or in a different color if you have a color system).

To move the block of text you place the cursor where you want the text to go and type the sequence CTRL-K V. This removes the previously defined block of text from its current position and places it at the new location. To copy a block you type the sequence CTRL-K C. To delete the currently marked block you type the sequence CTRL-K Y.

You can mark a single word as a block by positioning the cursor under the first character in the word and typing CTRL-K T.

More on Cursor Movement

The Turbo C editor has a number of special cursor commands, which are summarized in Table 13-1. The best way to learn these commands is to practice them a little each day until you have them memorized.

Find and Find with Replace

To find a specific sequence of characters you type CTRL-Q F. You are prompted at the status line for the string of charac-

Command	Action
CTRL-A	Move to the start of the word to the left of the cursor
CTRL-S	Move left one character
CTRL-D	Move right one character
CTRL-F	Move to the start of the word to the right of the cursor
CTRL-E	Move the cursor up one line
CTRL-R	Move the cursor up one full screen
CTRL-X	Move the cursor down one line
CTRL-C	Move the cursor down one full screen
CTRL-W	Scroll screen down
CTRL-Z	Scroll screen up
PGUP	Move the cursor up one full screen
PGDN	Move the cursor down one full screen
HOME	Move the cursor to the start of the line
END	Move the cursor to the end of the line
CTRL-Q E	Move the cursor to the top of the screen
CTRL-Q X	Move the cursor to the bottom of the screen
CTRL-Q R	Move the cursor to the top of the file
CTRL-Q C	Move the cursor to the bottom of the file

Table 13-1.   The Cursor Commands

ters you wish to find. Enter the string you are looking for and then press ENTER. You are once again prompted for search options. The search options modify the way the search is conducted. The options are shown in Table 13-2. For example, typing **G2** causes Turbo C to find the second occurrence of the string. No options need to be specified; you can simply press ENTER. If no options are present, the search proceeds from the current cursor position forward with case sensitivity and substring matches allowed.

You can repeat a search by typing CTRL-L. This is very convenient when you are looking for something specific in the file.

Option	Effect
B	Search the file backwards starting from the current cursor position
G	Search the entire file regardless of where the cursor is located
N	Replace without asking; for find-and-replace mode only
U	Match either upper- or lowercase
W	Match only whole words, not substrings within words
n	Where n is an integer, causes the nth occurrence of the string to be found

Table 13-2.   The Options to the Find Command

To activate the find-and-replace command you type CTRL-Q A. Its operation is identical to the find command except that it allows you to replace the string you are looking for with another. If you specify the **N** option you will not be asked whether to replace each occurrence of the search string with the replacement string. Otherwise you will be prompted for a decision each time a match occurs.

You can enter control characters into the search string by typing CTRL-P and the control character you want.

Setting and Finding Place Markers

You can set up to four place markers in your file by typing CTRL-K n, where n is the number of the place marker (0 to 3).

After a marker has been set, the command CTRL-Q *n*, where
n is the marker number, causes the cursor to go to that
marker.

Saving and Loading Your File

There are three ways to save your file. Two of the ways save it
to a file that has the same name as that shown on the status
line. The third way saves the file to a disk file of a different
name and then makes that name the current name of your
file. Let's look at how each method works.

The first way you can save your file is to exit the editor
(by pressing F10) and select the **File** main menu option. In
the **File** submenu, choosing the **Save** option saves what is
currently in the editor to a disk file by the name shown on
the status line.

The second way to save the file does not require you to
exit the editor. If you press the F2 key while you are using the
editor, the file is saved with the current name.

If you want to use a different file name, select the **Write
to** option. This allows you to enter the name of the file you
wish to write the current contents of the editor to. It also
makes this name the default file name.

To load a file you can either press F3 while inside the
editor or select the **Load** option in the **File** menu. Once you
have done that, you are prompted for the name of the file you
wish to load. There are two ways to specify the file name:

1. If you know the name, you can type it in at this time.

2. If you are unsure of the name, do not enter anything
   and Turbo C will display all files with the .C extension,
   from which you can choose one. You use the arrow keys
   to highlight the file you want and then press ENTER.

Understanding Autoindentation

Good programmers use indentation to help make the programs they write clearer and easier to understand. To assist you in this practice, after you press ENTER the Turbo C editor automatically places the cursor at the same indentation level as the line previously typed, assuming that autoindentation is on. (Remember that you toggle this feature by typing CTRL-O I.) For example, enter the following few lines exactly as they are shown here:

```
main()
{
  int i;

  for(i=0; i<100; i++) {
    printf("this is i: ");
    printf("%d\n", i);
  }
}
```

As you write Turbo C programs, you will find this feature quite handy.

Moving Blocks of Text to and from Disk Files

It is possible to move a block of text into a disk file for later use. This is done by first defining a block and then typing CTRL-K W. After you have done this, you are prompted for the name of the file you wish to save the block in. The original block of text is not removed from your program.

To read a block in, type CTRL-K R. You are prompted for the file name, and the contents of that file are read in at the current cursor location.

These two commands are most useful when you are moving text between two or more files, as is so often the case during program development.

Pair Matching

Several delimiters in C work in pairs, including { }, [ ], and (). In very long or complex programs, it is sometimes difficult to find the proper companion to a delimiter. Starting with Version 1.5 of Turbo C it is possible to have the editor find the corresponding companion delimiter automatically.

The Turbo C editor finds the companion delimiter for the following delimiter pairs:

```
{ }
[ ]
( )
< >
/* */
" "
' '
```

To find the matching delimiter, place the cursor on the delimiter you wish to match and type CTRL-Q [for a forward match or CTRL-Q] for a backward match. The editor moves the cursor to the matching delimiter.

Some delimiters are nestable, and some are not. The nestable delimiters are: {}, [ ], (), < >, and sometimes the comment symbols (when the nested comments option is enabled). The editor finds the proper matching delimiter according to C syntax. For example, in Figure 13-3 the lines indicate which curly braces match.

If for some reason the editor cannot find a proper match, the cursor is not moved.

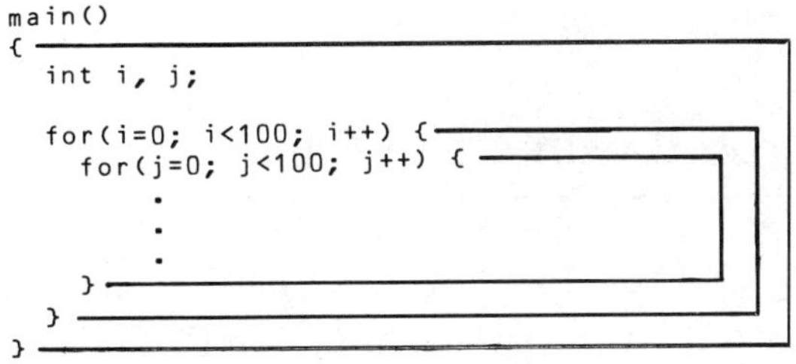

```
main()
{
  int i, j;

  for(i=0; i<100; i++) {
    for(j=0; j<100; j++) {
      .
      .
      .
    }
  }
}
```

Figure 13-3.   How the editor matches the curly braces

Miscellaneous Commands

You can abort any command that requests input by typing CTRL-U at the prompt. For example, if you execute the find command and then change your mind, you simply type CTRL-U.

If you wish to enter a control character into the file you first type CTRL-P followed by the control character you want. Control characters are displayed in either low intensity or reverse intensity depending on how your system is configured.

To undo changes made to a line before you have moved the cursor off that line, you type CTRL-Q L. Remember that once the cursor has been moved off the line all changes are final.

If you wish to go to the start of a block, you type CTRL-Q B. Typing CTRL-Q K takes you to the end of a block.

One particularly useful command is CTRL-Q P, which puts the cursor back to its previous position. This is handy if you want to search for something and then return to where you were.

Invoking Turbo C with a File Name

As mentioned earlier, you can specify the name of the file you want to edit when you invoke Turbo C. To do this you simply put the name of the file after the **TC** on the command line. For example, **TC MYFILE** executes Turbo C and loads MYFILE.C into the editor. The .C extension is added automatically by Turbo C. If MYFILE does not exist, it is created.

Command Summary

Table 13-3 shows all the Turbo C editor commands.

Cursor Commands

Command	Action
LEFT ARROW or CTRL-S	Left one character
RIGHT ARROW or CTRL-D	Right one character
CTRL-A	Left one word
CTRL-F	Right one word
UP ARROW or CTRL-E	Up one line
DOWN ARROW or CTRL-X	Down one line
CTRL-W	Scroll up
CTRL-Z	Scroll down

Table 13-3.   Turbo C Editor Command Summary by Category

Cursor Commands *(continued)*

Command	*Action*
PGUP or CTRL-R	Up one page
PGDN or CTRL-C	Down one page
HOME or CTRL-Q S	Go to start of line
END or CTRL-Q D	Go to end of line
CTRL-Q E	Go to top of screen
CTRL-Q X	Go to bottom of screen
CTRL-Q R	Go to top of file
CTRL-Q C	Go to bottom of file
CTRL-Q B	Go to start of block
CTRL-Q K	Go to end of block
CTRL-Q P	Go to last cursor position

Insert Commands

Command	*Action*
INS or CTRL-V	Toggle insert mode
ENTER or CTRL-N	Insert a blank line

Delete Commands

Command	*Action*
CTRL-Y	Entire line
CTRL-Q Y	To end of line
BACKSPACE	Character to left
DEL or CTRL-G	Character at cursor
CTRL-T	Word to the right

Block Commands

Command	*Action*
CTRL-K B	Mark beginning
CTRL-K K	Mark end
CTRL-K T	Mark a word
CTRL-K C	Copy a block
CTRL-K Y	Delete a block
CTRL-K H	Hide or display a block
CTRL-K V	Move a block
CTRL-K R	Write a block to disk
CTRL-K W	Read a block from disk

Table 13-3.   Turbo C Editor Command Summary by Category
(continued)

Find Commands

Command	*Action*
CTRL-Q F	Find
CTRL-Q A	Find and replace
CTRL-Q N	Find place marker
CTRL-L	Repeat find

Pair Matching

Command	*Action*
CTRL-Q [	Match pair forward
CTRL-Q]	Match pair reverse

Miscellaneous Commands

Command	*Action*
CTRL-U	Abort
CTRL-O I	Toggle autoindentation mode
CTRL-P	Control character prefix
F10	Exit editor
F3	New file
CTRL-Q W	Restore overwritten error message
F2	Save
CTRL-K N	Set place marker
CTRL-O T	Toggle tab mode
CTRL-Q L	Undo

Table 13-3.   Turbo C Editor Command Summary by Category *(continued)*

Compiler and Linker Options

Turbo C provides many options that affect the way programs are compiled and linked. Although Turbo C's default settings accommodate a wide variety of programming projects, there will almost certainly be times when you want to alter some of these settings to suit your specific application. This chapter will deal first with the compiler options available in the integrated environment, and then with the options used with the command line version of Turbo C. With the exception of the options and settings that deal exclusively with the integrated environment, all the options available in the integrated environment are also available for use by the command line version. However, there are a few options available in the command line version that are not supported by the integrated environment.

The chapter ends with a look at the standalone Turbo C linker called TLINK.

Integrated Development Environment Options

These are the options available in the **Options** menu:

Compiler
Linker
Environment
Directories
Args
Retrieve options
Store options

Each area will be examined in turn.

Compiler Options

After selecting **Compiler** you see these compiler options:

Model
Defines
Code generation
Optimization
Source
Errors
Names

Model

The **Model** option allows you to select which memory model is used to compile your program. The default is "small," which is adequate for most applications. For a complete discussion of the available memory models, refer to Chapter 10.

Defines

The **Defines** option allows you to define temporary preprocessor symbols to be used automatically by your program. You can define one or more macros by separating them with semicolons. This feature is most useful during program development and debugging. For example, in the following fragment, testing is performed with known input even though the final program uses a number generated by the random number generator **rand( )**. If you define the macro **RAND_ON** using the **Defines** option, the random number is used; otherwise the number is input from the keyboard. Remember that you could also define **RAND_ON** in the program by using the preprocessor command **define**.

```
main()
{
  int i;
```

```
#ifdef RAND_ON
i = rand();
#else
  /* for testing, read number from keyboard */
  printf("input number: ");
  scanf("%d", &i);
#endif
   .
   .
   .
}
```

Code Generation

Selecting **Code generation** presents you with a large number of switches that you can set. The options are

> Calling convention
> Instruction set
> Floating point
> Default char type
> Alignment
> Generate underbars
> Merge duplicate strings
> Standard stack frame
> Test stack overflows
> Line numbers

You can choose between the C calling convention and the Pascal calling convention. A calling convention is simply the method by which functions are called and arguments are passed. Generally, you should use the C calling convention.

If you know that the object code of your program will be used on a 80186/80286 processor, you can tell Turbo C to use the 80186/80286 extended instruction set using the **Instruction set** option. It will cause your program to execute a little faster, but it will not be able to run on 8088/8086-based computers. The default is 8088/8086 instructions.

You can control the way Turbo C implements floating point operations. The default—and most common—method is to use 8087/80287 emulation routines. The 8087 chip is the math coprocessor to the 8086 family of CPUs, while the 80287 is the math coprocessor for the 80286 CPU. When these coprocessors are in the system, they allow very rapid floating-point operations. However, if you don't have a math coprocessor or if your program will be used in a variety of computers, the 8087's operation must be emulated in software, which is much slower. The emulation mode uses the math coprocessor by default if one is in the system, or calls the emulation routines if no math coprocessor is installed. However, if you know in advance that the coprocessor is present in every system on which the program will run, you can select the 8087/80287 option, which generates in-line 8087/80287 code. This is the fastest way to implement floating-point operations. Finally, you can deselect floating point altogether when your program doesn't use it, thereby allowing the object code to be much smaller.

The **Default char type** option determines whether the type **char** is signed or unsigned. By default, **char** is signed in Turbo C.

The **Alignment** option determines whether data is aligned on byte or word boundaries. On the 8086 and 80286 processors memory accesses are quicker if data is word-aligned. However, there is no difference on the 8088. The default is word-alignment.

The **Generate underbars** option, which is on by default, determines whether an underscore is added to the start of each identifier in the link file. You should not turn this off unless you are an experienced programmer and understand the inner workings of Turbo C.

Elimination of duplicate string constants is a common compiler optimization that you can instruct Turbo C to perform. That is, all identical strings can be merged into one string, the result being smaller programs. You can control this by toggling the **Merge duplicate strings** option. It is off by default.

The **Standard stack frame** option is used to force Turbo C to generate standard calling and returning code for each function call to help in debugging. You will not generally have to worry about or use this option.

You can force Turbo C to check for stack overflows by turning on the **Test stack overflow** option. This makes your program run more slowly, but it may be necessary in order to find certain bugs. If your program crashes inexplicably from time to time, you might want to compile it with this test turned on to see if stack overflows are the problem.

Finally, you can force Turbo C to enter the number of each line of the source file into the object file. This is useful when using a debugger.

Optimization

The **Optimization** option contains four toggles:

Optimize for
Use register variables
Register optimization
Jump optimization

Turbo C is very efficient, but, for somewhat complicated reasons, some optimizations that make the object code smaller also make it slower. Other optimizations make the object code faster but larger. Turbo C lets you decide which is the most important consideration—speed or size—by toggling the **Optimize for** option. The default is size.

When the **Use register variables** option is on—its default state—Turbo C automatically uses registers to hold variables where applicable whether or not you have requested it explicitly using the **register** type modifier. When this option is turned off, no register variables are used, even when you explicitly request them. The main use for this option is to allow Turbo C to interface with other computer languages that may not recognize register variable types.

When the **Register optimization** option, which is off by default, is turned on, it allows Turbo C to perform some additional optimizations that prevent redundant load and store operations. However, Turbo C cannot know if a variable has been modified through a pointer, so you must use this option with care.

By toggling **Jump optimization** on, you allow Turbo C to rearrange the code within loops and switch statements. This can cause higher performance. You should turn this option off if you are using a debugger on your object code.

Source

The **Source** option lets you set the number of significant characters in an identifier, determine whether comments can be nested, and force Turbo C to accept only the ANSI keywords.

By default, Turbo C identifiers have 32 significant characters. However, may set this number anywhere in the range 1 through 32. You would most commonly want to reduce the number of significant characters when you are compiling source code written for a different compiler. Years ago it was common to have compilers recognize only the first 6 to 8 characters. Some programmers exploited this limitation by embedding "comments" into their variable to help with debugging. For example, programmers occasionally encoded the usage count into a variable's names as shown here:

```
/* Assuming 7 significant characters, the variables
   on the left side of the assignment statement all
   resolve to a single variable called counter.
*/

counter1 = 10;

counter2 = 20;

counter3 = 30;
```

This practice of encoding a usage count in the variable's name has been discredited, but some older source code may still contain instances of it.

Turbo C supports the ANSI standard, but it has added various enhancements to the language to support the 8086 processor better. If you want to make sure that you are writing code that uses only the ANSI keywords, toggle on the option **ANSI keywords only**. Otherwise leave it in its default (off) position.

In its standard form, C (including Turbo C) does not allow one comment to be inside another. For example, in standard C, the following code causes a compile time error:

```
/* In standard ANSI C this will not compile. */

/*
  if(x<10) printf("all OK"); /* signal status */
  else printf("failure in port 102");
*/
```

Here the programmer attempted to "comment out" a section of code but failed to notice that a nested comment was created. By selecting the **Nested comments** option, you can tell Turbo C to allow situations like the preceding example and allow the entire block to be ignored. This can be very useful when you wish to remove a section of code temporarily. Note that the standard and portable way to do this is to use an #**ifdef** preprocessor command. The use of the **Nested comments** option is best reserved for special exceptions encountered while debugging.

Errors

The **Errors** option lets you determine how errors are reported during the compilation process. There are seven options in this menu:

    Errors: stop after
    Warnings: stop after
    Display warnings
    Portability warnings
    ANSI violations
    Common errors
    Less common errors

You can set how many fatal errors can be reported

before the compilation process stops by using the **Errors: stop after** option. The default is 25.

You can set how many warning errors can be reported before compilation stops by using the **Warnings: stop after** option. The default setting is 100. Turbo C is very forgiving and tries to make sense out of your source code no matter how unusual it may seem. However, if Turbo C has a suspicion that what you have written is incorrect, it will display a warning error. A warning error does not stop compilation; it simply informs you of Turbo C's concerns about a certain construct. It is for you to decide whether Turbo C is correct in its concern.

Several types of warning errors can be generated. The first are portability errors, which reflect coding methods that would render the program nonportable to another type of processor. The second type of warning error is generated by non-ANSI code practices. The third group consists of common programming errors, and the final group consists of less common programming errors. These categories are summarized in Table 14-1.

You can choose whether warning errors are displayed by using the **Display warnings** option.

Names

The **Names** option lets you change the names Turbo C uses for the various memory segments used by your program. You will need to change these only in unusual situations. Don't change the names unless you really know what you are doing.

Linker Options

If you select the **Linker** options, you see the following list of choices:

Map file
Initialize segments
Default libraries
Warn duplicate symbols
Stack warning
Case-sensitive link

Let's examine each area in turn.

Map File

By default, Turbo C's linker does not create a map file of your compiled program. A map file shows the relative positions of the variables and functions that make up your program and where they reside in memory. You may need to create a map file for debugging certain programs in complex situations. You can create a map file in three ways. The first shows only the segments. The second shows the public (global) symbols. The third creates a detailed (complete) map.

Initialize Segments

By default, **Initialize segments** is off. It is turned on in highly specialized situations to force the linker to initialize segments, but this is seldom necessary.

Default Libraries

The **Default libraries** option applies only when you are linking modules compiled by other C compilers. By default this option is off. If you turn it on, the linker searches the libraries defined in the separately compiled modules before searching Turbo C's libraries. Again, this is a highly specialized situation that you will probably never need to worry about.

Portability Errors

Error	Default
Nonportable pointer conversion	On
Nonportable pointer assignment	On
Nonportable pointer comparison	On
Constant out of range in comparison	On
Constant is long	Off
Conversion may lose significant digits	Off
Mixing pointers to signed and unsigned char	Off

ANSI Violations

Error	Default
Identifier not part of structure	On
Zero length structure	On
Void functions may not return a value	On
Both return and return of a value used	On
Suspicious pointer conversion	On
Undefined structure identifier	On
Redefinition of an identifier is not identical	On

Common Errors

Error	Default
Function should return a value	On
Unreachable code	On
Code has no effect	On
Possible use of an identifier before definition	On
Identifier assigned a value which is never used	On
Parameter identifier is never used	On
Possibly incorrect assignment	On

Less Common Errors

Error	Default
Superfluous & with function or array	Off
Identifier declared but never used	Off
Ambiguous operators need parentheses	Off
Structure passed by value	Off
No declaration for function	Off
Call to function with no prototype	Off

Table 14-1.   Types of Warning Errors Issued by Turbo C

Warn Duplicate Symbols

By default, **Warn duplicate symbols** is on. This means that the linker warns you if you have multiple-defined global identifiers. By turning it off, you do not see this message and the linker chooses which one to use.

Stack Warning

If you are using Turbo C to create routines to link with external assembly language programs, you might receive the link-time message **No stack specified**. You can eliminate this message by turning **Stack warning** off.

Case-Sensitive Link

Case-sensitive link is on by default because C is case-sensitive. However, if you are trying to link Turbo C modules with FORTRAN modules, for example, you may need to turn this option off.

Environment Options

By selecting the **Environment** option from the **Options** menu you can change the way Turbo C's integrated environment works. The following selections are available:

    Backup source files
    Edit auto save
    Config auto save
    Zoomed windows
    Tab size
    Screen size

When you save a file, Turbo C automatically renames the previous version of that file from a .C extension to a

.BAK extension. In this way, you always have the previous version as a backup. You can turn off this option by toggling **Backup source files**. About the only reason for turning this option off is to save disk space if it is very limited.

When **Edit auto save** is on, the editor automatically saves your source file to disk each time you run the program or use the OS shell command. If the option is off, your file is saved only when you specifically command it. It is off by default.

When **Config auto save** is on, any changes made to the configuration file are automatically saved each time you run a program, use the OS shell command, or exit Turbo C. If it is off, the configuration is saved only on your command. This option is off by default.

If **Zoomed windows** is on, the editor window occupies the entire screen. The option is off by default.

The default tab size is 8; you can change it by using the **Tab size** option.

Finally, if you have an EGA or VGA video adapter you can tell Turbo C to use a 43-line display. If you have a VGA, you can use a 50-line display. These settings are specified using the **Screen size** option. A 25-line display is used by default.

The Directories Option

After selecting the **Directories** option you are presented with a menu consisting of six entries:

> Include directories
> Library directories
> Output directory
> Turbo C directory
> Pick file name

This option also reports the current pick file.

If you select the **Include directories** option, you can specify a list of directories to be searched for your include files. The list can be up to 127 characters long, and the file names must be separated by semicolons.

If you select the **Library directories** option, you can specify a list of directories to be searched for your library files. This list can also be up to 127 characters long, and the file names must be separated by semicolons.

Selecting the **Output directory** option allows you to specify the directory used for output. The file and path name must not be longer than 63 characters.

You can specify where Turbo C looks for its help files and the TCCONFIG.TC file by using the **Turbo C directory** option. This file and path name must not be longer than 63 characters.

You can specify the path for pick files using the **Pick file name** option.

Args

As you know, when you run a program in the interactive environment you do not type the program name as you do from the DOS system prompt. Hence, it is not possible to specify command line arguments directly when running a program in the integrated environment. However, Turbo C allows you to run programs that use the command line arguments in the IDE by using the **Args** option.

When you select **Args** you are prompted to enter the command line parameters your program requires. Enter the parameters desired—but not the program name. Then, each time you run the program, the command line parameters you specified will be used.

Saving and Loading Options

Once you have customized Turbo C by changing various options, you have two choices: You can use your chosen options during your current session only, or you can save them. The two entries **Retrieve options** and **Store options** in the **Options** menu allow you to save and load the options. Let's see how.

The TCCONFIG.TC File

The first thing that Turbo C does when it begins executing the integrated environment is to look for a file called TCCONFIG.TC. This file holds the configuration information for the system. You can change the contents of this file by using the **Store** option. In this way, the changes you make to Turbo C will still be there the next time you execute it.

Turbo C looks for the TCCONFIG.TC file first in the current working directory. If it is not found it then looks in the TURBO directory, should one exist. If you are going to modify TCCONFIG.TC, it is best to keep a copy of the unmodified file handy in case you need to go back to the default settings for some reason.

Using Other Configuration Files

When you save the changes you have made to Turbo C, you don't have to save them into the TCCONFIG.TC file. You can specify any file you desire. When Turbo C begins executing the integrated environment it uses the default settings. To load the options you want, simply select the **Options** menu and select **Retrieve options**. Then specify the name of the file that contains the settings you want to use. The advantage of this approach is that Turbo C's default settings are always available if you need them, but you can easily customize Turbo C to your liking.

The Command Line Version of Turbo C

If you are new to C, there is no doubt that you will find Turbo C's integrated environment the easiest way to develop programs. However, if you have been programming and using your own editor for some time, you might find the command line version of Turbo C more to your liking. For long-time C programmers, the command line version represents the traditional method of compilation and linking. Also, the command line version of the compiler can do a few things that the integrated environment version can't. For example, if you wish to generate an assembly language listing of the code generated by Turbo C or if you want to use in-line assembly code, you must use the command line version. The name of the command line compiler is TCC.EXE.

Compiling with the Command Line Compiler

Assume that you have a program called X.C. To compile this program using the command line version of Turbo C, your command line will look like this:

```
C>TCC X.C
```

Assuming that there are no errors in the program, this causes X.C to be compiled and linked with the proper library files. This is the simplest form of the command line.

The general form of the command line is

TCC [*option1 option2 ... optionN*] fname1 fname2 ... fnameN

where *option* is a compiler or linker option and **fname** is either a C source file, an .OBJ file, or a library. Additional .OBJ or .LIB files on the command line are passed along to the linker for inclusion in the final program. Remember, however, that Turbo C automatically includes its standard libraries, so they need not be specified.

All compiler-linker options begin with a dash (minus sign). Generally, following an option with a dash turns that option off. Table 14-2 shows the options available in the command line version of Turbo C. Keep in mind that the options are case-sensitive.

Option	Meaning
−A	Recognize ANSI keywords only
−a	Use word alignment for data
−a−	Use byte alignment for data
−B	In-line assembly code in source file
−C	Accept nested comments
−c	Compile to .OBJ only
−Dname	Define a macro name
−Dname=string	Define and give a value to a macro name
−d	Merge duplicate strings
−efname	Specify project name
−f	Use floating point emulation
−f−	No floating point
−f87	Use 8087
−G	Optimize code for speed
−gN	Stop after N warning errors
−Ipath	Specify the path to the include directory
−iN	Specify identifier length
−jN	Stop after N fatal errors
−K	**char** unsigned
−K−	**char** signed
−Lpath	Specify library directory
−M	Create map file
−mc	Use compact memory model
−mh	Use huge memory model
−ml	Use large memory model
−mm	Use medium memory model
−ms	Use small memory model
−mt	Use tiny memory model
−N	Check for stack overflows
−npath	Specify output directory
−O	Optimize for size
−p	Use Pascal calling conventions
−p−	Use C calling conventions
−r	Use register variables
−S	Generate assembly code output
−Uname	Undefine a macro name

Table 14-2.   Turbo C's Command Line Options

Option	Meaning
−w	Display warning errors
−w−	Do not display warning errors
−K	Use standard stack frame
−y	Embed line numbers into object code
−Z	Register optimization on
−z	Specify segment names
−1	Generate 80186/80286 instructions
−1−	Do not generate 80186/80286 instructions

Table 14-2.   Turbo C's Command Line Options (*continued*)

To compile X.C with the stack checked for overflow, your command line would look like

```
C>TCC -N X.C
```

The −**w**, enable warning messages option, allows you to set which types of warning messages are displayed by the command line version of the compiler. By default, the command line compiler displays the same messages as the integrated version. The exact form of the −**w** command is shown in Table 14-3. For example, to enable the identifier declared but not used message, when compiling a file called TEST.C, you would use this command line:

```
TCC -wuse TEST.C
```

On the other hand, to tell the command line compiler not to display a suspicious pointer conversion, you would use this option:

```
-wsus
```

Portability Errors

Error	Command Line Option
Nonportable pointer assignment	—wapt
Nonportable pointer comparison	—wcpt
Constant out of range in comparison	—wdgn
Constant is long	—wcln
Conversion may lose significant digits	—wsig
Nonportable return type conversion	—wrpt
Mixing pointers to signed and unsigned char	—wucp

ANSI Violations

Error	Command Line Option
Identifier not part of structure	—wstr
Zero length structure	—wxst
Void functions may not return a value	—wvoi
Both return and return of a value used	—wret
Suspicious pointer conversion	—wsus
Undefined structure identifier	—wstu
Redefinition of an identifier is not identical	—wdup

Common Errors

Error	Command Line Option
Function should return a value	—wrvl
Unreachable code	—wrch
Code has no effect	—weff
Possible use of an identifier before definition	—wdef
Identifier assigned a value that is never used	—waus
Parameter identifier is never used	—wpar
Possibly incorrect assignment	—wpia

Table 14-3. The Command Line Warning Message Options

Less Common Errors

Error	*Command Line Option*
Superfluous & with function or array	−wamp
Identifier declared but never used	−wuse
Ambiguous operators need parentheses	−wamb
Structure passed by value	−wstv
No declaration for function	−wnod
Call to function with no prototype	−wpro

Table 14-3.   The Command Line Warning Message Options
(*continued*)

What's in a File Name?

The Turbo C command line version does not require the .C extension. For example, both of these command lines are functionally the same:

```
C>TCC X.C
C>TCC X
```

You can compile a file with an extension other than .C by specifying its extension. For example, to compile X.TMP, the command line would look like

```
C>TCC X.TMP
```

You can specify additional object files to be linked with the source file you are compiling by specifying them after the source file. All included files must have been previously compiled and have an .OBJ extension. For example, if your program consists of the files P1, P2, and P3, and if P2 and P3 have already been compiled to .OBJ files, the following command line first compiles P1.C and then links it with the P2.OBJ and P3.OBJ:

```
C>TCC P1 P2.OBJ P3.OBJ
```

If you have additional libraries other than those supplied with Turbo C, you can specify them by using the .LIB extension.

In the foregoing example, it was assumed the P2.OBJ and P3.OBJ existed. The way to produce these files starting from their .C source files is to compile each using the −c compiler option. This option causes the compiler to create .OBJ files, but no link process takes place.

The executable output file produced by the linker is generally the name of the source file being compiled with an .EXE extension. However, you can specify a different name using the −e option. The name that follows the −e is the name the compiler uses as the executable file. There can be no spaces between the −e and the file name. For example, the following compiles the file TEST.C and creates an executable file called MYPROG.EXE:

```
C>TCC -eMYPROG test
```

TLINK: The Turbo C Standalone Linker

Unlike the integrated development environment, which has a built-in linker, the command line version of Turbo C uses a standalone linker called TLINK. You may not be aware of TLINK because it is loaded automatically by the command line compiler upon conclusion of a successful compilation. However, it is possible to use TLINK by itself. This section explores TLINK's use as a standalone linker.

TLINK is run completely from the command line and takes this general form:

TLINK OBJ files, output filename, map filename, libraries

In the first field you list all the .OBJ files you want to link, using spaces to separate the list. The second field specifies the name of the .EXE file that holds the output. If it is not specified, the name of the first .OBJ file is used. The map file name holds the map file. The map file has the extension .MAP. If the map file name is not specified, the name of the .EXE file is used. Finally, the libraries field holds a space-separated list of libraries. For example, the following links the files MYFILE1.OBJ and MYFILE2.OBJ with TEST.-EXE as the output file and MYMAP as the map file name. No libraries are used.

```
TLINK MYFILE1 MYFILE2, TEST, MYMAP,
```

Notice that you need not explicitly use the .EXE or .MAP extensions for the output or map file. TLINK supplies these for you.

Although the output file name and the map file name are optional, you must be sure to include the proper number of commas; otherwise TLINK does not know which field is which.

Linking Turbo C Programs

Some special instructions apply to TLINK when you want to use it manually to link object files produced by Turbo C into an executable program. First, every time a Turbo C program is linked, the first object file on the link line must be one of Turbo C's initialization modules. There is a module for each memory model supported by Turbo C, which must agree with the type of memory model used to compile the program.

The module names and their associated memory models are shown here:

Initialization Module Name	Memory Model
C0T.OBJ	Tiny
C0S.OBJ	Small
C0C.OBJ	Compact
C0M.OBJ	Medium
C0L.OBJ	Large
C0H.OBJ	Huge

You also need to ensure that the proper standard library file is linked. Like the initialization module, it must agree with the memory model used to compile the program. The library files are shown here:

Library Name	Memory Model
CT.LIB	Tiny
CS.LIB	Small
CC.LIB	Compact
CM.LIB	Medium
CL.LIB	Large
CH.LIB	Huge

If your program uses any floating point, you must include either EMU.LIB or FP87.LIB on the link line. If you have an 8087/80287, use FP87.LIB; otherwise use EMU.LIB.

The mathematics routines are contained in MATHx.LIB where x is one of the following letters and corresponds to the proper memory model: **t, s, c, m, l, h**. Remember, the memory model used to compile your program must agree with that of the library.

Given this information, to link a program file called

TCTEST that uses floating-point emulation (but no math routines) using the small memory model, use the following link line:

```
TLINK COS TCTEST, , , EMU CS
```

TLINK Options

TLINK supports eight options, summarized in Table 14-4. Each option consists of a slash followed by a letter. These options can be placed at any point in the TLINK command line. For example, the following link line does not produce a map file and causes source code line numbers to be included in the executable file:

```
TLINK /x /l COS MYFILE, , , CS
```

Option	Meaning
/c	Case is significant in PUBLIC and EXTRN symbols
/d	Display warning if duplicate symbols are found in the libraries
/i	Initialize all segments
/l	Include source line numbers for debugging
/m	Include public symbols in map file
/n	Ignore the default libraries
/s	Include detailed segment map in map file
/x	Do not create a map file

Table 14-4.   The TLINK Options

The Turbo C Library

Part Three examines the Turbo C library. It covers the standard library as defined by the proposed ANSI standard in addition to the de facto UNIX standard functions and Turbo C's additions. Chapter 15 begins with a discussion of linking, libraries, and header files. Chapters 16 through 24 describe the functions found in the library, with each chapter concentrating on a specific group.

**P
A
R
T

T
H
R
E
E**

Linking, Libraries, and Header Files

If you have never been involved with the creation of a C compiler, it is sometimes hard to understand that the compiler itself is actually fairly easy to develop. It is the library functions that take the most time and effort because the C standard library defines such a large and diverse set of functions, and many of them must interface with the operating system. Indeed, it is the richness and flexibility of the standard library that sets C above many other languages. Given the fact that Turbo C supplies a great many more functions in its library than are specified by the ANSI standard, it is difficult to imagine the hours of effort that went into its creation.

To understand the nature of the executable program produced by Turbo C, it is important to understand how the linker works, how libraries differ from object files, and the role of header files.

The Linker

The output of the compiler is a relocatable object file, and the output of the linker is an executable file. The role the linker plays is twofold:

1. It physically combines the files specified in the link list into one program file.

2. It resolves external references and memory addresses.

An external reference is created anytime the code in one file refers to code found in another file through either a function call or a reference to a global variable. For example, when the two files shown here are linked, file two's reference to **count** must be resolved. It is the linker that "tells" the code in file two where **count** will be found in memory.

```
file one:

int count;

main()
{
  count = 10;
  display();
}


file two:

extern int count;

display()
{
  printf("%d", count);
}
```

In a similar fashion, the linker also "tells" file one where the function **display()** is located so that it can be called.

When Turbo C generates the object code for file two, it substitutes a place-holder for the address of **count** because it has no way of knowing where **count** is located in memory. The same sort of thing occurs when file one is compiled. The address of **display()** is not known so a place-holder is used. This process forms the basis for *relocatable code*.

To understand relocatable code, you must first understand *absolute code*. Although it is seldom done today, in the earlier days of computers it was not uncommon for a program to run at a specific memory location. When compiled in this way, all addresses are fixed at compile time. (This of course, that the entire program must be in one file, a distinct drawback.) Because the addresses are fixed, the program can be loaded into and executed at only one exact region of memory: the one for which it was compiled. By contrast, relocatable code is compiled so that the address information is not fixed. In a relocatable object file, the address of each call, jump, or global variable is relative to an offset. When the file is loaded into memory for execution, the loader automatically resolves the relative addresses into addresses that will work for the location in memory into which it is being loaded. This means that a relocatable program can be loaded and run from many different memory locations.

The C Standard Library

The proposed ANSI standard has defined both the content and the form of the C standard library. To allow the fullest possible use and control of the computer, however, Turbo C contains many additional functions. For example, Turbo C supplies a complete set of screen and graphics functions. As long as you will not be porting the programs you write to a new environment, it is perfectly acceptable to use these enhanced functions.

Library Files Versus Object Files

Although libraries are similar to object files, they have one crucial difference: Not all the code in the library is added to your program. When you link a program that consists of several object files, all the code in each object file becomes part of the finished executable program. This happens whether the code is actually used or not. In other words, all object files specified at link time are "added together" to form the program. This is not the case with library files.

A library is a collection of functions. Unlike an object file, a library file stores the name of each function, the function's object code, and relocation information necessary to the linking process. When your program references a function contained in a library, the linker looks up that function and adds the code to your program. Only functions that you actually use in your program are added to the executable file.

Because functions are added to your program selectively when a library is used, the Turbo C functions are contained in a library rather than object files. (If they were in object files, every program you wrote would be several hundred thousand bytes long!)

Header Files

Many functions found in the Turbo C library work with their own specific data types and variables to which your program must have access. These variables and types are defined in *header files* supplied with the compiler, and they must be included (using **#include**) in any file that uses the specific functions they refer to. In addition, all functions in Turbo C's library have their prototypes defined in a header file to provide a means of stronger type-checking. By including the header files that correspond to the standard functions used by your program, you can catch potential type mismatch errors. For example, including **string.h**, the string function's header, will cause the following code to produce a warning message when compiled:

```
#include "string.h"

char s1[20] = "hello ";
char s2[] = "there.";

main()
{
  int p;
```

```
p = strcat(s1, s2);

}
```

Because **strcat( )** is declared as returning a character pointer in its header file, Turbo C can now flag as a possible error the assignment of that pointer to the integer **p**.

The standard header files used by Turbo C are shown in Table 15-1. Some header files are redundant: For example, all the declarations found in ALLOC.H are duplicated in STDLIB.H. The redundant header files are included to allow source code written prior to the ANSI standard to compile without change. In the remaining chapters of Part Three, the description of each function will specify which header file is associated with it.

Macros in Header Files

Many of the Turbo C library functions are not functions at all but macro definitions contained in a header file. For example, **abs( )**, which returns the absolute value of its integer argument, could be defined as a macro, as shown here:

```
#define abs(i)  (i<0) ? -i : i
```

Generally, whether a standard function is defined as a macro or as a regular C function is of no consequence. In rare situations where a macro definition is unacceptable — for example, where code size is to be minimized — you will have to create a real function and substitute it for the macro.

To force the compiler to use the real function (either from the library or written by you), you must prevent the compiler from substituting the macro when the function name is encountered. Although there are several possible ways to do this, by far the best is simply to undefine the macro name by using **#undef**. For example, to force the compiler to substitute the real function for the **abs( )** macro defined previously, you would insert this line of code near the beginning of your program:

```
#undef abs
```

Then, since **abs( )** is no longer defined as a macro, the function version will be used.

Header File	Purpose or Use
ALLOC.H	Dynamic allocation functions
ASSERT.H	Defines the **assert( )** macro
BIOS.H	ROM-BIOS functions
CONIO.H	Screen-handling functions
CTYPE.H	Character-handling functions
DIR.H	Directory-handling functions
DOS.H	DOS interfacing functions
ERRNO.H	Defines error codes
FCNTL.H	Defines constants used by **open( )**
FLOAT.H	Defines implementation-dependent floating-point values
GRAPHICS.H	Graphics functions
IO.H	UNIX-like I/O routines
LIMITS.H	Defines implementation-dependent various limits
MATH.H	Various definitions used by the math library
MEM.H	Memory manipulation functions
PROCESS.H	**spawn( )** and **exec( )** functions
SETJMP.H	Nonlocal jumps
SHARE.H	File sharing
SIGNAL.H	Defines signal values
STDARG.H	Variable length argument lists
STDDEF.H	Defines some commonly used constants
STDIO.H	For stream-based I/O
STDLIB.H	Miscellaneous declarations
STRING.H	String functions
TIME.H	System time functions
VALUES.H	Machine-dependent constants

Table 15-1.   The Standard Header Files

I/O Functions

The functions that comprise the C input/output system can be grouped into three major categories: console I/O, buffered file I/O, and the UNIX-like unbuffered file I/O. Strictly speaking, console I/O is made up of functions that are special case versions of the more general functions found in the buffered file system. However, in general usage, console I/O and file I/O have enough differences that they are often thought of as conceptually separate, especially by beginners. In the first part of this guide, the console and buffered file I/O were treated as somewhat separate as a means of emphasizing their differences. In this section, however, no such distinction is made because they use a common logical interface.

The unbuffered UNIX-like I/O system is not defined by the proposed ANSI standard and is expected to decline in popularity. The UNIX-like I/O system functions are included in Turbo C's library to ensure compatibility with existing programs.

For an overview of the C I/O system, see Chapter 8.

The I/O Functions

The rest of this chapter describes each of the I/O functions, including the UNIX-like ones. (Remember that the non-standard UNIX-like I/O functions include **open()**, **close()**, **read()**, **write()**, **creat()**, and **unlink()**.)

For the ANSI standard I/O system functions the header **stdio.h** is required. For the UNIX-like routines the header **io.h** is required. Many of the I/O functions set the predefined global integer variable **errno** to an appropriate error code when an error occurs. This variable is declared in **errno.h**.

int access(char *filename, int mode)

Description

The prototype for **access( )** is found in **io.h**.

The **access( )** function belongs to the UNIX-like file system and is not defined by the ANSI standard. It is used to see if a file exists. It can also be used to tell whether the file is write-protected and if it can be executed. The name of the file in question is pointed to by *filename*. The value of *mode* determines exactly how **access( )** functions. The legal values are

0	Check for file existence
1	Check for executable file
2	Check for write access
4	Check for read access
6	Check for read/write access

The **access( )** function returns 0 if the specified access is allowed; otherwise it returns −1. Upon failure, the predefined global variable **errno** is set to one of these values:

ENOENT	Path or file name not found
EACCES	Access denied

Example

The following program checks to see if the file TEST.TST is present in the current working directory:

```
#include "io.h"
main()
{
  if(!access("TEST.TST", 00))
    printf("file present");
  else printf("file not found");
}
```

Related Function

chmod( )

int —chmod(char *filename, int get—set, int attrib)

Description

The prototype for **—chmod()** is found in **io.h**.

The **—chmod()** function is not defined by the ANSI standard. It is used to read or set the attribute byte associated with the file pointed to by *filename* as allowed by DOS. If *get—set* is 0, **—chmod()** returns the current file attribute and *attrib* is not used. If *get—set* is 1, the file attribute is set to the value of *attrib*. The *attrib* argument can be one of these macros:

FA—RDONLY	Set file to read only
FA—HIDDEN	Make hidden file
FA—SYSTEM	Mark as a system file

The **—chmod()** function returns the file attribute if successful. Upon failure, it returns a −1 and sets **errno** either to **ENOENT** if the file does not exist or to **EACCES** if access to the file is denied.

Example

This line of code sets the file TEST.TST to read only:

```
if(_chmod("TEST.TST", 1, FA_RDONLY)==FA_RDONLY)
  printf("file set to read-only mode");
```

Related Functions

chmod( ), access( )

int chmod(char *filename, int mode)

Description

The prototype for **chmod()** is found in **io.h**.

The **chmod()** function is not defined by the ANSI standard. It changes the access mode of the file pointed to by *filename* to that specified by *mode*. The value of *mode* must be one or both of the macros **S_IWRITE** and **S_IREAD**, which correspond to write access and read access, respectively. To change a file's mode to read/write status, call **chmod( )** with *mode* set to **S_IWRITE | S_IREAD**.

The **chmod( )** function returns 0 if successful and −1 if unsuccessful.

Example

This call to **chmod( )** attempts to set the file TEST.TST to read/write access:

```
if(!chmod("TEST.TST", S_IREAD | S_IWRITE))
  printf("file set to read/write access");
```

Related Functions

access( ), **_chmod( )**

void clearerr(FILE *stream)

Description

The prototype for **clearerr( )** is found in **stdio.h**.

The **clearerr( )** function is used to reset the file error flag pointed to by *stream* to zero (off). The end-of-file indicator is also reset.

The error flags for each stream are initially set to zero by a successful call to **fopen( )**. Once an error has occurred, the flags stay set until an explicit call to either **clearerr( )** or **rewind( )** is made.

File errors can occur for a wide variety of reasons, many of which are system dependent. The exact nature of the error can be determined by calling **perror( )**, which displays what error has occurred (see **perror( )**).

Example

This program copies one file to another. If an error is encountered, a message is printed and the error is cleared.

```c
#include "stdio.h"

main(argc,argv)  /* copy one file to another */
int argc;
char *argv[];
{
  FILE *in, *out;
  char ch;

  if(argc!=3) {
    printf("You forgot to enter a filename\n");
    exit(0);
  }

  if((in=fopen(argv[1],"rb")) == NULL) {
    printf("cannot open file\n");
    exit(0);
  }
  if((out=fopen(argv[2],"wb")) == NULL) {
    printf("cannot open file\n");
    exit(0);
  }

  while(!feof(in)) {
    ch = getc(in);
    if(ferror(in)) {
      printf("read error");
      clearerr(in);
    } else {
      putc(ch, out);
      if(ferror(out)) {
        printf("write error");
        clearerr(out);
      }
    }
  }
  fclose(in);
  fclose(out);

}
```

Related Functions

feof( ), ferror( ), and perror( )

int close(int fd)
int —close(int fd)

Description

The prototypes for close( ) and —close( ) are found in io.h.

The **close( )** function belongs to the UNIX-like file system and is not defined by the proposed ANSI standard. When **close( )** is called with a valid file descriptor, it closes the file associated with it and flushes the write buffers if applicable. (File descriptors are created through a successful call to **open( )** or **creat( )** and do not relate to streams or file pointers.)

If successful, **close( )** returns a 0; if unsuccessful it returns a −1. Although there are several reasons why you might not be able to close a file, the most common is the premature removal of the medium. For example, if you remove a diskette from the drive before the file is closed, an error will result.

The **—close( )** function works exactly like **close( )** except that it does not write a CTRL-Z to the file.

Example

This program opens and closes a file using the UNIX-like file system:

```
#include "io.h"
#include "fcntl.h"
#include "sys\stat.h"

main(argc,argv)
int argc;
char *argv[];
{
  int fd;

  if((fd=open(argv[1],O_RDONLY))==-1) {
    printf("cannot open file");
    exit(1);
  }

  printf("file is existent\n");

  if(close(fd)) printf("error in closing file\n");
}
```

Related Functions

open( ), **creat( )**, **read( )**, **write( )**, **unlink( )**

int creat(char *filename, int pmode)
int —creat(char *filename, int attrib)
int creatnew(char *filename, int attrib)
int creattemp(char *filename, int attrib)

Description

The prototypes for these functions are found in **io.h**.

The **creat( )** function is part of the UNIX-like file system and is not defined by the proposed ANSI standard. Its purpose is to create a new file with the name pointed to by *filename* and to open it for writing. On success **creat( )** returns a file descriptor that is greater than or equal to 0; on failure it returns a −1. (File descriptors are integers and do not relate to streams or file pointers.)

The value of *pmode* determines the file's access setting, sometimes called its *permission mode*. The value of *pmode* is highly dependent upon the operating system. Use the macros **S_IWRITE** (write only) and **S_IREAD** (read only) as values for *pmode*.

If, at the time of the call to **creat( )**, the specified file already exists, it is erased and all previous contents are lost unless the original file was write-protected.

The **_creat( )** function works like **creat( )** but uses a DOS attribute byte. The *attrib* argument may be one of these macros:

FA_RDONLY	Set file to read-only
FA_HIDDEN	Make hidden file
FA_SYSTEM	Mark as a system file

The **creatnew( )** function is the same as **_creat( )** except that if the file already exists on disk, **creatnew( )** returns an error and does not erase the original file.

The **creattemp( )** function is used to create a unique temporary file. You call **creattemp( )** with *filename* pointing to the pathname ending with a backslash. Upon return, *filename* contains the name of a unique file. You must make sure that *filename* is large enough to hold the file name.

In the case of an error in any of these functions, **errno** is set to one of these values.

ENOENT	Path or file does not exist
EMFILE	Too many files are open
EZCCES	Access denied

Example

The following code fragment creates a file called **test:**

```
#include "io.h"

main()
{
  int fd;

  if((fd=creat("test",S_IWRITE))==-1) {
    printf("cannot open file\n");
    exit(1);
  }
  .
  .
  .
```

Related Functions

open( ), close( ), read( ), write( ), unlink( ), eof( )

int dup(int handle)
int dup2(int old—handle, int new—handle)

Description

The prototypes for **dup( )** and **dup2( )** are found in **io.h.**

The **dup( )** function returns a new file descriptor that fully describes the state of the file associated with *handle*. It returns nonnegative on success, −1 on failure.

The **dup2( )** function returns the value of *new_handle*. If there is a file associated with *new_handle* prior to the call to **dup2( )**, it is closed.

Example

This fragment assigns **fp2** a new file descriptor:

```
FILE *fp, *fp2;
.
.
.
fp2 = dup(fp);
```

Related Functions

close( ), **creat( )**

int eof(int fd)

Description

The prototype for **eof( )** is found in **io.h**.

The **eof( )** function is part of the UNIX-like file system and is not defined by the proposed ANSI standard. When called with a valid file descriptor, **eof( )** returns 1 if the end of the file has been reached; otherwise it returns a 0. If an error has occurred, it returns −1, and **errno** is set to **EBADF** (bad file number).

Example

The following program displays a text file on the console using **eof( )** to determine when the end of the file has been reached.

```
#include "io.h"
#include "fcntl.h"

main(argc,argv)
int argc;
char *argv[];
{
  int fd;
  char ch;

  if((fd=open(argv[1],O_RDWR))==-1) {
    printf("cannot open file\n");
    exit(1);
  }

  while(!eof(fd)) {
    read(fd, &ch, 1);    /* read one char at a time */
    printf("%c", ch);
  }

  close(fd);
}
```

Related Functions

open( ), **close( )**, **read( )**, **write( )**, **unlink( )**

int fclose(FILE *stream)
int fcloseall(void)

Description

The prototypes for **fclose( )** and **fcloseall( )** are found in
stdio.h.

The **fclose( )** function closes the file associated with
stream and flushes its buffer. After an **fclose( )**, *stream* is no
longer connected with the file and any automatically allocated buffers are deallocated.

If **fclose( )** is successful, a 0 is returned; otherwise a nonzero number is returned. Trying to close a file that has
already been closed is an error.

The **fcloseall( )** closes all open streams except **stdin,**
stdout, and **stderr.** It is not defined by the ANSI standard.

Example

The following code opens and closes a file:

```
#include "stdio.h"

main()
{
  FILE *fp;

  if((fp=fopen("test","rb"))==NULL) {
    printf("cannot open file\n");
    exit(1);
  }
  .
  .
  .
  if(fclose(fp)) printf("file close error\n");
}
```

Related Functions

fopen( ), freopen( ), fflush( )

FILE *fdopen(int handle, char *mode)

Description

The prototype for **fdopen( )** is found in **stdio.h**.

The **fdopen( )** function is not defined by the ANSI standard. It returns a stream that shares the same file that is associated with *handle*, where *handle* is a valid file descriptor obtained through a call to one of the UNIX-like I/O routines. In essence, **fdopen( )** is a bridge between the ANSI stream-based file system and the UNIX-like file system. The value of *mode* must be the same as that of the mode that originally opened the file.

See **open ( )** and **fopen( )** for details.

Related Functions

open( ), fopen( ), creat( )

int feof(FILE *stream)

Description

The prototype for **feof( )** is found in **stdio.h**.

The **feof( )** function checks the file position indicator to determine if the end of the file associated with *stream* has been reached. A nonzero value is returned if the file position indicator is at the end of the file; a 0 is returned otherwise.

Once the end of the file has been reached, subsequent read operations will return **EOF** until either **rewind( )** is called or the file position indicator is moved using **fseek( )**.

The **feof( )** function is particularly useful when working with binary files because the end-of-file marker is also a valid binary integer. You must make explicit calls to **feof( )** rather than simply testing the return value of **getc( )**, for example, to determine when the end of the file has been reached.

Example

This code fragment shows the proper way to read to the end of a binary file:

```
/*
   Assume that fp has been opened as a binary file
   for read operations.
*/

while(!feof(fp)) getc(fp);
```

Related Functions

clearerr( ), **ferror( )**, **perror( )**, **putc( )**, **getc( )**

int ferror(FILE *stream)

Description

The prototype for **ferror( )** is found in **stdio.h**.

The **ferror( )** function checks for a file error on the given *stream*. A return value of 0 indicates that no error has occurred while a nonzero value indicates an error.

The error flags associated with *stream* will stay set until either the file is closed or **rewind( )** or **clearerr( )** is called.

Use the **perror( )** function to determine the exact nature of the error.

Example

The following code fragment aborts program execution if a file error occurs:

```
/*
   Assume that fp points to a stream opened for write
   operations.
*/

while(!done) {
  putc(info,fp);
  if(ferror(fp)) {
    printf("file error\n");
    exit(1);
  }
  .
  .
  .
}
```

Related Functions

clearerr( ), **feof( )**, **perror( )**

int fflush(FILE *stream)

Description

The prototype for **fflush( )** is found in **stdio.h**.

If *stream* is associated with a file opened for writing, a call to **fflush( )** causes the contents of the output buffer to be physically written to the file. If *stream* points to an input file, the input buffer is cleared. In either case the file remains open.

A return value of 0 indicates success, while nonzero means a write error has occurred.

All buffers are automatically flushed upon normal termination of the program or when they are full. Closing a file also flushes its buffer.

Example

The following code fragment flushes the buffer after each write operation:

```
/*
  Assume that fp is associated with an output file.
*/
   .
   .
   .
fwrite(buf,sizeof(data_type),1,fp);
fflush(fp);
   .
   .
   .
```

Related Functions

fclose( ), fopen( ), fread( ), fwrite( ), getc( ), putc( )

int fgetc(FILE *stream)

Description

The prototype for **fgetc( )** is found in **stdio.h**.

The **fgetc( )** function returns the next character from the input *stream* from the current position and increments the file position indicator. The character is read as an **unsigned char** that is converted to an integer.

If the end of the file is reached, **fgetc( )** returns **EOF**. However, since **EOF** is a valid integer value, when working with binary files you must use **feof( )** to check for end-of-file. **EOF** is also returned if **fgetc( )** encounters an error. Again, when working with binary files you must use **ferror( )** to check for file errors.

Example

This program reads and displays the contents of a text file:

```
#include "stdio.h"

main(argc,argv)
int argc;
char *argv[];
{
  FILE *fp;
  char ch;

  if((fp=fopen(argv[1],"r"))==NULL) {
    printf("cannot open file\n");
    exit(1);
  }

  while((ch=fgetc(fp))!=EOF) {
    printf("%c",ch);
  }

  fclose(fp);
}
```

Related Functions

fputc( ), getc( ), putc( ), fopen( )

int fgetchar(void)

Description

The prototype for **fgetchar( )** is found in **stdio.h.**

The **fgetchar( )** function is functionally equivalent to fgetc(stdin). Refer to **fgetc( )** for details.

char *fgets(char *str, int num, FILE *stream)

Description

The prototype for **fgets( )** is found in **stdio.h.**

The **fgets( )** function reads up to **num−1** characters from *stream* and places them into the character array pointed to by *str*. Characters are read until a newline or an EOF is received or until the specified limit is reached. After the characters have been read, a null is placed in the array immediately after the last character read. A newline character will be retained and will be part of *str*.

If successful, **fgets( )** returns *str*; a null pointer is returned upon failure. If a read error occurs, the contents of the array pointed to by *str* are indeterminate. Because a null pointer is returned when an error occurs or the end of the file is reached, you should use **feof( )** or **ferror( )** to determine what has actually happened.

Example

This program uses **fgets( )** to display the contents of the text file specified in the first command line argument:

```
#include "stdio.h"

main(argc,argv)
int argc;
char *argv[];
{
  FILE *fp;
  char str[128];

  if((fp=fopen(argv[1],"r"))==NULL) {
    printf("cannot open file\n");
    exit(1);
  }

  while(!feof(fp)) {
    if(fgets(str,126,fp)) printf("%s",str);
  }

  fclose(fp);
}
```

Related Functions

fputs( ), **fgetc( )**, **gets( )**, **puts( )**

long filelength(int handle)

Description

The prototype for **filelength( )** is found in **io.h**.

The **filelength( )** function is not defined by the proposed ANSI standard. It returns the length, in bytes, of the file associated with the file descriptor *handle*. Remember that the return value is of type **long**. If an error occurs, $-1L$ is returned and **errno** is set to **EBADF**, which means bad file number.

Example

This fragment prints the length of a file whose file descriptor is called **fd**:

```
printf("The file is %ld bytes long.", filelength(fd));
```

Related Function

open( )

int fileno(FILE *stream)

Description

The prototype for **fileno( )** is found in **stdio.h**.

The **fileno( )** function is not defined by the proposed ANSI standard. It is used to return a file descriptor to the specified stream.

Example

After this fragment has executed, **fd** is associated with the file pointed to by **stream**.

```
FILE *stream;
int fd;

if(!(stream=fopen("TEST", "r"))) {
  printf("cannot open TEST file");
  exit(1);
}

fd = fileno(stream);
```

Related Function

fdopen( )

FILE *fopen(char *fname, char *mode)

Description

The prototype for **fopen( )** is found in **stdio.h**.

The **fopen( )** function opens a file whose name is pointed to by *fname* and returns the stream associated with it. The type of operations that will be allowed on the file are defined by the value of *mode*. The legal values for *mode* are shown in Table 16-1. The parameter *fname* must be a string of characters that comprise a valid file name and may include a path specification.

If **fopen( )** is successful in opening the specified file, a **FILE** pointer is returned. If the file cannot be opened, a null pointer is returned.

As Table 16-1 shows, a file can be opened in either text or binary mode. In text mode, carriage-return-linefeed sequences are translated to newline characters on input. On output, the reverse occurs: newlines are translated to carriage-return-linefeeds. No such translations occur on binary files.

The correct method of opening a file is illustrated by this code fragment:

```
FILE *fp;

if (!(fp = fopen("test","w"))) {
  printf("cannot open file\n");
  exit(1);
}
```

This method detects any error in opening a file, such as a write-protected or a full disk, before attempting to write to it. A null, which is 0, is used because no file pointer ever has that value.

Mode	Meaning
"r"	Open text file for reading
"w"	Create a text file for writing
"a"	Append to text file
"rb"	Open binary file for reading
"wb"	Create binary file for writing
"ab"	Append to a binary file
"r+"	Open text file for read/write
"w+"	Create text file for read/write
"a+"	Open text file for read/write
"rb+"	Open binary file for read/write
"wb+"	Create binary file for read/write
"ab+"	Open binary file for read/write

Table 16-1.   Legal Values for Mode

If you use **fopen( )** to open a file for write, then any preexisting file by that name is erased and a new file is started. If no file by that name exists, one is created. If you want to add to the end of the file, you must use mode **a**. If the file does not exist, an error is returned. Opening a file for read operations requires an existing file. If no file exists, an error is returned. Finally, if a file is opened for read/write operations it is not erased if it exists; however, if no file exists one is created.

Example

This fragment opens a file called **test** for binary read/write operations:

```
FILE *fp;

if(!(fp=fopen("test","r+"))) {
  printf("cannot open file\n");
  exit(1);
}
```

Related Functions

fclose( ), fread( ), fwrite( ), putc( ), getc( )

int fprintf(FILE *stream, char *format, arg-list)

Description

The prototype to **fprintf( )** is found in **stdio.h.**

The **fprintf( )** function outputs the values of the arguments that comprise *arg-list* as specified in the *format* string to the stream pointed to by *stream*. The return value is the number of characters actually printed. If an error occurs, a negative number is returned.

The operations of the format control string and commands are identical to those in **printf( )**; see the **printf( )** function for a complete description.

Example

This program creates a file called **test** and writes the string **"this is a test. 10 20.01"** into the file using **fprintf( )** to format the data:

```
#include "stdio.h"

main()
{
  FILE *fp;

  if(!(fp=fopen("test","wb"))) {
    printf("cannot open file\n");
    exit(1);
  }

  fprintf(fp,"this is a test %d %f", 10, 20.01);

  fclose(fp);
}
```

Related Functions

printf( ), fscanf( )

int fputc(int ch, FILE *stream)

Description

The prototype to **fputc( )** is found in **stdio.h**.

The **fputc( )** function writes the character *ch* to the specified stream at the current file position and then advances the file position indicator. Even though *ch* is declared to be an **int** for historical purposes, it is converted by **fputc( )** into an **unsigned char**. Because all character arguments are elevated to integers at the time of the call, you generally see character variables used as arguments. If an integer is used, the high-order byte is simply discarded.

The value returned by **fputc( )** is the value of the character written. If an error occurs, **EOF** is returned. For files opened for binary operations, the **EOF** may be a valid character and the function **ferror( )** must be used to determine whether an error has actually occurred.

Example

This function writes the contents of a string to the specified stream:

```
write_string(char *str, FILE *fp)
{
  while(*str) if(!ferror(fp)) fputc(*str++, fp);
}
```

Related Functions

fgetc( ), **fopen( )**, **fprintf( )**, **fread( )**, **fwrite( )**

int fputchar(int ch)

Description

The prototype for **fputchar( )** is found in **stdio.h**.

The **fputchar( )** function writes the character *ch* to **stdout**. Even though *ch* is declared to be an **int** for historical purposes, it is converted by **fputchar( )** into an **unsigned char**. Because all character arguments are elevated to integers at the time of the call, you generally see character variables used as arguments. If an integer is used, the high-order byte is simply discarded. A call to **fputchar( )** is the functional equivalent of a call to **fputc(ch, stdout)**.

The value returned by **fputchar( )** is the value of the character written. If an error occurs, **EOF** is returned. For files opened for binary operations, the **EOF** may be a valid character and the function **ferror( )** must be used to determine whether an error has actually occurred.

Example

This function writes the contents of a string to **stdout**:

```
write_string(char *str)
{
  while(*str) if(!ferror(fp)) fputchar(*str++);
}
```

Related Functions

fgetc( ), **fopen( )**, **fprintf( )**, **fread( )**, **fwrite( )**

int fputs(char *str, FILE *stream)

Description

The prototype for **fputs( )** is found in **stdio.h**.

The **fputs( )** function writes the contents of the string pointed to by *str* to the specified stream. The null terminator is not written.

The **fputs( )** function returns 0 on success, nonzero on failure.

If the stream is opened in text mode, certain character translations may take place. This means that there may not be a one-to-one mapping of the string onto the file. However, if opened in binary mode, no character translations occur and one-to-one mapping exists between the string and the file.

Example

This code fragment writes the string **"this is a test"** to the stream pointed to by **fp:**

```
fputs("this is a test",fp);
```

Related Functions

fgets( ), gets( ), puts( ), fprintf( ), fscanf( )

int fread(void ∗buf, int size, int count, FILE ∗stream)

Description

The prototype for **fread( )** is found in **stdio.h.**

The **fread( )** function reads *count* number of objects— each object being *size* number of characters in length—from the stream pointed to by *stream* and places them in the character array pointed to by *buf.* The file position indicator is advanced by the number of characters read.

The **fread( )** function returns the number of items actually read. If fewer items are read than are requested in the call, either an error has occurred or the end of the file has been reached. You must use **feof( )** or **ferror( )** to determine what has taken place.

If the stream is opened for text operations, carriage-return-linefeed sequences are automatically translated into newlines.

Example

This program reads 10 floating-point numbers from a disk file called **test** into the array **bal**:

```
#include "stdio.h"

main()
{
  FILE *fp;
  float bal[10];

  if(!(fp=fopen("test","rb"))) {
    printf("cannot open file\n");
    exit(1);
  }

  if(fread(bal, sizeof(float), 10, fp)!=10) {
    if(feof(fp)) printf("premature end of file");
    else printf("file read error");
  }

  fclose(fp);
}
```

Related Functions

fwrite( ), fopen( ), fscanf( ), fgetc( ), getc( )

FILE *freopen(char *fname, char *mode, FILE *stream)

Description

The prototype for **freopen( )** is found in **stdio.h**.

The **freopen( )** function is used to associate an existing stream with a different file. The new file's name is pointed to by *fname*, the access mode is pointed to by *mode*, and the stream to be reassigned is pointed to by *stream*. The string *mode* uses the same format as **fopen( )**; a complete discussion is found in the **fopen( )** description.

When called, **freopen( )** first tries to close a file that is currently associated with *stream*. Failure to achieve a successful closing is ignored, and the attempt to reopen continues.

The **freopen( )** function returns a pointer to *stream* on success and a null pointer otherwise.

The main use of **freopen( )** is to redirect the system-defined files **stdin, stdout,** and **stderr** to some other file.

Example

The program shown here uses **freopen( )** to redirect the stream **stdout** to the file called OUT. Because **printf( )** writes to **stdout,** the first message is displayed on the screen and the second is written to the disk file.

```
#include "stdio.h"

main()
{
  FILE *fp;
  char str[128];

  printf("This will display on the screen\n");

  if(!(fp=freopen("OUT","w",stdout))) {
    printf("cannot open file\n");
    exit(1);
  }

  printf("this will be written to the file OUT");

  fclose(fp);
}
```

Related Functions

fopen( ), fclose( )

int fscanf(FILE *stream, char *format, arg-list)

Description

The prototype for **fscanf( )** is found in **stdio.h.**

The **fscanf( )** function works exactly like the **scanf( )** function except that it reads the information from the stream specified by *stream* instead of **stdin.** See the **scanf( )** function for details.

The **fscanf( )** function returns the number of arguments actually assigned values. This number does not include skipped fields. A return value of **EOF** means that an attempt was made to read past the end of the file.

Example

This code fragment reads a string and a **float** number from the stream **fp**:

```
char str[80];
float f;

fscanf(fp, "%s%f", str, &f);
```

Related Functions

scanf( ), fprintf( )

int fseek(FILE *stream, long offset, int origin)

Description

The prototype for **fseek( )** is found in **stdio.h**.

The **fseek( )** function sets the file-position indicator associated with *stream* according to the values of *offset* and *origin*. Its main purpose is to support random I/O operations. The *offset* is the number of bytes from *origin* to make the new position. The *origin* is either 0, 1, or 2, with 0 being the start of the file, 1 the current position, and 2 the end of the file. Turbo C also defines the following macros in **stdio.h** for *origin:*

Origin	Name
Beginning of file	SEEK_SET
Current position	SEEK_CUR
End of file	SEEK_END

A return value of 0 means that **fseek()** succeeded. A nonzero value indicates failure.

As specified by the proposed ANSI standard, *offset* must be a **long int** in most implementations to support files larger than 64K bytes.

You may use **fseek()** to move the position indicator anywhere in the file, even beyond the end. However, it is an error to attempt to set the position indicator before the beginning of the file.

The **fseek()** function clears the end-of-file flag associated with the specified stream. Furthermore, it nullifies any prior **ungetc()** on the same stream. (See **ungetc()**.)

Example

The function shown here seeks to the specified structure of type **addr**. Notice the use of **sizeof** both to obtain the proper number of bytes to seek and to ensure portability.

```
struct addr {
  char name[40];
  char street[40];
  char city[40];
  char state[3];
  char zip[10];
} info;

find(long client_num)
{
  FILE *fp;

  if(!(fp=fopen("mail","rb"))) {
    printf("cannot open file\n");
    exit(1);
  }

  /* find the proper structure */
  fseek(fp, client_num*sizeof(struct addr), 0);

  /* read the data into memory */
  fread(&info, sizeof(struct addr), 1, fp);

  fclose(fp);
}
```

Related Functions

ftell(), rewind(), fopen()

long ftell(FILE *stream)

Description

The prototype for **ftell( )** is found in **stdio.h**.

The **ftell( )** function returns the current value of the file-position indicator for the specified stream. This value is the number of bytes the indicator is from the beginning of the file.

The **ftell( )** function returns −1L when an error occurs. If the stream is incapable of random seeks—if it is the console, for instance—the return value is undefined.

Example

This code fragment returns the current value of the file-position indicator for the stream pointed to by **fp**:

```
long i;
if((i=ftell(fp))==-1L) printf("A file error has occurred\n");
```

Related Function

fseek( )

int fwrite(void *buf, int size, int count, FILE *stream)

Description

The prototype for **fwrite( )** is found in **stdio.h**.

The **fwrite( )** function writes *count* number of objects— each object being *size* number of characters in length—to the stream pointed to by *stream*, from the character array pointed to by *buf*. The file-position indicator is advanced by the number of characters written.

The **fwrite( )** function returns the number of items actually written that, if the function is successful, equals the number requested. If fewer items are written than are requested, an error has occurred.

Example

This program writes a **float** to the file **test**. Notice that **sizeof** is used both to determine the number of bytes in a **float** variable and to ensure portability.

```
#include "stdio.h"

main()
{
  FILE *fp;
  float f=12.23;

  if(!(fp=fopen("test","wb"))) {
    printf("cannot open file\n");
    exit(1);
  }

  fwrite(&f, sizeof(float), 1, fp);

  fclose(fp);
}
```

Related Functions

fread( ), fscanf( ), getc( ), fgetc( )

int getc(FILE *stream)

Description

The prototype for **getc( )** is found in **stdio.h**.

The **getc( )** macro returns the next character from the current position in the input *stream* and increments the file-position indicator. The character is read as an **unsigned char** that is converted to an integer.

If the end of the file is reached, **getc( )** returns EOF. However, since EOF is a valid integer value, when working with binary files you must use **feof( )** to check for the end of the file. If **getc( )** encounters an error, EOF is also returned. Remember that if you are working with binary files you must use **ferror( )** to check for file errors.

Example

This program reads and displays the contents of a text file:

```
#include "stdio.h"

main(int argc, char *argv[]
{
  FILE *fp;
  char ch;

  if(!(fp=fopen(argv[1],"r"))) {
    printf("cannot open file\n");
    exit(1);
  }

  while((ch=getc(fp))!=EOF) {
    printf("%c", ch);
  }

  fclose(fp);
}
```

Related Functions

fputc( ), **fgetc( )**, **putc( )**, **fopen( )**

int getch(void)
int getche(void)

Description

The prototypes for **getch( )** and **getche( )** are found in **stdio.h**.

The **getch( )** function returns the next character read from the console but does not echo that character to the screen.

The **getche( )** function returns the next character read from the console and echos that character to the screen.

Example

This fragment uses **getch()** to read the user's menu selection for a spelling checker program:

```
do {
  printf("1: check spelling\n");
  printf("2: correct spelling\n");
  printf("3: lookup a word in the dictionary\n");
  printf("4: quit\n");

  printf("\nEnter your selection: ");
  choice = getch();
} while(!strchr("1234", choice);
```

Related Functions

getc( ), getchar( ), fgetc( )

int getchar(void)

Description

The prototype for **getchar()** is found in **stdio.h**.

The **getchar()** macro returns the next character from **stdin**. The character is read as an **unsigned char** that is converted to an integer. If the end-of-file marker is read, **EOF** is returned.

The **getchar()** function (or macro) is functionally equivalent to **getc(stdin).**

Example

This program reads characters from **stdin** into the array **s** until a carriage return is entered and then displays the string:

```
#include "stdio.h"

main()
{
```

```
    char s[256], *p;

    p=s;

    while((*p++=getchar())!='\n') ;
    *p = '\0';  /* add null terminator */
    printf(s);
}
```

Related Functions

fputc( ), fgetc( ), putc( ), fopen( )

char *gets(char *str)

Description

The prototype for **gets( )** is found in **stdio.h**.

The **gets( )** function reads characters from **stdin** and places them into the character array pointed to by *str*. Characters are read until a newline or an **EOF** is reached. The **EOF** or newline character is not made part of the string but is translated into a null to terminate the string.

If successful, **gets( )** returns *str;* if unsuccessful, it returns a null pointer. If a read error occurs the contents of the array pointed to by *str* are indeterminate. Because a null pointer is returned when either an error has occurred or the end of the file is reached, you should use **feof( )** or **ferror( )** to determine what has actually happened.

There is no limit to the number of characters that **gets( )** will read; it is the programmer's job to make sure that the array pointed to by *str* is not overrun.

Example

This program uses **gets( )** to read a filename:

```
#include "stdio.h"

main()
{
  FILE *fp;
  char fname[128];
```

```
  printf("Enter filename: ");
  gets(fname);

  if(!(fp=fopen(fname,"r"))) {
    printf("cannot open file\n");
    exit(1);
  }
    .
    .
    .
  fclose(fp);
}
```

Related Functions

fputs( ), fgetc( ), fgets( ), puts( )

int getw(FILE *stream)

Description

The prototype for **getw( )** is found in **stdio.h**.

The **getw( )** function is not defined by the proposed ANSI standard.

The **getw( )** function returns the next integer from *stream* and advances the file-position indicator appropriately.

Because the integer read may have a value equal to **EOF**, you must use **feof( )** and/or **ferror( )** to determine when the end-of-file marker is reached or an error has occurred.

Example

This program reads integers from the file **inttest** and displays their sum:

```
#include "stdio.h"

main()
{
  FILE *fp;
  int sum = 0;

  if(!(fp=fopen("inttest","rb")) {
    printf("cannot open file\n");
    exit(1);
```

```
    }
    while(!feof(fp))
      sum = getw(fp)+sum;

    printf("the sum is %d",sum);

    fclose(fp);
}
```

Related Functions

putw( ), fread( )

int isatty(int handle)

Description

The prototype for **isatty( )** is found in **io.h**.

The function **isatty( )** is not defined by the proposed ANSI standard. It returns nonzero if *handle* is associated with either a terminal, console, printer, or serial port; otherwise it returns 0.

Example

This fragment reports whether the device associated with **fd** is a character device:

```
if(isatty(fd)) printf("is a character device");
else printf("is not a character device");
```

Related Functions

open( )

int lock(int handle, long offset, long length)

Description

The prototype for **lock( )** is found in **io.h**.

The **lock( )** function is not defined by the proposed ANSI standard. It is used to lock a region of a file, thus preventing another program from using it until the lock is removed. To unlock a file use **unlock( )**. These functions provide control for file sharing in network environments.

The file to be locked is associated with *handle*. The portion of the file to be locked is determined by the starting *offset* from the beginning of the file and the *length*.

If **lock( )** is successful, 0 is returned; on failure, −1 is returned.

Example

This fragment locks the first 128 bytes of the file associated with **fd**:

```
lock(fd, 0, 128);
```

Related Function

unlock( )

long lseek(int handle, long offset, int origin)

Description

The prototype for **lseek( )** is found in **io.h**.

The **lseek( )** function is part of the UNIX-like I/O system and is not defined by the proposed ANSI standard.

The **lseek( )** function sets the file-position indicator to the location specified by *offset* and *origin* for the file specified by *handle*.

How **lseek( )** works depends on the values of *origin* and *offset*. The *origin* may be either 0, 1, or 2. The chart shown next explains how the *offset* is interpreted for each *origin* value.

Origin	Effect of Call to lseek( )
0	Count the offset from the start of the file
1	Count the offset from the current position
2	Count the offset from the end of the file

The following macros are defined in **io.h**. They can be used for a value of *origin* in order of 0 through 2.

SEEK—SET
SEEK—CUR
SEEK—END

The **lseek( )** function returns *offset* on success. Therefore, **lseek( )** will be returning a **long** integer and must be declared as such at the top of your program. Upon failure, a −1L is returned.

Example

The example shown here allows you to examine a file a sector at a time using the UNIX-like I/O system. You will want to change the buffer size to match the sector size of your system.

```
#include "stdio.h"
#include "fcntl.h"
#include "sys\stat.h"

#define BUF_SIZE   128

long int lseek();

/* read buffers using lseek() */
main(int argc, char *argv[])
{
  char buf[BUF_SIZE+1], s[10];
  int fd, sector;

  buf[BUF_SIZE+1]='\0'; /* null terminate buffer for printf */
  if((fd=open(argv[1],O_RDONLY))==-1) { /* open for read */
    printf("cannot open file\n");
    exit(0);
  }
  do {
```

```
printf("buffer: ");
gets(s);

sector = atoi(s); /* get the sector to read */

if(lseek(fd, (long)sector*BUF_SIZE,0)==-1L)
  printf("seek error\n");

if(read(fd, buf, BUF_SIZE)==0) {
  printf("sector out of range\n");
}
else
  printf(buf);
} while(sector>0);
close(fd);
}
```

Related Functions

read( ), write( ), open( ), close( )

int open(char *filename, int access, int mode)
int — open(char *filename, int access)

Description

The prototypes for **open( )** and **—open( )** are found in **io.h**.

The **open( )** function is part of the UNIX-like I/O system and is not defined by the proposed ANSI standard.

Unlike the buffered I/O system, the UNIX-like system does not use file pointers of type **FILE** but file descriptors of type **int**. The **open( )** function opens a file with the name **fname** and sets its access mode as specified by *access*. You can think of *access* as being constructed of a base mode of operation plus modifiers. The following base modes are allowed:

Base	Meaning
O—RDONLY	Open for read only
O—WRONLY	Open for write only
O—RDWR	Open for read/write

After selecting one of these values, you may **OR** it with one or more of the following access modifiers:

Access Modifiers	Meaning
O_NDELAY	Not used; included for UNIX compatibility
O_APPEND	Causes the file pointer to be set to the end of the file prior to each write operation
O_CREAT	If the file does not exist, creates one with its attribute set to the value of *mode*
O_TRUNC	If the file exists, truncates it to length zero but retains its file attributes
O_EXCL	Not used; included for UNIX compatibility
O_BINARY	Opens a binary file
O_TEXT	Opens a text file

The *mode* argument is required only if the **O_CREAT** modifier is used. In this case, *mode* may be one of three values:

Mode	Meaning
S_IWRITE	Write access
S_IREAD	Read access
S_IWRITE | S_IREAD	Read/write access

A successful call to **open()** returns a positive integer that is the file descriptor associated with the file. A return value of

−1 means that the file cannot be opened and **errno** is set to one of these values:

ENOENT	Path or file does not exist
EMFILE	Too many open files
EACCES	Access denied
EINVACC	Invalid access code

The function **_open( )** accepts a larger number of modifiers for the *access* parameter if executing under DOS 3.x or greater. These additional values are

Access Modifier	Meaning
O_NOINHERIT	File not passed to child programs
O_DENYALL	Only the current file descriptor has access to the file
O_DENYWRITE	Only read access to the file allowed by another open
O_DENYREAD	Only write access to the file allowed by another open
O_DENYNONE	Allows shared files

Example

You usually see the call to **open( )** like this:

```
if((fd=open(filename, mode)) == -1)  {
  printf("cannot open file\n");
  exit(1);
}
```

Related Functions

close( ), read( ), write( )

void perror(char *str)

Description

The prototype for the **perror( )** function is found in **stdio.h**.

The **perror( )** function maps the value of the global **errno** onto a string and writes that string to **stderr**. If the value of *str* is not null, the string is written first, followed by a colon, and then the proper error message as determined by the value of **errno**.

Example

This program purposely generates a domain error by calling **asin( )** with an out-of-range argument. The output is **Program Error Test: Math argument**.

```
#include "stdio.h"
#include "math.h"

extern int errno;

main()
{
    /* this will generate a domain error */
    asin(10.0);
    if(errno==EDOM) perror("Program Error Test");
}
```


Related Function

ferror( )

int printf(char *format, arg-list)

Description

The prototype to **printf( )** is found in **stdio.h**.

The **printf( )** function writes to **stdout** the arguments that comprise *arg-list* under the control of the string pointed to by *format*.

The string pointed to by *format* consists of two types of items. The first type is made up of characters that will be printed on the screen. The second type contains format commands that define the way the arguments are displayed. A format command begins with a percent sign and is followed by the format code. The format commands are shown in Table 16-2. There must be exactly the same number of arguments as there are format commands, and the format commands and

Code	Format
%c	A single character
%d	Decimal
%i	Decimal
%e	Scientific notation
%f	Decimal floating-point
%g	Uses %e or %f, whichever is shorter
%o	Octal
%s	String of characters
%u	Unsigned decimal
%x	Hexadecimal
%%	Prints a % sign
%p	Displays a pointer
%n	The associated argument will be an integer pointer into which is placed the number of characters written so far

Table 16-2.   **printf( )** Format Commands

the arguments are matched in order. For example, this **printf( )** call

```
printf("Hi %c %d %s",'c',10,"there!");
```

displays **Hi c 10 there!**

If there are insufficient arguments to match the format commands, the output is undefined. If there are more arguments than format commands, the remaining arguments are discarded.

The **printf( )** function returns the number of characters actually printed. A negative return value indicates that an error has taken place.

The format commands may have modifiers that specify the field width, the number of decimal places, and a left-justification flag. An integer placed between the percent sign and the format command acts as a *minimum field-width specifier*. This pads the output with blanks or zeros to ensure that it is at least a certain minimum length. If the string or number is greater than that minimum, it will be printed in full even if it overruns the minimum. The default padding is done with spaces. If you wish to pad with zeros, place 0 before the field-width specifier. For example, **%05d** will pad a number of fewer than five digits with zeros so that its total length is five.

To specify the number of decimal places printed for a floating-point number, place a decimal point after the field-width specifier followed by the number of decimal places you wish to display. For example, **%10.4f** displays a number at least ten characters wide with four decimal places. When this kind of format is applied to strings or integers, the number following the period specifies the maximum field length. For example, **%5.7s** displays a string that is at least five characters long and no longer than seven. If the string is longer than the maximum field width, the characters will be truncated at the end.

By default, all output is right-justified: If the field width is larger than the data printed, the data will be placed on the right edge of the field. You can force the information to be left-justified by placing a minus sign directly after the %. For example, **%−10.2f** left-justifies a floating-point number with two decimal places in a ten-character field.

There are two format command modifiers that allow **printf( )** to display **short** and **long** integers. These modifiers can be applied to the **d, i, o, u,** and **x** type specifiers. The **l** modifier tells **printf( )** that a **long** data type follows. For example, **%ld** means that a **long int** is to be displayed. The **h** modifier instructs **printf( )** to display a **short int.** Therefore, **%hu** indicates that the data is of type **short unsigned int.**

The **l** modifier can also prefix the floating-point commands of **e, f,** and **g** and indicates that a **double** follows.

The **%n** command causes the number of characters that have been written at the time the **%n** is encountered to be placed in an integer variable whose pointer is specified in the argument list. For example, this code fragment displays the number 14 after the line **this is a test**:

```
int i;

printf("this is a test%n",&i);
printf("%d",i);
```

Example

This program displays the output shown in its comments:

```
#include "stdio.h"

main()
{
  /* This prints "this is a test" left justified
     in 20 character field.
  */
  printf("%-20s", "this is a test");

  /* This prints a float with 3 decimal places in a 10
     character field. The output will be "    12.234".
  */
  printf("%10.3f", 12.234657);
}
```

Related Functions

scanf( ), fprintf( )

int putc(int ch, FILE *stream)

Description

The prototype for **putc( )** is found in **stdio.h**.

The **putc( )** function writes the character contained in the least significant byte of *ch* to the output stream pointed to by *stream*. Because character arguments are elevated to integers at the time of the call, you can use character variables as arguments to **putc( )**.

If successful, **putc( )** returns the character written; if an error occurs, it returns **EOF**. If the output stream has been opened in binary mode, **EOF** is a valid value for *ch*. This means that you must use **ferror( )** to determine whether an error has occurred.

Example

The following loop writes the characters in string **str** to the stream specified by **fp**. The null terminator is not written.

```
for(; *str; str++) putc(*str, fp);
```

Related Functions

fgetc( ), fputc( ), getchar( ), putchar( )

int putchar(int ch)

Description

The prototype for **putchar( )** is found in **stdio.h**.

The **putchar( )** macro writes the character contained in the least significant byte of *ch* to **stdout**. It is functionally equivalent to **putc(ch,stdout)**. Because character arguments are elevated to integers at the time of the call, you can use character variables as arguments to **putchar( )**.

If successful, **putchar( )** returns the character written; if an error occurs, it returns **EOF**. If the output stream has been opened in binary mode, **EOF** is a valid value for *ch*. This means that you must use **ferror( )** to determine whether an error has occurred.

Example

The following loop writes the characters in string **str** to **stdout**. The null terminator is not written.

```
for(; *str; str++) putchar(*str);
```

Related Functions

fputchar( ), putc( )

int puts(char *str)

Description

The prototype for **puts( )** is found in **stdio.h**.

The **puts( )** function writes the string pointed to by **str** to the standard output device. The null terminator is translated to a newline.

The **puts( )** function returns a newline if successful and an **EOF** if unsuccessful.

Example

The following writes the string **this is an example** to stdout:

```
#include "stdio.h"

main()
{
    char str[80];

    strcpy(str, "this is an example");

    puts(str);
}
```

Related Functions

putc( ), **gets( )**, **printf( )**

int putw(int i, FILE *stream)

Description

The **putw( )** function is not defined by the proposed ANSI standard and may not be fully portable.

The **putw( )** function writes the integer i to *stream* at the current file position and increments the file-position pointer appropriately.

The **putw( )** function returns the value written. A return value of **EOF** means an error has occurred in the stream if it is in text mode. Because **EOF** is also a valid integer value, you must use **ferror( )** to detect an error in a binary stream.

Example

This code fragment writes the value 100 to the stream pointed to by **fp**:

```
putw(100, fp);
```

Related Functions

getw( ), **printf( )**, **fwrite( )**

int read(int fd, void *buf, int count)
int —read(int fd, void *buf, int count)

Description

The prototypes for **read( )** and **—read( )** are found in **io.h**.

Neither the **read( )** nor the **—read( )** function is defined by the proposed ANSI standard. The **read( )** function is part of the UNIX-like I/O system. The **—read( )** function is specific to Turbo C and the MS-DOS operating system.

The **read( )** function reads *count* number of bytes from the file described by *fd* into the buffer pointed to by *buf*. The file-position indicator is incremented by the number of bytes read. If the file is opened in text mode, character translations may take place.

The return value is the number of bytes actually read. This number may be smaller than *count* if either an end-of-file or an error is encountered. A value of -1 means an error, and a value of 0 means the end of the file has been reached.

The difference between **read()** and **_read()** is that **read()** removes carriage returns and returns **EOF** when a CTRL-Z is read from a text file. The **_read()** function does not perform these actions.

Example

This program reads the first 100 bytes from the file TEST. TST into the array **buffer**:

```
#include "stdio.h"
#include "io.h"
#include "fcntl.h"

main()
{
  int fd;
  char buffer[100];

  if((fd=open("TEST.TST",O_RDONLY))==-1) {
    printf("cannot open file\n");
    exit(1);
  }

  if(read(fd, buffer, 100)!=100)
    printf("Possible read error.");

}
```

Related Functions

open(), **close()**, **write()**, **lseek()**

int remove(char *fname)

Description

The prototype for **remove()** is found in **stdio.h**.

The **remove()** function erases the file specified by

fname. It returns 0 if the file was successfully deleted and a
−1 if an error occurred.

Example

This program removes the file specified on the command
line:

```
#include "stdio.h"

main(int argc, char *argv[])
{
   if(remove(argv[1])==-1) printf("remove error");
}
```

Related Function

rename( )

int rename(char *oldfname, char *newfname)

Description

The prototype for **rename( )** is found in **stdio.h**.

The **rename( )** function changes the name of the file
specified by *oldfname* to *newfname*. The *newfname* must not
match any existing directory entry.

The **rename( )** function returns 0 if successful and nonzero if an error has occurred.

Example

This program renames the file specified as the first command line argument to that specified by the second command line argument. Assuming the program is called
change, a command line consisting of **change this that** will
change the name of a file called **this** to **that**.

```
#include "stdio.h"

main(int argc, char *argv[])
{
   if(rename(argv[1], argv[2])!=0) printf("rename error");
}
```

Related Function

remove( )

int rewind(FILE *stream)

Description

The prototype for **rewind( )** is found in **stdio.h**.

The **rewind( )** function moves the file position indicator to the start of the specified stream. It also clears the end-of-file and error flags associated with *stream*. It returns 0 if successful and nonzero otherwise.

Example

This function reads the stream pointed to by **fp** twice, displaying the file each time:

```
re_read(FILE *fp)
{
   /* read once */
   while(!feof(fp)) putchar(getc(fp));

   rewind(fp);

   /* read twice */
   while(!feof(fp)) putchar(getc(fp));
}
```

Related Function

fseek( )

int scanf(char *format, arg-list)

Description

The prototype for **scanf( )** is in **stdio.h**. The **scanf( )** function is a general-purpose input routine that reads the stream **stdin**. It can read all the built-in data types and automatically convert them into the proper internal format. It is much like the reverse of **printf( )**.

The control string pointed to by *format* consists of three classifications of characters:

- Format specifiers
- White-space characters
- Non-white-space characters

The input format specifiers are preceded by a percent sign and tell **scanf( )** what type of data is to be read next. These codes are listed in Table 16-3. For example, **%s** reads a string, while **%d** reads an integer.

The format string is read left to right, and the format codes are matched, in order, with the arguments that comprise the argument list.

A white-space character in the control string causes **scanf( )** to skip over one or more white-space characters in the input stream. A white-space character is either a space, a tab, or a newline. In essence, one white-space character in the control string causes **scanf( )** to read, but not store, any number (including 0) of white-space characters up to the first non-white-space character.

A non-white-space character causes **scanf( )** to read and discard a matching character. For example, "**%d,%d**" causes **scanf( )** first to read an integer, then to read and discard a comma, and finally to read another integer. If the specified character is not found, **scanf( )** terminates.

Code	Meaning
%c	Read a single character
%d	Read a decimal integer
%i	Read a decimal integer
%e	Read a floating-point number
%f	Read a floating-point number
%h	Read a short integer
%o	Read an octal number
%s	Read a string
%x	Read a hexadecimal number
%p	Read a pointer
%n	Receive an integer value equal to the number of characters read so far

Table 16-3.   scanf( ) Format Codes

All the variables used to receive values through **scanf( )** must be passed by their addresses. This means that all arguments must be pointers to the variables used as arguments. This is C's way of creating a "call by reference," and it allows a function to alter the contents of an argument. For example, if you wish to read an integer into the variable **count**, you use the following **scanf( )** call:

```
scanf("%d",&count);
```

Strings are read into character arrays, and the array name, without any index, is the address of the first element of the array. To read a string into the character array **address** you would use

```
scanf("%s",address);
```

In this case **address** is already a pointer and need not be preceded by the **&** operator.

The input data items must be separated by spaces, tabs, or newlines. Commas, semicolons, and other punctuation marks do not count as separators. This means that

```
scanf("%d%d",&r,&c);'
```

will accept an input of **10 20**, but fail with **10,20**. As in **printf( )**, the **scanf( )** format codes are matched in order with the variables receiving the input in the argument list.

An * placed after the % and before the format code will read data of the specified type but suppress its assignment. Thus, given the input **10/20**,

```
scanf("%d%*c%d",&x,&y);
```

places the value 10 into **x**, discards the divide sign, and gives **y** the value 20.

The format commands can specify a maximum field-length modifier. This is an integer number placed between the % and the format-command code that limits the number of characters read for any field. For example, if you wish to read no more than 20 characters into **address**, you write

```
scanf("%20s",address);
```

If the input stream was greater than 20 characters, a subsequent call to input would begin where this call left off. For example, if

ABCDEFGHIJKLMNOPQRSTUVWXYZ

had been entered as the response to the earlier **scanf( )** call, only the first 20 characters—up to the **T**—would have been placed into **address** because of the maximum size specifier. This means that the remaining six characters, UVWXYZ, have not yet been used. If another **scanf( )** call is made, such as the following,

```
scanf("%s", str);
```

UVWXYZ is placed into **str**. Input for a field can terminate before the maximum field length is reached if a white-space character is encountered. In this case, **scanf( )** moves on to the next field.

Although spaces, tabs, and newlines are used as field separators, when reading a single character they are read like any other character. For example, with an input stream of **x y,**

```
scanf("%c%c%c", &a, &b, &c);
```

returns the character **x** in **a,** a space in **b,** and the character **y** in **c.**

Be careful: Any other characters in the control string—including spaces, tabs, and newlines—are used to match and discard characters from the input stream. Any character that matches is discarded. For example, given the input stream **10t20,**

```
scanf("%st%s", &x, &y);
```

places 10 into **x** and 20 into **y.** The **t** is discarded because of the **t** in the control string. As another example,

```
scanf("%s ", name);
```

does *not* return until you type a character *after* you type a terminator because the space after the **%s** has instructed **scanf( )** to read and discard spaces, tabs, and newline characters.

The **scanf( )** function returns a number equal to the number of fields that were successfully assigned values. This number does not include fields that were read but not assigned using the * modifier to suppress the assignment. A return value of **EOF** is returned if an attempt is made to read at the end-of-file mark; 0 is returned if no fields were assigned.

Example

The operation of these **scanf( )** statements is explained in their comments:

```
char str[80];
int i;

/* read a string and an integer */
scanf("%s%d", str, &i);

/* read up to 79 chars into str */
scanf("%79s", str);

/* skip the integer between the two strings */
scanf("%s%*d%s", str, &i, str);
```

Related Functions

printf( ), fscanf( )

void setbuf(FILE *stream, char *buf)

Description

The prototype to **setbuf( )** is found in **stdio.h**.

The **setbuf( )** function is used either to specify the buffer the specified stream will use or, if called with *buf* set to null, to turn off buffering. If a programmer-defined buffer is to be specified, it must be **BUFSIZ** characters long. BUFSIZ is defined in **stdio.h**.

The **setbuf( )** function returns no value.

Example

The following fragment associates a programmer-defined buffer with the stream pointed to by **fp**:

```
char buffer[BUFSIZ];
 .
 .
 .
setbuf(fp,buffer);
```

Related Functions

fopen( ), fclose( ), setvbuf( )

int setmode(int handle, unsigned mode)

Description

The prototype for **setmode( )** is found in **io.h**.

The **setmode( )** function is not defined by the proposed ANSI standard. It is used to reset the mode of an already open file given its file descriptor and the new mode desired. The only valid modes are **O—BINARY** and **O—TEXT**.

It returns 0 on success and −1 on error.

Example

This line of code sets the file associated with **fd** to text-only operation:

```
setmode(fd, O_TEXT)
```

Related Functions

open( ), creat( )

int setvbuf(FILE *stream, char *buf, int mode, unsigned size)

Description

The prototype for **setvbuf( )** is found in **stdio.h**.

The **setvbuf( )** function allows the programmer to specify the buffer, its size, and its mode for the specified stream. The character array pointed to by *buf* is used as *stream*'s buffer for I/O operations. The size of the buffer is set by *size*, and *mode* determines how buffering is to be handled. If *buf* is null, no buffering takes place.

The legal values of *mode* are _IOFBF, _IONBF, and _IOLBF. These are defined in **stdio.h**. When the mode is set to _IOFBF, full buffering takes place. This is the default setting. When set to _IONBF, the stream is unbuffered regardless of the value *buf*. If mode is _IOLBF, the stream is line-buffered, which means that the buffer is flushed each time a newline character is written for output streams; for input streams an input request reads all characters up to a newline. In either case, the buffer is also flushed when full.

The value of *size* must be greater than 0.

The **setvbuf( )** function returns 0 on success; nonzero on failure.

Example

This fragment sets the stream **fp** to line-buffered mode with a buffer size of 128:

```
#include "stdio.h"
char buffer[128];
  .
  .
  .
setvbuf(fp , buffer, _IOLBF, 128);
```

Related Function

setbuf( )

int sprintf(char *buf, char *format, arg-list)

Description

The prototype for **sprintf( )** is found in **stdio.h.**

The **sprintf( )** function is identical to **printf( )** except that the output generated is placed into the array pointed to by *buf*. See the **printf( )** function.

The return value is equal to the number of characters actually placed into the array.

Example

After this code fragment executes, **str** holds **one 2 3**:

```
char str[80];

sprintf(str,"%s %d %c","one",2,'3');
```

Related Functions

printf( ), **fsprintf( )**

int sscanf(char *buf, char *format, arg-list)

Description

The prototype for **sscanf( )** is found in **stdio.h.**

The **sscanf( )** function is identical to **scanf( )** except that data is read from the array pointed to by *buf* rather than stdin. See **scanf( )**.

The return value is equal to the number of fields that were actually assigned values. This number does not include fields that were skipped through the use of the * format-command modifier. A value of 0 means that no fields were assigned, and **EOF** indicates that a read was attempted at the end of the string.

Example

This program prints the message **hello 1** on the screen:

```
#include "stdio.h"

main()
{
  char str[80];
  int i;

  sscanf("hello 1 2 3 4 5","%s%d",str,&i);
  printf("%s %d",str,i);
}
```

Related Functions

scanf( ), fscanf( )

long tell(int fd)

Description

The prototype for **tell( )** is found in **io.h**.

The **tell( )** function is part of the UNIX-like I/O system and is not defined by the ANSI standard.

The **tell( )** function returns the current value of the file-position indicator associated with the file descriptor *fd*. This value is the number of bytes the position indicator is from the start of the file. A return value of −**1L** indicates an error.

Example

This fragment prints the current value of the position indicator for the file described by *fd:*

```
int pos;
  .
  .
  .
pos = tell(fd);
printf("Position indicator is %d bytes from the start", pos);
```

Related Functions

lseek( ), open( ), close( ), read( ), write( )

FILE *tmpfile(void)

Description

The prototype for the **tmpfile( )** function is found in **stdio.h**.

The **tmpfile( )** function opens a temporary file for update and returns a pointer to the stream. The function automatically uses a unique file name to avoid conflicts with existing files.

The **tmpfile( )** function returns a null pointer on failure; otherwise it returns a pointer to the stream.

The temporary file created by **tmpfile( )** is automatically removed when the file is closed or when the program terminates.

Example

This fragment creates a temporary working file:

```
FILE *temp;

if(!(temp=tmpfile())) {
  printf("cannot open temporary work file\n");
  exit(1);
}
```

Related Function

tmpnam( )

char *tmpnam(char *name)

Description

The prototype for **tmpnam( )** is found in **stdio.h.**

The **tmpnam( )** function generates a unique file name and stores it in the array pointed to by *name.* The main purpose of **tmpnam( )** is to generate a temporary file name that is different from any other filename in the directory.

The function can be called up to **TMP__MAX** times, defined in **stdio.h.** Each time it generates a new temporary file name.

A pointer to *name* is returned on success; otherwise a null pointer is returned.

Example

This program displays three unique temporary file names:

```
#include "stdio.h"

main()
{
  char name[40];
  int i;            .

  for(i=0; i<3; i++) {
    tmpnam(name);
    printf("%s ", name);
  }
}
```

Related Function

tmpfile( )

int ungetc(int ch, FILE *stream)

Description

The prototype for **ungetc()** is found in **stdio.h**.

The **ungetc()** function returns the character specified by the low-order byte of *ch* back onto the input *stream*. This character is then returned by the next read operation on *stream*. A call to **fflush()** or **fseek()** undoes an **ungetc()** operation and discards the character put back.

Only one character can be put back between subsequent read operations.

You cannot unget an **EOF**.

A call to **ungetc()** clears the end-of-file flag associated with the specified stream. The value of the file-position indicator for a text stream is undefined until all pushed-back characters are read, in which case it is the same as it was prior to the first **ungetc()** call. For binary streams, each **ungetc()** call decrements the file-position indicator.

The return value is equal to *ch* on success and **EOF** on failure.

Example

This function reads words from the input stream pointed to by **fp**. The terminating character is returned to the stream for later use. For example, given input of **count/10**, the first call to **read_word()** returns **count** and puts the / back on the input stream.

```
read_word(FILE *fp, char *token)
{
  while(isalpha(*token=getc(fp))) token++;

  ungetc(fp, *token);
}
```

Related Function

getc( )

int unlink(char *fname)

Description

The prototype for **unlink( )** is found in **dos.h.**

The **unlink( )** function is part of the UNIX-like I/O system and is not defined by the proposed ANSI standard.

The **unlink( )** function removes the specified file from the directory. It returns 0 on success and −1 on failure and sets **errno** to one of the following values:

Error	Meaning
ENOENT	Invalid path or file name
EACCES	Access denied

Example

This program deletes the file specified as the first command line argument:

```
#include "dos.h"

main(int argc, char *argv[])
{
  if(unlink(argv[1])==-1) printf("cannot remove file");
}
```

Related Functions

open( ), close( )

int vprintf(char *format, va—list arg—ptr)
int vfprintf(FILE *stream, CHAR *format, va—list arg—ptr)
int vsprintf(char *buf, char *format, va—list arg—ptr)

Description

The prototypes for these functions are in the file **stdio.h**. You also need to include the file **stdarg.h**.

The functions **vprintf( )**, **vfprintf( )**, and **vsprintf( )** are equivalent to **printf( )**, **fprintf( )**, and **sprintf( )**, respectively, except that the argument list has been replaced by a pointer to a list of arguments. This pointer must be of type **va—list** and is defined in **stdarg.h**. See the proper related function. Also see **va—arg( )**, **va—start( )**, and **va—end( )** in Chapter 24 for further information.

Example

This fragment shows how to set up a call to **vprintf( )**. The call to **va—start( )** creates a variable length argument pointer to the start of the argument list. This pointer must be used in the call to **vprint( )**. The call to **va—end( )** clears the variable length argument pointer.

```
#include "stdio.h"
#include "stdarg.h"

main()
{
  print_message("cannot open file %s","test");
}
print_message (format)
char *format;
{
  va_list ptr; /* get an arg ptr */

  /* initialize ptr to point to the first argument after the format
     string
  */
  va_start( ptr,format);
```

```
/* print out message*/
vprintf(format, ptr);
va_end(ptr);
}
```

Related Functions

va—list( ), va—start( ), va—end( )

int write(int handle, void *buf, int count)
int —write(int handle, void *buf, int count)

Description

The prototypes for **write( )** and **—write( )** are found in **io.h**.

The **write( )** function is part of the UNIX-like I/O system and is not defined by the proposed ANSI standard.

The **write( )** function writes **count** number of bytes to the file described by *handle* from the buffer pointed to by *buf*. The file-position indicator is incremented by the number of bytes written. If the file is opened in text mode, linefeeds are automatically expanded to carriage-return-linefeed combinations. However, **—write( )** does not perform this expansion.

The return value will be equal to the number of bytes actually written. This number may be smaller than *count* if an error is encountered. A value of −1 means an error has occurred, and **errno** is set to one of the following values:

Value	Meaning
EACCES	Access denied
EBADF	Bad file number

Example

This program writes the 100 bytes from **buffer** to the file
test:

```
#include "stdio.h"
#include "io.h"
#include "fcntl.h"

main()
{
  int fd;
  char buffer[100];

  if((fd=open("test",O_WRONLY))==-1) {
    printf("cannot open file\n");
    exit(1);
  }

  gets(buffer);

  if(write(fd,buffer,100)!=100) printf("write error");
  fclose(fd);

}
```

Related Functions

read( ), close( ), write( ), lseek( )

SEVENTEEN

String, Memory, and Character Functions

The Turbo C standard library has a rich and varied set of string-, memory-, and character-handling functions. In C a string is a null-terminated array of characters, memory is a block of contiguous RAM, and a character is a single byte value. The string functions require the header file **string.h** to provide their declarations. The memory manipulation functions use **mem.h**, but several may also use **string.h**. The character functions use **ctype.h** as their header file.

Because C has no bounds checking on array operations, it is the programmer's responsibility to prevent an array overflow. As the proposed ANSI standard puts it, if an array has overflowed, "the behavior is undefined," which is a nice way of saying that your program is about to crash!

In Turbo C a *printable character* is one that can be displayed on a terminal. These are the characters between a space (0x20) and a tilde (0xfE). *Control characters* have values between (0) and (0x1F) as well as DEL (0x7F). The ASCII characters are between 0 and 0x7F.

The character functions are declared to take an integer argument. While this is true, only the low-order byte is used by the function. Generally, you are free to use a character argument because it is automatically elevated to **int** at the time of the call.

int isalnum(int ch)

Description

The prototype for **isalnum( )** is found in **ctype.h**.

The **isalnum( )** function returns nonzero if its argument is either a letter of the alphabet (upper- or lowercase) or a digit. If the character is not an alphanumeric, 0 is returned.

Example

This program checks each character read from **stdin** and reports all alphanumeric ones:

```
#include "ctype.h"
#include "stdio.h"

main()
{
  char ch;

  for(;;) {
    ch = getchar();
    if(ch==' ') break;
    if(isalnum(ch)) printf("%c is alphanumeric\n", ch);
  }
}
```

Related Functions

isalpha(), isdigit(), iscntrl(), isgraph(), isprint(), ispunct(), isspace()

int isalpha(int ch)

Description

The prototype for **isalpha()** is found in **ctype.h**.

The **isalpha()** function returns nonzero if *ch* is a letter of the alphabet (upper- or lowercase); otherwise it returns 0.

Example

This program checks each character read from **stdin** and reports all those that are letters of the alphabet:

```
#include "ctype.h"
#include "stdio.h"

main()
{
  char ch;

  for(;;) {
    ch = getchar();
    if(ch==' ') break;
    if(isalpha(ch)) printf("%c is a letter\n", ch);
  }
}
```

Related Functions

isalnum( ), isdigit( ), iscntrl( ), isgraph( ), isprint( ),
ispunct( ), isspace( )

int isascii(int ch)

Description

The prototype for **isascii( )** is found in **ctype.h**.

The **isascii( )** function returns nonzero if *ch* is in the range 0 through 0x7F; otherwise it returns 0.

Example

This program checks each character read from **stdin** and reports all those that are defined by ASCII:

```
#include "ctype.h"
#include "stdio.h"

main()
{
  char ch;

  for(;;) {
    ch = getchar();
    if(ch==' ') break;
    if(isascii(ch)) printf("%c is ASCII defined\n", ch);
  }
}
```

Related Functions

isalnum( ), isdigit( ), iscntrl( ), isgraph( ), isprint( ),
ispunct( ), isspace( )

int iscntrl(int ch)

Description

The prototype for **iscntrl( )** is found in **ctype.h**.

The **iscntrl( )** function returns nonzero if *ch* is between 0 and 0x1F or is equal to 0x7F (DEL); otherwise it returns 0.

Example

This program checks each character read from **stdin** and reports all those that are control characters:

```
#include "ctype.h"
#include "stdio.h"

main()
{
  char ch;

  for(;;) {
    ch = getchar();
    if(ch==' ') break;
    if(iscntrl(ch)) printf("%c is a control character\n", ch);
  }
}
```

Related Functions

isalnum( ), isdigit( ), isalpha( ), isgraph( ), isprint( ), ispunct( ), isspace( )

int isdigit(int ch)

Description

The prototype for **isdigit( )** is found in **ctype.h**.

The **isdigit( )** function returns nonzero if *ch* is a digit, that is, 0 through 9; otherwise it returns 0.

Example

This program checks each character read from **stdin** and reports all those that are digits:

```
#include "ctype.h"
#include "stdio.h"

main()
{
  char ch;

  for(;;) {
    ch = getchar();
    if(ch==' ') break;
    if(isdigit(ch)) printf("%c is a digit\n", ch);
  }
}
```

Related Functions

isalnum( ), iscntrl( ), isalpha( ), isgraph( ), isprint( ), ispunct( ), isspace( )

int isgraph(int ch)

Description

The prototype for **isgraph( )** is found in **ctype.h**.

The **isgraph( )** function returns nonzero if *ch* is any printable character other than a space; otherwise it returns 0. These characters are in the range 0x21 through 0x7E.

Example

This program checks each character read from **stdin** and reports all those that are printable characters:

```
#include "ctype.h"
#include "stdio.h"

main()
{
  char ch;

  for(;;) {
    ch = getchar();
    if(ch==' ') break;
    if(isgraph(ch)) printf("%c is a printing character\n", ch);
  }
}
```

Related Functions

isalnum( ), iscntrl( ), isalpha( ), isdigit( ), isprint( ), ispunct( ), isspace( )

int islower(int ch)

Description

The prototype for **islower( )** is found in **ctype.h**.

The **islower( )** function returns nonzero if *ch* is a lowercase letter (a-z); otherwise it returns 0.

Example

This program checks each character read from **stdin** and reports all those that are lowercase letters:

```
#include "ctype.h"
#include "stdio.h"

main()
{
  char ch;

  for(;;) {
    ch = getchar();
    if(ch==' ') break;
    if(islower(ch)) printf("%c is lowercase\n", ch);
  }
}
```

Related Function

isupper()

int isprint(int ch)

Description

The prototype for **isprint()** is found in **ctype.h**.

The **isprint()** function returns nonzero if *ch* is a printable character, including a space; otherwise it returns 0. The printable characters are in the range 0x20 through 0x7E.

Example

This program checks each character read from **stdin** and reports all those that are printable:

```
#include "ctype.h"
#include "stdio.h"

main()
{
  char ch;

  for(;;) {
    ch = getchar();
    if(ch==' ') break;
    if(isprint(ch)) printf("%c is printable\n", ch);
  }
}
```

Related Functions

isalnum( ), iscntrl( ), isalpha( ), isdigit( ), isgraph( ),
ispunct( ), isspace( )

int ispunct(int ch)

Description

The prototype for **ispunct( )** is found in **ctype.h**.

The **ispunct( )** function returns nonzero if *ch* is a punctuation character or a space; otherwise it returns 0.

Example

This program checks each character read from **stdin** and reports all those that are punctuation:

```
#include "ctype.h"
#include "stdio.h"

main()
{
  char ch;

  for(;;) {
    ch = getchar();
    if(ch==' ') break;
    if(ispunct(ch)) printf("%c is punctuation\n", ch);
  }
}
```

Related Functions

isalnum( ), iscntrl( ), isalpha( ), isdigit( ), isgraph( ),
isprint( ), isspace( )

int isspace(int ch)

Description

The prototype for **isspace( )** is found in **ctype.h**.

The **isspace( )** function returns nonzero if *ch* is either a space, tab, or newline character; otherwise it returns 0.

Example

This program checks each character read from **stdin** and reports all those that are white-space characters:

```
#include "ctype.h"
#include "stdio.h"

main()
{
  char ch;

  for(;;) {
    ch = getchar();
    if(ch==' ') break;
    if(isspace(ch)) printf("%c is white-space\n", ch);
  }
}
```

Related Functions

isalnum( ), iscntrl( ), isalpha( ), isdigit( ), isgraph( ), isprint( ), ispunct( )

int isupper(ch)

Description

The prototype for **isupper()** is found in **ctype.h**.

The **isupper()** function returns nonzero if *ch* is an uppercase letter (A-Z); otherwise it returns 0.

Example

This program checks each character read from **stdin** and reports all those that are uppercase letters:

```
#include "ctype.h"
#include "stdio.h"

main()
{
  char ch;

  for(;;) {
    ch = getchar();
    if(ch==' ') break;
    if(isupper(ch)) printf("%c is uppercase\n", ch);
  }
}
```

Related Function

islower( )

int isxdigit(int ch)

Description

The prototype for **isxdigit( )** is found in **ctype.h**.

The **isxdigit( )** function returns nonzero if *ch* is a hexadecimal digit; otherwise it returns 0. A hexadecimal digit will be in one of these ranges: A-F, a-f, or 0-9.

Example

This program checks each character read from **stdin** and reports all those that are hexadecimal digits:

```
#include "ctype.h"
#include "stdio.h"

main()
{
  char ch;

  for(;;) {
    ch = getchar();
    if(ch==' ') break;
    if(isxdigit(ch)) printf("%c is hexadecimal \n", ch);
  }
}
```

Related Functions

isalnum( ), iscntrl( ), isalpha( ), isdigit( ), isgraph( ),
isspace( ), ispunct( )

void *memccpy(void *dest, void *source, unsigned char ch, unsigned count)

Description

The prototype for **memccpy( )** is found in both **string.h** and **mem.h**.

The **memccpy()** function copies the contents of the memory pointed to by *source* into the memory pointed to by *dest*. The copy operation stops either when *count* number of bytes have been copied or after the first occurrence of *ch* has been copied.

Example

After this fragment has executed, **hello** will be in array **out** because the space is used to terminate the copy operation:

```
char str[20], out[20];
strcpy(str, "hello there");
memccpy(out, str, ' ', 20);
```

Related Functions

memcpy(), strcpy()

void *memchr(void *buffer, char ch, unsigned count)

Description

The prototype for the **memchr()** function is found in both **string.h** and **mem.h**.

The **memchr()** function searches *buffer* for the first occurrence of *ch* in the first *count* characters.

The **memchr()** function returns a pointer to the first occurrence of *ch* in *buffer*, or a null pointer if *ch* is not found.

Example

This program prints **is a test** on the screen:

```
#include "string.h"
main()
```

```
{
  void *p;

  p = memchr("this is a test", ' ', 14);
  printf((char *) p);
}
```

Related Functions

memmove( ), memcpy( )

int memcmp(void *buf1, void *buf2, unsigned count)
int memicmp(void *buf1, void *buf2, unsigned count)

Description

The prototypes for the **memcmp( )** and **memicmp( )** functions are found in both **string.h** and **mem.h**.

The **memcmp( )** function compares the first *count* characters of the arrays pointed to by *buf1* and *buf2*. The comparison is done lexicographically.

The **memcmp( )** function returns an integer that is interpreted as indicated here:

Value	Meaning
Less than 0	*buf1* is less than *buf2*
0	*buf1* is equal to *buf2*
Greater than 0	*buf1* is greater than *buf2*

The **memicmp( )** function is identical to **memcmp( )** except that case is ignored when comparing letters.

Example

The next program shows the outcome of a comparison of its two command line arguments.

```
#include "string.h"

main(int argc, char *argv[])

{
  int outcome,len,l1,l2;

  /* find the length of shortest */
  len=(l1=strlen(argv[1]))<(l2=strlen(argv[2])) ? l1:l2;

  outcome = memcmp(argv[1], argv[2], len);
  if(!outcome) printf("equal");
  else if(outcome<0) printf("first less than second");
  else printf("first greater than second");
}
```

Related Functions

memcpy( ), memchr( ), strcmp( )

void *memcpy(void *dest, void *source, unsigned count)

Description

The prototype for **memcpy( )** is found in both **string.h** and **mem.h**.

The **memcpy( )** function copies *count* characters from the array pointed to by *source* into the array pointed to by *dest*. If the arrays overlap, the behavior of **memcpy( )** is undefined.

The **memcpy( )** function returns a pointer to *dest*.

Example

This program copies the contents of **buf1** into **buf2** and displays the result:

```
#include "string.h"
#define SIZE 80

main()
{
  char buf1[SIZE], buf2[SIZE];
```

```
strcpy(buf1, "When, in the course of...");
memcpy(buf2, buf1, SIZE);
printf(buf2);
}
```

Related Function

memmove( )

void *memmove(void *dest, void *source,
unsigned count) unsigned int count

Description

The prototype for **memmove( )** is found in both **string.h** and **mem.h**.

The **memmove( )** function copies *count* characters from the array pointed to by *source* into the array pointed to by *dest*. If the arrays overlap, the copy takes place correctly, placing the correct contents into *dest* but leaving *source* modified.

The **memmove( )** function returns a pointer to *dest*.

Example

This program copies the contents of **str1** into **str2** and displays the result:

```
#include "string.h"
#define SIZE 80

main()
{
  char str1[SIZE], str2[SIZE];

  strcpy(str1,"When, in the course of...");
  memmove(str2,str1,SIZE);
  printf(str2);
}
```

Related Function

memcpy( )

void *memset(void *buf, char ch, unsigned count)

Description

The prototype to **memset( )** is found in both **string.h** and **mem.h**.

The **memset( )** function copies the low-order byte of *ch* into the first *count* characters of the array pointed to by *buf*. It returns *buf*.

The most common use of **memset( )** is to initialize a region of memory to some known value.

Example

This fragment first initializes to null the first 100 bytes of the array pointed to by *buf* and then sets the first 10 bytes to '**X**' and displays the string "**XXXXXXXXXX**":

```
memset(buf, '\0', 100);
memset(buf, 'X', 10);
printf((char *) buf);
```

Related Functions

memcpy( ), memcmp( ), memmove( )

char *strcat(char *str1, char *str2)

Description

The prototype for **strcat( )** is found in **string.h**.

The **strcat( )** function concatenates a copy of *str2* to *str1* and terminates *str1* with a null. The null terminator originally ending *str1* is overwritten by the first character of *str2*. The string *str2* is untouched by the operation.

The **strcat( )** function returns *str1*.

Remember that no bounds checking takes place, so it is

the programmer's responsibility to ensure that *str1* is large enough to hold both its original contents and the contents of *str2*.

Example

This program appends the first string read from **stdin** to the second. For example, assuming the user enters **hello** and **there**, the program prints **therehello**.

```
#include "string.h"

main()
{
  char s1[80], s2[80];

  gets(s1);
  gets(s2);

  strcat(s2, s1);
  printf(s2);
}
```

Related Functions

strchr(), strcmp(), strcpy()

char *strchr(char *str, char ch)

Description

The prototype for **strchr()** is found in **string.h**.

The **strchr()** function returns a pointer to the first occurrence of *ch* in the string pointed to by *str*. If no match is found, it returns a null pointer.

Example

This program prints the string **is a test**:

```
#include "string.h"

main()
{
  char *p;

  p = strchr("this is a test", ' ');
  printf(p);
}
```

Related Functions

strpbrk( ), strstr( ), strtok( ), strspn( )

int strcmp(char *str1, char *str2)

Description

The prototype for the **strcmp( )** function is found in **string.h**.

The **strcmp( )** function lexicographically compares two null-terminated strings and returns an integer based on the outcome, as shown here:

Value	Meaning
Less than 0	*str1* is less than *str2*
0	*str1* is equal to *str2*
Greater than 0	*str1* is greater than *str2*

Example

The following function can be used as a password-verification routine. It returns 0 on failure and 1 on success.

```
password()
{
  char s[80],*strcmp();

  printf("enter password: ");
  gets(s);

  if(strcmp(s, "pass")) {
    printf("invalid password\n");
    return 0;
  }
  return 1;
}
```

Related Functions

strchr( ), strcpy( ), strncmp( )

char *strcpy(char *str1, char *str2)

Description

The prototype for **strcpy( )** is found in **string.h**.

The **strcpy( )** function is used to copy the contents of *str2* into *str1; str2* must be a pointer to a null-terminated string. The **strcpy( )** function returns a pointer to *str1*.

If *str1* and *str2* overlap, the behavior of **strcpy( )** is undefined.

Example

The following code fragment copies **hello** into string *str:*

```
char str[80];
strcpy(str, "hello");
```

Related Functions

strchr( ), strcmp( ), memcpy( ), strncmp( )

int strcspn(char *str1, char *str2)

Description

The prototype for the **strcspn( )** function is found in **string.h**.

The **strcspn( )** function returns the length of the initial substring of the string pointed to by *str1* that is made up only of those characters not contained in the string pointed to by *str2*. Stated differently, **strcspn( )** returns the index of the first character in the string pointed to by *str1* that matches any of the characters in the string pointed to by *str2*.

Example

This program prints the number 8:

```
#include "string.h"

main()
{
  int len;

  len = strcspn("this is a test", "ab");
  printf("%d", len);
}
```

Related Functions

strpbrk(), strstr(), strtok(), strrchr()

char *strdup(char *str)

Description

The prototype for **strdup()** is found in **string.h**.

The **strdup()** function allocates enough memory, through a call to **malloc()**, to hold a duplicate of the string pointed to by *str* and then copies that string into the allocated region and returns a pointer to it.

Example

This fragment duplicates the string *str:*

```
char str[80], *p;

strcpy(str, "this is a test");

p = strdup(str);
```

Related Function

strcpy()

char *strerror(char *str)

Description

The prototype for the **strerror()** function is found in **string.h**.

The **strerror()** function lets you display your own error message followed by a colon and the most recent error message generated by the program. It returns a pointer to the entire string.

Example

This fragment prints that the function called **swap()** encountered an error:

```
swap()
{
   .
   .
   .

   if(error) printf(strerror("error in swap"));
```

Related Function

perror()

unsigned strlen(char *str)

Description

The prototype for **strlen()** is found in **string.h**.

The **strlen()** function returns the length of the null-terminated string pointed to by *str*. The null is not counted.

Example

The next code fragment prints the number **5** on the screen.

```
strcpy(s, "hello");
printf("%d", strlen(s));
```

Related Functions

strchr( ), strcmp( ), memcpy( ), strncmp( )

char *strlwr(char *str)

Description

The prototype for **strlwr( )** is found in **string.h**.
    The **strlwr( )** function converts the string pointed to by *str* to lowercase.

Example

This program prints **this is a test** on the screen:

```
#include  "string.h"
main()
{
  char s[80];
  strcpy(s, "THIS IS A TEST");
  strlwr(s);
  printf(s); }
```

Related Function

strupr( )

char *strncat(char *str1, char *str2, int count)

Description

The prototype for the **strncat( )** function is found in **string.h**.
    The **strncat( )** function concatenates no more than *count* characters of the string pointed to by *str2* to the string

pointed to by *str1* and terminates *str1* with a null. The null terminator originally ending *str1* is overwritten by the first character of *str2*. The string *str2* is untouched by the operation.

The **strncat( )** function returns *str1*.

Remember that no bounds checking takes place, so it is the programmer's responsibility to ensure that *str1* is large enough to hold both its original contents and those of *str2*.

Example

This program appends the first string read from **stdin** to the second and prevents an array overflow from occurring in *str1*. For example, if the user enters **hello** and **there**, the program prints **therehello**.

```
#include "string.h"

main()
{
  char s1[80], s2[80];
  unsigned int len;

  gets(s1);
  gets(s2);

  /* compute how many chars will actually fit */
  len = 79-strlen(s2);

  strncat(s2, s1, len);
  printf(s2);
}
```

Related Functions

strnchr( ), strncmp( ), strncpy( ), strcat( )

int strncmp(char *str1, char *str2, int count)

Description

The prototype for the **strncmp( )** function is found in **string.h**.

The **strncmp( )** function lexicographically compares no more than *count* characters from the two null-terminated strings and returns an integer based on the outcome, as shown here:

Value	Meaning
Less than 0	*str1* is less than *str2*
0	*str1* is equal to *str2*
Greater than 0	*str1* is greater than *str2*

If there are fewer than *count* characters in either string, the comparison ends when the first null is encountered.

Example

The following function compares the first eight characters of the two file names specified on the command line to determine if they are the same:

```
#include "string.h"

main(int argc, char *argv[])
{
  if(!strncmp(argv[1], argv[2],8))
    printf("the filenames are the same\n");
}
```

Related Functions

strnchr( ), strcmp( ), strncpy( )

char *strncpy(char *dest, char *source, int count)

Description

The prototype for **strncpy( )** is found in **string.h**.

The **strncpy( )** function is used to copy up to *count* characters from the string pointed to by *source* into the string pointed to by *dest*. The *source* must be a pointer to a null-terminated string. The **strncpy()** function returns a pointer to *dest*.

If *dest* and *source* overlap, the behavior of **strncpy()** is undefined.

If the string pointed to by *source* has fewer than *count* characters, nulls are added to the end of *dest* until *count* characters have been copied.

Alternately, if the string pointed to by *source* is longer than *count* characters, the resulting string pointed to by *dest* is not null-terminated.

Example

The following code fragment copies at most 79 characters of *str1* into *str2*, thus ensuring that no array boundary overflow will occur:

```
char str1[128], str2[80];
gets(str1);
strncpy(str2, str1, 79);
```

Related Functions

strchr(), **strncmp()**, **memcpy()**, **strncat()**

char *strnset(char *str, char ch, unsigned count)

Description

The prototype for **strnset()** is found in **string.h**.

The **strnset()** function sets the first *count* characters in the string pointed to by *str* to the value of *ch*.

Example

This fragment sets the first 10 characters of *str* to the value '**x**':

```
strnset(str, 'x', 10);
```

Related Function

strset( )

char *strpbrk(char *str1, char *str2)

Description

The prototype for **strpbrk( )** is found in **string.h**.

The **strpbrk( )** function returns a pointer to the first character in the string pointed to by *str1* that matches any character in the string pointed to by *str2*. The null terminators are not included. If there are no matches, a null pointer is returned.

Example

This program prints the message s **is a test** on the screen:

```
#include "string.h"

main()
{
   char *p;

   p = strpbrk("this is a test", " absj");
   printf(p);
}
```

Related Functions

strrchr( ), strstr( ), strtok( ), strspn( )

char *strrchr(char *str, char ch)

Description

The prototype to **strrchr( )** is found in **string.h**.

The **strrchr( )** function returns a pointer to the last

occurrence of the low-order byte of *ch* in the string pointed to by *str*. If no match is found, it returns a null pointer.

Example

This program prints the string **is a test**:

```
#include "string.h"

main()
{
  char *p;

  p = strrchr("this is a test", 'i');
  printf(p);
}
```

Related Functions

strpbrk(), strstr(), strtok(), strspn()

char *strrev(char *str)

Description

The prototype for **strrev()** is found in **string.h**.

The **strrev()** function reverses all characters, except the null terminator, in the string pointed to by *str*.

Example

This program prints **hello** backward on the screen:

```
#include "string.h"

char s[] = "hello"

main()
{
  strrev(s);

  printf(s);
}
```

Related Function

strset( )

char *strset(char *str, char ch)

Description

The prototype for **strset( )** is found in **string.h**.

The **strnset( )** function sets all characters in the string pointed to by *str* to the value of *ch*.

Example

This fragment fills the string *str* with the value 'x'.

```
strnset(str, 'x');
```

Related Function

strnset( )

int strspn(char *str1, char *str2)

Description

The **strspn( )** function returns the length of the initial substring of the string pointed to by *str1* that is made up only of those characters contained in the string pointed to by *str2*. Stated differently, **strspn( )** returns the index of the first character in the string pointed to by *str1* that does not match any of the characters in the string pointed to by *str2*.

Example

This program prints the number 8:

```
#include "string.h"
main()
{
   int len;

   len = strspn("this is a test", "siht ");
   printf("%d",len);
}
```

Related Functions

strpbrk( ), strstr( ), strtok( ), strrchr( )

char *strstr(char *str1, char *str2)

Description

The prototype for **strstr( )** is found in **string.h.**

The **strstr( )** function returns a pointer to the first occurrence in the string pointed to by *str1* of the string pointed to by *str2* (except *str2's* null terminator). It returns a null pointer if no match is found.

Example

This program displays the message **is is a test:**

```
#include "string.h"

main()
{
   char *p;

   p = strstr("this is a test", "is");
   printf(p);
}
```

Related Functions

strpbrk( ), strspn( ), strtok( ), strrchr( ), strchr( ), strcspn( )

char *strtok(char *str1, char *str2)

Description

The prototype for **strtok( )** is in **string.h**.

The **strtok( )** function returns a pointer to the next token in the string pointed to by *str1*. The characters making up the string pointed to by *str2* are the delimiters that determine the token. A null pointer is returned when there is no token to return.

The first time **strtok( )** is called, *str1* is actually used in the call. Subsequent calls use a null pointer for the first argument. In this way the entire string can be reduced to its tokens.

It is important to understand that the **strtok( )** function modifies the string pointed to by *str1*. Each time a token is found, a null is placed where the delimiter was found. In this way **strtok( )** continues to advance through the string.

It is possible to use a different set of delimiters for each call to **strtok( )**.

Example

This program tokenizes the string **"The summer soldier, the sunshine patriot"** with spaces and commas as the delimiters. The output is **The|summer|soldier|the|sunshine| patriot**.

```
#include "string.h"

main()
{
  char *p;

  p = strtok("The summer soldier, the sunshine patriot"," ");
  printf(p);
  do {
    p=strtok('\0', ", ");
    if(p) printf("|%s", p);
  } while(p);
}
```

Related Functions

strpbrk( ), strspn( ), strtok( ), strrchr( ), strchr( ), strcspn( )

char ∗strupr(char ∗str)

Description

The prototype for **strupr( )** is found in **string.h**.

The **strupr( )** function converts the string pointed to by *str* to uppercase.

Example

This program prints **THIS IS A TEST** on the screen:

```
#include "string.h"
main()
{
  char s[80];
  strcpy(s, "this is a test");
  strupr(s);
  printf(s); }
```

Related Functions

strlwr( )

int tolower(int ch)

Description

The prototype for **tolower( )** is found in **ctype.h**.

The **tolower** function returns the lowercase equivalent of *ch* if *ch* is a letter; otherwise it returns *ch* unchanged.

Example

This code fragment displays **q**:

```
putchar(tolower('Q'));
```

Related Functions

toupper( )

int toupper(int ch)

Description

The prototype for **toupper( )** is found in **ctype.h**.

The **toupper** function returns the uppercase equivalent of *ch* if *ch* is a letter; otherwise it returns *ch* unchanged.

Example

This displays **A**:

```
putchar(toupper('a'));
```

Related Functions

tolower( )

Mathematical Functions

The Turbo C library defines several mathematical functions that fall into the following categories:

- Trigonometric functions
- Hyperbolic functions
- Exponential and logarithmic functions
- Miscellaneous functions

All the math functions require the header **math.h** to be included in any program using them because they all return data of type **double**. In addition to declaring the math functions, this header defines three macros called **EDOM**, **ERANGE**, and **HUGE_VAL**. If an argument to a math function is not in the domain for which it is defined, an implementation-defined value is returned and the global **errno** is set equal to **EDOM**. If a routine produces a result that is too large to be represented by a **double** an overflow occurs. This causes the routine to return **HUGE_VAL** and **errno** is set to **ERANGE**, indicating a range error. If an underflow happens, the routine returns 0 and sets **errno** to **ERANGE**.

double acos(double arg)

Description

The prototype for **acos()** is in **math.h**.

The **acos()** function returns the arc cosine of *arg*. The argument to **acos()** must be in the range −1 to 1; otherwise a domain error occurs. The return value is also in the range −1 to 1. The value of *arg* is specified in radians.

Example

This program prints the arc cosines, in one-tenth increments, of the values −1 through 1:

```
#include "math.h"

main()
{
  double val = -1.0;

  do {
    printf("arc cosine of %f is %f\n", val, acos(val));
    val += 0.1;
  } while(val <= 1.0);
}
```

Related Functions

asin(), atan(), atan2(), sin(), cos(), tan(), sinh(), cosh(), tanh()

double asin(double arg)

Description

The prototype for **asin()** is in **math.h**.

The **asin()** function returns the arc sine of *arg*. The argument to **asin()** must be in the range −1 to 1; otherwise a derror occurs. Its return value is in the range −**pi/2** to **pi/2**. The value of *arg* is specified in radians.

Example

This program prints the arc sines, in one-tenth increments, of the values −1 through 1:

```
#include "math.h"

main()
{
  double val =- 1.0;
```

```
do {
   printf("arc sine of %f is %f\n", val, asin(val));
   val += 0.1;
} while(val <= 1.0);
}
```

Related Functions

asin( ), atan( ), atan2( ), sin( ), cos( ), tan( ), sinh( ), cosh( ), tanh( )

double atan(double arg)

Description

The prototype for **atan( )** is in **math.h**.

The **atan( )** function returns the arc tangent of *arg*. The value of *arg* must be in the range −1 to 1; otherwise a domain error occurs. The value of *arg* is specified in radians.

Example

This program prints the arc tangents, in one-tenth increments, of the values −1 through 1:

```
#include "math.h"

main()
{
  double val =- 1.0;

  do {
    printf("arc tangent of %f is %f\n", val, atan(val));
    val += 0.1;
  } while(val <= 1.0);
}
```

Related Functions

asin( ), acos( ), atan2( ), tan( ), cos( ), sin( ), sinh( ), cosh( ), tanh( )

double atan2(double y, double x)

Description

The prototype for **atan2()** is in **math.h**.

The **atan2()** function returns the arc tangent of **y/x**. It uses the signs of its arguments to compute the quadrant of the return value.

Example

This program prints the arc tangents, in one-tenth increments, of y, from −1 through 1:

```
#include "math.h"

main()
{
  double y = -1.0;

  do {
    printf("atan2 of %f is %f\n", y, atan2(y, 1.0));
    y += 0.1;
  } while(y <= 1.0);
}
```

Related Functions

asin(), acos(), atan(), tan(), cos(), sin(), sinh(), cosh(), tanh()

double cabs(struct complex znum)

Description

The prototype for **cabs()** is in **math.h**.

The **cabs()** macro returns the absolute value of a complex number. The structure **complex** is defined as

```
struct complex {
  double x;
  double y;
}
```

If an overflow occurs, **HUGE—VAL** is returned and **errno** is set to **ERANGE** (out of range).

Example

This code prints the absolute value of a complex number that has a real part equal to 1 and an imaginary part equal to 2:

```
#include "math.h"

main()
{
  struct complex z;

  z.x = 1;
  z.y = 2;

  printf("%f", cabs(z));
}
```

Related Function

abs( )

double ceil(double num)

Description

The prototype for **ceil( )** is in **math.h**.

The **ceil( )** function returns the smallest integer (represented as a **double( )** not less than *num*. For example, given 1.02, **ceil( )** would return 2.0. Given −1.02, **ceil( )** would return −1.

Example

This fragment prints **10** on the screen:

```
printf("%f", ceil(9.9));
```

Related Functions

floor( ), **fmod( )**

double cos(double arg)

Description

The prototype for **cos( )** is in **math.h**.

The **cos( )** function returns the cosine of *arg*. The value of *arg* must be in radians. The return value is in the range −1 to 1.

Example

This program prints the cosines, in one-tenth increments, of the values −1 through 1:

```
#include "math.h"

main()
{
  double val =- 1.0;

  do {
    printf("cosine of %f is %f\n", val, cos(val));
    val += 0.1;
  } while(val <= 1.0);
}
```

Related Functions

asin( ), **acos( )**, **atan2( )**, **atan( )**, **tan( )**, **sin( )**, **sinh( )**, **cosh( )**, **tanh( )**

double cosh(double arg)

Description

The prototype for **cosh( )** is in **math.h**.

The **cosh( )** function returns the hyperbolic cosine of *arg*.

The value of *arg* must be in radians.

Example

This program prints the hyperbolic cosines, in one-tenth increments, of the values −1 through 1:

```
#include "math.h"

main()
{
  double val =- 1.0;

  do {
    printf("hyperbolic cosine of %f is %f\n", val, cosh(val));
    val += 0.1;
  } while(val <= 1.0);
}
```

Related Functions

asin( ), acos( ), atan2( ), atan( ), tan( ), sin( ), cosh( ), tanh( )

double exp(double arg)

Description

The prototype for **exp( )** is in **math.h**.

The **exp( )** function returns the natural logarithm *e* raised to the *arg* power.

Example

This fragment displays the value of *e* (rounded to 2.718282):

```
printf("value of e to the first: %f", exp(1.0));
```

Related Function

log( )

double fabs(double num)

Description

The prototype for **fabs()** is in **math.h**.
The **fabs()** function returns the absolute value of *num*.

Example

This program prints **1.0 1.0** on the screen:

```
#include "math.h"

main()
{
   printf("%1.1f %1.1f", fabs(1.0), fabs(-1.0));
}
```

Related Function

abs()

double floor(double num)

Description

The prototype for **floor()** is in **math.h**.
The **floor()** function returns the largest integer (represented as a **double**) not greater than *num*. For example, given 1.02, **floor()** would return 1.0. Given −1.02, **floor()** would return −2.0.

Example

This fragment prints **10** on the screen:

```
printf("%f",floor(10.9));
```

Related Functions

fceil(), **fmod()**

double fmod(double x, double y)

Description

The prototype for **fmod()** is in **math.h**.
The **fmod()** function returns the remainder of **x/y**.

Example

This program prints **1.0** on the screen, which represents the remainder of 10/3:

```
#include "math.h"

main()
{
   printf("%1.1f", fmod(10.0, 3.0));
}
```

Related Functions

ceil(), floor(), fabs()

double frexp(double num, int *exp)

Description

The prototype for **frexp()** is in **math.h**.
The **frexp()** function decomposes the number *num* into a mantissa in the range 0.5 to less than 1, and an integer exponent such that **num=mantissa*2@+(exp)**. The mantissa is returned by the function, and the exponent is stored at the variable pointed to by *exp*.

Example

This code fragment prints **0.625** for the mantissa and **4** for the exponent:

```
int e;
double f;

f = frexp(10.0, &e);
printf("%f %d", f, e);
```

Related Function

ldexp( )

double hypot(double x, double y)

Description

The prototype for **hypot( )** is in **math.h**.

The **hypot( )** function returns the length of the hypotenuse of a right triangle given the lengths of the other two sides.

Example

This prints the value **2.236068**:

```
printf("%f", hypot(2, 1));
```

double ldexp(double num, int exp)

Description

The prototype for **ldexp( )** is in **math.h**.

The **ldexp( )** returns the value of **num*2@+(exp)**. If overflow occurs, **HUGE_VAL** is returned.

Example

This program displays the number **4**:

```
#include "math.h"

main()
{
   printf("%f", ldexp(1, 2));
}
```

Related Functions

frexp( ), modf( )

double log(double num)

Description

The prototype for **log( )** is in **math.h**.

The **log( )** function returns the natural logarithm for *num*. A domain error occurs if *num* is negative and a range error occurs if the argument is 0.

Example

This program prints the natural logarithms for the numbers 1 through 10:

```
#include "math.h"

main()
{
  double val = 1.0;

  do {
    printf("%f %f\n", val, log(val));
    val++;
  } while (val < 11.0);
}
```


Related Function

log10( )

double log10(double num)

Description

The prototype for **log10( )** is in **math.h**.

The **log10( )** function returns the base 10 logarithm for *num*. A domain error occurs if *num* is negative, and a range error occurs if the argument is 0.

Example

This program prints the base 10 logarithms for the numbers 1 through 10:

```
#include "math.h"

main()
{
  double val = 1.0;

  do {
    printf("%f %f\n", val, log10(val));
    val++;
  } while (val < 11.0);
}
```

Related Function

log( )

int matherr(struct exception *err)

Description

The prototype for **matherr( )** is in **math.h**.

The **matherr( )** function allows you to create custom math error-handling routines. The **matherr( )** function is called by **—matherr( )** whenever a math error occurs. (You should never call **—matherr( )** or **matherr( )** directly.) If **matherr( )** returns 0, **—matherr( )** reports the problem in the normal way. However, if **matherr( )** returns nonzero, no error message is printed and the value of **errno** is unchanged. By default, Turbo C provides a dummy **matherr( )** function that returns 0.

The **matherr( )** function is called with an argument of type **exception**, which is shown here:

```
struct exception {
  int type;
  char *name;
  double arg1, arg2;
  double retval;
}
```

The *type* element holds the type of the error that occurred. Its value will be one of the following enumerated values.

Symbol	Meaning
DOMAIN	Domain error
SING	Result is a singularity
OVERFLOW	Overflow error
UNDERFLOW	Underflow error
TLOSS	Total loss of significant digits

The *name* element holds a pointer to a string that holds the name of the functions in which the error took place. The *arg1* and *arg2* elements hold the arguments to the function that caused the error. If the function takes only one argument, it will be in *arg1*. Finally, *retval* holds the default return value for **matherr( )**. You can modify this value.

double modf(double num, int *i)

Description

The prototype for **modf( )** is in **math.h**.

The **modf( )** function decomposes *num* into its integer and fractional parts. It returns the fractional portion and places the integer part in the variable pointed to by *i*.

Example

This fragment prints **10** and **0.123** on the screen:

```
int i;
double f;

f = modf(10.123, &i);
printf("%d %f", i, f);
```

Related Functions

frexp( ), **ldexp( )**

double poly(double x, int n, double c[])

Description

The prototype for **poly( )** is in **math.h**.

The **poly( )** function evaluates a polynomial in n of degree x with coefficients *c[0]* through *c[n]* and returns the result. For example, if $n=3$, the polynomial evaluated is

$$c[3]x + c[2]x + c[1]x + c[0]$$

Example

This program prints 6 on the screen:

```
#include "math.h"

main()
{
  double c[2];

  c[0] = 3;
  c[1] = 2;
  c[2] = 1;

  printf("%f", poly(1, 2, c));
}
```

Related Function

hypot( )

double pow(double base, double exp)

Description

The prototype for **pow( )** is in **math.h**.

The **pow( )** function returns *base* raised to the **exp** power (**base@+(exp)**). A domain error occurs if *base* is 0 and **exp** is less than or equal to 0. An overflow produces a range error.

Example

This program prints the first ten powers of 10:

```
#include "math.h"

main()
{
  double x=10.0, y=0.0;

  do {
    printf("%f", pow(x, y));
    y++:
  } while(y<11);
}
```

Related Functions

exp( ), log( ), sqrt( )

double sin(double arg)

Description

The prototype for **sin( )** is in **math.h**.

The **sin( )** function returns the sine of *arg*. The value of *arg* must be in radians.

Example

This program prints the sines, in one-tenth increments, of the values −1 through 1.

```
#include "math.h"

main()
{
  double val =- 1.0;

  do {
    printf("sine of %f is %f\n", val, sin(val));
    val += 0.1;
  } while(val <= 1.0);
}
```

Related Functions

asin(), acos(), atan2(), atan(), tan(), cos(), sinh(), cosh(), tanh()

double sinh(double arg)

Description

The prototype for **sinh()** is in **math.h**.

The **sinh()** function returns the hyperbolic sine of *arg*. The value of *arg* must be in radians.

Example

This program prints the hyperbolic sines, in one-tenth increments, of the values −1 through 1:

```
#include "math.h"

main()
{
  double val =- 1.0;

  do {
    printf("hyperbolic sine of %f is %f\n", val, sinh(val));
    val += 0.1;
  } while(val <= 1.0);
}
```

Related Functions

asin( ), acos( ), atan2( ), atan( ), tan( ), cos( ), tanh( ), cosh( )

double sqrt(double num)

Description

The prototype for **sqrt( )** is in **math.h**.

The **sqrt( )** function returns the square root of *num*. If the function is called with a negative argument, a domain error occurs.

Example

This fragment prints 4 on the screen:

```
printf("%f", sqrt(16.0));
```

Related Functions

exp( ), log( ), pow( )

double tan(double arg)

Description

The prototype for **tan( )** is in **math.h**.

The **tan( )** function returns the tangent of *arg*. The value of *arg* must be in radians.

Example

This program prints the tangent, in one-tenth increments, of the values −1 through 1:

```
#include "math.h"

main()
```

```
{
  double val =- 1.0;

  do {
    printf("tangent of %f is %f\n", val, tan(val));
    val += 0.1;
  } while(val <= 1.0);
}
```

Related Functions

asin( ), atan( ), atan2( ), cos( ), sin( ), sinh( ), cosh( ), tanh( )

double tanh(double arg)

Description

The prototype for **tanh( )** is in **math.h.**

The **tanh( )** function returns the hyperbolic tangent of *arg*. The value of *arg* must be in radians.

Example

This program prints the hyperbolic tangent, in one-tenth increments, of the values −1 through 1:

```
#include "math.h"

main()
{
  double val =- 1.0;

  do {
    printf("Hyperbolic tangent of %f is %f\n", val, tanh(val));
    val += 0.1;
  } while(val <= 1.0);
}
```

Related Functions

asin( ), atan( ), atan2( ), cos( ), cosh( ), sin( )

Time-, Date-, and System-Related Functions

This chapter covers those functions that in one way or another are more operating-system sensitive than others. Of the functions defined by the proposed ANSI standard, these include the time and date functions, which relate to the operating system by using its time and date information.

Also discussed in this chapter is a category of functions that allow direct operating system interfacing. None of these functions is defined by the proposed ANSI standard, because each operating environment is different. However, Turbo C provides extensive DOS and BIOS interfacing functions.

The functions that deal with the system time and date require the header file **time.h** for their prototypes. This header also defines two types. The type **time_t** is capable of representing the system time and date as a long integer. This is referred to as the *calendar time*. The structure type **tm** holds the date and time broken down into elements. The **tm** structure is defined as shown here:

```
struct tm {
   int tm_sec;   /* seconds, 0-59 */
   int tm_min;   /* minutes, 0-59 */
   int tm_hour;  /* hours, 0-23 */
   int tm_mday;  /* day of the month, 1-31 */
   int tm_mon;   /* months since Jan, 0-11 */
   int tm_year;  /* years from 1900 */
   int tm_wday;  /* days since Sunday, 0-6 */
   int tm_yday;  /* days since Jan 1, 0-365 */
   int tm_isdst  /* Daylight Savings Time indicator */
}
```

The value of **tm—isdst** will be positive if daylight savings time is in effect, 0 if it is not in effect, and negative if no information is available. This form of the time and date is called *broken-down time*.

Turbo C also includes some nonstandard time and date functions that bypass the normal time and date system and interface more closely with DOS. The functions use structures of type **time** or **date**, which are defined in **dos.h**. Their declarations are

```
struct date {
  int da_year; /* year */
  char da_day; /* day of month */
  char da_mon; /* month, Jan=1 */
}

struct time {
  unsigned char ti_min;  /* minutes */
  unsigned char ti_hour; /* hours */
  unsigned char ti_hund; /* hundredths of seconds */
  unsigned char ti_sec;  /* seconds */
}
```

The DOS interfacing functions require the header **dos.h**. The file **dos.h** defines a union that corresponds to the registers of the 8088/86 CPU and is used by some of the system interfacing functions. It is defined as the union of two structures to allow each register to be accessed by either word or byte.

```
/*
        Copyright (c) Borland International Inc. 1987
        All Rights Reserved.
*/


struct WORDREGS
        {
        unsigned int    ax, bx, cx, dx, si, di, cflag;
        };
```

```
struct BYTEREGS
        {
        unsigned char    al, ah, bl, bh, cl, ch, dl, dh;
        };

union   REGS   {
        struct  WORDREGS x;
        struct  BYTEREGS h;
        };
```

Also defined in **dos.h** is the structure type **SREGS**, which is used by some functions to set the segment registers. It is defined as

```
struct  SREGS   {
   unsigned int  es;
   unsigned int  cs;
   unsigned int  ss;
   unsigned int  ds;
};
```

Several of the functions described here interface directly to the ROM-BIOS—the lowest level of the operating system. These functions require the header **bios.h**.

A few functions require predefined structures that have not been discussed. Definitions for these structures will be described as needed.

int absread(int drive, int numsects, int sectnum, void *buf)
int abswrite(int drive, int numsects, int sectnum, void *buf)

Description

The prototypes for **absread( )** and **abswrite( )** are in **dos.h**.

The functions **absread( )** and **abswrite( )** perform absolute disk read and write operations, respectively. They bypass the logical structure of the disk and ignore files or directories. Instead they operate on the disk at the sector specified in *sectnum*. The drive is specified in *drive* with drive A being equal to 0. The number of sectors to read or write is specified in *numsects*, and the information is read into or from the region of memory pointed to by *buf*.

These functions return 0 on success and nonzero on failure. The return value is determined by DOS, and you will need DOS technical documentation to determine the nature of any error that occurs.

You must use great caution when calling **abswrite( )** because it is very easy to corrupt the disk directory or a file.

Example

This program displays the contents of the specified disk sector in both hexadecimal and character form:

```c
#include "dos.h"

main()
{
  char buf[512];
  int sector, i, j;

  for(;;) {
    printf("Enter sector: ");
    scanf("%d", &sector);
    if(sector==-1) exit(0);
    absread(3, 1, sector, buf); /* read drive C */
    for(i=0, j=0; i<512; i++) {
      printf("%x ", buf[i]);
      if(!(i%16)) {
        for( ; j<i; j++) printf("%c", buf[j]);
        printf("\n");
      }
    }
  }
}
```

Related Functions

read( ), fread( ), write( ), fwrite( )

char *asctime(struct tm *ptr)

Description

The prototype for **asctime( )** is in **time.h**.

The **asctime( )** function returns a pointer to a string that is the conversion of the information stored in the structure pointed to by *ptr* into the following form:

day month date hours:minutes:seconds year \n \0

For example:

Wed Jun 19 12:05:34 1999

The structure pointer passed to **asctime( )** is generally obtained from either **localtime( )** or **gmtime( )**.

The buffer used by **asctime( )** to hold the formatted output string is a statically allocated character array and is overwritten each time the function is called. If you wish to save the contents of the string, it is necessary to copy it elsewhere.

Example

This program displays the local time defined by the system:

```
#include "time.h"
#include "stddef.h"

main()
{
  struct tm *ptr;
  time_t lt;

  lt=time(NULL);
  ptr=localtime(&lt);
  printf(asctime(ptr));
}
```

Related Functions

localtime( ), gmtime( ), time( ), ctime( )

int bdos(int fnum, unsigned dx, unsigned al)
int bdosptr(int fnum, void *dsdx, unsigned al)

Description

The prototype for **bdos** is in **dos.h**.

This function is not part of the proposed ANSI standard.

The **bdos( )** function is used to access the DOS system call specified by *fnum*. It first places the values *dx* and *al* into the **DX** and **AL** registers and then executes an INT 21H instruction.

If you will be passing a pointer argument to DOS, use the **bdosptr( )** function instead of **bdos( )**. Although for the tiny, small, and medium memory models the two functions are operationally equivalent, when the larger memory models are used, 20-bit pointers are required. When this is the case, the pointer will be passed in **DS:DX**.

Both the **bdos( )** and **bdosptr( )** functions return the value of the **AX** register, which is used by DOS to return information.

Example

This program reads characters directly from the keyboard, bypassing all of C's I/O functions, until a **q** is typed:

```
/* do raw keyboard reads */
#include "dos.h"

main()
{
  char ch;

  while((ch=bdos(1, 0, 0))!='q') ;
  /* ... */
}
```

Related Functions

intdos( ), intdosx( )

int bioscom(int cmd, char byte, int port)

Description

The prototype for **bioscom( )** is in **bios.h**.

The **bioscom( )** function is used to manipulate the RS232 asynchronous communication port specified in *port*. Its operation is determined by the value of *cmd*, whose values are shown here:

Command	Meaning
0	Initialize the port
1	Send a character
2	Receive a character
3	Return the port status

Before using the serial port you will probably want to initialize it to something other than its default setting. To do this, call **bioscom( )** with *cmd* set to 0. The exact way the port is set up is determined by the value of *byte*, which is encoded with initialization parameters, as shown here:

```
Bit Numbers:        7 6 5  4 3  2  1 0
baud ───────────────────┘    │  │   │
parity ──────────────────────┘  │   │
stop bits ──────────────────────┘   │
data bits ──────────────────────────┘
```

The baud is encoded as shown here:

Baud	Bit Pattern
9600	1 1 1
4800	1 1 0
2400	1 0 1
1200	1 0 0
600	0 1 1

300	0 1 0
150	0 0 1
110	0 0 0

The parity bits are encoded as shown here:

Parity	Bit Pattern
No parity	0 0 or 1 0
Odd	0 1
Even	1 1

The number of stop bits is determined by bit 2 of the serial port initialization byte. If it is 1, 2 stop bits are used; otherwise 1 stop bit is used. Finally, the number of data bits is set by the code in bits 1 and 0 of the initialization byte. Of the four possible bit patterns, only two are valid. If bits 1 and 0 contain the pattern 1 0, 7 data bits are used. If they contain 1 1, 8 data bits are used.

For example, if you want to set the port to 9600 baud, even parity, 1 stop bit, and 8 data bits, you would use this bit pattern:

```
Bit Numbers:      1 1 1   1 1   0   1 1
baud──────────────────┘     │   │   │
parity────────────────────────┘   │   │
stop bits──────────────────────────┘   │
data bits──────────────────────────────┘
```

In decimal, this works out to 251.

The return value of **bioscom( )** is always a 16-bit quantity. The high-order byte contains the status bits, and they have the following values.

Meaning When Set	Bit
Data ready	0
Overrun error	1
Parity error	2
Framing error	3
Break-detect error	4
Transfer holding register empty	5
Transfer shift register empty	6
Time-out error	7

If *cmd* is set to 0, 1, or 3, the low-order byte is encoded as shown here:

Meaning When Set	Bit
Change in clear-to-send	0
Change in data-set-ready	1
Trailing-edge ring detector	2
Change in line signal	3
Clear-to-send	4
Data-set-ready	5
Ring indicator	6
Line signal detected	7

When *cmd* has a value of 2, the lower-order byte contains the value received by the port.

Example

This initializes port 0 to 9600 baud, even parity, 1 stop bit, and 8 data bits:

```
bioscom(0, 251, 0);
```

int biosdisk(int cmd, int drive, int head, int track, int sector, int nsects, void *buf)

Description

The prototype for **biosdisk( )** is in **bios.h**.

The **biosdisk( )** function performs BIOS-level disk operations using interrupt 0x13. These operations ignore the logical structure of the disk including files. All operations take place on sectors.

The drive affected is specified in *drive* with 0 corresponding to A, 1 to B, and so on for floppy drives. The first fixed disk is drive 0x80, the second 0x81, and so on. The part of the disk that is operated on is specified in *head*, *track*, and *sector*. You should refer to the IBM PC technical reference manual for details of operation and options of the BIOS-level disk routines. Keep in mind that direct control of the disk requires thorough and intimate knowledge of both the hardware and DOS. It is best avoided except in unusual situations.

Related Functions

absread( ), **abswrite( )**

int biosequip(void)

Description

The prototype for **biosequip( )** is found in **bios.h**.

The **biosequip( )** function returns what equipment is in the computer encoded as a 16-bit value. This value is encoded as shown here:

Bit	Equipment
0	Must boot from the floppy drive
1	80×87 math coprocessor installed
2, 3	Motherboard RAM size

	0 0: 16KB
	0 1: 32KB
	1 0: 48KB
	1 1: 64KB
4, 5	Initial video mode
	0 0: unused
	0 1: 40×25 BW, color adapter
	1 0: 80×25 BW, color adapter
	1 1: 80×25, monochrome adapter
6, 7	Number of floppy drives
	0 0: one
	0 1: two
	1 0: three
	1 1: four
8	DMA chip installed
9, 10, 11	Number of serial ports
	0 0 0: zero
	0 0 1: one
	0 1 0: two
	0 1 1: three
	1 0 0: four
	1 0 1: five
	1 1 0: six
	1 1 1: seven
12	Game adapter installed
13	Serial printer installed (PCjr only)
14, 15	Number of printers
	0 0: zero
	0 1: one
	1 0: two
	1 1: three

Example

The program on the following page displays the number of floppy drives installed in the computer.

```
#include "bios.h"
main()
{
  unsigned eq;
  eq = biosequip();
  eq >>= 6; /* shift bits 6 and 7 into lowest position */
  printf("number of disk drives: %d", eq & 3)+1;
}
```

Related Function

bioscom( )

int bioskey(int cmd)

Description

The prototype for **bioskey( )** is in **bios.h**.

The **bioskey( )** function performs direct keyboard operations. The value of *cmd* determines what operation is executed.

If *cmd* is 0, **bioskey( )** returns the next key pressed on the keyboard. (It will wait until a key is pressed.) It returns a 16-bit quantity that consists of two different values. The low-order byte contains the ASCII character code if a "normal" key is pressed. It will contain 0 if a "special" key is pressed. Special keys include the arrow keys, the function keys, and the like. The high-order byte contains the scan code of the key. This value corresponds loosely to the position the key has on the keyboard.

If *cmd* is 1, **bioskey( )** checks to see if a key has been pressed. It returns nonzero if a key has been pressed and 0 otherwise.

When *cmd* is 2, the shift status is returned. The status of the various keys that shift a state is encoded into the low-order part of the return value, as shown here:

Bit	Meaning
0	Right shift pressed
1	Left shift pressed
3	CTRL pressed
4	ALT pressed
5	SCROLL LOCK on
6	NUM LOCK on
7	CAPS LOCK on
8	Insert on

Example

This fragment generates random numbers until a key is pressed:

```
while(!bioskey(1)) rand();
```

Related Functions

getche( ), **kbhit( )**

int biosmemory(void)

Description

The prototype for **biosmemory( )** is in **bios.h**.

The **biosmemory( )** function returns the amount of memory (in units of 1KB) installed in the system.

Example

The following program reports the amount of memory in the system.

```
#include "bios.h"
main()
{
    printf("%dK bytes of ram", biosmemory());
}
```

Related Function

biosequip( )

int biosprint(int cmd, int byte, int port)

Description

The prototype for **biosprint( )** is in **bios.h**.

The **biosprint( )** function controls the printer port specified in *port*. If *port* is 0, LPT1 is used; if *port* is 1, LPT2 is accessed. The exact function performed depends on the value of *cmd*. The legal values for *cmd* are shown here:

Value	Meaning
0	Print the character in *byte*
1	Initialize the printer port
2	Return the status of the port

The printer port status is encoded into the low-order byte of the return value as shown here:

Bit	Meaning
0	Time-out error
1	Unused
2	Unused
3	Unused
4	I/O error
5	Printer selected
6	Out-of-paper error
7	Acknowledge
8	Print not busy

Example

The fragment prints the string **hello** on the printer connected to LPT1:

```
char p[]="hello";
while(*p) biosprint(0, *p++, 0);
```

Related Function

bioscom( )

long biostime(int cmd, long newtime)

Description

The prototype for **biostime( )** is in **bios.h**.

The **biostime( )** function reads or sets the BIOS clock. The BIOS clock ticks at a rate of about 18.2 ticks per second. Its value is 0 at midnight and increases until reset at midnight or manually set to some value. If *cmd* is 0, **biostime( )** returns the current value of the timer. If *cmd* is 1, it sets the timer to the value of *newtime*.

Example

This program prints the current value of the timer:

```
#include "bios.h"

main()
{
  printf("the current timer value is %ld", biostime(0,0));
}
```

Related Functions

time( ), ctime( )

struct country *country(int countrycode, struct country *countryptr)

Description

The prototype for **country( )** is in **dos.h.**

The **country( )** function sets several country-dependent items, such as the currency symbol and the way the date and time are displayed.

The structure **country** is defined like this:

```
struct country {
  int co_date;                 /* date format */
  char co_curr[5];             /* currency symbol */
  char co_thsep[2];            /* thousand separator */
  char co_desep[2];            /* decimal separator */
  char co_dtsep[2];            /* date separator */
  char co_tmsep[2];            /* time separator */
  char co_currstyle;           /* currency style */
  char co_digits;              /* significant digits in currency */
  int (far *co_case)();        /* case map function */
  char so_dasep;               /* data separator */
  char co_fill[10];            /* filler */
}
```

If *countrycode* is set to 0, the country-specific information is put in the structure pointed to by *countryptr*. If *countrycode* is nonzero, the country-specific information is set to the value of the structure pointed to by *countryptr*.

The value of **co—date** determines the date format. If it is 0, the U.S. style (month, day, year) is used. If it is 1, the European style (day, month, year) is used. If it is 2, the Japanese style (year, month, day) is used.

The way currency is displayed is determined by the value of **co—currstyle**. The legal values for **co—currstyle** are shown here:

Value	Meaning
0	Currency symbol immediately precedes the value
1	Currency symbol immediately follows the value

2   Currency symbol precedes the value with a space between the symbol and the value

3   Currency symbol follows the value with a space between the symbol and the value

The function returns a pointer to the *countryptr* argument.

Example

This program displays the currency symbol:

```
#include "dos.h"

main()
{
  struct country c;

  country(0, &c);

  printf(c.co_curr);
}
```


Related Functions

time.h, ctime( )

char *ctime(long *time)

Description

The **ctime( )** function returns a pointer to a string of the form

day month date hours:minutes:seconds year \n \0

given a pointer to the calendar time. The calendar time is generally obtained through a call to **time( )**. The **ctime( )** function is equivalent to

```
asctime(localtime(time))
```

The buffer used by **ctime( )** to hold the formatted output string is a statically allocated character array and is over-written each time the function is called. If you wish to save the contents of the string, it is necessary to copy it elsewhere.

Example

This program displays the local time defined by the system:

```
#include "time.h"
#include "stddef.h"

main()
{
  time_t lt;

  lt = time(NULL);
  printf(ctime(&lt));
}
```

Related Functions

localtime( ), **gmtime( )**, **time( )**, **asctime( )**

void ctrlbrk(int (*fptr)(void))

Description

The prototype for **ctrlbrk( )** is in **dos.h**.

The **ctrlbrk( )** function is used to replace the control-break handler called by DOS when the CTRL-BRK key combination is pressed. A control-break generates an interrupt 0x23.

Turbo C automatically replaces the old control-break handler when your program exits.

Example

This program prints the numbers 0 to 31,999 unless the CTRL-BRK key combination is pressed, which causes the program to abort:

```
#include "dos.h"

int break_handler();

main()
{
  register int i;

  ctrlbrk(break_handler);

  for(i=0; i<32000; i++)  printf("%d ", i);
}

break_handler()
{
  printf("this is the new break handler");
  return 0;
}
```

Related Function

geninterrupt( )

double difftime(time—t time2, time—t time1)

Description

The prototype for **difftime( )** is in **time.h**.

The **difftime( )** function returns the difference in seconds between *time1* and *time2*, that is, *time2—time1*.

Example

This program times the number of seconds that it takes for the empty **for** loop to go from 0 to 500000. (On an IBM model 60, this displays **loop required 3.00000 seconds.**)

```
#include "time.h"
#include "stddef.h"

main()
{
  time_t start,end;
  long unsigned int t;

  start = time(NULL);
  for(t=0; t<500000; t++) ;
  end = time(NULL);
  printf("loop required %f seconds\n", difftime(end, start));
}
```

Related Functions

localtime( ), **gmtime( )**, **time( )**, **asctime( )**

void disable(void)

Description

The prototype for **disable( )** is in **dos.h**.

The **disable( )** macro disables interrupts. The only interrupt that it allows is the NMI (nonmaskable interrupt). Use this function with care because many devices in the system use interrupts.

Related Functions

enable( ), **geninterrupt( )**

int dosexterr(struct DOSERR *err)

Description

The prototype for **dosexterr( )** is in **dos.h**.

The **dosexterr( )** fills the structure pointed to by *err* with extended error information when a DOS call fails. The **DOSERR** structure is defined like this:

```
struct DOSERR {
  int exterror;        /* error code */
  int class;           /* class of error */
  char action;         /* suggested action */
  char locus;          /* location of error */
}
```

For the proper interpretation of the information returned by DOS, refer to the DOS technical reference manual.

Related Function

ferror( )

long dostounix(struct date *d, struct time *t)

Description

The prototype for **dostounix( )** is in **dos.h**.

The function **dostounix( )** returns the system time as returned by **gettime( )** and **getdate( )** into a form compatible with the UNIX time format (also compatible with the ANSI standard's format).

Example

See **getdate( )** for an example.

Related Functions

unixtodos( ), ctime( ), time( )

void enable(void)

Description

The prototype for **enable** is in **dos.h**.

The **enable( )** function enables interrupts.

Related Functions

disable( ), geninterrupt( )

unsigned FP—OFF(void far *ptr)
unsigned FP—SEG(void far *ptr)

Description

The prototypes for **FP—OFF( )** and **FP—SEG( )** are in **dos.h**.

The **FP—OFF( )** macro returns the offset portion of the far pointer *ptr*. The **FP—SEG( )** macro returns the segment of the far pointer *ptr*.

Example

This program prints the segment and offset of the far pointer *ptr*.

```
#include "dos.h"

main()
{
  char far *ptr=0xB0000;

  printf("segment:offset of ptr: %u %u", FP_SEG(ptr),
         FP_OFF(ptr));
}
```

Related Function

MK—FP( )

void geninterrupt(int intr)

Description

The prototype for **geninterrupt( )** is in **dos.h**.

The **geninterrupt( )** macro generates a software interrupt. The number of the interrupt generated is determined by the value of *intr*.

Example

This generates interrupt 5, the print screen function:

```
#include "dos.h"

main()
{
  geninterrupt(5); /* print screen function */
}
```

Related Functions

enable( ), **disable( )**

int getcbrk(void)

Description

The prototype for **getcbrk( )** is in **dos.h**.

The **getcbrk( )** function returns 0 if extended control-break checking is off and 1 if extended control-break checking is on. When extended control-break checking is off, the only time DOS checks to see if the CTRL-BRK key combination has been pressed is when console, printer, or auxiliary communication devices are performing I/O operations. When the extended checking is on, the control-break combination is checked for by each DOS call.

Example

This prints the current state of control-break checking:

```
printf("The current cbrk setting is %d", getcbrk());
```

Related Function

setcbrk( )

void getdate(struct date *d)
void gettime(struct time *t)

Description

The prototypes for **getdate( )** and **gettime( )** are in **dos.h**.

The **getdate( )** function fills the **date** structure pointed to by d with the DOS form of the current system date. The **gettime( )** function fills the **time** structure pointed to by t with the DOS form of the current system time.

Example

This converts the DOS version of time and date into the form that can be used by the standard ANSI time and date routines and displays the time and date on the screen:

```
#include "time.h"
#include "stddef.h"
#include "dos.h"

main()
{
  time_t t;
  struct time dos_time;
  struct date dos_date;
  struct tm *local;

  getdate(&dos_date);
  gettime(&dos_time);

  t = dostounix(&dos_date, &dos_time);
  local = localtime(&t);
  printf("time and date: %s\n", asctime(local));
}
```

Related Functions

settime( ), setdate( )

void getdfree(int drive, struct dfree *dfptr)

Description

The prototype for **getdfree( )** is in **dos.h**.

The **getdfree( )** function returns the amount of free disk space in the structure pointed to by *dfptr* for the drive specified by *drive*. The drives are numbered from 1 beginning with drive A. You can specify the default drive by calling **getdfree( )** with a value of 0. The **dfree** structure is defined like this:

```
struct dfree {
  unsigned df_avail;   /* unused clusters */
  unsigned df_total;   /* total number of clusters */
  unsigned df_bsec;    /* number of bytes per sector */
  unsigned df_sclus;   /* number of sectors per cluster */
};
```

If an error occurs, the **df—sclus** field is set to −1.

Example

This program prints the number of free clusters available for use in drive C:

```
#include "dos.h"

main()
{
  struct dfree p;

  getdfree(3, &p); /* drive C */

  printf("Number of free clusters is %d.", p.df_avail);
}
```

Related Function

getfat( )

char far *getdta(void)

Description

The prototype for **getdta( )** is in **dos.h.**

The **getdta( )** function returns a pointer to the disk transfer address (DTA). A *far* pointer is returned because you cannot assume that the disk transfer address will always be located within the data segment of your program.

Example

This fragment assigns the DTA to the far pointer *ptr*:

```
char far *ptr;
ptr = getdta();
```

Related Function

setdta( )

void getfat(int drive, struct fatinfo *fptr)
void getfatd(struct fatinfo *fptr)

Description

The prototypes for **getfat( )** and **getfatd( )** are in **dos.h.**

The **getfat( )** function returns various information about the disk in *drive* that is gathered from that drive's file allocation table (FAT). If the value *drive* is 0, the default drive is used. Otherwise, 1 is used for drive A, 2 for B, and so on. The structure pointed to by **fptr** is loaded with the information from the FAT. The structure **fatinfo** is defined as

```
struct fatinfo {
  char fi_sclus; /* number of sectors per cluster */
  char fi_fatid; /* FAT ID */
  int fi_nclus;  /* total number of clusters */
  int fi_bysec;  /* number of bytes per sector */
```

The **getfatd( )** function is the same as **getfat( )** except that the default drive is always used.

Example

This program displays the total storage capacity in bytes of the default drive:

```
#include "dos.h"

main()
{
  long total;
  struct fatinfo p;

  getfat(0, &p);

  total = (long) p.fi_sclus * (long) p.fi_nclus * (long) p.fi_bysec;

  printf("total storage capacity: %ld.", total);
}
```


Related Function

getdfree( )

int getftime(int handle, struct ftime *ftptr)

Description

The prototype for **getftime( )** is in **dos.h**.

The function **getftime( )** returns the time and date of creation for the file associated with *handle*. The information is loaded into the structure pointed to by *ftptr*. The bit field structure **ftime** is defined like this:

```
struct ftime {
  unsigned ft_tsec: 5;      /* seconds */
  unsigned ft_min: 6;       /* minutes */
  unsigned ft_hour: 5;      /* hours */
  unsigned ft_day: 5;       /* days */
  unsigned ft_month: 4      /* month */
  unsigned ft_year: 7        /* year from 1980 */
}
```

The **getftime( )** function returns 0 if successful. If an error occurs, −1 is returned and **errno** is set to either **EINVFNC** (invalid function number) or **EBADF** (bad file number).

Remember that files associated with file descriptors (handles) use the UNIX-like I/O system, which is not defined by the ANSI standard.

Example

This program prints the year the file TEST.TST was created:

```
#include "io.h"
#include "dos.h"
#include "fcntl.h"

main()
{
  struct ftime p;
  int fd;

  if((fd=open("TEST.TST", O_RDONLY))==-1) {
    printf("cannot open file");
    exit(1);
  }

  getftime(fd, &p);

  printf("%d", p.ft_year + 1980);

}
```

Related Function

open( )

unsigned getpsp(void)

Description

The prototype for **getpsp( )** is in **dos.h**.

The **getpsp( )** function returns the segment of the program segment prefix (PSP). This function works only with DOS Version 3.0 or later.

The PSP is also set in the global variable _psp_, which can be used with versions of DOS more recent than 2.0.

Related Function

biosdisk( )

void interrupt(*getvect(int intr))(void)

Description

The prototype for **getvect( )** is in **dos.h**.

The **getvect( )** function returns the address of the interrupt service routine associated with the interrupt specified in _intr_. This value is returned as a far pointer.

Example

This fragment returns the address of the print screen function (which is associated with interrupt 5):

```
void interrupt(*p)(void);
p = getvect(5);
```

Related Function

setvect( )

int getverify(void)

Description

The prototype for **getverify( )** is in **dos.h**.

The **getverify( )** function returns the status of the DOS verify flag. When this flag is on, all disk writes are verified against the output buffer to ensure that the data was properly written. If the verify flag is off, no verification is performed.

If the verify flag is off, 0 is returned; otherwise 1 is returned.

Example

This program prints the value of the DOS verify flag:

```
#include "dos.h"

main()
{
  printf("The verify flag is set to %d.", getverify());
}
```

Related Function

setverify( )

struct tm *gmtime(time—t *time)

Description

The prototype for **gmtime( )** is in **time.h**.

The **gmtime( )** returns a pointer to the broken-down *time* in the form of a **tm** structure. The time is represented in Greenwich mean time. The *time* value is generally obtained through a call to **time( )**.

The structure used by **gmtime( )** to hold the broken-down time is statically allocated and is overwritten each time the function is called. If you wish to save the contents of the structure, it is necessary to copy it elsewhere.

Example

This program prints both the local time and the Greenwich mean time of the system:

```
#include "time.h"
#include "stddef.h"

/* print local and GM time */
main()
{
  struct tm *local, *gm;
  time_t t;

  t = time(NULL);
  local = localtime(&t);
  printf("Local time and date: %s", asctime(local));
  gm = gmtime(&t);
  printf("Greenwich mean time and date: %s", asctime(gm));
}
```

Related Functions

localtime( ), time( ), asctime( )

void harderr(int (*int—handler)( ))
void hardresume(int code)
void hardretn(code)

Description

The prototypes for **harderr( )**, **hardresume( )**, and **hardretn( )** are in **dos.h**.

The function **harderr( )** allows you to replace DOS's default hardware error handler with one of your own. The function is called with the address of the function that is to become the new error-handling routine. It will be executed each time an interrupt 0x24 occurs.

Assuming the name of the error-handling function is **err__handler( )**, it must have the following prototype:

err__handler(*int errnum, int ax, int bp, int si*);

Here, *errnum* is DOS's error code and *ax, bp,* and *si* contain the values of the **AX**, **BP**, and **SI** registers. If *ax* is nonnegative, a disk error has occurred. When this is the case, ANDing *ax* with 0xFF yields the number of the drive that failed with **A** being equal to 1. If *ax* is negative, a device failed. You must consult a DOS technical reference guide for complete interpretation of the error codes. The **BP** and **SI** registers contain the address of the device driver from the device that sustained the error.

You must follow two very important rules when creating your own error handlers:

1. The interrupt handler must not use any of Turbo C's standard or UNIX-like I/O functions. Attempting to do so will crash the program.

2. You can use only DOS calls numbers 1 through 12.

The error interrupt handler can exit in one of two ways:

1. The **hardresume( )** function causes the handler to exit to DOS, returning the value of *code*.

2. The handler can return to the program via a call to **hardretn( )** with a return value of *code*.

In either event, the value returned must be 0 for ignore, 1 for retry, or 2 for abort.

Due to the complex nature of interrupt service functions, no example is shown.

Related Function

geninterrupt( )

int inport(int port)
int intportb(int port)

Description

The prototypes for **inport( )** and **inportb( )** are in **dos.h**.

The **inport( )** function returns the word value read from the port specified in *port*.

The **inportb( )** macro returns a byte read from the specified port.

Example

The following fragment reads a word from port 1:

```
unsigned int i;
i = inport(1);
```

Related Functions

outport( ), **outportb( )**

int intdos(union REGS ∗in—regs, union REGS ∗out—regs)
int intdosx(union REGS ∗in—regs, union REGS ∗out—regs, struct SREGS ∗segregs)

Description

The prototypes for **intdos( )** and **intdosx( )** are in **dos.h**.

The **intdos( )** function is used to access the DOS system call specified by the contents of the union pointed to by *in—regs*. It executes an INT 21H instruction and places the outcome of the operation in the union pointed to by *out—regs*. The **intdos( )** function returns the value of the **AX** register used by DOS to return information. On return, if the carry flag is set, an error has occurred.

The **intdos( )** function is used to access those system calls that either require arguments in registers other than **DX** or **AL** or return information in a register other than **AX**.

The union **REGS** defines the registers of the 8088/86 family of processors and is found in the **dos.h** header file.

For **intdosx( )**, the value of *segregs* specifies the **DS** and **ES** registers. This is principally for use in programs compiled using the large data models.

Example

This program reads the time directly from the system clock, bypassing all of C's time functions:

```
#include "dos.h"

main()
{
  union REGS in, out;

  in.h.ah=0x2c;  /* get time function number */
  intdos(&in, &out);
  printf("time is %.2d:%.2d:%.2d", out.h.ch, out.h.cl, out.h.dh);
}
```

Related Functions

bdos( ), int86( )

int **int86(int int—num, union REGS ∗in—regs, union REGS ∗out—regs)**

int **int86x(int int—num, union REGS ∗in—regs, union REGS ∗out—regs, struct SREGS ∗segregs)**

Description

The prototypes for **int86( )** and **int86x( )** are in **dos.h**.

The **int86( )** function is used to execute a software interrupt specified by *int—num*. First the contents of the union *in—regs* are copied into the registers of the processor, and then the proper interrupt is executed.

Upon return, the union *out—regs* will contain the values of the registers that the CPU has upon return from the interrupt. If the carry flag is set, an error has occurred. The value of the **AX** register is returned.

The **int86x( )** function copies the values of *segregs—>ds* into the **DS** register and *segregs—>es* into the **ES** register. This allows programs compiled for the large data model to specify which segments to use during the interrupt.

The union **REGS** and structure **SREGS** are defined in the header **dos.h**.

Example

The **int86( )** function is often used to call ROM routines in the IBM PC. For example, this function executes an INT 10H function code 0 that sets the video mode to the value specified by the argument mode:

```
#include "dos.h"

/* Set the video mode */
set_mode(mode)
char mode;
{
  union REGS in, out;

  in.h.al = mode;
  in.h.ah = 0;  /* set mode function number */

  int86(0x10, &in, &out);
}
```

Related Functions

intdos( ), bdos( )

void intr(int intr—num, struct REGPACK *reg)

Description

The prototype for **intr( )** is in **dos.h**.

The **intr( )** function executes the software interrupt specified by *intr—num*. It provides an alternative to the **int86( )** function, but has no other function.

The values of the registers in the structure pointed to by *reg* are copied into the CPU registers before the interrupt occurs. After the interrupt returns, the structure contains the values of the register as set by the interrupt service routine. The structure **REGPACK** is defined as shown here:

```
struct REGPACK {
  unsigned r_ax, r_bx, r_cx, r_dx;
  unsigned r_bp, r_si, r_di, r_ds, r_es;
  unsigned r_flags;
};
```

Any registers not used by the interrupt are ignored.

Example

This program prints the screen via interrupt 5, the print screen interrupt:

```
#include "dos.h"

main()
{
  struct REGPACK r;

  intr(5, &r);
}
```

Related Functions

int86( ), intdos( )

void keep(int status, int size)

Description

The prototype for **keep( )** is in **dos.h**.

The **keep( )** function executes an interrupt 0×31, which causes the current program to terminate but stay resident.

The value of *status* is returned to DOS as a return code. The size of the program that is to stay resident is specified in *size*. The rest of the memory is freed for use by DOS.

Because the subject of terminate and stay resident programs is quite complex, no example is presented here. The interested reader is referred to *C: Power User's Guide* (by Herbert Schildt, Osborne/McGraw-Hill, 1987), which provides coverage of this topic.

Related Function

geninterrupt( )

struct tm *localtime(time—t *time)

Description

The prototype for **localtime( )** is in **time.h**.

The **localtime( )** function returns a pointer to the broken-down *time* in the form of a **tm** structure. The time is represented in local time. The *time* value is generally obtained through a call to **time( )**.

The structure used by **localtime( )** to hold the broken-down time is statically allocated and is overwritten each time the function is called. If you wish to save the contents of the structure, it is necessary to copy it elsewhere.

Example

This program prints both the local time and the Greenwich mean time of the system:

```
#include "time.h"
#include "stddef.h"

/* print local and Greenwich mean time */
main()
{
  struct tm *local, *gm;
  time_t t;
```

```
t = time(NULL);
local = localtime(&t);
printf("Local time and date: %s", asctime(local));
gm = gmtime(&t);
printf("Greenwich mean time and date: %s", asctime(gm));
}
```

Related Functions

gmtime( ), time( ), asctime( )

void far *MK—FP(unsigned seg, unsigned off)

Description

The prototype for **MK—FP( )** is in **dos.h**.

The **MK—FP( )** macro returns a far pointer given the segment *seg* and the offset *off*.

Example

This returns the appropriate far pointer given a segment value of 16 and an offset of 101:

```
void far *p;

p = MK_FP(16, 101);
```

Related Functions

FP—OFF( ), FP—SEG( )

void outport(int port, int word)
void outportb(int port, char byte)

Description

The prototypes for **outport( )** and **outportb( )** are in **dos.h**.

The **outport( )** function outputs the value of *word* to the port specified in *port*. The macro **outportb( )** outputs the specified byte to the specified port.

Example

This fragment writes the value 0xFF to port 0x10:

```
outport(0x10, 0xFF);
```

Related Functions

inport( ), **inportb( )**

char *parsfnm(char *fname, struct fcb *fcbptr, int option)

Description

The prototype for **parsfnm( )** is in **dos.h**.

The **parsfnm( )** function converts a file name contained in a string into the form required by the file control block (FCB) and places it into the one pointed to by *fcbptr*. This function is frequently used with command line arguments. The function uses DOS function 0x29. The *option* parameter is used to set the **AL** register prior to the call to DOS. Refer to a DOS programmer's manual for complete information on the 0x29 function. The **fcb** structure is defined as

```
struct  fcb  {
  char    fcb_drive;      /* 0 = default, 1 = A, 2 = B */
  char    fcb_name[8];    /* File name */
  char    fcb_ext[3];     /* File extension */
  short   fcb_curblk;     /* Current block number */
  short   fcb_recsize;    /* Logical record size in bytes */
  long    fcb_filsize;    /* File size in bytes */
  short   fcb_date;       /* Date file was last written */
  char    fcb_resv[10];   /* Reserved for DOS */
  char    fcb_currec;     /* Current record in block */
  long    fcb_random;     /* Random record number */
};
```

If the call to **parsfnm( )** is successful, a pointer to the next byte after the file name is returned; if there is an error, 0 is returned.

Related Function

fopen( )

int peek(int seg, unsigned offset)
char peekb(int seg, unsigned offset)
void poke(int seg, unsigned offset, int word)
void pokeb(int seg, unsigned offset, char byte)

Description

The prototypes for **peek( )**, **peekb( )**, **poke( )**, and **pokeb( )** are in **dos.h**.

The **peek( )** macro returns the 16-bit value at the location in memory pointed to by *seg:offset*.

The **peekb( )** macro returns the 8-bit value at the location in memory pointed to by *seg:offset*.

The **poke( )** macro stores the 16-bit value of *word* at the address pointed to by *seg:offset*.

The **pokeb( )** macro stores the 8-bit value of *byte* at the address pointed to by *seg:offset*.

Example

This program displays the value of the byte stored at location 0000:0100:

```
#include "dos.h"

main()
{
  printf("%d", peekb(0, 0x0100));
}
```

Related Functions

FP—OFF( ), FP—SEG( ), MK—FP( )

int randbrd(struct fcb *fcbptr, int count)
int randbwr(struct fcb *fcbptr, int count)

Description

The prototypes for **randbrd( )** and **randbwr( )** are in **dos.h**.

The **randbrd( )** function reads *count* number of records into the memory at the current disk transfer address. The actual records read are determined by the values of the structure pointed to by *fcbptr*. The **fcb** structure is defined as

```
struct   fcb  {
  char    fcb_drive;      /* 0 = default, 1 = A, 2 = B */
  char    fcb_name[8];    /* File name */
  char    fcb_ext[3];     /* File extension */
  short   fcb_curblk;     /* Current block number */
  short   fcb_recsize;    /* Logical record size in bytes */
  long    fcb_filsize;    /* File size in bytes */
  short   fcb_date;       /* Date file was last written */
  char    fcb_resv[10];   /* Reserved for DOS */
  char    fcb_currec;     /* Current record in block */
  long    fcb_random;     /* Random record number */
};
```

The **randbrd( )** function uses DOS function 0x27 to accomplish its operation. Refer to a DOS programmer's guide for details.

The **randbwr( )** writes *count* records to the file associated with the **fcb** structure pointed to by *fcbptr*. The **randbwr( )** function uses DOS function 0x28 to accomplish its operation. Refer to a programmer's DOS guide for details.

The following values are returned by the functions:

0   All records successfully transferred

1   EOF encountered but the last record is complete

2   Too many records

3   EOF encountered and the last record is incomplete

Related Function

parsfnm( )

void segread(struct SREGS *sregs)

Description

The prototype for **segread( )** is in **dos.h**.

The **segread( )** function copies the current values of the segment registers into the structure of **SREGS** pointed to by *sregs*. This function is intended for use by the **intdosx( )** and **int86x( )** functions. Refer to these functions for further information.

void setdate(struct date *d)
void settime(struct time *t)

Description

The prototypes for **setdate( )** and **settime( )** are in **dos.h**.

The **setdate( )** function sets the DOS system date as specified in the structure pointed to by *d*. The **settime( )** function sets the DOS system time as specified in the structure pointed to by *t*.

Example

This fragment sets the system time to 10:10:10.0:

```
struct time t;

t.ti_hour = 10;
t.ti_min  = 10;
t.ti_sec  = 10;
t.ti_hund = 0;

settime(&t);
```

Related Functions

gettime( ), getdate( )

void setdta(char far *dta)

Description

The prototype for **setdta( )** is in **dos.h.**

The **setdta( )** function sets the disk transfer address (DTA) to that specified by *dta*.

Example

This sets the disk transfer address to location 0000:A000:

```
char far *p;
p = MK_FP(0xA000, 0)
setdta(p);
```

Related Function

getdta( )

void setvect(int intr, void interrupt(*isr)( ))

Description

The prototype for **setvect( )** is in **dos.h.**

The **setvect( )** function puts the address of the interrupt service routine, *isr*, into the vectored interrupt table at the location specified by *intr*.

Related Function

getvect( )

void setverify(int value)

Description

The prototype for **setverify( )** is in **dos.h**.

The **setverify( )** function sets the state of the DOS verify flag. When this flag is on, all disk writes are verified against the output buffer to ensure that the data was properly written. If the verify flag is off, no verification is performed.

To turn on the verify flag, call **setverify( )** with *value* set to 1. Set *value* to 0 to turn it off.

Example

This program turns on the DOS verify flag:

```
#include "dos.h"

main()
{
  printf("Turning the verify flag on.", setverify(1));
}
```

Related Function

getverify( )

void sleep(unsigned time)

Description

The prototype for **sleep( )** is in **dos.h**.

The **sleep( )** function suspends program execution for *time* number of seconds.

Example

This program waits 10 seconds between messages.

```
#include "dos.h"

main()
{
  printf("hello");

  sleep(10);

  printf(" there");
}
```

Related Function

time( )

time—t time(time—t *time)

Description

The prototype for **time( )** is in **time.h**.

The **time( )** function returns the current calendar time of the system.

The **time( )** function can be called either with a null pointer or with a pointer to a variable of type **time—t**. If the latter is used, the argument is also assigned the calendar time.

Example

This program displays the local time defined by the system:

```
#include "time.h"
#include "stddef.h"

main()
{
  struct tm *ptr;
  time_t lt;

  lt = time(NULL);
  ptr = localtime(&lt);
  printf(asctime(ptr));
}
```

Related Functions

localtime( ), gmtime( ), strftime( ), ctime( )

void tzset(void)

Description

The prototype for **tzset( )** is in **time.h**.

The **tzset( )** function is included in Turbo C for UNIX compatibility, but it does nothing whatsoever.

void unixtodos(time__t utime, struct date *d, struct time *t)

Description

The prototype for **unixtodos( )** is in **dos.h**.

The **unixtodos( )** function converts a UNIX time format into a DOS format. The UNIX and ANSI standard time formats are the same. The *utime* argument holds the UNIX time format. The structures pointed to by *d* and *t* are loaded with the corresponding DOS date and time.

Example

This converts the time contained in **timeandday** into its corresponding DOS format:

```
struct time t;
struct date d;

unixtodos(timeandday, &d, &t)
```

Related Function

dostounix( )

TWENTY

Dynamic Allocation

There are two primary ways in which a Turbo C program can store information in the main memory of the computer. The first uses *global* and *local variables*, including arrays and structures. In the case of global and static local variables, the storage is fixed throughout the run time of your program. For dynamic local variables, storage is allocated from the stack space of the computer. Although these variables are very efficiently implemented in Turbo C, they require the programmer to know in advance how much storage is needed for every situation.

The second way information can be stored is through the use of Turbo C's dynamic allocation system. In this method, storage for information is allocated from the free memory area as it is needed and returned to free memory when it has served its purpose. The free memory region lies between the permanent storage area of your program and the stack. This region, called the *heap*, is used to satisfy a dynamic allocation request. The heap is contained in the data segment.

One advantage of using dynamically allocated memory to hold data is that the same memory can be used for several different purposes in the course of a program's execution. Because memory can be allocated for one purpose and freed when that use has ended, it is possible for another part of the program to use the same memory for something else at a different time. Another advantage of dynamically allocated storage is that it allows the creation of linked lists.

At the core of C's dynamic allocation system are the functions **malloc( )** and **free( )**, which are part of the standard C library. Each time a **malloc( )** memory request is made, a portion of the remaining free memory is allocated. Each time a **free( )** memory release call is made, memory is returned to the system.

The proposed ANSI standard defines only four functions for the dynamic allocation system: **calloc( )**, **malloc( )**, **free( )**, and **realloc( )**. However, Turbo C contains several other dynamic allocation functions. Some of these additional functions are necessary to support the segmented architecture of the 8086 family of processors.

The proposed ANSI standard specifies that the header information necessary to the dynamic allocation functions defined by the standard will be in **stdlib.h**. Turbo C lets you use either **stdlib.h** or **alloc.h**. This guide uses **stdlib.h** because it is more portable. Some of the other Turbo C dynamic allocation functions require the header **alloc.h**, and two of them require the **dos.h** header. You should pay special attention to which header file is used with which function.

One final point: Some of Turbo C's allocation functions allocate memory from the *far heap*, which lies outside the program's default data segment. This provides for two very important features:

1. All the RAM in the system can be allocated — not just that within the data segment.

2. Blocks of memory larger than 64KB can be allocated.

Memory in the far heap must be accessed with far pointers.

int allocmem(unsigned size, unsigned *seg)

Description

The prototype for **allocmem( )** is in **dos.h**.

The **allocmem( )** function executes a DOS 0x48 function call to allocate a paragraph-aligned block of memory. It puts the segment address of the block into the unsigned integer pointed to by *seg*. The *size* argument specifies the number of paragraphs to be allocated. (A paragraph is 16 bytes.)

If the requested memory can be allocated, a −1 is returned. If insufficient free memory exists, no assignment is made to the unsigned integer pointed to by *seg*, and the size of the largest available block is returned.

Example

This fragment allocates 100 paragraphs of memory:

```
unsigned i;

i = 0;

if(i=(allocmem(100, &i))==-1) printf("allocate successful");
else
  printf("allocation failed, only %u paragraphs available", i);
```

Related Functions

freemem( ), **setblock( )**

int brk(void *eds)

Description

The prototype for **brk( )** is in **alloc.h**.

The **brk( )** function dynamically changes the amount of memory for use by the data segment. If successful, the end of data segment is *eds* and 0 is returned. If unsuccessful, −1 is returned and **errno** is set to **ENOMEM** (insufficient memory).

Because the application of **brk( )** is highly specialized, no example is presented here.

Related Function

sbrk( )

void *calloc(unsigned num, unsigned size)

Description

The prototype for **calloc( )** is in **stdlib.h**.

The **calloc( )** function returns a pointer to the allocated memory. The amount of memory allocated is equal to **num* size** where *size* is in bytes. That is, **calloc( )** allocates sufficient memory for an array of *num* objects of size *size*.

The **calloc( )** function returns a pointer to the first byte of the allocated region. If there is not enough memory to satisfy the request, a null pointer is returned. It is always important to verify that the return value is not a null pointer before attempting to use the pointer.

Example

This function returns a pointer to a dynamically allocated array of 100 **float**s:

```
#include "stdlib.h"

float *get_mem()
{
  float *p;

  p = (float *) calloc(100, sizeof(float));
  if(!p) {
    printf("allocation failure - aborting");
    exit(1);
  }
  return p;
}
```

Related Functions

malloc( ), realloc( ), free( )

unsigned coreleft(void); /* small data models */
unsigned long coreleft(void); /* large data models */

Description

The prototype for **coreleft( )** is in **alloc.h**.

The **coreleft( )** function returns the number of bytes of unused memory left on the heap. For programs compiled using a small memory model, the function returns an **unsigned** integer. For programs compiled using a large data model, **coreleft( )** returns an **unsigned long** integer.

Example

This program displays the size of the heap when compiled for a small data model:

```
#include "alloc.h"

main()
{
  printf("The size of the heap is %u", coreleft());
}
```

Related Function

malloc( )

void far *farcalloc(unsigned long num, unsigned long size)

Description

The prototype for **farcalloc( )** is in **alloc.h**.

The **farcalloc( )** function is the same as **calloc( )** except that memory is allocated from outside the current data segment by using the far heap.

See **calloc( )** for additional details.

long farcoreleft(void)

Description

The prototype for **farcoreleft( )** is in **alloc.h**.

The function **farcoreleft( )** returns the number of bytes of free memory left in the far heap.

Example

This program prints the number of bytes of available memory left in the far heap:

```
#include "alloc.h"

main()
{
   printf("far heap free memory: %ld", farcoreleft());
}
```

Related Function

coreleft( )

void farfree(void far *ptr)

Description

The prototype for **farfree( )** is in **alloc.h**.

The function **farfree( )** is used to release memory allocated from the far heap via a call to **farmalloc( )** or **farcalloc( )**.

You must use great care to call **farfree( )** only with a valid pointer into the far heap. Doing otherwise will corrupt

the far heap. You cannot free a far heap pointer with the
free() function or a regular heap pointer with **farfree()**.

Example

This program allocates and then frees a 100-byte region in
the far heap:

```
#include "alloc.h"

main()
{
  char far *p;

  p = farmalloc(100);

  /* only free it if there was no allocation error */
  if(p) farfree(p);
}
```

Related Function

free()

void far *farmalloc(unsigned long size)

Description

The prototype for **farmalloc()** is in **alloc.h**.

The **farmalloc()** function returns a pointer into the far
heap that is the first byte in a region of memory *size* bytes
long. It is the same as **malloc()** except that the far heap is
used instead of the heap within the default data segment.

See **malloc()** for further details.

void far *farrealloc(void far *ptr, unsigned long newsize)

Description

The prototype for **farrealloc()** is in **alloc.h**.

The **farrealloc()** function resizes the block of memory previously allocated from the far heap and pointed to by *ptr* to the new size specified in *newsize*. It is functionally equivalent to **realloc()** except that it operates on the far heap instead of the heap within the default data segment.

See **realloc()** for further details.

void free(void *ptr)

Description

The prototype for **free()** is in **stdlib.h**.

The **free()** function returns the memory pointed to by *ptr* back to the heap. This makes the memory available for future allocation.

It is imperative that **free()** be called only with a pointer that was previously allocated by using one of the dynamic allocation system's functions, such as **malloc()** or **calloc()**. Using an invalid pointer in the call will most likely destroy the memory-management mechanism and cause a system crash.

Example

This program first allocates room for strings entered by the user and then frees them:

```
#include "stdlib.h"

main()
{
  char *str[100];
  int i;

  for(i=0; i<100; i++) {
    if((str[i]=(char *)malloc(128))==NULL) {
      printf("allocation error - aborting");
      exit(0);
    }
    gets(str[i]);
  }

  /* now free the memory */
  for(i=0; i<100; i++) free(str[i]);
}
```

Related Functions

malloc( ), realloc( ), calloc( )

int freemem(unsigned seg)

Description

The prototype for **freemem( )** is in **dos.h**.

The **freemem( )** function frees the block of memory whose first byte is at *seg*. This memory must have been previously allocated using **allocmem( )**. The function returns 0 on success. On failure, it returns −1.

Example

This fragment illustrates how to allocate and free memory using **allocmem( )** and **freemem( )**:

```
unsigned i;

if(allocmem(some, &i)!=-1)
  printf("allocation error");
else
  freemem(i);
```

Related Functions

allocmem( ), setblock( )

void *malloc(unsigned size)

Description

The prototype for **malloc( )** is in **stdlib.h**.

The **malloc( )** function returns a pointer to the first byte of a region of memory of size *size* that has been allocated from the heap. If there is insufficient memory in the heap to satisfy the request, **malloc( )** returns a null pointer. It is always important to verify that the return value is not a null pointer before attempting to use the pointer. Attempting to use a null pointer usually causes a system crash.

Example

This function allocates sufficient memory to hold structures of type **addr**:

```
#include "stdlib.h"

struct addr {
  char name[40];
  char street[40];
  char city[40];
  char state[3];
  char zip[10];
};
  .
  .
  .
struct addr *get_struct()
{
  struct addr *p;

  if(!(p=(struct addr *)malloc(sizeof(addr)))) {
    printf("allocation error - aborting");
    exit(0);
  }
  return p;
}
```

Related Functions

free( ), realloc( ), calloc( )

void *realloc(void *ptr, unsigned newsize)

Description

The prototype for **realloc( )** is in **stdlib.h**.

The **realloc( )** function changes the size of the allocated memory pointed to by *ptr* to that specified by *newsize*. The value of *newsize* can be greater or less than the original. A pointer to the memory block is returned because it may be necessary for **realloc( )** to move the block to increase its size. If this occurs, the contents of the old block are copied into the new block and no information is lost.

If there is not enough free memory in the heap to allocate *newsize* bytes, a null pointer is returned and the original block is freed (lost). Thus it is important to verify the success of a call to **realloc( )**.

Example

This program allocates 17 characters of memory, copies the string **"this is 16 chars"** into them, and then uses **realloc( )** to increase the size to 18 in order to place a period at the end:

```
#include "stdlib.h"

main()
{
  char *p;

  p = (char *) malloc(17);
  if(!p) {
    printf("allocation error - aborting");
    exit(1);
  }

  strcpy(p, "this is 16 chars");

  p = (char *) realloc(p,18);
  if(!p) {
    printf("allocation error - aborting");
    exit(1);
  }

  strcat(p, ".");

  printf(p);

  free(p);
}
```

Related Functions

free( ), malloc( ), calloc( )

char *sbrk(int amount)

Description

The prototype for **sbrk()** is in **alloc.h**.

The **sbrk()** function increments (or decrements, if a negative value is used) the amount of memory allocated to the data segment by *amount* number of bytes.

Because the use of **sbrk()** is highly specialized, no example is given.

Related Function

brk()

int setblock(int seg, int size)

Description

The prototype for **setblock()** is in **dos.h**.

The **setblock()** function changes the size of the block of memory whose segment address is *seg*. The *size* is specified in paragraphs (16 bytes). The block of memory must have been previously allocated using **allocmem()**.

If the size adjustment cannot be made, **setblock()** returns the largest block that can be allocated. On success, it returns −1.

Example

This fragment attempts to resize to 100 paragraphs the block of memory whose segment address is in *seg:*

```
if(setblock(seg, 100)!=-1) printf("resize error");
```

Related Functions

allocmem(), **freemem()**

Directory Functions

Turbo C has a number of directory manipulation functions in its library. Although none of these functions is defined by the ANSI standard, they are included in Turbo C to allow easy access to the DOS disk-file directory. The functions discussed in this chapter all use the **dir.h** header file.

int chdir(char *path)

Description

The prototype for **chdir()** is in **dir.h**.

The **chdir()** function causes the directory whose path name is pointed to by *path* to become the current working directory. The path name may include a drive specifier. The directory must exist.

If successful, **chdir()** returns 0; if unsucessful, it returns −1 and sets **errno** to **ENOENT** (invalid path name).

Example

This fragment makes the WP/FORMLET directory on drive C the current working directory:

```
chdir("C:\\WP\\ FORMLET");
```

Related Functions

mkdir(), rmdir()

int findfirst(char *fname, struct ffblk *ptr, int attrib)
int findnext(struct ffblk *ptr);

Description

The prototypes for **findfirst( )** and **findnext( )** are in **dir.h**. However, you also need to include the **dos.h** header, which contains macros that can be used as values for *attrib*.

The **findfirst( )** function searches for the first file name that matches that pointed to by *fname*. The file name may include both a drive specifier and a path name. The file name may also include the wildcard characters * and ?. If a match is found, the structure pointed to by *ptr* is filled with information about the file, and the DTA is set to the address of the **ffblk** structure.

The **ffblk** structure is defined as

```
struct ffblk {
  char ff_reserved[2]; /* used by DOS */
  char ff_attrib;      /* attribute of file */
  int ff_ftime;        /* creation time */
  int ff_fdate;        /* create date */
  long ff_fsize;       /* size in bytes */
  char ff_name[13];    /* filename */
};
```

The *attrib* parameter determines the type of files to be found by **findfirst**. If *attrib* is 0, all types of files that match the desired filename are acceptable. To cause a more selective search, *attrib* can be one of the following macros:

Macro	Meaning
FA—RDONLY	Read-only file
FA—HIDDEN	Hidden file
FA—SYSTEM	System file
FA—LABEL	Volume label
FA—DIREC	Subdirectory
FA—ARCH	Archive byte set

The **findnext( )** function continues a search started by **findfirst( )**.

Both the **findfirst()** and **findnext()** functions return 0 on success and −1 on failure. On failure, **errno** is set to either **ENOENT** (file name not found) or **ENMFILE** (no more files in directory).

Example

This program displays all files with a .C extension (and their sizes) in the current working directory:

```
#include "dos.h"
#include "dir.h"

main()
{
  struct ffblk f;
  register int done;

  done = findfirst("*.c", &f, 0);
  while(!done) {
    printf("%s %ld\n", f.ff_name, f.ff_fsize);
    done = findnext(&f);
  }
}
```

Related Function

fnmerge()

void fnmerge(char *path, char *drive, char *dir, char *fname, char *ext)
int fnsplit(char *path, char *drive, char *dir, char *fname, char *ext)

Description

The prototypes for **fnmerge()** and **fnsplit()** are in **dir.h**.

The **fnmerge()** function constructs a file name from the specified individual components and puts that name into the string pointed to by *path*. For example, if *drive* is C:, *dir* is

\TC\, *fname* is TEST, and *ext* is .C, the file name C:\TC\TEST.C is produced.

The **fnsplit( )** function decomposes into its component parts the file name pointed to by *path*.

The array size needed for each parameter is shown here, along with a macro defined in **dir.h** that can be used in place of the actual number:

Parameter	Size	Macro Name
path	80	MAXPATH
drive	3	MAXDRIVE
dir	66	MAXDIR
fname	9	MAXFILE
ext	5	MAXEXT

The **fnsplit( )** function puts the colon after the drive specifier in the string pointed to by *drive*. It puts the period preceding the extension into the string pointed to by *ext*. Leading and trailing spaces are retained.

The two functions **fnmerge( )** and **fnsplit( )** are complementary; the output from one can be used as input to the other.

The **fnsplit( )** function returns an integer that has five flags encoded into it. The flags have these macro names associated with them (defined in **dir.h**):

Macro Name	Meaning When Set
EXTENSION	Extension present
FILENAME	File name present
DIRECTORY	Directory path present
DRIVE	Drive specifier present
WILDCARD	One or more wild card characters present

To determine if a flag is set, AND the flag macro with the return value and test the result. If the result is 1, the flag is set; otherwise it is off.

Example

This program illustrates how **fnmerge()** encodes a file name. Its output is **C:TEST.C**:

```
#include "dir.h"

main()
{
  char path[MAXPATH];

  fnmerge(path, "C:", "", "TEST", ".C");
  printf(path);
}
```

Related Functions

findfirst(), **findnext()**

int getcurdir(int drive, char *dir)

Description

The prototype for **getcurdir()** is in **dir.h**.

The **getcurdir()** function copies the name of the current working directory of the drive specified in *drive* into the string pointed to by *dir*. A 0 value for *drive* specifies the default drive. For drive A, use 1; for B, 2; and so on.

The string pointed to by *dir* must be at least **MAXDIR** bytes in length. **MAXDIR** is a macro defined in **dir.h**. The directory name will not contain the drive specifier and will not include leading backslashes.

The **getcurdir()** function returns 0 if successful and -1 if not.

Example

The next program prints the current directory on the default drive.

```
#include "dir.h"

main()
{
  char dir[MAXDIR];

  getcurdir(0, dir);
  printf("current directory is %s", dir);
}
```

Related Function

getcwd( )

char *getcwd(char *dir, int len)

Description

The prototype for **getcwd( )** is in **dir.h**.

The **getcwd( )** function copies the full path name (up to *len* characters) of the current working directory into the string pointed to by *dir*. An error occurs if the full path name is longer than *len* characters. The **getcwd( )** function returns a pointer to *dir*.

If **getcwd( )** is called with *dir*'s value being null, **getcwd( )** automatically allocates a buffer using **malloc( )** and returns a pointer to this buffer. You can free the memory allocated by **getcwd( )** by using **free( )**.

Example

This program prints the full path name of the current working directory:

```
#include "dir.h"

main()
{
  char dir[MAXDIR];

  getcwd(dir, MAXDIR);
  printf("current directory is %s", dir);
}
```

Related Function

getcurdir( )

int getdisk(void)

Description

The prototype for **getdisk( )** is in **dir.h**.

The **getdisk( )** function returns the number of the current drive. Drive A corresponds to 0, drive B is 1, and so on.

Example

This program displays the name of the current drive:

```
#include "dir.h"

main()
{
  printf("current drive is %c", getdisk()+'A');
}
```

Related Functions

setdisk( ), getcwd( )

int mkdir(char *path)

Description

The prototype for **mkdir( )** is in **dir.h**.

The **mkdir( )** function creates a directory using the path name pointed to by *path*.

The **mkdir( )** function returns 0 if successful; if unsuccessful, it returns a −1 and sets **errno** to either **EACCES** (access denied) or **ENOENT** (invalid path name).

Example

This program creates a directory called FORMLET:

```
#include "dir.h"

main()
{
  mkdir("FORMLET");
}
```

Related Function

rmdir( )

char *mktemp(char *fname)

Description

The prototype for **mktemp( )** is in **dir.h**.

The **mktemp( )** function creates a unique file name and copies it into the string pointed to by *fname*. When you call **mktemp( )**, the string pointed to by *fname()* must contain six Xs followed by a null terminator. The **mktemp( )** function transforms that string into a unique file name. It does not create the file, however.

If successful, **mktemp( )** returns a pointer to *fname;* otherwise it returns a null.

Example

This program displays a unique file name:

```
#include "dir.h"

char fname[7] = "XXXXXX";

main()
{
  mktemp(fname);
  printf(fname);
}
```

Related Function

findfirst( ), findnext( )

int rmdir(char *path)

Description

The prototype for **rmdir( )** is in **dir.h**.

The **rmdir( )** function removes the directory whose path name is pointed to by *path*. To be removed, a directory must be empty, must not be the current working directory, and must not be the root.

If **rmdir( )** is successful, 0 is returned; otherwise, a −1 is returned and **errno** is set to either **EACCES** (access denied) or **ENOENT** (invalid path name).

Example

This removes the directory called FORMLET:

```
#include "dir.h"

main()
{
   if(!rmdir("FORMLET")) printf("FORMLET removed");
}
```

Related Function

mkdir( )

char *searchpath(char *fname)

Description

The prototype for **searchpath( )** is in **dir.h**.

The **searchpath( )** function tries to find the file whose name is pointed to by *fname* using the DOS PATH environmental variable. If it finds the file, it returns a pointer to the entire path name. This string is statically allocated and is overwritten by each call to **searchpath( )**. If the file cannot be found, a null is returned.

Example

This program displays the path name for the file TCC.EXE.

```
#include "dir.h"

main()
{
   printf(searchpath("TCC.EXE"));
}
```

Related Function

mktemp( )

int setdisk(int drive)

Description

The prototype for **setdisk( )** is in **dir.h**.

The **setdisk( )** function sets the current drive to that specified by *drive*. Drive A corresponds to 0, drive B to 1, and so on. It returns the total number of drives in the system.

Example

This program switches to drive A and reports the total number of drives in the system:

```
#include "dir.h"

main()
{
  printf("%d drives", setdisk(0));
}
```

Related Function

getdisk( )

Process Control Functions

This chapter covers a number of functions that are used to control the way a program executes, terminates, or invokes the execution of another program. Aside from **abort()**, **atexit()**, and **exit()**, none of the functions described here is defined by the ANSI standard. However, all allow your program greater flexibility in its execution.

The process control functions have their prototypes in **process.h**. The functions defined by the ANSI standard also have their prototypes in the **stdlib.h** header file.

void abort( )

Description

The prototype for **abort()** is in **process.h** and **stdlib.h**.

The **abort()** function causes immediate termination of a program. No files are flushed. It returns a value of 3 to the calling process (usually the operating system).

The primary use of **abort()** is to prevent a runaway program from closing active files.

Example

This program terminates if the user enters an **A**:

```
#include "process.h"

main()
{
  for(;;)
    if(getch()=='A') abort();
}
```

Related Functions

exit( ), atexit( )

int atexit(func) void (*func)( )

Description

The prototype for **atexit( )** is in **stdlib.h**.

The **atexit( )** function establishes the function pointed to by *func* as the function to be called on normal program termination. That is, the specified function is called at the end of a program run. The act of establishing the function is referred to as *registration* by the ANSI standard.

The **atexit( )** function returns 0 if the function is registered as the termination function and nonzero otherwise.

Up to 32 termination functions can be established. They are called in the reverse order of their establishment: that is, first in, last out.

Example

This program prints **hello there** on the screen:

```
#include "stdlib.h"

/* example using atexit() */
main()
{
  void done();

  if(atexit(done)) printf("error in atexit()");
}

void done()
{
  printf("hello there");
}
```

Related Functions

exit( ), abort( )

**int execl(char *fname, char *arg0, . . ., char *argN,
    NULL)**

**int execle(char *fname, char *arg0, . . ., char *argN,
    NULL, char *envp[])**

**int execlp(char *fname, char *arg0, . . ., char *argN,
    NULL)**

**int execlpe(char *fname, char *arg0, . . ., char *argN,
    NULL, char *envp[])**

int execp(char *fname, char *arg[])

int execpe(char *fname, char *arg[], char *envp[])

int execv(char *fname, char *arg[])

int execve(char *fname, char *arg[], char *envp[])

Description

The prototypes for these functions are in **process.h**.

The **exec** group of functions is used to execute another program. This other program, called the *child process*, is loaded over the one that contains the **exec** call. The name of the file that contains the child process is pointed to by *fname*. Any arguments to the child process are pointed to either individually by *arg0* through *argN* or by the array *arg[]*. An environment string must be pointed to by *envp*. (The arguments are pointed to by **argv** in the child process.)

If no extension or period is part of the string pointed to by *fname*, a search is first made for a file by that name. If that fails, the .EXE extension is added and the search is tried again. When an extension is specified, only an exact match will satisfy the search. Finally, if a period but no extension is present, a search is made for only the file specified by the left side of the file name.

The exact way the child process is executed depends on which version of **exec** you use. You can think of the **exec** function as having different suffixes that determine its operation. A suffix can consist of either one or two characters.

Functions that have a **p** in the suffix search for the child process in the directories specified by the DOS PATH command. If a **p** is not in the suffix, only the current and root directories are searched.

An **l** in the suffix specifies that the arguments to the child process will be passed individually. You use this method when you know in advance how many arguments will be passed. Notice that the last argument must be a **NULL**. (**NULL** is defined in **stdio.h**.)

A **v** in the suffix means that the arguments to the child process will be passed in an array. This is the way you must pass arguments when you do not know in advance how many there will be.

An **e** in the suffix specifies that one or more environmental strings will be passed to the child process. The **envp( )** parameter is an array of string pointers. Each string pointed to by the array must have the form

environment variable = value

The last pointer in the array must be **NULL**. If the first element in the array is **NULL**, the child retains the same environment as the parent.

It is important to remember that files open at the time of an **exec** call are also open in the child program.

When successful, the **exec** functions return no value. On failure, they return −1 and set **errno** to one of the following values:

Macro	Meaning
E2BIG	Too many arguments
EACCES	Access to child process file denied
EMFILE	Too many files
ENOENT	File not found
ENOEXEC	Exec format error
ENOMEM	Not enough free memory

Example

The first program that follows invokes the second, which displays its arguments. Remember that the programs must be in separate files.

```
/* first file  - parent */

#include "stdio.h"
#include "process.h"

main()
{
  execl("test.exe", "test.exe", "hello", "10", NULL);
}


/* second file - child */
main(int argc, char *argv[])
{
  printf("this program is executed with these command line ");
  printf("arguments: ");
  printf(argv[1]);
  printf(" %d", atoi(argv[2]));
}
```

Related Function

spawn( )

void exit(int status)
void —exit(int status)

Description

The prototypes for **exit( )** and **—exit( )** are in **process.h**.

The **exit( )** function causes immediate, normal termination of a program. The value of *status* is passed to the calling process. By convention, if the value of *status* is 0, normal program termination is assumed. A nonzero value can be used to indicate an implementation-defined error. Calling **exit( )** flushes and closes all open files, writes any buffered output, and calls any program termination functions registered using **atexit( )**.

The __exit( )__ program does not close any files, flush any buffers, or call any termination functions.

Example

This function performs menu selection for a mailing-list program. If Q is pressed, the program is terminated.

```
menu()
{
  char choice;

  do {
    printf("Enter names (E)\n");
    printf("Delete name (D)\n");
    printf("Print (P)\n");
    printf("Quit (Q)\n");
  } while(!strchr("EDPQ",toupper(ch)));
  if(ch=='Q') exit(0);
  return ch;
}
```

Related Functions

atexit( ), abort( )

int spawnl(int mode, char *fname, char *arg0, . . ., char *argN, NULL)

int spawnle(int mode, char *fname, char *arg0, . . . ,char *argN, NULL, char *envp[])

int spawnlp(int mode, char *fname, char *arg0, . . . ,char *argN, NULL)

int spawnlpe(int mode, char *fname, char *arg0, . . ., char *argN, NULL, char *envp[])

int spawnp(int mode, char *fname, char *arg[])

int spawnpe(int mode, char *fname, char *arg[], char *envp[])

int spawnv(int mode, char *fname, char *arg[])

int spawnve(int mode, char *fname, char *arg[], char *envp[])

Description

The prototypes for these functions are in **process.h**.

The **spawn** group of functions is used to execute another program. This other program, the child process, does not necessarily replace the parent program (unlike the child process executed by the **exec** group of functions). The name of the file that contains the child program is pointed to by *fname*. The arguments to the child program, if any, are pointed to either individually by *arg0* through *argN* or by the array *arg[]*. If you pass an environment string, it must be pointed to by *envp*. (The arguments will be pointed to by *argv* in the child process.) The mode parameter determines how the child process will be executed. It can have one of these three values (defined in **process.h**):

Macro	Execution Mode
P—WAIT	Suspends parent process until the child has finished executing
P—NOWAIT	Executes both the parent and the child concurrently — not implemented in Turbo C
P—OVERLAY	Replaces the parent process in memory

Since the **P—NOWAIT** option is currently unavailable, you will almost always use **P—WAIT** as a value for mode. (If you want to replace the parent program, it is better to use the **exec** functions instead.) If you use the **P—WAIT** option, when the child process terminates, the parent process is resumed at the line after the call to **spawn**.

If no extension or period is part of the string pointed to by *fname*, a search is made for a file by that name. If that fails, then the .EXE extension is added and the search is tried again. If an extension is specified, only an exact match satisfies the search. If a period but no extension is present, a search is made for only the file specified by the left side of the file name.

The exact way the child process is executed depends on which version of **spawn** you use. You can think of the **spawn** function as having different suffixes that determine its operation. A suffix can consist of either one or two characters.

Functions that have a **p** in the suffix search for the child process in the directories specified by the DOS PATH command. If a **p** is not in the suffix, only the current and root directories are searched.

An **l** in the suffix specifies that the arguments to the child process will be passed individually. You use this method when you know in advance how many arguments will be passed. Notice that the last argument must be a **NULL**. (**NULL** is defined in **stdio.h**.)

A **v** in the suffix means that the arguments to the child process will be passed in an array. This is the way you must pass arguments when you do not know in advance how many there will be.

An **e** in the suffix specifies that one or more environmental strings will passed to the child process. The **envp()** parameter is an array of string pointers. Each string pointed to by the array must have the form

environment variable = value

The last pointer in the array must be **NULL**. If the first element in the array is **NULL**, the child retains the same environment as the parent.

It is important to remember that files open at the time of a **spawn** call are also open in the child process.

When successful, the **spawn** functions return no value. On failure, they return −1 and set **errno** to one of the following values:

Macro	Meaning
EINUAL	Bad argument
E2BIG	Too many arguments
ENOENT	File not found
ENOEXEC	**spawn** format error
ENOMEM	Not enough free memory

A **spawn**ed process can **spawn** another process. The level of nested **spawn**s is limited by the amount of available RAM and the size of the programs.

Example

The first program that follows invokes the second, which displays its arguments and invokes a third program. After the third program terminates, the second is resumed. When the second program terminates, the parent program is resumed. Remember that the three programs must be in separate files.

```
/* parent process */

#include "stdio.h"
#include "process.h"

main()
{
  printf("In parent\n");
  spawnl(P_WAIT, "test.exe", "test.exe", "hello", "10", NULL);
  printf("\nBack in parent");
}


/* first child */
#include "stdio.h"
#include "process.h"

main(int argc, char *argv[])
{
  printf("First child process executing with these command line ");
  printf("arguments: ");
  printf(argv[1]);
  printf(" %d\n", atoi(argv[2]));
  spawnl(P_WAIT, "test2.exe", NULL);
  printf("\nBack in first child process.");
}


/* second child */
main()
{
  printf("In second child process.");
}
```

Related Function

exec()

Text Screen
and Graphics
Functions

The proposed ANSI standard does not define any text screen or graphics functions, mainly because the capabilities of diverse hardware environments preclude standardization across a wide range of machines. However, Turbo C provides extensive screen and graphics support systems for the PC environment. As long as you will not be porting your code to a different computer system, you should feel free to use them because they can add substantial appeal to any application. In fact, intensive screen control is a must for most successful commercial programs.

The prototypes and header information for the text screen handling functions are in **conio.h**. The prototypes and related information for the graphics system are in **graphics.h**.

The graphics system requires that the **graphics.lib** library be linked with your program. If you are using the command line version, you need to include its name on the command line. For example, if your program is called **test**, the command line looks like this:

```
tcc test graphics.lib
```

For the integrated development environment, you need to place the line

```
test graphics.lib
```

into the TEST.PRJ file.

Central to both the text screen manipulation and graphics functions is the concept of the *window*, the active part of the screen within which output is displayed. A window can be as large as the entire screen, as it is by default, or as small as your specific needs require. Turbo C uses slightly different terminology between the text screen and graphics systems to help keep the two systems separate. The text screen functions refer to *windows*; the graphics system refers to *viewports*. However, the concept is the same.

It is important to understand that most of the screen and graphics functions are window (viewport) relative. For example, the **gotoxy( )** text screen cursor location function sends the cursor to the specified x,y position relative to the window, not the screen.

All of the graphics functions are **far** functions.

One last point: When the screen is in a text mode, the upper left corner is location 1,1. In a graphics mode, the upper left corner is 0,0.

Refer to Chapter 11 for an overview of how the text screen and graphics systems operate and for background material on the various video modes.

void far arc(int x, int y, int start, int end, int radius)

Description

The prototype for **arc( )** is in **graphics.h**.

The **arc( )** function draws an arc from *start* to *end* (given in degrees) along the invisible circle centered at x,y with the radius *radius*. The color of the arc is determined by the current drawing color.

Example

This fragment draws an arc from 0 to 90 degrees on an imaginary circle centered at 100,100 with the radius 20:

```
#include "graphics.h"

main()
{
  int driver, mode;

  driver = DETECT; /* autodetect */
  mode = 0;
  initgraph(&driver, &mode, "");

  setcolor(WHITE);
  arc(100, 100, 0, 90, 20);

  getch(); /* wait until keypress */
  restorecrtmode();
}
```

Related Functions

circle( ), ellipse( ), getarccoords( )

void far bar(int left, int top, int right, int bottom)
void far bar3d(int left, int top, int right, int bottom, int depth, int topflag)

Description

The prototypes for **bar( )** and **bar3d( )** are in **graphics.h**.

The **bar( )** function draws a rectangular bar that has its upper left corner defined by *left-top* and its lower right corner defined by *right-bottom*. The bar is filled with the current fill pattern and color. (You set the current fill pattern and color using **setfillpattern( )**. The bar is not outlined.)

The **bar3d( )** function is the same as **bar( )** except that it produces a three-dimensional bar of *depth* pixels. The bar is outlined in the current drawing color. This means that if you want a two-dimensional bar that is outlined, use **bar3d( )** with a depth of 0. If the *topflag* is nonzero, a top is added to the bar; otherwise, the bar has no top.

Example

This program draws a two-dimensional and a three-dimensional bar:

```
#include "graphics.h"

main()
{
  int driver, mode;
  driver = DETECT; /* autodetect */
  mode = 0;
  initgraph(&driver, &mode, "");

  /* display a green 2-d bar */
  setfillstyle(SOLID_FILL, GREEN);
  bar(100, 100, 120, 200);

  /* now show a red 3-d bar */
  setfillstyle(SOLID_FILL, RED);
  bar3d(200, 100, 220, 200, 10, 1);

  getch();
  restorecrtmode();
}
```

Related Function

rectangle( )

void far circle(int x, int y, int radius)

Description

The prototype for **circle( )** is in **graphics.h**.

The **circle( )** function draws a circle centered at x,y with the radius as *radius* (expressed in pixels) in the current drawing color.

Example

This program draws five concentric circles centered on location 200,200:

```
#include "graphics.h"

main()
{
  int driver, mode;
  driver = DETECT; /* autodetect */
  mode = 0;
  initgraph(&driver, &mode, "");
```

```
circle(200, 200, 20);
circle(200, 200, 30);
circle(200, 200, 40);
circle(200, 200, 50);
circle(200, 200, 60);

getch();
restorecrtmode();
}
```

Related Functions

arc(), ellipse()

void far cleardevice(void)
void far clearviewport(void)

Description

The prototypes for **cleardevice()** and **clearviewport()** are in **graphics.h**.

The **cleardevice()** function clears the screen and resets the current position (CP) to 0,0. This function is used only with the graphics screen modes.

The **clearviewport()** function clears the current viewport and resets the current position (CP) to 0,0. After **clearviewport()** has executed, the viewport no longer exists.

Example

This program creates a viewport, writes some text into it, and then clears it:

```
#include "graphics.h"

void box(int, int, int, int, int);

main()
{
  int driver, mode;

  driver = DETECT; /* autodetect */
  mode = 0;
  initgraph(&driver, &mode, "");
```

```
/* frame the screen for perspective */
box(0, 0, 639, 349, WHITE);

setviewport(20, 20, 200, 200, 1);
box(0, 0, 179, 179, RED);

outtext("this is a test of the view port");

outtextxy(20, 10, "press a key");
getch();
/* clear the current viewport but not the entire screen */
clearviewport();

getch();
restorecrtmode();
}

/* Draw a box given the coordinates of its two corners. */
void box(int startx, int starty, int endx, int endy,
         int color)
{
  setcolor(color);

  line(startx, starty, startx, endy);
  line(startx, starty, endx, starty);
  line(endx, starty, endx, endy);
  line(endx, endy, startx, endy);
}
```

Related Function

getviewsettings( )

void far closegraph(void)

Description

The prototype for **closegraph( )** is in **graphics.h**.

The **closegraph( )** function deactivates the graphics environment, which includes returning to the system memory that was used to hold the graphics drivers and fonts. This function should be used when your program uses both graphics and nongraphics output. It also returns the system video mode to what it was prior to the call to **initgraph( )**. You may also use **restorecrtmode( )** in place of **closegraph( )** if your program is terminating. In this case, any allocated memory is automatically freed.

Example

This fragment turns off the graphics system:

```
closegraph()
printf("this is not in graphics");
```

Related Function

initgraph()

void clreol(void)
void clrscr(void)

Description

The prototypes for **clreol()** and **clrscr()** are in **conio.h**.

The **clreol()** function clears from the current cursor position to the end of the line in the active text window. The cursor position remains unchanged.

The **clrscr()** function clears the entire active text window and locates the cursor in the upper left corner (1,1).

Example

This program illustrates **clreol()** and **clrscr()**:

```
#include "conio.h"

main()
{
    register int i;

    gotoxy(10, 10);
    printf("This is a test of the clreol() function.");
    getch();
    gotoxy(10, 10);
    clreol();

    for(i=0; i<20; i++) printf("Hello there\n");
    getch();

    /* clear the screen */
    clrscr();
}
```

Related Functions

delline( ), window( )

int cputs(const char *str)

Description

The prototype for **cputs( )** is in **conio.h**.

The **cputs( )** function outputs the string pointed to by *str* to the current text window. Its output cannot be redirected, and it automatically prevents the boundaries of the window from being overrun. It returns the last character written if successful and EOF if unsuccessful.

Example

This program creates a window and uses **cputs( )** to write a line longer than will fit in the window. The line is automatically wrapped at the end of the window instead of spilling over into the rest of the screen.

```
#include "conio.h"

void border(int, int, int, int);

main()
{
  clrscr();

  /* create first window */
  window(3, 2, 40, 9);
  border(3, 2, 40, 9);
  gotoxy(1,1);
  cputs("This line will be wrapped at the end of the window.");
  getche();
}

/* Draws a border around a text window. */
void border(startx, starty, endx, endy)
int startx, starty, endx, endy;
{
  register int i;

  gotoxy(1, 1);
  for(i=0; i<=endx-startx; i++)
    putch('-');

  gotoxy(1, endy-starty);
```

```
for(i=0; i<=endx-startx; i++)
  putch('-');

for(i=2; i<endy-starty; i++) {
  gotoxy(1, i);
  putch('|');
  gotoxy(endx-startx+1, i);
  putch('|');
}
}
```

Related Functions

cprintf( ), window( )

void delline(void)

Description

The prototype for **delline( )** is in **conio.h**.

The **delline( )** function deletes the line in the active window that contains the cursor. All lines below the deleted line are moved up to fill the void. Remember that if the current window is smaller than the entire screen, only the text inside the window is affected.

Example

This program prints 24 lines on the screen and then deletes line 3:

```
#include "conio.h"

main()
{
  register int i;

  clrscr();

  for(i=0; i<24; i++) printf("Line %d\n", i);
  getch();

  gotoxy(1, 3);
  delline();

  getch();
}
```

Related Functions

clreol( ), insline( )

void far detectgraph(int far *driver, int far *mode)

Description

The prototype for **detectgraph( )** is in **graphics.h**.

The function **detectgraph( )** determines what type of graphics adapter, if any, the computer contains. If the system has a graphics adapter, **detectgraph( )** returns the number of the appropriate graphics driver for the adapter in the integer pointed to by *driver*. It sets the variable pointed to by *mode* to the highest resolution supported by the adapter. If no graphics hardware is in the system, the variable pointed to by *driver* contains a −2.

You can use **detectgraph( )** to determine what type of video graphics hardware is in the system.

Example

This fragment tests for the presence of a video adapter:

```
int driver, mode;

detectgraph(&driver, &mode);
if(driver==-2) {
  printf("no graphics adapter in the system.");
  exit(1);
}
```

Related Function

initgraph( )

void far drawpoly(int numpoints, int far *points)

Description

The prototype for **drawpoly( )** is in **graphics.h**.

The **drawpoly( )** function draws a polygon using the current drawing color. The number of end points in the polygon is equal to *numpoints*. Since each point consists of both x and y coordinates, the integer array pointed to by *points* must be at least as large as 2 times the number of points. Within this array, each point is defined by its x,y coordinate pairs with the x coordinate first.

Example

This program draws the polygon defined in the array **shape:**

```
#include "graphics.h"

main()
{
  int driver, mode;
  int shape[10] = { /* five points * 2 */
    10, 10,
    100, 80,
    200, 200,
    350, 90,
    0, 0
  };

  driver = DETECT; /* autodetect */
  mode = 0;
  initgraph(&driver, &mode, "");

  drawpoly(5, shape);

  getch();
  restorecrtmode();
}
```

Related Functions

fillpoly( ), line( ), circle( )

void far ellipse(int x, int y, int start, int end, int xradius, int yradius)

Description

The prototype for **ellipse( )** is in **graphics.h**.

The **ellipse( )** function draws an ellipse in the current

drawing color. The center of the ellipse is at *x,y*. The length of the *x* and *y* radiuses is specified by *xradius* and *yradius*. The amount of the ellipse actually displayed is determined by the values for *start* and *end*, which are specified in degrees. If *start* equals 0 and *end* equals 360, the entire ellipse is shown.

Example

This program draws an egg-shaped ellipse on the screen:

```
#include "graphics.h"

main()
{
  int driver, mode;

  driver = DETECT; /* autodetect */
  mode = 0;
  initgraph(&driver, &mode, "");

  ellipse(100, 100, 0, 360, 80, 40);

  getch();
  restorecrtmode();
}
```

Related Functions

arc( ), **circle( )**

void far fillpoly(int numpoints, int far *points)

Description

The prototype for **fillpoly( )** is in **graphics.h**.

The **fillpoly( )** first draws the object, in the current drawing color, consisting of *numpoints* points defined by the *x,y* coordinates in the array pointed to by *points*. (See **drawpoly( )** for details on the construction of a polygon.) It then proceeds to fill the object using the current fill pattern and color. The fill pattern can be set by calling **setfillpattern( )**.

Example

This program fills a triangle with magenta interleaving:

```
#include "graphics.h"

main()
{
   int driver, mode;
   int shape[] = {
     100, 100,
     100, 200,
     200, 200,
     100, 100
   };

   driver = DETECT; /* autodetect */
   mode = 0;
   initgraph(&driver, &mode, "");

   setfillstyle(INTERLEAVE_FILL, MAGENTA);
   fillpoly(4, shape);

   getch();
   restorecrtmode();
}
```

Related Function

floodfill()

void far floodfill(int x, int y, int border)

Description

The prototype for **floodfill()** is in **graphics.h**.

The **floodfill()** function fills an object with the current fill color and pattern given the coordinates of any point within that object and the color of the border of the object (the color of the lines or arcs that make up the object). You must make sure that the object you are filling is completely enclosed. If it isn't, area outside the shape will also be filled. The background color is used by default, but you can change the way objects are filled using **setfillstyle()**.

Example

This program uses **floodfill( )** to fill an ellipse with magenta cross-hatching:

```
#include "graphics.h"

main()
{
  int driver, mode;

  driver = DETECT; /* autodetect */
  mode = 0;
  initgraph(&driver, &mode, "");

  ellipse(100, 100, 0, 360, 80, 40);

  setfillstyle(XHATCH_FILL, MAGENTA);
  floodfill(100, 100, WHITE);

  getch();
  restorecrtmode();
}
```

Related Function

fillpoly( )

void far getarccoords(struct arccoordstype far *coords)

Description

The prototype for **getarccoords( )** is in **graphics.h.**

The **getarccoords( )** function fills the structure pointed to by *coords* with coordinates related to the last call to **arc( )**. The *arccoordstype* structure is defined as

```
struct arccoordstype {
  int x, y;
  int xstart, ystart, xend, yend;
};
```

Here, x and y are the center of the imaginary circle about which the arc was drawn. The starting and ending x,y coordinates are stored in *xstart, ystart* and *xend, yend.*

Example

This program draws a quarter of a circle about point 100,100 and then connects a line between the arc's endpoints:

```
#include "graphics.h"

main()
{
  int driver, mode;
  struct arccoordstype ac;

  driver = DETECT; /* autodetect */
  mode = 0;
  initgraph(&driver, &mode, "");

  arc(100, 100, 0, 90, 100);

  /* now, draw a line between the endpoints of the arc */
  getarccoords(&ac);  /* get the coordinates */
  line(ac.xstart, ac.ystart, ac.xend, ac.yend);

  getch();
  restorecrtmode();
}
```

Related Functions

line( ), pieslice( )

void far getaspectratio(int far *xasp, int far *yasp)

Description

The prototype for **getaspectratio( )** is in **graphics.h**.

The **getaspectratio( )** copies the x aspect ratio into the variable pointed to by $xasp$ and the y aspect ratio into the variable pointed to by $yasp$. You can manipulate these aspect ratios to alter the way objects are displayed on the screen.

Example

This fragment prints the aspect ratios:

```
int xasp, yasp;

getaspectratio(&xasp, &yasp);

printf("X,Y aspect ratios %d %d", xasp, yasp);
```

Related Functions

circle( ), ellipse( ), arc( )

int far getbkcolor(void)

Description

The prototype for **getbkcolor( )** is in **graphics.h**.

The **getbkcolor( )** function returns the current background color. The values and their corresponding macros (defined in **graphics.h**) are shown here:

Macro	Integer Equivalent
BLACK	0
BLUE	1
GREEN	2
CYAN	3
RED	4
MAGENTA	5
BROWN	6
LIGHTGRAY	7
DARKGRAY	8
LIGHTBLUE	9
LIGHTGREEN	10
LIGHTCYAN	11
LIGHTRED	12
LIGHTMAGENTA	13
YELLOW	14
WHITE	15

Example

This fragment displays the current background color:

```
printf("background color is %d", getbkcolor());
```

Related Function

setbkcolor( )

int far getcolor(void)

Description

The prototype for **getcolor( )** is in **graphics.h**.

The **getcolor( )** function returns the current drawing color.

Example

This fragment displays the current drawing color:

```
printf("drawing color is %d", getcolor());
```

Related Function

setcolor( )

void far getfillpattern(char far *pattern)

Description

The prototype for **getfillpattern( )** is in **graphics.h**.

The **getfillpattern( )** fills the array pointed to by *pattern* with the 8 bytes that comprise the current fill pattern. The array must be at least 8 bytes long. The pattern is arranged as an 8-bit by 8-byte pattern.

Example

This program displays the bytes that comprise the current fill pattern:

```
#include "graphics.h"

main()
{
  int driver, mode;
  struct arccoordstype ac;
  char f[8];
  int i;

  driver = DETECT; /* autodetect */
  mode = 0;
  initgraph(&driver, &mode, "");

  getfillpattern(f);

  /* display each byte in fill pattern */
  for(i=0; i<8; i++) printf("%d ", f[i]);

  getch();
  restorecrtmode();
}
```

Related Functions

setfillpattern( ), setfillstyle( )

void far getfillsettings(struct fillsettingstype far *info)

Description

The prototype for **getfillsettings( )** is in **graphics.h**.

The **getfillsettings( )** function fills the structure pointed to by *info* with the number of the fill pattern and the color currently in use. The **fillsettingstype** structure is defined in **graphics.h** as

```
struct fillsettingstype {
  int pattern;
  int color;
}
```

The values for *pattern* are shown here along with their macro equivalents (defined in **graphics.h**):

Macro	Value	Meaning
EMPTY—FILL	0	Fill with background color
SOLID—FILL	1	Fill with solid color
LINE—FILL	2	File with lines
LTSLASH—FILL	3	Fill with light slashes
SLASH—FILL	4	Fill with slashes
BKSLASH—FILL	5	Fill with backslashes
LTBKSLASH—FILL	6	Fill with light backslashes
XHATCH—FILL	8	Fill with hatching
INTERLEAVE—FILL	9	Fill with interleaving
WIDEDOT—FILL	10	Fill with widely spaced dots
CLOSEDOT—FILL	11	Fill with closely spaced dots
USER—FILL	12	Fill with custom pattern

The color will be one of the colors valid in the video mode currently in use.

Example

This fragment reads the current fill pattern and color:

```
struct fillsettingstype p;
getfillsettings(&p);
```

Related Function

setfillsettings( )

int far getgraphmode(void)

Description

The prototype for **getgraphmode( )** is in **graphics.h**.

The **getgraphmode( )** function returns the current graphics mode. The value returned does *not* correspond to the actual value BIOS associates with the active video mode. Instead, the value returned is relative to the current video driver. The value returned will be one of these values (defined in **graphics.h**):

Macro	Value	Resolution
CGAC0	0	320×200
CGAC1	1	320×200
CGAC2	2	320×200
CGAC3	3	320×200
CGAHI	4	640×200
MCGAC0	0	320×200
MCGAC1	1	320×200
MCGAC2	2	320×200
MCGAC3	3	320×200
MCGAMED	4	640×200
MCGAHI	5	640×480
EGALO	0	640×200
EGAHI	1	640×350
EGA64LO	0	640×200
EGA64HI	1	640×350

Macro	Value	Resolution
EGAMONOHI	3	640×350
HERCMONOHI	0	720×348
ATT400C0	0	320×200
ATT400C1	1	320×200
ATT400C2	2	320×200
ATT400C3	3	320×200
ATT400CMED	4	640×200
ATT400CHI	5	640×400
VGALO	0	640×200
VGAMED	1	640×350
VGAHI	2	640×480
PC3270HI	0	720×350

Example

This fragment displays the number of the current graphics mode relative to the active graphics driver:

```
printf("graphics mode is %d", getgraphmode());
```

Related Function

setgraphmode()

void far getimage(int left, int top, int right, int bottom, void far *buf)

Description

The prototype for **getimage()** is in **graphics.h**.

The **getimage()** function copies the portion of the

graphics screen whose upper left corner has the coordinates *left,top* and lower right corner the coordinates *right,bottom* into the region of memory pointed to by *buf*.

To determine the number of bytes needed to store an image, use the **imagesize( )** function. An image stored using **getimage( )** can be written to the screen using the **putimage( )** function.

Example

This fragment copies a rectangle with two diagonal lines to other screen locations:

```
/* This program demonstrates how a graphics image can be
   moved using getimage(), imagesize(), and putimage().
*/
#include "conio.h"
#include "graphics.h"
#include "stdlib.h"

void box(int, int, int, int, int);

main()
{
  int driver, mode;
  unsigned size;
  void *buf;

  driver = DETECT; /* autodetect */
  mode = 0;
  initgraph(&driver, &mode, "");

  box(20, 20, 200, 200, 15);

  setcolor(RED);
  line(20, 20, 200, 200);
  setcolor(GREEN);
  line(20, 200, 200, 20);
  getch();

  /* move the image */

  /* first, get the image's size */
  size = imagesize(20, 20, 200, 200);
  if(size !=-1) { /* alloc memory for the image */
    buf = malloc(size);
    if(buf) {
      getimage(20, 20, 200, 200, buf);
      putimage(100, 100, buf, COPY_PUT);
      putimage(300, 50, buf, COPY_PUT);
    }
  }
}
```

```
  outtext("press a key");
  getch();
  restorecrtmode();
}

/* Draw a box given the coordinates of its two corners. */
void box(int startx, int starty, int endx, int endy,
         int color)
{
  setcolor(color);

  line(startx, starty, startx, endy);
  line(startx, starty, endx, starty);
  line(endx, starty, endx, endy);
  line(endx, endy, startx, endy);
}
```

Related Functions

putimage( ), imagesize( )

void far getlinesettings(struct linesettingstype far *info)

Description

The prototype for **getlinesettings( )** is in **graphics.h**.

The **getlinessettings( )** function fills the structure pointed to by *info* with the current line style. The structure **linesettingstype** is defined as

```
struct linesettingstype {
  int linestyle;
  unsigned upattern;
  int thickness;
};
```

The *linestyle* element holds the style of the line. It will be one of these enumerated values (defined in **graphics.h**):

Value	Meaning
SOLID—LINE	Unbroken line
DOTTED—LINE	Dotted line
CENTER—LINE	Centered line
DASHED—LINE	Dashed line
USERBIT—LINE	User-defined line

If *linestyle* is equal to **USERBIT—LINE**, the 16-bit pattern in *upattern* determines how the line appears. Each bit in the pattern corresponds to 1 pixel. If that bit is set, the pixel is turned on; otherwise it is turned off.

The *thickness* element will have one of these values:

Value	Meaning
NORM—WIDTH	1 pixel wide
THICK—WIDTH	3 pixels wide

Example

This fragment reads the current line settings:

```
struct linesettingstype info;

getlinesettings(&info);
```

Related Function

setlinestyle()

int far getmaxcolor(void)

Description

The prototype for **getmaxcolor()** is in **graphics.h**.

The **getmaxcolor()** function returns the largest valid color value for the current video mode. For example, in four-color CGA mode, this number will be 3. (The valid colors for this mode are 0 through 3.)

Example

This program displays the largest valid color value:

```
#include "graphics.h"

main()
{
  int driver, mode;

  driver = DETECT; /* autodetect */
  mode = 0;
  initgraph(&driver, &mode, "");

  printf("largest color: %d", getmaxcolor());
  getch();
  restorecrtmode();
}
```

Related Functions

getbkcolor( ), getpalette( )

int far getmaxx(void)
int far getmaxy(void)

Description

The prototypes for **getmaxx( )** and **getmaxy( )** are in **graphics.h**.

The **getmaxx( )** function returns the largest valid x value for the current graphics mode.

The **getmaxy( )** function returns the largest valid y value for the current graphics mode.

Example

This fragment displays the maximum x and y coordinates supported by the graphics hardware in the system:

```
#include "graphics.h"

main()
{
  int driver, mode;

  driver = DETECT; /* autodetect */
```

```
mode = 0;
initgraph(&driver, &mode, "");

printf("max X,Y: %d,%d", getmaxx(), getmaxy());
getch();
restorecrtmode();
}
```

Related Function

getmaxcolor( )

void far getmoderange(int driver, int far *lowmode, int far *himode)

Description

The prototype for **getmoderange( )** is in **graphics.h**.

The **getmoderange( )** function determines the lowest and highest modes supported by the graphics driver specified by *driver* and puts these values at the variable pointed to by *lowmode* and *himode*, respectively. The valid values of *driver* are shown here along with their macro names:

Macro	Value
CGA	1
MCGA	2
EGA	3
EGA64	4
EGAMONO	5
RESERVED	6
HERCMONO	7
ATT400	8
VGA	9
PC3270	10

Example

This program displays the value of the video mode range for the graphics hardware currently installed in the system:

```
#include "graphics.h"

main()
{
  int driver, mode;
  int high, low;

  driver = DETECT; /* autodetect */
  mode = 0;
  initgraph(&driver, &mode, "");

  getmoderange(driver, &low, &high);
  printf("mode range: %d - %d", low, high);
  getch();
  restorecrtmode();
}
```

Related Function

getgraphmode()

void far getpalette(struct palettetype far *pal)

Description

The prototype for **getpalette()** is in **graphics.h**.

The **getpalette()** function loads the structure pointed to by *pal* with the number of the current palette. The **palettetype** structure is defined as

```
#define MAXCOLORS 15
struct palettetype {
  unsigned char size;
  signed char colors[MAXCOLORS + 1];
};
```

The **size** element holds the number of colors available in the current palette. The **colors** array holds the values for the colors available in the palette. The available colors, along with their macro names, are shown here:

CGA codes (background only):

Macro	Value
BLACK	0
BLUE	1
GREEN	2
CYAN	3
RED	4
MAGENTA	5
BROWN	6
LIGHTGRAY	7
DARKGRAY	8
LIGHTBLUE	9
LIGHTGREEN	10
LIGHTCYAN	11
LIGHTRED	12
LIGHTMAGENTA	13
YELLOW	14
WHITE	15

EGA and VGA:

Macro	Value
EGA_BLACK	0
EGA_BLUE	1
EGA_GREEN	2
EGA_CYAN	3
EGA_RED	4

Macro	Value
EGA—MAGENTA	5
EGA—BROWN	20
EGA—LIGHTGRAY	7
EGA—DARKGRAY	56
EGA—LIGHTBLUE	57
EGA—LIGHTGREEN	58
EGA—LIGHTCYAN	59
EGA—LIGHTRED	60
EGA—LIGHTMAGENTA	61
EGA—YELLOW	62
EGA—WHITE	63

Example

This program prints the number of colors supported by the default video mode:

```
#include "graphics.h"

main()
{
  int driver, mode;
  struct palettetype p;

  driver = DETECT; /* autodetect */
  mode = 0;
  initgraph(&driver, &mode, "");

  getpalette(&p);
  printf("number of colors in palette: %d", p.size);
  getch();
  restorecrtmode();
}
```

Related Function

setpalette( )

int far getpixel(int x, int y)

Description

The prototype for **getpixel( )** is in **graphics.h**.

The **getpixel( )** function returns the color of the pixel located at the specified x,y position.

Example

This fragment puts the value of the color at location 10,20 into the variable **color**:

```
color = getpixel(10, 20);
```

Related Function

putpixel( )

int gettext(int left, int top, int right, int bottom, void *buf)

Description

The prototype for **gettext( )** is in **conio.h**.

The **gettext( )** function copies the text from the rectangle with the upper left corner coordinates *left,top* and lower right corner coordinates *right,bottom* into the buffer pointed to by *buf*. The coordinates are screen, not window, relative.

The amount of memory needed to hold a region of the screen is computed by the formula **num_bytes = rows $\times$ columns $\times$ 2**. The reason you must multiply the number of rows times the number of columns by 2 is that each character displayed on the screen requires 2 bytes of storage: 1 for the character itself and 1 for its attributes.

The function returns 1 on success and 0 on failure.

Example

This fragment copies a region of the screen into the memory pointed to by **buf**:

```
buf = (char *) malloc(10 * 10 *2);

gettext(10, 10, 20, 20, buf);
```

Related Functions

puttext( ), movetext( )

void far gettextsettings(struct textsettingstype far *info)

Description

The prototype for **gettextsettings( )** is in **graphics.h**.

The **gettextsettings( )** function loads the structure pointed to by *info* with information about the current graphics text settings. The structure **textsettingstype** is defined in **graphics.h** and is shown here:

```
struct textsettingstype {
  int font;          /* font type */
  int direction;     /* horizontal or vertical */
  int charsize;      /* size of characters */
  int horiz;         /* horizontal justification */
  int vert;          /* vertical justification */
};
```

The *font* element will contain one of these values (as defined in **graphics.h**):

Value	Font
0	Default 8×8 bit-mapped font
1	Stroked triplex font
2	Stroked small font
3	Stroked sans serif font
4	Stroked gothic font

The *direction* element must be set to either **HORIZ_DIR**
(the default) for horizontal text or **VERT_DIR** for vertical
text. The *charsize* element is a multiplier used to scale the
size of the output text. The values of *horiz* and *vert* indicate
how text will be justified relative to the current position
(CP). They will be one of the following values (macros
defined in **graphics.h**):

Macro	Value	Meaning
LEFT_TEXT	0	CP at left
CENTER_TEXT	1	CP in the center
RIGHT_TEXT	2	CP at right
BOTTOM_TEXT	3	CP at the bottom
TOP_TEXT	4	CP at the top

Example

This fragment reads the current text settings:

```
struct textsettingstype t;

gettextsettings(&t);
```

Related Function

settextstyle( )

void far getviewsettings(struct viewporttype far *info)

Description

The prototype for **getviewsettings( )** is in **graphics.h**.

The **getviewsettings( )** function loads information about
the current viewport into the structure pointed to by *info*.
The structure **viewporttype** is defined as

```
struct viewporttype {
  int left, top, right , bottom;
  int clipflag;
}
```

The fields **left**, **top**, **right**, and **bottom** hold the coordinates of the upper left and lower right corners of the viewport. When **clipflag** is 0, there is no clipping of output that overruns the viewport boundaries. Otherwise, clipping is performed to prevent boundary overrun.

Example

This fragment prints the dimensions of the current screen:

```
struct viewporttype info;

getviewsettings(&info);

printf("view port is %dx%x by %dx%d", info.left, info.right,
        info.top, info.bottom);
```

Related Function

setviewport( )

int far getx(void)
int far gety(void)

Description

The prototypes for **getx( )** and **gety( )** are in **graphics.h**.

The functions **getx( )** and **gety( )** return the current position's (CP's) x and y location on the graphics screen.

Example

This fragment displays the CP's current location:

```
printf("CP's loc: %d, %d", getx(), gety());
```

Related Function

moveto( )

void gotoxy(int x, int y)

Description

The prototype for **gotoxy( )** is in **conio.h**.

The **gotoxy( )** function sends the text screen cursor to the location specified by x,y. If either or both of the coordinates are invalid, no action takes place.

Example

This program prints **X**s diagonally across the screen:

```
#include "conio.h"

main()
{
  register int i, j;

  clrscr();

  /* print diagonal Xs */
  for(i=1, j=1; j<24; i+=3, j++) {
    gotoxy(i, j);
    printf("X");
  }
  getche();
  clrscr();
}
```

Related Functions

wherex( ), wherey( )

void far graphdefaults(void)

Description

The prototype for **graphdefaults( )** is in **graphics.h**.

The **graphdefaults( )** function resets the graphics system to its default settings. Specifically, the entire screen becomes the viewport with the CP located at 0,0. The palette, drawing color, and background color are reset; the fill style, fill pattern, text font, and justification are returned to their original values.

Example

This resets the graphics system:

```
graphdefaults();
```

Related Functions

initgraph( ), setpalette( )

char far *far grapherrormsg(int errcode)

Description

The prototype for **grapherrormsg( )** is in **graphics.h**.

The **grapherrormsg( )** function returns a pointer to the error message that corresponds to *errcode*. The error code is obtained by a call to **graphresult( )**.

See **graphresult( )** for details of the error conditions.

Example

Assuming that *errcode* was returned by a call to **graphresult( )**, this fragment displays in text form the error message associated with that code:

```
printf("%s", grapherrormsg(graphresult()));
```

Related Function

graphresult( )

void far —graphfreemem(void far *ptr, unsigned size)
void far *far —graphgetmem(unsigned size)

Description

The prototypes for **—graphfreemem( )** and **—graph-getmem( )** are in **graphics.h**.

The **—graphgetmem( )** function is called by Turbo C's graphics system to allocate memory for the graphics drivers and other graphics system needs. The **—graphfreemem( )** function frees this memory.

These functions should not generally be called directly by your programs.

int far graphresult(void)

Description

The prototype for **graphresult( )** is in **graphics.h**.

The function **graphresult( )** returns a value that represents the outcome of the last graphics operation. This value will be one of the following enumerated values:

Name	Value	Meaning
grOk	0	Successful
grNoInitGraph	−1	No driver installed
grNotDetected	−2	No graphics hardware in system
grFileNotFound	−3	Driver file not found
grInvalidDriver	−4	Invalid driver file
grNoLoadMem	−5	Not enough memory
grNoScanMem	−6	Insufficient memory for scan fill
grNoFloodMem	−7	Insufficient memory for flood fill

Name	Value	Meaning
grFontNotFound	−8	Font file not found
grNoFontMem	−9	Insufficient memory for font
grInvalidMode	−10	Invalid mode
grError	−11	General graphics error
grIOerror	−12	I/O error
grInvalidFont	−13	Invalid font file
grInvalidFontNum	−14	Invalid font number
grInvalidDeviceNum	−15	Invalid device number

Use **grapherrormsg( )** to display a graphics error message given its error number.

Example

This fragment displays the outcome of the last graphics operation:

```
printf("%s", grapherrormsg(graphresult()));
```

Related Function

grapherrormsg( )

void highvideo(void)

Description

The prototype for **highvideo( )** is in **conio.h**.

After a call to **highvideo( )**, characters written to the

screen are displayed in high-intensity video. This function works only for text screens.

Example

This fragment turns on high-intensity output:

```
highvideo();
```

Related Functions

lowvideo( ), normvideo( )

unsigned far imagesize(int left, int top, int right, int bottom)

Description

The prototype for **imagesize( )** is in **graphics.h**.

The **imagesize( )** function returns the number of bytes of storage necessary to hold a portion of the screen with upper left corner at location *left,top* and lower right corner at *right, bottom*. This function is generally used in conjunction with **getimage( )**.

Example

This fragment determines the number of bytes needed to hold an image at the specified location:

```
unsigned size;
size = imagesize(10, 10, 100, 100);
```

Related Function

getimage( )

void far initgraph(int far *driver, int far *mode, char far *path)

Description

The prototype for **initgraph( )** is in **graphics.h**.

The **initgraph( )** function is used to initalize the graphics system and load the appropriate graphics driver. The **initgraph( )** function loads into memory a graphics driver that corresponds to the number pointed to by *driver*. Without a graphics driver loaded into memory, no graphics functions can operate. The video mode used by the graphics functions is specified by an integer pointed to by *mode*. Finally, a path to the driver can be specified in the string pointed to by *path*. If no path is specified, the current working directory is searched.

The graphics drivers are contained in .BGI files, which must be available on the system. However, you need not worry about the actual name of the file because you only have to specify the driver by its number. The header **graphics.h** defines several macros that you can use for this purpose. They are shown here:

Macro	Equivalent
DETECT	0
CGA	1
MCGA	2
EGA	3
EGA64	4
EGAMONO	5
RESERVED	6
HERCMONO	7
ATT400	8
VGA	9
PC3270	10

When you use **DETECT**, **initgraph()** automatically detects the type of video hardware present in the system and selects the video mode with the greatest resolution.

The value of *mode* must be one of the graphics modes shown here. Notice that the value pointed to by *mode* is not the same as the value recognized by the BIOS routine that actually sets the mode. Instead the value used to call BIOS to initialize a video mode is created by **initgraph()** using both the driver and the mode.

Driver	Mode	Equivalent	Resolution
CGA	CGAC0	0	320×200
	CGAC1	1	320×200
	CGA2	2	320×200
	CGAC3	3	320×200
	CGAHI	4	640×200
MCGA	MCGAC0	0	320×200
	MCGAC1	1	320×200
	MCGAC2	2	320×200
	MCGAC3	3	320×200
	MCGAMED	4	640×200
	MCGAHI	5	640×480
EGA	EGALO	0	640×200
	EGAHI	1	640×350
EGA64	EGA64LO	0	640×200
	EGA64HI	1	640×350
EGAMONO	EGAMONOHI	3	640×350
HERC	HERCMONOHI	0	720×348

Drive	Mode	Equivalent	Resolution
ATT400	ATT400C0	0	320×200
	ATT400C1	1	320×200
	ATT400C2	2	320×200
	ATT400C3	3	320×200
	ATT400CMED	4	640×200
	ATT400CHI	5	640×400
VGA	VGALO	0	640×200
	VGAMED	1	640×350
	VGAHI	2	640×480
PC3270	PC3270HI	0	720×350

Example

This fragment uses **initgraph( )** to autodetect the graphics
hardware and select the mode of greatest resolution:

```
int driver, mode;

driver = DETECT; /* autodetect */
mode = 0;
initgraph(&driver, &mode, "");
```

Related Function

getgraphmode( )

void insline(void)

Description

The prototype for **insline( )** is in **conio.h**.
   The **insline( )** function inserts a blank line at the current

cursor position. All lines below the cursor move down. This function is for text mode only, and it operates relative to the current text window.

Example

This program illustrates the use of **insline()**:

```
#include "conio.h"

main()
{
   register int i;

   clrscr();

   /* print diagonal X's */
   for(i=1; i<24; i++) {
      gotoxy(1, i);
      printf("this is line %d\n", i);
   }
   getche();
   gotoxy(1, 10);
   insline();
   getch();
}
```

Related Function

delline()

void far line(int startx, int starty, int endx, int endy)
void far lineto(int x, int y)
void far linerel(int deltax, int deltay)

Description

The prototypes for **line()**, **lineto()**, and **linerel()** are in graphics.h.

The **line()** function draws a line in the current drawing color from *startx,starty* to *endx,endy*. The current position is unchanged.

The **lineto( )** function draws a line in the current drawing color from the current position (CP) to x,y and locates the CP at x,y.

The **linerel( )** function draws a line from the CP to the location that is *deltax* units away in the x direction and *deltay* units away in the y direction. The CP is moved to the new location.

Example

This program illustrates the line functions:

```
#include "graphics.h"

main()
{
  int driver, mode;
  struct palettetype p;

  driver = DETECT; /* autodetect */
  mode = 0;
  initgraph(&driver, &mode, "");

  line(100, 100, 200, 200);

  lineto(100, 50);

  linerel(30, 40);

  getch();
  restorecrtmode();
}
```

Related Functions

circle( ), **drawpoly( )**

void lowvideo(void)

Description

The prototype for **lowvideo( )** is in **conio.h**.

After a call to **lowvideo( )**, characters written to the

screen are displayed in low-intensity video. This function works only for text screens.

Example

This fragment turns on low-intensity output:

```
lowvideo();
```

Related Functions

highvideo( ), normvideo( )

void far moverel(int deltax, int deltay)

Description

The prototype for **moverel( )** is in **graphics.h**.

The **moverel( )** function advances the current position (CP) on a graphics screen by the magnitudes of *deltax* and *deltay*.

Example

If the CP is at location 10,10 prior to execution of the following statement, it will be at 20,30 after the statement executes:

```
moverel(10, 20);
```

Related Function

moveto( )

int movetext(int left, int top, int right, int bottom, int newleft, int newtop)

Description

The prototype for **movetext( )** is in **conio.h**.

The **movetext( )** function moves the portion of a text screen with the upper left corner at *left,top* and lower right corner at *right,bottom* to the region of the screen that has *newleft,newtop* as the coordinates of its upper left corner. This function is screen, not window, relative.

The **movetext( )** function returns 0 if one or more coordinates are out of range and 1 otherwise.

Example

This fragment moves the contents of a rectangle with upper left corner coordinates of 1,1 and lower right corner coordinates of 8,8 to 10,10:

```
movetext(1, 1, 8, 8, 10, 10);
```

Related Function

gettext( )

void far moveto(int x, int y)

Description

The prototype for **moveto( )** is in **graphics.h**.

The **moveto( )** function moves the current position (CP) to the location specified by *x,y*, relative to the current viewport.

The **moveto( )** graphics function corresponds to the text screen **gotoxy( )** function in operation.

Example

This fragment moves the CP to location 100,100:

```
moveto(100, 100);
```

Related Function

moverel( )

void normvideo(void)

Description

The prototype for **normvideo( )** is in **conio.h.**

After a call to **normvideo( )**, characters written to the screen are displayed in normal-intensity video. This function works only for text screens.

Example

This turns on normal-intensity output:

```
normvideo();
```

Related Functions

highvideo( ), lowvideo( )

void far outtext(char far *str)
void var outtextxy(int x, int y, char *str)

Description

The prototypes for **outtext( )** and **outtextxy( )** are in **graphics.h.**

The **outtext( )** function displays a text string on a graphics mode screen at the current position (CP) using the active text settings (direction, font, size, and justification). If the active direction is horizontal, the CP is increased by the length of the string; otherwise no change is made in the CP. In graphics modes, there is no visible cursor, but the current position on the screen is maintained as if there were an invisible cursor.

To change the style of the text refer to **settextstyle()**.

Example

This program illustrates the use of **outtext()** and **outtextxy()**:

```
#include "graphics.h"

main()
{
  int driver, mode;
  struct palettetype p;
  int i;

  driver = DETECT; /* autodetect */
  mode = 0;
  initgraph(&driver, &mode, "");

  /* write two lines at CP */
  outtext("this is an example ");
  outtext("another line");

  /* use "cursor" positioning */
  for(i=100; i<200; i+=8) outtextxy(200, i, "hello");

  getch();
  restorecrtmode();
}
```

Related Function

settextstyle()

void far pieslice(int x, int y, int start, int end, int radius)

Description

The prototype for **pieslice()** is in **graphics.h**.

The **pieslice()** function draws a pie slice, using the current drawing color, covering an angle equal to *end–start*. The beginning and ending points of the angle are specified in degrees. The center of the "circle" that the slice is "cut" from is at *x,y* and has a radius equal to *radius*. The slice is filled with the current fill pattern and color.

Example

This program prints a full circle of pieslices, each 45 degrees wide and each in a different color. (This program requires an EGA or VGA.)

```c
#include "graphics.h"

main()
{
  int driver, mode;
  struct palettetype p;
  int i, start, end;

  driver = DETECT; /* autodetect */
  mode = 0;
  initgraph(&driver, &mode, "");

  /* demonstrate pieslice() */

  start = 0; end = 45;
  for(i=0; i<8; i++) {
    setfillstyle(SOLID_FILL, i);
    pieslice(300, 200, start, end, 100);
    start += 45;
    end += 45;
  }

  getch();
  restorecrtmode();
}
```

Related Functions

arc( ), **circle( )**

void far putimage(int x, int y, void var *buf, int op)

Description

The prototype for **putimage( )** is in **graphics.h**.

The **putimage( )** function copies an image previously

saved (by using **getimage()**) in the memory pointed to by *buf* to the screen beginning at location *x,y*. The value of *op* determines exactly how the image is written to the screen. Its valid enumerated values are

Name	Value	Meaning
COPY_PUT	0	Copy as is
XOR_PUT	1	Exclusive-OR with destination
OR_PUT	2	Inclusive-OR with destination
AND_PUT	3	AND with destination
NOT_PUT	4	Invert source image

Example

The following program demonstrates the **getimage()**, **imagesize()**, and **putimage()** functions:

```
/* This program demonstrates how a graphics image can be
   moved using getimage(), imagesize(), and putimage().
*/
#include "conio.h"
#include "graphics.h"
#include "stdlib.h"

void box(int, int, int, int, int);

main()
{
  int driver, mode;
  unsigned size;
  void *buf;

  driver = DETECT; /* autodetect */
  mode = 0;
  initgraph(&driver, &mode, "");

  box(20, 20, 200, 200, 15);

  setcolor(RED);
  line(20, 20, 200, 200);
  setcolor(GREEN);
  line(20, 200, 200, 20);
  getch();

  /* move the image */

  /* first, get the image's size */
  size = imagesize(20, 20, 200, 200);
  if(size !=-1) { /* alloc memory for the image */
    buf = malloc(size);
```

```
     if(buf) {
       getimage(20, 20, 200, 200, buf);
       putimage(100, 100, buf, COPY_PUT);
       putimage(300, 50, buf, COPY_PUT);
     }
   }
   outtext("press a key");
   getch();
   restorecrtmode();
}

/* Draw a box given the coordinates of its two corners. */
void box(int startx, int starty, int endx, int endy,
         int color)
{
   setcolor(color);

   rectangle(startx, starty, endx, endy);
}
```

Related Functions

getimage( ), imagesize( )

void far putpixel(int x, int y, int color)

Description

The prototype for **putpixel( )** is in **graphics.h**.

The **putpixel( )** function writes the color specified by *color* to the pixel at location *x,y*.

Example

This fragment makes the pixel at location 10,20 green, assuming that green is supported by the current video mode:

```
putpixel(10, 20, GREEN);
```

Related Function

getpixel( )

int puttext(int left, int top, int right, int bottom, void *buf)

Description

The prototype for **puttext()** is in **conio.h**.

The **puttext()** function copies text previously saved by **gettext()** from the buffer pointed to by *buf* into the region whose upper left and lower right corners are specified by *left,top* and *right,bottom*.

The **puttext()** functions use screen-absolute, not window-relative, coordinates.

Example

This fragment copies a region of the screen into the memory pointed to by *buf* and puts the text in a new location:

```
buf = (char *) malloc(10 * 10 *2);

gettext(10, 10, 20, 20, buf);

puttext(0, 0, 30, 30, buf);
```

Related Functions

gettext(), movetext()

void far rectangle(int left, int top, int right, int bottom)

Description

The prototype for **rectangle()** is in **graphics.h**.

The **rectangle** function draws a box defined by the coordinates *left,top* and *right,bottom* in the current drawing color.

Example

This program draws some sample rectangles:

```
#include "graphics.h"

main()
{
   int driver, mode;

   driver = DETECT; /* autodetect */
   mode = 0;
   initgraph(&driver, &mode, "");

   rectangle(100, 100, 300, 300);
   rectangle(150, 90, 34, 300);
   rectangle(0, 0, 2, 2);

   getch();
   restorecrtmode();
}
```

Related Functions

bar( ), bar3d( ), line( )

int registerbgidriver(void (*driver)(void))
int registerbgifont(void (*font)(void))

Description

The prototypes for **registerbgidriver( )** and **registerbgi-font( )** are in **graphics.h**.

These functions are used to notify the graphics system that a graphics driver, a font, or both have been linked in and there is no need to look for a corresponding disk file.

The actual registration process is somewhat difficult, and you should consult your Turbo C user's manual for details.

void far restorecrtmode(void)

Description

The prototype for **restorecrtmode()** is in **graphics.h**.

The **restorecrtmode()** function restores the screen to the mode that it had prior to the call to **initgraph()**.

Example

This restores the screen to its original video mode:

```
restorecrtmode();
```

Related Function

initgraph()

void far setactivepage(int page)

Description

The prototype for **setactivepage()** is in **graphics.h**.

The **setactivepage()** function determines the video page that will receive the output of Turbo C's graphics functions. Turbo C uses video page 0 by default. If you call **setactivepage()** with another page, subsequent graphics output is written to the new page, not necessarily the one currently displayed. In graphics modes, only the EGA and VGA support multiple pages. However, even for these adapters, not all modes have multiple pages.

Example

This fragment makes page 1 the active page:

```
setactivepage(1);
```

Related Function

setvisualpage()

void far setallpalette(struct palettetype far *pal)

Description

The prototype for **setallpalette()** is in **graphics.h**.

The **setallpalette()** function changes all the colors in an EGA/VGA palette. The structure **palettetype** is defined as

```
struct palettetype {
  unsigned char size;
  signed char colors[16];
}
```

You must set *size* to the number of colors in the palette and then load the color for each index into its corresponding element in the array **colors**.

Refer to **setcolor()** for the valid colors for the various adapters.

Example

This fragment changes the 16-color palette for an EGA/VGA adapter to the first 16 colors:

```
struct palettetype p;
int i;

for(i=0; i<16; i++) p.colors[i] = i;
p.size = 16;

setallpalette(&p);
```

Related Function

setpalette( )

void far setbkcolor(int color)

Description

The prototype for **setbkcolor( )** is in **graphics.h**.

The **setbkcolor( )** function changes the background color to the color specified in *color*. The valid values for *color* are

Number	Macro Name
0	BLACK
1	BLUE
2	GREEN
3	CYAN
4	RED
5	MAGENTA
6	BROWN
7	LIGHTGRAY
8	DARKGRAY
9	LIGHTBLUE
10	LIGHTGREEN
11	LIGHTCYAN
12	LIGHTRED
13	LIGHTMAGENTA
14	YELLOW
15	WHITE

Example

This program sets the background to light gray before drawing some rectangles:

```c
#include "graphics.h"

main()
{
  int driver, mode;

  driver = DETECT; /* autodetect */
  mode = 0;
  initgraph(&driver, &mode, "");

  setbkcolor(LIGHTGRAY);

  rectangle(100, 100, 300, 300);
  rectangle(150, 90, 34, 300);
  rectangle(0, 0, 2, 2);

  getch();
  restorecrtmode();
}
```

Related Function

setcolor()

void far setcolor(int color)

Description

The prototype for **setcolor()** is in **graphics.h**.

The **setcolor()** function sets the current drawing color to the color specified by *color*. For the valid colors for each video adapter refer to **setpalette()**.

Example

Assuming an EGA/VGA adapter, this program prints 16 line segments in 16 different colors. (The first is the same color as the background.)

```c
#include "graphics.h"

main()
{
```

```
  int driver, mode;
  int i;

  driver = DETECT; /* autodetect */
  mode = 0;
  initgraph(&driver, &mode, "");

  moveto(0, 200);

  for(i=0; i<16; i++) {
    setcolor(i);
    linerel(20, 0);
  }

  getch();
  restorecrtmode();
}
```

Related Function

setpalette( )

void far setfillpattern(char far *pattern, int color)

Description

The prototype for **setfillpattern( )** is in **graphics.h**.

The **setfillpattern( )** function sets the fill pattern used by various functions, such as **floodfill( )**, to the pattern pointed to by *pattern*. The array must be at least 8 bytes long. The pattern is arranged as an 8-bit by 8-byte pattern. When a bit is on, the color specified by *color* is displayed; otherwise the background color is used.

Example

This program creates an unusual fill pattern and uses it to fill a rectangle:

```
#include "graphics.h"

main()
{
  int driver, mode;
  /* define a fill pattern */
  char p[8] = {10, 20, 30, 40, 50, 60, 70, 80};

  driver = DETECT; /* autodetect */
```

```
    mode = 0;
    initgraph(&driver, &mode, "");

    setcolor(GREEN);
    rectangle(100, 200, 200, 300);

    setfillpattern(p, RED);
    floodfill(150, 250, GREEN);

    getch();
    restorecrtmode();
}
```

Related Function

setfillstyle( )

void far setfillstyle(int pattern, int color)

Description

The prototype for **setfillstyle( )** is in **graphics.h**.

The **setfillstyle( )** function sets the style and color of the fill used by various graphics functions. The value of *color* must be valid for the current video mode. The values for *pattern* are shown here along with their macro equivalents (defined in **graphics.h**):

Macro	Value	Meaning
EMPTY_FILL	0	Fill with background color
SOLID_FILL	1	Fill with solid color
LINE_FILL	2	File with lines
LTSLASH_FILL	3	Fill with light slashes
SLASH_FILL	4	Fill with slashes
BKSLASH_FILL	5	Fill with backslashes
LTBKSLASH_FILL	6	Fill with light backslashes

Macro	Value	Meaning
XHATCH—FILL	8	Fill with hatching
INTERLEAVE—FILL	9	Fill with interleaving
WIDEDOT—FILL	10	Fill with widely spaced dots
CLOSEDOT—FILL	11	Fill with closely spaced dots
USER—FILL	12	Fill with custom pattern

You define a custom fill pattern by using **setfillpattern( )**.

Example

This program fills a box using **LINE—FILL**:

```
#include "graphics.h"

main()
{
  int driver, mode;
  /* define a fill pattern */
  char p[8] = {10, 20, 30, 40, 50, 60, 70, 80};

  driver = DETECT; /* autodetect */
  mode = 0;
  initgraph(&driver, &mode, "");

  rectangle(100, 200, 200, 300);

  setcolor(GREEN);
  setfillstyle(LINE_FILL, RED);
  floodfill(150, 250, GREEN);

  getch();
  restorecrtmode();
}
```

Related Function

setfillpattern( )

unsigned far setgraphbufsize(unsigned size)

Description

The prototype for **setgraphbufsize( )** is in **graphics.h**.

The **setgraphbufsize( )** function is used to set the size of the buffer used by many of the graphics functions. You generally do not need to use this function. If you do use it, you must call it before **initgraph( )**.

Related Function

_getgraphmem( )

void far setgraphmode(int mode)

Description

The prototype for **setgraphmode( )** is in **graphics.h**.

The **setgraphmode( )** function sets the current graphics mode to that specified by _mode_, which must be a valid mode for the graphics driver.

Example

This fragment sets a CGA adapter to CGAHI mode:

```
/* after graphics system has been intialized */
setgraphmode(CGAHI);
```

Related Function

getmoderange( )

void far setlinestyle(int style, unsigned pattern, int width)

Description

The prototype for **setlinestyle( )** is in **graphics.h**.

The **setlinestyle( )** function determines the way a line

looks when drawn with any graphics function that draws lines.

The *style* element holds the style of the line. It will be one of these enumerated values (defined in **graphics.h**):

Value	Meaning
SOLID—LINE	Unbroken line
DOTTED—LINE	Dotted line
CENTER—LINE	Centered line (dash-dot-dash)
DASHED—LINE	Dashed line
USERBIT—LINE	User-defined line

If *style* is equal to **USERBIT—LINE**, the 16-bit pattern in *pattern* determines how the line appears. Each bit in the pattern corresponds to 1 pixel. If that bit is set, the pixel is turned on; otherwise it is turned off.

The *thickness* element will have one of these values:

Value	Meaning
NORM—WIDTH	1 pixel wide
THICK—WIDTH	3 pixels wide

The value of *pattern* is important only if the **USERBIT— LINE** is the value of *style*.

Example

This program displays the Turbo C built-in line styles:

```
#include "graphics.h"

main()
{
  int driver, mode;
  int i;

  driver = 0; /* autodetect */
  mode = 0;
  initgraph(&driver, &mode, "");

  for(i=0; i<4; i++) {
    setlinestyle(i, 0, 1);
    line(i*50, 100, i*50+50, 100);
```

```
   }
   getch();
   restorecrtmode();
}
```

Related Function

setfillstyle()

void far setpalette(int index, int color)

Description

The prototype for **setpalette()** is in **graphics.h**.

The **setpalette()** function changes the colors displayed by the video system. The operation of this function is a little difficult to understand at first. Essentially, it associates the value of *color* with an index into a table that Turbo C uses to map the color actually shown on the screen with the color being requested. The values for the *color* codes are shown here:

CGA codes (background only):

Macro	Value
BLACK	0
BLUE	1
GREEN	2
CYAN	3
RED	4
MAGENTA	5
BROWN	6
LIGHTGRAY	7
DARKGRAY	8
LIGHTBLUE	9
LIGHTGREEN	10

Macro	Value
LIGHTCYAN	11
LIGHTRED	12
LIGHTMAGENTA	13
YELLOW	14
WHITE	15

EGA and VGA:

Macro	Value
EGA_BLACK	0
EGA_BLUE	1
EGA_GREEN	2
EGA_CYAN	3
EGA_RED	4
EGA_MAGENTA	5
EGA_BROWN	20
EGA_LIGHTGRAY	7
EGA_DARKGRAY	56
EGA_LIGHTBLUE	57
EGA_LIGHTGREEN	58
EGA_LIGHTCYAN	59
EGA_LIGHTRED	60
EGA_LIGHTMAGENTA	61
EGA_YELLOW	62
EGA_WHITE	63

Only the background color can be changed for CGA modes. The background color is always index 0. For CGA modes, this code changes the background color to green:

```
setpalette(0, GREEN);
```

The EGA can display 16 colors at a time with the total number of different colors being 64. You can use **setpalette()** to map a color onto one of the 16 different indexes.

Example

This sets the value of color 5 to cyan:

```
setpalette(5, EGA_CYAN);
```

Related Function

setcolor()

void far settextjustify(int horiz, int vert)

Description

The prototype for **settextjustify()** is in **graphics.h.**

The **settextjustify()** function sets the way text is aligned relative to the CP. The values of *horiz* and *vert* determine the effect of **settextjustify()**, as shown here (macros defined in **graphics.h**):

Macro	Value	Meaning
LEFT_TEXT	0	CP at left
CENTER_TEXT	1	CP in the center
RIGHT_TEXT	2	CP at right
BOTTOM_TEXT	3	CP at the bottom
TOP_TEXT	4	CP at the top

The default settings are **LEFT—TEXT** and **TOP—TEXT**.

Example

This fragment places the CP on the right:

```
settextjustify(RIGHT_TEXT, TOP_TEXT);
```

Related Function

settextstyle( )

void far settextstyle(int font, int direction, int size)

Description

The prototype for **settextstyle( )** is in **graphics.h**.

The **settextstyle( )** function sets the active font used by the graphics text output functions. It also sets the direction and size of the characters.

The *font* parameter determines the type of font used. The default is the hardware-defined 8×8 bit-mapped font. You can give *font* one of these values (macros defined in **graphics.h**):

Font	Value	Meaning
DEFAULT—FONT	0	8×8 bit-mapped
TRIPLEX—FONT	1	Stroked triplex
SMALL—FONT	2	Small stroked font
SANSSERIF	3	Stroked sans serif
GOTHIC—FONT	4	Stroked gothic

The direction in which the text is displayed—either left to right or bottom to top—is determined by the value of *direction*, which can be either **HORIZ—DIR** (0) or **VERT—DIR** (1).

The *size* parameter is a multiplier that increases the character size. It can have a value of 0 through 10.

Example

The following program illustrates the use of the **settextstyle()** function:

```
/* Demonstrate some different text fonts and sizes. */
#include "graphics.h"
#include "conio.h"

main()
{
  int driver, mode;
  register int i;

  driver = DETECT; /* autodetect */
  mode = 0;
  initgraph(&driver, &mode, "");

  outtext("Normal ");

  /* Gothic font, twice normal size */
  settextstyle(GOTHIC_FONT, HORIZ_DIR, 2);
  outtext("Gothic ");

  /* Triplex font, twice normal size */
  settextstyle(TRIPLEX_FONT, HORIZ_DIR, 2);
  outtext("Triplex ");

  /* Sans serif font, 7 times normal size*/
  settextstyle(TRIPLEX_FONT, HORIZ_DIR, 7);
  outtext("Sans serif");

  getch();
  restorecrtmode();
}
```

Related Function

settextjustify()

setusercharsize(int mulx, int divx, int muly, int divy)

Description

The prototype for **setusercharsize()** is in **graphics.h**.

The **setusercharsize()** function specifies multipliers

and divisors that scale the size of graphics text characters. In essence, after a call to **setusercharsize( )**, each character displayed on the screen has its default size multiplied by *mulx/divx* for its x dimension and *muly/divy* for its y dimension.

Example

This fragment writes text in both normal and large letters:

```
#include "graphics.h"

main()
{
  int driver, mode;

  driver = 0; /* autodetect */
  mode = 0;
  initgraph(&driver, &mode, "");

  outtext("normal ");
  settextstyle(TRIPLEX_FONT, HORIZ_DIR, USER_CHAR_SIZE);

  /* make very big letters */
  setusercharsize(5, 1, 5, 1);
  outtext("big");

  getch();
  restorecrtmode();
}
```

Related Function

gettextsettings( )

void far setviewport(int left, int top, int right, int bottom, int clip)

Description

The prototype for **setviewport( )** is in **graphics.h**.

The **setviewport( )** function creates a new viewport using the upper left and lower right corner coordinates specified by *left*, *top*, *right*, and *bottom*. If *clip* is 1, output is automatically clipped at the edge of the viewport and prevented from spilling into other parts of the screen. If *clip* is 0, no clipping takes place.

Example

This fragment creates a viewport with corners at 10,10 and 40,40 and with clipping:

```
setviewport(10, 10, 40, 40, 1);
```

Related Function

clearviewport( )

void far setvisualpage(int page)

Description

The prototype for **setvisualpage( )** is in **graphics.h**.

For some video modes, there is enough memory in video adapters to have two or more complete screens' worth of information stored at the same time. The RAM that holds the information displayed on the screen is called a *page*. Turbo C uses page 0 by default. However, you can use any of the video pages supported by your hardware, switching between them as desired. Although only one screenful of data can be displayed at one time, it is occasionally useful to build an image as a background task in a page that is not currently displayed so that it is ready when needed without delay. To activate the image, simply switch to that display page. This method is particularly useful in cases where complex images take a long time to construct. To support this sort of approach, Turbo C supplies the functions **setactivepage( )** and **setvisualpage( )**.

The **setactivepage( )** function determines the video page that output of Turbo C's graphics functions will be directed to. If you call **setactivepage( )** with another page, subsequent graphics output is written to the new page, not necessarily the one currently displayed. To display pages other than 0, use the **setvisualpage()** function. For example, to display video page 1 you would call **setvisualpage()** with an argument of 1.

Example

This fragment selects page 1 to be displayed:

```
setvisualpage(1);
```

Related Function

setactivepage()

void textattr(int attr)

Description

The prototype for **textattr()** is in **conio.h**.

The **textattr()** function sets both the foreground and background colors in a text screen at one time. The value of *attr* represents an encoded form of the color information, as shown here:

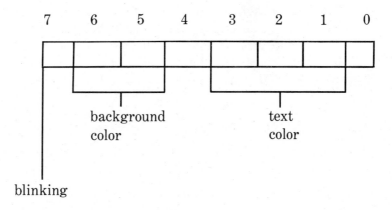

If bit 7 is set, the text blinks. Bits 6 through 4 determine the background color. Bits 3 through 0 set the color for the text. The easiest way to encode the background color into the attribute byte is to multiply the number of the color you desire by 16 and then OR that with the text color. For example, to create a green background with blue text you would use **GREEN * 16 | BLUE**. To cause the text to blink, OR the text color, background color, and BLINK (128) together.

Example

This fragment displays the text in blinking red with a blue background:

```
textattr(RED | BLINK | BLUE*16);
```

Related Functions

textbackground( ), **textcolor( )**

void textbackground(int color)

Description

The prototype for **textbackground( )** is in **conio.h**.

The **textbackground( )** function sets the background color of a text screen. A call to **textbackground( )** affects only the background color of subsequent write operations. The valid colors are shown here along with their macro names (defined in **conio.h**):

Macro	Integer Equivalent
BLACK	0
BLUE	1

Macro	Integer Equivalent
GREEN	2
CYAN	3
RED	4
MAGENTA	5
BROWN	6

The new background color takes effect after the call to **textbackground( )**. The background of characters currently on the screen is not affected.

Example

This fragment sets the background color of a text screen to cyan:

```
textbackground(CYAN);
```

Related Function

textcolor( )

void textcolor(int color)

Description

The prototype for **textcolor( )** is in **conio.h**.

The **textcolor( )** function sets the color in which characters are displayed in a text screen. It may also be used to specify blinking characters. The valid values for *color* are shown here, along with their macro names (defined in **conio.h**):

Macro	Integer Equivalent
BLACK	0
BLUE	1
GREEN	2
CYAN	3
RED	4
MAGENTA	5
BROWN	6
LIGHTGRAY	7
DARKGRAY	8
LIGHTBLUE	9
LIGHTGREEN	10
LIGHTCYAN	11
LIGHTRED	12
LIGHTMAGENTA	13
YELLOW	14
WHITE	15
BLINK	128

The color of characters on the screen is not changed by **text-color( )**; it affects only the color of characters written after it has executed.

Example

This fragment displays subsequent output in blinking characters:

```
textcolor(BLINK);
```

Related Function

textattr()

int far textheight(char far *str)

Description

The prototype for **textheight()** is in **graphics.h**.

The **textheight()** function returns the height, in pixels, of the string pointed to by *str* relative to the current font and size.

Example

This program displays the number 8 for the text height:

```
#include "graphics.h"

main()
{
  int driver, mode;

  driver = 0; /* autodetect */
  mode = 0;
  initgraph(&driver, &mode, "");

  printf("height: %d", textheight("hello"));

  getch();
  restorecrtmode();
}
```

Related Function

textwidth()

void textmode(int mode)

Description

The prototype for **textmode()** is in **conio.h**.

The **textmode()** function is used to change the video

mode of a text screen. The argument *mode* must be one of the values shown in the following table. You can use either the integer value or the macro name (defined in **conio.h**).

Macro Name	Integer Equivalent	Description
BW40	0	40-column black and white
C40	1	40-column color
BW80	2	80-column black and white
C80	3	80-column color
MONO	7	80-column mono-chrome
LAST	−1	Previous mode

After a call to **textmode( )** the screen is reset and all text screen attributes are returned to their default settings.

Example

This fragment puts the video hardware into 80-column color mode:

```
textmode(C80);
```

Related Function

gettextinfo( )

int far textwidth(char far *str)

Description

The prototype for **textwidth( )** is in **graphics.h**.

The **textwidth( )** function returns the width, in pixels, of the string pointed to by *str* relative to the current font and size.

Example

This program displays 40 as the pixel length of the string **hello**:

```
#include "graphics.h"

main()
{
  int driver, mode;

  driver = 0; /* autodetect */
  mode = 0;
  initgraph(&driver, &mode, "");

  printf("width: %d", textwidth("hello"));

  getch();
  restorecrtmode();
}
```

Related Function

textheight()

int wherex(void)
int wherey(void)

Description

The prototypes for **wherex()** and **wherey()** are in **conio.h**.

The **wherex()** and **wherey()** functions return the current x and y cursor coordinates relative to the current text window.

Example

This fragment loads the variables **xpos** and **ypos** with the current x,y coordinates:

```
int xpos, ypos;

xpos = wherex();
ypos = wherey();
```

Description

gotoxy( )

void window(int left, int top, int right, int bottom)

Description

The prototype for **window( )** is in **conio.h**.

The **window( )** function is used to create a rectangular text window whose upper left and lower right coordinates are specified by *left,top* and *right,bottom*. If any coordinate is invalid, **window( )** takes no action. Once a call to **window( )** has been successfully completed, all references to location coordinates are interpreted relative to the window, not the screen.

Example

This fragment of code creates a window and writes a line of text at location 2,3 inside that window:

```
window(10, 10, 60, 15);
gotoxy(2, 3);
cprintf("at location 2, 3");
```

Related Function

clrscr( )

Miscellaneous Functions

The functions discussed in this chapter are all the standard functions that don't easily fit in any other category. They include various conversion, variable length argument processing, sorting, and other functions.

Many of the functions covered here require the use of the header **stdlib.h**. This header defines two types of values: **div—t** and **ldiv—t**, which are the types of the values returned by **div( )** and **ldiv( )** respectively. The following macros are also defined:

- ERANGE: the value assigned to errno if a range error occurs

- HUGE—VAL: the largest value representable by the floating-point routines

- RAND—MAX: the maximum value that can be returned by the **rand( )** function

Different header files will be discussed in the descriptions of the functions that require them.

int abs(int num)

Description

The prototype for **abs( )** is in **stdlib.h**.

The **abs( )** function returns the absolute value of the integer *num*.

Example

This function converts the user-entered numbers into their absolute values:

```
#include "stdlib.h"

get_abs()
{
  char num[80];

  gets(num);

  return abs(atoi(num));
}
```

Related Function

labs()

void assert(int exp)

Description

The prototype for **assert()** is in **assert.h**.

The **assert()** function writes error information to **stderr** and aborts program execution if the expression *exp* evaluates to 0. Otherwise, **assert()** does nothing. The output of the function is in this general form:

Assertion failed: file (*file*), line (*linenum*)

The **assert()** macro is generally used to help verify that a program is operating correctly; the expression is so devised that it evaluates true only when no errors have taken place.

It is not necessary to remove the **assert()** statements from the source code once a program is debugged because if the macro **NDEBUG** is defined (as anything), the **assert()** macros are ignored.

Example

This code fragment is used to test whether the data read from a serial port is ASCII (that is, that it does not use the 7th bit):

```
    .
    .
    .
ch = read_port();
assert(!(ch & 128)); /* check bit 7 */
    .
    .
    .
```

Related Function

abort( )

double atof(char *str)

Description

The prototype for **atof( )** is in **math.h**.

The **atof( )** function converts the string pointed to by *str* into a **double** value. The string must contain a valid floating-point number. If this is not the case, 0 is returned.

The number may be terminated by any character that cannot be part of a valid floating-point number. This includes white space, punctuation (other than periods), and characters other than **E** or **e**. This means that if **atof( )** is called with **100.00HELLO**, the value 100.00 is returned.

Example

The following program reads two floating-point numbers and displays their sum.

```
#include "stdlib.h"

main()
{
  char num1[80], num2[80];

  printf("enter first: ");
  gets(num1);
  printf("enter second: ");
  gets(num2);
  printf("the sum is: %f",atof(num1)+atof(num2));
}
```

Related Functions

atoi( ), atol( )

int atoi(char *str)

Description

The prototype for **atoi( )** is in **stdlib.h**.

The **atoi( )** function converts the string pointed to by *str* into an **int** value. The string must contain a valid integer number. If this is not the case, 0 is returned.

The number can be terminated by any character that cannot be part of an integer number. This includes white space, punctuation, and characters other than **E** or **e**. This means that if **atoi( )** is called with **123.23**, the integer value 123 is returned and the 0.23 ignored.

Example

This program reads two integer numbers and displays their sum:

```
#include "stdlib.h"

main()
{
  char num1[80], num2[80];

  printf("enter first: ");
```

```
    gets(num1);
    printf("enter second: ");
    gets(num2);
    printf("the sum is: %d",atoi(num1)+atoi(num2));
}
```

Related Functions

atof( ), atol( )

long atol(char *str)

Description

The prototype for **atol( )** is in **stdlib.h**.

The **atol( )** function converts the string pointed to by *str* into a **long int** value. The string must contain a valid long integer number. If this is not the case, 0 is returned.

The number can be terminated by any character that cannot be part of an integer number. This includes white space, punctuation, and characters other than **E** or **e**. This means that if **atol( )** is called with **123.23**, the integer value 123 is returned and the 0.23 ignored.

Example

This program reads two long integer numbers and displays their sum:

```
#include "stdlib.h"

main()
{
  char num1[80], num2[80];

  printf("enter first: ");
  gets(num1);
  printf("enter second: ");
  gets(num2);
  printf("the sum is: %ld",atol(num1)+atol(num2));
}
```

Related Functions

atof( ), atoi( )

void ∗bsearch(const void ∗key, const void ∗base, size—t num, size—t size, int (∗compare)(const void ∗, const void ∗))

Description

The prototype for **bsearch( )** is in **stdlib.h**.

The **bsearch( )** function performs a binary search on the sorted array pointed to by *base* and returns a pointer to the first member that matches the key pointed to by *key*. The number of elements in the array is specified by *num*, and the size (in bytes) of each element is described by *size*.

The type **size—t** is defined as an **unsigned int** in **stdlib.h**.

The function pointed to by *compare* is used to compare an element of the array with the key. The form of the function must be

```
func_name(arg1, arg2)
void *arg1, *arg2;
```

It must return the following values:

- If *arg1* is less than *arg2*, less than 0
- If *arg1* is equal to *arg2*, 0
- If *arg1* is greater than *arg2*, greater than 0

The array must be sorted in ascending order with the lowest address containing the lowest element.

If the array does not contain the key, a null pointer is returned.

Example

This program reads characters entered at the keyboard (assuming buffered keyboard I/O) and determines whether they belong to the alphabet:

Related Function

qsort( )

```
#include "stdlib.h"
#include "ctype.h"

char *alpha="abcdefghijklmnopqrstuvwxyz";

main()
{
  char ch;
  char *p;
  int comp();

  do {
    printf("enter a character: ");
    scanf("%c%*c", &ch);
    ch = tolower(ch);
    p = (char *)bsearch(&ch,alpha, 26, 1, comp);
    if(p) printf("is in alphabet\n");
    else printf("is not in alphabet\n");
  } while(p);
}

/* compare two characters */
comp(char *ch, char *s)
{
  return *ch-*s;
}
```

unsigned in —clear87(void)

Description

The prototype for **—clear87( )** is in **float.h**.

The **—clear87( )** function resets the 8087/80287 hardware floating-point coprocessor's status word.

You must have an 8087/80287 math coprocessor installed

in your system in order to use any of the 8087/80287-based functions.

Related Function

__status87( )

div__t div(int numer, int denom)

Description

The prototype for **div( )** is in **stdlib.h**.

The **div( )** function returns the quotient and the remainder of the operation *numer/denom*.

The structure type **div__t** is defined in **stdlib.h** and has these two fields:

```
int quot;  /* the quotient */
int rem;   /* the remainder */
```

Example

This program displays the quotient and remainder of 10/3:

```
#include "stdlib.h"

main()
{
  div_t n;

  n=div(10,3);

  printf("quotient and remainder: %d %d\n", n.quot, n.rem);
}
```

Related Function

ldiv( )

char *ecvt(double value, int ndigit, int *dec, int *sign)

Description

The prototype for **ecvt()** is in **stdlib.h**.

The **ecvt()** function converts *value* into a string *ndigit* long. After the call, the value of the variable pointed to by *dec* indicates the position of the decimal point. If the decimal point is to the left of the number, the number pointed to by *dec* is negative. If the variable pointed to by *sign* is negative, the number is negative.

The **ecvt()** function returns a pointer to a static data area that holds the string representation of the number.

Example

This call converts the number 10.12 into a string:

```
int decpnt, sign;
char *out;

out = ecvt(10.12, 5, &decpnt, &sign);
```

Related Functions

fcvt(), gcvt()

char *fcvt(double value, int ndigit, int *dec, int *sign)

Description

The prototype for **fcvt()** is in **stdlib.h**.

The **fcvt()** function is the same as **ecvt()** except that the output is rounded into the FORTRAN-compatible F-format.

The **fcvt()** function returns a pointer to a static data area that holds the string representation of the number.

Example

This call converts the number 10.12 into a string:

```
int decpnt, sign;
char *out;

out = fcvt(10.12, 5, &decpnt, &sign);
```

Related Functions

ecvt( ), gcvt( )

void —fpreset(void)

Description

The prototype for —fpreset( ) is in **float.h**.

The —**fpreset( )** function resets the floating-point arithmetic system. You may need to reset the floating-point routines after a **system( )**, **exec( )**, **spawn( )**, or **signal( )** function executes. Refer to the Turbo C user manuals for details.

Example

This fragment ensures that the floating-point arithmetic routines are reset after **system( )** returns

```
/* compute and print payroll checks */
system("payroll");

_fpreset();
```

Related Function

—status87( )

char *gcvt(double value, int ndigit, char *buf)

Description

The prototype for **gcvt( )** is in **stdlib.h**.

The **gcvt( )** function converts *value* into a string *ndigit* long. The converted string output is stored in the array pointed to by *buf* in FORTRAN F-format if possible, E-format otherwise. A pointer to *buf* is returned.

Example

This call converts the number 10.12 into a string:

```
char buf[80];

gcvt(10.12, 5, buf);
```

Related Functions

fcvt( ), **ecvt( )**

char *getenv(char *name)

Description

The prototype for **getenv( )** is in **stdlib.h**.

The **getenv( )** function returns a pointer to environmental information associated with the string pointed to by *name* in the DOS environmental information table. The string returned must never be changed by the program.

The environment of a program may include such things as path names and devices online. The exact meaning of this data is defined by DOS.

If a call is made to **getenv( )** with an argument that does not match any of the environment data, a null pointer is returned.

Example

The following fragment returns a pointer to the list of devices:

```
    .
    .
    .
p = getevn("DEVICES");
    .
    .
    .
```

Related Functions

putenv( ), system( )

int gsignal(int signal)

Description

The prototype for **gsignal( )** is in **signal.h**.

The **gsignal( )** function sends the signal specified by *signal* to an executing program and executes the function associated with that signal. Signals are associated with functions by scsignal( ).

If **gsignal( )** is successful, 0 is returned. Otherwise non-zero is returned.

Related Function

ssignal( )

char *itoa(int num, char *str, int radix)

Description

The prototype for **itoa( )** is in **stdlib.h**.

The **itoa( )** function converts the integer *num* into its string equivalent and places the result in the string pointed to by *str*. The base of the output string is determined by *radix*, which can be in the range 2-36.

The **itoa( )** function returns a pointer to *str*. Generally there is no error-return value. Be sure to call **itoa( )** with a string of sufficient length to hold the converted result. The maximum length needed is 17 bytes.

Example

This program displays the value of 1423 in hexadecimal (58F):

```
#include "stdlib.h"

main()
{
  char p[17];

  itoa(1423, p, 16);

  printf(p);
}
```

Related Functions

atoi( ), **sscanf( )**

long labs(long num)

Description

The prototype for **labs( )** is in **stdlib.h**.

The **labs( )** function returns the absolute value of the **long int** *num*.

Example

The following function converts the user-entered numbers into their absolute values.

```
#include "stdlib.h"

long int get_labs()
{
  char num[80];

  gets(num);

  return labs(atol(num));
}
```

Related Function

abs( )

ldiv—t ldiv(long numer, long denom)

Description

The prototype for **ldiv( )** is in **stdlib.h**.

The **ldiv( )** function returns the quotient and the remainder of the operation *numer/denom*.

The structure type **ldiv—t** is defined in **stdlib.h** and has these two fields:

```
long quot;  /* the quotient */
long rem;   /* the remainder */
```

Example

This program displays the quotient and remainder of 100000L/3L:

```
#include "stdlib.h"

main()
{
  ldiv_t n;

  n = ldiv(100000L,3L);

  printf("quotient and remainder: %ld %ld\n", n.quot, n.rem);
}
```

Related Function

div( )

void ∗lfind(const void ∗key, const void ∗base, size—t ∗num, size—t size, int (∗compare)(const void ∗, const void ∗))
void ∗lsearch(const void ∗key, const void ∗base, size—t ∗num, size—t size, int (∗compare)(const void ∗, const void ∗))

Description

The prototypes for **lfind( )** and **lsearch( )** are in **stdlib.h**.

The **lfind( )** and **lsearch( )** functions perform a linear search on the array pointed to by *base* and return a pointer to the first element that matches the key pointed to by *key*. The number of elements in the array is specified by *num*, and the size (in bytes) of each element is described by *size*.

The type **size—t** is defined as an **unsigned int** in **stdlib.h**.

The function pointed to by *compare* compares an element of the array with the key. The form of the function must be

```
func_name(arg1, arg2)
void *arg1, *arg2;
```

It must return the following values:

- If *arg1* does not equal *arg2*, nonzero

- If *arg1* is equal to *arg2*, 0

The array being searched does not have to be sorted.

If the array does not contain the key, a null pointer is returned.

The difference between **lfind( )** and **lsearch( )** is that if the item being searched for does not exist in the array, **lsearch( )** adds it to the end of the array; **lfind( )** does not.

Example

This program reads characters entered at the keyboard (assuming buffered keyboard I/O) and determines whether they belong to the alphabet:

```
#include "stdlib.h"
#include "ctype.h"

char *alpha="abcdefghijklmnopqrstuvwxyz";

main()
{
  char ch;
  char *p;
  int comp();
  int num=26;

  do {
    printf("enter a character: ");
    scanf("%c%*c", &ch);
    ch = tolower(ch);
    p = (char *)lfind(&ch,alpha, &num, 1, comp);
    if(p) printf("is in alphabet\n");
    else printf("is not in alphabet\n");
  } while(p);
}

/* compare two characters */
comp(char *ch, char *s)
{
  return *ch-*s;
}
```

Related Function

qsort( )

void longjmp(jmp—buf envbuf, int val)

Description

The prototype for **longjmp()** is in **setjmp.h**.

The **longjmp()** instruction causes program execution to resume at the point of the last call to **setjmp()**. These two functions are Turbo C's way of providing for a jump between functions. Notice that the header **setjmp.h** is required.

The **longjmp()** function operates by resetting the stack to *envbuf*, which must have been set by a prior call to **setjmp()**. This causes program execution to resume at the statement following the **setjmp()** invocation. That is, the computer is "tricked" into thinking that it never left the function that called **setjmp()**. (As a somewhat graphic explanation, the **longjmp()** function "warps" across time and space (memory) to a previous point in your program without having to perform the normal function return process.)

The buffer *evnbuf* is of type **jmp—buf**, which is defined in the header **setjmp.h**. The buffer must have been set through a call to **setjmp()** prior to calling **longjmp()**.

The value of *val* becomes the return value of **setjmp()** and can be interrogated to determine where the long jump came from. The only value not allowed is 0.

It is important to understand that the **longjmp()** function must be called before the function that called **setjmp()** returns. If not, the result is technically undefined. (Actually a crash will almost certainly occur.)

By far the most common use of **longjmp()** is to return from a deeply nested set of routines when a catastrophic error occurs.

Example

The following program prints **1 2 3**:

```
#include "setjmp.h"

jmp_buf ebuf;

main()
{
  char first=1;
  int i;

  printf("1 ");
  i = setjmp(ebuf);
  if(first) {
    first =! first;
    f2();
    printf("this will not be printed");
  }
  printf("%d", i);
}

f2()
{
 printf("2 ");
 longjmp(ebuf, 3);
}
```

Related Function

setjmp( )

char *ltoa(long num, char *str, int radix)

Description

The prototype for **ltoa( )** is in **stdlib.h**.

The **ltoa( )** function converts the long integer *num* into its string equivalent and places the result in the string pointed to by *str*. The base of the output string is determined by *radix,* which is generally in the range 2-36.

The **ltoa( )** function returns a pointer to *str*. There is no error-return value. Be sure to call **ltoa( )** with a string of sufficient length to hold the converted result. The longest string you need is 33 bytes.

Example

This program displays the value of 1423 in hexadecimal (58F):

```
#include "stdlib.h"

main()
{
   char p[33];

   ltoa(1423, p, 16);

   printf(p);
}
```

Related Functions

itoa( ), sscanf( )

int putenv(char *evar)

Description

The prototype for **putenv( )** is in **stdlib.h**.

The **putenv( )** function puts an environmental variable into DOS.

Refer to **getenv( )** and to a DOS manual for information about DOS environmental variables.

Related Function

getenv( )

void qsort(void *base, int num, int size, int (*compare)( ))

Description

The prototype for **qsort( )** is in **stdlib.h**.

The **qsort( )** function sorts the array pointed to by *base* using a quicksort (developed by C.A.R. Hoare). The quicksort is generally considered the best general-purpose sorting algorithm. Upon termination, the array will be sorted. The number of elements in the array is specified by *num*, and the size (in bytes) of each element is described by *size*.

The function pointed to by *compare* compares the array elements. The form of the *compare* function must be

```
func_name(arg1, arg2)
void *arg1, *arg2;
```

It must return the following values:

- If *arg1* is less than *arg2*, less than 0
- If *arg1* is equal to *arg2*, 0
- If *arg1* is greater than *arg2*, greater than 0

The array is sorted into ascending order with the lowest address containing the lowest element.

Example

This program sorts a list of integers and displays the result:

```
#include "stdlib.h"   /* "search.h" in some systems */

int num[10]= {
  1,3,6,5,8,7,9,6,2,0
};

main()
{
  int i, comp();

  printf("original array: ");
  for(i=0; i<10; i++) printf("%d ",num[i]);

  qsort(num, 10, sizeof(int), comp);

  printf("sorted array: ");
  for(i=0; i<10; i++) printf("%d ", num[i]);
}

/* compare the integers */
comp(int *i, int *j)
{
  return *i-*j;
}
```

Related Function

bsearch()

int rand(void)

Description

The prototype for **rand( )** is in **stdlib.h**.

The **rand( )** function generates a sequence of pseudorandom numbers. Each time it is called it returns an integer between 0 and **RAND—MAX**.

Example

This program displays ten pseudorandom numbers:

```
#include "stdlib.h"

main()
{
  int i;

  for(i=0; i<10; i++)
    printf("%d ", rand());
}
```

Related Function

srand( )

int random(int num)
void randomize(void)

Description

The prototypes for **random( )** and **randomize( )** are in **stdlib.h**.

The **random( )** macro returns a random number in the range 0-*num*.

The **randomize( )** macro initializes the random number generator to some random value. It uses the **time( )** function, so you may want to include **time.h** in any program that uses **randomize( )**.

Example

This program prints 10 random numbers between 0 and 25:

```
#include "time.h"
#include "stdlib.h"

main()
{
  int i;

  randomize();

  for(i=0; i<10; i++) printf("%d ", random(25));
}
```

Related Functions

rand( ), **srand( )**

int setjmp(jmp—buf envbuf)

Description

The prototype for **setjmp( )** is in **stdlib.h**.

The **setjmp( )** function saves the contents of the system stack in the buffer *envbuf* for later use by **longjmp( )**.

The **setjmp( )** function returns 0 upon invocation. However, when it executes, **longjmp( )** passes an argument (always nonzero) to **setjmp( )**, which appears to be **setjmp( )**'s value.

See **longjmp( )** for additional information.

Example

This program prints **1 2 3**:

```
#include "setjmp.h"

jmp_buf ebuf;

main()
{
```

```
    char first=1;
    int i;

    printf("1 ");
    i = setjmp(ebuf);
    if(first) {
      first =! first;
      f2();
      printf("this will not be printed");
    }
    printf("%d", i);
}

f2()
{
 printf("2 ");
 longjmp(ebuf, 3);
}
```

Related Function

longjmp( )

void srand(unsigned seed)

Description

The prototype for **srand( )** is in **stdlib.h**.

The **srand( )** function is used to set a starting point for the sequence generated by **rand( )**. (The **rand( )** function returns pseudorandom numbers.)

The **srand( )** function allows multiple program runs using different sequences of pseudorandom numbers.

Example

This program uses the system time to initialize the **rand( )** function randomly by using **srand( )**:

```
#include "stdio.h"
#include "stdlib.h"
#include "time.h"

/* Seed rand with the system time
   and display the first 100 numbers.
*/
```

```
main()
{
  int i,stime;
  long ltime;

  /* get the current calendar time */

  ltime = time(NULL);
  stime = (unsigned int) ltime/2;
  srand(stime);
  for(i=0; i<10; i++) printf("%d ", rand());
}
```

Related Function

rand( )

int (*ssignal(int signal, int (*func)( )))( )

Description

The prototype for **ssignal( )** is in **signal.h**.

The **ssignal( )** function defines the *function* to be executed if the specified *signal* is received. The value for *func* must be the address of a function or one of the following macros (defined in **signal.h**):

Macro	Meaning
SIG—DFL	Use default signal handling
SIG—IGN	Ignore the signal

If a function address is used, the specified function is executed.

Related Function

gsignal( )

unsigned int —status87(void)

Description

The prototype for —**status87( )** is in **float.h.**

The —**status87( )** function returns the value of the floating-point status word. You must have an 8087/80287 math coprocessor installed in the computer before using this function.

Related Functions

—**clear87( )**, —**fpreset( )**

double strtod (char *start, char **end)

Description

The prototype for **strtod( )** is in **stdio.h.** The **strtod( )** function converts the string representation of a number stored in the string pointed to by *start* into a **double** and returns the result.

The **strtod( )** function works as follows: First, any leading white space in the string pointed to by *start* is stripped. Next, each character that comprises the number is read. Any character that cannot be part of a floating-point number stops the process. This includes white space, punctuation other than periods, and characters other than **E** or **e.** Finally, *end* is set to point to the remainder, if any, of the original string. This means that if **strtod( )** is called with **100.00 Pliers**, the value 100.00 is returned and *end* points to the space that precedes Pliers.

If a conversion error occurs, **strtod( )** returns either **HUGE—VAL** for overflow, or −**HUGE—VAL** for underflow. If no conversion could take place, 0 is returned.

Example

This program reads floating-point numbers from a character array:

```
#include "stdlib.h"
#include "ctype.h"

main()
{
  char *end, *start="100.00 pliers 200.00 hammers";

  end=start;
  while(*start) {
    printf("%f, ",strtod(start,&end));
    printf("remainder: %s\n",end);
    start=end;
    /* move past the non-digits */
    while(!isdigit(*start) && *start) start++;
  }
}
```

The output is:

```
100.00000, remainder: pliers 200.00 hammers
200.00000, remainder: hammers
```

Related Function

atof( )

long int strtol(char *start, char **end, int radix)

Description

The prototype for **strtol( )** is in **stdlib.h**.

The **strtol( )** function converts the string representation of a number stored in the string pointed to by *start* into a **long int** and returns the result. The base of the number is determined by *radix*. If *radix* is 0, the base is determined by rules that govern constant specification. If *radix* is other than 0, it must be in the range 2-36.

The **strtol( )** function works as follows. First, any leading white space in the string pointed to by *start* is stripped.

Next, each character that comprises the number is read. Any character that cannot be part of a long integer number stops the process. This includes white space, punctuation, and characters. Finally, *end* is set to point to the remainder, if any, of the original string. This means that if **strtol( )** is called with **100 Pliers**, the value 100L is returned and *end* points to the space that precedes **Pliers**.

If a conversion error occurs, **strtol( )** returns either **LONG—MAX** for overflow, or **LONG—MIN** for underflow. If no conversion could take place, 0 is returned.

Example

This function reads base 10 numbers from standard input and returns their **long** equivalents:

```
#include "stdlib.h"

long int read_long()
{
  char *start[80], *end;

  printf("enter a number: ");
  gets(start);
  return strtol(start, &end, 10);
}
```

Related Function

atol( )

void swab(char *source, char *dest, int num)

Description

The prototype for **swab( )** is in **stdlib.h**.

The **swab( )** function copies *num* bytes from the string pointed to by *source* into *dest*, switching the position of each even/odd pair of bytes as it goes.

Example

This fragment prints **iH**:

```
char dest[3];

swab("Hi", dest, 2);
printf(dest);
```

int system(char *str)

Description

The prototype for **system()** is in **stdlib.h**.

The **system()** function passes to DOS as a command the string pointed to by *str* and returns the exit status of the command.

Example

This program displays the contents of the current working directory:

```
#include "stdlib.h"

main()
{
   system("dir");
}
```


Related Function

exit()

void va—start(va—list argptr, last—parm)
void va—end(va—list argptr)
type va—arg(va—list argptr, type)

Description

The prototypes for these functions are in **stdarg.h**.

The **va—arg()**, **va—start()**, and **va—end()** functions work together to allow a variable number of arguments to be passed to a function. The most common example of a function that takes a variable number of arguments is **printf()**. The type **va—list** is defined by **stdarg.h**.

The general procedure for creating a function that can take a variable number of arguments is as follows. The function must have at least one known parameter, but may have more, prior to the variable parameter list. The rightmost known parameter is called the *last—parm*. Before any of the variable length parameters can be accessed, the argument pointer *argptr* must be initialized through a call to **va— start()**. After that, parameters are returned via calls to **va— arg()** with *type* being the type of the next parameter. Finally, once all the parameters have been read and prior to returning from the function, a call to **va—end()** must be made to ensure that the stack is properly restored. If **va— end()** is not called, a program crash is very likely.

Example

This program uses **sum—series()** to return the sum of a series of numbers. The first argument contains a count of the number of arguments to follow. This fragment displays the sum of the first five elements of the series $1/2 + 1/4 + 1/8 + 1/16 \ldots + 1/2^n$:

```c
#include "stdio.h"
#include "stdarg.h"

/* variable length argument example - sum a series */
main()
{
  double d, sum_series();

  d = sum_series(5, 0.5, 0.25, 0.125, 0.0625, 0.03125);

  printf("sum of series is %f\n",d);
}

double sum_series(int num)
{
  double sum = 0.0, t;
  va_list argptr;

  /* initialize argptr */
```

```
va_start(argptr,num);

/* sum the series */
for(; num; num--) {
  t = va_arg(argptr,double);
  sum += t;
}

/* do orderly shutdown */
va_end(argptr);
return sum;
}
```

The output displayed is **0.968750**.

Related Function

vprintf( )

Turbo C Applications

The chapters in this section apply Turbo C to three widely divergent programming tasks. The goal is to give you the flavor of Turbo C programming in a variety of situations. Each chapter was adapted from one of my previous books on C as being representative of a class of applications to which Turbo C can be applied with great success. The applications were also chosen because of their general interest and applicability to many mainstream programming projects.

Chapter 25 deals with the basic building blocks of database management programs: queues, stacks, linked lists, and binary trees. This chapter is taken from *Advanced Turbo C* (by Herbert Shildt, Osborne/McGraw-Hill, 1987), which covers a wide range of the common programming situations likely to confront the Turbo C programmer and provides a wealth of algorithms and routines to deal with them effectively.

Chapter 26 covers AI-based problem solving. As you are probably aware, artificial intelligence is becoming increasingly important in many applications. The chapter illustrates several of the basic techniques used to solve problems that do not lend themselves to "normal" solutions. This chapter is taken from *Artificial Intelligence Using C* (by Herbert Shildt, Osborne/McGraw-Hill, 1987). If you are interested in applying C to AI-based problems, you will be interested in this book.

Finally, Chapter 27 discusses language interpreters and expression parsers. A Small BASIC is developed in this chapter to illustrate how language interpreters can be created. This chapter is from *C: Power User's Guide* (by Herbert Schildt, Osborne/McGraw-Hill, 1988), which explores and explains the programming secrets the pros use to create world-class software.

675

Queues, Stacks, Linked Lists, and Trees

Programs consist of two things: algorithms and data structures. A good program is a blend of both. The choice and implementation of a data structure is as important as the routines that manipulate it. How information is organized and accessed is usually determined by the nature of the programming problem. It is important for a programmer to know the right storage and retrieval method for a variety of situations.

How closely the logical concept of an item of data is bound with its physical machine representation is in inverse correlation to its abstraction. That is, as data types become more complex, the way the programmer thinks of them bears an ever-decreasing resemblance to the way they are actually represented in memory. For example, simple types, such as **char** and **int**, are tightly bound to their machine representation. In this case, for example, the value that an integer has in its machine representation closely approximates the programmer's conception of it. Simple arrays, which are organized collections of the simple data types, are not quite as tightly bound as the simple types themselves because an array may not appear in memory the way the programmer thinks of it. Still less tightly bound are **floats** because the actual representation inside the machine is a little like the average programmer's conception of a floating-point number. The structure, which is a conglomerate data type accessed under one name, is even more abstracted from the machine representation. The final level of abstraction transcends the mere physical aspects of the data and concentrates instead upon the sequence in which the data will be accessed, that is, *stored* and *retrieved*. In essence, the physical data is linked with a "data engine" that controls the way information can be accessed by your program. The basic engines are

- A queue
- A stack
- A linked list
- A binary tree

Each of these methods provides a solution to a class of problems. These methods are essentially "devices" that perform a specific storage and retrieval operation on the information they are given and the requests they receive. They share two operations, *store an item* and *retrieve an item,* where an item is one informational unit. The rest of this chapter will show you how to implement these operations for use in your own Turbo C programs.

Queues

A *queue* is simply a linear list of information that is accessed in *first-in, first-out* order, sometimes called FIFO. That is, the first item placed in the queue is the first item retrieved, the second item put in is the second retrieved, and so on. This is the only means of storage and retrieval; random access of any specific item is not allowed.

Queues are very common in real life. For example, lines at a bank or a fast-food restaurant are queues. To visualize how a queue works, consider two functions: **qstore( )** and **qretrieve( )**. The **qstore( )** function places an item on the end of the queue, and **qretrieve( )** removes the first item from the queue and returns its value. Figure 25-1 shows the effect of a series of these operations.

Action	Contents of Queue
qstore(A)	A
qstore(B)	A B
qstore(C)	A B C
qretrieve( ) returns A	B C
qstore(D)	B C D
qretrieve( ) returns B	C D
qretrieve( ) returns C	D

Figure 25-1.   A queue in action

Remember that a retrieve operation removes an item from the queue and, if it is not stored elsewhere, destroys it. Therefore, a queue may be empty, even though the program using it is still active, because all its items have been removed.

Queues are used in many types of programming situations. One of the most common uses is for simulations. Two other main uses are for event scheduling, such as a PERT or Gantt chart, and I/O buffering.

Let's develop a simple appointment scheduling program as an example. This program allows you to enter a number of appointments, which will be removed from the list as they are performed. You might use a program like this to organize a day's appointments. For the sake of simplicity the program uses an array of pointers to the event strings and limits each appointment description to 256 characters. The number of entries is arbitrarily limited to 100 and is represented by the macro **MAX**. First, the functions **qstore()** and **qre-**

trieve( ) are needed for the simple scheduling program. They are shown here:

```
/* Store an appointment. */
void qstore(char *q)
{
  if(spos==MAX) {
    printf("List full\n");
    return;
  }
  p[spos]=q;
  spos++;
}

/* Retrieve an appointment. */
char *qretrieve()
{
  if(rpos==spos) {
    printf("No (more) appointments.\n");
    return NULL;
  }
  rpos++;
  return p[rpos-1];
}
```

Notice that these functions require two global variables: **spos**, which holds the index of the next free storage location, and **rpos**, which holds the index of the next item to retrieve. It is possible to use these functions to maintain a queue of other data types by simply changing the base type of the array they operate on.

The function **qstore( )** places pointers to new appointments on the end of the list and checks to see if the list is full. The **qretrieve( )** function takes appointments off the queue as they occur. With each new appointment scheduled, **spos** is incremented, and with each appointment removed **rpos** is incremented. In essence, **rpos** chases **spos** through the queue. Figure 25-2 shows how this appears in memory as the program executes. If **rpos** and **spos** are equal, there are no appointments left in the schedule. Keep in mind that even though the information stored in the queue is not actually destroyed by the **qretrieve( )** function, it can never be accessed again and thus is effectively destroyed.

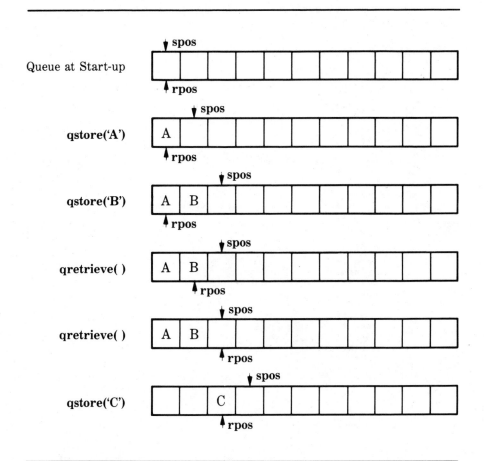

Figure 25-2.   The retrieve index chasing a store index

The entire program for this simple appointment scheduler is listed here. You may find it fun to enhance this program for your own use.

```
#include "stdlib.h"
#include "stdio.h"
#define MAX 100

char *p[MAX], *qretrieve();
int spos;
int rpos;
void enter(void), qstore(char *), review(void), delete(void);

main()  /* Mini Appointment-Scheduler */
{
  char s[80];
  register int t;

  for(t=0; t<MAX; ++t) p[t]=NULL; /* init array to nulls */
  spos=0; rpos=0;

  for(;;) {
    printf("Enter, List, Remove, Quit: ");
    gets(s);
    *s = toupper(*s);

    switch(*s) {
      case 'E':
        enter();
        break;
      case 'L':
        review();
        break;
      case 'R':
        delete();
        break;
      case 'Q':
        exit(0);
    }
  }
}

/* Enter appointments in queue. */
void enter()
{
  char s[256], *p;

  do {
    printf("enter appointment %d: ", spos+1);
    gets(s);
    if(*s==0) break;  /* no entry */
    p=malloc(strlen(s));
    if(!p) {
      printf("out of memory.\n");
      return;
    }
    strcpy(p, s);
    if(*s) qstore(p);
  }while(*s);
}
```

```
/* See what's in the queue. */
void review()
{
  register int t;

  for(t=rpos; t<spos; ++t)
    printf("%d. %s\n", t+1, p[t]);
}

/* Delete an appointment from the queue. */
void delete()
{
  char *p;

  if(!(p=qretrieve())) return;
  printf("%s\n", p);
}

/* Store an appointment. */
void qstore(char *q)
{
  if(spos==MAX) {
    printf("List full\n");
    return;
  }
  p[spos]=q;
  spos++;
}

/* Retrieve an appointment. */
char *qretrieve()
{
  if(rpos==spos) {
    printf("No (more) appointments.\n");
    return NULL;
  }
  rpos++;
  return p[rpos-1];
}
```

A sample run of the appointment scheduler is shown here:

```
Enter, List, Remove, Quit: E
enter appointment 1: Jon at 9 about the phone system
enter appointment 2: Ted at 10:30 - wants that raise...humm.
enter appointment 3: lunch with Mary and Tom at Harry's
enter appointment 4: <cr>
Enter, List, Remove, Quit: L
1. Jon at 9 about the phone system
2. Ted at 10:30 - wants that raise...humm.
3. lunch with Mary and Tom at Harry's
Enter, List, Remove, Quit: R
```

```
Jon at 9 about the phone system
Enter, List, Remove, Quit: L
2. Ted at 10:30 - wants that raise...humm.
3. lunch with Mary and Tom at Harry's
Enter, List, Remove, Quit:
```

The Circular Queue

In studying the appointment scheduler program in the previous section, an improvement may have occurred to you. Instead of having the program stop when the limit of the array used to store the queue is reached, you could have both the store index, **spos**, and the retrieve index, **rpos**, loop back to the start of the array. In this way, any number of items could be placed on the queue as long as items were also being taken off. This method of implementing a queue is called a *circular queue* because it uses its storage array like a circle rather than a linear list.

To create a circular queue for use in the appointment scheduler program, the functions **qstore()** and **qretrieve** need to be changed as shown here:

```
void qstore(char *q)
{
  /* The queue is full if either spos is one less than rpos
     or if spos is at the end of the queue array and rpos
     is at the beginning.
  */
  if(spos+1==rpos || (spos+1==MAX && !rpos)) {
    printf("list full\n");
    return;
  }
  p[spos] = q;
  spos++;
  if(spos==MAX) spos=0; /* loop back */
}

char *qretrieve()
{
  if(rpos==MAX) rpos=0; /* loop back */
  if(rpos==spos) {
    printf("No events to perform.\n");
    return NULL;
  }
  rpos++;
  return p[rpos-1];
}
```

In essence, the queue is full only when both the store index and the retrieve index are equal; otherwise there is room in the queue for another event. However, this means that when the program starts, the retrieve index, **rpos** must be set not to 0, but to **MAX**, so that the first call to **qstore( )** does not produce the **list full** message. It is important to note that the queue will hold only **MAX**−1 elements because **rpos** and **spos** must always be at least one element apart. Otherwise it would be impossible to know whether the queue was full or empty. Conceptually, the array used for the circular version of the appointment scheduler program looks like Figure 25-3.

Perhaps the most common use of a circular queue is in operating systems to hold the information that is read from and written to disk files or the console. Another very common

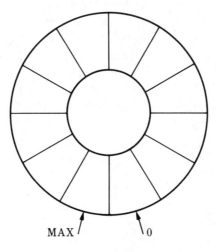

Figure 25-3.   The circular array for the mini-scheduler program

use of the circular queue is in real-time application programs that must continue to process information while buffering I/O requests. Many word processors do this when they reformat a paragraph or justify a line. There is a brief time during which what is being typed is not displayed until after that other process is completed. To accomplish this, the application program needs to continue to check for keyboard entry during the other process's execution. If a key has been typed, it is quickly placed in the queue, and the process continues. Once the process is complete, the characters are retrieved from the queue.

To see how this can be done, look at the following simple program that contains two processes. The first process in the program prints the numbers 1-32,000 on the screen. The second process places characters into a circular queue as they are typed, without echoing them to the screen, until a semicolon is typed. The characters you type are not displayed because the first process is given priority over the screen at this time. Once the semicolon has been typed, the characters in the queue are retrieved and printed. The proposed ANSI standard does not define library functions that check keyboard status or read keyboard characters without echoing them to the display because these functions are highly operating-system dependent. However, Turbo C does supply routines to do these things. The short program shown here will work with the IBM PC and uses the Turbo C **kbhit( )** and **getch( )** functions to determine the keyboard status and read a character without echoing it to the screen.

```
/* A circular queue example using a keyboard buffer. */
#include "stdio.h"

#define MAX 80

char buf[MAX+1];
int spos=0;
int rpos=MAX;

void qstore(char);
char qretrieve();
```

```
main()
{
  register char ch;
  int t;

  buf[80]=NULL;

  for(ch=' ',t=0; t<32000 && ch!=';'; ++t) {
    printf("%d", kbhit());
    if(kbhit()) {
      ch = getch();
      qstore(ch);
    }
    printf("%d ", t);
  }

  while((ch=qretrieve())!=NULL) putchar(ch); /* display buf */
}

/* Store characters in the queue. */
void qstore(char q)
{
  if(spos+1==rpos || (spos+1==MAX && !rpos)) {
    printf("List full\n");
    return;
  }
  buf[spos] = q;
  spos++;
  if(spos==MAX) spos = 0; /* loop back */
}

/* Retrieve a character. */
char qretrieve()
{
  if(rpos==MAX) rpos=0; /* loop back */
  if(rpos==spos) {
    return NULL;
  }
  rpos++;
  return buf[rpos-1];
}
```

Stacks

A *stack* is the opposite of a queue because it uses *last-in, first-out* accessing, sometimes called LIFO. To visualize a stack you need only imagine a stack of plates. The first plate on the table is the last to be used and the last plate placed on the stack is the first to be used. Stacks are used a great deal in system software, including compilers and interpreters. In fact, Turbo C uses the computer's stack when passing arguments to functions.

The two basic operations, *store* and *retrieve* are, for historical reasons, usually called *push* and *pop*, respectively. To implement a stack you need two functions: **push()**, which places a value on the stack, and **pop()**, which retrieves a value from the stack. You also need a region of memory to use as the stack. You can either use an array for this purpose or allocate a region of memory by using Turbo C's dynamic memory allocation functions. Like the queue, the retrieval function takes a value off the list and, if it is not stored elsewhere, destroys it. The general form of **push()** and **pop()** using an integer array is shown here. You can maintain stacks of other data types by changing the base type of the array that the **push()** and **pop()** functions operate on.

```
int stack[MAX];
int tos=0;    /* top of stack */

/* Put an element on the stack. */
void push(int i)
{
  if(tos>=MAX) {
    printf("stack full\n");
    return;
  }
  stack[tos] = i;
  tos++;
}

/* Retrieve the top element from the stack. */
int pop()
{
  tos--;
  if(tos<0) {
    printf("stack underflow\n");
    return HUGE_VAL;
  }
  return stack[tos];
}
```

The size of the stack is determined by the value you choose for **MAX**. In the example that follows, the value 100 is used. The variable **tos** is the index of the next open stack location. When implementing these functions, you must always remember to prevent overflow and underflow. In these routines, the stack is empty if **tos** is 0, and full if **tos** is greater than the last storage location. To see how a stack works, see Figure 25-4.

An excellent example of stack use is a four-function calculator. Most calculators today accept a standard form of expression called *infix* notation, which takes the general form operand-operator-operand. For example, to add 100 to 200, you enter **100, +, 200**, and then =. However, in an effort to save memory (which used to be expensive), many early calculators used a form of expression evaluation called *postfix* notation, in which both operands are entered first, and then the operator is entered. For example, using postfix to add 100 to 200, you enter **100, 200**, and then **+**. In postfix, as

Action	Contents of Stack
push(A)	A
push(B)	B A
push(C)	C B A
pop( ) retrieves C	B A
push(F)	F B A
pop( ) retrieves F	B A
pop( ) retrieves B	A
pop( ) retrieves A	*empty*

Figure 25-4.   A stack in action

operands are entered, they are placed on a stack. Each time an operator is entered, two operands are removed from the stack, and the result is pushed back on the stack. The advantage of the postfix form is that very complex expressions can easily be evaluated by the calculator without much code.

Before the full four-function calculator for postfix expressions is developed, the basic **push( )** and **pop( )** functions need to be modified. The program uses Turbo C's dynamic memory allocation routines to provide memory for the stack. These functions are shown here as they are used in the calculator example:

```
int *p;    /* will point to a region of free memory */
int *tos; /* points to top of stack */
int *bos; /* points to bottom of stack */

/* Store an element on the stack. */
void push(int i)
{
   if(p>bos) {
     printf("stack full\n");
     return;
   }
   *p = i;
   p++;
}

/* Retrieve the top element from the stack. */
pop()
{
   p--;
   if(p<tos) {
     printf("stack underflow\n");
     return 0;
   }
   return *p;
}
```

Before these functions can be used, a region of free memory must be allocated using **malloc( )**, the address of the beginning of that region assigned to **tos**, and the address of the end assigned to **bos**.

The entire calculator program is shown here. In addition to the operators +, −, ×, /, you may also enter a period, which displays the current value on the top of the stack.

```
/* A simple four-function calculator. */

#include "stdlib.h"
#define MAX 100

int *p;    /* will point to a region of free memory */
int *tos; /* points to top of stack */
int *bos; /* points to bottom of stack */
void push(int);

main()
{
  int a,b;
  char s[80];

  p = (int *) malloc(MAX*sizeof(int));  /* get stack memory */
  if(!p) {
    printf("allocation failure\n");
    exit(1);
  }
  tos = p;
  bos = p+MAX-1;

  printf("Four Function Calculator\n");

  do {
    printf(": ");
    gets(s);
    switch(*s) {
      case '+':
        a = pop();
        b = pop();
        printf("%d\n", a+b);
        push(a+b);
        break;
      case '-':
        a = pop();
        b = pop();
        printf("%d\n", b-a);
        push(b-a);
        break;
      case '*':
        a = pop();
        b = pop();
        printf("%d\n", b*a);
        push(b*a);
        break;
      case '/':
        a = pop();
        b = pop();
        if(a==0) {
          printf("divide by 0\n");
          break;
        }
        printf("%d\n", b/a);
```

```
              push(b/a);
              break;
          case '.': /* show  contents of top of stack */
              a = pop();
              push(a);
              printf("Current value on top of stack: %d\n", a);
              break;
          default:
              push(atoi(s));
      }
  } while(*s!='q');
}

/* Put an element on the stack. */
void push(int i)
{
  if(p>bos) {
    printf("stack full\n");
    return;
  }
  *p = i;
  p++;
}

/* Retrieve the top element from the stack. */
pop()
{
  p--;
  if(p<tos) {
    printf("stack underflow\n");
    return 0;
  }
  return *p;
}
```

A sample session at the calculator is shown here:

```
Four Function Calculator
: 10<cr>
: 10<cr>
: +<cr>
20
: 5<cr>
: /<cr>
4
: .<cr>
Current value on top of stack: 4
: q<cr>
```

Linked Lists

Queues and stacks share two traits:

1. They have very strict rules for referencing the data stored in them.

2. Their retrieval operations are consumptive by nature. That is, accessing an item in a stack or queue requires its removal and, unless stored elsewhere, its destruction.

In addition, stacks and queues both use a contiguous region of memory to operate. Unlike a stack or a queue, a *linked list* can access its storage in a random fashion because each piece of information carries with it a *link* to the next data item in the chain. That is, a linked list requires a complex data structure, unlike a stack or queue, which can operate on both simple and complex data items. Also, a linked list retrieval operation does not remove and destroy an item from the list. In fact, a specific *deletion* operation has to be added to do this.

Linked lists are used for two main purposes. The first purpose is to create arrays of unknown size in memory. If the amount of storage is knowable in advance, an array could be used, but if the actual size of a list is not knowable, a linked list must be used. The second purpose is for disk file storage of databases. The linked list allows items to be inserted and deleted quickly and easily without rearranging the entire disk file. For these reasons linked lists are used extensively in database managers.

Linked lists can be linked either singly or doubly. A singly linked list contains a link to the next data item. A doubly linked list contains links to both the next and the previous element in the list. You use one or the other depending on your application.

Singly Linked Lists

A singly linked list requires each item of information to contain a link to the next element in the list. Each data item generally consists of a structure that contains both information fields as well as a link pointer. Conceptually, a singly linked list looks like Figure 25-5.

There are two ways to build a singly linked list. The first is simply to put each new item on the end of the list. The second is to add items in specific places in the list: in ascending sorted order, for example. How you build the list determines the way the **store( )** function is coded. First, let's look at the simpler case of creating a linked list by adding items at the end.

Before beginning, you need to define a data structure to hold the information and the links. Because mailing lists are common let's use one here. The data structure for each element in the mailing list is defined as

```
struct address {
   char name[40];
   char street[40];
   char city[20];
   char state[3];
   char zip[10];
   struct address *next;
} info;
```

The function **slstore( )** builds a singly linked list by placing each new element at the end. It must be passed a pointer to a structure of type **address** as shown here:

```
void slstore(struct address *i)
struct address *i;
{
   static struct address *last=NULL; /* start with null link */

   if(!last) last = i; /* first item in list */
   else last->next = i;
   i->next = NULL;
   last = i;
}
```

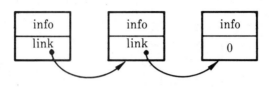

Figure 25-5.   Singly linked list in memory

Notice the use of the **static** variable *last*. Because initialization of a **static** variable occurs once, at the start of the program, it can be used to start the list-building process.

Although it is possible to sort the list created with the function **slstore( )** as a separate operation, it would be easier simply to sort the list while building it by inserting each new item in the proper sequence of the chain. If the list is already sorted, it would also be advantageous to keep it sorted by inserting new items in their proper locations. This is done by scanning the list sequentially until the proper location is found, inserting the new address at that point, and rearranging the links as necessary.

Three possible situations can occur when inserting an item in a singly linked list:

1. The item may become the new first item.

2. It may go in the middle, between two other items.

3. It may become the last item.

Figure 25-6 shows how the links are changed for each case.

Remember that if you change the first item in the list you must update the entry point to the list elsewhere in your program. To avoid this overhead, it is possible to use a *sentinel* as a first item. In this case, a special value is chosen

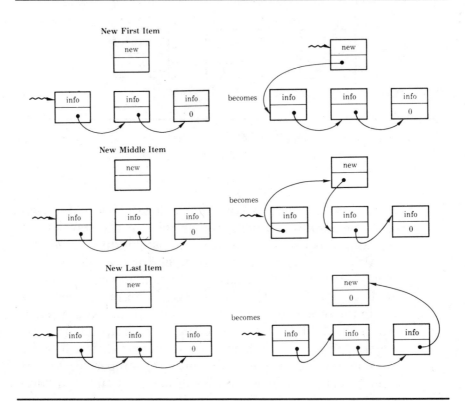

Figure 25-6.   Inserting an item into a singly linked list

that is always first in the list. In this way, the entry point to the list never changes. One disadvantage of this method is that one extra storage location is needed to hold the sentinel. A more important problem, however, is that it requires a value that can never constitute valid data—a difficult thing to guarantee in certain situations.

The function **sls_store()** in the following program inserts addresses into the mailing list in ascending order based on the **name** field. It returns a pointer to the first element in the list and also requires that the pointer to the start of the list be passed to it. When the first element is inserted, both **top** and **i** are the same.

```
/* store in sorted order */
struct address *sls_store(struct address *i, /* new element to store */
                          struct address *top) /* start of list */
{
  static struct address *last=0; /* start with null link */
  struct address *old,*start;

  start=top;

  if(!last) {  /* first element in list */
    i->next = NULL;
    last = i;
    return i;
  }

  old = NULL;
  while(top) {
    if(strcmp(top->name,i->name)<0) {
      old = top;
      top = top->next;
    }
    else {
      if(old) {  /* goes in middle */
        old->next = i;
        i->next = top;
        return start;
      }
      i->next = top; /* new first element */
      return     i;
    }
  }
  last->next = i; /* put on end */
  i->next = NULL;
  last = i;
  return start;
}
```

In a linked list, it is uncommon to find a specific function dedicated to the retrieve process, that is, returning item after item in list order. Usually this code is so short that it is simply placed inside another routine such as a search, delete, or display function. For example, the routine shown here displays all the names in a mailing list:

```
void display(struct address *top)
{
  while(top) {
    printf(top->name);
    top=top->next;
  }
}
```

Here, **top** is a pointer to the first structure in the list. It must be initialized to 0 elsewhere in the program. Retrieving items from the list is as simple as following a chain. A search routine based on the **name** field could be written like this:

```
struct address *search(struct address *top, char *n)
{
  while(top) {
    if(!strcmp(n,top->name)) return top;
    top = top->next;
  }
  return NULL;  /* no match */
}
```

Because **search( )** is returning a pointer to the list item that matches the search name, it must be declared to be returning a structure pointer of type **address**. If there is no match, a null is returned.

The process of deleting an item from a singly linked list is straightforward. As with insertion, there are three possibilities: deleting the first item, deleting an item in the middle, and deleting the last item. Figure 25-7 shows each of these operations diagrammatically.

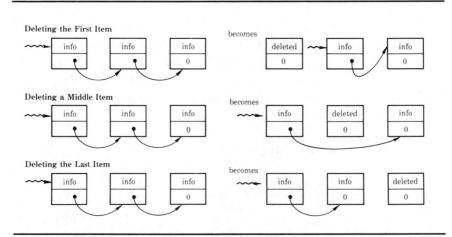

Figure 25-7. The three cases of deleting an item from a singly linked list

The function shown here deletes a given item from a list of structures of type **address**:

```
struct address *sldelete(
   struct address *p, /* previous item */
   struct address *i, /* item to delete */
   struct address *top)  /* start of list */
{
   if(p) p->next = i->next;
   else   top = i->next;

   return top;
}
```

The **sldelete()** function must be sent pointers to the deleted item, the item before it in the chain, and the start of the list. If the first item is to be removed, the previous pointer must be null. The function must return a pointer to the start of the list because, if the first item is deleted, the program must know where the new first element is located.

Singly linked lists have one major drawback: The list cannot be followed in reverse order. For this reason, doubly linked lists are generally used.

Doubly Linked Lists

Doubly linked lists consist of data plus links to both the next item and the preceding item. Figure 25-8 shows how these links are arranged.

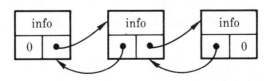

Figure 25-8.   A doubly linked list

Having two links has two major advantages:

1. The list can be read in either direction. This not only simplifies sorting the list but also, in the case of a database, allows a user to scan the list in either direction.

2. In case of equipment failure, if one of the links becomes invalid, the list can be reconstructed using the other because either the forward links or the backward links can read the entire list.

The three basic operations that can be performed on a doubly linked list are inserting a new first element, inserting an element in the middle, and inserting a new last element. These operations are shown diagrammatically in Figure 25-9.

Building a doubly linked list is similar to building a singly linked list except that two links are maintained. Therefore the structure needs to have room for both links. Using the mailing list example again, we can modify structure **address** as shown here to accommodate double linking:

```
struct address {
  char name[40];
  char street[40];
  char city[20];
  char state[3];
  char zip[10];
  struct address *next;
  struct address *prior;
} info;
```

Using structure **address** as the basic data item, the **dlstore( )** function shown here builds a doubly linked list:

```
void dlstore(struct address *i)
{
  static struct address *last=NULL; /* start with null link */

  if(last==NULL) last = i; /* first item in list */
  else last->next = i;
  i->next = NULL;
  i->prior = last;
  last = i;
}
```

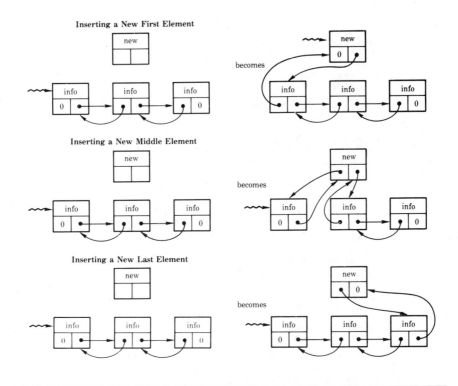

Figure 25-9.   The three cases of inserting an item into a doubly linked list

This function places each new entry on the end of the list.

Like the singly linked list, a doubly linked list can have a function that stores each element in a specific location in the list as it is built instead of always placing each new item on the end. The **dls_store( )** function shown here creates a list that is sorted in ascending order:

```
/* Create a doubly linked list in sorted order.
   A pointer to the first element is returned because
   it is possible that a new element will be inserted
   at the start of the list.
```

```
*/
struct address *dls_store(struct address *i, /* new element */
                struct address *top) /* first element in list */
{
  struct address *old,*p;

  if(last==NULL) {   /* first element in list */
    i->next = NULL;
    i->prior = NULL;
    last = i;
    return i;
  }

  p = top; /* start at top of list */

  old = NULL;
  while(p) {
    if(strcmp(p->name, i->name)<0){
      old = p;
      p = p->next;
    }
    else {
      if(p->prior) {
        p->prior->next = i;
        i->next = p;
        i->prior = p->prior;
        p->prior = i;
        return top;
      }
      i->next = p; /* new first element */
      i->prior = NULL;
      p->prior = i;
      return    i;
    }
  }
  old->next = i; /* put on end */
  i->next = NULL;
  i->prior = old;
  last = i;
  return start;
}
```

Because an item can be inserted at the top of the list, this function must return a pointer to the first item in the list so that other parts of the program will know where the list begins.

As with the singly linked list, retrieving a specific data item is simply the process of following the links until the proper element is found.

The three cases to consider when deleting an element from a doubly linked list are deleting the first item, deleting an item from the middle, and deleting the last item. Figure 25-10 shows how the links are rearranged.

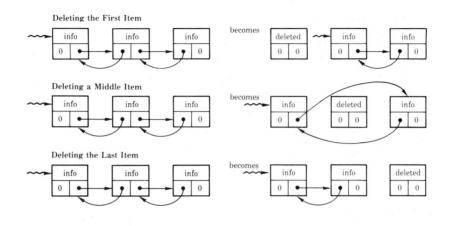

Figure 25-10.   Deletion in a doubly linked list

The following function deletes an item of type **address** from a doubly linked list:

```
struct address *dldelete(
  struct address *i, /* item to delete */
  struct address *top)  /* first item in list */
{
  if(i->prior) i->prior->next = i->next;
  else { /* new first item */
    top = i->next;
    /* if deleting only element in list skip */
      if(top) top->prior=0;
  }

  if(i->next) i->next->prior = i->prior;
  return top;
}
```

As you can see, this function requires one less pointer to be passed to it than the singly linked list version because the data item being deleted already carries with it a link to the previous and next element. Again, because the first element in the list could change, the pointer to the top element is passed back to the calling routine.

A Mailing List Example

The following is a simple but complete mailing list program that shows the use of a doubly linked list. The entire list is kept in memory while in use. However, it can be stored in a disk file and loaded for later use.

```
#include "stdio.h"
#include "stdlib.h"

struct address {
  char name[30];
  char street[40];
  char city[20];
  char state[3];
  char zip[10]; /* hold US and Canadian zips */
  struct address *next;  /* pointer to next entry */
  struct address *prior;  /* pointer to previous record */
} list_entry;

struct address *start;  /* pointer to first entry in list */
struct address *last;  /* pointer to last entry */

void enter(), display(), search(), save(), load(), list();
struct address *dls_store(struct address *, struct address *);

main()
{

  start=last=NULL;  /* zero length list */
  for(;;) {
    switch(menu_select()) {
      case 1: enter();
        break;
      case 2: delete();
        break;
      case 3: list();
        break;
      case 4: search(); /* find a street */
        break;
      case 5: save();  /* save list to disk */
        break;
      case 6: load();  /* read from disk */
        break;
      case 7: exit(0);
    }
  }
}

/* select an operation */
menu_select()
{
  char s[80];
  int c;
```

```
    printf("1. Enter a name\n");
    printf("2. Delete a name\n");
    printf("3. List the file\n");
    printf("4. Search\n");
    printf("5. Save the file\n");
    printf("6. Load the file\n");
    printf("7. Quit\n");
    do {
      printf("\nEnter your choice: ");
      gets(s);
      c = atoi(s);
    } while(c<0 || c>7);
    return c;
}

/* Enter names and addresses. */
void enter()
{
  struct address *info;

  for(;;) {
    info = (struct address *)malloc(sizeof(list_entry));
    if(!info) {
      printf("\nout of memory");
      return;
    }

    inputs("enter name: ", info->name,30);
    if(!info->name[0]) break;  /* stop entering */
    inputs("enter street: ", info->street,40);
    inputs("enter city: ", info->city,20);
    inputs("enter state: ", info->state,3);
    inputs("enter zip: ", info->zip,10);

    start = dls_store(info, start);
  } /* entry loop */
}

/* This function will input a string up to
   the length in count and will prevent
   the string from being overrun.  It will also
   display a prompting message. */
inputs(char *prompt, char *s, int count)
{
  char p[255];

  do {
    printf(prompt);
    gets(p);
    if(strlen(p)>count) printf("\ntoo long\n");
  } while(strlen(p)>count);
  strcpy(s,p);
}

/* Create a doubly linked list in sorted order.
   A pointer to the first element is returned because
   it is possible that a new element will be inserted
   at the start of the list.
```

```
*/
struct address *dls_store(
  struct address *i,    /* new element */
  struct address *top   /* first element in list */
)
{
  struct address *old,*p;

  if(last==NULL) {  /* first element in list */
    i->next = NULL;
    i->prior = NULL;
    last = i;
    return i;
  }

  p = top; /* start at top of list */

  old = NULL;
  while(p) {
    if(strcmp(p->name, i->name)<0){
      old = p;
      p = p->next;
    }
    else {
      if(p->prior) {
        p->prior->next = i;
        i->next = p;
        i->prior = p->prior;
        p->prior = i;
        return top;
      }
      i->next = p; /* new first element */
      i->prior = NULL;
      p->prior = i;
      return i;
    }
  }
  old->next = i; /* put on end */
  i->next = NULL;
  i->prior = old;
  last = i;
  return start;
}

/* Remove an element from the list. */
delete()
{
  struct address *info, *find();
  char s[80];

  printf("enter name: ");
  gets(s);
  info=find(s);
  if(info) {
    if(start==info) {
      start=info->next;
```

```
          if(start) start->prior = NULL;
          else last = NULL;
        }
      else {
        info->prior->next = info->next;
        if(info!=last)
            info->next->prior = info->prior;
        else
          last = info->prior;
      }
      free(info);  /* return memory to system */
    }
}

/* Find an address. */
struct address *find( char *name)
{
  struct address *info;

  info = start;
  while(info) {
    if(!strcmp(name, info->name)) return info;
    info = info->next;  /* get next address */
  }
  printf("name not found\n");
  return NULL;  /* not found */
}

/* Display the entire list. */
void list()
{
  struct address *info;

  info = start;
  while(info) {
    display(info);
    info = info->next;  /* get next address */
  }
  printf("\n\n");
}

/*This function actually prints the fields in each address.*/
void display(struct address *info)
{
    printf("%s\n", info->name);
    printf("%s\n", info->street);
    printf("%s\n", info->city);
    printf("%s\n", info->state);
    printf("%s\n", info->zip);
    printf("\n\n");
}

/* Look for a name in the list. */
void search()
{
  char name[40];
```

```
    struct address *info, *find();

    printf("enter name to find: ");
    gets(name);
    if(!(info=find(name))) printf("not found\n");
    else display(info);
}

/* Save the file to disk. */
void save()
{
    struct address *info;

    FILE *fp;
    if((fp=fopen("mlist","wb"))==NULL) {
        printf("cannot open file\n");
        exit(1);
    }
    printf("\nsaving file\n");

    info = start;
    while(info) {
        fwrite(info, sizeof(struct address),1,fp);
        info = info->next;  /* get next address */
    }
    fclose(fp);
}

/* Load the address file. */
void load()
{
    struct address *info, *temp=NULL;
    FILE *fp;

    if((fp=fopen("mlist","rb"))==NULL) {
        printf("cannot open file\n");
        exit(1);
    }

    while(start) {
        info = start->next;
        free(info);
        start = info;
    }

    printf("\nloading file\n");

    start = (struct address *) malloc(sizeof(struct address));
    if(!start) {
        printf("out of memory\n");
        return;
    }
    info = start;
    while(!feof(fp)) {
        if(1!=fread(info,sizeof(struct address),1,fp)) break;
```

```
  /* get memory for next */
  info->next = (struct address *)
  malloc(sizeof(struct address));
  if(!info->next) {
    printf("out of memory\n");
    return;
  }
  info->prior = temp;
  temp = info;
  info = info->next;
}
temp->next = NULL;  /* last entry */
last = temp;

start->prior = NULL;
fclose(fp);
}
```

Binary Trees

Although there are many different types of trees, *binary trees* are special because when sorted they lend themselves to rapid searches, insertions, and deletions. Each item in a tree consists of information and links to both left and right members. Figure 25-11 shows a small tree.

Special terminology is needed when discussing trees. Computer scientists are not known for their grammar, and terminology for trees is a classic case of mixed metaphors! The *root* is the first item in the tree. Each data item is called a *node* (or sometimes a *leaf*) of the tree, and any piece of the tree is called a *subtree*. A node that has no subtrees attached to it is called a *terminal node*. The *height* of the tree is equal to the number of layers deep its roots grow. Throughout this discussion we will think of binary trees looking in memory the way they do on paper, but remember that a tree is only a

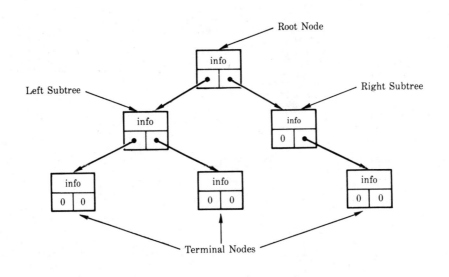

Figure 25-11.   A sample binary tree of height of 3

way to structure data in memory, and memory is linear in form.

In a sense, the binary tree is a special form of linked list. Items can be inserted, deleted, and accessed in any order, and the retrieval operation is nondestructive. Although trees are visually easy to understand, they present some very difficult programming problems of which we can only scratch the surface here.

Most functions that use trees are recursive because the tree itself is a recursive data structure. That is, each subtree is itself a tree. Therefore, the routines that we develop are recursive as well. Nonrecursive versions of these functions exist, but their code is much harder to understand.

How a tree is ordered depends on how it is going to be referenced. The process of accessing each node in a tree is called a *tree traversal*. Consider the following tree:

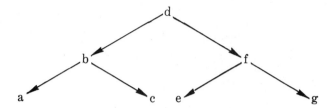

There are three ways to traverse a tree: *inorder, preorder,* and *postorder.* Using inorder, you visit the left subtree, visit the root, and then visit the right subtree. In preorder, you visit the root, then the left subtree, then the right subtree. With postorder, you visit the left subtree, then the right subtree, then the root. For the tree shown the order of access using each method is

Method	Order
inorder	a b c d e f g
preorder	d b a c f e g
postorder	a c b e g f d

Although a tree need not be sorted, most uses require it. Of course, what constitutes a sorted tree depends on how you will traverse the tree. For the rest of this chapter we will access the tree inorder. Therefore, a sorted binary tree is one where the subtree on the left contains nodes that are less than or equal to the root, while those on the right are greater than the root. The following **stree( )** function builds a sorted binary tree:

```
struct tree *stree(
  struct tree *root,
  struct tree *r,
  char info)
{
  if(!r) {
    r = (struct tree *) malloc(sizeof(struct tree));
    if(!r) {
      printf("out of memory\n");
      exit(0);
```

```
      }
      r->left = NULL;
      r->right = NULL;
      r->info = info;
      if(!root) return r; /* first entry */
      if(info<root->info) root->left = r;
      else root->right = r;
      return r;
    }

  if(info<r->info) stree(r,r->left,info);
  else
  if(info>r->info) stree(r,r->right,info);
}
```

This algorithm simply follows the links through the tree going left or right based on the **info** field. To use this function you need a global variable that holds the root of the tree. This global is initially set to null and a pointer to the root is assigned on the first call to **stree()**. Subsequent calls do not need to reassign the root. Assuming the name of this global is **rt**, to call the **stree()** function you use

```
/* call stree() */
if(!rt) rt=stree(rt,rt,info);
else stree(rt,rt,info);
```

In this way, both the first and subsequent elements can be inserted correctly.

The **stree()** function is a recursive algorithm, as are most tree routines. The same routine would be several times longer if straight iterative methods were employed. The function must be called with a pointer to the root, the left or right node, and the information. Although for the sake of clarity a single character is used as the information, you could substitute any simple or complex data type you like.

To traverse the tree built by **stree()** inorder, printing the *info* field of each node, you could use **inorder()** as shown here:

```
void inorder(struct tree *root)
{
  if(!root) return;
```

```
  inorder(root->left);
  printf("%c ",root->info);
  inorder(root->right);
}
```

This recursive function returns when a terminal node (a null pointer) is encountered. The functions to traverse the tree in preorder and postorder are shown here:

```
void preorder(struct tree *root)
{
  if(!root) return;

  printf("%c ", root->info);
  preorder(root->left);
  preorder(root->right);
}

void postorder(struct tree *root)
{
  if(!root) return;

  postorder(root->left);
  postorder(root->right);
  printf("%c ", root->info);
}
```

A short but interesting program can be written to build a sorted binary tree and print that tree sideways on the screen of your computer. To accomplish this you need only a small modification to the **inorder( )** function. The new function, called **print—tree( )**, which prints a tree in inorder fashion is shown here:

```
void print_tree(struct tree *r, int l)
{
  int i;

  if(r==NULL) return;

  print_tree(r->left, l+1);
  for(i=0; i<l; ++i) printf("   ");
  printf("%c\n", r->info);
  print_tree(r->right, l+1);
}
```

The entire tree-printing program is given here. Try

entering various trees to see how each one is built.

```c
#include "stdlib.h"
#include "stdio.h"

struct tree {
  char info;
  struct tree *left;
  struct tree *right;
};

struct tree *root;  /* first node in tree */
struct tree *stree(struct tree *,
                    struct tree *, char);
void print_tree(struct tree *, int);

main()  /* printtree program */
{
  char s[80];

  root = NULL;  /* initialize the root */

  do {
    printf("enter a letter: ");
    gets(s);
    if(!root) root = stree(root, root, *s);
    else stree(root, root, *s);
  } while(*s);

  print_tree(root, NULL);

}

struct tree *stree(
  struct tree *root,
  struct tree *r,
  char info)
{

  if(!r) {
    r = (struct tree *) malloc(sizeof(struct tree));
    if(!r) {
      printf("out of memory\n");
      exit(0);
    }
    r->left = NULL;
    r->right = NULL;
    r->info = info;
    if(!root) return r; /* first entry */
    if(info<root->info) root->left = r;
    else root->right = r;
    return r;
  }

  if(info<r->info) stree(r, r->left, info);
  else
  if(info>r->info) stree(r, r->right, info);
```

```
}
void print_tree(struct tree *r, int l)
{
  int i;

  if(!r) return;

  print_tree(r->left, l+1);
  for(i=0; i<l; ++i) printf("   ");
  printf("%c\n", r->info);
  print_tree(r->right, l+1);
}
```

You may not have thought about it, but this program actually is sorting the information you are giving it. For the average case its performance can be quite good, but the quicksort is still a better general-purpose sorting method because it uses less memory and has lower processing overhead. However, if you have to build a tree from scratch or maintain an already sorted tree, you should always insert new entries in sorted order using the **stree()** function.

If you have run the **Treeprint** program you have probably noticed that some trees are *balanced* —that is, each subtree is the same or nearly the same height as any other —and that others are very far out of balance. In fact, if you entered the tree **abcd**, it would have been built looking like this:

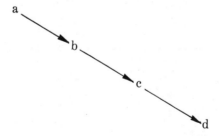

There would have been no left subtrees. This is called a *degenerate tree*, because it has degenerated into a linear list. In general, if the data you use to build a binary tree is fairly random, the tree produced approximates a balanced tree.

However, if the information is already sorted, a degenerate tree results. (It is possible to readjust the tree with each insertion to keep the tree in balance. The algorithms to do this are fairly complex, and interested readers are referred to books on advanced programming algorithms.)

Search functions are very easy to implement for binary trees. The following fragment returns a pointer to the node in the tree that matches the key; otherwise it returns null.

```
struct tree *search_tree(struct tree *root, char key)
{
  if(!root) return root;  /* empty tree */
  while(root->info!=key) {
    if(key<root->info) root = root->left;
    else root = root->right;
    if(root==NULL) break;
  }
  return root;
}
```

Unfortunately, deleting a node from a tree is not as simple as searching the tree. The deleted node may be either the root, a left node, or a right node. The node may also have from 0 to 2 subtrees attached to it. The process of rearranging the pointers lends itself to a recursive algorithm, as shown here:

```
struct tree *dtree(struct tree *root, char key)
{
  struct tree *p,*p2;

  if(root->info==key) { /* delete root */
    /* this means an empty tree */
    if(root->left==root->right){
      free(root);
      return NULL;
    }
    /* or if one subtree is null */
    else if(root->left==NULL) {
      p = root->right;
      free(root);
      return p;
    }
    else if(root->right==NULL) {
      p = root->left;
      free(root);
      return p;
```

```
      }
      /* or both tree present */
      else {
        p2 = root->right;
        p = root->right;
        while(p->left) p = p->left;
        p->left = root->left;
        free(root);
        return p2;
      }
    }
    if(root->info<key) root->right = dtree(root->right, key);
    else root->left = dtree(root->left, key);
    return root;
}
```

Remember to update the pointer to the root in the rest of your program's code because the node deleted could be the root of the tree.

Binary trees offer tremendous power, flexibility, and efficiency when used with database management programs because the information for these databases must reside on disk and access times are important. Because a balanced binary tree has, as a worst case, **$\log_2 n$** comparisons in searching, it is far better than a linked list, which must rely on a sequential search.

AI-Based
Problem Solving

The field of artificial intelligence (AI) is made up of of several different exciting areas.[1] Fundamental to most AI applications, however, is problem solving.

There are basically two types of problems. The first type can be solved by using some sort of deterministic procedure that is guaranteed success. In other words, a computation. Computational solutions apply only to the types of problems for which such procedures exist, such as mathematics. The methods used to solve these types of problems are often easily translated into an algorithm that can be executed by a computer. However, few real-world problems lend themselves to computational solutions; the others must be placed in the second category: non-computational problems. These types of problems are solved by searching for a solution. It is this method of problem solving that AI is concerned with.

It is interesting to note that one of the "dreams" of AI research is the creation of a *general problem solver*. A general problem solver is a program that produces solutions when given all sorts of different problems about which it has no specific designed-in knowledge. In the course of this chapter you will see why the dream is as tantalizing as it is difficult to realize.

---

1. If you are interested in AI, see *Artificial Intelligence Using C* (by Herbert Schildt, Osborne/McGraw-Hill, 1987), which discusses such things as expert systems, robotics, natural language processing, vision, and logic.

In the early days of AI research, developing good search methods was a primary goal. One of the most difficult obstacles to overcome when trying to apply AI techniques to real-world problems is the sheer magnitude and complexity of most situations. To solve these problems required good search techniques. In addition, it was and still is believed that searching is central to problem solving, which is a crucial ingredient of intelligence.

Representation and Terminology

Imagine that you have lost your car keys. You know that they are somewhere in your house, which looks like this:

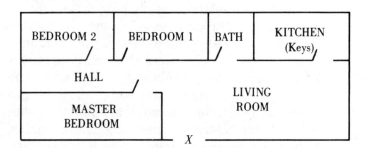

You are standing at the front door (where the X is). As you begin your search you first check the living room. Then you go down the hall to the first bedroom, back to the hall and to the second bedroom, back to the hall again, and then to the master bedroom. Not yet having found your keys, you go back through the living room and finally find your keys in the kitchen. This situation is easily represented by a graph, as shown in Figure 26-1.

The fact that problems can be represented as graphs is important because a graph is a simple way to visualize the

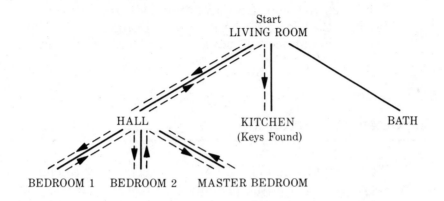

Figure 26-1.   Solution path for the lost keys

way the different search techniques work. (Being able to represent problems as graphs also allows an AI researcher to apply various theorems from graph theory, but that is beyond the scope of this book.) Keep this in mind while reading the following definitions:

Node: a discrete point and possible goal

Terminal node: a node that ends a path

Search space: the set of all nodes

Goal: the node that is the object of the search

Heuristic: information about the likelihood that a specific node is a better choice to try next rather than another

Solution path: a directed graph of the nodes visited that lead to the solution

In the lost keys example, each room in the house is a node; the entire house is the search space; and the goal, as it turns out, is the kitchen. The solution path is shown in Figure 26-1. The bedrooms and the bath are terminal nodes because they lead nowhere. In this example, no heuristics were used, but you will see some later on in this chapter.

Combinatorial Explosions

At this point, you may think that searching for a solution is easy. Just start at the beginning and work your way to the conclusion. In the extremely simple case of the lost keys, this is not a bad way to do it. But in most problems that you would want to use a computer to solve, the situation is much different. Generally, you use the computer to solve problems where the number of nodes in the search space is very large. As the search space grows, so does the number of different possible paths to the goal. The trouble is that each node added to the search space adds more than one path. That is, the number of pathways to the goal increases faster as each node is added.

To understand this, consider the number of ways three objects, called A, B, and C, can be arranged on a table. The six possible different arrangements are

A B C
A C B
B C A
B A C
C B A
C A B

Although you can quickly prove to yourself that these are all the ways A, B, and C can be arranged, the same number can be derived using a theorem from the branch of mathematics called *combinatorics,* which is the study of the way things can be combined. The theorem states that the number of ways that N objects can be combined (or arranged) is equal to $N!$ (N factorial). The factorial of a number is the product of all whole numbers equal to or less than itself down to 1. Therefore, 3! is $3 \times 2 \times 1$, or 6. Given this information, you can see that if you had 4 objects to arrange, there would be 4! or 24 combinations. With 5 objects, the number is 120, and with 6 it is 720. With, say, 1000 objects the number of possible combinations is huge! The graph in Figure 26-2 gives you a visual feel for what AI researchers commonly refer to as a *combinatoric explosion.* Once there are more than a handful of possibilities, it quickly becomes impossible to examine (or even enumerate) all the combinations.

Relative to problem solving, the point is that each additional node added to the search space increases the number of possible solutions by a number far greater than 1. Hence, at some point there are too many possibilities to work with. Because the number of possibilities grows so quickly, only the simplest of problems lend themselves to exhaustive searches. An *exhaustive search* is one that examines all nodes. While the "brute force" technique always works in theory, it is not often practical because it consumes far too much time, computing resources, or both. Therefore, other search techniques have been developed.

There are several ways to search for a possible solution. The most important and common are

- Depth-first searching
- Breadth-first searching
- Hill climbing
- Least-cost searching

We will examine each of these in turn later in the chapter.

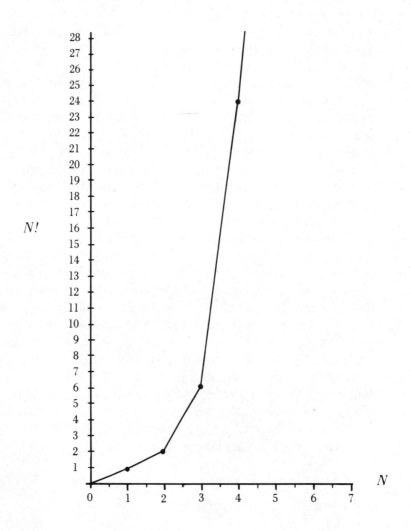

Figure 26-2.   A graph that shows a combinatorial explosion with factorials

Evaluating a Search

Evaluating the performance of a search technique can be very complicated. In fact, the evaluation of searches forms a very large part of AI. For our purposes the two basic measurements that are important are

1. How quickly the search finds a solution

2. How good the solution is

There are several types of problems for which all that matters is that any solution be found with the minimum effort. For those types of problems the first measurement is important. In other situations, however, the solution must be good, perhaps even optimal.

The speed of a search is determined by both the length of the solution path and the actual number of nodes traversed. Remember that backtracking from dead-ends is essentially wasted effort; what is desired is a search that backtracks little.

It is important to understand that there is a difference between finding an optimal solution and finding a good solution. The difference lies in the fact that finding an optimal solution usually entails an exhaustive search because that is the only way to be sure that the best solution has been found. But finding a good solution means finding a solution within a set of constraints; it doesn't matter if a better solution exists.

As you will see, all the search techniques described in this chapter work better in certain specific situations than in others; it is difficult to say whether one search method is always superior to another. But some search techniques are more likely to be better for the average case. Keep in mind that the way a problem is defined sometimes helps you choose an appropriate searching method.

Before starting, let's define a problem that we can use various searches to solve. Imagine that you are a travel agent and a rather quarrelsome customer wants you to book a flight from New York to Los Angeles with XYZ Airlines. You try to tell the customer that XYZ does not have a direct flight from New York to Los Angeles, but the customer insists that XYZ is the only airline he will fly! Looking at XYZ's scheduled flights, you find the following information:

New York to Chicago	1000 miles
Chicago to Denver	1000 miles
New York to Toronto	800 miles
New York to Denver	1900 miles
Toronto to Calgary	1500 miles
Toronto to Los Angeles	1800 miles
Toronto to Chicago	500 miles
Denver to Urbana	1000 miles
Denver to Houston	1500 miles
Houston to Los Angeles	1500 miles
Denver to Los Angeles	1000 miles

You quickly see that there is a way to fly from New York to Los Angeles using XYZ if connecting flights are used. And you book the fellow a flight.

However, our task is to write Turbo C programs that do the same thing—perhaps even better!

A Graphic Representation

The flight information given in XYZ's schedule book can be translated into the directed graph shown in Figure 26-3.

A directed graph is simply a graph where the lines connecting each node have an arrow attached to them indicating

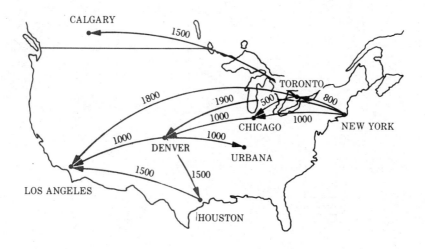

Figure 26-3.   A directed graph of XYZ's flight schedule

the direction of motion. In a directed graph it is impossible to travel in the opposite direction from the arrow.

To make things a little easier to understand, this graph can be redrawn as a tree as shown in Figure 26-4. We will refer to this version throughout the rest of this chapter. The goal, Los Angeles, is circled. Also notice that various cities appear more than once in the graph to simplify its construction.

Now you are ready to develop various search programs to find paths from New York to Los Angeles.

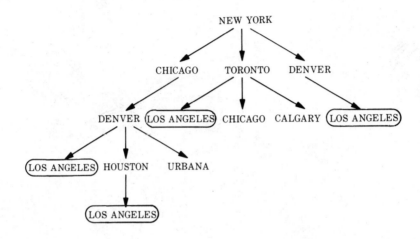

Figure 26-4. A tree version of XYZ's flight schedule

Depth-First Searching

A *depth-first* search explores each possible path to its conclusion (or goal) before another path is tried. To understand exactly how this works, consider the tree shown here where F is the goal:

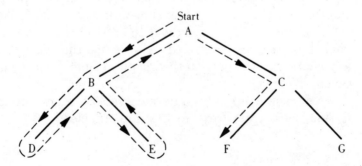

A depth-first search traverses this graph in the following order: ABDBEBACF. Those of you familiar with trees can see that this type of search is essentially the same as an inorder tree traversal. That is, go left until a terminal node is reached or the goal is found. If a terminal node is reached, back up one level, go right, then left until either the goal or a terminal node is encountered. Repeat this procedure until the goal is found or the last node in the search space has been examined.

As you can see, a depth-first search is certain to find the goal because as a worst case it degenerates into an exhaustive search, which is what would happen if G were the goal.

In order to write a Turbo C program to find a route from New York to Los Angeles you need a database that contains the information about XYZ's flights. Each entry in the database will contain departure and destination cities, the distance between them, and a flag to aid in backtracking. The following structure holds the information:

```
#define MAX 100

/* structure of the flight database */
struct FL {
  char from[20];
  char to[20];
  int distance;
  char skip;  /* used in backtracking */
};

struct FL flight[MAX];  /* array of db structures */

int f_pos=0; /* number of entries in flight db */
int find_pos=0; /* index for searching flight db */
```

Entries are placed into the database, and **assert_flight( )** and **setup( )** are used to initialize the information. The global **f_pos** holds the index of the last item in the database. These routines are shown here:

```
void setup()
{
  assert_flight("New York", "Chicago", 1000);
  assert_flight("Chicago", "Denver", 1000);
```

```
   assert_flight("New York", "Toronto", 800);
   assert_flight("New York", "Denver", 1900);
   assert_flight("Toronto", "Calgary", 1500);
   assert_flight("Toronto", "Los Angeles", 1800);
   assert_flight("Toronto", "Chicago", 500);
   assert_flight("Denver", "Urbana", 1000);
   assert_flight("Denver", "Houston", 1500);
   assert_flight("Houston", "Los Angeles", 1500);
   assert_flight("Denver", "Los Angeles", 1000);
}

/* Put facts into the database. */
void assert_flight(char *from, char *to, int dist)
{

   if(f_pos<MAX) {
     strcpy(flight[f_pos].from, from);
     strcpy(flight[f_pos].to, to);
     flight[f_pos].distance = dist;
     flight[f_pos].skip = 0;
     f_pos++;
   }
   else printf("Flight database full.\n");
}
```

In keeping with the spirit of AI, the database should be thought of as containing facts. The program to be developed will use these facts to arrive at a solution. For this reason, many AI researchers refer to the database as a *knowledge base;* this book uses the terms interchangeably.

Before you can write the actual code to find a route between New York and Los Angeles you need several support functions. First, you need a routine to determine if there is a flight between two cities. This function is called **match( )**, and it returns 0 if no such flight exists or the distance between the two cities if there is a flight. The routine is shown here:

```
/* If flight between from and to, then return
   the distance of flight; otherwise, return 0. */
match(char *from, char *to)
{
   register int t;

   for(t=f_pos-1; t>-1; t--)
     if(!strcmp(flight[t].from, from) &&
       !strcmp(flight[t].to, to)) return flight[t].distance;

   return 0;  /* not found */
}
```

Another necessary function is called **find( )**; given a city, it searches the database for any connection. If a connection is found, the name of the destination city and its distance are returned; otherwise 0 is returned. The **find()** function is shown here:

```
/* Given from, find anywhere. */
find(char *from, char *anywhere)
{
  find_pos = 0;
  while(find_pos<f_pos) {
    if(!strcmp(flight[find_pos].from, from) &&
    !flight[find_pos].skip) {
      strcpy(anywhere, flight[find_pos].to);
      flight[find_pos].skip = 1; /* make active */
      return flight[find_pos].distance;
    }
    find_pos++;
  }
  return 0;
}
```

As you can see by examining the code to **find()**, cities that have the *skip* field set to 1 are not valid connections. If a connection is found, its *skip* field is marked as active. As you will see, this is used to control backtracking from dead-ends.

Backtracking is a crucial ingredient in many AI techniques. Backtracking is accomplished by using recursive routines and a backtrack stack. Virtually all backtracking situations are stack-like in operation—that is, first in, last out. In simple terms, as a path is explored, nodes are pushed onto the stack as they are encountered. At each dead-end, the last node is popped off the stack, and a new path is tried from that point. This process continues until either the goal is reached or all paths have been exhausted. The functions **push()** and **pop()** are shown here. They use the globals **tos** and **bt—stack** to hold the top-of-stack pointer and the stack array, respectively.

```
/* stack routines */
void push(char *from, char *to, int dist)
{
  if(tos<MAX) {
    strcpy(bt_stack[tos].from, from);
    strcpy(bt_stack[tos].to, to);
```

```
        bt_stack[tos].dist = dist;
        tos++;
    }
    else printf("Stack full.\n");
}

void pop(char *from, char *to, int *dist)
{
    if(tos>0) {
        tos--;
        strcpy(from, bt_stack[tos].from);
        strcpy(to, bt_stack[tos].to);
        *dist = bt_stack[tos].dist;
    }
    else printf("Stack underflow.\n");
}
```

Now that the required support routines have been developed, the key function in finding a route between New York and Los Angeles is called **isflight( )**, and is shown here:

```
/* Determine if there is a route between from and to. */
isflight(char *from, char *to)
{
    int d, dist;
    char anywhere[20];

    /* see if at destination */
    if(d=match(from, to)) {
        push(from, to, d);
        return;
    }

    /* try another connection */
    if(dist=find(from, anywhere)) {
        push(from, to, dist);
        isflight(anywhere, to);
    }
    else if(tos>0) {
        /* backtrack */
        pop(from, to, &dist);
        isflight(from, to);
    }
}
```

The routine works like this. First, the database is checked by **match( )** to see if there is a flight between **from** and **to**. If there is, the goal has been reached, the connection is pushed onto the stack, and the function returns. Otherwise, **find( )** is used to see if there is a connection between **from** and anyplace else. If there is, the connection is pushed onto the stack and **isflight( )** is called recursively. Otherwise, backtracking takes place. The previous node is removed from the stack, and **isflight( )** is called recursively. This process continues until the goal is found. It is important to understand that the *skip* field is necessary in backtracking to prevent the same connections from being tried over and over again.

Hence, if called with "Denver" and "Houston," the first part of the routine succeeds and **isflight( )** terminates. However, suppose **isflight( )** is called with "Chicago" and "Houston." The first part fails because there is no direct flight connecting these two cities, so the second part is tried by attempting to find a connection between the origin city and any other city. In this case, Chicago connects with Denver, so **isflight( )** is called recursively with "Denver" and "Houston." Once again the first condition is tested and this time a connection is found. Finally, the recursive calls unravel and **isflight( )** terminates. As **isflight( )** is presented here, it performs a depth-first search of the knowledge base.

It is important to understand that **isflight( )** does not actually return the solution—it generates it. The key point is that, on exit from **isflight( )**, *the backtrack stack contains the route, that is, the solution, between Chicago and Houston.* In fact, the success or failure of **isflight( )** is determined by the state of the stack. An empty stack indicates failure; otherwise it holds a solution. Hence the function needed to complete the entire program is called **route( )**, and it prints both the path to follow and the total distance. It is shown here:

```
/* Show the route and total distance. */
route(char *to)
{
  int dist, t;

  dist = 0;
  t = 0;
  while(t<tos) {
    printf("%s to ", bt_stack[t].from);
    dist += bt_stack[t].dist;
    t++;
  }
  printf("%s\n", to);
  printf("distance is %d\n", dist);
}
```

The entire depth-first search program is shown here. You should enter this program into your computer at this time.

```c
/* Depth-first search */
#include "stdio.h"

#define MAX 100

/* structure of the flight database */
struct FL {
  char from[20];
  char to[20];
  int distance;
  char skip;  /* used in backtracking */
};

struct FL flight[MAX];  /* array of db structures */

int f_pos=0; /* number of entries in flight db */
int find_pos=0; /* index for searching flight db */

int tos=0;        /* top of stack */
struct stack {
  char from[20];
  char to[20];
  int dist;
} ;
struct stack bt_stack[MAX]; /* backtrack stack */

void setup(void), route(char *);
void assert_flight(char *, char *, int);
void push(char *, char *, int);
void pop(char *, char *, int *);
void isflight(char *, char *);
int find(char *, char *);
int match(char *, char *);

main()
{
  char from[20], to[20];

  setup();

  printf("from? ");
  gets(from);
  printf("to? ");
  gets(to);

  isflight(from,to);
  route(to);
}
```

```
void setup()
{
  assert_flight("New York","Chicago",1000);
  assert_flight("Chicago","Denver",1000);

  assert_flight("New York","Toronto", 800);
  assert_flight("New York","Denver", 1900);
  assert_flight("Toronto","Calgary",1500);
  assert_flight("Toronto","Los Angeles",1800);
  assert_flight("Toronto","Chicago",500);
  assert_flight("Denver","Urbana",1000);
  assert_flight("Denver","Houston",1500);
  assert_flight("Houston","Los Angeles",1500);
  assert_flight("Denver","Los Angeles",1000);
}

/* Put facts into the database. */
void assert_flight(char *from, char *to, int dist)
{

  if(f_pos<MAX) {
    strcpy(flight[f_pos].from, from);
    strcpy(flight[f_pos].to, to);
    flight[f_pos].distance = dist;
    flight[f_pos].skip = 0;
    f_pos++;
  }
  else printf("Flight database full.\n");
}


/* Show the route and total distance. */
void route(char *to)
{
  int dist, t;

  dist = 0;
  t = 0;
  while(t<tos) {
    printf("%s to ", bt_stack[t].from);
    dist += bt_stack[t].dist;
    t++;
  }
  printf("%s\n", to);
  printf("distance is %d\n", dist);
}

/* If flight between from and to, then return
   the distance of flight; otherwise, return 0. */
match(char *from, char *to)
{
  register int t;

  for(t=f_pos-1; t>-1; t--)
    if(!strcmp(flight[t].from, from) &&
```

```
              !strcmp(flight[t].to, to)) return flight[t].distance;

   return 0;  /* not found */
}

/* Given from, find anywhere. */
find(char *from, char *anywhere)
{
   find_pos=0;
   while(find_pos<f_pos) {
     if(!strcmp(flight[find_pos].from,from) &&
       !flight[find_pos].skip) {
         strcpy(anywhere,flight[find_pos].to);
         flight[find_pos].skip=1; /* make active */
         return flight[find_pos].distance;
       }
     find_pos++;
   }
   return 0;
}

/* Determine if there is a route between from and to. */
void isflight(char *from, char *to)
{
   int d, dist;
   char anywhere[20];

   /* see if at destination */
   if(d=match(from, to)) {
     push(from, to, d);
     return;
   }

   /* try another connection */
   if(dist=find(from, anywhere)) {
     push(from, to, dist);
     isflight(anywhere, to);
   }
   else if(tos>0) {
     /* backtrack */
     pop(from, to, &dist);
     isflight(from, to);
   }
}

/* stack routines */
void push(char *from, char *to, int dist)
{
   if(tos<MAX) {
     strcpy(bt_stack[tos].from,from);
     strcpy(bt_stack[tos].to,to);
     bt_stack[tos].dist=dist;
     tos++;
   }
```

```
    else printf("Stack full.\n");
}

void pop(char *from, char *to, int *dist)
{
  if(tos>0) {
    tos--;
    strcpy(from,bt_stack[tos].from);
    strcpy(to,bt_stack[tos].to);
    *dist=bt_stack[tos].dist;
  }
  else printf("Stack underflow.\n");
}
```

Notice that **main( )** prompts you for both the city of origin and the destination. This means that you can use the program to find routes between any two cities. For the rest of this chapter it is assumed that New York is the origin and Los Angeles is the destination.

When the program is run with New York and Los Angeles, the solution is

New York to Chicago to Denver to Los Angeles
distance is 3000

If you refer to Figure 26-5, you will see that this is indeed the first solution that would be found using a depth-first search. It is not the optimal solution, which is New York to Toronto to Los Angeles with a distance of 2600 miles, but it is not bad.

Evaluating Depth-First Searches

As you can see in this example, the depth-first approach found a fairly good solution. Also, relative to this specific problem, depth-first searching succeeded in finding a solution on its first try with no backtracking—very good. But it would have had to traverse nearly all of the nodes to arrive at the optimal solution—not so good.

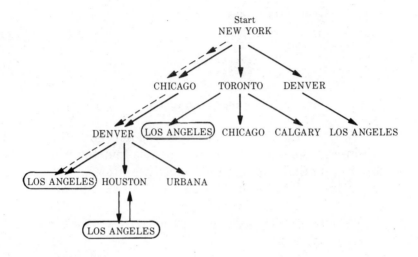

Figure 26-5.   The path of the depth-first search to a solution

It should be noted, however, that a depth-first search can be quite poor in situations where a particularly long branch is explored only to find that there is no solution at its end. In this case a depth-first search will waste considerable time, not only in exploring this chain, but also in backtracking to the goal. Situations like this lead us to breadth-first searching.

Breadth-First Searching

The opposite of depth-first searching is *breadth-first*. In this method each node on the same level is checked before proceeding to the next deeper level. This traversal method is shown here with C as the goal:

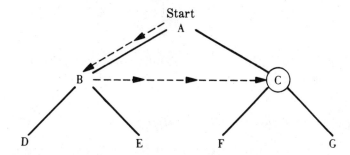

As you can see, the nodes A, B, and C are visited. Like depth-first, breadth-first searching guarantees a solution, if one exists, because it will eventually degenerate into an exhaustive search.

Transforming the route-seeking program to perform a breadth-first search requires only a simple alteration to the **isflight( )** procedure, as shown here:

```
void isflight(char *from, char *to)
{
  int d, temp, dist;
  char anywhere[20];

  while(dist=find(from, anywhere)) {
    /* breadth-first modification */
    if(d=match(anywhere, to)) {
      push(from, to, dist);
      push(anywhere, to, d);
      return;
    }
  }
  /* try any connection */
  if(dist=find(from, anywhere)) {
    push(from, to, dist);
    isflight(anywhere, to);
  }
  else if(tos>0) {
    pop(from, to, &dist);
    isflight(from, to);
  }
}
```

Only the first condition has been altered. Now all connecting cities to the departure city are checked to see if they connect with the destination city.

Substitute this version of **isflight( )** in the program and run the program. The solution is

New York to Toronto to Los Angeles
distance is 2600

which is optimal. Figure 26-6 shows the breadth-first path to
the solution.

Analysis of Breadth-First Searches

In this specific example, breadth-first searching has performed very well by finding the first solution without backtracking. As it turns out this is also the optimal solution. In
fact, the first three solutions that would be found are the best
three routes there are! You are cautioned, however, to
remember that this result does not generalize to other situations because it depends on the physical organization of the

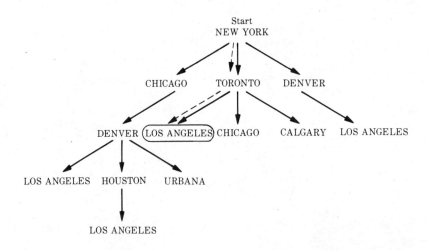

Figure 26-6.   The path of the breadth-first search to a solution

information as it is stored in the computer. However, it does illustrate how radically different depth-first and breadth-first searches are.

Breadth-first searching is at a disadvantage when the goal is located several layers deep. In this case, breadth-first searching expends substantial effort to find the goal. Generally the choice between depth-first and breadth-first searching is determined by the programmer based on an educated guess about the most likely position of the goal.

Adding Heuristics

You have probably guessed by now that both the depth-first and breadth-first search routines are blind. They are methods of looking for a solution that rely solely on moving from one goal to the other without the use of "educated guesses." While this may be fine for certain controlled situations where the programmer has knowledge that dictates the use of one method over another, what a generalized AI program needs is a search procedure that is generally superior to either of these two techniques. The only way to achieve such a search is to add heuristic capabilities.

As you recall, heuristics are simply rules that qualify the possibility that a search is proceeding in the correct direction. To understand this, imagine that you are lost in the woods and really need a drink of water. The woods are so thick that you cannot see very far ahead, and the trees are too big to climb to get a look around. However, you have four pieces of knowledge:

1. Rivers, streams, and ponds are most often in valleys.

2. Animals frequently make paths to their watering places.

3. When you are near water you can "smell" it.

4. You can hear running water.

To find your way to water, you begin moving downhill because water is likely to lie in that direction. Next you come across a deer trail that also runs downhill. Knowing that this may lead to water, you follow it. You begin to hear a slight rush off to your left. Knowing that this may be water, you cautiously move in that direction. As you move, you begin to detect increased humidity in the air—you can "smell" the water. Finally, you find a stream and have your drink of water. As you can see, heuristic information, although not precise or guaranteed, increases the chances that a search method will find a goal quickly, optimally, or both. In short, it increases the odds in favor of quick success.

You may be thinking that heuristic information could easily be included in programs designed for specific applications, but that it would be impossible to create generalized heuristic searches. However, this is not the case, as you will see.

Heuristic search methods are most often based on maximizing or minimizing some aspect of the problem. In fact, the two heuristic approaches that you will look at use opposite heuristics and yield different results. Both of these searches are built on the depth-first search basic routines.

Hill Climbing

Going back to the problem of scheduling a flight from New York to Los Angeles, there are two possible constraints that a passenger may want minimized: the number of connections that have to be made and the length of the route. Remember, the shortest route does not necessarily imply the fewest connections. A search algorithm that attempts to find as a first solution one that minimizes the number of connections will use the heuristics that the longer the distance covered the greater likelihood that it will take one closer to the destination, thereby reducing the number of connections. In the language of AI this is called *hill climbing*.

Formally, the hill-climbing algorithm chooses as its next step the node that appears to place it closest to the goal (that is, furthest away from the current position). It derives its name from the analogy of a hiker being lost in the dark halfway up a mountain. Assuming that the hiker's camp is at the top of the mountain, the hiker knows that each step up is a step in the right direction!

Relative to the flight-scheduling problem, and working only with the information contained in the knowledge base, we incorporate the following hill-climbing heuristic into the routing program. Choose the connecting flight that is as far away as possible from the current position in the hope that it will be closer to the destination. To do this you must modify the **find( )** function as shown:

```
/* Given from, find the farthest away "anywhere". */
find(char *from, char *anywhere)
{
  int pos, dist;

  pos=dist = 0;
  find_pos = 0;

  while(find_pos<f_pos) {
    if(!strcmp(flight[find_pos].from, from) &&
      !flight[find_pos].skip) {
        if(flight[find_pos].distance>dist) {
        pos = find_pos;
        dist = flight[find_pos].distance;
      }
    }
    find_pos++;
  }
  if(pos) {
    strcpy(anywhere, flight[pos].to);
    flight[pos].skip = 1;
    return flight[pos].distance;
  }
  return 0;
}
```

The **find()** function now searches the entire database, looking for the connecton that is farthest away from the departure city.

The entire hill-climbing program is shown here. You should enter this program into your computer at this time.

```c
/* Hill-climbing */
#include "stdio.h"

#define MAX 100

/* structure of the flight database */
struct FL {
  char from[20];
  char to[20];
  int distance;
  char skip; /* used for backtracking */
};

struct FL flight[MAX];   /* array of db structures */

int f_pos=0; /* number of entries in flight db */
int find_pos=0; /* index for searching flight db */

int tos=0;       /* top of stack */
struct stack {
  char from[20];
  char to[20];
  int dist;
} ;
struct stack bt_stack[MAX]; /* backtrack stack */

void setup(void), route(char *);
void assert_flight(char *, char *, int);
void push(char *, char *, int);
void pop(char *, char *, int *);
void isflight(char *, char *);
int find(char *, char *);
int match(char *, char *);

main()
{
  char from[20], to[20];

  setup();

  printf("from? ");
  gets(from);
  printf("to? ");
  gets(to);
```

```
      isflight(from,to);
      route(to);
}

void setup()
{
  assert_flight("New York", "Chicago", 1000);
  assert_flight("Chicago", "Denver", 1000);
  assert_flight("New York", "Toronto", 800);
  assert_flight("New York", "Denver", 1900);
  assert_flight("Toronto", "Calgary", 1500);
  assert_flight("Toronto", "Los Angeles", 1800);
  assert_flight("Toronto", "Chicago", 500);
  assert_flight("Denver", "Urbana", 1000);
  assert_flight("Denver", "Houston", 1500);
  assert_flight("Houston", "Los Angeles", 1500);
  assert_flight("Denver", "Los Angeles", 1000);
}

/* Put facts into the database. */
void assert_flight(char *from, char *to, int dist)
{

  if(f_pos<MAX) {
    strcpy(flight[f_pos].from, from);
    strcpy(flight[f_pos].to, to);
    flight[f_pos].distance = dist;
    flight[f_pos].skip = 0;
    f_pos++;
  }
  else printf("Flight database full.\n");
}

/* Show the route and the total distance. */
void route(char *to)
{
  int dist, t;

  dist = 0;
  t = 0;
  while(t<tos) {
    printf("%s to ", bt_stack[t].from);
    dist += bt_stack[t].dist;
    t++;
  }
  printf("%s\n", to);
  printf("distance is %d\n", dist);
}


/* If flight between from and to, then return
   the distance of flight; otherwise, return 0. */
match(char *from, char *to)
{
```

```
  register int t;

  for(t=f_pos-1; t>-1; t--)
    if(!strcmp(flight[t].from, from) &&
      !strcmp(flight[t].to, to)) return flight[t].distance;

  return 0;  /* not found */
}

/* Given from, find the farthest away "anywhere". */
find(char *from, char *anywhere)
{
  int pos, dist;

  pos=dist = 0;
  find_pos = 0;

  while(find_pos<f_pos) {
    if(!strcmp(flight[find_pos].from, from) &&
      !flight[find_pos].skip) {
        if(flight[find_pos].distance>dist) {
          pos = find_pos;
          dist = flight[find_pos].distance;
        }
    }
    find_pos++;
  }
  if(pos) {
    strcpy(anywhere, flight[pos].to);
    flight[pos].skip = 1;
    return flight[pos].distance;
  }
  return 0;
}

/* Determine if there is a route between from and to. */
void isflight(char *from, char *to)
{
  int d, dist;
  char anywhere[20];

  if(d=match(from, to)) {
    /* is goal */
    push(from, to, d);
    return;
  }

  /* find any connection */
  if(dist=find(from, anywhere)) {
    push(from, to, dist);
    isflight(anywhere, to);
  }
  else if(tos>0) {
```

```
        pop(from, to, &dist);
        isflight(from, to);
    }
}

/* stack routines */
void push(char *from, char *to, int dist)
{
  if(tos<MAX) {
    strcpy(bt_stack[tos].from, from);
    strcpy(bt_stack[tos].to, to);
    bt_stack[tos].dist = dist;
    tos++;
  }
  else printf("Stack full.\n");
}

void pop(char *from, char *to, int *dist)
{
  if(tos>0) {
    tos--;
    strcpy(from, bt_stack[tos].from);
    strcpy(to, bt_stack[tos].to);
    *dist = bt_stack[tos].dist;
  }
  else printf("Stack underflow.\n");
}
```

When the program is run, the solution found is

New York to Denver to Los Angeles
distance is 2900

This is quite good! It has the minimal number of stops on the way, only one, and is really quite close to the shortest route. Furthermore, it does this with no time or effort wasted through extensive backtracking.

However, if the Denver to Los Angeles connection did not exist, the solution would not be quite so good. In fact, it would be New York to Denver to Houston to Los Angeles—a distance of 4900 miles! In this solution a false peak is climbed because the route to Houston does not take us closer to the goal of Los Angeles. Figure 26-7 shows the solution as well as the false peak path.

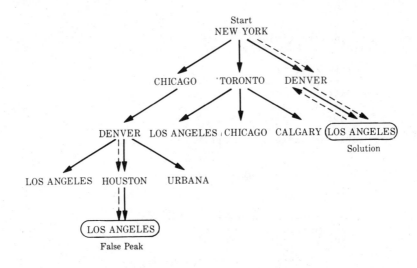

Figure 26-7.   The path of the hill-climbing search to the solution
and to a false peak

Analyzing Hill Climbing

Actually, hill climbing is fairly good in many circumstances because it has the tendency to reduce the number of nodes that need to be visited before a solution is reached. However, there are three possible drawbacks. First, there is the problem of false hills, as seen in the second solution in the example. In this case extensive backtracking is required to find the solution. The second is the problem of "plateaus," in which all next steps look equally good (or bad). In this case hill climbing is no better than depth-first searching. The final problem is that of a ridge. In this case, hill climbing really falls down because the algorithm causes the ridge to be "crossed" several times as backtracking occurs.

In spite of these potential troubles hill climbing generally leads to a closer-to-optimal solution quicker than any of the non-heuristic methods.

Least-Cost Searching

The opposite of hill climbing is *least-cost* searching. This strategy is similar to standing in the middle of a street on a big hill while wearing rollerskates. You have the definite feeling that it's a lot easier to go down than up! That is, least-cost searching takes the path of least effort.

Applying least-cost searching to the flight schedule problem implies that the shortest connecting flight will be taken in all cases so that the route found will have a good chance of having the shortest distance. Unlike hill climbing, which minimizes the number of connections, least-cost searching minimizes the number of miles traveled.

To use least-cost, you must alter **find( )** as shown:

```
/* Find closest "anywhere". */
find(char *from, char *anywhere)
{
  int pos, dist;

  pos = 0;
  dist = 32000;   /* larger than the longest route */
  find_pos = 0;

  while(find_pos<f_pos) {
    if(!strcmp(flight[find_pos].from, from) &&
      !flight[find_pos].skip) {
        if(flight[find_pos].distance<dist) {
        pos = find_pos;
        dist = flight[find_pos].distance;
      }
    }
    find_pos++;
  }
  if(pos) {
    strcpy(anywhere, flight[pos].to);
```

```
      flightCpos]].skip = 1;
      return flightCpos]].distance;
   }
   return 0;
}
```

As you can see, the only change between least-cost searching and hill climbing is that the former finds the shortest connecting flight each time.

Using this version of **find( )**, the solution is

New York to Toronto to Los Angeles
distance is 2600

As you can see, the least-cost search actually found the shortest route. Figure 26-8 shows the least-cost path to the goal.

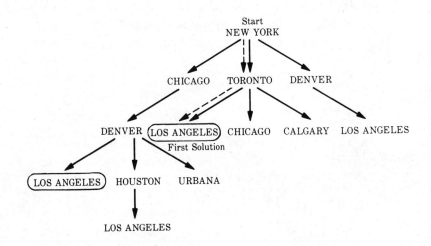

Figure 26-8. The path of the least-cost search to a solution

Analysis of Least-Cost Searches

Least-cost and hill-climbing searches have the same advantages and disadvantages, except in reverse. There can be false valleys, lowlands, and gorges, but overall least-cost searching tends to work fairly well. However, you should not make the assumption that least-cost searching is generally better just because it outperformed hill climbing in this problem.

Choosing a Search Technique

As you have seen, the heuristic techniques tend to work better than blind searching. However, it is not always possible to use a heuristic search because sometimes there is not enough information available to qualify the likelihood that the next node is on a path to the goal. Therefore, the rules for choosing a search method are separated into two categories: one for problems that can use a heuristic search, and one for those that cannot.

If it is not possible to apply heuristics to a problem, depth-first searching is often the best. The exception to this is when you have knowledge that tells you that a breadth-first search will be better.

The choice between hill climbing and least-cost searching is really one of deciding what constraint you are trying to minimize or maximize. Generally, hill climbing produces a solution with the least nodes visited, while a least-cost search finds a path that requires the least effort.

If you are seeking a near-optimal solution but cannot apply an exhaustive search, a very good method is to use each of the four searches and use the best solution. They all work in substantially different ways, and therefore one should produce better results than the others.

Finding Multiple Solutions

Sometimes it is valuable to find several solutions to the same problem. This is not the same as finding all the solutions (an exhaustive search). To understand why this can be important, think about designing your "dream house." You will want to sketch several different floor plans to help you decide on one to follow. In essence, multiple solutions can help you see many different ways to approach a solution before implementing it.

There are many ways to generate multiple solutions, but only two are examined here. The first is called path removal and the second node removal. As their names imply, generating multiple solutions without redundancy requires that found solutions be removed from the system. It is of the utmost importance to remember that neither of these methods attempts (or can even be used) to find all solutions. Finding all solutions is a different problem and is generally not used because it often implies an exhaustive search.

Path Removal

The *path removal* method of generating multiple solutions removes all nodes that form a current solution from the database and then attempts to find another. In essence, path removal prunes limbs from the tree.

The only modification necessary to the depth-first search to find multiple solutions using path removal is to alter **main( )** as shown here:

```
main()
{
  char from[20], to[20];

  setup();

  printf("from? ");
  gets(from);
```

```
printf("to? ");
gets(to);
do {
  isflight(from, to);
  route(to);
  tos = 0;  /* reset the backtrack stack */
} while(getche()!='q');
}
```

Because any connection that is part of a solution has its *skip* field marked, it can no longer be found by **find( )**. Hence, all connections in a solution are effectively removed. The only thing that needs to be done is to reset **tos**, which clears the backtrack stack.

Using this method, the following solutions are found:

New York to Chicago to Denver to Los Angeles
distance is 3000

New York to Toronto to Los Angeles
distance is 2600

New York to Denver to Los Angeles
distance is 2900

It is interesting that the three best solutions are found. However, this result cannot be generalized because it is based on how the data is placed in the database and the actual situation under study.

Node Removal

The *node removal* method of generating additional solutions simply removes the last node in the current solution path and tries again. To do this, the **main( )** function must pop the last node off the backtrack stack and remove it from the database by using a new function called **retract( )**. All the *skip* fields must also be reset by using **clearmarkers( )**, and the backtrack stack must be cleared. The **main( )**, **retract( )**, and **clearmarkers( )** functions are shown next.

```
main()
{
  char from[20], to[20], c1[20], c2[20];
  int d;

  setup();

  printf("from? ");
  gets(from);
  printf("to? ");
  gets(to);
  do {
    isflight(from, to);
    route(to);
    clearmarkers();  /* reset the database */
    if(tos>0) pop(c1, c2, &d);
    retract(c1, c2);  /* remove last node from database */
    tos = 0;  /* reset the backtrack stack */
  } while(getche()!='q');
}

/* Reset the "skip" field - i.e., re-activate all nodes, */
void clearmarkers()
{
  int t;

  for(t=0; t<f_pos; ++t) flight[t].skip = 0;
}


/* Remove an entry from the database. */
void retract(char *from, char *to)
{
  int t;

  for(t=0; t<f_pos; t++)
    if(!strcmp(flight[t].from, from) &&
      !strcmp(flight[t].to, to)) {
        strcpy(flight[t].from, "");
        return;
    }
}
```

As you can see, retracting an entry is accomplished by simply using 0 length strings for the names of the cities. For your convenience, the entire node removal program is shown here:

```
/* Depth-first with multiple solutions
   using node removal */
#include "stdio.h"

#define MAX 100
```

```
/* structure of the flight database */
struct FL {
  char from[20];
  char to[20];
  int distance;
  char skip;    /* used in backtracking */
};

struct FL flight[MAX];

int f_pos=0; /* number of entries in flight db */
int find_pos=0; /* index for searching flight db */

int tos=0;       /* top of stack */
struct stack {
char from[20];
char to[20];
int dist;
} ;
struct stack bt_stack[MAX]; /* backtrack stack */

void retract(char *, char *);
void clearmarkers();
void setup(void), route(char *);
void assert_flight(char *, char *, int);
void push(char *, char *, int);
void pop(char *, char *, int *);
void isflight(char *, char *);
int find(char *, char *);
int match(char *, char *);

main()
{
  char from[20],to[20], c1[20], c2[20];
  int d;

  setup();

  printf("from? ");
  gets(from);
  printf("to? ");
  gets(to);
  do {
    isflight(from,to);
    route(to);
    clearmarkers();  /* reset the database */
    if(tos>0) pop(c1,c2,&d);
    retract(c1,c2);  /* remove last node from database */
    tos=0;  /* reset the backtrack stack */
  } while(getche()!='q');
}


void setup()
{
  assert_flight("New York","Chicago",1000);
  assert_flight("Chicago","Denver",1000);
```

```
    assert_flight("New York","Toronto", 800);
    assert_flight("New York","Denver", 1900);
    assert_flight("Toronto","Calgary",1500);
    assert_flight("Toronto","Los Angeles",1800);
    assert_flight("Toronto","Chicago",500);
    assert_flight("Denver","Urbana",1000);
    assert_flight("Denver","Houston",1500);
    assert_flight("Houston","Los Angeles",1500);
    assert_flight("Denver","Los Angeles",1000);
}

/* Put facts into the database. */
void assert_flight(char *from, char *to, int dist)
{
  if(f_pos<MAX) {
    strcpy(flight[f_pos].from, from);
    strcpy(flight[f_pos].to, to);
    flight[f_pos].distance = dist;
    flight[f_pos].skip = 0;
    f_pos++;
  }
  else printf("Flight database full.\n");
}

/* Reset the "skip" field - i.e., re-activate all nodes. */
void clearmarkers()
{
  int t;

  for(t=0; t<f_pos; ++t) flight[t].skip = 0;
}


/* Remove an entry from the database. */
void retract(char *from, char *to)
{
  int t;

  for(t=0; t<f_pos; t++)
    if(!strcmp(flight[t].from, from) &&
      !strcmp(flight[t].to, to)) {
        strcpy(flight[t].from,"");
        return;
    }
}

/* Show the route and the total distance. */
void route(char *to)
{
  int dist, t;

  dist=0;
  t=0;
  while(t<tos) {
  printf("%s to ", bt_stack[t].from);
  dist += bt_stack[t].dist;
```

```c
      t++;
    }
  printf("%s\n",to);
  printf("distance is %d\n", dist);
}

/* Given from, find anywhere. */
find(char *from, char *anywhere)
{
  find_pos = 0;
  while(find_pos<f_pos) {
    if(!strcmp(flight[find_pos].from, from) &&
      !flight[find_pos].skip) {
        strcpy(anywhere, flight[find_pos].to);
        flight[find_pos].skip = 1;
        return flight[find_pos].distance;
      }
    find_pos++;
  }
  return 0;
}

/* If flight between from and to, then return
   the distance of flight; otherwise, return 0. */
match(char *from, char *to)
{
  register int t;

  for(t=f_pos-1; t>-1; t--)
    if(!strcmp(flight[t].from, from) &&
      !strcmp(flight[t].to, to)) return flight[t].distance;

  return 0;  /* not found */
}

/* Determine if there is a route between from and to. */
void isflight(char *from, char *to)
{
  int d, dist;
  char anywhere[20];

  if(d=match(from, to)) {
    push(from, to, d); /* distance */
    return;
  }

  if(dist=find(from, anywhere)) {
    push(from, to, dist);
    isflight(anywhere, to);
  }
  else if(tos>0) {
    pop(from, to, &dist);
    isflight(from, to);
  }
}
```

```
/* stack routines */
void push(char *from, char *to, int dist)
{
  if(tos<MAX) {
    strcpy(bt_stack[tos].from, from);
    strcpy(bt_stack[tos].to, to);
    bt_stack[tos].dist = dist;
    tos++;
  }
  else printf("Stack full.\n");
}

void pop(char *from, char *to, int *dist)
{
  if(tos>0) {
    tos--;
    strcpy(from, bt_stack[tos].from);
    strcpy(to, bt_stack[tos].to);
    *dist = bt_stack[tos].dist;
  }
  else printf("Stack underflow.\n");
}
```

Using this method produces the following solutions:

New York to Chicago to Denver to Los Angeles
distance is 3000

New York to Chicago to Denver to Houston to Los Angeles
distance is 5000

New York to Toronto to Los Angeles
distance is 2600

In this case, the second solution is the worst possible route, but the optimal solution is still found. However, remember that it is impossible to generalize these results because they are based on both the physical organization of data in the database and the specific situation under study.

Finding the "Optimal" Solution

All of the previous search techniques were concerned with finding a solution. As you saw with the heuristic searches, efforts were made to improve the likelihood of finding a good (perhaps the optimal) solution. However, sometimes only the optimal solution is desired. Keep in mind that *optimal* as it is used here simply means the best route that can be found using one of the various multiple solution generation techniques; it may not actually be the best solution. (Finding the truly best solution would require either the prohibitively expensive exhaustive search or the use of some additional information that could be used to prove that no better solution could exist for the given situation.)

Before leaving our well-worked scheduling example, let's develop a program to find the optimal schedule, assuming that distance is to be minimized. The path removal method of generating multiple solutions will be employed, and the search technique will be least-cost to minimize distance.

The key to finding the shortest schedule is to keep a solution that has a distance that is less than the previous one. When there are no more solutions to generate, the best one found by the search is left. To accomplish this you must make a major change to the **route( )** function and create an additional stack. The new stack holds the current solution and, upon completion, the optimal solution. The new stack is held in an array called **solution**, and the **spush( )** function is used to put connections onto this stack. The global **stos** is used to index the solution stack. The **route( )** function is modified, as shown here, to try different routes. Whenever a route is shorter than the one already on the solution stack, the old route is removed (by resetting the solution stack index) and the new route is put on the stack.

```
/* Find the shortest distance. */
route()
{
  int dist, t;
  static int old_dist=32000;

  if(!tos) return 0;  /* all done */
  t = 0;
  dist = 0;
  while(t<tos) {
    dist += bt_stack[t].dist;
    t++;
```

```
}
/* if shorter, then make new solution */
if(dist<old_dist && dist) {
  t = 0;
  old_dist = dist;
  stos = 0; /* clear old route from location stack */
  while(t<tos)  {
    spush(bt_stack[t].from, bt_stack[t].to, bt_stack[t].dist);
    t++;
  }
}
return dist;
}
```

Be aware that **route( )** no longer takes an argument, and it now returns the total distance of the current route. When it returns 0, there are no more untried routes between the departure and destination points.

The entire program is shown here. Notice the changes in **main( )** and the addition of **spush( )**, which places the new solution nodes onto the solution stack.

```
/* Optimal solution using least-cost with
   route removal.
*/
#include "stdio.h"

#define MAX 100

/* structure of the flight database */
struct FL {
  char from[20];
  char to[20];
  int distance;
  char skip;  /* used for backtracking */
};

struct FL flight[MAX];  /* array of db structures */

int f_pos=0; /* number of entries in flight db */
int find_pos=0; /* index for searching flight db */

int tos=0;        /* top of stack */
int stos=0;       /* top of solution stack */

struct stack {
char from[20];
char to[20];
int dist;
} ;
```

```
struct stack bt_stack[MAX]; /* backtrack stack */
struct stack solution[MAX]; /* hold temporary solutions */

void setup(void);
void assert_flight(char *, char *, int);
void push(char *, char *, int);
void pop(char *, char *, int *);
void isflight(char *, char *);
void spush(char *, char *, int);
int find(char *, char *);
int match(char *, char *);
int route(void);

main()
{
  char from[20], to[20];
  int t, d;

  setup();

  printf("from? ");
  gets(from);
  printf("to? ");
  gets(to);
  do {
    isflight(from, to);
    d = route();
    tos = 0;  /* reset the backtrack stack */
  } while(d!=0);  /* while still finding solutions */

  t = 0;
  printf("Optimal solution is:\n");
  while(t<stos) {
    printf("%s to ", solution[t].from);
    d += solution[t].dist;
    t++;
  }
  printf("%s\n", to);
  printf("distance is %d\n", d);
}

void setup()
{
  assert_flight("New York", "Chicago", 1000);
  assert_flight("Chicago", "Denver", 1000);
  assert_flight("New York", "Toronto", 800);
  assert_flight("New York", "Denver", 1900);
  assert_flight("Toronto", "Calgary", 1500);
  assert_flight("Toronto", "Los Angeles", 1800);
  assert_flight("Toronto", "Chicago", 500);
  assert_flight("Denver", "Urbana", 1000);
  assert_flight("Denver", "Houston", 1500);
  assert_flight("Houston", "Los Angeles", 1500);
  assert_flight("Denver", "Los Angeles", 1000);
}
```

```
/* Put facts into the database. */
void assert_flight(char *from, char *to, int dist)
{
  if(f_pos<MAX) {
    strcpy(flight[f_pos].from, from);
    strcpy(flight[f_pos].to, to);
    flight[f_pos].distance = dist;
    flight[f_pos].skip = 0;
    f_pos++;
  }
  else printf("Flight database full.\n");
}

/* Find the shortest distance. */
route()
{
  int dist, t;
  static int old_dist=32000;

  if(!tos) return 0;   /* all done */
  t = 0;
  dist = 0;
  while(t<tos) {
    dist += bt_stack[t].dist;
    t++;
  }

  /* if shorter then make new solution */
  if(dist<old_dist && dist) {
    t = 0;
    old_dist = dist;
    stos = 0; /* clear old route from location stack */
    while(t<tos)  {
      spush(bt_stack[t].from, bt_stack[t].to, bt_stack[t].dist);
      t++;
    }
  }
  return dist;
}

/* If flight between from and to, then return
   the distance of flight; otherwise, return 0. */
match(char *from, char *to)
{
  register int t;

  for(t=f_pos-1; t>-1; t--)
    if(!strcmp(flight[t].from, from) &&
      !strcmp(flight[t].to, to)) return flight[t].distance;

  return 0;   /* not found */
}

/* Given from, find anywhere. */
find(char *from, char *anywhere)
{
```

```
    find_pos=0;
    while(find_pos<f_pos) {
      if(!strcmp(flight[find_pos].from, from) &&
        !flight[find_pos].skip) {
          strcpy(anywhere, flight[find_pos].to);
          flight[find_pos].skip = 1;
          return flight[find_pos].distance;
      }
      find_pos++;
    }
    return 0;
}

/* Determine if there is a route between from and to. */
void isflight(char *from, char *to)
{
  int d, dist;
  char anywhere[20];

  if(d=match(from, to)) {
    push(from, to, d); /* distance */
    return;
  }

  if(dist=find(from, anywhere)) {
    push(from, to, dist);
    isflight(anywhere, to);
  }
  else if(tos>0) {
    pop(from, to, &dist);
    isflight(from, to);
  }
}

/* stack routines */
void push(char *from, char *to, int dist)
{
  if(tos<MAX) {
    strcpy(bt_stack[tos].from, from);
    strcpy(bt_stack[tos].to, to);
    bt_stack[tos].dist = dist;
    tos++;
  }
  else printf("Stack full.\n");
}

void pop(char *from, char *to, int *dist)
{
  if(tos>0) {
    tos--;
    strcpy(from, bt_stack[tos].from);
    strcpy(to, bt_stack[tos].to);
    *dist = bt_stack[tos].dist;
  }
  else printf("Stack underflow.\n");
}
```

```
/* solution stack */
void spush(char *from, char *to, int dist)
{
  if(stos<MAX) {
    strcpy(solution[stos].from, from);
    strcpy(solution[stos].to, to);
    solution[stos].dist = dist;
    stos++;
  }
  else printf("Shortest distance stack full.\n");
}
```

The one inefficiency in this method is that all paths are followed to their conclusion. An improved method would stop following a path as soon as the length equaled or exceeded the current minimum. You might find it interesting to modify this program to include such an enhancement.

Back to the Lost Keys

To conclude this chapter on problem solving, it seems only fitting to provide a Turbo C program that finds the lost car keys described in the first part of this chapter. Even though it is a different problem from finding a route between two cities, it can employ the same techniques. By now you should have a fairly good understanding of how to use Turbo C to solve problems, so the program is presented for your enjoyment without further explanation!

```
/* Find the keys using a depth-first search. */
#include "stdio.h"

#define MAX 100

/* structure of the keys database */
struct FL {
  char from[20];
  char to[20];
  char skip;
};

struct FL keys[MAX];  /* array of db structures */
```

```
int f_pos=0; /* number of rooms in house */
int find_pos=0; /* index for searching keys db */

int tos=0;        /* top of stack */
struct stack {
  char from[20];
  char to[20];
} ;
struct stack bt_stack[MAX]; /* backtrack stack */

void setup(void), route(void);
void assert_keys(char *, char *);
void push(char *, char *);
void pop(char *, char *);
void iskeys(char *, char *);
int find(char *, char *);
int match(char *, char *);

main()
{

  setup();
  iskeys("front_door", "keys");
  route();
}

void setup()
{
  assert_keys("front_door", "lr");
  assert_keys("lr", "bath");
  assert_keys("lr", "hall");
  assert_keys("hall", "bd1");
  assert_keys("hall", "bd2");
  assert_keys("hall", "mb");
  assert_keys("lr", "kitchen");
  assert_keys("kitchen", "keys");
}

/* Put facts into the database. */
void assert_keys(char *from, char *to)
{
  if(f_pos<MAX) {
    strcpy(keys[f_pos].from, from);
    strcpy(keys[f_pos].to, to);
    keys[f_pos].skip = 0;
    f_pos++;
  }
  else printf("Keys database full.\n");
}

/* Show the route to the keys. */
void route()
{
  int t;

  t = 0;
```

```
    while(t<tos) {
      printf("%s", bt_stack[t].from);
      t++;
      if(t<tos) printf(" to ");
    }
    printf("\n");
}

match(char *from, char *to)
{
    register int t;

    for(t=f_pos-1; t>-1; t--)
      if(!strcmp(keys[t].from, from) &&
        !strcmp(keys[t].to, to)) return 1;

    return 0;  /* not found */
}

/* Given from, find anywhere. */
find(char *from, char *anywhere)
{
    find_pos = 0;
    while(find_pos<f_pos) {
      if(!strcmp(keys[find_pos].from, from) &&
        !keys[find_pos].skip) {
          strcpy(anywhere, keys[find_pos].to);
          keys[find_pos].skip = 1;
          return 1;
      }
      find_pos++;
    }
    return 0;
}

/* Determine if there is a route between from and to. */
void iskeys(char *from, char *to)

{
    char anywhere[20];

    if(match(from, to)) {
      push(from, to); /* distance */
      return;
    }

    if(find(from, anywhere)) {
      push(from, to);
      iskeys(anywhere, to);
    }
    else if(tos>0) {
      pop(from, to);
      iskeys(from, to);
    }
}
```

```
/* stack routines */
void push(char *from, char *to)
{
  if(tos<MAX) {
    strcpy(bt_stack[tos].from, from);
    strcpy(bt_stack[tos].to, to);
    tos++;
  }
  else printf("Stack full.\n");
}

void pop(char *from, char *to)
{
  if(tos>0) {
    tos--;
    strcpy(from, bt_stack[tos].from);
    strcpy(to, bt_stack[tos].to);
  }
  else printf("Stack underflow.\n");
}
```

Language
Interpreters

Have you ever wanted to create your own computer language? If you are like most programmers, you probably have. Most programmers find the idea of being able to create, control, enhance, and modify their own computer language very appealing. However, few programmers realize how easy and enjoyable the creation of a computer language can be. The development of a full-featured compiler is certainly a major undertaking, but the creation of a language interpreter is a much simpler task. The main problem is that the methods used to create language interpreters are often not taught, or are taught only as abstractions, in computer science classes. In this chapter, you will learn the secrets of language interpretation and expression parsing and see a working example.

Language interpreters are important for three widely separated reasons:

1. They can provide a truly interactive environment, as evidenced by the standard BASIC interpreter that comes with most microcomputers. Many novice users find an interactive environment easier to use than a compiler.

2. They can provide excellent interactive debugging facilities. Even seasoned veteran programmers sometimes resort to debugging a misbehaving routine with an interpreter because it is possible to set the value of variables and conditions dynamically.

3. Most database management programs interpret the query language accepted by the database.

This chapter develops an interpreter for a subset of BASIC, hereafter referred to as Small BASIC. The reason that BASIC is chosen over C is that BASIC is designed to be much easier to interpret than C or any other structured language. An interpreter for a structured language, such as C, is more difficult than one for BASIC because a structured language has standalone functions with local variables. These functions add significant complexity to an interpreter. However, the principles used to interpret BASIC also apply to any other language, and you can use the routines developed here as a starting point. Just as you must learn to crawl before you walk, it is necessary to learn the essentials of language interpretation before tackling the interpretation of something as complex as C. If you don't know BASIC, don't worry—the commands used in Small BASIC are easy to understand.

We will begin with the heart of any interpreter: the expression parser.

Expression Parsing

The most important part of a language interpreter is the expression parser. The *expression parser* transforms numeric expressions such as **(10−X)/23** into a form that the computer can understand and evaluate. In the book *C: The Complete Reference* (by Herbert Schildt, Osborne/McGraw-Hill, 1987), an entire chapter is devoted to expression parsing. The parser developed there is used here, with slight modifications, to support the Small BASIC interpreter. Therefore, this chapter presents only a brief explanation of expression parsing. For a detailed discussion, refer to *C: The Complete Reference*.

Expression parsing is not difficult and is a task like other programming tasks (in some ways it is easier because it works with the very strict rules of algebra). The expression parser developed in this chapter is commonly called a "recursive descent parser." Before developing the actual parser, it is necessary to understand how to think about expressions.

Expressions

Although expressions can be composed of all types of information, this chapter deals only with *numeric expressions*. For our purposes, numeric expressions can be composed of the following items:

- Numbers
- The operators $+ - / * ^\wedge \% = ( ) < > ; ,$
- Parentheses
- Variables

The $^\wedge$ indicates exponentiation. The $=$ is used as the assignment operator and for equality. These items can be combined in expressions according to the rules of algebra. Here are some examples:

```
7-8
(100-5) * 14/6
a+b-c
10^5
a=7-b
```

Although the $=$, $>$, $<$, ,, and ; are operators, the way BASIC treats them, they do not fit easily into the expression parser and are, instead, handled explicitly by the functions that process the IF, PRINT, and assignment statements. (A C language parser would contain these operators, however.) BASIC does not define the precedence of these operators. (You can think of them as having the highest precedence.) For the operators that are actually processed by the parser, assume this precedence:

highest: ()

$\wedge$

$* / \%$

$+ -$

lowest: $=$

Operators of equal precedence evaluate from left to right. Small BASIC makes the following assumptions:

• All variables are single letters; this means that 26 variables, the letters **A** through **Z**, are available for use.

• Although most BASIC interpreters support more variables by allowing a number to follow a letter, such as X27, in the interest of simplicity, the small BASIC interpreter developed here does not do so.

• The variables are not case-sensitive; **a** and **A** are treated as the same variable.

• All numbers are integers, although you could easily write the routines to handle other types of numbers.

• No string variables are supported, although quoted string constants can be used for writing messages to the screen.

These assumptions will be built into the parser.

Tokens

Before you can develop a parser to evaluate expressions, you must have some way to decompose the string that contains the expression into its components. For example, the expression **A∗B−(W+10)** has the components **A**, **∗**, **B**, **−**, **(**, **W**, **+**, **10**, and **)**. Each component represents an indivisible unit of the expression, which is called a *token*. In general, the function that breaks an expression into its component parts must do four things: (1) ignore spaces and tabs; (2) extract each token; (3) convert the token into an internal format, if necessary; and (4) and determine the type of the token.

Each token has two formats: external and internal. The external format is the string form that you use when writing a program. For example, PRINT is the external form of the BASIC PRINT command. Although it is possible for an interpreter to be designed so that each token is used in its external string format, this is seldom (if ever) done because it is horribly inefficient. Instead, the internal format of a token, which is simply an integer, is used. For example, the PRINT command might be represented by 1, the INPUT command by 2, and so on. The advantage of the internal representation is that much faster routines can be written using integers rather than strings. The function that returns the next token converts the token from its external format into its internal format. Keep in mind that not all tokens have different formats. For example, there is no advantage to converting the operators, for example, because they can be treated as characters or integers in their external form.

It is important to know what type of token is being returned. For example, the expression parser needs to know whether the next token is a number, an operator, or a variable. The importance of the token type will become evident as the interpreter is developed.

The function that returns the next token in the expression is called **get_token( )**. In Small BASIC, the program to be executed is stored as one null-terminated string. The **get_token( )** function progresses through the program a character at a time. The next character to be read is pointed to by a global character pointer. In the version of **get_token( )** shown here this pointer is called **prog**. The reason that **prog** is global is that it must maintain its value between calls to **get_token( )** and allow other functions to use it. The parser developed in this chapter uses six token types: DELIMITER, VARIABLE, NUMBER, COMMAND, STRING, and QUOTE. DELIMITER is used for both operators and parentheses. VARIABLE is used when a variable is

encountered. NUMBER is for numbers. The COMMAND
type is assigned when a BASIC command is found. STRING
is a temporary type used inside **get_token()** until a deter-
mination is made about a token. QUOTE is for quoted
strings. The global variable **token_type** holds the token
type. The internal representation of the token is placed into
the global **tok**. The **get_token()** function is shown here. Its
necessary support functions are found in the listing of the
entire parser.

```
#define DELIMITER  1
#define VARIABLE   2
#define NUMBER     3
#define COMMAND    4
#define STRING     5
#define QUOTE      6

extern char tok, token_type;
extern char *prog;  /* holds expression to be analyzed */

/* Get a token. */
get_token()
{
  register char *temp;

  token_type=0; tok=0;
  temp=token;

  if(*prog=='\0') { /* end of file */
    *token=0;
    tok = FINISHED;
    return(token_type=DELIMITER);
  }

  while(iswhite(*prog)) ++prog;  /* skip over white space */

  if(*prog=='\r') { /* crlf */
    ++prog; ++prog;
    tok = EOL; *token='\r';
    token[1]='\n'; token[2]=0;
    return (token_type = DELIMITER);
  }

  if(strchr("+-*^/%=;(),><", *prog)){ /* delimiter */
    *temp=*prog;
    prog++; /* advance to next position */
    temp++;
    *temp=0;
    return (token_type=DELIMITER);
  }
```

```
if(*prog=='"') { /* quoted string */
  prog++;
  while(*prog!='"'&& *prog!='\r') *temp++=*prog++;
  if(*prog=='\r') serror(1);
  prog++;*temp=0;
  return(token_type=QUOTE);
}

if(isdigit(*prog)) { /* number */
  while(!isdelim(*prog)) *temp++=*prog++;
  *temp = '\0';
  return(token_type = NUMBER);
}

if(isalpha(*prog)) { /* var or command */
  while(!isdelim(*prog)) *temp++=*prog++;
  token_type=STRING;
}

*temp = '\0';

/* see if a string is a command or a variable */
if(token_type==STRING) {
  tok=look_up(token); /* convert to internal rep */
  if(!tok) token_type = VARIABLE;
  else token_type = COMMAND; /* is a command */
}
return token_type;
}
```

Look closely at **get—token()**. Because people like to put spaces into expressions to add clarity but not meaning, leading spaces are skipped over using the function **iswhite()**, which returns true if its argument is a space or tab. Once the spaces have been skipped, **prog** points to a number, a variable, a command, a carriage-return-linefeed, an operator, or a null if trailing spaces end the expression. If a carriage return is next, **EOL** is returned. If the next character is an operator, it is returned as a string in the global variable **token**, and the type of DELIMITER is placed in **token— type**. Otherwise, the program checks for a quoted string and sees if the next token is a number. If the next character is a letter instead, it is either a variable or a command. The function **look—up()** compares the token against strings in a table and, if it finds a match, returns the appropriate internal representation. (The **look—up()** function is discussed later.)

If no match is found, the token is assumed to be a variable. If the token is not an operator, a number, or a variable, the interpreter assumes that the end of the expression has been reached and **token** is null, signaling the end of the expression.

To better understand how **get_token( )** works, study what it returns for each token and type for the following expression:

PRINT A + 100 −(B∗C)/2

Token	Token Type
PRINT	COMMAND
A	VARIABLE
+	DELIMITER
100	NUMBER
−	DELIMITER
(	DELIMITER
B	VARIABLE
∗	DELIMITER
C	VARIABLE
)	DELIMITER
/	DELIMITER
2	NUMBER
null	FINISHED

Remember that **token** always holds a null-terminated string, even if it contains just a single character.

Some of the functions in the interpreter need to look ahead one token to determine the next course of action. In some of these cases, it is necessary to return the token to the input stream if it is not needed by the routine. The function **putback( )** performs this task.

```
/* Return a token to input stream. */
void putback()
{
  char *t;

  t = token;
  for(; *t; t++) prog--;
}
```

How Expressions Are Constructed

There are a number of possible ways to parse and evaluate an expression. For use with a recursive descent parser, you should think of expressions as *recursive data structures*, that is, expressions that are defined in terms of themselves. If, for the moment, expressions can use only +, −, *, /, and (), all expressions can be defined using the following rules:

Expression => Term [+ Term] [− Term]
Term => Factor [* Factor] [/ Factor]
Factor => Variable, Number, or (Expression)

Any part of these expressions can be null.

Here the square brackets mean "optional" and the => means "produces." In fact, these rules are usually called the *production rules* of the expression. Therefore, you could say that "Term produces Factor times Factor or Factor divided by Factor" for the definition of *term*. You should notice that the precedence of the operators is implicit in the way an expression is defined.

The expression **10+5*B** has two terms: 10 and 5*B. It has three factors: 10, 5, and B. These factors consist of two numbers and one variable.

On the other hand, the expression **14*(7−C)** has two terms, 14 and (7−C), consisting of one number and one parenthesized expression. The parenthesized expression evaluates to one number and one variable.

You can transform the production rules for expressions into a set of mutually recursive, chainlike functions that form a recursive descent parser. At each appropriate step the parser performs the specified operations in the algebraically correct sequence. To see how this process works, parse the following expression and perform the arithmetic operations at the right time.

Input expression: 9/3−(100+56)
Step 1. Get first Term: 9/3.
Step 2. Get each Factor and divide integers. That value is 3.
Step 3. Get second Term: (100+56). At this point recursively start analyzing the second expression.
Step 4. Get each Term and add. That value is 156.
Step 5. Return from recursive call and subtract 156 from 3, yielding the answer −153.

If you are a little confused at this point, don't feel bad! This fairly complex concept takes some getting used to. There are two basic things to remember about this recursive view of expressions:

1. The precedence of the operators is implicit in the way the production rules are defined.

2. This method of parsing and evaluating expressions is very similar to the way we humans do the same thing.

The Expression Parser

Here is the entire simple recursive descent parser for integer expressions along with some support functions. You should put this code into its own file. (Together the code for the parser and the interpreter make a fairly large file, so two separately compiled files are recommended.) The meaning and use of the external variables are described shortly, when the interpreter is discussed.

```
/* Recursive descent parser for integer expressions
   which may include variables.  */
#include "stdio.h"
#include "string.h"
#include "setjmp.h"
#include "math.h"
#include "ctype.h"
#include "stdlib.h"

#define DELIMITER  1
#define VARIABLE   2
#define NUMBER     3
#define COMMAND    4
#define STRING     5
#define QUOTE      6

#define EOL    9
#define FINISHED  10

extern char *prog;  /* holds expression to be analyzed */
extern jmp_buf e_buf; /* hold environment for longjmp() */
extern int variables[26]; /* variables */
extern struct commands {
  char command[20];
  char tok;
} table[];

extern char token[80]; /* holds string representation of token */
extern char token_type; /* contains type of token */
extern char tok; /* holds the internal representation of token */

void get_exp(int *), level2(int *), level3(int *);
void level4(int *), level5(int *);
void level6(int *), primitive(int *), unary(char, int *);
void arith(char, int *, int *);
void serror(int), putback(void);
int find_var(char *), look_up(char *), isdelim(char);
int iswhite(char);
int get_token(void);

/* Entry point into parser. */
void get_exp(int *result)
{
  get_token();
  if(!*token) {
    serror(2);
    return;
  }
  level2(result);
  putback(); /* return last token read to input stream */
}

/*  Add or subtract two terms. */
void level2(int *result)
{
  register char  op;
  int hold;

  level3(result);
  while((op = *token) == '+' || op == '-') {
    get_token();
```

```
      level3(&hold);
      arith(op, result, &hold);
    }
}

/* Multiply or divide two factors. */
void level3(int *result)
{
  register char  op;
  int hold;

  level4(result);
  while((op = *token) == '*' || op == '/' || op == '%') {
    get_token();
    level4(&hold);
    arith(op, result, &hold);
  }
}

/* Process integer exponent. */
void level4(int *result)
{
  int hold;

  level5(result);
  if(*token== '^') {
    get_token();
    level4(&hold);
    arith('^', result, &hold);
  }
}

/* Is a unary + or -. */
void level5(int *result)
{
  register char  op;

  op = 0;
  if((token_type==DELIMITER) && *token=='+' || *token=='-') {
    op = *token;
    get_token();
  }
  level6(result);
  if(op)
    unary(op, result);
}

/* Process parenthesized expression. */
void level6(int *result)
{
  if((*token == '(') && (token_type == DELIMITER)) {
    get_token();
    level2(result);
    if(*token != ')')
      serror(1);
```

```
      get_token();
  }
  else
    primitive(result);
}

/* Find value of number or variable. */
void primitive(int *result)
{

  switch(token_type) {
  case VARIABLE:
    *result = find_var(token);
    get_token();
    return;
  case NUMBER:
    *result = atoi(token);
    get_token();
    return;
  default:
    serror(0);
  }
}

/* Perform the specified arithmetic. */
void arith(char o, int *r, int *h)
{
  register int t, ex;

  switch(o) {
    case '-':
      *r = *r-*h;
      break;
    case '+':
      *r = *r+*h;
      break;
    case '*':
      *r = *r * *h;
      break;
    case '/':
      *r = (*r)/(*h);
      break;
    case '%':
      t = (*r)/(*h);
      *r = *r-(t*(*h));
      break;
    case '^':
      ex = *r;
      if(*h==0) {
        *r = 1;
        break;
      }
      for(t=*h-1; t>0; --t) *r = (*r) * ex;
      break;
  }
```

```
}

/* Reverse the sign. */
void unary(char o, int *r)
{
    if(o=='-') *r = -(*r);
}

/* Find the value of a variable. */
int find_var(char *s)
{
    if(!isalpha(*s)){
        serror(4); /* not a variable */
        return 0;
    }
    return variables[toupper(*token)-'A'];
}

/* display an error message */
void serror(int error)
{
    static char *e[]= {
        "syntax error",
        "unbalanced parentheses",
        "no expression present",
        "equals sign expected",
        "not a variable",
        "Label table full",
        "duplicate label",
        "undefined label",
        "THEN expected",
        "TO expected",
        "too many nested FOR loops",
        "NEXT without FOR",
        "too many nested GOSUBs",
        "RETURN without GOSUB"
    };
    printf("%s\n", e[error]);
    longjmp(e_buf, 1); /* return to save point */
}

/* Get a token. */
get_token()
{

    register char *temp;

    token_type=0; tok=0;
    temp=token;

    if(*prog=='\0') { /* end of file */
        *token=0;
        tok = FINISHED;
        return(token_type=DELIMITER);
    }
```

```
  while(iswhite(*prog)) ++prog;   /* skip over white space */

  if(*prog=='\r') { /* crlf */
    ++prog; ++prog;
    tok = EOL; *token='\r';
    token[1]='\n'; token[2]=0;
    return (token_type = DELIMITER);
  }

  if(strchr("+-*^/%=;(),><", *prog)){ /* delimiter */
    *temp=*prog;
    prog++; /* advance to next position */
    temp++;
    *temp=0;
    return (token_type=DELIMITER);
  }

  if(*prog=='"') { /* quoted string */
    prog++;
    while(*prog!='"'&& *prog!='\r') *temp++=*prog++;
    if(*prog=='\r') serror(1);
    prog++;*temp=0;
    return(token_type=QUOTE);
  }

  if(isdigit(*prog)) { /* number */
    while(!isdelim(*prog)) *temp++=*prog++;
    *temp = '\0';
    return(token_type = NUMBER);
  }

  if(isalpha(*prog)) { /* var or command */
    while(!isdelim(*prog)) *temp++=*prog++;
    token_type=STRING;
  }

  *temp = '\0';

  /* see if a string is a command or a variable */
  if(token_type==STRING) {
    tok=look_up(token); /* convert to internal rep */
    if(!tok) token_type = VARIABLE;
    else token_type = COMMAND; /* is a command */
  }
  return token_type;
}

/* Return a token to input stream. */
void putback()
{

  char *t;

  t = token;
```

```
      for(; *t; t++) prog--;
}

/* Look up a a token's internal representation in the
   token table.
*/
look_up(char *s)
{
   register int i;
   char *p;

   /* convert to lowercase */
   p = s;
   while(*p){ *p = tolower(*p); p++; }

   /* see if token is in table */
   for(i=0; *table[i].command; i++)
      if(!strcmp(table[i].command, s)) return table[i].tok;
   return 0; /* unknown command */
}

/* Return true if c is a delimiter. */
isdelim(char c)
{
   if(strchr(" ;,+-<>/*%^=()", c) || c==9 || c=='\r' || c==0)
      return 1;
   return 0;
}

/* Return 1 if c is space or tab. */
iswhite(char c)
{
   if(c==' ' || c=='\t') return 1;
   else return 0;
}
```

The parser shown can handle the following operators: +, −, *, /, %, integer exponentiation (^), and the unary minus. It can also deal correctly with parentheses. Notice that it has six levels as well as the **primitive( )** function, which returns the value of a number. Also included are routines for performing the various arithmetic operations, **arith( )** and **unary( )**, as well as the **get_token( )** code.

To evaluate an expression, set the pointer **prog** to point to the beginning of the string that holds the expression and call **get_exp( )** with the address of the variable you want to hold the result.

You should pay special attention to the **serror( )** function, which is used to report errors. When a syntax error is detected, **serror( )** is called with the number of the error. Error 0, which displays the message **syntax error**, is a sort of catchall message used when nothing else applies. Otherwise, the specific error is reported. Notice that **serror( )** ends with a call to **longjmp( )**. The **longjmp( )** function performs a nonlocal goto, returning to the point defined by its companion function **setjmp( )** — presumably a safe place. (The **setjmp( )** function is found in the interpreter code, not the parser code.) The first argument in **longjmp( )** is an environment buffer that is initialized by **setjmp( )** and resets the state of the computer to what it was at the time of the **setjmp( )** call. The second argument is a value that appears to be "returned" by **setjmp( )**. You will see how it is used later. The use of **longjmp( )** simplifies error handling because the routines do not explicitly abort when errors occur; instead they can execute a **longjmp( )** and return to a stable point in the program.

How the Parser Handles Variables

As stated earlier, the Small BASIC interpreter will recognize only the variables **A** through **Z**. Each variable uses one array location in a 26-element array of integers called **variables**. This array is defined in the interpreter code shown here with each variable initialized to 0:

```
int variables[26]= {     /* 26 user variables,  A-Z */
  0, 0, 0, 0, 0, 0, 0, 0, 0, 0,
  0, 0, 0, 0, 0, 0, 0, 0, 0, 0,
  0, 0, 0, 0, 0, 0
};
```

Because the variable names are the letters **A** through **Z**, they can easily be used to index the array **variables** by subtracting the ASCII value for **A** from the variable name. The function **find_var( )**, which finds a variable's value, is shown next.

```
/* Find the value of a variable. */
int find_var(char *s)
{
  if(!isalpha(*s)){
    serror(4); /* not a variable */
    return 0;
  }
  return variables[toupper(*token)-'A'];
}
```

As this function is written, it actually accepts long variable names, but only the first letter is significant. You can modify it to enforce single letter variable names if you like.

The Small BASIC Interpreter

Now that expressions can be parsed and evaluated, it is time to develop the actual Small BASIC interpreter. The Small BASIC interpreter recognizes the following BASIC keywords:

PRINT
INPUT
IF
THEN
FOR
NEXT
TO
GOTO
GOSUB
RETURN
END

The internal representation of these commands—plus **EOL** for end-of-line and **FINISHED**, which signals the end of the program—are defined as shown here:

```
#define PRINT 1
#define INPUT 2
```

```
#define IF       3
#define THEN     4
#define FOR      5
#define NEXT     6
#define TO       7
#define GOTO     8
#define EOL      9
#define FINISHED   10
#define GOSUB 11
#define RETURN 12
#define END 13
```

Although **#define** statements are used for these values, you can use an enumeration if you prefer.

For the external representation of a token to be converted into the internal representation, both the external and the internal formats are held in a table of structures called **table**, as shown here:

```
struct commands { /* keyword lookup table */
  char command[20];
  char tok;
} table[] = {        /* Commands must be entered lowercase */
  "print", PRINT, /* in this table. */
  "input", INPUT,
  "if", IF,
  "then", THEN,
  "goto", GOTO,
  "for", FOR,
  "next", NEXT,
  "to", TO,
  "gosub", GOSUB,
  "return", RETURN,
  "end", END,
  "", END  /* mark end of table */
};
```

Notice that a null string marks the end of the table.

The function **look_up( )**, shown here, returns either a token's internal representation or a null if no match is found.

```
/* Look up token's internal representation in the
   token table.
*/
look_up(char *s)
{
  register int i;
  char *p;

  /* convert to lowercase */
```

```
    p = s;
    while(*p){ *p = tolower(*p); p++; }

    /* see if token is in table */
    for(i=0; *table[i].command; i++)
        if(!strcmp(table[i].command, s)) return table[i].tok;
    return 0; /* unknown command */
}
```

No integral editor is supported by the Small BASIC interpreter. Instead, you must create a BASIC program using a standard test editor. The program is then loaded and executed by the interpreter. The function that loads the program is called **load—program( )** and is shown here:

```
/* Load a program. */
load_program(char *, char *fname)
{
    FILE *fp;
    int i=0;

    if(!(fp=fopen(fname, "rb"))) return 0;

    i = 0;
    do {
      *p = getc(fp);
      p++; i++;
    } while(!feof(fp) && i<PROG_SIZE);
    *(p-2) = '\0'; /* null terminate the program */
    fclose(fp);
    return 1;
}
```

The Main Loop

All interpreters are driven by a top-level loop that operates by reading the next token from the program and selecting the right function to process it. The main loop for the Small BASIC interpreter looks like this:

```
do {
  token_type = get_token();
  /* check for assignment statement */
  if(token_type==VARIABLE) {
    putback(); /* return the var to the input stream */
    assignment(); /* must be assignment statement */
  }
```

```
    else /* is a command, execute it */
      switch(tok) {
        case PRINT:
          print();
          break;
        case GOTO:
          exec_goto();
          break;
        case IF:
          exec_if();
          break;
        case FOR:
          exec_for();
          break;
        case NEXT:
          next();
          break;
        case INPUT:
          input();
          break;
        case GOSUB:
          gosub();
          break;
        case RETURN:
          greturn();
          break;
        case END:
          exit(0);
      }
  } while (tok != FINISHED);
```

First, a token is read from the program. For reasons that will become clear, that token is always the first token on each line. Assuming no syntax errors have been made, if the token is a variable, an assignment statement occurs. (The Small BASIC interpreter does not support the antiquated LET command.) Otherwise, the token must be a command and the appropriate **case** statement is selected based on the value of *tok*. Let's see how each of these commands work.

The Assignment Function

In BASIC, the general form of an assignment statement is

$$<var\text{-}name> = <expression>$$

The **assignment( )** function shown next supports this type of assignment:

```
/* Assign a variable a value. */
assignment()
{
  int var, value;

  /* get the variable name */
  get_token();
  if(!isalpha(*token)) {
    serror(4); /* not a variable */
    return;
  }

  /* find the index of the variable */
  var = toupper(*token)-'A';

  /* get the equals sign */
  get_token();
  if(*token!='=') {
    serror(3);
    return;
  }

  /* get the value to assign to var */
  get_exp(&value);

  /* assign the value */
  variables[var] = value;
}
```

The first thing **assignment( )** does is read a token from
the program. This is the variable that will have its value
assigned. If it is not a valid variable, an error is reported.
Next, the equal sign is read. Then **get—exp( )** is called to
compute the value to assign the variable. Finally, the value is
assigned to the variable. The function is surprisingly simple
and uncluttered because the expression parser and the **get—
token( )** function do much of the "messy" work.

The PRINT Command

The standard BASIC PRINT command is actually quite
powerful and flexible, especially when PRINT USING is employed. Although it is beyond the scope of this chapter to
create a function that supports all the functionality of the
PRINT command, the one developed here embodies its most

important essential functions. The general form of the Small BASIC PRINT command is

   PRINT <*arg-list*>

where *arg-list* is a comma- or semicolon-separated list of variables or quoted strings. The function **print( )**, shown here, executes a BASIC PRINT command:

```
/* Execute a simple version of the BASIC PRINT statement */
void print()
{
  int answer;
  int len=0, spaces;
  char last_delim;

  do {
    get_token(); /* get next list item */
    if(tok==EOL || tok==FINISHED) break;
    if(token_type==QUOTE) { /* is string */
      printf(token);
      len += strlen(token);
      get_token();
    }
    else { /* is expression */
      putback();
      get_exp(&answer);
      get_token();
      len += printf("%d", answer);
    }
    last_delim = *token;

    if(*token==';') {
      /* compute number of spaces to move to next tab */
      spaces = 8 - (len % 8);
      len += spaces; /* add in the tabbing position */
      while(spaces) {
        printf(" ");
        spaces--;
      }
    }
    else if(*token==',') /* do nothing */;
    else if(tok!=EOL && tok!=FINISHED) serror(0);
  } while (*token==';' || *token==',');

  if(tok==EOL || tok==FINISHED) {
    if(last_delim != ';' && last_delim!=',') printf("\n");
  }
  else serror(0); /* error is not , or ; */

}
```

The PRINT command can be used to print a list of variables and quoted strings on the screen. If two items are separated by a comma, no space is printed between them. If two items are separated by a semicolon, the second item is displayed beginning at the next tab position. If the list ends in a comma or semicolon, no newline is issued. Here are some examples of valid PRINT statements:

```
PRINT X; Y; "THIS IS A STRING"

PRINT 10 / 4

PRINT
```

The last example simply prints a newline.

Notice that **print( )** makes use of the **putback( )** function to return a token to the input stream because **print( )** must look ahead to see whether the next item to be printed is a quoted string or a numeric expression. If the next item is an expression, the first term in the expression must be replaced on the input stream so that the expression parser can correctly compute the value of the expression.

The INPUT Command

In BASIC, the INPUT command is used to read information from the keyboard into a variable. It has two general forms. The first is

INPUT <*var-name*>

which displays a question mark and waits for input. The second is

INPUT "<*prompt-string*>", <*var-name*>

which displays a prompting message and waits for input. The function **input( )**, shown here, implements the BASIC INPUT command:

```
/* Execute a simple form of the BASIC INPUT command */
void input()
{
  char var;
  int i;

  get_token(); /* see if prompt string is present */
  if(token_type==QUOTE) {
    printf(token); /* if so, print it and check for comma */
    get_token();
    if(*token!=',') serror(1);
    get_token();
  }
  else printf("? "); /* otherwise, prompt with ? */

  var = toupper(*token)-'A'; /* get the input var */

  scanf("%d", &i); /* read input */

  variables[var] = i; /* store it */
}
```

The operation of this function is straightforward and should be clear after reading the comments.

The GOTO Command

Now that you have seen the way a few simple commands work, it is time to develop a somewhat more difficult command. In BASIC, the most important form of program control is the lowly GOTO. In standard BASIC, the object of a GOTO must be a line number. In Small BASIC, this traditional approach is preserved. However, Small BASIC does not require a line number for each line; a number is needed only if that line is the target of a GOTO. The general form of the GOTO is

GOTO <line-number>

The main complexity associated with the GOTO is that both forward and backward jumps must be allowed. To satisfy this constraint in an efficient manner, the entire program must be scanned prior to execution and the location of each label must be placed in a table. Then each time a GOTO is executed, the location of the target line can be looked up and program control transferred to that point. The table that holds the labels is declared like this:

```
struct label {
  char name[LAB_LEN]; /* name of label */
  char *p;  /* points to place of label in source file*/
};
struct label label_table[NUM_LAB];
```

The routine that scans the program and puts each label's location in the table is called **scan_labels( )** and is shown here along with several of its support functions:

```
/* Find all labels. */
void scan_labels()
{
  register int loc;
  char *temp;

  label_init();  /* zero all labels */
  temp = prog;   /* save pointer to top of program */

  /* if the first token in the file is a label */
  get_token();
  if(token_type==NUMBER) {
    strcpy(label_table[0].name,token);
    label_table[0].p=prog;
  }

  find_eol();
  do {
    get_token();
    if(token_type==NUMBER) {
      loc=get_next_label(token);
      if(loc==-1||loc==-2) {
          (loc==-1) ?serror(5):serror(6);
      }
      strcpy(label_table[loc].name, token);
      label_table[loc].p = prog;  /* current point in program */
    }
    /* if not on a blank line, find next line */
    if(tok!=EOL) find_eol();

  } while(tok!=FINISHED);
  prog = temp;  /* restore to original */
}

/* Initialize the array that holds the labels.
   By convention, a null label name indicates that
   array position is unused.
*/
```

```
void label_init()
{
  register int t;

  for(t=0;t<NUM_LAB;++t) label_table[t].name[0]='\0';
}

/* Find the start of the next line. */
void find_eol()
{
  while(*prog!='\n'  && *prog!='\0') ++prog;
  if(*prog) prog++;
}

/* Return index of next free position in label array.
   A -1 is returned if the array is full.
   A -2 is returned if a duplicate label is found.
*/
get_next_label(char *s)
{
  register int t;

  for(t=0;t<NUM_LAB;++t) {
    if(label_table[t].name[0]==0) return t;
    if(!strcmp(label_table[t].name,s)) return -2; /* dup */
  }

  return -1;
}
```

Two types of errors are reported by **scan_labels( )**. The first is "duplicate labels." In BASIC (and most other languages), no two labels can be the same. The second error is "label table full." The table's size is defined by **NUM_LAB**, which you can set to any size you desire.

Once the label table has been built, it is quite easy to execute a GOTO instruction as shown here in **exec_goto( )**:

```
/* Execute a GOTO statement. */
void exec_goto()
{

  char *loc;

  get_token(); /* get label to go to */
  /* find the location of the label */
  loc = find_label(token);
  if(loc=='\0')
    serror(7); /* label not defined */

  else prog=loc;  /* start program running at that loc */
}
```

```
/* Find location of given label.  A null is returned if
   label is not found; otherwise a pointer to the position
   of the label is returned.
*/
char *find_label(char *s)
{
  register int t;

  for(t=0; t<NUM_LAB; ++t)
    if(!strcmp(label_table[t].name,s)) return label_table[t].p;
  return '\0'; /* error condition */
}
```

The support function **find_label()** looks a label up in the label table and returns a pointer to it. If the label is not found, a null—which can never be a valid pointer—is returned. If the address is not null, it is assigned to the global **prog** causing execution to resume at the location of the label. (Remember, **prog** is the pointer that keeps track of where the program is currently being read.) If the label is not found, an **undefined label** message is issued.

The IF Statement

The Small BASIC interpreter executes a subset of the standard BASIC IF statement. In Small BASIC, no ELSE is allowed and only the conditions greater than, less than, or equal to are supported. (However, you can easily enhance the IF once you understand its operation.) The IF statement takes this general form:

IF *<expression>* *<operator>* *<expression>*
THEN *<statement>*

The statement that follows THEN is executed only if the relational expression is true. The following function, called **exec_if()**, executes this form of the IF statement:

```
/* Execute an IF statement. */
void exec_if()
{
  int x , y, cond;
  char op;

  get_exp(&x); /* get left expression */

  get_token(); /* get the operator */
```

```
if(!strchr("=<>", *token)) {
  serror(0); /* not a legal operator */
  return;
}
op=*token;

get_exp(&y); /* get right expression */

/* determine the outcome */
cond=0;
switch(op) {
    case '=':
  if(x==y) cond=1;
  break;
    case '<':
  if(x<y) cond=1;
  break;
    case '>':
  if(x>y) cond=1;
  break;
}
if(cond) { /* is true so process target of IF */
  get_token();
  if(tok!=THEN) {
    serror(8);
    return;
  }/* else prog exec starts on next line */
}
else find_eol(); /* find start of next line */
}
```

The **exec—if( )** function operates as follows. First, the value of the left expression is computed, then the operator is read and the value of the right expression is computed. Next, the relational operation is evaluated. If the condition is true, the target of THEN is executed; otherwise, **find—eol( )** finds the beginning of the next line.

The FOR Loop

The implementation of the BASIC FOR loop presents a challenging problem that lends itself to a rather elegant solution. The general form of the FOR loop is

FOR <control var-name> = <initial value> TO <target value>

.
.
.

statement sequence

.

.

.

NEXT

The Small BASIC version of the FOR allows only positively running loops that increment the control variable by 1 each iteration. The STEP command is not supported.

In BASIC, as in C, FOR loops can be nested to several levels. The main challenge presented by this is keeping the information associated with nested FOR loops straight. That is, how does the interpreter "know" which NEXT is associated with which FOR? Giving this a little thought, you should be able to see that a FOR loop is a stack-based algorithm. The alogrithm works like this. At the top of a FOR loop, information about the status of the control variable, the target value, and the location of the top of the loop in the program is pushed onto a stack. Each time NEXT is encountered, the information on the top of the stack is popped, the control variable is updated, and its value is checked against the target value. If the control value exceeds the target, the loop stops, and execution continues with the next line following the NEXT statement. Otherwise, the updated information is placed on the stack and execution resumes at the top of the loop. Implementing a FOR loop in this way works not only for a single loop but also for loops nested to any level. The stacklike nature of the loop causes each NEXT to be associated with the nearest FOR.

To support the FOR loop, a stack must be created to hold the loop information, as shown here:

```
struct for_stack {
   int var; /* counter variable */
   int target;  /* target value */
   char *loc;
} fstack[FOR_NEST]; /* stack for FOR/NEXT loop */
int ftos;  /* index to top of FOR stack */
```

The value of **FOR_NEST** defines how deeply nested the FOR loops can be. (Generally 25 is more than adequate.) The

ftos variable holds the index to the top of the stack.

You need two stack routines called **fpush( )** and **fpop( )**, which follow:

```
/* Push function for the FOR stack. */
void fpush(struct for_stack i)
{
    if(ftos>FOR_NEST)
     serror(10);

   fstack[ftos]=i;
   ftos++;
}

struct for_stack fpop()
{
   ftos--;
   if(ftos<0) serror(11);
   return(fstack[ftos]);
}
```

Now that the necessary support is in place, the functions that execute the FOR and NEXT statements can be developed as shown here:

```
/* Execute a FOR loop. */
void exec_for()
{
  struct for_stack i;
  int value;

  get_token(); /* read the control variable */
  if(!isalpha(*token)) {
    serror(4);
    return;
  }

  i.var=toupper(*token)-'A'; /* save its index */

  get_token(); /* read the equals sign */
  if(*token!='=') {
    serror(3);
    return;
  }

  get_exp(&value); /* get initial value */

  variables[i.var]=value;

  get_token();
  if(tok!=TO) serror(9); /* read and discard the TO */

  get_exp(&i.target); /* get target value */
```

```
/* if loop can execute at least once, push info on stack */
if(value>=variables[i.var]) {
  i.loc = prog;
  fpush(i);
}
else { /* otherwise, skip loop code altogether */
  while(tok!=NEXT) get_token();
}
}

/* Execute a NEXT statement. */
void next()
{
  struct for_stack i;

  i = fpop(); /* read the loop info */

  variables[i.var]++; /* increment control variable */
  if(variables[i.var]>i.target) return;  /* all done */
  fpush(i);  /* otherwise, restore the info */
  prog = i.loc;  /* loop */
}
```

You should be able to follow the operation of these routines by reading the comments. As the code stands, it does not prevent you from writing a GOTO out of a FOR loop. However, doing so corrupts the FOR stack and should be avoided.

The stack-based solution to the FOR loop problem can be generalized to all loops. Although Small BASIC does not implement any other types of loops, you can apply the same sort of procedure to WHILE and DO/WHILE loops. Also, as you will see in the next section, the stack-based solution can be applied to any language element that can be nested, including calls to subroutines.

The GOSUB

Although BASIC does not support true standalone subroutines, it does allow portions of a program to be called and returned from using the GOSUB and RETURN statements. The general form of a GOSUB/RETURN is

GOSUB <line-num>

.

.

.

<line-num>

.

. subroutine code

.

RETURN

Calling a subroutine, even as simply as subroutines are implemented in BASIC, requires the use of a stack. The reason for this is similar to that given for the FOR statement. Because it is possible to have one subroutine call another, a stack is required to ensure that a RETURN statement is associated with the proper GOSUB. The GOSUB stack is defined as

```
char *gstack[SUB_NEST]; /* stack for gosub */

int gtos;  /* index to top of GOSUB stack */
```

The function **gosub( )** and its support routines are shown here:

```
/* Execute a GOSUB command. */
void gosub()
{
  char *loc;

  get_token();
  /* find the label to call */
  loc = find_label(token);
  if(loc=='\0')
    serror(7); /* label not defined */
  else {
    gpush(prog); /* save place to return to */
    prog = loc;  /* start program running at that loc */
  }
}

/* Return from GOSUB. */
void greturn()
{
  prog = gpop();
}

/* GOSUB stack push function. */
void gpush(char *s)
{
  gtos++;

  if(gtos==SUB_NEST) {
```

```
      serror(12);
      return;
   }

   gstack[gtos]=s;
}

/* GOSUB stack pop function. */
char *gpop()
{
   if(gtos==0) {
      serror(13);
      return 0;
   }

   return(gstack[gtos--]);
}
```

The GOSUB command works like this. A current value of **prog** is pushed onto the GOSUB stack. The target line number is looked up and the address associated with it is assigned to **prog**. This causes program execution to resume at the start of the specified line. When a RETURN is encountered, the GOSUB stack is popped and this value is assigned to **prog**, causing execution to continue on the next line after the GOSUB statement. The process allows GO-SUBs to be nested to any depth by always associating each RETURN statement with its corresponding GOSUB.

The Entire Interpreter File

All the code for the Small BASIC interpreter—except the routines found in the expression parser file—is shown here. Once you have entered it into your computer, you should compile both the interpreter and the parser files and link them together.

```
/* A small BASIC interpreter */

#include "string.h"
#include "stdio.h"
#include "setjmp.h"
#include "math.h"
#include "ctype.h"
#include "stdlib.h"
```

```
#define NUM_LAB 100
#define LAB_LEN 10
#define FOR_NEST 25
#define SUB_NEST 25
#define PROG_SIZE 10000

#define DELIMITER  1
#define VARIABLE   2
#define NUMBER     3
#define COMMAND    4
#define STRING     5
#define QUOTE      6

#define PRINT 1
#define INPUT 2
#define IF     3
#define THEN   4
#define FOR    5
#define NEXT   6
#define TO     7
#define GOTO   8
#define EOL    9
#define FINISHED   10
#define GOSUB 11
#define RETURN 12
#define END 13

char *prog;  /* holds expression to be analyzed */
jmp_buf e_buf; /* hold environment for longjmp() */

int variables[26]= {     /* 26 user variables,  A-Z */
  0, 0, 0, 0, 0, 0, 0, 0, 0, 0,
  0, 0, 0, 0, 0, 0, 0, 0, 0, 0,
  0, 0, 0, 0, 0, 0
};

struct commands { /* keyword lookup table */
  char command[20];
  char tok;
} table[] = { /* Commands must be entered lowercase */
  "print", PRINT, /* in this table. */
  "input", INPUT,
  "if", IF,
  "then", THEN,
  "goto", GOTO,
  "for", FOR,
  "next", NEXT,
  "to", TO,
  "gosub", GOSUB,
  "return", RETURN,
  "end", END,
  "", END  /* mark end of table */
};

char token[80];
char token_type, tok;

struct label {
  char name[LAB_LEN];
  char *p;  /* points to place to go in source file*/
};
struct label label_table[NUM_LAB];
```

```
struct for_stack {
  int var; /* counter variable */
  int target;  /* target value */
  char *loc;
} fstack[FOR_NEST]; /* stack for FOR/NEXT loop */
struct for_stack fpop(void);

char *gstack[SUB_NEST]; /* stack for gosub */

int ftos;  /* index to top of FOR stack */
int gtos;  /* index to top of GOSUB stack */

void print(void), scan_labels(void), find_eol(void);
void exec_goto(void), exec_if(void), input(void);
void exec_for(void), next(void), fpush(struct for_stack);
void gosub(void), greturn(void), gpush(char *), label_init(void);
void assignment(void);
int load_program(char *, char *), get_next_label(char *);
char *find_label(char *), *gpop(void);
void get_exp(int *), serror(int), putback(void);
int get_token(void);

main(argc, argv)
int argc;
char *argv[];
{
  char *p_buf;

  if(argc!=2) {
    printf("usage: run <filename>\n");
    exit(1);
  }

  /* allocate memory for the program */
  if(!(p_buf=(char *) malloc(PROG_SIZE))) {
    printf("allocation failure");
    exit(1);
  }

  /* load the program to execute */
  if(!load_program(p_buf,argv[1])) exit(1);

  if(setjmp(e_buf)) exit(1); /* initialize the long jump buffer */

  prog = p_buf;
  scan_labels(); /* find the labels in the program */
  ftos = 0; /* initialize the FOR stack index */
  gtos = 0; /* initialize the GOSUB stack index */
  do {
    token_type = get_token();
    /* check for assignment statement */
    if(token_type==VARIABLE) {
      putback(); /* return the var to the input stream */
      assignment(); /* must be assignment statement */
    }
```

```
      else /* is command */
        switch(tok) {
          case PRINT:
            print();
            break;
          case GOTO:
            exec_goto();
            break;
          case IF:
            exec_if();
            break;
          case FOR:
            exec_for();
            break;
          case NEXT:
            next();
            break;
          case INPUT:
            input();
            break;
          case GOSUB:
            gosub();
            break;
          case RETURN:
            greturn();
            break;
          case END:
            exit(0);
        }
  } while (tok != FINISHED);
}

/* Load a program. */
load_program(char *p, char *fname)
{
  FILE *fp;
  int i=0;

  if(!(fp=fopen(fname, "rb"))) return 0;

  i = 0;
  do {
    *p = getc(fp);
    p++; i++;
  } while(!feof(fp) && i<PROG_SIZE);
  *(p-2) = '\0'; /* null terminate the program */
  fclose(fp);
  return 1;
}

/* Assign a variable a value. */
void assignment()
{
  int var, value;

  /* get the variable name */
```

```
    get_token();
    if(!isalpha(*token)) {
      serror(4);
      return;
    }

    var = toupper(*token)-'A';

    /* get the equals sign */
    get_token();
    if(*token!='=') {
      serror(3);
      return;
    }

    /* get the value to assign to var */
    get_exp(&value);

    /* assign the value */
    variables[var] = value;
}

/* Execute a simple version of the BASIC PRINT statement */
void print()
{
  int answer;
  int len=0, spaces;
  char last_delim;

  do {
    get_token(); /* get next list item */
    if(tok==EOL || tok==FINISHED) break;
    if(token_type==QUOTE) { /* is string */
      printf(token);
      len += strlen(token);
      get_token();
    }
    else { /* is expression */
      putback();
      get_exp(&answer);
      get_token();
      len += printf("%d", answer);
    }
    last_delim = *token;

    if(*token==';') {
      /* compute number of spaces to move to next tab */
      spaces = 8 - (len % 8);
      len += spaces; /* add in the tabbing position */
      while(spaces) {
        printf(" ");
        spaces--;
      }
    }
    else if(*token==',') /* do nothing */;
    else if(tok!=EOL && tok!=FINISHED) serror(0);
  } while (*token==';' || *token==',');
```

```
    if(tok==EOL || tok==FINISHED) {
      if(last_delim != ';' && last_delim!=',') printf("\n");
    }
    else serror(0); /* error is not , or ; */

}

/* Find all labels. */
void scan_labels()
{
  int addr;
  char *temp;
  label_init();  /* zero all labels */
  temp = prog;   /* save pointer to top of program */

  /* if the first token in the file is a label */
  get_token();
  if(token_type==NUMBER) {
    strcpy(label_table[0].name,token);
    label_table[0].p=prog;
  }

  find_eol();
  do {
    get_token();
    if(token_type==NUMBER) {
      addr = get_next_label(token);
      if(addr==-1 || addr==-2) {
          (addr==-1) ?serror(5):serror(6);
      }
      strcpy(label_table[addr].name, token);
      label_table[addr].p = prog;  /* current point in program */
    }
    /* if not on a blank line, find next line */
    if(tok!=EOL) find_eol();
  } while(tok!=FINISHED);
  prog = temp;  /* restore to original */
}

/* Find the start of the next line. */
void find_eol()
{
  while(*prog!='\n'  && *prog!='\0') ++prog;
  if(*prog) prog++;
}

/* Return index of next free position in label array.
   A -1 is returned if the array is full.
   A -2 is returned when duplicate label is found.
*/
get_next_label(char *s)
{
  register int t;

  for(t=0;t<NUM_LAB;++t) {
    if(label_table[t].name[0]==0) return t;
    if(!strcmp(label_table[t].name,s)) return -2; /* dup */
```

```
  }

  return -1;
}

/* Find location of given label.  A null is returned if
   label is not found; otherwise a pointer to the position
   of the label is returned.
*/
char *find_label(char *s)
{
  register int t;

  for(t=0; t<NUM_LAB; ++t)
    if(!strcmp(label_table[t].name,s)) return label_table[t].p;
  return '\0'; /* error condition */
}

/* Execute a GOTO statement. */
void exec_goto()
{

  char *loc;

  get_token(); /* get label to go to */
  /* find the location of the label */
  loc = find_label(token);
  if(loc=='\0')
    serror(7); /* label not defined */

  else prog=loc;  /* start program running at that loc */
}

/* Initialize the array that holds the labels.
   By convention, a null label name indicates that
   array position is unused.
*/
void label_init()
{
  register int t;

  for(t=0; t<NUM_LAB; ++t) label_table[t].name[0]='\0';
}

/* Execute an IF statement. */
void exec_if()
{
  int x , y, cond;
  char op;

  get_exp(&x); /* get left expression */

  get_token(); /* get the operator */
  if(!strchr("=<>", *token)) {
    serror(0); /* not a legal operator */
    return;
  }
```

```
  op=*token;

  get_exp(&y); /* get right expression */

  /* determine the outcome */
  cond = 0;
  switch(op) {
    case '<':
      if(x<y) cond=1;
      break;
    case '>':
      if(x>y) cond=1;
      break;
    case '=':
      if(x==y) cond=1;
      break;
  }
  if(cond) { /* is true so process target of IF */
    get_token();
    if(tok!=THEN) {
      serror(8);
      return;
    }/* else program execution starts on next line */
  }
  else find_eol(); /* find start of next line */
}

/* Execute a FOR loop. */
void exec_for()
{
  struct for_stack i;
  int value;

  get_token(); /* read the control variable */
  if(!isalpha(*token)) {
    serror(4);
    return;
  }

  i.var=toupper(*token)-'A'; /* save its index */

  get_token(); /* read the equals sign */
  if(*token!='=') {
    serror(3);
    return;
  }

  get_exp(&value); /* get initial value */

  variables[i.var]=value;

  get_token();
  if(tok!=TO) serror(9); /* read and discard the TO */

  get_exp(&i.target); /* get target value */

  /* if loop can execute at least once, push info on stack */
```

```
   if(value>=variables[i.var]) {
     i.loc = prog;
     fpush(i);
   }
   else  /* otherwise, skip loop code altogether */
     while(tok!=NEXT) get_token();
}

/* Execute a NEXT statement. */
void next()
{
   struct for_stack i;

   i = fpop(); /* read the loop info */

   variables[i.var]++; /* increment control variable */
   if(variables[i.var]>i.target) return;  /* all done */
   fpush(i);  /* otherwise, restore the info */
   prog = i.loc;  /* loop */
}

/* Push function for the FOR stack. */
void fpush(struct for_stack i)
{
   if(ftos>FOR_NEST)
     serror(10);

   fstack[ftos]=i;
   ftos++;
}

struct for_stack fpop()
{
   ftos--;
   if(ftos<0) serror(11);
   return(fstack[ftos]);
}

/* Execute a simple form of the BASIC INPUT command */
void input()
{
   char  var;
   int i;

   get_token(); /* see if prompt string is present */
   if(token_type==QUOTE) {
     printf(token); /* if so, print it and check for comma */
     get_token();
     if(*token!=',') serror(1);
     get_token();
   }
   else printf("? "); /* otherwise, prompt with / */
   var = toupper(*token)-'A'; /* get the input var */
```

```
    scanf("%d", &i); /* read input */

    variables[var] = i; /* store it */
}
/* Execute a GOSUB command. */
void gosub()
{
  char *loc;

  get_token();
  /* find the label to call */
  loc = find_label(token);
  if(loc=='\0')
    serror(7); /* label not defined */
  else {
    gpush(prog); /* save place to return to */
    prog = loc;  /* start program running at that loc */
  }
}

/* Return from GOSUB. */
void greturn()
{
    prog = gpop();
}

/* GOSUB stack push function. */
void gpush(char *s)
{
  gtos++;

  if(gtos==SUB_NEST) {
    serror(12);
    return;
  }

  gstack[gtos]=s;

}

/* GOSUB stack pop function. */
char *gpop()
{
  if(gtos==0) {
    serror(13);
    return 0;
  }

  return(gstack[gtos--]);
}
```

Using Small BASIC

Here are some sample programs that Small BASIC will execute. Notice that both upper- and lowercase are supported.

```
PRINT "This program demostrates all commands."
FOR X = 1 TO 100
PRINT X, X/2; X, X*X
NEXT
GOSUB 300
PRINT "hello"
INPUT H
IF H<11 THEN GOTO 200
PRINT 12-4/2
PRINT 100
200 A = 100/2
IF A>10 THEN PRINT "this is ok"
PRINT A
PRINT A+34
INPUT H
PRINT H
INPUT "this is a test ",y
PRINT H+Y
END
300 PRINT "this is a subroutine"
    RETURN
```

```
PRINT "This program demonstrates nested GOSUBs."
INPUT "enter a number: ", I
GOSUB 100

END

100 FOR T = 1 TO I
  X = X + I
  GOSUB 150
NEXT
RETURN

150 PRINT X;
    RETURN
```

```
print "This program computes the volume of a cube."
input "Enter length of first side ", l
input "Enter length of second side ", w
input "Enter length of third side ", d
t = l * w * d
print "Volume is ",t
```

```
PRINT "This program demostrates nested FOR loops."
FOR X = 1 TO 100
  FOR Y = 1 TO 10
    PRINT X; Y; X*Y
  NEXT
NEXT
```

Enhancing and Expanding the Interpreter

The most important thing to understand about expanding or enhancing the interpreter is that you are not limited to the BASIC language. The techniques described in this chapter will work on any procedural language. You can even invent a language that reflects your own programming style and personality.

To add commands, just follow the general format of the ones presented in the chapter. To add different variable types, use an array of structures to hold the variables with one field in the structure indicating the type of the variable and the other field holding the value. To add strings, establish a string table. The easiest approach is to require fixed length strings, each of which is allocated 255 bytes of storage.

One final thought: The types of statements that you can interpret are limited only by your imagination.

Software Development Using C

This final section of the book will examine various issues and aspects of the software development process as they relate to the Turbo C programming environment. At the top of the list is the use of assembly language subroutines and optimizations. This is followed by an overview of the design process in Turbo C, including discussions of code and data hiding, the use of function prototypes, and the use of utility programs such as **MAKE** and **TLIB**. The section ends with a look at porting, efficiency, and debugging.

PART FIVE

Interfacing to Assembly Language Routines

Although the subject of assembly language interfacing is covered in significant detail in the Turbo C user manual, it is such a difficult and confusing subject that it will be examined here from a different perspective.

As efficient and powerful as Turbo C is, you must sometimes write a routine using assembler to

- Increase speed and efficiency of the routine

- Perform some machine-specific function unavailable in Turbo C

- Use third-party routines

Although Turbo C produces extremely fast, compact object code, no compiler consistently creates code as fast or compact as the code written by an excellent programmer using assembler. Most of the time the small difference does not matter or does not warrant the extra time needed to write in assembler. However, there are special cases where a specific function is coded in assembler to decrease its execution time. For example, a floating-point math package might be coded in assembler because it is used frequently and has great effect on the execution speed of a program that uses it. There are also situations in which special hardware devices need exact timing, and you must code in assembler to meet this strict timing requirement. Stated another way, even though Turbo C produces very fast, efficient code, in run-time-sensitive tasks, you will want to *hand optimize* various critical sections. Remember that you the programmer know

817

what the code is actually doing, so you can often perform optimizations that the compiler cannot.

Certain instructions cannot be executed by a Turbo C program. For example, it is not possible to change data segments or perform an efficient rotate on a byte or word.

It is very common in professional programming environments to purchase subroutine libraries for things like graphics, floating-point math, and the like. Sometimes it is necessary to take these in object format because the developer will not sell the source code. Occasionally it is possible simply to link these routines in with code compiled by your compiler; at other times you must write an interface module to correct any differences in the interface used by Turbo C and the routines you purchased.

A word of warning: The interfacing of Turbo C code with assembly code is definitely an advanced topic. This chapter is intended for readers who have some familiarity with assembly language programming. (This chapter does not teach how to program in assembler; it assumes you know how.) If you do not fall into this category, you will still find the material interesting, but please do not try the examples! It is very easy to do something slightly wrong and create a disaster, such as erasing your hard disk.

Each processor has a different assembly language. In this chapter the examples use the 8086/8088/80286 processor, assuming a PC-DOS environment.

To try the examples in this chapter, you must have a copy of Microsoft's MASM macro-assembler program Version 3.0 or greater. This is needed to assemble the assembly language programs.

There are two ways of combining assembly code routines with Turbo C. The first involves the creation, assembly, and linkage of a separate assembly language routine with C functions. The second method uses Turbo C's nonstandard extension called **asm** to embed in-line assembly code instructions directly into C functions. Before we begin, you need to know something about the way Turbo C calls functions.

Calling Conventions

A *calling convention* is the method that the implementors of a C compiler choose to pass information into functions and to return values. The usual solutions use either the internal register of the CPU or the system stack to pass information between functions. Generally, C compilers use the stack to pass arguments to functions and registers to hold function return values. If an argument is one of the basic data types, the actual value is placed on the stack. If the argument is an array, its address is placed on the stack. When a C function begins execution, it retrieves its argument's values from the stack. On termination, it passes back to the calling routine a return value in the register of the CPU. (Although it could, in theory, pass the return value to the stack, this is seldom done.)

In addition to defining the way parameters and return values are handled, the calling convention determines exactly which registers must be preserved and which ones you can use freely. Often a compiler produces object code that needs only a portion of the registers available in the processor. You must preserve the contents of the registers used by your compiler, generally by pushing their contents onto the stack before using them. Any other registers are generally free for your use.

When you write an assembly language module that must interface to code compiled by Turbo C, you must follow all the conventions defined and used by Turbo C. Only by doing this can you hope to have assembly language routines correctly interfaced to your C code.

The Calling Conventions of Turbo C

In this section you will learn how Turbo C passes arguments to and returns values from a function. Only the default C parameter-passing method is examined (the seldom used, optional **pascal** is not), since it is by far the most common. Like most C compilers, Turbo C passes arguments to functions on the stack. The arguments are pushed onto the stack right to left. That is, given the call **func**(*a,b,c*), *c* is pushed first, followed by *b*, and then *a*. The number of bytes occupied on the stack by each type is shown in Table 28-1.

Upon entry into an assembly code procedure, the contents of the **BP** register must be saved on the stack, and the current value of the stack pointer (**SP**) must be placed into

Type	Number of Bytes
char	2
short	2
signed char	2
signed short	2
unsigned char	2
unsigned short	2
int	2
signed int	2
unsigned int	2
long	4
unsigned long	4
float	4
double	8
(near) pointer	2 (offset only)
(far) pointer	4 (segment and offset)

Table 28-1.   Number of Bytes on Stack Required for Each Data Type When Passed to a Function

BP. The only other registers that you must preserve are **SI** and **DI** if your routine uses them.

Before returning, your assembly language function must restore the value of **BP**, **SI**, and **DI** and reset the stack pointer.

If your assembly language function returns a value, it is placed in the **AX** register if it is a 16-bit value. Otherwise it is returned according to Table 28-2.

Type	Register(s) and Meaning
char	AX
unsigned char	AX
short	AX
unsigned short	AX
int	AX
unsigned int	AX
long	Low-order word in AX
	High-order word in DX
unsigned long	Low-order word in AX
	High-order word in DX
float	Low-order word in AX
	High-order word in DX
double	Return on 8087 stack or at TOS in emulator
struct and union	Address to value
(near) pointer	AX
(far) pointer	Offset in AX, segment in DX

Table 28-2.   Register Usage for Return Values

Creating an Assembly Code Function

Without a doubt, the easiest way to learn to create assembly language functions is to see how Turbo C generates code by using the −S compiler option with the command-line version of Turbo C. (It is not possible to produce an assembly language listing from the integrated development environment.) This option outputs an assembly language listing of the code that it generates. By examining this file you can learn a great deal about how to interface to the compiler and how Turbo C actually works.

Let's begin with the following short program:

```
int sum;
main()
{
  sum = add(10, 20);
}

add(int a, int b)
{
  int t;

  t = a+b;
  return t;
}
```

The variable **sum** is intentionally declared as global so that you can see examples of both local and global data. If this program is called **test**, this command line creates **test.asm**:

```
>tcc -S test
```

The contents of **test.asm** are shown here:

```
          name     test
_text     segment  byte public 'code'
dgroup    group    _bss,_data
          assume   cs:_text,ds:dgroup,ss:dgroup
_text     ends
_data     segment  word public 'data'
_da       label    byte
_data     ends
```

```
_bss      segment word public 'bss'
_b@       label   byte
_bss      ends
_text     segment byte public 'code'
_main     proc    near
; Line 4
          mov     ax,20
          push    ax
          mov     ax,10
          push    ax
          call    near ptr _add
          pop     cx
          pop     cx
          mov     word ptr dgroup:_sum,ax
; Line 5
@1:
          ret
_main     endp
_add      proc    near
          push    si
          push    bp
          mov     bp,sp
; Line 9
; Line 10
; Line 11
; Line 12
          mov     si,word ptr [bp+6]
          add     si,word ptr [bp+8]
; Line 13
          mov     ax,si
@2:
; Line 14
          pop     bp
          pop     si
          ret
_add      endp
_text     ends
_bss      segment word public 'bss'
          public  _sum
_sum      label   word
          db      2 dup (?)
_bss      ends
_data     segment word public 'data'
_s@       label   byte
_data     ends
_text     segment byte public 'code'
          public  _add
          public  _main
_text     ends
          end
```

The program begins by establishing the various segments required by a Turbo C program. These vary between the different memory models. (This file was produced by the small model compiler. The other examples in this chapter also use the small model.) Notice that two bytes are allocated in the __bss__ segment for the global variable **sum** near the end of the listing. The underscore in front of **sum** is added by the compiler to avoid confusion with any internal compiler names. It is added to the front of all function and global variable names. After this the code to the program begins. In Turbo C the code segment is called __text__.

The first thing that happens inside the __main__ procedure is that the two arguments to __add__ are pushed on the stack and __add__ is called. On return from the __add__ function, the two **pop cx** instructions restore the stack to its original state. The next line moves the return value from __add__ into **sum**. Finally, __main__ returns.

The function __add__ begins by saving **SI** and **BP** on the stack and then placing the value of **SP** into **BP**. At this point the stack looks like this:

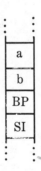

The next three lines of code add the numbers together. Notice that Turbo C is using the register **SI** to hold the value of the local variable **t**. Even though the program did not specify that **t** should be a **register** type, Turbo C automatically made it one as part of Turbo C's compiler optimizations. If the program had had more than two register variables, space for them would have been made on the stack. Finally, the answer is placed into **AX**, **BP** and **SI** are popped, and __add__ returns.

You can literally assemble this assembly language file using the Microsoft macro-assembler MASM, link it using **TLINK**, and run it. If you want to try this, use the following link line (assuming that the file is called **addit**):

```
TLINK C0s addit,,,Cs
```

The file **C0s.obj** contains startup and DOS specific header information. The library **Cs.lib** is Turbo C's standard small model library. (Refer to the Turbo C manual for more information on these files.) What is more interesting is that you can modify it to make it run faster but leave the C source code untouched. For example, you could remove the instructions that pushed and popped **SI** inside the **_add** function (because it is apparent that **SI** is not used elsewhere in the program) and then assemble the file. Doing this is called *hand optimization*.

Now that you have seen how Turbo C compiles functions, it is a short step to writing your own assembly language functions. One of the easiest ways to do this is to let the compiler generate an assembly language skeleton for you. Once you have the skeleton, all you have to do is fill in the details. For example, suppose it is necessary to create an assembly routine that multiplies two integers together. To have the compiler generate a skeleton for this function, first create a file containing only this function:

```
mul(int a, b)
{
}
```

Next, compile the file with the −S option so that an assembly language file is produced. The file looks like this:

```
        name    mul
_text   segment byte public 'code'
dgroup  group   _bss,_data
        assume  cs:_text,ds:dgroup,ss:dgroup
_text   ends
_data   segment word public 'data'
_d@     label   byte
_data   ends
_bss    segment word public 'bss'
_b@     label   byte
_bss    ends
_text   segment byte public 'code'
_mul    proc    near
        push    bp
        mov     bp,sp
```

```
@1:
          pop       bp
          ret
_mul      endp
_text     ends
_data     segment word public 'data'
_s@       label     byte
_data     ends
_text     segment byte public 'code'
          public    _mul
_text     ends
          end
```

In this skeleton, the compiler has done all the work of defining the proper segments and setting up the stack and registers. All you have to do is fill in the details. The finished **mul( )** function is shown here:

```
          name      _mul
_text     segment byte public 'code'
dgroup    group     _bss,_data
          assume    cs:_text,ds:dgroup,ss:dgroup
_text     ends
_data     segment word public 'data'
_d@       label     byte
_data     ends
_bss      segment word public 'bss'
_b@       label     byte
_bss      ends
_text     segment byte public 'code'
; *********************************************
; this is added to let the C program know about _mul
          public _mul
;
_mul      proc      near
          push      bp
          mov       bp,sp
; *********************************************
; here is the code to multiply the numbers
          mov       ax,[bp+4]          ;a
          imul      word ptr [bp+6] ;b
;*********************************************
@1:
          pop       bp
          ret
_mul      endp
_text     ends
_data     segment word public 'data'
_s@       label     byte
_data     ends
_text     segment byte public 'code'
          public    _mul
_text     ends
          end
```

MASM converts all external names into uppercase by default, but Turbo C does not. The best thing to do is to use lowercase for function names and use the −ml **MASM** option, which causes MASM to generate lowercase external names.

Once this file is assembled, it can be linked to any C program that requires it. For example, this program prints the number 10 on the screen (remember to link in **mul()**):

```
main()
{
  printf("%d ", mul(2, 5));
}
```

Notice that a line of code has been added directly before the first code of the procedure **_mul**. It is the line **public _mul**. This statement tells the assembler that the identifier **_mul** should be made available to any routine that needs it. This enables the C program to call **_mul**. You have to do this with any function that you want to be able to call from a C program. If there is data that the C program must know about, it should also be made public. The rule is very simple. Place the names of functions that you want public in the **CODE** segment and the names of variables in the **DATA** segment.

The opposite of this is when you want to call a C function or access a variable defined in a C program from an assembly language function. In this case you must declare external the objects your assembly language routine needs by using the **extrn** assembler command. The general form of the **extrn** statement is

extern <*object*> : <*attribute*>

If *object* is a function, *attribute* can be either **near** or **far**. If you are using a small code model, use **near**; otherwise, use **far**. For variables, *attribute* can be one of the following values:

Value	Size in Bytes
byte	1
word	2
dword	4
qword	8
tbyte	10

For example, if your assembler routine needed to access the global integer variable **count** and the function **search( )**, you would place these statements at the start of the assembly language file:

```
extrn _count : word
extrn _search : near
```

Keep in mind that the name of any assembly language function or external data to be called by a Turbo C program must have an underscore in front of it.

A slightly more challenging situation arises when pointers are passed to a function. In this case, to access and alter the value of the argument requires indirect addressing methods. For example, assume that you need to create an assembly language function that negates the integer pointed to by the argument to the function. Assuming that this function is called **neg( )**, the following fragment prints the number 10 on the screen:

```
x = 10;

neg(&x);

printf("%d", neg);   /* prints -10 */
```

In C, the **neg( )** function looks like this:

```
neg(a)
int *a;
{
   *a = -*a;
}
```

The **neg()** function coded in assembler looks like this, assuming that the small data model is used:

```
              name     neg
_text     segment byte public 'code'
dgroup    group    _bss,_data
              assume   cs:_text,ds:dgroup,ss:dgroup
_text     ends
_data     segment word public 'data'
_d@       label    byte
_data     ends
_bss      segment word public 'bss'
_b@       label    byte
_bss      ends
_text     segment byte public 'code'
              public   _neg
_neg      proc     near
              push     bp
              mov      bp,sp
; ************************************************
; The negate code
              mov      bx, word ptr [bp+4] ; get the address
              mov      ax, word ptr [bx]   ; load the arg
              neg      ax                   ; negate it
              mov      word ptr [bx],ax     ; store it
;
@1:
              pop      bp
              ret
_neg      endp
_text     ends
_data     segment word public 'data'
_s@       label    byte
_data     ends
_text     segment byte public 'code'
              public   _neg
_text     ends
              end
```

The key lines of code are

```
mov      bx, word ptr [bp+4] ; get the address
mov      ax, word ptr[bx]    ; load the arg
neg      ax                   ; negate it
mov      word ptr [bx],ax     ; store it
```

First, the address of the argument is loaded from the stack. Next, the relative addressing mode of the 8086 is used to load the integer to be negated. The **neg** instruction reverses the sign, and the last instruction places the value back at the location pointed to by **BX**.

The best way to learn more about interfacing assembly language code with your C programs is to write short functions in C that do something similar to what you want the assembly language version to do, and create an assembly language file by using the assembly language compiler option. Most of the time all you have to do is hand optimize this code instead of actually creating an assembly language routine from the ground up.

As you have seen, it is really quite easy to use assembly language functions with your Turbo C code if you follow the rules precisely.

Using asm

Although the keyword **asm** is not supported by the proposed ANSI standard, Turbo C has added it to allow in-line assembly code to be made part of a C program without using a completely separate assembly language module. This has two advantages:

1. You are not required to write and maintain all the interface code.

2. All the code is in "one place," making support a little easier.

To put in-line assembly code in a Turbo C function, you simply place the keyword **asm** at the beginning of each line of assembly code and then enter the assembly language statement. All code that follows the **asm** must be correct assembly code for the computer that you are using. Turbo C simply passes this code through, untouched, to the MASM assembler. You should use Turbo C's **−B** option, which informs Turbo C that in-line assembly code occurs in the program. If you don't, Turbo C will have to restart itself by first calling MASM. (You must have the Microsoft macro-assembler Version 4.0 or greater to use this option.)

A very simple example of in-line assembly code is shown here. It is used to output information to a port, presumably for initialization purposes.

```
init_port1()
{
  printf("Initializing Port\n");
asm      out 26,255
asm      out 26,0
}
```

Here, the C compiler automatically provides the code to save registers and to return from the function. Notice that **asm** statements do not require a semicolon to terminate; an assembly language statement is terminated by the end of the line.

You could use in-line assembly code to create **mul()**, from the previous section, without actually creating a separate assembly language file. Using this approach, the code for **mul()** is shown here:

```
mul(int a, b)
{
asm      mov ax,word ptr 4[bp]
asm      word ptr 6[bp]
}
```

Remember that Turbo C provides all customary support for setting up and returning from a function call. All you have to do is provide the body of the function and follow the calling conventions to access the arguments. Although the use of a nonstandard feature certainly reduces portability, the use of assembly code probably reduces it more. So the use of **asm** can be recommended, especially for short assembly code fragments.

If you wish to place comments in **asm** statements you *must use* the standard C /* and */ method. Do not use the semicolon convention used by most assemblers; it confuses Turbo C.

Assembly code statements that are found inside a function are placed in the **CODE** segment. Those found outside any function are placed in the **DATA** segment.

Whatever method you use, remember that you are creating machine dependencies that make your program difficult to port to a new machine. However, for the demanding situations that require assembly code it is usually worth the effort.

When to Code in Assembler

Because of the difficulty of coding in assembler, most programmers do it only when absolutely necessary. The general rule is, don't do it; it creates too many problems! With this warning in mind, there are two times when coding in assembler makes sense: (1) when there is absolutely no other way to do it—for example, when you have to interface directly to a hardware device that cannot be handled using C; and (2) when a C program's execution time must be reduced.

When you need to speed up a program, you should choose carefully which functions you code in assembler. If you code the wrong ones you will see very little increase in speed. If you choose the right one, your program will fly! It is easy to determine which functions to recode by reviewing how your program runs. The functions that are used inside loops are generally the ones to program in assembler because they are executed repeatedly. For example, consider the following **main( )** function:

```
main()
{
  register int t;

  init();

  for(t=0; t<1000; ++t) {
    phase1();
    phase2();
    if(t==10) phase3();
  }

  byebye();
}
```

Clearly, recoding **init( )** and **byebye( )** will not measurably affect the speed of this program because they execute only once. The **phase3( )** function is executed only once, so even though it is inside the loop this function should not be recoded into assembler either. However, both **phase1( )** and **phase2( )** are executed a thousand times; coding them in assembler will have a major effect on the run time of this program.

With careful thought, it is possible to make major speed improvements to your program by recoding only a few functions in assembler. Remember, however, that the greatest speed increases come from better algorithms, not hand-optimized assembly routines. You should consider assembly code only after you have optimized the underlying algorithm.

Software Engineering
Using Turbo C

It is strange to think about how quickly the entire discipline of computer science has come into existence. In the early days, before 1970, little distinction was made between engineers who could design computers and those who could program them. It was assumed that if you understood computers you could engineer both hardware and software. This situation changed radically during the 1970s, and now most colleges offer separate curricula for computer engineers and software engineers.

The art and science of software engineering encompass a wide range of topics. Creating a large computer program is a little like designing a large building. There are so many bits and pieces that it seems impossible for everything to work together. Of course, what makes the creation of a large program possible is the application of the proper engineering methods. This chapter examines several techniques and utilities that relate specifically to the Turbo C programming environment and make the creation and maintenance of a program much easier.

Top-Down Design

Without a doubt, the single most important thing that you can do to simplify the creation of a large program is to apply a solid approach to it. There are three general approaches to writing a program: top-down, bottom-up, and ad hoc. In the *top-down* approach you start with the top-level routine and move down to the low-level routines. The *bottom-up* approach works in the opposite direction: You begin with specific routines and build them progressively into more complex structures, ending at the top-level routine. The *ad hoc* approach has no predetermined method.

As a structured language C lends itself to a top-down approach. The top-down method produces clean, readable code that is easily maintained. A top-down approach also helps you clarify the overall structure and operation of the program before you code low-level functions. This can reduce time wasted by false starts.

Outlining Your Program

Like outlining, the top-down method starts with a general description and works toward specifics. In fact, a good way to design a program is to define exactly what the program is going to do at the top level. For example, assume that you have to write a mailing list program. Your first task should be to make a list of what the program will do. Each entry in the list should contain only one functional unit. A functional unit can be thought of as a black box that performs a single task. For example, your list might look like this:

- Enter a new name.

- Delete a name.

- Print the list.

- Search for a name.

- Save the list to a disk file.

- Load the list.

- Quit the program.

These functional units can form the basis of functions in the program.

After the overall functionality of the program has been defined, you can begin to sketch in the details of each functional unit, beginning with the main loop. The main loop of this program is

```
main loop
{
  do {
    display menu
    get user selection
    process the selection
  } while selection does not equal quit
}
```

The use of this type of algorithmic notation can help you clarify the general structure of your program even before you sit down at the computer. The C syntax has been used because it is familiar, but any type of syntax is acceptable.

You should give a similar definition to each functional area. For example, the function that writes the mailing list to a disk file can be defined like this:

```
save to disk {
  open disk file
  while data left to write {
    write data to disk
  }
  close disk file
}
```

At this point, the save-to-disk function has created new, more specific functional units. Each of these must be defined. If in the course of their definition new functional units are created, they must also be defined, and so on. This process stops when no new functional units are created and all that is left is actually to code the routine. For example, if the open-file functional unit is coded as follows, no new functional units need to be resolved.

```
FILE *fp;

if((fp=fopen("mlist","r+"))==NULL) {
  printf("cannot open MLIST file\n");
  exit(1);
}
```

Notice that the definition does not mention data structure or variables. This is intentional. At this point you are interested only in defining what your program will do, not how it actually will do it. This definition process helps you determine the actual structure of the data, a task that must be done before all functional units can be coded.

Choosing a Data Structure

After you have determined the general outline of your program, the next step is to decide how to structure the data used by your program. The selections of both the data structure and its implementation are critical because they help determine the design limits of your program.

Again, using a top-down approach, a mailing list deals with collections of information: names and addresses. This immediately suggests the use of a **struct** to hold the information. However, the question now becomes how those structures should be stored and manipulated. For a mailing list program, a fixed size array of structures could be used. But a fixed size array has two serious drawbacks:

1. The size of the array limits the length of the mailing list by placing an arbitrary limit on the program.

2. A fixed size array does not take advantage of any additional memory you may add to your computer. On the other hand, if memory is subtracted (for example, a memory card fails), the program may not work because the fixed array does not fit.

Therefore, a mailing list program should use dynamic memory allocation so that the list can be as large as free memory allows.

Although the dynamic storage allocation has been chosen over a fixed size array, the exact form of the data has not yet been decided. There are several possibilities. You could use a singly linked list, a doubly linked list, a binary tree, or even a hashing method. Each method has its merits and drawbacks. If you decide to use a binary tree for its fast search times, you can define a structure to hold each name and address in the list, as shown here:

```
struct addr {
   char name[30];
   char street[40];
   char city[20];
   char state[3];
   char zip[10]; /* hold US and Canadian zips */
   struct addr *left;   /* pointer to left subtree */
   struct addr *right;  /* pointer to right subtree */
};
```

If you follow the top-down approach, your programs will not only be much easier to read, but will also take less time to develop and less effort to maintain.

Bulletproof Functions

In large programs, especially those that control potentially life-threatening events, it is important that the potential for error be very slight. Although small programs can be verified as correct, this is not the case for large ones. (A verified program is proved to be free of errors and will never malfunction, at least in theory.) To understand the problem, consider a program that controls the wing flaps of a 767 jet airplane. It is not possible to test all the ways the numerous forces exerted on the plane will interact. This means that the program cannot be exhaustively tested. At best, all that can be said is that it performed correctly in such-and-such situations. In a program of this type, the last thing that you (as a passenger or programmer) want is a crash (of the program or the plane)! After you have been a programmer for a few years you learn that most program crashes after the initial development stage occur because one function inadvertently "messes" with another function's code or data. Therefore, to reduce the chance of a catastrophic failure, you want your functions and their data to be as "bulletproof" as possible. The most important way to achieve this is to keep the code and data related to each function hidden from the rest of the program. This is sometimes called *hiding code and data*.

The process of hiding code and data is similar to the way a secret is told only to those who "need to know." Simply put, if a function does not need to know about another function or variable, don't let it have access to it. There are three rules you must follow to accomplish this.

1. Each functional unit has one entry point and one exit point.

This means that although a functional unit can contain several functions, the rest of the program communicates through only one of them. To understand this, think about the mailing list program discussed earlier. There are seven functional areas. All the functions needed by each functional area could be placed in their own files and compiled separately. If done correctly, the only way in or out of each functional unit is through its top-level function. In the mailing list program, these top-level functions are called only by **main()**, which prevents any functional unit from accidentally damaging another. This situation is depicted in Figure 29-1.

2. Wherever possible, functions are passed information instead of using global variables.

Although it decreases performance, the best way to reduce the possibility of side effects is always to pass all information needed by a function to that function. Never use global data. If you have ever written a large program in BASIC, where every variable is global, you already understand the importance of this rule.

3. When global variables are required by a few related functions, both the variables and the functions should be

placed in a separate file. Also, the global variables must be declared as **static**.

Keep in mind that strict adherence to these rules is not necessary in every situation, but they are required in situations where the highest degree of fault tolerance is required. The goal of this approach is to create a program that has the highest likelihood of recovering unharmed from an error condition. For example, if the program that controls the flaps on the 767 experiences an out-of-range condition, it is important that it does not crash. It should simply wait a couple of clock ticks and try again.

Even if you follow these rules it is still possible to have a program crash, but it is less likely. And even though you will still not be able to prove that your program is correct, you can more easily verify that it should be correct because of the controls you have in place.

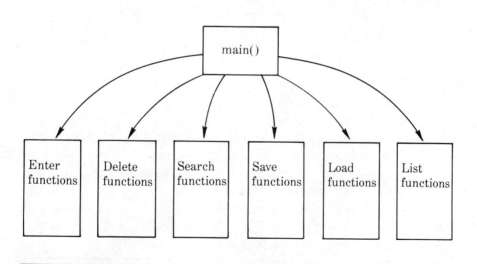

Figure 29-1.   Each functional unit has only one entry point

Function Prototypes

The proposed ANSI standard supports an extension to the way a function can be defined prior to use. As you know, a function returning a value other than **int** must be defined prior to its use. The proposed standard takes this idea one step further by allowing you also to declare the number and types of the function's arguments. This expanded definition is called a *function prototype*, and it allows stronger type-checking than is normally provided by C. When function prototypes are used, Turbo C issues a compile-time error if the number of arguments used to call a function does not match the number of arguments specified in its prototype or if an illegal type conversion is attempted. For example, this program issues an error message because there is an attempt to call **func( )** with one argument instead of the two specified by the prototype:

```
float func(int, int);

main()
{
  int x;

  x=10;
  func(x);   /* number of arguments mismatch */
}

float func(int x, int y)
{
  printf("%f", y*x);
}
```

The use of function prototypes not only helps you trap bugs before they occur, but also helps you verify that your program is working correctly by not allowing functions to be called with mismatched arguments.

Compiling Multiple File Programs

As has been mentioned several times in this book, most real-world C programs are too large to fit easily into one file, mostly because of efficiency considerations. Extremely large files are difficult to edit, and making a small change in a program requires that the entire program be recompiled. Although Turbo C is very fast at compiling, at some point the time it takes to compile a long program will become unbearable.

The solution to these types of problems is to break the program into smaller pieces, compile the pieces, and link them together. This process is known as *separate compilation and linking*, and it forms the backbone of most development efforts.

The manner of creating, compiling, and linking multiple-file programs differs between the integrated environment and the command-line version of Turbo C. This section concentrates on the integrated environment. The next section illustrates the command-line approach.

Projects and the Project Option

In the Turbo C integrated environment, multiple-file programs are called *projects*. Each project is associated with a *project file*, which determines what files are part of the project. The main menu **Project** option lets you specify a project file. All project files must end with a .PRJ extension.

Once you have defined a project file inside the **Project** menu, you place in it the names of the files that form the project. For example, if the project file is called MYPROJ.PRJ, and your project contains the two files TEST1.C and TEST2.C, you would edit MYPROJ.PRJ and enter the two files TEST1.C and TEST2.C. That is, MYPROJ.OBJ will look like this:

```
TEST1.C
TEST2.C
```

For the sake of discussion, assume that neither TEST1.C nor TEST2.C have yet been compiled. There are two ways to compile and link these files:

1. You can select the **Run** main menu option. When there is a .PRJ file specified in the **Project** option, this

file is used to guide Turbo C in compiling your program. The contents of .PRJ are read, and each file that needs to be compiled is compiled to an .OBJ file. Next, those files are linked and the program is executed.

2. You can use the built-in **Make** facility. By pressing F9, or by selecting the **Make** option under the **Compile** main menu option, you cause Turbo C to compile and link all files specified in the project file. The only difference between this and the **Run** option is that the program is not executed. In fact, you can think of the **Run** option as first performing a **Make** and then executing the .EXE file.

Whenever you **Make** a program, only those files that need to be compiled are actually compiled. Turbo C determines this by checking the time and date associated with each source file and its .OBJ file. If the .C file is newer than the .OBJ file, Turbo C knows that the .C has been changed, and it recompiles it. Otherwise, it simply uses the .OBJ file. In this situation, the *target* .OBJ file is said to be dependent on the .C file. The same sort of thing is true of the .EXE file. As long as the .EXE file is newer than all the .OBJ files in the project, nothing is recompiled. Otherwise, the necessary file is compiled and the project relinked.

Trying It Yourself

To see how this process works, first select the **Project** option from the main menu and select **(Project name)**. You will be prompted for the name of the project. Use MYPROJ.PRJ. Next, using the **File** option, load the file TEST1.C. (This should be a new file. If not, use a different name.) Enter and save the following code:

```
/* file TEST1.C */

main()
{
```

```
  printf("This is file 1.\n");

  count(); /* this is in TEST2.C */
}
```

Next, edit TEST2.C. Enter and save this code.

```
/* file TEST2.C */

count()
{
  int i;

  for(i=0; i<10; i++)
    printf("%d ", i);
}
```

Now you can compile and run the program by selecting the **Run** option. Do so at this time. As you can see, Turbo C compiles both files and links them automatically. If you select **Run** again, Turbo C merely checks the dates on the files, sees that nothing needs to be recompiled, and runs the program.

Specifying Additional Dependencies

Just as the standard library functions have header files, so may your program. In fact, customized header files are very common in C programs that use multiple files because they are used to declare **external** variables as well as any #**defines** needed by your program. Since a change to a header file means that any file depending on that header must be recompiled, it is important to specify this relationship.

To specify a dependency like this, you place the name of the file (or files) inside parentheses on the same line as the dependent file. For example, assume that MYPROG.H is a header file necessary to TEST2.C from the previous example. In this case MYPROJ.PRJ looks like this:

```
TEST1
TEST2 (MYPROG.H)
```

To see how this might actually work, make MYPROJ.PRJ

look as shown above and then modify TEST1.C and TEST2.C as shown here (remember to keep them separate):

```
/* file TEST1.C */
int max;

main()
{
  printf("This is file 1.\n");

  max = 100;
  count(); /* this is in TEST2.C */
}



/* file TEST2.C */

#include "myprog.h"  /* read in the header file */

count()
{
  int i;

  for(i=0; i<max; i++)
    printf("%d ", i);
}
```

Finally, create the header file MYPROG.H as shown here:

```
/* header file MYPROG.H */

extern int max;
```

As you can see, the keyword **extern** is used to prevent Turbo C from creating two separate copies of **max**. The header file simply specifies that somewhere a variable named **max** is declared as an integer.

Now, select the **Run** option. Assuming you entered everything correctly, the program runs fine. Now edit the header file, change nothing, but save it back to disk. This causes the date of the header file to be newer than its dependent file TEST2.C. Now when you select **Run**, TEST2.C is automatically recompiled and the program relinked.

Without a doubt, the project capabilities of Turbo C are among its most important aspects because they let you manage multiple-source-file programs with little difficulty.

The Standalone MAKE

Turbo C comes with a standalone version of **MAKE** for use with the command line version of the Turbo C. Frankly, **MAKE** is a very sophisticated program and this section is here just to introduce you to it. If you intend to use the command line compiler, you will want to study Appendix D of *The Turbo C Reference Guide*, which fully describes **MAKE**.

The **MAKE** program automates the recompilation process for large programs composed of several files when you are using the command-line version of the Turbo C. Its operation is similar to the **project/make** facilities of the integrated environment except that it is more flexible. As you probably know, in the course of program development many small changes are made to some of the files and then the program is recompiled and tested. Unfortunately, it is easy to forget which of the files need to be recompiled. This situation leads either to a recompilation of all the files—a waste of time—or to failure to recompile a file that should be recompiled, potentially adding several hours of frustrating debugging. The **MAKE** program solves this problem by automatically recompiling only the files that have been altered.

The **MAKE** program is driven by a *make file*, which contains a list of *target files*, *dependent files*, and commands. A target file requires its dependent file(s) to produce it. For example, T.C would be the dependent file of T.OBJ because T.C is required to make T.OBJ. Like its cousin in the integrated environment, **MAKE** works by comparing the date and time between a dependent file and its target file. If the target file has an older date than its dependent file, or if it does not exist, the specified command sequence is executed.

The general form of the make file is

    target-file1 : dependent-file list
        command-sequence
    target-file2 : dependent-file list
        command-sequence
    target-file3 : dependent-file list
        command-sequence
        .
        .
        .
    target-fileN : dependent-file list
        command-sequence

The target filename must start in the leftmost column and be
followed by a colon and its list of dependent files. The command sequence associated with each target must be preceded by at least one space or a tab. Comments are preceded
by a # and may follow the dependent file list and the command sequence. If they appear on a line of their own, they
must start in the leftmost column. Each target file specification must be separated from the next by at least one blank
line.

The following very simple program shows how **MAKE**
works. The program is divided into four files called **test.h**,
test.c, **test2.c**, and **test3.c**. This situation is illustrated in
Figure 29-2.

A make file that can be used to recompile the program
when changes are made looks like this:

```
tcc test.exe: test.h # recreate if header file changed
        tcc -c test2
        tcc -c test3
        tcc test test2.obj test3.obj

test.obj: test.c # test.c changed
        tcc test test2.obj test3.obj

test2.obj: test2.c # test2.c changed
        tcc -etest test2 test.obj test3.obj

test3.obj: test3.c # test3.c changed
        tcc -etest test3 test.obj test2.obj
```

test.h
```
extern int count;
```

test.c
```
int count=0;

main()
{
  printf("count=%d\n",count);
  test2();
  printf("count=%d\n",count);
  test3();
  printf("count=%d\n",count);
}
```

test2.c
```
#include "test.h"

test2()
{
  count=30;
}
```

test3.c
```
#include "test.h"

test3()
{
  count=-100;
}
```

Figure 29-2.   A simple four-file program

If the name of this file is MAKEFILE, your command line would look like

```
C>MAKE
```

to compile the necessary modules and create an executable program. When no other file name is specified, **MAKE** executes whatever is in the file called MAKEFILE, if it exists.

To specify a different make file, use the **-f** option, which tells **MAKE** to use the file that follows as its make file. For example, this line tells **MAKE** to use the MYMAKE make file:

```
C>MAKE -fMYMAKE
```

Order is very important in the make file because **MAKE** moves through the list in the forward direction only. Suppose the make file were changed to look like this:

```
# this is an incorrect make file

test.obj: test.c # test.c changed
      tcc test test2.obj test3.obj

test2.obj: test2.c # test2.c changed
      tcc -etest test2 test.obj test3.obj

test3.obj: test3.c # test3.c changed
      tcc -etest test3 test.obj test2.obj

tcc test.exe: test.h # recreate if header file changed
      tcc -c test2
      tcc -c test3
      tcc test test2.obj, test3.obj
```

It would no longer work correctly when the file **test.h** and any other source file were changed because the changing of a source file causes a new **test.exe** to be created. Therefore its date would no longer be older than that of **test.h**.

As stated, **MAKE** only recreates the files whose dates are earlier than the files they depend on. In some situations, such as when the system clock is in error, you may wish to force **MAKE** to reconstruct a file that does not appear out of date. To do this use the **TOUCH** program, which updates the specified file's creation date. The **TOUCH** program makes use of this command line:

```
TOUCH filename [filename...filename]
```

TLIB, the Turbo C Librarian

Beginning with Version 1.5, Turbo C has included **TLIB**, the Turbo C librarian. The **TLIB** program allows you to create libraries containing functions that you have created. As you probably know, a library is a collection of functions in object format. Although in many ways a library is like a separately compiled module, it differs from an .OBJ file in one very special way: When a separately compiled file is linked with other files, all the functions contained in that file become part of the executable program whether they are actually used by the program or not, but when a library file is linked with other files, the executable program contains only those library functions that are actually used by the program. For example, the Turbo C standard library contains hundreds of functions, but your programs contain only the functions actually called by your program.

The ability to build your own libraries is very helpful when you are working on a large project that contains several programs. For example, imagine that you are creating a system of programs to run a nuclear power plant. You need a set of routines to monitor the core temperature, to insert and retract the control rods, and to watch for faults in the system. You will probably want to put the routines that perform these functions into a library so that they can be linked into each program that you write as needed. For example, the program that runs pre-startup-system diagnostics on the reactor may not need to monitor the control rods, so that code will not be linked into this program.

It is quite easy to create your own libraries using **TLIB**. In essence, there are three operations: Add a module to a library, remove a module from a library, and extract an .OBJ file from a library. The general form of the **TLIB** command line is

TLIB libraryname [*op*]module—name [*op*]module—
name ...

where *op* is an operator that specifies the **TLIB** action and
module—name is the name of the module that will be acted
on. The library affected is specified by **libraryname**. The
valid values of *op* are shown here:

Operator	Action
+	Adds a module to the specified library
−	Removes a module from the specified library
*	Extracts an .OBJ file from the specified library
−+ or +−	Replaces the specified module with a new copy (this is shorthand for remove and add)
−* or *−	Extracts the specified module and removes it from the library (this is shorthand for extract and remove)

The **TLIB** program assumes the extension .LIB for the **libraryname** and the extension .OBJ for the **module—names**.
In fact, in order to add a module to a library it must be in
.OBJ format. The file may contain as few as one function or
as many as are practical for your specific application.
Although each function in the module is treated separately
when linked into a program, only the entire module can be
manipulated by **TLIB**. For example, it is not possible to
extract one function from a module using **TLIB**.

To create a library, you simply specify the name of a
nonexistent library and add modules to it. For example, this
line creates the library NEWLIB.LIB and adds the module
MYMOD to it:

```
TLIB NEWLIB +MYMOD
```

This next example adds the modules **RODS**, **LEAKS**, and **PANIC** to NEWLIB:

```
TLIB NEWLIB +RODS +LEAKS +PANIC
```

This line removes **MYMOD** from the library:

```
TLIB NEWLIB -MYMOD
```

A Short Example Using **TLIB**

The best way to understand how **TLIB** works is to try a short example. To begin, enter these functions into a file called TEST.C:

```
/* A very trivial library of functions. */
func1()
{
  printf("this is function 1\n");

}

func2()
{
  printf("this is function 2\n");
}

func3()
{
  printf("this is function 3\n");
}

func4()
{
  printf("this is function 4\n");
}
```

After you have entered the functions, compile TEST.C to a .OBJ file. If you are using the integrated environment, select the **Compile to .OBJ** option. If you are using the command-line version of Turbo C, use the following command line.

```
TCC -c TEST
```

Now enter this **TLIB** command:

```
TLIB MYLIB +TEST
```

This creates the file MYLIB.LIB.

To try the library, enter this program into a file called T.C:

```
main()
{
    func1();
    func2();
    func3();
}
```

Compile it using this command line:

```
TCC T MYLIB.LIB
```

To use MYLIB.LIB from the integrated environment, you must create a project file that includes a list of all the object modules and libraries needed by your program. For the example at hand, the project file must contain this line:

```
T MYLIB.LIB
```

If you want to see what functions are in a library, use this basic **TLIB** command:

```
TLIB library_name, outputfile.1st
```

Notice that the comma is essential in this command. The names of the functions in the library are placed in the file specified by **outputfile.lst**. For example, the command

```
TLIB MYLIB, OUT.LST
```

produces a file named OUT.LST that contains this information:

```
Publics by module

TEST               size = 116
        _func1                              _func2
        _func3                              _func4
```

One last point about libraries: Although they can provide a great deal of control and structure in a complicated programming situation, it is important not to give in to the "garbage can" syndrome. It is very easy to continue adding new functions to a library while old ones go unused or to add a repaired function by calling it a slightly different name than its misbehaving cousin. The point is that in order to receive all the benefits of custom libraries, you must put some effort into managing them. If you don't, your libraries will soon degenerate into uncontrollable collections of forgotten code.

The GREP Utility

Turbo C Version 1.5 and greater include a utility program called **GREP**, which is essentially a more powerful version of the DOS FIND command. The **GREP** program finds which files contain strings that match a specified string. A brief overview of **GREP** is given here. You will find a complete description in Appendix C of the *Turbo C Additions and Enhancements* supplemental manual.

The basic form of the **GREP** command is

GREP search_string file_list

In its default mode of operation, **GREP** searches for occurrences of **search_string** in the files whose names appear in the file list. If a match is found, the name of the file and the line containing the match are printed. For example, this code searches the files F1.C, F2.C, and F3.C for the string "**printf**":

```
GREP printf F1.C F2.C F3.C
```

Notice that unlike **FIND**, **GREP** does not require that the search string be contained between double quotes. Also unlike **FIND**, **GREP** accepts wild card characters in a file name. For example, this line searches all files ending in .C for the string "**close_files()**".

```
GREP close_files() *.c
```

The **GREP** utility allows many options and variations and is an important programming tool for the serious programmer. For complete details, refer to your Turbo C user's manuals.

Efficiency,
Porting, and Debugging

The mark of a professional programmer is the ability to write programs that make efficient use of system resources and are bug free and transportable to a new computer. Computer science becomes the "art of computer science" in these areas because so few formal techniques are available to ensure success. This chapter presents some of the methods by which you can achieve efficiency, debugging, and portability.

Efficiency

When used in connection with a computer program, efficiency can refer to the speed of execution, the use of system resources, or both. System resources include such things as RAM, disk space, and printer paper—anything that can be allocated and used up. Whether a program is efficient is sometimes a subjective judgment that changes from situation to situation. For example, consider a sorting program that uses 128KB of RAM, requires 2MB of disk space, and averages 7 hours run time. If this program is sorting only 100 addresses in a mailing list database, the program is not very efficient. However, if the program is sorting the New York telephone directory, it is probably quite efficient.

Another point to consider when trying to make your programs efficient is that optimizing one aspect of a program often degrades another. For example, making a program execute faster often means making it bigger when in-line code is used to eliminate the overhead of a function call.

857

Making a program smaller by replacing in-line code with function calls makes the program run slower. Making more efficient use of disk space means compacting the data, which often makes disk access slower. This problem even affects Turbo C's code generator, which is why Turbo C lets you decide whether to optimize for speed or for memory. These and other types of efficiency trade-offs can be very frustrating, especially to the nonprogrammer end user who cannot see why one thing should affect the other.

In light of these problems, you might be wondering how one can discuss efficiency at all. The answer lies in the fact that some programming practices are always efficient or at least more efficient than others. Also, a few techniques make programs both faster and smaller. We will look at these techniques.

The Increment and Decrement Operators

Discussions of the efficient use of C almost always start with a consideration of the increment and decrement operators. In case you have forgotten, the increment operator, ++, increases its argument by one, and the decrement operator, −−, decreases its argument by one. In essence, the increment operator replaces the following type of assignment statement:

```
x = x + 1;
```

The decrement operator replaces assignment statements of this type:

```
x = x - 1;
```

Aside from the obvious advantage to the programmer of reducing the number of keystrokes needed, the increment and decrement operators have the glorious advantage of both executing faster and needing less RAM than their statement counterparts! The reason for this is based on the way object code is generated by the compiler. Often, as is the case for most common microcomputers, it is possible to increment or decrement a word of memory using explicit load and store instructions. For Turbo C to take advantage of this requires that you use the ++ or −− operators. If you don't, unneeded load and store instructions are used. For example, this program

```
main()
{
  int t=0;

  t++;

  t = t+1;
}
```

produces the following assembly language code when compiled with the −S (generate assembly listing) option. (The comments that begin with asterisks are added by the author.)

```
          name    test
_text     segment byte public 'code'
dgroup    group   _bss,_data
          assume  cs:_text,ds:dgroup,ss:dgroup
_text     ends
_data     segment word public 'data'
_d@       label   byte
_data     ends
_bss      segment word public 'bss'
_b@       label   byte
_bss      ends
_text     segment byte public 'code'
_main     proc    near
          push    si
; Line 3
; Line 4
; Line 5
          xor     si,si
; Line 6
; Line 7
; ***** This is the t++ statement
          inc     si
; Line 8
;***** This is the t=t+1 statement.  Notice that
;***** three instructions are used: one to load t into a
;***** register, one to increment it, and one to store it.
          mov     ax,si
          inc     ax
          mov     si,ax
```

```
; Line 9
@1:
            pop      si
            ret
_main       endp
_text       ends
_data       segment word public 'data'
_s@         label    byte
_data       ends
_text       segment byte public 'code'
            public   _main
_text       ends
            end
```

As you can see, both the load and store instructions that are present in the **t = t+1** assignment statement are absent from the increment statement. This means that the code will execute faster and be smaller.

Using Register Variables

There are two reasons why you should use **register** variables for loop control whenever possible:

1. Because the variable is held in an internal register of the CPU, its access time is very short—much shorter than if it were held in memory.

2. The speed with which the critical loops of a program execute sets the overall speed of the program.

To show how the code differs for **register** and regular memory variables, this program was compiled to an assembly language:

```
int j;

main()
{
  register int i;

  for(i=0; i<100 ;i++) ;

  for(j=0; j<100; j++) ;

}
```

The assembly code file produced is shown here (comments beginning with asterisks were added by the author):

```
          name    test
_text     segment byte public 'code'
dgroup    group   _bss,_data
          assume  cs:_text,ds:dgroup,ss:dgroup
_text     ends
_data     segment word public 'data'
_da       label   byte
_data     ends
_bss      segment word public 'bss'
_ba       label   byte
_bss      ends
_text     segment byte public 'code'
_main     proc    near
          push    si
; Line 4
; Line 5
; Line 6
;******* This is the initialization of the register
;******* controlled loop.  Notice that SI is cleared
;******* using a subtract instruction.
          xor     si,si
          jmp     short '5
@4:
@3:
;******* a register increment
          inc     si
@5:

;******* Only a register comparison is necessary
;******* to access SI's value.
          cmp     si,100
          jl      '4
@2:
; Line 7
;******* Here is the initialization of the memory
;******* controlled loop.  Notice that a memory access
;******* is required to clear the variable.
          mov     word ptr dgroup:_j,0
          jmp     short '9
@8:
@7:
;******* Here, a memory access increment is needed.
          inc     word ptr dgroup:_j
@9:
;******* Another memory access required to check the
;******* control variable's value.
          cmp     word ptr dgroup:_j,100
          jl      '8
@6:
; Line 8
@1:
          pop     si
          ret
```

```
_main    endp
_text    ends
_bss     segment word public 'bss'
         public  _j
_j       label   word
         db      2 dup (?)
_bss     ends
_data    segment word public 'data'
_s@      label   byte
_data    ends
_text    segment byte public 'code'
         public  _main
_text    ends
         end
```

To get an idea of the time differences, assume an 8088 processor executes this program. The register-controlled loop uses the instruction **inc si** to increment the control variable. This requires only two system clock ticks. On the other hand, the memory-controlled loop must use **inc word ptr dgroup:** —**j**, which requires 29 clock ticks—almost a 15-to-1 increase!

Turbo C automatically makes the first two integer variables in a function into **register** types if no other **register** variables are present. This process is called a compiler optimization and is used to increase the overall speed of execution. Remember: Global variables cannot be placed in registers.

Because you can have only two register variables, it is important to choose the correct loops for their use. For example, given the following fragment, you would use **register** variables for the two inner loops, but not for the outer loop:

```
for(i=0; i<100; i++) {
  .
  .
  .
  for(j=0; j<1000; j++) {
    .
    .
    .
  }
  for(k=0; k<10; k++) ...;
}
```

The reason for choosing the inner loops is that they are both executed 100 times. This means that **j** is accessed 100,000 times and **k**, 1000 times, while **i** is accessed only 100 times.

Pointers Versus Array Indexing

Another optimization that produces both smaller and faster code is substituting pointer arithmetic for array indexing. The use of pointers always makes your code run faster and take up less space. Take a look at the following two code fragments that do the same thing:

```
array indexing            pointer arithmetic

                          p=array;
for(;;) {                 for(;;) {
    a=array[t++];             a=*(p++);
         .                         .
         .                         .
         .                         .
}                         }
```

The advantage of the pointer method is that once **p** has been loaded with the address of **array**, only an increment must be performed each time the loop repeats. However, the array index version must always compute the array index based on the value of **t** —a more complex task. The disparity in execution speeds between array indexing and pointer arithmetic gets wider as multiple indexes are used. Each index requires its own sequence of instructions, whereas the pointer arithmetic equivalent can use simple addition.

Be careful, though, to use array indexes when the index is derived through a very complex formula and the use of pointer arithmetic would obscure the meaning of the program. It is usually better to degrade performance slightly rather than sacrifice clarity.

Use of Functions

Always remember that using standalone functions with local variables is the basis of structured programming. Functions are the building blocks of C programs and are one of C's strongest assets. Do not let anything that is discussed in this section be construed otherwise. That being said, there are a few things you should know about C functions and the effects they have on the size and speed of your code.

First and foremost, Turbo C is a stack-oriented language. This means that all local variables and parameters to functions use the stack for temporary storage. When a function is called, the return address of the calling routine is also placed on the stack. This enables the subroutine to return to the location from which it was called. When a function returns, this address and all local variables and parameters have to be removed from the stack. The process of pushing this information is generally called the *calling sequence*, and the popping process is called the *returning sequence*. These sequences take time—sometimes quite a bit of time.

To understand how a function call can slow down your program, look at the two code fragments shown here:

```
version 1                          version 2

for(x=1;x<100;++x) {               for(x=1;x<100;++x) {
  t=compute(x);                       t=abs(sin(q)/100/3.1416);
}                                  }

float compute(q)
int q;
{
  return abs(sin(q)/100/3.1416);
}
```

Although each loop performs the same function, Version 2 will be much faster because the overhead of the calling and returning sequence has been eliminated through the use of in-line code.

Let's look at another example. When this program is compiled using the −S option, it produces the following assembly code listing:

```
main()
{
   int x;

   x=max(10,20);
}

max(a,b)
int a,b;
{
   return a>b ? a : b;
}
```

The assembly code produced by this program is shown next. The calling and returning sequences are indicated by comments beginning with asterisks added by the author. As you can see, they amount to a sizable amount of the code in the program.

```
           name      test
_text      segment   byte public 'code'
dgroup     group     _bss,_data
           assume    cs:_text,ds:dgroup,ss:dgroup
_text      ends
_data      segment   word public 'data'
_d@        label     byte
_data      ends
_bss       segment   word public 'bss'
_b@        label     byte
_bss       ends
_text      segment   byte public 'code'
_main      proc      near
           push      bp
           mov       bp,sp
           dec       sp
           dec       sp
; Line 3
; Line 4
; Line 5
; *******************************************************
; ***** the calling sequence:
           mov       ax,20
           push      ax
           mov       ax,10
           push      ax
; *******************************************************
           call      near ptr _max
; *******************************************************
; ***** end of the returning sequence
           pop       cx
           pop       cx
; *******************************************************
           mov       word ptr [bp-2],ax
```

```
; Line 6
@1:
        mov     sp,bp
        pop     bp
        ret
_main   endp
_max    proc    near
; ************************************************************
; ***** more of the calling sequence
        push    bp
        mov     bp,sp
; ************************************************************
; Line 10
; Line 11
        mov     ax,word ptr [bp+6]
        cmp     word ptr [bp+4],ax
        jle     @4
        mov     ax,word ptr [bp+4]
        jmp     short @3
@4:
        mov     ax,word ptr [bp+6]
@3:
@2:
; Line 12
; ************************************************************
; ***** the returning sequence
        pop     bp
        ret
; ************************************************************
_max    endp
_text   ends
_data   segment word public 'data'
_s@     label   byte
_data   ends
_text   segment byte public 'code'
        public  _max
        public  _main
_text   ends
        end
```

You may be thinking now that you should write programs that have just a few very large functions so that they will run quickly. In the vast majority of cases, however, the slight time differential is not meaningful and the loss of structure is acute! But there is another problem. Replacing functions that are used by several routines with in-line code makes your program very large because the same code is duplicated several times. Keep in mind that subroutines were invented largely as a way to make efficient use of memory. In fact, this is the reason that the rule of thumb is: Making a program faster makes it bigger, and making it smaller makes it slower.

In the final analysis, it makes sense to use in-line code instead of a function call only when speed is the overriding priority. Otherwise, the liberal use of functions is definitely recommended.

Porting Programs

It is very common for a program written on one machine to be transported to another computer with a different processor, operating system, or both. This process is called *porting* and can be very easy or extremely hard, depending on how the program was originally written. A program that can be easily ported is called *portable*. When a program is not easily portable, it is usually because it contains numerous *machine dependencies*, which means that it has code fragments that work only with one specific operating system or processor. Turbo C has been designed to allow the creation of portable code, but it requires care and attention to detail actually to achieve that goal. In this section we examine a few specific problem areas and offer some solutions.

Using #define

Perhaps the simplest way to make programs portable is to make *every* system or processor-dependent "magic number" a #**define** macro-substitution directive. These "magic numbers" include things like buffer sizes for disk accesses, special screen and keyboard commands, and memory allocation information—that is, anything that has even the slightest possibility of changing when the program is ported. These #**define**s not only make all "magic numbers" obvious to the person doing the porting, but also simplify the editing job because their values have to be changed only once instead of throughout the program.

For example, here are two functions that use **fread()** and **fwrite()** to read and write information from a disk file:

```
f1()
{
   fwrite(buf, 128, 1, fp);
}

f2()
{
   fread(buf, 128, 1, fp);
}
```

The problem here is that the buffer size, 128, is hard coded into both the **fread()** and the **fwrite()** statements. This might be fine for one operating system but be less than optimal for another. A better way to code this function is shown here:

```
#define buf_size 128

f1()
{
   fwrite(buf, buf_size, 1, fp);
}

f2()
{
   read(buf, buf_size, 1, fp);
}
```

In this case, only the #**define** would have to change and all references to **buf_size** would automatically be corrected. This not only makes it easier to change but also avoids many editing errors. Remember that there are generally many references to **buf_size** in a real program, so the gain in portability is often quite great.

Operating System Dependencies

Virtually all commercial programs have code that is specific to the operating system. For example, a spreadsheet program might make use of the IBM PC's video memory to allow fast switching between screens, or a graphics package might use special commands that are applicable only to that operating system. The point is that some operating system dependencies are necessary for truly good, fast, commercially viable programs. However, there is no reason to hard code any more dependencies than necessary.

As hinted in the preceding section, disk-file functions can sometimes contain implicit machine dependencies. For example, the **fread()** and **fwrite()** functions found in the standard library work with various buffer sizes, but usually an operating system requires even multiples of some number (at least for efficient operation). Therefore, a buffer size of 128 might be fine for CP/M 2.2 but not great for MS-DOS. In this case, the buffer size should be defined as discussed earlier.

When you must use system calls to access the operating system, it is best to do them all through one master function so that it needs to be changed only to accommodate a new operating system, leaving the rest of the code intact. For example, if system calls are needed to clear the screen, clear end-of-line, and locate the cursor at an x,y coordinate, you should create a master function, such as **op—sys—call()**, as shown here:

```
void op_sys_call(char op, int x, int y)
{
  switch(op) {
    case 1: clear_screen();
    break;
    case 2: clear_eol();
    break;
    case 3: goto_xy(x,y);
    break;
  }
}
```

In this way, only the code that forms the actual functions would have to change, leaving a common interface intact.

Differences in Data Sizes

As you may know, in a 16-bit processor the size of a word is 16 bits; in a 32-bit processor it is 32 bits. Because the size of a word tends to be the size of an integer, if you wish to write portable code you must never make assumptions about the size of a data type. Therefore, you should use **sizeof** whenever your program needs to know how many bytes long something is. For example, this function writes an integer to a disk file and works on any computer:

```
void write_int(int i)
{
   fwrite(&i, sizeof(int), 1, stream);
}
```

Sometimes, however, it is not possible to create portable code even with **sizeof**. For example, the following function, which swaps the bytes in an integer, works on an 8088-based computer but not on a 68000. The reason this function cannot be made portable is that it is based on the fact that in the 8088, integers are 2 bytes long. In the 68000, integers are 4 bytes long.

```
void swap_bytes(int *x)
{
   union sb {
     int t;
     unsigned char c[2];
   } swap;

   unsigned char temp;

   swap.t = *x;
   temp = swap.c[1];
   swap.c[1] = swap.c[0];
   swap.c[0] = temp;
   *x = swap.t;
}
```

Debugging

To paraphrase Thomas Edison, programming is 10% inspiration and 90% debugging! All really good programmers are good debuggers. Certain types of bugs occur easily when you use C, and these bugs are the topic of this section.

Order-of-Process Errors

The increment and decrement operators are used in most C programs, and the order in which the operation takes place is affected by whether these operators precede or follow the variable. Consider the following:

```
y = 10;              y = 10;

x = y++;             x = ++y;
```

The two statements are not the same. The first one assigns the value of 10 to **x** and then increments **y**. The second increments **y** to 11 and then assigns the value 11 to **x**. In the first case **x** contains 10; in the second case **x** contains 11. The rule is that increment and decrement operations occur before other operations if they precede the operand; otherwise they happen afterward.

An order-of-process error usually occurs through changes to an existing statement. For example, you may enter the statement

```
x = *p++;
```

which assigns the value pointed to by **p** to **x** and then increments the pointer **p**. However, let's say that later you decide that **x** really needs the value pointed to by **p** times the value pointed to by **p**. To do this you try

```
x = *p++ * (*p);
```

but this can't work because **p** has already been incremented. The proper solution is to write

```
x = *p * (*p++);
```

Errors like this can be very hard to find. There may be clues such as loops that don't run right or routines that are off by one. If you have any doubt about a statement, recode it in a way that you are sure about.

Pointer Problems

A very common error in C programs is the misuse of pointers. Pointer problems fall into two general categories:

1. Misunderstanding of indirection and the pointer operators

2. Accidental use of invalid pointers

The solution to the first problem is to understand the C language; the solution to the second is always to verify the validity of a pointer before it is used.

The following is a typical error C programmers make:

```
#include "stdlib.h"

main()  /* this program is WRONG */
{
  char *p;

  *p = (char *) malloc(100); /* this line is wrong */

  gets(p);
  printf(p);

}
```

This program will most likely crash, probably taking the operating system with it. The reason is that the address returned by **malloc()** was not assigned **p** but the memory location pointed to by **p**, which in this case is completely unknown. This is most certainly not what is wanted. To make this program correct you must substitute

```
p = (char *) malloc(100); /* this is correct */
```

for the wrong line.

The program also has a second, more insidious error. There is no run-time check on the address returned by **malloc()**. Remember, if memory is exhausted, **malloc()** will return **NULL**, which is never a valid pointer in C. The malfunction caused by this type of bug is difficult to find because it occurs only rarely, when an allocation request fails. The best way to handle this is to prevent it. A corrected version of the program, including a check for pointer validity, is shown here:

```
#include "stdlib.h"
#include "stdio.h"

main()  /* this program is now correct */
{
  char *p;

  p = (char *) malloc(100); /* this is correct */

  if(p==NULL) {
    printf("out of memory\n");
    exit(1);
  }

  gets(p);
  printf(p);
}
```

The terrible thing about "wild" pointers is that they are so hard to track down. If you are making assignments to a pointer variable that does not contain a valid pointer address, your program may appear to function correctly some of the time and crash at other times. The smaller your program the more likely it is to run correctly, even with a stray pointer, because very little memory is in use and the odds of that memory being used by something else are statistically small.

As your program grows, failures become more common, but you are thinking about current additions or changes to your program, not about pointer errors. Hence, you tend to look in the wrong spot for the bug.

The way to recognize a pointer problem is that errors tend to be erratic. Your program works right one time, wrong another. Sometimes other variables contain garbage for no explainable reason. If these problems begin to occur, check your pointers. As a matter of procedure you should always check all pointers when bugs begin to occur.

As consolation, remember that although pointers can be troublesome, they are also one of the most powerful and useful aspects of the C language and worth whatever trouble they may, from time to time, cause you. Make the effort early on to learn to use them correctly.

One final point to remember about pointers is that you must initialize them before they are used. Consider the following code fragment:

```
int *x;
*x = 100;
```

This is a disaster because you don't know where **x** is pointing, and assigning a value to that unknown location will probably destroy something of value—like other code or data for your program.

Redefining Functions

You can, but you should not, call your functions by the same names as those in the C standard library. Turbo C will use your function over the one in the library. One of the worst occurrences of the redefinition problem is when a standard library function is redefined and the standard function is not used directly in the program but indirectly by another standard function. Consider the following:

```
char text[1000];

main()
{
  int x;

  scanf("%d",&x);
        .
        .
        .
}

getc(p)   /* return char from array */
{
  return text[p];
}
        .
        .
        .
```

This program does not work with most compilers because **scanf( )**, a standard C function, will most likely call **getc( )**, a standard C function that has been redefined in the program. This can be a very frustrating problem to find because there is no clue that you have created a side effect. It simply seems that **scanf( )** is not working correctly.

The only way to avoid these problems is never to give a function you write the same name as one in the standard library. If you are unsure, append your initials to the start of the name, such as **hs̲getc( )** instead of **getc( )**.

On-Off Errors

As you should know by now, in C all array indexes start at 0. A common error involves the use of a **for** loop to access the elements of an array. Consider the following program, which is supposed to initialize an array of 100 integers:

```
main()  /* this program will not work */
{

  int x, num[100];

  for(x=1; x<=100; ++x) num[x]=x;
}
```

The **for** loop in this program is wrong in two ways:

1. It does not initialize **num[0]**, the first element of array **num**.

2. It goes one past the end of the array because **num[99]** is the last element in the array and the loop runs to 100.

The correct way to write this program is

```
main()   /* this is right */
{
  int x, num[100];

  for(x=0; x<100; ++x) num[x]=x;
}
```

Remember that an array of 100 has elements 0 through 99.

Boundary Errors

The Turbo C run-time environment and many standard library functions have little or no run-time bounds checking. For example, it is possible to index an array beyond its dimensions. Consider the following program, which is supposed to read a string from the keyboard and display it on the screen:

```
main()
{
  int var1;
  char s[10];
  int var2;

  var1 = 10;  var2 = 10;
  get_string(s);
  printf("%s %d %s", s, var1, var2);
}

get_string(char *string)
{
  register int t;
```

```
printf("enter twenty characters\n");
for(t=0; t<20; ++t) {
  *s++ = getchar();
}
}
```

Here there are no direct coding errors. Indirectly, however, calling **get_string( )** with s causes a bug. s is declared to be 10 characters long, but **get_string( )** reads 20 characters. This causes s to be overwritten. The real problem is that s may display all 20 characters perfectly well, but either **var1** or **var2** will not contain the correct value. Here's why. Turbo C allocates memory for local variables from the stack. The variables **var1**, **var2**, and s are located in memory, as shown in Figure 30-1.

When s is overwritten, the additional information is placed in the area that is supposed to be **var2**, destroying any previous contents. Therefore, instead of printing the number 10 for both integer variables, the one destroyed by the overrun of s displays something else. This makes you look for the problem in the wrong place. In this specific instance, the return address of the function call may also be overwritten, which causes a crash.

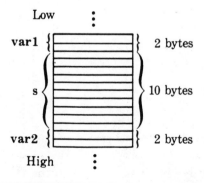

Figure 30-1.   The variables **var1**, **var2**, and s in memory

Function Declaration Omissions

Any time a function returns a value type other than **int**, the function must be declared as such inside each function that uses it. Consider the following program, which multiplies two floating-point numbers together:

```
main() /* this is wrong */
{
  float x, y;

  scanf("%f%f", &x, &y);
  printf("%f", mul(x, y));

}

float mul(float a, b)
{
  return a*b;
}
```

Here **main()** expects an integer value back from **mul()**, but **mul()** returns a floating-point number. Although the compiler will catch this error if these functions are both in the same file, it cannot if they are in separately compiled modules.

The way to correct this program is to declare **mul()** in **main()**. The corrected version follows.

```
main() /* this is correct */
{
  float x, y, mul();

  scanf("%f%f", &x, &y);
  printf("%f", mul(x, y));
}
float mul(a, b)
float a, b;
{
  return a*b;
}
```

Here **mul()** has been added to the **float** declaration list, which tells **main()** to expect a floating-point value to be returned from **mul()**.

An even better way to correct the program is to use the full prototype for **mul( )** at the start of the program. In this way Turbo C catches all types of mismatch errors.

Calling Argument Errors

You must be sure to match whatever type of argument a function expects with the type you give it. An important example is **scanf( )**. Remember that **scanf( )** expects to receive the addresses of its arguments, not their values. For example,

```
int x;
char string[10];

scanf("%d%s", x, string);
```

is wrong, while

```
scanf("%d%s",&x,string);
```

is correct. Remember that strings already pass their addresses to functions, so you should not use the **&** operator on them.

Stack-Heap Collisions

When the stack runs into the heap a *stack-heap collision* occurs. When this happens, the program either completely dies or continues executing at a bizarre point. This second symptom is due to data being used accidentally as a return address. The worst thing about stack-heap collisions is that they generally occur without any warning and kill the program so completely that debug code cannot execute. Another problem is that a stack-heap collision often appears like a wild pointer and thus misleads you. The only piece of advice that can be offered is that most stack-heap collisions are caused by runaway recursive functions. If your program uses recursion and you experience unexplainable failures, check the terminating conditions in your recursive functions.

Using Prototypes to Prevent Bugs

Although not required by C, function prototypes can shorten debugging time in certain situations by allowing the computer to catch a greater number of errors. Many long-time C programmers scoff at function prototypes because they were not part of the original K&R C. Like a fine wine, however, C has gotten better with age. If you are writing a program that has more than a few hundred lines, you really should be using function prototypes.

Debugging Theory in General

Everyone has a different approach to programming and debugging. Over time, however, certain techniques have proven to be better than others. In the case of debugging, incremental testing is considered to be the most cost- and time-effective method, even though it can appear to slow the development process at first. To understand what incremental testing is, you must first see what it is not.

In the early days of computers, programmers were taught to prepare their programs in advance, submit them for execution, and then interpret results. This is called batch programming. It was necessary when computers were scarce, but it is seldom used today because there are many computers that support an interactive programming environment. Batch programming is one of those things that helped give computers a bad image in the early 1960s because it required programmers to expend an enormous amount of time and mental energy developing a program. It is, indeed, a painful experience. Because all testing had to be done in batch mode as well, it was very difficult to try all possible conditions a program could fail in. This lack of thorough testing led to the pervasive "computer error" problems so common in many early computer installations.

Batch programming is virtually extinct today because it cannot support an interactive *incremental testing* environment. Incremental testing is the process of always having a working program. That is, very early in the development process, an operational unit is established. (An operational unit is simply a piece of working code.) As new code is added to this unit, it is tested and debugged. In this way the programmer can find errors easily because the errors most likely occur in the newly added code or in the way that it interacts with the operational unit.

Debugging time can be computed according to the formula **DebugTime** = **(NumOfLines+X)**^{2}, where **NumOfLines** is the total number of lines of code that a bug could be in and **X** is some constant (programmer dependent). As you can see, debugging time is a squared quantity. With incremental testing it is possible to restrict the number of lines of code to those that are newly added, that is, not part of the operational unit. This situation is shown in Figure 30-2.

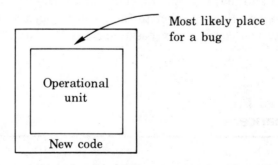

Figure 30-2.   The most likely location of a bug when incremental testing is used

Incremental testing theory is generally based on probability and areas. As you know, area is a squared dimension. As your program grows, there is an n squared area you must search for bugs. As a programmer, you want the smallest possible area to deal with while debugging. Through incremental testing, you are able to subtract the area already tested from the total area, thereby reducing the region where a bug may be found.

In large projects, there are often several modules that have only mild interaction. In these cases, it is possible to establish several operational units to allow concurrent development.

There are two reasons that incremental testing is so important:

1. It greatly reduces debugging time because errors are easier to find.

2. It speeds up the development process because design errors can be caught early in the project — before all the code is written. (This should never, of course, take the place of a good design!)

Incremental testing is simply the process of always having working code. As soon as it is possible to run a piece of your program, you should do so, testing that section completely. As you add to the program, continue to test the new sections and the way they connect to the known operational code. In this way you confine any possible bugs to a small area of code.

The Art of Program Maintenance

Once a program has been written, tested, debugged, and finally judged ready for use, the program's development phase is over and its maintenance phase begins. Most programmers like the glamour and excitement of developing a new program but try to avoid being the one to maintain it, partly because the maintenance phase never ends. When a program (even a very large one) is being developed, there is always light at the end of the tunnel. Someday the program will be done. However, the maintenance phase is a never-ending daily grind of quirks, anomalies, errors, and bugs. The maintenance programmer may never feel the thrill of accomplishment, and the only good part of the day may be quitting time. As bleak as it seems, however, program maintenance can be a challenging and rewarding task if it is approached correctly.

The maintenance programmer is in charge of two things: (1) correcting bugs and (2) protecting source code. Let's examine each of these areas now.

Fixing Bugs

All nontrivial programs have bugs. This is one of the unprovable but irrefutable truths of computer science. The hard part of maintaining a program is that all the easy bugs are found during the development stage. The bugs that the maintenance programmer must find and fix are often very obscure and turn up only under devilishly complex and difficult-to-recreate circumstances. If you like real challenges, perhaps program maintenance is for you.

There are basically three types of bugs: (1) those that you must fix, (2) those that you would like to fix, and (3) those that you just plain aren't going to worry about. Category 1 bugs crash the system, scribble on the disk, or destroy data. For example, the bug that occasionally causes a database program to trash the database disk file must be fixed because it renders the program unusable. Category 2 bugs get fixed only when there are no category 1 bugs to fix. An example of this type is the bug that on rare occasions causes a word processor to reformat a paragraph incorrectly. Nothing is lost, the program doesn't die, and the user makes a manual adjustment. Category 2 bugs are for the most part annoyances, but the user can work around them. They should and will be fixed, but they are not a top priority. Finally, category 3 bugs are general nuisances, such as a word processor that always spits out an extra sheet of paper at the end of a print session. (Sure, paper costs money, but not that much.) Another type of category 3 bug is really not a bug at all but a difference between the way the documentation says the program works and the way it actually works. These types of bugs are rarely fixed, not because they shouldn't be, but because there are always too many category 1 and 2 bugs to fix first.

If you can organize the reported bugs into the three categories described above, you will be able to budget your time accordingly.

Protecting Source Code

It is often the maintenance programmer's job to be in charge of the source code for the program. Although most companies place a copy of the source of the current version of the program in a bank box, it is usually out of date when it is needed (if ever). The code in the bank is generally viewed as the code of last resort, and the maintenance programmer is actually in charge of protecting the company's source code. What this really means is *not losing it!*

Source code is most commonly lost during the bug-fixing process. It works like this. Programmer A "fixes" a bug. In the process A inadvertently makes an editing error that deletes five lines of code elsewhere in the file. Programmer A compiles the program and checks to see if the bug is fixed. The bug appears fixed, so — and here is the important part — A copies the "fixed" source code from the work directory back into the storage directory. Now five lines of code are missing and the program definitely has a new bug. But before this is discovered, programmer B, whose job it is to back up the hard disk, copies the new, mutilated copy of the program onto the offsite storage disk. Now the old source code is really gone.

There is only one way to prevent the above scenario: Never destroy old versions of the program. The real error that occurred, aside from sloppy editing, was not that programmer A copied the "fixed" source code back into the storage directory, but that programmer B overwrote the offsite storage media.

Here is the way the source code to an evolving program must be handled to prevent its loss.

1. Create three directories. The first holds the currently released version of the program. This directory is only updated when a new release is made. The second directory contains the latest stable, but unreleased, version of the program. The third directory contains the evolving code.

2. Perform offsite storage backups on a regular basis, perhaps weekly, always using a new diskette (or tape). Keep all previous backups on file. In this way, the offsite storage will never be more than five days out of date if it is needed for a recovery.

Differences Between
ANSI C and K&R C

If you have programmed in C for a number of years, you've probably been using a version of C that corresponds to the de facto standard defined by Brian W. Kernighan and Dennis M. Ritchie in their book *The C Programming Language* (Prentice-Hall, 1978). Now that you are using Turbo C, it is important to be aware of some crucial differences between it and the C that you are accustomed to. As has been mentioned numerous times in this book, the proposed ANSI standard has defined a slightly different and expanded version of C than the K&R de facto standard. Turbo C follows the ANSI standard and thus differs in some ways from K&R C. Each of these differences is thoroughly covered in the chapters of this book. This appendix provides a convenient, quick reference for the most important differences, leaving the in-depth discussions to the book proper. It is intended for the experienced C programmer migrating from a K&R environment to Turbo C.

As you may already know, Turbo C supplies some extensions to C that are not defined by the ANSI standard. These extensions are discussed in Part One of this book and are not the subject of this appendix.

Keyword Deletions

The proposed ANSI standard has deleted the unused—but previously reserved for future use—keyword **entry**.

Keyword Extensions

The proposed ANSI standard has added the following five keywords:

const
enum
signed
void
volatile

Each is examined briefly in turn.

const

The **const** type modifier is used to inform the compiler that the value of the variable that follows it may not be changed except for an initialization. For example,

```
const int version=2;
```

informs the compiler that **version** may not occur on the left-hand side of an assignment statement and sets its initial value to 2.

The main use for **const** is to ensure that arguments to functions are not modified by that function. Consider this:

```
char *find_first_space(const char* p)
{
    .
    .
    .
}
```

Because **p** is declared as a **const**, no code in the function can modify its value.

enum

The **enum** type specifier is used to create *enumeration types*. An enumeration is a list of named constants that a variable of that type can have. For example, the following declaration defines an enumeration type and two variables:

```
enum names = {Herb, Sherry, Jon, Rachel, Sasha, Josselyn};

enum names child, parent;
```

Now the following statements are legal:

```
parent = sherry;

child = Jon;

if(child == Jon &&  parent != Herb) ...;
```

The values associated with the named constants are integer values.

signed

The **signed** type modifier was added to the proposed ANSI standard mostly to allow the type **signed char** to be specified explicitly. The **signed** modifier helps standardize the use of type **char**.

void

The **void** type is used in two ways:

1. Functions that do not return values may be declared to be of type **void**, which tells the compiler that no value will be returned. This prevents any accidental usage in an expression.

2. Generic pointers can be created as **void** * variables. You then use an explicit type cast to a pointer of the type you desire.

volatile

The **volatile** type modifier is used to tell the compiler that the variable that follows can be modified in ways that are not under the direct control of the program. For example, a variable may be updated by the system clock every 1/10 second. Variables are declared **volatile** to prevent certain compiler optimizations that might prevent the value of the variable from being accessed precisely as the expression indicates. For example, given this fragment,

```
volatile int clck;
int time1;

time1=clck;
if(time1==clck) ...;
```

if **clck** was not declared **volatile**, it would be legal for Turbo C to optimize the two expressions so that the value of **clck** is examined only once.

Passing Structures

Some early versions of C were not capable of passing structures to functions. They would pass only the address of the structure in much the same way that arrays are passed. How-ever, Turbo C follows the method described in the proposed ANSI standard: passing entire structures on the stack to a function. If you wish to pass the address of a structure instead, you must precede the structure name with the & operator.

Function Prototypes

The proposed ANSI standard allows the types of the arguments and the return type of a function to be declared in advance so that strong type-checking can be enforced for arguments as well as return values. This is called function *prototyping*. For example, the function **func1()** is prototyped in this example:

```
float func1(int, float);   /* function prototype */

main()
{
  int x,
  float y;

  x = 10;
  y = 10.12;

  printf("%f", func1(x, y));
}

float func1(int a, float b)
{
  return (float) a + b;
}
```

Additional Preprocessor Directives

The following C preprocessor directives have been added by the proposed ANSI standard to those normally provided by the old UNIX standard:

#elif
#error
#line
#pragma

The ANSI standard also defines these built-in macros.

Macro	**Meaning**
__LINE__	Number of current line
__FILE__	Name of source file
__DATE__	Current system date
__TIME__	Current system time
__STDC__	1 if a standard implementation

Apple II+™	Apple Computer, Inc.
Color Graphics Adapter™	International Business Machines Corporation
CP/M®	Digital Research, Inc.
DEC™	Digital Equipment Corporation
IBM®	International Business Machines Corporation
MicroPro®	MicroPro International Corporation
Microsoft®	Microsoft Corporation
MS-DOS®	Microsoft Corporation
PCjr™	International Business Machines Corporation
SideKick®: The Desktop Organizer	Borland International, Inc.
Turbo C®	Borland International, Inc.
Turbo Pascal®	Borland International, Inc.
Turbo Prolog®	Borland International, Inc.
UNIX®	AT&T
WordStar®	MicroPro International Corporation

T R A D E M A R K S

The manuscript for this book was prepared and submitted to Osborne/McGraw-Hill in electronic form. The acquisitions editor for this project was Jeffrey Pepper, the technical reviewer was Robert Goosey, and the project editor was Fran Haselsteiner.

Text body in Century Expanded and display in Eras Demi.

Cover art by Bay Graphics Design Associates. Color separation by Colour Image. Cover supplier, Phoenix Color Corp. Book printed and bound by R.R. Donnelley & Sons Company, Crawfordsville, Indiana.